FROMMER'S

WASHINGTON, D.C., AND HISTORIC VIRGINIA ON $40 A DAY

by Rena Bulkin

1988–89 Edition

Published by Prentice Hall Press
A Division of Simon & Schuster, Inc.
Gulf + Western Building
One Gulf + Western Plaza
New York, NY 10023

ISBN 0-13-944430-0

Manufactured in the United States of America

CONTENTS

MAPS

INFLATION ALERT: We don't have to tell you that inflation has hit the United States as it has everywhere else. In researching this book we have made every effort to obtain up-to-the-minute prices, but even the most conscientious researcher cannot keep up with the current pace of inflation. As we go to press, we believe we have obtained the most reliable data possible. Nonetheless, in the lifetime of this edition—particularly its second year (1989)—the wise traveler will add 10% to 15% to the prices quoted throughout these pages.

WASHINGTON, D.C., ON $40 A DAY

THE ONLY AMERICAN CITY that belongs to all Americans is Washington, D.C. As a nation, our Union has always been an uneasy one. From its earliest days, agrarian South has looked askance at citified North, and by expanding our frontiers we added the friction of ostensibly intellectual East and rugged down-to-earth West. But in Washington we're all represented, and we all come together as one. Whether we hail from L.A. or Oshkosh, we visit the city as schoolchildren and grow up with a proprietary feeling about the White House, the Capitol, the cherry blossoms, and even the FBI. Probably we come again as adults—for pleasure or for protest, or to acquaint our own kids with their national heritage. Americans from all regions are united in their allegiance to Washington, and further united in their profound suspicion of its every move. "North and South," says Russell Baker, "Washington is generally despised as an unworthy place where men of mean talents but cunning proclivities conspire to inconvenience decent people beyond its frontiers." And it better watch its step, because we—and the entire world—never cease watching it. Reams are written about the city daily, and would-be Woodwards and Bernsteins keep a sharp and hopeful eye out for trouble. But this is nothing new. Our pride in the capital has always been mingled with cynicism and distrust—so much so that Washington's very survival is cause for the rosiest optimism.

1. Background

Today, whatever people choose to criticize about Washington, they're bound to admit it's one of the most beautiful cities in the nation. But it hasn't always been a showplace city of gleaming marble monuments and beautiful tree-lined thoroughfares. For most of the first century of its existence, the world only wondered why America had chosen as its capital city "a howling, malarious wilderness."

A WANDERING CONGRESS: To say that Washington got off to a shaky start is putting it mildly. For openers, our capital came about as the result of a mutiny. In 1783, 250 Revolutionary War soldiers, understandably angered because Congress was ignoring their petitions for back pay, stormed the temporary capitol, the State House in Philadelphia, demanding justice. The city of Philadelphia, sympathizing with the soldiers, ignored congressional pleas for protection, and as the soldiers rioted outside, the lawmakers locked the doors and huddled within. When the soldiers finally returned to their barracks, Congress deemed it politic to move on to Princeton. They also decided that they needed a capital city whose business was government and the protection thereof.

This was not an altogether new idea. Congress was so nomadic in its first decade of existence that when a statue of George Washington was authorized in 1783, satirist Francis Hopkinson suggested putting it on wheels so it could follow the government around. Before settling into Washington, Congress met at various times in New York, Baltimore, Philadelphia, Lancaster, Princeton, Annapolis, York, and Trenton.

YOU PLAY BALL WITH ME . . . : When Congress proposed that a city be designed and built for the sole purpose of housing the government of the new nation, fresh difficulties arose. There was a general feeling that wherever the capital went up a great commercial center would arise, and many cities vied for the honor. Then too, northerners were strongly opposed to a southern capital—and vice versa. Finally, after seven years of bickering, New Yorker Alexander Hamilton and Virginian Thomas Jefferson worked out a compromise over dinner one night in New York. The North would support a southern site for the capital in return for southern assumption of debts incurred by the states during the Revolution. As a further sop to the North, it was agreed that the seat of government would remain in Philadelphia through 1800 to allow suitable time for surveying, purchasing lands, and constructing government buildings.

ENTER L'ENFANT TERRIBLE: An act passed in 1790 specified a site "not exceeding 10 miles square" (that's 100 square miles) to be located on the Potomac. President and experienced surveyor George Washington was charged with selecting the exact site and appointing building commissioners. He chose a part of the Potomac Valley where the river becomes tidal and is joined by the Anacostia. Maryland gladly provided 69¼ square miles and Virginia 30¾ for the new Federal District. Virginia, whose portion included Arlington and Alexandria, later complained that it was developing too slowly. Her 30¾ square miles were deemed unnecessary, and were returned in 1846. Hence the District today covers about 69¼ square miles.

President Washington hired French military engineer Pierre Charles L'Enfant to lay out the new Federal City. It has since been said that "it would have been hard to find a man better qualified artistically and less fitted by temperament" for the job. L'Enfant arrived in 1791 and immediately declared Jenkins Hill (today Capitol Hill) "a pedestal waiting for a monument." He surveyed every inch of the new Federal District and began his plans by selecting dominant sites for major buildings. He designed broad, 160-foot-wide avenues radiating from squares and circles centered on monumental sculptures and fountains (much like Paris). The Capitol, the "presidential palace," and an equestrian statue where today the Washington Monument stands, were to be the focal points. Pennsylvania Avenue would be the major thoroughfare, and the Mall was conceived as a bustling ceremonial avenue of embassies and other distinguished buildings. L'Enfant was a genius, his plan a masterpiece, but he was also a temperamental *artiste* with no patience for the workings of a bureaucracy or the exigencies of politics. And he was difficult to get along with. He refused to cooperate with Washington's appointed surveyor, Andrew Ellicott, or the building commissioners in charge of the Federal City. Worse yet, he went out of his way to offend one of the latter. Without so much as a by-your-leave (in fact, in spite of an injunction to the contrary) he tore down the manor house commissioner Daniel Carroll was building because it blocked one of his cherished vistas. George Washington diplomatically assuaged Carroll and arranged compensation, but L'Enfant continued to create difficulties. His plan itself dismayed landowners who had been promised $66.66 per acre for land donated for buildings, while land for avenues was to be donated free. L'Enfant's 160-foot-wide avenues and two-mile-long Mall were therefore not appreciated. Of the 6611 acres to be included in the boundaries of the Federal City about half would be avenues and the Mall. A more likable man might have won over the landowners and commissioners, inspiring them with his dreams and his passion, but L'Enfant exhibited only a peevish and condescending secretiveness that alienated one and all. The price of genius became too high when L'Enfant ignored Washington's repeated urgings to produce at least a preliminary blueprint so that fundraising could begin. A year after he had been hired, L'Enfant was fired. For the next few decades he was a familiar figure "haunting the lobbies of the Capitol . . . pacing the newly marked avenues"—keeping a bitter and lonely vigil (with a mangy dog for company) over the developing city. Capitol architect Benjamin Latrobe wrote in his diary: "Daily through the city stalks the picture of famine, L'Enfant and his dog." A grateful Congress offered him $2500 compensation for his year of work, and James Monroe urged him to accept a professorship at West Point. Insulted, he spurned all offers, suing the government for $95,500 instead. He lost and died a pauper in 1825. In 1909, in belated recognition for his services, his remains were brought to Arlington National Cemetery. Some 118 years after he had conceived it, his vision of the Federal City would be a reality.

HOME NOT-SO-SWEET HOME: In 1800 the government (106 representatives and 32 senators) and its effects arrived, according to schedule. What they found bore little resemblance to a city. "One might take a ride of several hours within the precincts without meeting with a single individual to disturb one's meditation," commented one early resident. Pennsylvania Avenue was a mosquito-infested swamp, and there were fewer than 400 habitable houses. Disgruntled Secretary of the Treasury Oliver Wolcott wrote his wife, "I do not perceive how the members of Congress can possibly secure lodgings, unless they will consent to live like Scholars in a college or Monks in a monastery. . . ." The solution was a boom in boarding houses.

Abigail Adams was dismayed at the condition of her new home. The damp caused her rheumatism to act up, the main stairs were not yet constructed, not a single room was finished, and there were not even enough logs for all the fireplaces. And since there was "not the least fence, yard, or other convenience," she hung the presidential laundry in the unfinished East Room. To attend presidential affairs or visit one another, Washington's early citizens had to drive through mud and slush, their vehicles often becoming embedded in bogs and gullies—not a pleasant state of affairs, but one that would go on for many decades. There were many hitches in building the capital. Money, as always, was in short supply, as were materials and labor. The home of the world's most enlightened democracy was built largely by slaves. And always, in the background, there was talk of abandoning the city and starting over somewhere else.

REDCOATS REDUX: Then came the War of 1812. At first the fighting centered on Canada and the West—both too far away to affect daily life in the capital. (In the early 1800s it was a 33-hour ride from Washington to Philadelphia—if you made good time.) In May 1813 the flamboyant British Rear Admiral Cockburn sent word to the executive mansion that "he would make his bow" in the Madisons' drawing room shortly. On August 23, 1814, alarming news reached the capital: the British had landed troops in Maryland. On August 24, James Madison was at the front, most of the populace had fled, and Dolley created a legend by refusing to leave the White House without Gilbert Stuart's famous portrait of George Washington. As the British neared her gates she was calmly writing a blow-by-blow description to her sister, "Our kind friend, Mr. Carroll, has come to hasten my departure, and is in a very bad humour with me because I insist on waiting until the large picture of General Washington is secured, and it requires to be unscrewed from the wall. This process was found too tedious for these perilous moments; I have ordered the frame to be broken, and the canvas taken out; it is done. . . . And now, dear sister, I must leave this house, or the retreating army will make me a prisoner in it, by filling up the road I am directed to take." When the British arrived early that evening, they found dinner set up on the table (Dolley had hoped for the best until the last), and according to some accounts, ate it before torching the mansion. They also burned the Capitol, the Library of Congress, and newly built ships and naval stores. A thunderstorm later that night saved the city from total destruction, while a tornado the next day added to the damage but daunted the British troops.

It seemed that the new capital was doomed. Margaret Bayard Smith, wife of the owner of the influential *National Intelligencer,* lamented, "I do not suppose the Government will ever return to Washington. All those whose property was invested in that place, will be reduced to general poverty. . . . The consternation about us is general. The despondency still greater." But the *Intelligencer* was among the voices speaking out against an even temporary move. Editorials warned that it would be a "treacherous breach of faith" with those who had "laid out fortunes in the purchase of property in and about the city." To move the capital would be "kissing the rod an enemy has wielded." Washingtonian pride rallied and the city was saved once again. Still, it was a close call; Congress came within nine votes of abandoning the place!

In 1815 leading citizens erected a brick building in which Congress could meet in relative comfort until the Capitol was restored. The Treaty of Ghent, establishing peace with Great Britain, was ratified at Octagon House, where the Madisons were temporarily ensconced. And Thomas Jefferson donated his books to replace the destroyed contents of the Library of Congress. Confidence was restored, and the city began to prosper. When the Madisons moved into the rebuilt mansion its exterior had been painted gleaming white to cover the charred walls. From then on it would be known as the White House.

THE CITY OF MAGNIFICENT INTENTIONS: Between the War of 1812 and the Civil War few people evinced any great enthusiasm for Washington. European visitors especially looked at the capital and found it wanting. It was still a provincial backwater, Pennsylvania Avenue and the Mall remaining muddy messes inhabited by pigs, goats, cows, and geese. Many were repelled by the slave auctions openly taking place in the backyard of the White House. The best that could be said—though nobody said it—was that the young capital was picturesque. Merriwether Lewis kept the bears he had brought back from his 4000-mile expedition up the Missouri in cages on the president's lawn. Indian chiefs in full regalia were oft seen negotiating with the white man's government. And matching them in splendor were magnificently attired European court visitors. The only foreigner who praised Washington was Lafayette, who visited in 1825 and was feted with lavish balls and dinners throughout his stay. Charles Dickens gave us the raspberry in 1842. "It is sometimes called the City of Magnificent Distances," he said, "but it might with greater propriety be termed the City of Magnificent Intentions. . . . Spacious avenues, that begin in nothing and lead nowhere; streets, miles long, that only want houses, roads, and inhabitants;

public buildings that need but a public to be complete; and ornaments of great thoroughfares, which only lack great thoroughfares to ornament—are its leading features." Tobacco chewing and sloppy senatorial spitting particularly appalled him. "Both houses are handsomely carpeted," he reported, "but the state to which these carpets are reduced by the universal disregard of the spittoon with which every honorable member is accommodated, and the extraordinary improvements on the pattern which are squirted and dabbled upon it in every direction, do not admit of being described. I will merely observe, that I strongly recommend all strangers not to look at the floor; and if they happen to drop anything . . . not to pick it up with an ungloved hand on any account."

But Dickens's critique was mild compared to Anthony Trollope's, who declared Washington in 1860 "as melancholy and miserable a town as the mind of man can conceive."

A NATION DIVIDED: During the Civil War the capital became an armed camp, with thousands of camp followers. It was the principal supply depot for the Union Army, and an important medical center. Parks became campgrounds, churches became hospitals, and forts ringed the town. The population doubled from 60,000 to 120,000, including about 40,000 former slaves who streamed into the city seeking federal protection. Over 3000 soldiers slept in the Capitol, and a bakery was set up in the basement. The streets were filled with the wounded, and Walt Whitman was a familiar figure, making daily rounds to succor the ailing soldiers. In spite of everything, Lincoln insisted on continuing work on the Capitol. "If people see the Capitol going on, it is a sign we intend the Union shall go on," he said. When the giant dome was completed in 1863 and a 35-star flag was flown overhead, Capitol Hill's field battery fired a 35-gun salute, honoring the Union's then 35 states.

There was joy in Washington and an 800-gun salute in April 1865 when news of the fall of the Confederacy reached the capital. The joy was short-lived. Five days after Appomattox, President Lincoln was shot at Ford's Theatre while attending a performance of *Our American Cousin.* Black replaced the festive tricolored draperies, and the city went into mourning.

The war had enlarged the city's population while doing nothing to improve its facilities. Agrarian, uneducated ex-slaves stayed on, and poverty, unemployment, and disease were rampant. A red-light district remained, the parks were trodden bare, and tenement slums arose within a stone's throw of the Capitol. Horace Greeley suggested that the capital go west.

LED BY A SHEPHERD: As swashbuckling and friendly as L'Enfant had been aloof and introverted, Alexander "Boss" Shepherd was nevertheless destined to implement after 70 years the French architect's glorious vision. A real estate speculator who had made his money in a plumbing firm, Shepherd shouldered a musket in the Union Army and became one of Gen. Ulysses S. Grant's closest intimates. When Grant became president he wanted to appoint Shepherd governor, but blueblood opposition ran too high. Washington high society considered him a parvenu and feared his ambitions for civic leadership. Instead Grant named the more popular Henry D. Cooke (a secret Shepherd ally) governor and named Shepherd vice-president of the Board of Public Works. No one was fooled. Shepherd made all the governor's decisions, and a joke went around the capital: "Why is the new governor like a sheep? Because he is led by A. Shepherd." He became the actual governor in 1873.

Shepherd vowed that his "comprehensive plan of improvement" would make the city a showplace. But an engineer he wasn't. Occasionally, newly paved streets had to be torn up because he had forgotten to install the sewers first. But he was a first-rate orator and politician. He began by hiring an army of laborers and starting them on projects all over town. Congress would have had to halt work on half-finished sidewalks, streets, and sewers throughout the District in order to stop him. It would have been a mess. The press liked and supported the colorful Shepherd; people forced out of their homes because they couldn't pay the high assessments for improvements hated him. Between 1871 and 1874 he established parks, paved and lighted the streets, installed sewers, filled in sewage-laden Tiber Creek, and planted over 50,000 trees. He left the city bankrupt—over $20 million in debt! But he did get the job done.

L'ENFANT REBORN: Through the end of the 19th century Washington continued to make great aesthetic strides. The Washington Monument, long a truncated obelisk and major eyesore, was finally completed in 1884. Pennsylvania Avenue was beginning to develop into the ceremonial thoroughfare L'Enfant had envisioned as important buildings rose up one after another. Shepherd had done a great deal, but much was still left undone. In 1887 L'Enfant's "Plan for the City of Washington" was resurrected. In 1900 Michigan Sen. James McMillan—a retired railroad mogul with architectural and engineering skills—determined to complete the job L'Enfant had started a century earlier. A tireless lobbyist for government-sponsored municipal improvements, he persuaded his colleagues to appoint an advisory committee to create "the city beautiful." At his personal expense, McMillan sent this illustrious committee—landscapist Frederick Law Olmsted (designer of New York's Central Park), sculptor Augustus Saint-Gaudens, and noted architects Daniel Burnham and Charles McKim—to Europe for seven weeks to study the landscaping and architecture of that continent's great capitals. Assembled at last was a force combining L'Enfant's artistic genius and Shepherd's political savvy. "Make no little plans," counseled Burnham. "They have no magic to stir men's blood, and probably themselves will not be realized. Make big plans, aim high in hope and work, remembering that a noble and logical diagram once recorded will never die, but long after we are gone will be a living thing, asserting itself with ever growing insistency." The committee's big plans—almost all of which were accomplished—included the development of a complete park system, selection of sites for government buildings, and the designing of the Lincoln Memorial, the Arlington Memorial Bridge, and the Reflecting Pool (the last inspired by Versailles). They also got to work on the improving Mall, the first step being to remove the tracks, train sheds, and stone depot that the Baltimore and Potomac Railroad had constructed there; in return for the railroad's sacrifice, Congress authorized money for monumental Union Station, inspired by the Baths of Diocletian. Throughout the McMillan Commission years, the House was under the hostile leadership of Speaker "Uncle Joe" Cannon of Illinois who, among other things, swore he would "never let a memorial to Abraham Lincoln be erected in that goddamned swamp" (West Potomac Park). Cannon caused some problems and delays, but on the whole the committee's prestigious membership added weight to their usually accepted recommendations. McMillan, however, did not live to see most of his dreams accomplished. He died in 1902.

By the 20th century Washington was no longer an object of ridicule. And it has continued to develop apace. The Library of Congress, Union Station, and the Corcoran Gallery had been completed before the turn of the century. The Museum of Natural History went up in 1911 (already extant Smithsonian buildings included Arts and Industries, the Old Patent Office Building, and the Castle), the Lincoln Memorial was completed in 1922, the Freer Gallery in 1923. A Commission of Fine Arts was appointed in 1910 by President Taft to create monuments and fountains, once again with Olmsted as a member. Thanks to Mrs. Taft the famous cherry trees presented to the United States by the Japanese in 1912 were planted in the Tidal Basin. And thanks to Taft's commission, neoclassic architecture and uniform building height became the order of the day.

WASHINGTON TODAY: It's been a long while since people have plotted to move the capital. Today Americans are proud of their showplace Federal City—its museums, monuments, parks, memorials, and beaux-arts buildings. It's a capital worthy of a great and powerful nation, complete with fine restaurants, lively nightlife, and a cultural scene dominated by the prestigious Kennedy Center. Artists make pilgrimages to D.C. to visit its famous museums and galleries.

It is, and always has been, a company town, and the business at hand is politics, described by Russell Baker as "an occult art practiced by the city's famous, and incessantly discussed, though rarely understood by everyone else." The government employs a large percentage of Washingtonians, so it's only natural that people talk about their work.

The second-largest industry is us—tourists; over 10 million of us flock to the capital each year. What we find is a clean, friendly city (Washingtonians are invariably hospitable and helpful) offering seemingly endless sightseeing options. We're impressed—especially if we come from the Big Apple—with how civilized it all is. The subways are safe, efficient, and free of graffiti; everyone is well (albeit conservatively) dressed; everyone behaves (at least in public). This is a city that works.

$40 A DAY—WHAT IT MEANS: Is it still possible to visit Washington on a $40-a-day budget? The answer is yes and to do that you have to begin with a moderate per-day cost of living. By living costs I refer to basic necessities: your hotel room and three meals. That $40 a day allowance is maintained by spending no more than $20 to $25 per person in a double-occupancy room, $2 for breakfast, $5 for lunch, $8 for dinner. Obviously your transportation, sightseeing, and entertainment costs will all be in addition to this, but I'll show you how to enjoy these other activities with a reasonable expenditure of money. The following chapters will tell you about hostel rooms for $13 a night (less for AYH members), B&B accommodations for under $100 a week, and a guest house where a double room costs under $20 per person. There are excellent cafeterias in town serving full meals for under $4. And almost all of the sightseeing attractions are free. I've also included budget-priced hotels and restaurants that don't fit precisely into the title category, but are part of the wide spectrum of low-cost Washington. This book is for everyone who is trying to keep travel expenses down while having the best possible time. And in these inflationary days that includes almost everyone. You'll find in the pages to come the information you need to get the most for your money in D.C. And equally important, you'll find informative and, I hope, entertaining commentary on all aspects of the nation's capital and its attractions. Here's wishing you a happy, trouble-free, and rewarding Washington vacation.

AN INVITATION TO READERS: Like the other books in the $$$-A-Day series, *Washington D.C., on $40 a Day* hopes to list the establishments that offer the best value for budget-conscious travelers. In achieving this goal, your comments and suggestions can be of tremendous help. Therefore if you come across a particularly appealing lodging, restaurant, store, even sightseeing attraction, please don't keep it to yourself. In fact, I encourage you to write to me on any

PRESIDENTS OF THE UNITED STATES	TERMS
George Washington	1789–1797
John Adams	1797–1801
Thomas Jefferson	1801–1809
James Madison	1809–1817
James Monroe	1817–1825
John Quincy Adams	1825–1829
Andrew Jackson	1829–1837
Martin Van Buren	1837–1841
William Henry Harrison	1841
John Tyler	1841–1845
James K. Polk	1845–1849
Zachary Taylor	1849–1850
Millard Fillmore	1850–1853
Franklin Pierce	1853–1857
James Buchanan	1857–1861
Abraham Lincoln	1861–1865
Andrew Johnson	1865–1869
Ulysses S. Grant	1869–1877
Rutherford B. Hayes	1877–1881
James A. Garfield	1881
Chester A. Arthur	1881–1885
Grover Cleveland	1885–1889
Benjamin Harrison	1889–1893
Grover Cleveland	1893–1897
William McKinley	1897–1901
Theodore Roosevelt	1901–1909
William Howard Taft	1909–1913
Woodrow Wilson	1913–1921
Warren G. Harding	1921–1923
Calvin Coolidge	1923–1929
Herbert Hoover	1929–1933
Franklin Delano Roosevelt	1933–1945
Harry S. Truman	1945–1953
Dwight D. Eisenhower	1953–1961
John F. Kennedy	1961–1963
Lyndon B. Johnson	1963–1969
Richard M. Nixon	1969–1974
Gerald R. Ford	1974–1977
Jimmy Carter	1977–1980
Ronald Reagan	1980–

matter dealing with this book. Every now and then a change of management, staff, or ownership will affect the quality of an establishment, and if you find this is the case with any recommended place, let me know so I can look it over extra carefully for the following edition. And if you find a suggestion of mine particularly good, or find the book helpful in general, I don't mind hearing that either! Finally, you might want to share your experiences with other readers.

You have my word that every letter will be read by me personally, although I find it well-nigh impossible to answer each and every one. Send your notes to Rena Bulkin, c/o Frommer Books, Prentice Hall Press, Gulf + Western Building, One Gulf + Western Plaza, New York, NY 10023.

2. The $35-A-Day Travel Club—How to Save Money on All Your Travels

In this book we'll be looking at how to get your money's worth in Washington, D.C., but there is a "device" for saving money and determining value on *all* your trips. It's the popular, international $35-A-Day Travel Club, now in its 26th successful year of operation. The Club was formed at the urging of numerous readers of the $$$-A-Day and Dollarwise Guides, who felt that such an organization could provide continuing travel information and a sense of community to value-minded travelers in all parts of the world. And so it does!

In keeping with the budget concept, the annual membership fee is low and is immediately exceeded by the value of your benefits. Upon receipt of $18 (U.S. residents), or $20 U.S. by check drawn on a U.S. bank or via international postal money order in U.S. funds (Canadian, Mexican, and other foreign residents) to cover one year's membership, we will send all new members the following items.

(1) Any *two* of the following books

Please designate in your letter which two you wish to receive:

Frommer's $-A-Day Guides
> Europe on $30 a Day
> Australia on $25 a Day
> Eastern Europe on $25 a Day
> England on $40 a Day
> Greece (including Istanbul and Turkey's Aegean Coast) on $25 a Day
> Hawaii on $50 a Day
> India on $15 & $25 a Day
> Ireland on $30 a Day
> Israel on $30 & $35 a Day
> Mexico (plus Belize and Guatemala) on $20 a Day
> New York on $50 a Day
> New Zealand on $40 a Day
> Scandinavia on $50 a Day
> Scotland and Wales on $40 a Day
> South America on $30 a Day
> Spain and Morocco (plus the Canary Is.) on $40 a Day
> Turkey on $25 a Day
> Washington, D.C. (including Historic Virginia) on $40 a Day

Frommer's Dollarwise Guides
> Dollarwise Guide to Austria and Hungary
> Dollarwise Guide to Belgium, Holland, & Luxembourg
> Dollarwise Guide to Bermuda and The Bahamas
> Dollarwise Guide to Canada
> Dollarwise Guide to the Caribbean
> Dollarwise Guide to Egypt
> Dollarwise Guide to England and Scotland
> Dollarwise Guide to France

Dollarwise Guide to Germany
Dollarwise Guide to Italy
Dollarwise Guide to Japan and Hong Kong
Dollarwise Guide to Portugal, Madeira, and the Azores
Dollarwise Guide to the South Pacific
Dollarwise Guide to Switzerland and Liechtenstein
Dollarwise Guide to Alaska
Dollarwise Guide to California and Las Vegas
Dollarwise Guide to Florida
Dollarwise Guide to the Mid-Atlantic States
Dollarwise Guide to New England
Dollarwise Guide to New York State
Dollarwise Guide to the Northwest
Dollarwise Guide to Skiing USA—East
Dollarwise Guide to Skiing USA—West
Dollarwise Guide to the Southeast and New Orleans
Dollarwise Guide to the Southwest
Dollarwise Guide to Texas
(Dollarwise Guides discuss accommodations and facilities in all price ranges, with emphasis on the medium-priced.)

Frommer's Touring Guides
Egypt
Florence
London
Paris
Venice
(These new, color illustrated guides include walking tours, cultural and historic sites, and other vital travel information.)

A Shopper's Guide to Best Buys in England, Scotland, and Wales
(Describes in detail hundreds of places to shop—department stores, factory outlets, street markets, and craft centers—for great quality British bargains.)

A Shopper's Guide to the Caribbean
(Two experienced Caribbean hands guide you through this shopper's paradise, offering witty insights and helpful tips on the wares and emporia of more than 25 islands.)

Bed & Breakfast—North America
(This guide contains a directory of over 150 organizations that offer bed & breakfast referrals and reservations throughout North America. The scenic attractions, and major schools and universities near the homes of each are also listed.)

Dollarwise Guide to Cruises
(This complete guide covers all the basics of cruising—ports of call, costs, fly-cruise package bargains, cabin selection booking, embarkation and debarkation and describes in detail over 60 or so ships cruising the waters of Alaska, the Caribbean, Mexico, Hawaii, Panama, Canada, and the United States.)

Dollarwise Guide to Skiing Europe
(Describes top ski resorts in Austria, France, Italy, and Switzerland. Illustrated with maps of each resort area plus full-color trail maps.)

Fast 'n' Easy Phrase Book
(French, German, Spanish, and Italian—all in one convenient, easy-to-use phrase guide.)

Honeymoon Guide
(A special guide for that most romantic trip of your life, with full details on planning and choosing the destination that will be just right in the U.S. [California, New England, Hawaii, Florida, New York, South Carolina, etc.], Canada, Mexico, and the Caribbean.)

How to Beat the High Cost of Travel
(This practical guide details how to save money on absolutely all travel items—accommodations, transportation, dining, sightseeing, shopping, taxes, and more. Includes special budget information for seniors, students, singles, and families.)

Marilyn Wood's Wonderful Weekends
(This very selective guide covers the best mini-vacation destinations within a 175-mile radius of New York City. It describes special country inns and other accommodations, restaurants, picnic spots, sights, and activities—all the information needed for a two- or three-day stay.)

Motorist's Phrase Book
(A practical phrase book in French, German, and Spanish designed specifically for the English-speaking motorist touring abroad.)

Swap and Go—Home Exchanging Made Easy
(Two veteran home exchangers explain in detail all the money-saving benefits of a home exchange, and then describe precisely how to do it. Also includes information on home rentals and many tips on low-cost travel.)

The Candy Apple: New York for Kids
(A spirited guide to the wonders of the Big Apple by a savvy New York grandmother with a kid's-eye view to fun. Indispensable for visitors and residents alike.)

Travel Diary and Record Book
(A 96-page diary for personal travel notes plus a section for such vital data as passport and traveler's check numbers, itinerary, postcard list, special people and places to visit, and a reference section with temperature and conversion charts, and world maps with distance zones.)

Where to Stay USA
(By the Council on International Educational Exchange, this extraordinary guide is the first to list accommodations in all 50 states that cost anywhere from $3 to $30 per night.)

(2) A one-year subscription to *The Wonderful World of Budget Travel*

This quarterly eight-page tabloid newspaper keeps you up to date on fast-breaking developments in low-cost travel in all parts of the world bringing you the latest money-saving information—the kind of information you'd have to pay $25 a year to obtain elsewhere. This consumer-conscious publication also features columns of special interest to readers: **Hospitality Exchange** (members all over the world who are willing to provide hospitality to other members as they pass through their home cities—); **Share-a-Trip** (offers and requests from members for travel companions who can share costs and help avoid the burdensome single supplement); and **Readers Ask . . . Readers Reply** (travel questions from members to which other members reply with authentic firsthand information).

(3) A copy of *Arthur Frommer's Guide to New York*

This is a pocket-size guide to hotels, restaurants, nightspots, and sightseeing attractions in all price ranges throughout the New York area.

(4) Your personal membership card

Membership entitles you to purchase through the Club all Arthur Frommer publications for a third to a half off their regular retail prices during the term of your membership.

So why not join this hardy band of international budgeteers and participate in its exchange of travel information and hospitality? Simply send your name and address, together with your annual membership fee of $18 (U.S. residents) or $20 U.S. (Canadian, Mexican, and other foreign residents), by check drawn on a U.S. bank or via international postal money order in U.S. funds to: $35-A-Day Travel Club, Inc., Frommer Books, Gulf + Western Building, One Gulf + Western Plaza, New York, NY 10023. And please remember to specify which *two* of the books in section (1) above you wish to receive in your initial package of members' benefits. Or, if you prefer, use the last page of this book, simply checking off the two books you select and enclosing $18 or $20 in U.S. currency.

Once you are a member, there is no obligation to buy additional books. No books will be mailed to you without your specific order.

Chapter I

GETTING TO KNOW THE CAPITAL

1. Before You Leave Home
2. Getting There
3. Getting Oriented
4. Getting Around

IF YOU'RE GOING TO a beach resort, there's little need to plan your vacation. You can wing it. But when visiting a city where dozens of sightseeing attractions vie for your time, planning is the key to optimum enjoyment. Moreover, in Washington, some of the most comprehensive and least crowded tours are available only to those who have contacted congressional representatives or senators for special advance passes (see below). My suggestion is to read the sightseeing chapter carefully and decide on your own not-to-be-missed imperatives. Then map out each vacation day, taking into consideration geographic proximity (don't jump around town; see sights near each other on the same day) and caveats about best times to visit (for instance, you must be at the National Air and Space Museum at opening time in order to get tickets for the spectacular IMAX films during tourist season). Make sure to plan some leisure time into each day; it's better to miss an attraction or two than turn your trip into a sightseeing marathon. And consider the Virginia and Maryland chapters—do you want to schedule a few days in Williamsburg, Alexandria, Charlottesville, see the U.S. Naval Academy, Potomac Plantations, the Pentagon, etc.?

1. Before You Leave Home

CHOOSE A HOTEL: Note that advance hotel bookings often allow you to take advantage of low weekend rates at first-class properties. For a free booklet listing over 65 hotels that offer special weekend deals, contact the **Hotel Association of Washington, D.C.,** P.O. Box 33578, Washington, D.C. 20033 (tel. 202/833-3350), and request a copy of their free *Washington Weekends* brochure.

Also call or write **Taj International Hotels,** 1315 16th St. NW, Washington, DC. 20036 (tel. 202/462-7104 or toll free 800/DC-VISIT). Owners and operators of five Washington properties that run the gamut from moderate- to luxury-class hotels, the Taj group offers some of the most advantageous weekend rates and packages in town. And they extend those "weekend" rates to include off-season weekdays (November to February and July and August) as well. Because they have so many rooms, Taj is sure to be able to place you at a good price. Contact them for details.

Finally, do consider the services of **Capitol Reservations** (details in Chapter II).

WRITE YOUR SENATOR OR CONGRESSPERSON: Your senators and/or congressional representatives can provide you with passes for several VIP tours of the Capitol, the White House, the FBI, and the Kennedy Center. This is no secret. Thousands of people know about it and do write, so make your request as far in advance as possible—even six months is not too soon. Their allotment of tickets for each sight is limited so there's no guarantee, but it's worth a try. At the very least you can get some general information about Washington. Address requests to your representative (or senator), U.S. House of Representatives (or Senate), Washington, DC 20515 (for the House) or 20510 (for the Senate). Be sure to include the exact dates of your Washington trip.

When you write, also request tourist information and literature. Most members of the House and Senate keep some on hand for constituents.

The Capitol

The 8 a.m. weekday VIP tour of the Capitol is 15 minutes longer than the regular tour and visits both the House and Senate chambers (the regular tour visits only one).

The White House

Between 8 and 8:45 a.m. the doors of the White House are open for special VIP tours to those with tickets. Once again, write far, far in advance, because each senator gets only 15 tickets a week to distribute, and each congressperson gets only 10. These early tours ensure your entrance in the busy tourist season when thousands line up during the two hours daily the White House is open to the public. They're also more extensive than later tours, with guides providing explanatory commentary as you go; on later tours guides are on hand to answer questions but don't give actual talks in each room.

The FBI

The line for this very popular tour can get extremely long. One way to beat the system is to have your senator or representative set up a reservation for you for a scheduled time. Then you can just waltz right in.

The Kennedy Center

The VIP tour offered Monday to Saturday at 9:30 a.m. once again allows you to avoid a long wait with the thronging masses who did not take the trouble to write to their senators and congresspeople.

VISITOR INFORMATION SOURCES: The **Washington, D.C., Convention and Visitors Association,** 1575 I St. NW, Suite 250, Washington, DC 20005 (tel. 202/789-7000), will send you the following brochures free upon request: *Washington, DC, Attractions;* a *Calendar of Events; Washington, DC, Accommodations;* a visitor map; *Washington, DC: A Capital City;* and the *Washington, DC, Dining/Shopping Guide.* They'll also be happy to answer your specific questions.

Write to the **D.C. Department of Recreation,** 3149 16th St. NW, Washington, DC 20010 (tel. 202/673-7660), enclose a self-addressed stamped envelope, and request their calendar of events called *Do You Know* for the month you'll be visiting. It will acquaint you with a wide variety of events—theatrical productions, big-name concerts (a typical issue listed D.C. vicinity appearances by Paul Anka, Kenny Loggins, Al Jarreau, Bette Midler, and Harry Belafonte, among others), free outdoor entertainment, children's theater, athletic events, lectures, art exhibits, watermelon-eating contests, square dances, cookouts, symphonies, craft shows, and more.

WHEN TO VISIT: Probably you'll visit when you have vacation time or when the kids are out of school, but assuming you have the luxury of choice I'd recommend the **fall.** The weather is lovely, Washington's abundant natural areas are awash in fall foliage colors, and the tourists have thinned out.

If you really hate crowds, and want to get the most out of Washington sights, **winter** is your season. It's not that cold (see chart below), there are no long lines or early-morning dashes to avoid them; and hotel prices are lower.

Spring weather is delightful, and of course there are those cherry blossoms. Along with autumn, it's the nicest time to enjoy D.C.'s outdoor attractions, to get around to museums in comfort, to laze away an afternoon or evening at the ubiquitous Washington street cafés. But the city is also crowded with millions of tourists.

The throngs remain in **summer,** and anyone who's ever spent a D.C. summer will tell you how hot and steamy it is. Though there's occasional relief, those 90° days do seem to arrive with amazing frequency. The advantage: this is the season to enjoy hundreds of outdoor events—free concerts, festivals, parades, Revolutionary War reenactments, and more. There's something doing almost every night and day. And, of course, Independence Day in the Capital is a spectacular celebration.

Whenever you visit, you can be sure there's plenty going on around town.

Average Temperatures in Washington, D.C.

	High		Medium		Low	
	F	C	F	C	F	C
January	44.6°	7.0°	35.0°	1.6°	27.4°	−2.6°
February	44.4	6.8	36.2	2.3	28.0	−2.2
March	53.0	11.6	44.0	6.7	35.0	1.6
April	64.2	17.8	54.2	12.3	44.2	6.8
May	74.9	23.8	64.7	18.2	54.5	12.5
June	82.8	28.2	73.1	22.8	63.4	17.4
July	86.8	30.4	77.4	25.2	68.0	20.0
August	84.4	29.1	75.3	24.0	66.1	18.9
September	78.4	25.7	69.0	20.5	59.6	15.3
October	67.5	19.7	57.8	14.3	48.0	8.8
November	55.1	12.8	46.5	8.0	37.9	3.3
December	44.8	7.1	37.3	2.9	29.8	−1.2

ANNUAL EVENTS: The festival spirit runs strong in D.C., and nary a week goes by without a celebration or two, be it feast or fair or historic birthday bash. Listed below are major annual events. For up-to-the-minute information, when in town call the National Park Service hotline number (tel. 485-PARK), check the *Washington Post*, especially the Friday "Weekend" section, and pick up a copy of *Sights & Sounds* at the Convention and Visitors Association (CVA) on Pennsylvania Avenue (tel. 789-7000).

January

Congress convenes on the first Monday of the month; senators and congresspeople get back to work.

Special excitement on January 20 if it's an election year and a new or recycled president is inaugurated on the Capitol steps. After the swearing-in, the crowd follows the new chief executive's motorcade down Pennsylvania Avenue to the White House. Parades, concerts, puppet shows, plays, parties, and other festivities highlight the event.

Antique lovers will want to peruse the wares of some 50 East Coast dealers at the **Washington Antique Show,** in the Shoreham Hotel (tel. 234-0700), in early or mid-January. Admission (about $5) is charged, and profits go to thrift-shop charities. This is a high-toned event with displays of artifacts relating to the show's annual theme (like Historical Preservations) and catalogs containing articles by museum curators and scholars.

Martin Luther King, Jr.'s Birthday is celebrated the third Monday of January. It's highlighted by dance, theater, and choral performances; speeches by prominent civil rights leaders and politicians; prayer vigils; concerts; special readings; and other events, some of them taking place at the Martin Luther King Memorial Library, 901 G St. NW (tel. 727-1186). Call the Convention and Visitors Association (tel. 789-7000) for additional details.

Chinese New Year in late January or early February (it depends on the lunar calendar) is celebrated in D.C.'s tiny Chinatown for ten days with the traditional dragon dance and endless firecrackers. Some restaurants offer special menus. The area is bounded by H and I Streets between 5th and 8th Streets NW. A friendship archway, topped by 300 painted dragons and lit up at night, marks the entrance to Chinatown at 7th and H Streets.

February

Black History Month, February is a time of celebrating Afro-American contributions to American life. Call the Anacostia Neighborhood Museum (tel. 287-3369) to find out about their special events. Get additional information from the Convention and Visitors Association (tel. 789-7000) and the Smithsonian (tel. 357-2700).

Abraham Lincoln's Birthday is marked by the laying of a wreath at the Lincoln Memorial (noon), followed by band music and political speeches. Citywide sales are of equal interest to the populace.

Similar celebrations at the Washington Monument mark **Washington's Birthday,** usually on the Monday closest to February 22. Call 485-9666 for details. The biggest to-dos are in nearby Alexandria (see Chapter VIII for details).

March

In early March the B'nai B'rith Museum, 1640 Rhode Island Ave. NW (tel. 857-6583), usually (budget permitting) celebrates **Purim** with masks, costumes, puppets, and a reenactment of the Purim story. Participants learn how to make traditional foods like *hamantashen* (triangular pastries filled with prune jam or poppy seeds)—fun for kids. Admission is charged.

The annual **St. Patrick's Day Parade** on Constitution Ave. NW from 7th to 17th Sts. takes place the Sunday before March 17 with floats, bagpipes, bands, and the wearin' o' the green. In past years, its illustrious grand marshals have included Tip O'Neill, Eunice Shriver, and Helen Hayes. For additional parade information, call 424-2200. Get into the spirit of things with a preparade brunch at the Dubliner, 4 F St. NW at N. Capitol St. (tel. 737-3773)—rashers of bacon, sage sausage, and Cashel Cottage eggs. Return again postparade for live traditional Gaelic entertainment (Irish and Celtic reels, jigs, ballads, and protest songs), 16-ounce tumblers of imported Guinness stout, and classic Irish coffee. The party continues next door at Irish Times, 14F St. NW (tel. 543-5433).

In honor of **Johann Sebastian Bach's birthday** (March 21) 16 organists play his music (each for a half hour) on the massive pipe organ at Chevy Chase Presbyterian Church, 1 Chevy Chase Circle NW (tel. 363-2202). Admission is free, and the concert begins at 1 p.m. on a selected March Sunday.

Smithsonian Kite Day (tel. 357-3030 for details) brings throngs of kite-makers and kite-flyers to the Washington Monument grounds. Enthusiasts with handcrafted kites compete for ribbons and trophies. It's usually the third or fourth Saturday in March.

Call the **National Cathedral** (tel. 537-6200) for information on Holy Week services and concerts.

Easter also brings **Ringling Bros. and Barnum & Bailey Circus** (tel. 364-5000) to town for a two-week engagement.

The official beginning of spring is heralded by the blooming of the famous **Japanese cherry trees** in late March or early April with parades, pageants, and princesses. Details are in Chapter V.

April

It's still—or finally—cherry blossom time. You can attend 6 a.m. **Easter Sunrise Services** at the Memorial Amphitheater in Arlington; sunrise services too at the Carter Barron Amphitheater.

Get to the White House early on Easter Monday for the traditional **Easter Egg Roll.** In past years the entertainment has included clog dancers, Ukrainian egg decorators, puppet shows, magic, military drill teams, and prizes. All children age 8 and under are welcome with their accompanying adults. Enter at the southeast gate on East Executive Avenue. The Roll takes place between 10 a.m. and 2 p.m. Call 456-2200 for details.

Spring flowers bloom in profusion at the United States Botanic Garden, Maryland Ave. between 1st and 2nd Sts. SW (tel. 225-8333), during the annual **Spring Flower Show,** beginning Palm Sunday and running for several weeks thereafter.

The creator of the Declaration of Independence is honored on **Thomas Jefferson's Birthday,** April 13, with a noon wreath-laying ceremony and military drills at the Jefferson Memorial.

See the beautiful **White House gardens** when they're open to the public for two days in mid-April between 2 and 5 p.m. Call 456-2200 for exact dates.

My favorite spring event (usually the last Saturday in April) is the **Justice Douglas Reunion Hike** on the C&O Canal. Douglas once walked the entire 184½-mile path in protest against a plan to build a scenic parkway along the canal. The annual hike covers about 12 miles (always on a different section). Shuttle service back is free, and a buffet banquet wraps up the day's activities. For details contact the C&O Canal Association, P.O. Box 66, Glen Echo, MD 20812. Call 301/739-4200 for details.

Old Georgetown homes are open for viewing on the **Georgetown House Tour** late in April. The admission fee (about $10) includes high tea at St. John's Church (tel. 338-1796). **Georgetown gardens** are on view in mid- or late April, usually, including a guided tour of Dumbarton Oaks and tea (tel. 333-4953). Admission is about $10.

May

On a Saturday early in May the **Asian Pacific American Heritage Festival** (tel. 223-5500) honors America's first Japanese settlement and the completion of the transcontinental railroad, constructed largely by Chinese workers. All of

Washington's Asian communities participate—Chinese, Japanese, Koreans, Indians, Vietnamese, Hawaiians, Thais, and others. There are cultural displays, crafts booths, ethnic foods, dragon dances, martial arts exhibitions, and other festivities at the Sylvan Theater on the south side of the Washington Monument grounds.

The **Washington National Cathedral Annual Flower Mart** (tel. 537-6200), the first Friday and Saturday in May, includes displays of flowering plants, vegetables, and herbs (all for sale, but you can come look for free) on the cathedral grounds. Lunch is available, and there's an antique carousel ride for kids.

Also at the cathedral in early May is the **Kirkin' o' the Tartan,** a colorful Scottish Presbyterian religious event featuring bagpipers and twirling kilts. Call 537-6200 for details.

Still hungry? There's more ethnic fare at the **Greek Spring Festival** in late May at Saints Constantine and Helen Greek Orthodox Church, 4115 16th St. NW (tel. 829-2910). Souvlaki, baklava, Greek wine, dances, games, arts and crafts, and more.

On **Memorial Day** at 11 a.m. (tel. 475-0856 for details), a wreath-laying ceremony at the Tomb of the Unknown Soldier in Arlington National Cemetery is followed by military band music, a service, and an address by a high-ranking government official (sometimes the president). There's also a ceremony—color guard, wreath laying, speakers, and the playing of "Taps"—at the Vietnam Memorial at 1 p.m. In the evening the National Symphony Orchestra gives a free Memorial Day concert on the west lawn of the Capitol.

June

A day in mid-June is set aside for the **Irish Feis** (pronounced "fesh"), a 4000-year-old traditional Irish event of competitions in Gaelic recitation, dancing (reels, jigs, and hornpipes), doll-making, Irish bread baking, singing, and music. It's sponsored by the Irish-American Club (tel. 567-9332).

The **Smithsonian Institution's Festival of American Folklife,** the last week of June and the first week of July, is a major grass-roots celebration with folk artists, performers, concerts, crafts, games, exhibits, and ethnic food. Most of it takes place on the Mall. Call 357-2700 for program information. All events are free.

In mid-June the Revolutionary War and history of America are traced through music and skits at military band **Spirit of America Concerts** at the Capital Centre (tel. 475-0856).

Every June and July the **Men's Tennis Classics** are held at courts in Rock Creek Park. Top-seeded players compete. Call 269-7200 for details.

July

No city celebrates **July 4th** in grander style than the nation's capital. A mammoth parade of floats, princesses, marching groups, and military bands beginning at 10 a.m. on Constitution Avenue kicks off the day's events—baseball games, dances, arts and crafts exhibits, star entertainers, numerous concerts, and all-American foods. A Revolutionary War encampment is set up on the lawn of the National Archives, where the program includes military demonstrations, music of the period, and a reading of the Declaration of Independence. In the evening the National Symphony Orchestra plays on the steps of the Capitol Building with guest artists like Leontyne Price. And of course there's a fabulous fireworks display over the Washington Monument.

The annual **Hispanic Festival** takes place the last week in July with reggae, salsa, Xaragua bands, Cuban rumba, and African music and dance up and down Columbia Road in Adams Morgan. Also a parade, over 100 ethnic food kiosks, crafts, plays, and special Hispanic events around town the entire week. Over 100,000 people attend. Call 789-7000 for details.

August

Head down to Alexandria for **August Tavern Days** (determined annually) when Colonial life is recreated via food, music, and entertainment. Call 703/549-0205 for details.

September

Bring the kids to Wolf Trap Farm Park in Vienna, Va. (tel. 703/941-1527) for the **International Children's Festival** in early September. Mimes, clowns, musical performances, and puppet shows entertain. Admission is charged.

The round-robin elimination trials at the **Annual Croquet Tournament** are open to anyone 16 or older. Instruction is available, and the winner gets a trophy. This mid-September event is held on the 17th Street side of the Ellipse (tel. 234-4602).

Washington National Cathedral's Open House Day, held on a Saturday late in the month (sometimes early in October), includes a tour, an organ demonstration, exhibits, and performances by dancers, choirs, and puppeteers (tel. 537-6200). It's the only time visitors are allowed to ascend to the top of the tower to see the carillon—a strenuous climb, but a spectacular view makes it worthwhile.

A great late-September party is **Rock Creek Park Day** (tel. 485-9666), celebrating the birthday (its centennial's coming up in 1990) of Washington's largest park. Highlights include music, folk dancing, balloons, pony riding, and international crafts and food booths.

October

On a selected Sunday you can watch a centuries-old sport—jousting—on the Washington Monument grounds (tel. 485-9660).

The **Supreme Court** term begins. Visitors can watch cases argued before the justices. Call 479-3211 for information.

October brings another chance to see the Rose Garden, the South Lawn, and other usually off-limits areas of the executive mansion grounds during two days of **White House Garden Tours** (tel. 426-2200). Music by a military band accompanies the tours.

Rock Creek Foliage Day takes place late in October, with hiking, milling demonstrations, music, nature films, and other activities. The day's events begin at the Shoreham Hotel. Phone 485-9666 for details.

November

Veteran's Day, in commemoration of the signing of the armistice ending World War I and in honor of all veterans, is marked by the laying of a wreath (by the president or a high-ranking government official) at the Tomb of the Unknown Soldier. Military bands play. The ceremony begins at 11 a.m. Phone 475-0856 for more information. At the Vietnam Memorial, observances include speakers, wreath laying, a color guard, and the playing of "Taps" at 1 p.m.

The **Marine Corps Marathon** (tel. 485-9660), a 26-mile jaunt past some of Washington's most famous monuments, takes place on the first Sunday in November. World-class runners compete. The race begins at the Iwo Jima Memorial in Arlington.

December

At the **Annual Carol Sing and Band Concert,** the U.S. Marine Band and local choirs lead the audience in singing Yuletide favorites and a candlelight procession at Wolf Trap Farm Park (tel. 255-1900). It's outdoors, so bundle up. BYOB (Bring Your Own Bell).

The **Christmas Greens Show** at the United States Botanical Gardens (tel. 225-7099) in early December features beautifully decorated trees, wreaths, and table and hearth arrangements contributed by the National Capital Area Federation of Garden Clubs. It's followed by the annual poinsettia show which lasts through the second week in January.

The B'nai B'rith Museum, 17th St. and Rhode Island Ave. NW (tel. 857-6583), usually celebrates **Hannukah** with music, storytelling, crafts, films, gallery talks, potato latkes, and more. Admission is charged.

The **Christmas Pageant of Peace/National Tree Lighting** (tel. 485-9666). On a selected Thursday in December between 5 and 6 p.m., the president lights the National Christmas Tree at the northern end of the Ellipse. The lighting, to the accompaniment of orchestral and choral music, inaugurates the two-week Pageant of Peace, a tremendous Yule celebration with seasonal music, caroling, nightly choral performances, a Nativity scene, 50 state trees, and a burning Yule log.

Call the **National Cathedral** (tel. 537-6200) to find out about their Christmas services, concerts, pageants, and special children's activities.

The Museum of American History (tel. 357-2700) puts on an annual **Trees of Christmas exhibition** from mid-December through New Year's. It features trees decorated with ornaments from countries around the world.

White House Candlelight Tours in late December allow visitors to see the Christmas holiday decorations by candlelight; tours are enhanced by string music. Call 456-2200 for information.

2. Getting There

BY AIR: Washington is served by three major airports—**Washington National Airport,** just across the Potomac in Virginia and a 15-minute drive from downtown; **Dulles International Airport,** about 45 minutes from downtown, also in Virginia; and **Baltimore-Washington International Airport,** between Baltimore and Washington about 45 minutes from downtown. Numerous domestic carriers have flights into all three airports.

Call your travel agent to find out which airline is offering the lowest fares at the time you intend to travel. Often restricted fares (e.g. those involving advance purchase or specifying a given day of return) are the most advantageous, so don't wait until the last minute to find out. When evaluating airfares, also take into consideration bus and taxi fares to and from departure and arrival airports. A low-cost flight between Newark and Baltimore–Washington Airports, for instance, might end up costing a New Yorker more in ground transportation that a slightly higher-priced—and probably more convenient—fare between LaGuardia and National. Taxi and bus fares listed below will help you make these computations.

One carrier that serves not only Washington, D.C., but many of the other destinations detailed in this book is **Piedmont Airlines** (tel. 212/489-1460 or 800/251-5720). In Virginia it serves Charlottesville, Williamsburg (via Newport News, the closest airport), and Richmond, and in Maryland, Baltimore.

Getting to and from the Airports

Taxi fare to downtown from Washington National Airport is about $7, from Dulles International it's about $30, and from Baltimore-Washington, about $40.

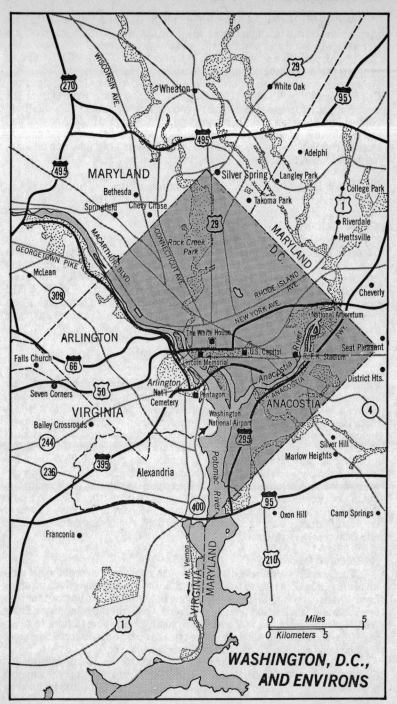

WASHINGTON, D.C.,
AND ENVIRONS

Washington National Airport is right on the Blue and Yellow Metro lines from which you can reach just about any point in town. Courtesy van service is provided between the airport terminal and the Metro station.

The **Airport Connection** (tel. 685-1400 or toll free 800/431-5472) runs buses between two hotels (the Capitol and Washington Hiltons) and the Baltimore-Washington Airport, with departures about every 45 minutes in each direction. Call for exact times. The fare is $12 each way; children under 6 travel free. The same company operates **Washington Flyer** buses between five D.C. hotels (both Hiltons, the Sheraton, the Shoreham, and J. W. Marriott) and National and Dulles Airports, once again with departures about every 45 minutes in each direction. For National, the fare is $5 one way, $9 round trip (children under 6, free); for Dulles, $11 one way, $19 round trip (children under 6, free).

BY TRAIN: Historic **Union Station** at Massachusetts Ave. and North Capitol St. is the **Amtrak** terminal here. It's conveniently located, and connects with Metro service. There are also plenty of taxis available at all times. For rail reservations, contact Amtrak (tel. toll free 800/USA-RAIL).

BY BUS: Both Greyhound and Trailways buses connect just about the entire country with Washington, D.C. Compare prices, and do inquire about moneysaving excursion fares. **Greyhound** buses pull in at 1110 New York Ave. NW (tel. 565-2662), **Trailways** buses at 1st and L Sts. NE (tel. 737-5800). The closest Metro station to Greyhound is Metro Center; to Trailways, Union Station. Neither terminal is in a showplace neighborhood, so if you arrive at night, a taxi is advisable.

3. Getting Oriented

VISITOR INFORMATION: The spiffy **Washington Tourist Information Center** opened in 1983 in the Great Hall of the Department of Commerce Building, between 14th and 15th Sts. on Pennsylvania Avenue NW (tel. 789-7000). A block from the White House, it provides information on every aspect of Washington tourism and stocks a vast supply of free maps, brochures, and promotional literature of interest to visitors. On hand are volunteers from Travelers Aid and International Visitors Information Service (more about both of these immediately below). The center's friendly and knowledgeable staff can answer all your Washington-related questions. This service is operated by the Washington, D.C., Convention and Visitors Association, and is open from 9 a.m. to 5 p.m. daily mid-April through the end of September, Monday to Saturday the rest of the year. Phones are answered on weekdays only. A gift shop on the premises sells quality souvenir items.

For Troubled Travelers

The **Travelers Aid Society** is a nationwide, voluntary nonprofit social service agency providing help to travelers in difficulty. This might include anything from emotional counseling to straightening out of ticket mix-ups, not to mention reuniting families accidentally separated while traveling, locating missing relatives (sometimes just at the wrong airport), and helping retrieve lost baggage (also sometimes at the wrong airport). They even offer financial assistance for food and/or shelter if you're stranded without cash.

In addition to the above-mentioned location at the Tourist Information Center, Travelers Aid has a central office at 1015 12th St. NW, open 9 a.m. to 5 p.m. weekdays, and has a 24-hour phone number (tel. 347-0101) manned by professionals.

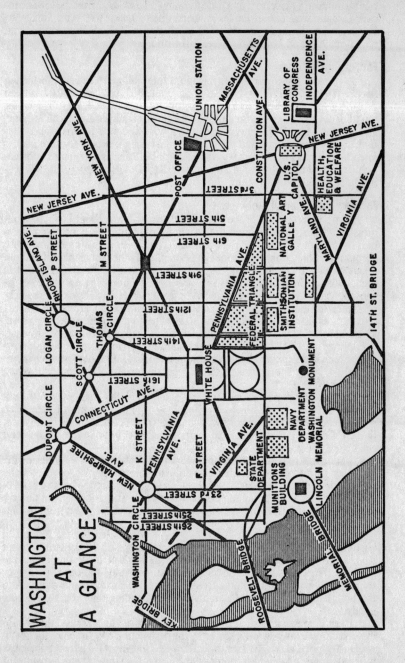

WASHINGTON AT A GLANCE

There are also **Travelers Aid** desks at National Airport, open 9 a.m. to 9 p.m. Sunday to Friday, to 6 p.m. on Saturday (tel. 684-3472); on the lower concourse at the west end of Dulles Airport, open 10 a.m. to 9 p.m. Sunday to Friday, to 6 p.m. on Saturday (tel. 661-8636); and at Union Station, open seven days from 9:30 a.m. to 5:30 p.m. (tel. 347-0101).

For Foreign Visitors

A private, not-for-profit organization, **International Visitors Information Service (IVIS),** 733 15th St. NW, at H St., Suite 300 (tel. 783-6540), has been providing special services to foreign visitors for over two decades. They offer multilingual assistance (volunteers who speak 55 languages are on call 24 hours a day—after 11 p.m., for emergencies only), with accommodations, transportation, sightseeing, dining, and other traditional tourist needs. The office itself is open Monday to Friday from 9 a.m. to 5 p.m. IVIS also maintains an information desk at the International Arrivals Area of Dulles Airport (tel. 703/661-8747). It's open every day from noon to 7 p.m.

For Servicepeople on Active Duty

If you're in the service, you probably already know about **USO,** the congressionally chartered, nonprofit agency representing civilian concern for members of the armed forces and their families. You can stop by for assistance with accommodations, transportation, sightseeing, and other travel needs; find out about dozens of cultural events and recreational activities in the Washington area, many of them USO-sponsored for service families (these include barbecues, bowling nights, lectures, wine and cheese parties, etc.); pick up free tickets (when available) to theaters and sporting events; and learn about District discounts available on tours and travel, at hotels, restaurants, and elsewhere. Or perhaps you'd just like a free cup of coffee in the lounge and a friendly chat. The lounge has a TV, books, magazines, stationery, phones, lockers, and showers for men and women. Whatever your problems, USO is here to solve them. Call 879-4700 for information on theater/sporting events tickets and VIP White House tours.

The Washington headquarters, the Bob Hope USO Building at 601 Indiana Ave., near the Archives Metro (tel. 783-8117), is open from 10 a.m. to 6 p.m. weekdays, to 5 p.m. weekends (you can write for information in advance; the ZIP Code is 20004). Weekend hours are subject to volunteer availability; call before you go.

There's also a USO Center complete with TV lounge and free coffee on the first floor of the North Terminal of National Airport (tel. 920-6990). At the same airport, also in the North Terminal, is a USO information booth (tel. 920-2705). They're staffed by volunteers, so hours do vary occasionally, but they try to keep one or the other of these airport facilities open seven days from 10 a.m. to 9 p.m.

GETTING YOUR BEARINGS: Though explanations of Washington's layout have a way of sounding impossibly complicated, it's actually a pretty simple business. The city is laid out on a graph paper-like grid, and once you understand how it works, you're home free (or at least able to find your way back to the hotel). It will help immeasurably if, when reading this, you have a map handy.

Even if you've never been to the capital, you've likely noticed that Washington addresses are always followed by the designation NW (it stands for northwest), NE (northeast), SW (southwest), or SE (southeast). These are the city's four quadrants, all of which center on the Capitol building. If you look at your map, you'll see that some addresses, say, the corner of G and 7th Streets, appear in four different places. That's why you must pay careful attention to the quadrant designation.

East Capitol Street (conveniently located east of the Capitol) divides the city north and south. Streets below it and above it are alphabetically named, in both cases beginning with A. There are two important exceptions. In most of the District, what should be South B Street is called Independence Avenue (it's the southern border of the Mall), and what should be North B Street is called Constitution Avenue (it's the northern border of the Mall).

Numbered streets, beginning with East 1st Street and West 1st Street begin on either side of the Capitol.

Lettered streets run east to west, and numbered streets run north to south.

That's the simple part. **Avenues** (named for states) run at angles across the grid pattern and often intersect at traffic circles (for instance, New Hampshire, Connecticut, and Massachusetts Avenues all intersect at Dupont Circle).

A few other things you should know: I Street is often written as "Eye" Street to prevent confusion with 1st Street—and there is no J Street. According to Washington legend, L'Enfant so disliked John Jay that he omitted a J Street in his city plan. Also, after W Street in both directions (X, Y, and Z Streets don't exist), a confusing system of two-syllable alphabetically named streets (like Adams, Bryant, College—but it's seldom that orderly) begins. However, chances are you won't be spending much time that far north or south.

Finding an Address

Finding a specific address is a piece of cake. The White House, for instance, at 1600 Pennsylvania Ave. NW, is in the northwest quadrant at 16th Street and Pennsylvania Avenue. If it were at 1625 Pennsylvania Ave. it would be between 16th and 17th Streets. Similarly, 1900 K St. NW is at the corner of 19th and K Streets in the northwest quadrant. An address like 1940 K St. NW would be between 19th and 20th Streets, 1730 K St. NW is between 17th and 18th Streets, 615 I St. NW is between 6th and 7th Streets. In other words, in a four-digit address the first two digits indicate the lower-numbered cross street, and in a three-digit address the first digit indicates the lower-numbered cross street.

To find an address on a numbered (north-south) street, you'll probably have to use your fingers. The blocks between A and B Streets (actually Constitution and Independence Avenues) going north or south are the 100 blocks, the blocks between B and C Streets going north or south are the 200 blocks, the blocks between C and D Streets going north or south are the 300 blocks, and so on. Hence an address like 819 15th St. NW is between H and I Streets in the northwest quadrant, H being the eighth letter in the alphabet. Get it? If not, just ask someone.

WASHINGTON AREAS: What do people mean when they talk about Capitol Hill, the Mall, downtown, etc.? The following brief paragraphs describe D.C.'s major areas.

The Mall

This lovely tree-lined stretch of open space between Constitution and Independence Avenues, extending for 2½ miles from the Capitol to the Lincoln Memorial, is the hub of tourist attractions. It includes nine Smithsonian Institution museums, and many other visitor attractions are close by. The 300-foot-wide Mall is used by natives as well as tourists—joggers, food vendors, kite-flyers, and picnickers among them. It's also the setting for festivals and occasional baseball games. In summer, an old-fashioned carousel in front of the Arts and Industries Building enhances its park-like atmosphere.

Downtown

Roughly the area between 7th and 22nd Streets NW going east to west, and P Street and Pennsylvania Avenue going north to south, downtown is a mix of Federal Triangle's government office buildings, K Street and Connec-ticut Avenue restaurants and shopping, F Street department stores, and much more. Too large an area to have a consistent character, it contains lovely Lafayette Park, Washington's tiny porno district, its slightly larger Chinatown, the Washington, D.C., Convention Center, and a half dozen or so sightseeing attractions.

Capitol Hill

Everyone's heard of "the Hill," the area crowned by the Capitol which L'Enfant dramatically located on what was then Jenkins Hill (he called it "a pedestal awaiting a monument"). When people speak of Capitol Hill they refer to a large section of town, extending from the western side of the Capitol to the RFK Memorial Stadium going east, bounded by H Street NE and the Southwest Freeway north and south. It contains not only the chief symbol of the nation's capital, but the Supreme Court building, the Library of Congress, the Folger Shakespeare Library, the Museum of African Art, Union Station, and the Botanic Gardens. Much of it is a quiet residential neighborhood of tree-lined streets and Victorian homes, and there are many good restaurants in the vicinity.

Foggy Bottom

The area west of the White House to the edge of Georgetown, Foggy Bottom was Washington's early industrial center. Its name comes from the foul fumes emitted in those days by a coal depot and gasworks, but its original name, Funkstown (for owner Jacob Funk), is perhaps even worse. There's nothing foul about the area today. The Kennedy Center and George Washington University are located here. Constitution and Pennsylvania Avenues are Foggy Bottom's southern and northern boundaries, respectively.

Dupont Circle

Generally, when Washingtonians speak of Dupont Circle they don't mean just the park, they mean the area around it. The park itself, named for navy Rear Adm. Samuel Francis Dupont, is centered around D.C.'s most famous fountain, at the intersection of Connecticut and Massachusetts Avenues, and is a popular rendezvous spot. Dupont Circle is one of the liveliest sections in town, rivaled only by Georgetown for nightspots, movie theaters, and restaurants.

Georgetown

This historic community dates back to colonial times. It was a thriving tobacco port long before the District of Columbia existed, and one of its attractions, the Old Stone House, dates to pre-Revolutionary days. Georgetown action centers on M and Wisconsin Streets NW, where you'll find numerous boutiques (see Chapter VII for details), chic restaurants, and popular pubs. But do get off the main drags and see the quiet tree-lined streets of restored Colonial row houses, stroll through the beautiful gardens of Dumbarton Oaks, and check out the C&O Canal. One of the reasons so much activity flourishes in Georgetown is that it also contains the campus of Georgetown University.

Adams-Morgan

This unconventional multiethnic neighborhood (it's easy to be unconventional in D.C.; all you have to do is not wear a suit and tie) is becoming increas-

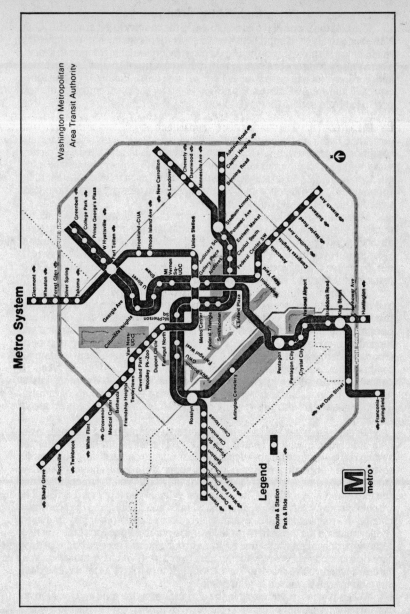

Metro System

Washington Metropolitan
Area Transit Authority

Legend

Route & Station
Park & Ride

M
metro.

ingly popular for its restaurants serving Jamaican, Ethiopian, Spanish, and other international cuisines. Try to plan at least one meal up here; it's a good opportunity to see an authentic untouristy Washington neighborhood. Adams-Morgan centers around Columbia Road and 18th Street NW.

4. Getting Around

Washington is one of the easiest towns in the country to get around in. Only New York rivals its comprehensive transportation system, but Washington's clean, efficient subways put the Big Apple's underground nightmare to shame. There's also a complex bus system with routes covering all major D.C. arteries, and it's easy to hail a taxi anywhere at any time. Finally, Washington— especially the areas of interest to tourists—is pretty compact, and often the best way to get from here to there is on foot.

BY METRORAIL: The stations are immaculate, cool, and attractive, with terracotta floors and high, vaulted ceilings; the sleek subway cars are air-conditioned, carpeted, furnished with upholstered seats, and fitted with picture windows; the tracks are rubber-cushioned so the ride is quiet; the service is frequent enough that you usually get a seat; for safety, each train has instant radio communications with police and security forces; and the system is so simply designed that a 10-year-old can understand it.

Metrorail's 64 stations and 70 miles of track (87 stations and 103 miles of track are the eventual goal) include locations at or near almost every sightseeing attraction and extend to suburban Maryland and northern Virginia. If you're in Washington even for a few days you'll probably have occasion to use the system, but if you don't, I suggest you create one—perhaps dinner at a Dupont Circle restaurant. Metro is a sightseeing attraction in its own right.

There are four lines in operation at this writing, the **Red, Blue, Orange, and Yellow Lines,** with a Green Line and extensions of the others in the works for the future. The lines connect at several points, making transfers easy. Metro stations are indicated by discreet brown columns bearing the station's name and topped by the letter "M." Below the "M," at most stations, is a colored stripe or stripes indicating which of the lines it serves. When entering a Metro station for the first time, ask the kiosk attendant for a free copy of *All About Metro*. It contains a map of the system, explains how it works, lists parking lots at Metrorail stations, and indicates the closest Metro stops to points of interest. The attendant can also answer any questions about routing or purchase of farecards.

To enter or exit a Metro station you need a computerized farecard, available at vending machines near the entrance. The minimum fare to enter the system is 80¢—it could go up—which pays for rides to and from any point within seven miles of boarding during non-rush hours; during rush hours (weekdays from 6 to 9:30 a.m. and 3 to 6:30 p.m.) 80¢ only takes you for three miles, and the maximum fare is $2.40. The maximum value allowed per card is $30. The machines take nickels, dimes, quarters, $1 bills, and $5 bills, and they can make change. If you plan to make several Metrorail trips during your stay, put more money value on the farecard to avoid having to purchase one each time you ride. Otherwise you might waste time standing on long lines. There's a bonus of a 5% fare discount on everything you purchase over $10. If you have money on your farecard when you're ready to leave town, just turn it in to a station attendant; the amount will be mailed to your home.

When you insert your card in the entrance gate, the time and location are recorded on its magnetic tape and your card is returned. Don't forget to snatch it up, and keep it handy. You have to reinsert it in the exit gate at your destination where the fare will automatically be deducted. Again the card will be returned if there's any value left on it. If you arrive at a destination and your farecard doesn't have enough money on it, add what's necessary at the Addfare machines near the exit gate.

If you're planning to continue your travel via Metrobus, pick up a transfer at the station where you enter the system (*not* your destination station) from the transfer machine on the mezzanine. It's good for full fare within D.C., and gives you a discount on bus fares in Maryland and Virginia. There are no bus-to-subway transfers.

Metrorail operates Monday to Friday from 6 a.m. to midnight, on Saturday from 8 a.m. to midnight, and on Sunday from 10 a.m. to midnight. A Saturday or Sunday schedule is in effect on most holidays.

BY METROBUS: While any 10-year-old could understand the Metrorail system, the Metrobus system would probably perplex Einstein. The 10,000 stops on the 2200-square-mile route (it operates on all major D.C. arteries and in the Virginia and Maryland suburbs) are indicated by red, white, and blue signs. However, the signs just tell you what buses pull into a given stop (if that), not where they go. For routing information, call 637-7000. Using a computer, a transit information agent can tell you the most efficient route from where you are to where you want to go (using bus and/or subway) almost instantly. Calls are taken daily between 6 a.m. and 11:30 p.m., but the line is often busy, so don't wait until the last minute to call.

If you travel the same route frequently and would like a free map and time schedule, ask the bus driver or call 637-7000 and request one. Information about free parking in Metrobus fringe lots is also available from this number.

Fares in the city are 75¢ during off-peak hours, 80¢ during rush hours (6 to 9:30 a.m. and 3 to 6:30 p.m. weekdays). During nonpeak hours the fare is $1.60 into Virginia and $1.25 into Maryland; more, depending on distance traveled, during rush hours. Transfers are available for one additional free or discounted bus ride; request one when you board. Bus drivers are not equipped to make change, so be sure to *carry exact change or tokens*. The latter are available at 250 ticket outlets (call the above number for locations and hours of operation). If you're going to be in Washington for a while, and plan to use the buses a lot, consider a two-week pass such as the $15 **D.C. Only Pass** good for unlimited Metrobus rides within the District and $4 worth of Metrorail rides. These are also available at ticket outlets. Others include zones in Virginia or Maryland.

Most buses operate daily between 6 a.m. and 11:30 p.m. Service is very frequent on weekdays, especially during rush hours. On weekends, your wait will be a bit longer.

There's a full bus information center at Metro Center Station (12th and F Sts.) where tokens, special bus tickets, and all else is available.

On Buses and Subways

Up to two children under 5 ride free with a paying passenger, and there are reduced fares for senior citizens (tel. 637-7000), and the handicapped (tel. 962-1245). Finally, should you leave something on a bus, on a train, or in a station, call Lost and Found at 962-1195.

BY CAR: Within the District a car is a luxury since public transportation is so comprehensive. It can even be an inconvenience, especially during spring and summer when traffic jams are frequent, parking spaces almost nonexistent, and parking lots ruinously expensive. But there's a great deal to see in the D.C. vicinity, and for most attractions in Virginia and Maryland you will want a car.

Budget Rent-a-Car, with a convenient downtown office at 1200 K St. NW (tel. 628-2750 or toll free 800/527-0700), is also represented at all three airports. You can reserve at any location via the 800 number. Budget offers some of the lowest prices in town and a fleet mix that runs the gamut from seven-passenger Dodge Caravans to luxury Lincoln town cars to a wide selection of economy cars. At this writing you can rent an economy car from Thursday noon to Monday noon for under $30 with 100 free miles a day! That's hard to beat. And in any Budget car you rent, at any time, a portable cellular phone is available for $3 a day plus 95¢ a minute for calls. Cars rented in town can be dropped at the airport at no extra charge and vice versa.

Also represented at all airports and in town at 12th and K Sts. NW and 1618 L St. NW is **National Car Rental** (tel. toll free 800/328-4567).

BY TAXI: Surprise! You can take taxis in Washington without busting your budget—at least in some cases. District cabs work on a zone system. If you take a trip from one point to another in the same zone, you pay just $2.10, regardless of the distance traveled. So it would cost you $2.10 to travel a few blocks from the U.S. Botanic Garden to the Museum of American History, the same $2.10 from the Botanic Garden all the way to Dupont Circle. They're both in Zone 1. Also in Zone 1 are most other tourist attractions: the Capitol, the White House, most of the Smithsonian, the Washington Monument, the FBI, the National Archives, the Supreme Court, the Library of Congress, the Bureau of Engraving and Printing, the Old Post Office, and Ford's Theatre. If your trip takes you into a second zone, the price is $3, $3.90 for a third zone, $4.75 for a fourth, $5.50 for a fifth, and so on. But you're unlikely to travel more than three zones unless you're staying in some remote section of town.

So far fares are pretty low. Here's how they can add up. There's a $1.25 charge for each additional passenger after the first, so a $2.10 Zone 1 fare becomes $5.85 for a family of four (though one child under 6 can ride free). There's also a rush-hour surcharge of $1 per trip between 4 and 6:30 p.m. weekdays. And there are charges for large pieces of luggage ($1.25 per piece) and for calling a taxi (65¢).

It's generally quite easy to hail a taxi in the District; there are about 9000 cabs, and drivers are allowed to pick up as many passengers as they can comfortably fit in. Expect to share. You can also call a taxi. Try **Diamond Cab Company** (tel. 387-6200), **Yellow Cab** (tel. 544-1212), or **Capitol Cab** (tel. 546-2400).

BY TOURMOBILE: What, you may ask, are those blue-and-white tourist-filled trams you see throughout the Mall area? They're Tourmobiles, sightseeing buses run by Landmark Services under contract to the National Parks Service that makes stops at major sightseeing attractions. Tourmobile's unique feature is unlimited free reboarding throughout the day. You can begin your tour at any stop.

There are six Tourmobile tours to choose from. The most popular is the **Washington and Arlington Cemetery Tour,** a fully narrated service (all Tourmobile tours provide informative commentary) with stops at 15 historic sites:

The White House
The Washington Monument
The Arts and Industries Building
The National Air and Space Museum
Union Station
The Capitol
The National Gallery of Art
The Museum of Natural History
The Museum of American History
The Bureau of Engraving and Printing
The Jefferson Memorial
West Potomac Park

The Kennedy Center
The Lincoln Memorial
Arlington Cemetery Visitors Center: Gravesites of John F. and Robert
F. Kennedy/Tomb of the Unknowns/Arlington House, the Robert E. Lee
Memorial

A fare of $7 for adults, $3.50 for children ages 3 to 11, allows you to get off
or on at any stop as many times as you like from 9 a.m. to 6:30 p.m. June 15
through Labor Day (from 9:30 a.m. to 4:30 p.m. the rest of the year). Tickets
can be purchased from any Tourmobile driver or at Tourmobile ticket booths at
some sites.

Is It Worth It?

The Washington and Arlington Cemetery Tour can be a great convenience, but its value depends largely on your sightseeing itinerary. You can always save time and money by planning to see close-together attractions on the
same day. If most of your sights are clustered, and only one or two are out of the
way, consider whether cabs would be cheaper. Remember, you can't see all 18
sights in one day. Also, in tourist season lines are so long that you might miss the
first Tourmobile that pulls in and have to wait for another. You can sometimes
waste valuable vacation time in this manner.

Other Tourmobile Tours

The **Arlington National Cemetery Tour.** If you get to Arlington on your
own steam, you'll probably want to spend the $2.25 for adults, $1 for children,
to ride around this 617-acre cemetery and make stops at the gravesites and memorials. As on any Tourmobile excursion, you can get off at any site for as long
as you like and reboard when you're ready. Without Tourmobile, you're in for a
lot of walking here, which could be very nice or practically devastating, depending on the weather. In summer I'd definitely opt for Tourmobile. It operates
from 8 a.m. to 6:30 p.m. April to September, till 4:30 p.m. the rest of the year.
This ticket is sold only at Arlington Cemetery.

If you don't have a car, another good deal is the **Mount Vernon Tour,** departing daily from Arlington National Cemetery, the Lincoln Memorial, and
the Washington Monument at 10 a.m., noon, and 2 p.m., April through October. The round-trip fare of $13.50 for adults and $6.25 for children includes admission to George Washington's estate and a scenic 17-mile drive (in an
air-conditioned vehicle) along the Potomac and through Alexandria's Old
Town. You must make reservations (at any of the three departure sites) at least
an hour in advance.

The **Combination Tour of Washington, Arlington Cemetery, and Mount
Vernon** combines everything described above and gives you two consecutive
days to see it. It operates from 9 a.m. to 6 p.m. April to October, and tickets can
be purchased from Tourmobile drivers or at a ticket booth. Adults pay $21; chil-
dren $10.

Finally, there's the **Frederick Douglass Home Tour,** which includes a
guided tour of Cedar Hill, the home of ex-slave, abolitionist, orator, statesman,
and author Frederick Douglass. Departures are from Arlington National Cemetery, the Lincoln Memorial, and the Washington Monument at 10 a.m. and 1
p.m. daily between June 15 and Labor Day. Like the Mount Vernon tour, reservations must be made at least an hour in advance. Adults pay $5; children,
$2.50. A two-day **Combination Frederick Douglass Home and Washington, Ar-
lington Cemetery Tour** is also available at $13 for adults, $6.50 for children.

For further Tourmobile information, call 554-7020.

Chapter II

FINDING BUDGET LODGINGS

IT GETS HARDER EVERY YEAR, but savvy tourists can still find clean, comfortable, low-cost lodgings in Washington, D.C. One boon to budgeteers are the weekend rates offered at so many otherwise high-priced establishments. Many are specified in the following pages.

A good idea is to utilize the free service offered by **Capitol Reservations,** 1201 K St. NW, Washington, DC 20005 (tel. 202/842-4187 or toll free 800/VISIT-DC). They'll find a hotel to suit your specific requirements, and procure the best possible rates. "Because of the high volume of room nights we book," explains owner Thom Hall, "some properties offer discounts to the public available only through this service." Their listings begin at about $55 a night for a double, all have been screened for cleanliness and general desirability, and all are in very safe neighborhoods. Calling Capitol Reservations is like checking with your travel agent for the lowest airfares.

WASHINGTON'S WONDERFUL WEEKENDS: Weekends, and sometimes off-season weekdays as well, D.C. hotel prices at properties ranging from budget to five-star are slashed 30% to 50%. That means you can stay at a top luxury property and pay the tariff of a medium-priced hotel, at a moderate hotel for budget rates—or at a budget hotel for peanuts, reserving your extra cash for good restaurants.

When you make reservations, always inquire about special rates and packages. Be sure to verify that your reservation has been made at weekend rates before hanging up, and check on it again when you register. At many hotels, you can't just turn up at the desk on Monday morning and expect to get weekend rates; you have to be so registered in advance.

Full details on over 65 lodging places featuring special weekend and holiday rates are available from the **Hotel Association of Washington, DC.,** P.O. Box 33578, Washington, DC 20033 (tel. 202/833-3350). Write or call for a gratis copy of their very helpful *Washington Weekends* brochure.

Taj International Hotels, 1315 16th St. NW, Washington, DC 20036 (tel. 202/462-7104 or toll free 800/DC-VISIT), are the owners of some of India's most posh hotels, among them Udaipur's Lake Palace which was featured in the James Bond movie *Octopussy* and the famed Taj Mahal Hotel in Bombay. So what has this to do with Washington, DC? In the 1970s Taj expanded operations to the U.S., and this prestige firm now operates five properties—ranging from the low moderate to the luxury class—right here in the District. And at all of these properties they offer weekend rates that are not only very competitive but are extended to include available weekdays November through February and during July and August. Some Taj hotels also feature frequent promotional packages with perks like champagne and chocolate upon arrival, discounted meals, etc. Over two thirds of the rooms in the Taj network are actually suites with complete kitchens, equipped for in-room cooking and dining upon request. When you call the above-listed toll free number, you put yourself in line for all 660-plus rooms of the Taj network, and the reservations person who takes your call will tell you the best deal to fit your budget. Sometimes, when occupancy is low, that will mean a luxury room at a surprisingly low price. In addition to the two Taj properties detailed in this chapter (the Quality Inn and Ramada Inn Central) the network includes the Marbury Hotel in the heart of Georgetown, offering a popular nightclub, lavish Sunday buffet brunches, and a swimming pool; the Canterbury, located on the site of Theodore Roosevelt's home; and the Hampshire, home of Lafitte, Washington's premier Créole restaurant. The latter two are exquisite residential-style hostelries. All offer very central locations.

FOR GROUPS ONLY: If you're planning a group function, meeting, or convention, there's a service in Washington you'll want to contact. **U.S.A. Groups** (tel. toll free 800/USA-GRPS) is a referral agency for function planners (both corporate and leisure) that represents over 12,000 hotel rooms in the District and surrounding areas, including Baltimore and Williamsburg. Their participating hotels run the gamut from low cost to luxury, and they'll work hard to match you up with the property that best fits your group's needs and budget. Unlike a hotel sales office, which is geared to filling rooms regardless of suitability, U.S.A. Groups is primarily interested in meeting your specifications. One call to this organization can save you dozens of phone inquiries about rates, facilities, location, etc. And best of all, whether you book through them or not, there's no charge for the service.

FINDING LODGINGS TO MEET YOUR BUDGET: Though it won't work in high season, one good tactic is to bargain at the desk, especially if it's late in the afternoon. You do, of course, take the risk of being snubbed, but at least half the time a hotel with vacant rooms will negotiate. The best way to ensure low rates is to reserve far in advance. The least expensive hostelries are the first to fill up. Plan ahead and you'll have the greatest number of options.

In budget hotels, the first room you see might be a bit disappointing (all right, maybe even dismal). Before you storm out, however, ask to see some other rooms. They often vary considerably.

Many hotels give discounts to students, government employees, senior citizens, and military personnel, so if you belong to one of those groups, be sure to inquire.

The following section is divided geographically, beginning with the most central locations and moving outward to the Virginia and Maryland suburbs. Most of these suburban listings are close to Metro stops, so you can whiz right into the center of town easily. Within each geographic category is a mix of low-cost hotels, guest houses, weekend specials, and student hostelries. Following those listings are special categories like bed-and-breakfast accommodations, a service for women only, and a roommate-finding service.

For your ease in writing for reservations, I have included the ZIP Code for each address, although I haven't repeated the words "Washington, D.C.," every time.

1. Downtown/Chinatown

COMFORT PLUS: The new Comfort Inn at 500 H St. NW, 20001 (tel. 202/289-5959 or toll free 800/228-5150), is part of a new chain created in late 1985. A lower-budget offshoot of the Quality Inn chain, the Comfort concept has caught on like wildfire, with 330 properties created in two years, 85% of them new constructions. The Washington Comfort Inn opened in December, 1986, and if you stay here, you'll quickly see the reason this venture is such a success. The theory behind it is that a low-cost hotel needn't be a no-frills hotel, nor need it be an aesthetic nonentity. The 197 rooms here (most of them double doubles) are very nicely decorated with light brown carpeting, muted blue cotton bedspreads and curtains, and grasspaper-look wall coverings. Each has a full bath with a large tub, a table with two chairs, color TV (with pay movies, Showtime, ESPN, and CNN stations), a digital alarm clock, direct-dial phone, and AM/FM radio. Even the hallways are notably nice, carpeted in forest green with Chinese-motif border. (You'll see other Oriental nuances here, all very appropriate since this hotel is in the heart of D.C.'s little Chinatown.) There are non-smoking and handicapped-equipped rooms, and on-premises facilities include a coin-op laundry, parking ($5 a day), even a sunny exercise room on the 10th floor with Universal equipment and a sauna. A restaurant on the premises, Cafe Express, offers reasonably priced fresh-cooked fare in a very pretty setting; decorated in teal and peach, it has a wall of windows hung with swagged floral-print drapes and tables adorned with fresh flowers. Of course, numerous Chinese restaurants are within a block's walk as well. From the minute you enter the well-lit lobby, furnished with plush sofas and chairs, you'll feel welcome and secure here. There's a Metro stop a little over a block away, and Smithsonian museums —plus many other tourist attractions—are also within easy walking distance. All in all, this is an excellent choice for the budget traveler.

Regular rates at the Comfort Inn are low moderate—$62 single, $72 double, $10 for an extra person, children under 18 free. But the weekend rate, offered Thursday through Sunday, is just $50 per room for up to four adults, with complimentary parking as an added bonus. Reserve as far in advance as possible.

Another excellent budget chain is **Days Inn,** here very centrally represented by the **Days Inn Downtown,** 1201 K St. NW, 20005 (tel. 202/842-1020 or toll free 800/562-3350), just three blocks from the Metro Center subway station. And the great news is that Days Inns around the country have inaugurated a Super Saver rate of just $39 a night, any night, single or double, if you reserve 30 days in advance via the above 800 number. That just can't be beat! This is a very well-run property. Its 220 rooms are cheerfully decorated in blue or rust color schemes and equipped with AM/FM radios, color TVs with HBO movie stations, and all the other expected motel amenities. They've all undergone a recent renovation, so paint, wallpaper, carpeting, drapes, and bedspreads are in top condition. Kids will enjoy the small rooftop pool with sundeck and video game room. Grown-ups will like the complimentary Happy Hour buffets served weekdays from 5 to 8 p.m. in the lounge. And everyone will like Buckley's Grill, the hotel's very affordable but excellent nautically themed restaurant specializing in mesquite-grilled seafood, baby back ribs, Creole specialties, and gourmet pizzas. Great desserts here, too. This is one hotel eatery much frequented by locals, myself included.

Regular rates are, once again, low moderate; $62 single, $68 for two people in a room with one double bed, $74 for two people in a room with two double beds, $6 for an extra person, free for children under 17. Weekend rate, offered Friday, Saturday, and Sunday nights, is $58 single or double. Valet parking is $4 a night.

Harrington Hotel, 11th and E Sts. NW, 20004 (tel. 202/628-8140 or toll free 800/424-8532). Right in the heart of downtown (Metro Center station is just two blocks away), the 11-story Harrington offers 300 budget rooms and a few pleasant extras. You'll find a chocolate mint on your bureau when you check in, and a free morning newspaper will be delivered daily. These are nice touches in a budget hotel, letting you know the management cares. The rooms are clean and adequately, if not aesthetically, furnished. Most have cream-colored walls, red shag carpeting, and cheerful prints that create a homey touch; some, on the other hand, have fluorescent lights. They vary, so if the hotel's not fully booked and the first room you see fails to please, ask to see another. All rooms have color TV, air conditioning, switchboard phone, and tub/shower bath. If you're traveling by car, it's nice to know that parking is free, though in-and-out privileges cost $1. You probably won't need your car much; the hotel is within easy walking distance of the Mall and other attractions. On-premises facilities include Kitcheteria, a cheerful cafeteria with red-leather furnishings and gaslight-style wall sconces. Open daily from 7 a.m. to 9 p.m. it offers budget fare (like roast beef, mashed potatoes, and lima beans at $4, and a dessert of fresh-baked Boston cream pie with a cup of coffee just $1.50 more). Low-priced food is also served at the fancier candlelit and red-leather-boothed Café and in Beefe 'n Rolle, a comfortable self-service coffeeshop. A pay laundry, barbershop, and gift shop round out the amenities.

Rates are $48 to $52 single, $60 to $66 double or twin, $6 for an extra bed; children stay free in a room with parents. The best deal is the Harrington's family rate: $65 for a large room that accommodates two adults and two children. On weekends, your rate includes a full breakfast.

Hotel Farragut West 1808 I St. NW, 20006 (tel. 202/393-2400). This centrally located 74-room hostelry (three blocks from the White House and close to the Farragut West Metro) is clean and cheerful. Both rooms and hallways have recently been redecorated with floral-design paneling, the former also fitted out with new gray carpeting and burgundy drapes and bedspreads. Each room is equipped with air conditioning, direct-dial phone, AM/FM radio, color TV, and full bath. There are no on-premises amenities, but you're within easy walking distance of many restaurants.

Rates are $59 single, $69 double or twin, $74 for a king-bedded room, $110 for a suite (two adjacent rooms with a king-size bed in one and two twin beds in the other or two twins in each). Weekend rate is $54 single or double if you stay both Friday and Saturday nights.

WASHINGTON'S BEST VALUE: The brand-new **Washington International**

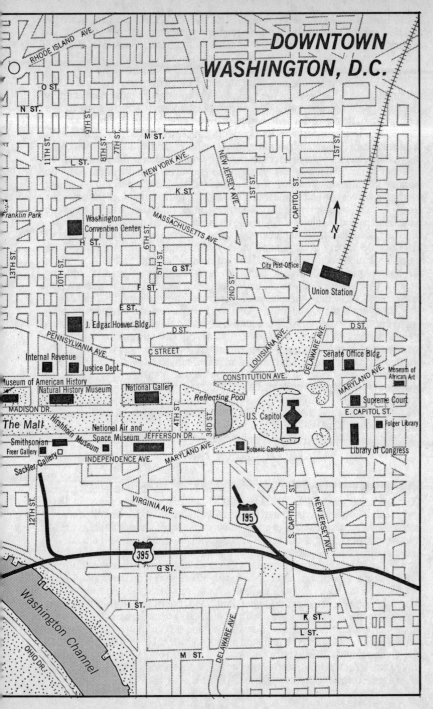

DOWNTOWN WASHINGTON, D.C.

RHODE ISLAND AVE.

O ST.

N ST.

M ST.

11TH ST.

9TH ST.

8TH ST.

7TH ST.

L ST.

NEW YORK AVE.

K ST.

MASSACHUSETTS AVE.

Franklin Park

Washington Convention Center

6TH ST.

5TH ST.

H ST.

13TH ST.

10TH ST.

G ST.

F ST.

NEW JERSEY AVE.

1ST ST.

1ST ST.

N. CAPITOL ST.

City Post Office

Union Station

E ST.

J. Edgar Hoover Bldg.

D ST.

D ST.

PENNSYLVANIA AVE.

Internal Revenue

Justice Dept.

C STREET

LOUISIANA AVE.

DELAWARE AVE.

Senate Office Bldg.

MARYLAND AVE.

Museum of African Art

CONSTITUTION AVE.

Museum of American History

Natural History Museum

National Gallery

Reflecting Pool

U.S. Capitol

Supreme Court

E. CAPITOL ST.

Folger Library

MADISON DR.

4TH ST.

3RD ST.

The Mall

Hirshhorn Museum

National Air and Space Museum

JEFFERSON DR.

Botanic Garden

Library of Congress

Smithsonian

Freer Gallery

Sackler Gallery

INDEPENDENCE AVE.

MARYLAND AVE.

12TH ST.

VIRGINIA AVE.

395

S. CAPITOL ST.

NEW JERSEY AVE.

395

G ST.

Washington Channel

I ST.

K ST.

L ST.

OHIO DR.

M ST.

DELAWARE AVE.

Youth Hostel, 1009 11th St. NW, 20001 (tel. 202/737-2333), is a very welcome addition to the District's budget lodging picture. Nearing completion at press-time, it will be fully operational by the time you read this. Therefore, though I was able to view only the gutted eight-story brick building that will house the new hostel, I'll describe it as a *fait accompli*. More details next edition.

Three blocks from Metro Center Station, a block from the Greyhound bus terminal, and six blocks from the Mall, WIYH couldn't be more conveniently placed. And though accommodations are in dorm rooms (four to eight beds to a room) with baths down the hall, it offers many facilities you won't find at a hotel. These include a comfortable lounge with armchairs and sofas, a huge self-service kitchen (stoves, refrigerators, sinks) where you can do your own cook-ing (basic foods and other necessaries can be purchased on the premises), an adjacent dining room with a wall of windows overlooking the street, coin-op laundry machines and storage lockers, and indoor bicycle parking. A dining room that serves cooked meals is in the works for the future. Near the entrance is an information center, staffed by knowledgeable volunteers, where guests can pick up maps and brochures. You'll also be given a free guidebook written espe-cially for hostellers detailing local sights and services. And WIYH itself gene-rates a wide variety of activities—movies, lectures, travel seminars, walking tours, cookouts, volleyball games, international nights, etc. Since the property has just opened, all rooms and public areas are freshly painted and spanking clean. As for your fellow guests, undesirables are weeded out, so this is a per-fectly safe place to stay—or send your grandmother or young adult kids to stay.

Rates are just $10 a night for AYH members; everyone else pays an addi-tional temporary membership fee (one time only) of three dollars. An annual membership in AYH is $20. Anyone can stay, but since dorms are for men or women only, couples are, of course, separated. Maximum stay is three nights, but that limit may be extended with permission, subject to available space. You must supply your own linens, towels, and soap (blankets and pillows are provided); sleeping bags are not allowed. You can rent the requisite sleep sheet here for $1 a night or buy one. Call as far in advance as possible to reserve (there are only 250 beds and they go fast), and guarantee your reservation with a 50% deposit. *Note:* There is a midnight curfew here.

2. Capitol Hill

FOR WOMEN ONLY: Thompson-Markward Hall, 235 2nd St. NE, between Maryland Ave. and C St., 20002 (tel. 202/546-3255), was established in 1887, and Eleanor Roosevelt dedicated its "new" building in 1932. The ambience is a bit old-fashioned: one might even call it ladylike. All of the public areas are at-tractively furnished and carpeted. There's a recreation room with a color TV and a refrigerator for guest use; a living room with piano, fireplace (ablaze in winter), comfortable armchairs and sofas; a dining room with white-shuttered windows; and a fairly extensive library with a Persian rug on the floor. A laun-dry room, a sun roof, and a delightful garden are additional amenities. Guest rooms (all singles) are air-conditioned and clean, but of the no-frills dormitory variety. Each is simply furnished with a twin bed, a dresser, a desk/chair set, a direct-dial phone, an armchair, a bookcase, and a floor lamp. Closet space is ample, bathrooms are in the hall, and guests provide their own sheets and tow-els. Thompson-Markward is for women ages 18 to 35 only. There's a minimum stay of two weeks, a maximum of two years. There's always a waiting list for the 117 rooms, so write as far in advance as possible.

Rates, including 13 substantial meals (breakfast and dinner Monday to Saturday and breakfast on Sunday): $231 for two weeks, with no reductions for longer stays. Female guests can spend the night on a cot in your room for $7, but men are not allowed above the lobby floor.

3. Dupont Circle

WEEKEND SPECIALS: The hotels listed below are first-class establishments.

Quality at a Discount

Since the Taj Group offers its weekend rates not just Friday through Sunday, but, subject to availability, weekdays much of the rest of the year as well, its two moderately priced properties, the Quality Inn Downtown and the Ramada Inn Central, merit serious consideration. Both are within walking distance of Dupont Circle, the White House, several Metro stations, K Street restaurants, and many other attractions. *Note:* Taj discount rates do fluctuate, depending on the season; you'll always do best by reserving as far in advance as possible.

The **Quality Inn Downtown,** 1315 16th St. NW (at Scott Circle), 20036 (tel. 202/232-8000 or toll free 800/368-5689), is much more luxurious than you might expect a Quality Inn to be. It has recently been charmingly redecorated throughout. The good news is that despite its plush new look, the Quality's rates remain moderate.

As at most Taj properties, its 135 rooms are actually suites, complete with dining areas and kitchens, the latter fully equipped upon request. Furnished in

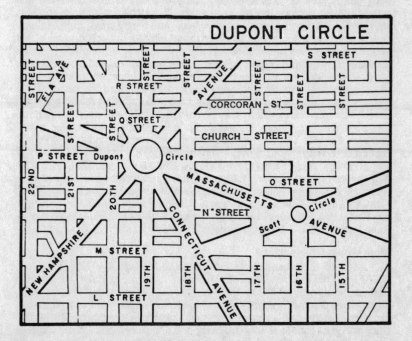

Chippendale-style cherrywood, mahogany, and pecan pieces, they're decorated in muted colors like teal blue and pale rose/mauve. Framed Chinese prints adorn raw-silk-covered walls, beds are covered in cotton chintz florals, and decorative moldings adorn the ceilings. Even the baths have been given shiny new brass fixtures and fitted out with hair dryers and phones; you'll also find a basket of fine toiletries. Other in-room amenities: a 19-inch color TV with free HBO movie channel concealed in a handsome armoire; AM/FM radio, dressing room, and a large walk-in closet. Some rooms have desks as well. The public areas of the Quality are also looking marvelous. The lobby has been refurnished with Louis XVI-style silk and velvet pieces, and hallways have raw silk wall coverings and flower-bordered forest-green carpeting. The on-premises restaurant here is the reasonably priced Bleeker's, its eclectic American menu running the gamut from delicious burritos to Maryland crabcakes (I love this restaurant's homemade brownie pie, too). It's a pleasant, plant-filled eatery, with daylight streaming in through a windowed wall (at night it's cozily candlelit). An underground parking garage, coin-op laundry, and free use of a swimming pool at a nearby hotel are other pluses here.

Regular rates are $69 to $109 single, $79 to $119 double, children under 18 free. But on weekends and off-season weekdays rates can plummet to as low as $26.50 per person per night, based on double occupancy.

The nearby **Ramada Inn Central,** 1430 Rhode Island Ave. NW, 20005 (tel. 202/462-7777 or toll free 800/368-5690), is on a quiet, tree-lined street. All but 20 of its 186 rooms are also equipped with full kitchens (request pots, pans, etc., when you check in if you want to prepare meals in your room), and the same amenities are offered. The rooms—recently redecorated with silk-look wallpapers, pearly gray or jade carpeting, pretty quilted cotton bedspreads, and framed botanical prints—are most attractive. They all have large walk-in closets with louvered doors, full-size or double beds, and dining areas. Eighteen one-bedroom suites have full sofabed living rooms plus adjoining bedrooms with a king-size bed and another sofa bed. Hallways, too, have been spiffed up in the renovation, with fresh carpeting, crystal lighting fixtures, and nice artworks. On-premises facilities are many; they include a basement laundry, a game room, and indoor parking, not to mention a rooftop pool and sundeck. Off the lobby is a pleasant, moderately priced American/continental restaurant called the Kitchen Cabinet, especially attractive when candlelit at dinner. A children's menu is a plus here. Guests enjoy cocktails in the Civil Servant Lounge, a cozy pub with a sofa and velvet-upholstered chairs grouped around a fireplace and framed historic prints and photos lining the walls.

Ramada's regular rates are moderate—$69 to $99 single, $79 to $109 double, children under 18 free. But once again, those weekend rates offered on weekdays half the year make this a very plausible budget option at just $55 per night, single or double, in any accommodation. Reserve in time and you might even get a one-bedroom suite for that price. With its swimming pool and in-room kitchens, this is a great choice for families with kids.

More Weekend Specials

At the 65-suite **General Scott Inn,** 1464 Rhode Island Ave. NW, 20005 (tel. 202/333-6700 or toll free 800/424-2496), rooms are exceptionally tasteful, with framed fine art prints (like David Hockney) adorning grasscloth-covered walls; hand-woven designer draperies on the windows; carpeted baths with plush towels, special soaps, and a shower massage; pantry kitchens equipped with fine china and glassware as well as cookware and appliances; and Breuer chairs at chrome-and-glass tables. Of course modern amenities—color TV, air conditioning, direct-dial phone, and clock radio—are present and accounted for. Weekdays, breakfast and dinner are served in a charming room adjoining the lobby. Laundry machines are available, and there's limited parking (not free) on the premises. Regular rates, including complimentary breakfast (croissants, danish, juice, and tea or coffee), are $70 single, $80 double, $10 per additional person (children under 16 free). But on weekends, if you stay two nights (Friday and Saturday or Saturday and Sunday), the rate is just $49 per night, single or double, with complimentary parking but no breakfast.

EUROPEAN STYLE, BUDGET PRICE: The **Gralyn,** 1745 N St. NW, 20036 (tel. 202/785-1515), is a European-style hotel in a four-story Georgian brick town house that once housed an embassy. Its somewhat faded old-world elegance begins in the burgundy-carpeted lobby with its plush velvet furnishings, a gilt-framed mirror, and fireplace. The 34 rooms vary considerably. Some have high ceilings, carved-wood fireplaces, oak wainscoting, ornate carved beds, or Victorian sofas; others are smaller and less charming. All have switchboard phones and ample closet space, and black-and-white TVs are available. The 15 rooms with private bath and air conditioning are priced at $50 to $60 single, $60 to $70 double. The bargain here is in the 19 bathless rooms (with sinks only; guests share hall baths) which are not air-conditioned, though they are equipped with electric fans. These go for $40 to $45 single, $50 to $55 double. An extra person in any room pays $10. Breakfast, not included in these rates, is served in a homey dining room with cheerful yellow-clothed tables or on the flagstone patio under the shade of an old oak tree; the latter locale is also nice for picnics. Though there's no elevator at the Gralyn—just a beautiful wide staircase—the management places older guests on the first floor (just one flight up) upon request.

Down the block at 1755 N St. (and a pretty, tree-lined residential street it is, by the way), the same owners have 20 apartments with fully equipped kitchens. Once again these vary, with furnishings ranging from antiques (some come from old estates) to the flea-market variety. Some rooms are larger than others, and have high ceilings, shuttered windows, and/or fireplaces. All are air-conditioned, have full baths, and contain switchboard phones and black-and-white TVs. The public areas are lovely. Rates are $50 to $60 single, $60 to $70 double, $10 per additional person.

Free parking is provided for both hotel and apartment guests. In all its aspects, the Gralyn is a good choice.

STUDENT ACCOMMODATIONS: For students of all ages (over 18) and nationalities, the **International Student House,** 1825 R St. NW, 20009 (tel. 202/232-4007), offers an unbeatable package—accommodations in a magnificent Tudor building on a tree-lined street just a few blocks from Dupont Circle, low rates, terrific facilities, and a relaxed, noninstitutional atmosphere. If you're American—as about 10 of the 60 guests usually are—you'll be encouraged to share a room with a foreign student, because ISH exists to foster international understanding and promote cross-cultural interaction. Residents share daily meals (breakfast and dinner plus tea on Sunday) in the wood-paneled dining room, though in good weather many students dine al fresco in the adjoining garden. Public areas include an oak-paneled library with leaded-glass windows, a comfortable TV room, a rec room with pool and Ping-Pong tables, a laundry room, a sitting room, and the exquisite oak-paneled Great Hall, complete with Persian rugs, antique furnishings, and a high, beamed, carved plaster ceiling;

the hall's fireplace is a copy of the one at Hatfield Hall, former residence of Queen Elizabeth I. The room has a grand piano which guests can use.

The rooms are in both the Tudor building and an adjoining newer building. Those in the former have leaded-glass windows, while the newer rooms are more modern with painted concrete walls. All are air-conditioned, and provided with linens, bedding, and towels. There are phones in the halls for incoming calls, as well as pay phones, and the desk takes phone messages between 9 a.m. and midnight. No maid service—you do your own cleaning. Furnishings are modest but functional; most students personalize their rooms with posters and possessions.

A month is usually the minimum stay permitted, but there are exceptions subject to availability. Rates, including daily breakfast and dinner, are $440 per month for a bed in a four-person dorm with shared bath, $685 to $715 for a private room with bath.

There's an informal recreation program (parties at holidays and such-like), and a house car is used for day and weekend trips to area attractions like Charlottesville and Williamsburg.

FOR FOREIGN VISITORS (OCCASIONALLY AMERICANS): Though it has only space for nine residents, **Davis House**, 1822 R St. NW, 20009 (tel. 202/232-3196), is a fortunate choice for those who do manage to find space. Run by the American Friends Service Committee as an international hospitality center since the 1940s, it offers rooms (three singles, three twins) to foreign visitors here for work, study, or leisure. And though foreigners and people traveling on Quaker business are given priority, if there is an empty bed, they will occasionally put up an American tourist as well. The white rooms are immaculate and homey, furnished with antiques and flea-market finds, and public areas include a cozy living room with a color TV, a large and lovely dining room (where tea and coffee are available throughout the day), and an outdoor deck with umbrella tables. Rooms are air conditioned, phones are in the hall (the switchboard takes incoming calls from 7:30 a.m. to 10 p.m.), and baths are shared. The atmosphere in the house is friendly and warm, and the location is very central. Inexpensive meals are available at the above-mentioned International Student House, just across the street. No smoking is permitted in the house. If you're from another country, reserve as far in advance as possible. Americans can try the last minute. Maximum stay is two weeks. No curfew.

Rates: $18 per bed per night.

NO-FRILLS BUDGET: I wouldn't recommend the **Marifex**, 1523 22nd St. NW, between P and Q Sts., 20037 (tel. 202/293-1885), to everyone. The location couldn't be better—two blocks from Dupont Circle—but though it's perfectly safe and charges rock-bottom rates, its rundown rooms won't meet the standards of the most fastidious among you. They number 45, mostly singles with shared bath (50% have sinks), on four floors; there is an elevator. Rooms are painted flat white with brown painted-wood floors and are minimally furnished in vintage Salvation Army pieces. You get a bed, dresser, chair, telephone table, and night table. On the plus side, accommodations in this converted apartment building tend to be spacious and reasonably clean, and they're equipped with switchboard phones. On the debit, there's no air conditioning, and you don't get a TV. A laundry room and soda machine are among the Marifex's public amenities, there's daily maid service, and the front desk is manned round the clock. The registration area, in fact, is quite pleasant, its white walls hung with framed prints. Owners (since 1957) Maurice and June

Coja make sure there are no undesirable elements among guests. The rates: $25 single, $35 double. Weekly rates are $90 and $100, respectively.

A big plus is a restaurant/bar on the premises called the Brickskellar, a popular hangout of area professionals, students, and embassy people. Open for lunch and dinner weekdays, dinner only weekends, and for drinks till the wee hours every night, it's a warm and cozy place. The dining area, with its red-and-white checkered-clothed tables, exposed-brick walls, and large stone fireplace is charming, and the bar claims to serve the largest selection of beers in the world —over 500 brands including everything from Chinese Tsingtao to Welsh Double Dragon. The menu features moderately priced fare: burgers and deli sandwiches, plus entrees like tempura vegetables, baby back ribs, and grilled rainbow trout. Buffalo steaks and stew are house specialties.

4. Foggy Bottom

WEEKEND SPECIALS: Hotel Lombardy, 2019 I St. NW, 20006 (tel. 202/828-2600 or toll free 800/424-5486), in an elegant 11-story Tudor brick building, offers 125 rooms and suites, about 70% of them with fully equipped kitchens. From the lavishly paneled entrance with its carved plaster ceiling to the beautifully furnished rooms, this hotel is a delight. And the location, a few blocks from the White House and convenient to Farragut West Metro station, is excellent. The room decor reflects the good taste and attention to detail that is evident throughout. Immaculate, newly redecorated accommodations feature fine cherrywood furnishings, dusty rose carpeting, Casablanca fans overhead, cotton chintz floral drapes and curtains, and off-white walls hung with attractive artworks and gilt-framed mirrors. Baths have gleaming brass fixtures, and kitchens feature little dining nooks. The remaining soon-to-be-redecorated rooms have a different decor (mahogany furnishings, gold or brown carpets, etc.) but are still charmingly residential in feel. The Lombardy's old-world charm is complemented by all the usual modern amenities—air conditioning, direct-dial phone, color TV, radio, and full bath, plus a VCR on your TV; a wide selection of movies is available at the desk. A free newspaper is delivered to your room daily, laundry facilities are in the basement, and a sunshiny, café-curtained restaurant with oak floors and tables, the Lombardy Café, is open weekdays from 7 a.m. to 9 p.m., weekends for brunch and dinner only.

Though regular Lombardy rates are in the $100-and-up range, on weekends (Friday and Saturday nights) they plummet to just $55 for one or two people for any accommodation, $10 for each additional person, and no charge for children under 16. If a weekend is included in your stay, you must request the weekend rates when you reserve to obtain it. Reduced weekly and monthly rates are also available.

FEW FRILLS, LOW BUDGET: A four-story gleaming white brick building (with elevator), the **Allen Lee Hotel,** 2224 F St. NW 20037 (tel. 202/331-1224), is located in the heart of the George Washington University area. It's popular with European tourists, State Department workers visiting from overseas, and impecunious Kennedy Center performers. It's a European-style hotel, with about half its 90 rooms sharing hall baths. The rooms vary considerably in size and decor, but they're reasonably pleasant and clean with freshly painted walls and an odd assortment of furnishings. Some have hexagonal windowed walls and/or pretty fireplaces; most have venetian blinds rather than curtains and full-length mirrors. All rooms are air-conditioned and equipped with color TVs and switch-

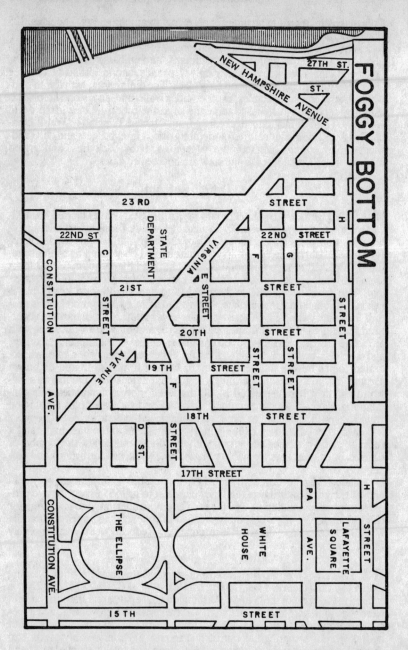

board phones. Free coffee and cookies are served in the lobby on Sunday mornings. Like the above-mentioned Marifex, the Allen Lee won't meet the standards of the fastidious guest. Public areas and rooms are on the shabby side, and most mattresses are decidedly lumpy. On a more positive note, the clientele is quite presentable (I saw no seedy types) and manager Richard Jordan tries hard to please his guests. Rates for bathless rooms (they do have sinks with hot and cold running water) are $22 to $24 single, $30 double, and $32 twin. For a room with bath you'll pay $35 single, $40 double, $42 twin. An extra person pays $5. There are no weekend or long-term rates, and credit cards are not accepted.

5. Upper Connecticut Avenue/North Washington

EMBASSY DISTRICT HOTELS: One block east of Connecticut Avenue, the **Rock Creek Hotel,** at 1925 Belmont Rd. NW, 20009 (tel. 202/462-6007), is in a quiet residential/embassy district convenient to Rock Creek Park, and Dupont Circle/Adams-Morgan eateries. Fronted by a towering elm, it's a clean and well-kept hostelry with 54 rooms on three floors. Rooms are painted white and gold, and have brown carpeting, orange bedspreads, and coordinated striped drapes. Furnishings are not fancy, but they're in good condition. Most rooms have two double beds, though some have twins, and all are equipped with modern bath, air conditioning, switchboard phone, and black-and-white TV. Ironing boards and irons are available, and there's free courtyard parking. A pleasant, reasonably priced coffeeshop is located off the lobby.

The rates are $40 single, $46 double, and $4 for each additional person. The Woodley Park Metro station is four blocks away, and Connecticut Avenue buses are even closer. A good choice.

The **Windsor Park,** 2116 Kalorama Rd. NW, near Connecticut Ave., 20008 (tel. 202/483-7700), is situated in the embassy district (the adjacent Tudor building is the Algerian Embassy), a lovely neighborhood of shady tree-lined streets. It offers 43 tidy but simply furnished rooms with two twins or one double bed, tub/shower bath, mini-refrigerator, color TV, air conditioning, and direct-dial phone. The white walls are freshly painted, bedspreads are gold, there's wall-to-wall carpeting, and windows are curtained. The Windsor Park isn't fancy, but it's homey. There are no dining facilities, but, once again, Adams-Morgan and Dupont Circle restaurants are close by. Soft-drink, coffee, and candy machines provide fare to assuage hunger pangs between meals, and complimentary coffee and tea are served in the lobby each morning.

Rates are $45 single, $55 double or twin, $63 for a suite accommodating up to four people, $4 a night per extra person; children under 12, free.

MARVELOUS MOTELS: Still farther north, the six-story **Connecticut Avenue Days Inn,** 4400 Connecticut Ave. NW, between Yuma and Albemarle Sts., 20008 (tel. 202/244-5600 or toll free 800/325-2525), offers 155 spiffy rooms that are always kept in top-notch condition. Grasspaper-covered walls are hung with modernistic art prints framed in brass (they match the brass lamps and mirror frames), furnishings are teak (Danish modern style), beds are made up with attractive floral-print spreads, and in-room accoutrements include direct-dial phone, full tub/shower bath with shower massage, color TV with HBO movies, AM/FM radio, and individual temperature controls. A sofa and coffee table in most rooms make things homier. For families there are parlor suites, which means the kids can have their own room with its own TV. Another type of accommodation, the "king leisure" room, has a king-size bed (the others have doubles or queens) and an alcove containing an attractive desk. All rooms are done up in one of two color schemes—tan and navy or tan and jade (I prefer the latter). The Days Inn's lobby/reception area, decorated in earth tones and comfortably furnished with plush chairs and sofas, would pass muster at a first-class hotel. Complimentary continental breakfast—coffee, tea, juice, and doughnuts —is served there each morning. With or without a car, this is a great choice. You can park free on the premises, and the Van Ness Metro stop is just a block away; that means you can be at Dupont Circle in less than 10 minutes, the Smithsonian in 15. There are plenty of restaurants and a coin laundry nearby. Rates are seasonal. April 1 through October 1 singles pay $75, doubles $80; the rest of the year singles pay $59 to $69, doubles $64 to $74. Suites for four are $85 year round. The weekend rate (offered Friday, Saturday and Sunday nights) is $59 per room. But even better: all Days Inns offer a Super Saver of $39 per night, any night, if you reserve 30 nights in advance (via the 800 number) and pay for the first night when you reserve. Children under 16 always stay free. Seniors (55 and older) should inquire about September Days Club discounts.

Continuing farther afield, four miles from the Mall, is the **Walter Reed Hospitality House,** 6711 Georgia Ave. NW at Aspen St., 20012 (tel. 202/722-1600 or toll free 800/222-8388). Here, too, parking is free, but the walk to the Metro is a bit longer (eight blocks), and from the station (Tokoma Park) the ride to the Smithsonian is about 20 minutes. You'll like the Walter Reed from the minute you enter its pleasant, plant-filled, oak-paneled lobby (a nice lobby is always very reassuring, I think). The hallways are also attractive and nicely lit with brass wall lamps. Rooms are handsomely furnished with sturdy oak pieces, and the decorator has chosen pretty fabrics for drapes and bedspreads. Some rooms have pull-out sofas, some have alcoves with "cuddle couches," and some have balconies. There are several different color schemes—beige, green, and russet, among them. In-room amenities include direct-dial phone, color TV with HBO movies, AM/FM radio, and full bath. On the premises are a swimming pool/ sundeck, and Mr. Chan's Szechuan Restaurant, strikingly decorated with ultrasuede walls, grass-green carpeting, Chinese artworks, and chrome-framed upholstered sienna chairs. It serves American breakfasts and offers a low-priced Chinese menu (with a few American selections) at lunch and dinner.

Rates at Walter Reed are $53 single, $63 double or twin, $75 for executive doubles and suites equipped with microwave ovens and small refrigerators. An extra person pays $10. Children under 16 stay free. Weekend rates here are $47 per night, single or double, on Friday and/or Saturday nights. Joggers and nature lovers will enjoy the proximity to Rock Creek Park.

GUEST HOUSES: The **2005 Guest House,** named for its location at 2005 Columbia Rd. NW, Washington, DC 20009, between 20th and California Sts. (tel. 202/265-4006), rents out six rooms in a formerly elegant white-painted three-story brownstone. The former elegance is reflected in beautiful fireplaces in most rooms, stately staircases, and wainscotted walls. The furnishings are a mix of good pieces ranging from crystal chandeliers and Indian carved sandlewood screens to funky flea-market pieces. Some rooms are air-conditioned (others have fans), some have black-and-white TVs, and most share hall baths. The property is reasonably clean and well cared for, and the price is right: $18 to $24 single, $25 to $40 double. Special rates are offered to students and youth hostel members. NOTE: The manager is not always on the premises; be sure to call first and let him know what time you'll be arriving.

A three-story turn-of-the-century brick building, the **Connecticut-Woodley Guest House,** 2647 Woodley Rd. NW, between Connecticut Ave. and 27th St., 20008 (tel. 202/667-0218), is in a residential area of embassies and luxurious private homes. The Woodley Park-Zoo Metro station is less than a block away. The 14 air-conditioned rooms—four singles and ten doubles—are furnished quite decently with pieces from the defunct Sheraton Park Hotel (it's now the Sheraton-Washington, and it's just across the street) and assorted others. All have direct-dial phones, but no TVs. Some of the "doubles" are large enough to accommodate five people. A lounge in the basement offers color TV, soft-drink machines, laundry facilities, and comfy furniture. Owner/manager Ray Knickel has been running this guest house efficiently since 1963.

Rates for rooms with shared bath are $30 to $33 single, $36 to $39 double. For rooms with private bath you pay $40 to $44 single, $45 to $50 double. An extra person is $6 a night. Family rates are available.

International Guest House, 1441 Kennedy St. NW, 20011 (tel. 202/726-5808), is just east of the Carter Barron Amphitheatre and Rock Creek Park. Situated on a tree-lined residential street, and run by the Mennonite church, IGH provides "temporary, clean, inexpensive housing for international visitors and their families in a home-like atmosphere." Since the opening in 1967, it has accommodated over 25,000 guests from 146 different countries—professionals, tourists, educators, and students among them. Americans are also welcome, but there is a quota (about 25% maximum), and they can stay only one week (foreign guests are allowed to stay for two weeks). IGH is a friendly place. Guests mingle in the comfortably furnished living/dining room, complete with piano, or in the basement lounge where a black-and-white TV, a soft-drink machine, a Ping-Pong table, and a refrigerator are supplied for guest use. Kids get acquainted in the backyard playground where there are swings and a badminton net. There's also a porch with an old-fashioned swing, and the living room is stocked with books and current magazines.

The no-frills rooms, mostly doubles, are clean, adequately furnished, air-conditioned, and carpeted. Pay phones are in the hall. No real maid service here, but towels and washcloths are changed daily, sheets once a week. You can park in a limited free-parking area; if it's full, street parking is plentiful in the neighborhood. And if you don't have a car, bus stops are less than a block away (figure on a 20- to 30-minute ride to or from downtown, depending on traffic). The house is locked up at 11 p.m. each night, so this is not a good choice for late-night revelers. The office also closes between 11 p.m. and 7:30 a.m., and no incoming calls are taken during those hours.

Rates, including breakfast (fresh-baked muffins with butter and jam, cold cereal, juice, and tea or coffee), are just $17 per person per night (including tax), $100 per week. Children 6 to 16 pay half price; those 5 and under, free. Single guests are expected to share a room with another person if the house is full. Reserve far in advance.

6. New York Avenue NE

New York Avenue in Ivy City is one of those classic American stretches of highway (it becomes Route 50) lined with gas stations, fast-food restaurants, and motels. It's not scenic, but it does offer budget accommodations just 15 minutes by bus (less by car) from downtown.

An excellent motel choice in this part of town is the AAA-approved **Master Hosts Inn,** 1917 Bladensburg Rd. NE, corner of New York Ave., 20002 (tel. 202/832-8600 or toll free 800/251-1962), advertising itself as "close to everything in Washington but miles away in price." Its 150 rooms, in three two-story motel buildings, are neat and clean—done up in cocoa and mauve color schemes and equipped with one or two double beds, a dressing room, modern tub/shower bath, air conditioning, direct-dial phone, and color TV with VCR movies. All two-bedded rooms have an extra sink in the dressing room. Particularly nice are the upstairs rooms with high sloped ceilings; many of the accommodations also overlook the pool (a nice-size one), which is surrounded by an expanse of lawn. Here, in an enclosed courtyard, you can work on your tan or retreat to the shade of maples, pines, and crab apple trees—or feed Willie, resident squirrel and inn mascot. There are also umbrella tables where you might enjoy a picnic lunch or fare from the New China Inn, an attractive Chinese-American eatery with a bar on the premises. It serves everything from American breakfasts, burgers, and steaks (even lobster tail) to Cantonese and Szechuan fare. Other amenities include a lobby gift shop, free parking (with all-night security patrol of the grounds), sightseeing buses that depart from the lobby twice daily, soda and ice machines in the halls, babysitting services, and a bus to the Mall right across the street. And the property adjoins the U.S. National Arboretum—444 acres of lawn, trees, flower gardens, shrubs, wildflowers, and boxwoods (details in Chapter V); it's great for nature walks and jogging.

Depending on the season, rates range from $46 to $52 for one person in a room with one double bed, $48 to $57 for two people in the same room, $52 to $59 for one or two people in a room with two double beds. An extra person pays $5, a rollaway or crib is another $5, and children under 12 stay free.

Another good bet out here is the **Econo Lodge** at 1600 New York Ave. NE, 20002 (tel. 202/832-3200 or toll free 800/446-6900), a seven-story hotel-like setup with 136 modern rooms situated off well-lit, cheerful, blue-carpeted hallways. The rooms have tan carpeting, with walls, bedspreads, and curtains in harmonizing earth tones. Everything is new and spiffy. You get all the expected amenities here—color TV, direct-dial phone, air conditioning, and full bath. There are ice and soft-drink machines on every floor, parking is free, and complimentary coffee is served in the lobby each morning. Families with kids will especially appreciate the nice-size indoor pool and adjacent Astroturf sundeck.

Rates: $43.95 for one person in a room with one double bed, $48.95 for two in a room with one or two double beds, $4 per additional person or rollaway; free for kids under 12. Discounts are available for senior citizens.

Just across the street is the AAA-approved **Budget Motor Inn,** 1615 New York Ave. NE, 20002 (tel. 202/529-3900), with 52 rooms offering amenities identical to the above—plus free satellite movies on your TV. It has a small freeform outdoor pool and sundeck with umbrella picnic tables, plus a Chinese-American restaurant that is about as exotic as McDonald's. In fact it even serves up burgers, fries, and shakes in addition to moo goo gai pan and the rest. A coin laundromat for guests is another convenience.

Rates are seasonal, ranging from a low of $43 single, $48 double during the off-season (mid-September through mid-March) to a high of $50 single, $58 double the rest of the year. An extra person pays $4 a night, and children under 12 stay free.

7. In Suburban Virginia

ARLINGTON: Don't be put off by an out-of-the-District location. Arlington is just across the Potomac, in some cases within walking distance of major D.C. attractions. All the following establishments offer easy access to Washington via Metro.

Moderately Priced Hotels/Motels

I very much like the **Clarendon Hotel Court,** 3824 Wilson Blvd., Arlington, VA 22203 (tel. 703/525-7200 or toll free 800/368-3082), just two blocks from the Virginia Square Metro station and a quick ride from downtown D.C. Its 111 units (54 hotel rooms and 57 completely furnished apartments, the latter rentable on a daily or weekly basis), are housed in two-story brick buildings with neat white trim, doors, and balcony railings. And though you're a hop, skip, and a jump from the city, this nicely landscaped property has a pleasant suburban feel (grass and trees can be observed). Each of the rooms is equipped with color TV (with HBO movies), direct-dial phone, and a digital alarm clock radio. Grasspaper-covered walls are hung with old-fashioned paintings and prints, and

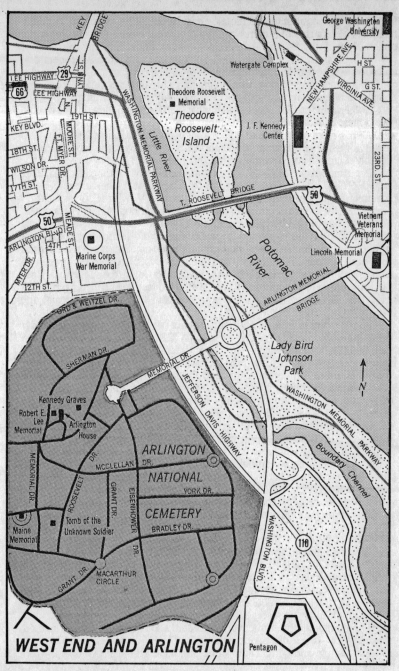

WEST END AND ARLINGTON

furnishings are of the standard motel genre. Hotel guests, of course, get daily maid service; apartment renters are given new linens twice a week and have the option of paying for daily maid service ($20/week). The apartments, by the way, have living rooms, dining rooms, and full kitchens with stoves, refrigerators, and sinks. Parking is free, and amenities include a playground for kids and a coin-op laundry. In addition, a complimentary breakfast of coffee, juice, and doughnuts is served in the pleasant plant-filled lobby each morning.

Hotel rooms are $45 single, $49 double, $50 king, $56 for a double double (two double beds, sleeps four), $62 for a suite. There's a discount if you stay a week. Apartments cost $60 daily, $220 weekly for an efficiency; $70 daily, $270 weekly for a one-bedroom unit, $80 and $325, respectively for two bedrooms. Monthly rentals are offered subject to availability.

The **Americana Motel,** 1400 Jefferson Davis Hwy., Arlington, VA 22202 (tel. 703/979-3772), has 102 standard motel rooms (color schemes are beige or pale green) equipped with tub/shower bath, color TV (with HBO movies and remote bedside control), direct-dial phone, and air conditioning. There are 72 rooms with one double bed and 30 with two double beds. The hotel is in Crystal City, a block from the Metro and Crystal Underground's numerous restaurants and shops. A nice touch: complimentary coffee and doughnuts are served in the lobby each morning. A room with one double bed is $50 a night for one or two people; a room with two double beds is priced at $60 for up to four people. Roll-aways and cribs are an additional $5 per night. Reduced weekend rates are available. There's free parking on the premises, and the staff is congenial and helpful.

Just 1½ blocks from the Virginia Square Metro station, the **Highlander Motor Inn,** 3336 Wilson Blvd., Arlington, VA 22201 (tel. 703/524-4300), is a low brick building with 45 rooms. They have different color schemes, but are all identically set up with two double beds, color TV (with HBO), tub/shower bath, direct-dial phone, air conditioning, and the rest. Free coffee is served in the lobby, and there's ample free parking. Many restaurants are close by. Singles are $47, doubles $52, and extra people are charged $5 each. Weekend rates are offered subject to availability.

Quality Inn Iwo Jima, 1501 Arlington Blvd., on Rte. 50, Arlington, VA 22209 (tel. 703/524-5000 or toll free 800/228-5151), is three blocks from the Roslyn Metro and about half a mile from Georgetown. It offers the usual Quality Inn amenities—air conditioning, color TV (with HBO movies), direct-dial phone, and tub/shower bath—plus a swimming pool with sundeck, a restaurant, washers and dryers, and free parking. Best rates are for double-bedded rooms ($49 to $54 for one or two people). Rooms with two double beds are $70 to $75, an extra person pays $5, and children under 17 stay free.

Weekend Special

Howard Johnson's National Airport Hotel, 2650 Jefferson Davis Hwy., Arlington, VA 22202 (tel. 703/684-7200 or toll free 800/654-2000), is not really a budget accommodation. The usual rate here is $89 to $108 a night for a double room. However, on Friday and Saturday nights this HoJo slashes prices, and you can stay for just $55 double (rollaways for additional people are $6). The further in advance you reserve, the better your chances. Rooms are standard motel accommodations, attractively decorated and equipped with all the modern amenities—direct-dial phone, cable color TV, HBO movies, AM/FM radio, air conditioning, and bath. There's free parking on the first five floors, which means that every room is at least six floors up and many provide a view of D.C. or the Potomac. A nice-sized swimming pool, health club (with Nautilus equipment), restaurant, and courtesy cars to and from National Airport are additional bonuses, and just across the street is Crystal City—a Metro stop and shopping mall with numerous restaurants (details in other chapters). The District is about 15 minutes away, National Airport even closer.

For Longer Stays

Motel 50, 1601 Arlington Blvd., between Pierce and Queen Sts., Arlington, VA 22209 (tel. 703/524-3400), has ten furnished apartments across the street available for longer rentals. A one-bedroom unit with fully equipped kitchen, bath, and living/dining room is $650 a month for one or two people. Two-bedroom units are $750 a month. These units offer color TVs but no phones. The Roslyn Metro is three blocks away.

Under the same management as the **Americana Motel** is an apartment building at 2868 South Fort Scott Dr. (tel. 703/979-3772), a little under a mile from the motel and the Crystal City Metro stop. Here, 30 fully furnished, air-conditioned apartments (15 one-bedroom units, 14 two-bedroom units, and one efficiency) are rented only on a monthly basis. They contain a living room, dining room, and bath, and are totally equipped, from color TV to pots and pans. There are even jacks, should you wish to install your own phone. Rates are $700 a month for a one-bedroom unit, $800 for two bedrooms, $400 for the efficiency.

And don't forget the one- and two-bedroom units at the **Clarendon Hotel Court,** 3824 Wilson Blvd. (tel. 703/525-7200, or east of the Mississippi, toll free 800/368-3082), available for nightly, weekly, and occasionally, monthly rental.

ALEXANDRIA: Most of the hotel/motel listings in the Alexandria section of this book (Chapter VIII) are practical only if you have a car. But **Alexandria Lodgings,** 10 Sunset Dr., Alexandria, VA 22301 (tel. 703/836-5575), located just half a block from the King Street Metro station, puts you within about ten minutes' riding distance from the Smithsonian and other Washington attractions. It's a great choice for many reasons. A small brick house fronted by a garden, it's in a very pleasant residential, suburban neighborhood. Owner/hostess Bette Gorman has decorated the rooms nicely. They're not fancy, but everything is very clean and in good condition, and there's well-chosen art on the freshly painted white walls. The front rooms are especially large and sunny. The smallest accommodation here is a room with a double bed adjoining a room with one twin that costs just $40 a night for one or two people; it's ideal if you're traveling with a friend or as an adult with one child and would like a bit of privacy come nightfall. There are also rooms with one double bed at the same price. A three-bedroom apartment (a whole floor, really) with fully equipped kitchen and private bath (the rest share) rents for just $65 a day for up to five people—great for families. There are also weekly rates of $200 for one or two people, $325 for the apartment. All rooms are air-conditioned and equipped with color TV and clock. And all guests have use of shared, fully equipped kitchens. Bette's laundry room has a washer and dryer, iron/ironing board, and folding table. You can do your laundry here at no charge; she even provides free detergent. A private pay phone is located on the first level, and guests can receive incoming calls via a round-the-clock answering service. The minimum stay is three days. No smoking is permitted in the house. No children under 6. No credit cards. A grocery store is three blocks away, and, of course, Alexandria's numerous restaurants are in easy walking distance. *Note:* The office is staffed at irregular hours. Best time to call is between 9 and 11 p.m.

8. In Suburban Maryland

COLLEGE PARK: An interesting mix of accommodations is offered at **Colonial**

Motel and Dormitories, 10203 Baltimore Blvd., College Park, MD 20740 (tel. 301/474-5678), just 12 miles or 25 minutes north of downtown Washington via U.S. 1 (Exit 25A). Most people will want a car here, though a bus outside the motel will take you right to the Rhode Island Avenue Metro station. Facilities include a large wooded area ideal for picnicking (ten acres of grass, trees, and flowers with barbecue setups and picnic tables); a TV room with jukebox, snack vending machines, and video games; a swimming pool and sundeck; an outdoor playground for kids; and plenty of free parking. Of interest to most tourists are the 30 motel units, each with two double beds, wall-to-wall carpeting, color TV, air conditioning, and private bath with shower, but no phone. They cost $38 a night for one or two people, $2 per extra person.

For groups, there are dorm rooms (mostly four-bedded) in over a dozen buildings, all of them air-conditioned, carpeted, attractively furnished, and equipped with linens and bedding. Groups of up to 350 can be accommodated at Colonial Plaza at about $6.50 per person with a minimum of 20 people. Book far in advance.

CHEVY CHASE: If you stay at the **Chevy Chase Motor Hotel,** 6800 Wisconsin Ave., Chevy Chase, MD 20815 (tel. 301/654-1400 or toll free 800/334-7218), you'll be just a quick 20-minute Metro hop from the District. You'll get a bit of exercise too, since the Bethseda station is five blocks away. The property is a two- to three-story white motel building made festive by bright orange doors, balcony railings, and window trim. Its 94 rooms are clean and attractive with floral-print bedspreads, tan or rose carpeting, and floral-themed prints on the walls. Most have two double beds; all have direct-dial phone, color TV, and tub/shower bath. On the premises is a swimming pool, a feature that makes this a good choice for families. A round-the-clock diner is adjacent, many shops and restaurants are nearby, and there's a laundromat a block away. The airport bus from National and Dulles stops right at the door. And if you drive, parking is free.

Rates are just $49 single, $55 double, $60 triple, $65 for four. Weekend rates are about 10% less across the board, and there are discounts for longer stays (seven days or more, payable in advance). There's no charge for two children under 12; additional children pay $6 extra.

ROCKVILLE: Though it's a bit far from the District (about 40 minutes by car from Dupont Circle) the **Pavilion Hotel,** 12000 Old Georgetown Rd., Rockville, MD 20852 (tel. 301/881-6900), offers so many pluses that it attracts quite a few Washington tourists—especially families. And it's two blocks equidistant from the White Flint and Twin Brook Metro stations, a trip that cuts at least ten minutes off driving time. All of its 145 rooms are actually large suites; each has a fully equipped and spacious eat-in kitchen, living room, and dining room. It's impossible to describe decor, since every room is different, but I inspected about 20 and all were very tastefully furnished. In-room frills include HBO movies on your color TV, individual climate control, call-waiting on your phone, and in some cases, dishwashers. Free underground parking, a sauna and immense swimming pool, an exercise room with Universal equipment, laundry facilities on each floor, a gift shop, a unisex hair salon, and mini-market that carries beer and wine as well as groceries are additional lures. And the White Flint Mall, just a few blocks away, gives you access to Bloomies, I. Magnin, Lord & Taylor, and much more. That's not all: the Pavilion's steak and seafood restaurant, James III, is exquisite, decorated in turn-of-the-century motif. Dinners are expensive, but lunches squeak by budget standards with entrees in the $6 to $7 range.

The rates: $60 single, $70 double; for an efficiency $75 single, $85 double for a one-bedroom unit; $100 for a two-bedroom apartment; $165 for a three-bedroom unit. There's no charge for children under 16.

LAUREL: Laurel, Maryland is about equidistant between Washington, D.C. and Baltimore, so for families who would like to divide their time between the Harbor (See Chapter IX) and the District, it might be a good choice. Ten miles from BWI Airport, the **Red Carpet Inn,** 9920 U.S. Rte. 1, between Rtes. 32 and 198, Laurel, MD 20707, (tel. 301/498-7750 or toll free 800/251-1962), built in 1986, has 79 spiffy new rooms with all the expected motel amenities, plus a low-priced on-premises restaurant and pool. Rates are $40 for a king single, $45 for two people in a room with one king bed, $48 for a double double, $5 for an extra person, children under 12 free.

GAITHERSBURG: The **Gaithersburg Quality Inn,** 80 Bureau Dr., at Firstfield Rd., Gaithersburg, MD 20878 (tel. 301/963-5900 or toll free 800/228-5151), is quite far afield—about a 40-minute drive from the center of D.C. You'll need a car if you stay here, and your best bet will be to park it at the nearby Shady Grove Metro station during the day and take the subway into town. Why recommend a property so far from town? Because staying out in the suburbs means a higher scale of accommodations for less money, and this property, furthermore, is offering our readers 10% off their regular rates of $56 to $68 single, $64 to $76 double, $48 single or double Friday and Saturday nights. Mention the book when you reserve, and show it at the desk when you register. The Quality offers guests 127 attractive rooms decorated in teal, burgundy, or cocoa color schemes, all equipped with handsome oak furnishings, color TVs with HBO movies and other cable stations, clock radios, and special bath amenities. Mini-refrigerators are available gratis on request, and all rooms have dining tables. A reasonably priced garden-decor restaurant, a small pool/sundeck, use of facilities (for a small fee) at a nearby health club (Nautilus machines, racquetball, a vast indoor pool, etc.), free parking, and a guest services desk that works hard to please are additional lures. If you like to get into town for full days of sightseeing, and don't mind not having access to your hotel midday, this can be a good choice.

9. Special Kinds of Accommodations

BED AND BREAKFAST: One of the most enjoyable ways to travel on a budget is to stay at B&B accommodations. Prices are reasonable, rooms are often charming, and you get an opportunity to meet local people.

In addition to specific B&B accommodations, I've listed several services under whose umbrellas are numerous homes renting out rooms on this basis. Reserve as early as possible to get the greatest selection of locations and lowest rates, and do specify your needs and preferences: for instance, discuss children, pets, smoking policy, preferred locations (do you require convenient public transportation), parking, availability of TV and/or phone, what your preferred breakfast consists of, how payment can be made, etc.

The **Bed & Breakfast League Ltd.,** 3639 Van Ness St. NW, 20008 (tel. 202/363-7767), has about 50 current listings in the D.C. area, some of them at extremely central locations like Capitol Hill and Dupont Circle, others further afield but close to Metro stops and in nearby Maryland and Virginia suburbs. They run the gamut from late Victorian mansions to a private cabin on a yacht.

Hosts are encouraged—though not required—to offer such niceties as fresh-baked muffins at breakfast. The accommodations are all screened, and guest reports are given serious consideration. Rates range from about $30 to $60 single, $40 to $70 for doubles. There's a booking fee of $10, and a two-night minimum stay is required.

A similar service operating primarily in the Washington, D.C., area is **Sweet Dreams & Toast,** P.O. Box 4835-0035, 20008 (tel. 202/483-9191). Director Ellie Chastain personally inspects every home she lists; there are about 70 to date, all convenient to public transportation. They range from modern Georgetown condos to antique-filled Victorian homes on Capitol Hill. There's no service charge here. B&B rooms range from $40 to $60 single, $55 to $70 double.

You might also contact **Bed 'n' Breakfast Ltd. of Washington, D.C.,** P.O. Box 12011, 20005 (tel. 202/328-3510), with about 100 rooms—in both homes and unhosted furnished apartments—on its rosters. All their accommodations are carefully checked out, and guest comments are solicited. Rates, including continental breakfast, are $35 to $70 single, $45 to $80 double. Apartments start at $50 a night for a studio.

The **Kalorama Guest House,** 1854 Mintwood Pl., between 19th St. and Columbia Rd. NW, 20009 (tel. 202/667-6369). In 1982, Roberta Pieczenik opened a charming six-bedroom B&B accommodation in this conveniently located Victorian town house. The combination she offered—lovely rooms and excellent service (all staff members live in, so they're very accessible)—proved so successful that she soon expanded, adding nine rooms next door and another eight across the street. The she added 11 rooms in another Victorian town house, this one at 2700 Cathedral Ave. NW at 27th St., 20008 (tel. 202/328-0860), and soon acquired a house across the street from it, giving her another eight rooms. And most recently, in 1986, she purchased another seven rooms at 1831 Mintwood Place. Since all her B&Bs are within eight blocks of Metro stops (or closer) and near many restaurants, and prices are most reasonable, you'll do well at any of them. Via either of the above-listed phone numbers, you can make reservations at all locations.

Roberta scours the city's flea markets, antique shops, and auctions on a regular basis in search of beautiful furnishings and knickknacks to enhance the rooms. Yours might feature a Singer sewing machine table, an oak mirror shelf with a display of antique bottles, a Victorian armoire, and/or turn-of-the-century framed sheet music and portraits. All rooms have brass beds with floral-print bedspreads and matching ruffled curtains, are heated in winter and air-conditioned in summer, and contain live plants and clock radios. Upon arrival you'll find a dish of candy and fresh flowers. At 1854 Mintwood, public areas include a cheerful shell-pink/exposed-brick breakfast room with garden furnishings (park benches at marble tables) and plant-filled windows. A meal of bagels, croissants, toast, orange juice, and tea or coffee is served here daily. In good weather you can enjoy it al fresco in a small flower-bordered garden at umbrella tables. The garden is also a pleasant setting for post-sightseeing relaxation over sherry or a picnic dinner. A barbecue grill is provided for guest use. Upstairs, there's a parlor with a working fireplace where magazines, games, and newspapers are provided, along with a decanter of sherry on the buffet for complimentary afternoon apéritifs. Additional on-premises amenities include a seldom-used TV, a phone (local calls are free), a coin phone for long distance calls, a vending machine for soft drinks, a washing machine and dryer, and a refrigerator. Though rooms have no phones, incoming calls are answered around the clock, so people can leave messages for you. Maid service is provided about every three days. Other locations are very similar in their offerings.

Rates throughout the Kalorama Guest House network range from $50 to $70 for a single with bath, $55 to $75 double. Bathless singles are $35 to $50, doubles $40 to $60. A two-room suite with private bath is $75 for up to three occupants, $5 for each additional. In other rooms an additional person pays $10. Weekly rates are available off season. Highest recommendation.

Very much in the Kalorama genre is the new **Windsor Inn,** 1842 16th St. NW, at T St., 20009 (tel. 202/667-0300 or toll free 800/423-9111), with 38 rooms in a neat brown brick building on a tree-lined residential street. It was built in the 1920s as a boarding house, later renovated and run as an inn through 1963. A wealthy owner then let the property lie empty and unused until the Windsor folks discovered and purchased it in 1985. Many of the rooms still have original windows with wavy hand-pressed glass. The Windsor's decor is strictly art deco, with the staff all actively engaged in a second career of antiquing in search of additional pieces to enhance rooms and public areas. The former are painted pale peach with gray trim and carpeting and period prints adorn the walls. Four rooms have day beds with bolsters. Guests here enjoy several amenities usually lacking at B&B accommodations. Rooms are equipped with color TVs, air conditioning, direct-dial phones, and AM/FM radios, and each has its own private bath, albeit with shower only. Lower level rooms face a skylit terrace with lawn furnishings and flower boxes, however I prefer the sunnier upstairs accommodations. A continental breakfast—danish, croissants, fresh fruit, cheeses, fruit juices, and tea/coffee—is served in the comfy mauve and gray art deco lobby, or, upon request, in your room. And during the day, complimentary coffee, tea, and hot chocolate are available. There are ice machines and a refrigerator for guest use. And upon checking in, you'll find a dish of candy and fresh flowers in your room. A very hospitable and friendly staff is a big plus here.

Rates range from $64 to $84 single, $74 to $94 double—a tad high for this book—but on weekends you can stay for just $50 a night single or double. At this writing the owners have already purchased a second building and will soon double their room count.

The **Adams Inn,** 1744 Lanier Pl. NW, between Calvert St. and Ontario Rd., 20009 (tel. 202/745-3600), offers ten homey rooms and a carriage house—all furnished in kitschy pieces culled from flea markets and auctions. They're brightened up by freshly painted or cheerfully papered walls and matching ruffled curtains and bedspreads. Some have oak floors, others are carpeted, and those that share baths (which are kept nice and clean, by the way), have in-room sinks. Most attractive of the inn's accommodations is the sunny carriage house, with its yellow/gold walls and printed patchwork drapes and bedspreads. It alone has a fully equipped kitchen. Guests mingle in a cozy parlor with lace-curtained windows (maps, books, games, and magazines are provided), and a continental breakfast—orange juice, coffee or tea, home-baked muffins or nut bread, and a fruit cup—is served daily in the dining room at a large mahogany table by a working fireplace. Weather permitting, one can also take this morning meal on the front porch or the flower-bordered garden patio where tables and chairs are provided. Coffee and doughnuts are available throughout the day. All rooms are heated and air-conditioned. There's a pay phone in the dining room and limited parking space on the premises (cost is $5 a night). You're just four blocks from the Woodley Park-Zoo Metro here, Adams-Morgan eateries offer numerous dining options, and it's only about a ten-block walk to Dupont Circle. For carriage house occupants, a Safeway supermarket just 100 feet away is a great convenience. Amiable English hostess Sybille Cooke extends herself to make guests comfortable.

Rates are $40 single, $45 double, for rooms with shared bath; $55 single, $60 double with private bath; $75 for one to four people in the carriage house.

All rates include the above-described breakfast. Thanksgiving through February, weekly rates are offered subject to availability. *Note:* No smoking is permitted inside the house.

FOR WOMEN ONLY: The **Women's Information Bank,** 3918 W St. NW, 20007 (tel. 202/338-8163), is a volunteer-staffed organization offering a number of services to women, among them help in finding safe, reasonably priced, long- and short-term accommodations. They often know of houses and apartments for rent, people who need roommates, and bed-and-breakfast places. In addition they'll assist with information on jobs, rides, and other problems, including any tourism-related inquiries. Best of all, there's no fee, though donations are accepted. There's generally someone on hand daily from 10 a.m. to 10 p.m., but call first. Sometimes they're slow at answering phone messages. Perservere.

FINDING A ROOMMATE: If you're planning on a longish stay in Washington and prefer an apartment or house to a hotel, one way to beat the high cost of renting is to share. In a transient city like D.C. roommates come and go, and over at **Roommates Preferred,** 904 Pennsylvania Ave. SE, 20003 (tel. 202/547-4666), Betsy Neal finds replacements. She keeps in close personal contact with clients, carefully screens applicants, and tries hard to match up compatible types. And she's been doing it successfully for over a decade. A personal interview is required; you'll discuss preferences, pets, smoking, lifestyles, etc. Betsy has clients throughout D.C. and in nearby Maryland and Virginia. Rents for listed apartments and houses range from about $300 (probably for a house shared by three or four people) on up. The fee is $50. If the first placement is unsatisfactory to either party, there's no additional charge for another placement if you notify Betsy within two months. Open weekdays from 9 a.m. to 8 p.m., on Saturday from 11 a.m. to 3 p.m.

Chapter III

EATING CHEAPLY
AND WELL

1. Capitol Hill
2. Near the White House
3. On and Near the Mall
4. Downtown
5. K Street Restaurant Row
6. Dupont Circle Area
7. The Kennedy Center
8. Georgetown
9. Adams-Morgan

THOUGH PLENTY OF PLUSH RESTAURANTS cater to Washington's wealthy power brokers, you won't have any trouble finding inexpensive fare. Low-level bureaucrats, impecunious students (though it's secondary to the business of government, D.C. is a college town), and hungry hordes of tourists have to eat too, and they have plenty of budget dining options.

One factor is unique to D.C. dining. Washington has more—and better—cafeterias than any other American city. They're ubiquitous—in museums, office buildings, government buildings, even in the Capitol and the Library of Congress, and many more are privately run. At any of these establishments you can enjoy a multicourse soup-to-nuts lunch or dinner for as little as $5 or $6, with no added expense for tipping either. Cafeteria dining in Washington is fast and convenient—a boon to busy sightseers—but it's by no means bleak. The trend here is toward high-quality, home-cooked fare (often you'll get fresh-from-the-oven breads and desserts) served in pleasant surroundings.

Also abounding are ethnic eateries catering not to tourists but to vast segments of the population—diplomats, students, and other residents—from foreign nations. In Ethiopian, Afghani, Vietnamese, Indian, and other foreign restaurants, you'll sample authentic and usually low-priced fare along with fellow diners from those countries. The U.N.-like aspect of Washington (home to about 140 foreign missions) is a definite plus when it comes to dining out.

Over the past decade Washington has made vast strides toward gastronomic sophistication. Time was when Americans returning from a sojourn abroad loudly bemoaned the difficulty of obtaining a decent croissant and espresso *petit déjeuner*. In today's Washington, I'd like to see them avoid one. Yet another manifestation of D.C.'s continental style is the ever-growing number of outdoor cafés. Every spare inch of sidewalk space near a restaurant is aclutter with umbrella tables from spring through fall.

Speaking of outdoor eating, keep in mind that the capital offers endless squares, parks, and grassy grounds—not to mention the Mall itself—that are perfect for picnicking.

Finally, it may be true that you are what you eat, but I've based this chapter on the premise that you eat where you are. Hence, restaurants listed below are grouped by geographic proximity.

1. Capitol Hill

BAGELMANIA: Following in the wake of Washington's croissant craze is bagelmania, evidenced by the tremendous popularity of bagel-centered eateries like the **Chesapeake Bagel Bakery,** 215 Pennsylvania Ave. SE (tel. 546-0994), a block from the Library of Congress and two blocks east of the Capitol. A fastfood restaurant with a little bit of Jewish soul, the Chesapeake is pristine and pleasant, with plenty of sunlight streaming in, white enamel lamps and fans overhead, white tile floors, blue-cushioned bentwood chairs at matching Formica tables, and changing art and photo exhibits on the walls. As you wait in line (it's cafeteria service) you can peruse the notices on two immense community bulletin boards. But it's hard to keep your mind off the food, since the bagels are baked on the premises, and the aroma is heavenly. You can see the open kitchen behind the counter.

The bagels—of the authentic New York variety, good enough to please the most meticulous *mavin*—come in nine varieties (plain, cinnamon-raisin, pumpernickel, whole-wheat, poppy, sesame, onion, garlic, and salt) with fillings like cream cheese, walnuts, raisins, and carrots; the traditional nova and cream cheese; hummus; chicken salad; kosher salami; shrimp salad; chopped liver; etc.—all for $3.50 or less. There are also low-priced homemade soups; blueberry, cranberry, and bran muffins; salads; and desserts like carrot cake, brownies, and blondies. Open weekdays 7 a.m. to 9 p.m., on weekends in summer till 10 p.m. No credit cards. A terrific choice for budget meals. There's another location in the Dupont Circle area at 1636 Connecticut Ave. NW, between Q and R Sts. (tel. 328-7985). Yet a third is at 818 18th St. between H and I Sts. (tel. 775-4690).

IN THE CAPITOL: There are several restaurants in the Capitol itself (lawmakers have to eat, too), and they're especially worth considering when you tour the building. All offer very reasonable prices for superior fare. Do note that hours of operation listed are sometimes curtailed or expanded for the public. These restaurants are primarily for Capitol staff members, and if there's a shortage of space you may be turned away. Not to worry. You're sure to find seating at one of the below-listed establishments.

Most impressive is the **House of Representatives Restaurant,** in Room H118 on the south end of the Capitol (tel. 225-6300). It consists of two plush dining rooms separated by a comfortable lounge. Both rooms are beautifully appointed, one with forest green carpeting, cream-colored walls hung with gilt-framed Federalist mirrors and historic prints, and lighting emanating from crystal sconces and graceful Georgian chandeliers. The other has high ceilings with beautiful moldings, a windowed wall hung with gorgeous moss green velvet draperies, and a very large gilt-framed painting of George Washington receiving Cornwallis's letter of surrender at Yorktown on the opposite wall. Throughout, seating is in Windsor chairs at tables clothed in champagne linen and adorned with small flower arrangements. Bean soup has been a featured item here since 1904 when then Speaker of the House Joseph G. Cannon ordered it only to find that it had been omitted from the menu because the day was too hot for hearty soups. "Thunderation," roared Cannon, "I had my mouth set for bean soup . . . From now on, hot or cold, rain, snow, or shine, I want it on the menu every day!" And so it's been ever since. Prices are very reasonable for such a lofty setting. A breakfast (served 9 to 11 a.m. weekdays) of two eggs, homemade biscuits, sausage patty, fresh-squeezed orange juice, and coffee is under $4. At lunch (served to the public from 1:30 to 2:30 p.m. weekdays) the famous bean soup is 90¢; hot entrees like roast prime rib of beef *au jus* and broiled filet of sole with lemon butter are mostly in the $5 to $7.50 range and come with vegetable and potato. Even less expensive are deli sandwiches and burgers. And several specials are offered each day—perhaps crêpes stuffed with creamed chicken and buttered succotash ($4.60). For dessert, apple pie seems appropriate. Who knows, you might even get to see your congressperson.

A terrific lunch option is the lavish all-you-can-eat meal served in the **Dirksen Senate Office Building South Buffet Room** (tel. 224-4249) weekdays from 11:30 a.m. to 2:30 p.m. Here, your chance of getting a seat is almost always 100%. It's fun to get here, too, involving a free ride on a subway that runs through the underbelly of the Capitol; ask Capitol police for directions. Like the House Restaurant, the Buffet Room offers a handsome setting—marble floors and columns and seating in red leather chairs at flower-bedecked tables clothed in forest green or gold linen. You can load up your plate with meat from a carvery station (perhaps roast beef or leg of lamb), a choice of about eight additional hot entrees, stir-fried vegetables, potatoes, pasta and rice dishes, a full salad and fruit bar, a wide choice of desserts, tea/coffee/milk, and soft drinks. The price: just $5.95 for adults, $3.95 for children under 12. A make-your-own-sundae bar is $1.95 additional.

For a lighter lunch, or for breakfast, you might consider the Buffet Room's adjoining **North Servery** (no phone), an attractive cafeteria with a low slatted oak ceiling, gallery white walls, carpeted floors, and red leather-upholstered Breuer chairs at matte-topped gray tables. Low priced breakfast choices here include a meal of eggs, home fries, bacon, juice, toast, and coffee for $2.29. At lunch the famed bean soup is just 65¢, and specials like fettuccine with haddock and clams, stuffed cabbage, beef enchiladas, and chicken pot pie are $2.50 to $3.50. Side orders of veggies—mashed potatoes, succotash, broccoli with cheese sauce, etc.—are 50¢ to $1. Hours: 9 a.m. to noon and 1:30 to 3:30 p.m. weekdays.

Another dining room reached via the Capitol subway system is the **Longworth Building Cafeteria** (tel. 225-4410), an art deco courtyard with ornate street lights, *trompe l'oeil* mirrored windows, pale-yellow walls, and yellow leather-upholstered garden furnishings. Many plants further the outdoorsy feel. At breakfast, two eggs with hotcakes and coffee cost about $2. At lunch there's a wide choice of items like macaroni and cheese casserole, salmon cakes with coleslaw, and baked chicken served with potato and carrots in the $2 to $4 range, not to mention a goodly selection of pies and cakes for dessert. Open to the public weekdays from 9 to 11:45 a.m. and 1:15 to 2:30 p.m.

You won't need a subway to get to the **Capitol Coffee Shop,** Room HB11, in the basement on the House Side of the building (tel. 225-3919). A small facility, it's quite pretty, with trellised cream-colored walls, dark beige carpeting, and graceful brass chandeliers and sconces. There are two especially nice alcoves with round windows in recessed walls. It's open to the public for inexpensive and tasty fare (e.g. a lunch of chicken in the basket, cherry pie, and coffee for about $4) from 9 to 11:30 a.m. and 1 to 2:30 p.m. Service is cafeteria style.

Take the Capitol subway to the **Rayburn Building Cafeteria** (tel. 225-7109), an immense room divided by colonnaded areas. Soft lighting, cocoa-mauve carpeting, and comfortable seating in tufted white leather chairs make this a pleasant facility. A breakfast of chipped beef, cornbread, and coffee here is $2.30. Lunch items under $3.50 include fried chicken with potato salad, veal parmigiana with spaghetti, and seafood cakes with whipped potatoes. Finish up with cheesecake and coffee. Hours: 9 to 11:45 a.m. and 1:15 to 2:30 p.m.

Finally, back on the first floor of the Senate side of the building is the **Refectory** (tel. 224-4870), an appealing little place under vaulted ceilings with wainscotted walls. A big breakfast—eggs, bacon, grits, juice, coffee, and toast—can be obtained here for $2.35. At lunch, entrees like a hot roast beef sandwich with mashed potatoes and gravy or a cold chunky chicken salad plate with seasonal fruits are under $5. Pecan pie and a hot fudge sundae are among your dessert options. Open weekdays 9 a.m. to 4 p.m.

Somehow dining in the Capitol is intrinsically exciting, the Washington glamor equivalent of Hollywood movie-lot restaurants. Adults will probably favor the House of Representatives Restaurant (first listing); kids do like those cafeterias reached by underground train.

IN THE LIBRARY OF CONGRESS: The **James Madison Memorial Building of the Library of Congress,** 101 Independence Ave. SE (tel. 287-8300), caters to researchers with a first-rate cafeteria, happily open to the public as well. On the sixth floor, it's immaculate and tasteful, with rust-colored carpeting and matching Breuer chairs, white draperies, and a row of comfortable brown-leather booths by a wall of windows overlooking the city. Everything served is fresh and prepared on the premises. There are six service areas: fast food (fried chicken, burgers, etc.); carved meats (two a day carved from the joint); deli sandwiches, hot entrees like Swedish meatballs over noodles or fried crab cakes; health food; and a salad bar where a plate of greens is $1.05 and additional toppings—tomato, egg salad, onion, mushroom, chickpeas, beans, sprouts, etc.—are 20¢ each. Prices are extremely reasonable: hot entrees are in the $1.75 to $2.50 range; sandwiches, $1.40 to $3.50; and desserts—pies, cakes, and puddings—75¢ to $1.25. Open weekdays from 8:30 to 10:30 a.m. for breakfast, 11 a.m. to 2 p.m. for lunch, and 2 to 3:30 p.m. for light fare. There's even a nonsmoking area.

Adjoining, and even better, is the **Montpelier Dining Room** serving $6.95 prix-fixe buffet lunches on weekdays from 11:30 a.m. to 2 p.m. It's a lovely carpeted room, with panoramic views (including the Capitol dome) from white-draped windows on two sides, tables adorned with fresh flowers, oak-paneled walls, and an elegant dessert display table with a floral centerpiece. Your meal might consist of cheddar cheese soup, prime rib, baked potato, vegetable, bread and butter, and selections from a stunning salad bar. There's always a choice of two or three entrees. Sumptuous desserts—or a glass of wine—are $1.25 and $1.35, respectively. Major credit cards are accepted.

AMERICAN FARE: One of my favorite Capitol Hill haunts is **Stevan's,** 231 Pennsylvania Ave. SE (tel. 543-8337), a rustic/comfy place with halaphane lamps suspended from a yellow pine ceiling, plank oak floors, exposed brick and mirrored walls, and philodendrons in clay pots and planters. *Big Chill*–era music is played, lighting is soft, seating comfortable, the bar lively, especially when sports events are being aired. A bistro-like dining room downstairs is used for overflow at lunch, becoming a fancier milieu at night when it caters largely to a post-theater crowd. Head downstairs evenings for wine bar offerings, cappuccino, espresso, and sinfully rich desserts—all served up by smartly tuxedoed waiters.

Lunch or dinner, I love the eight-ounce burgers here ($5) served with fresh-cut fries or superb beer-battered onion rings. Overstuffed deli sandwiches—corned beef, pastrami, ham, turkey, etc.—are in the $5.50 to $6.25 range, all made with meats fresh cooked on the premises. In the same price bracket are salads such as sliced duck over spinach topped with blanched almonds, mandarin oranges, enoki mushrooms, and crisp noodles in warm, tangy sesame dressing. Omelets, chili, crab cakes, and fried oysters are additional choices, always supplemented by daily specials (in the $6 to $8 range) as diverse as meat loaf with mashed potatoes and cold sesame noodles with chicken. Everything's made from scratch, and portions are hefty. There's an all-you-can-eat dinner offered Sunday nights from 5 to 9 p.m.—perhaps fried chicken and fish with homemade coleslaw, potato salad, fries, and three-bean salad for $8.25. The waiter will happily provide seconds, thirds, etc., so plan to pig out. Also noteworthy is Stevan's Saturday and Sunday brunch featuring items like homemade corned beef hash, creamed chipped beef, waffles, fresh-squeezed juices, and eggs Chesapeake (poached eggs topped with crabmeat, sliced tomato, and sauce Choron served on an English muffin with fresh broccoli). Prices are reasonable and include unlimited champagne. This brunch is very popular with fans heading out to RFK Stadium for Redskin games. Stevan's is open Monday to Thursday from 11:30 a.m. to 12:30 a.m., Friday from 11:30 a.m. to 2 a.m., Saturday 11 a.m. to 2 a.m., Sunday 10 a.m. to 12:30 a.m. The kitchen closes about two hours before the bar.

A local joke is that if Washington were ever nuked, **Sherrill's Bakery,** 233 Pennsylvania Ave. SE (tel. 544-2480), would remain standing. The *Washington Post* calls this unchanged-from-the-1940s luncheonette "a slice of Americana." It does seem like something out of a Hopper painting, with its sturdy wooden booths, coat-hook posts, mahogany paneling, soda counter complete with old-fashioned malted machine, even a scale that tells your weight and fortune. Sherrill's has been in the Revis family for 47 years, and they've changed nothing; even much of the staff dates from the early days. The handpainted oil murals of hunting and fishing scenes were a gift from a 1940s congressman. Since Sherrill's doubles as a bakery, be sure to ask for your sandwiches on homemade bread and your burgers on fresh-baked buns. The menu lists all the traditional luncheonette favorites for $2 to $3.50: burger and fries, egg salad sandwich, grilled cheese sandwich, and bacon, lettuce, and tomato sandwich, with which, of course, a milkshake ($1.25) is *de rigueur*. Or perhaps you should have a Coke with your sandwich and save room for a banana split ($2.60). Sherill's also serves full meals (platters, they're called) such as baked meat loaf, roast chicken with dressing, fresh roast ham, and fried filet of haddock, all served with two vegetables, bread, and butter, and all under $5. The bakery display counter, filled with fresh-from-the-oven strawberry shortcake, eclairs, napoleons, cream horns, brownies, and chocolate-chip cookies, also merits some attention. Open weekdays from 6 a.m. to 8:30 p.m., weekends from 7 a.m. to 8:30 p.m. No credit cards.

Capitol Hill has a branch of the **American Cafe** (details in Georgetown section) at 227 Massachusetts Ave. NE (tel. 547-8500). The newer of the two, it's ultramodern and theatrical-looking, with black metal Tinkertoy-like beams overhead, brass rails, Scandinavian furnishings, exposed brick walls, hanging white enamel lamps, and mirrors expanding perceived space into infinity. Large potted plants, fresh flowers on every table, and soft lighting save the decor from starkness. You can also sit outdoors on a brick terrace with umbrella tables. Friday and Saturday from 7 p.m. to midnight there's piano bar music, and a string quartet plays at Sunday brunch. The menu is identical to the Georgetown location (see below) and here too there's an adjoining market where you can "take out." Open for lunch/dinner/brunch Monday to Thursday from 11 a.m. to 1 a.m., on Friday and Saturday to 3 a.m., on Sunday from 10:30 a.m. to 1 a.m. The American Café also serves breakfast weekdays from 7:30 to 9:30 a.m., on weekends from 8:30 to 10 a.m.

Another favorite with Hill staffers is **The Delly of Capitol Hill,** 332 Pennsylvania Ave. SE (tel. 547-8668), catering to the congressional crowd with a mahogany-paneled "Caucus Room" and specialties like "Nancy's hunch—diet lunch" (a hamburger with cottage cheese, lettuce, and sliced tomato for $5.25). Served all day is the "congressional brunch": juice, two eggs, any style; choice of bacon, ham, sausage, or lox; french fries or home fries; assorted rolls, bagels, and English muffins; cream cheese, jelly, and butter; assorted danish; and coffee, tea, hot chocolate, or milk ($7.50, $1 for an extra plate if you share). Typical deli fare includes three stuffed cabbage rolls with choice of potato, coleslaw, vegetable, and roll and butter ($6.75); cheese blintzes with sour cream ($5.50); and moderately priced sandwiches (made with meats cooked on the premises) like corned beef brisket, and chopped liver and onion. Free with entrees (not sandwiches) are the salad bar offerings —fresh greens, mushrooms, chickpeas, tomatoes, sprouts, etc.—plus homemade soup. And this is also a place where you can get a terrific piece of chocolate mousse pie for dessert. The Delly is a pretty place, its wainscotted white walls hung with framed prints and posters, china, antique musical instruments, and memorabilia. Floors are carpeted, and there are often fresh flowers on every table. Open Monday to Friday from 8 a.m. to 10 p.m., Saturday and Sunday from 9 a.m. to 3 p.m. No credit cards. There's a full bar in the front room.

2. Near the White House

A SPECIAL LUNCHEONETTE: Though **Drake's Garden Café,** 801 18th St. NW, between H and I Sts. (tel. 293-2933), at first appears to be one of Washington's hundreds of tiny luncheonettes, a closer look tells you that this is someplace special. Not many luncheonettes have tastefully subdued gray walls, dark-green carpeting coordinated to match the Levolor blinds, and bentwood chairs at oak tables. Further enhancing the decor are many plants and flower boxes.

Drake's fare is also a cut above its competitors. Everything is fresh and homemade. For under $5, you can get a chef salad, a taco salad (seasoned beef, lettuce, cheddar, tomatoes, onions, bell peppers, chips, and salsa), or a crabmeat salad. The menu also features a wide choice of sandwiches, quiche of the day, a bowl of chili with grated cheddar, and burgundy beef stew (these items in the $2.50 to $4.25 range). And for dessert there are yummy choices like carrot cake with creamy icing and the "great American chocolate cake." Not only wine and beer, but, surprisingly, all other drinks are available; there's a full bar. Drake's, as any eatery in this district worth its salt, is mobbed at lunch. Open weekdays from 7 a.m. to 8 p.m. (later in summer), on Saturday from 9 a.m. to 5 p.m. This little eatery accepts major credit cards. And fresh-baked blueberry, cranberry, and bran muffins—not to mention danish and doughnuts —plus a wide choice of gourmet coffees (from French roast to Swiss chocolate almond decaf) make this a good breakfast choice.

Under the same ownership is **Primo's Deli Café** with locations at the Shops

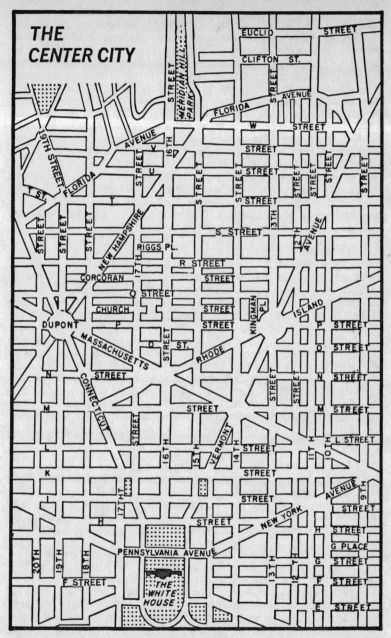

THE CENTER CITY

at National Place, second level, enter at 13th and F Sts. NW (tel. 737-7272) and at 3000 Connecticut Ave. NW, directly across from the main entrance to the zoo (tel. 332-8989). Prices and fare are similar to Drake's. The latter location is especially recommendable when you visit the zoo.

CONTINENTAL CUISINE, WITH ART: How can you go wrong with a restaurant that uses the *Mona Lisa* as its logo? **The Art Gallery,** 1712 I St. NW (tel. 298-6658), is a darling little eatery that utilizes its wall space for a changing art exhibit (it's all for sale) and places a plant in a clay pot on every table. It's really a mom-and-pop operation, run by Samia and Mo Fayyad. They make everything from scratch—desserts, fresh-cooked turkeys, chickens, pastrami, etc.—and offer the unbeatable combination of quality, quantity, and low prices. Samia's like-mother-used-to-make daily specials ($4.50 to $5.50) might include stuffed cabbage with salad, meat loaf with mashed potatoes and vegetable, and fabulous homemade falafel. There are delicious overstuffed deli sandwiches like pastrami, corned beef, fresh-roasted turkey on rye, and a Reuben that would pass muster in New York, plus salads, burgers, and omelets. For dessert, try Samia's superb pineapple Bavarian cream tarts or vanilla and chocolate ribbon mousse cake. Sometimes she even makes baked Alaska with Häagen-Dazs ice cream! If you crave it, call and order it in advance. Open from 7 a.m. (at breakfast, two eggs, hash browns, bacon, toast, and coffee cost $2.55, a bacon and egg sandwich just 99¢) to 3:30 p.m. weekdays only. Beer and wine are available.

A COFFEESHOP: Unbeknownst to the general public, office building coffeeshops abound in D.C., some of them, like **Copperfield's,** in the Brawner Building at 888 17th St. NW, at I St. (tel. 293-2217), offering quite good food at low prices. This eatery's attributes extend to a charming ambience, with low-ceilinged inn-like dining areas and soft lighting from lanterns and stained-glass fixtures. Some walls are adorned with pewter mugs, cooking implements, old photographs, and framed oil paintings; others are covered in red Scottish plaid. For about two decades, Copperfield's has been bucking up office drudges with midday home-cooked meals. A six-ounce New York strip steak sandwich smothered in onions and served with french fries is $6.25; a cream cheese and bacon burger with lettuce, tomato, and fries is $4.35; a ham-and-swiss sandwich on pumpernickel with coleslaw, $3.75. There's a full bar. Open weekdays only from 7 to 11 a.m. for breakfast, 11 a.m. to 3 p.m. for lunch, and 5 to 7 p.m. weekdays for Happy Hour featuring complimentary hors d'oeuvres and drink specials.

3. On and Near the Mall

I love the Smithsonian, but I'd like to store its eating facilities up in the nation's attic. Most Mall restaurants cater to hordes of tourists, and volume food is never great. If you want a really good meal, take an hour or two off and get yourself to another part of town. On the other hand, if you just need sufficient calories to continue making the museum rounds without passing out, there are plenty of options. Go early or late to avoid the most crowded times.

IN THE NATIONAL GALLERY: The **cafeteria** in the Concourse connecting the East and West Buildings of the National Gallery of Art is bright and cheerful, with green plastic furniture amid planters and potted palms. It overlooks a cascading waterfall, and good acoustics keep the noise level bearable. A good bet here is the create-your-own-salad bar, $1.70 for greens, 40¢ to 70¢ for additional items like mushrooms, ham, grated cheese, and chickpeas. Or ward off hunger with something like a chicken salad sandwich on croissant with potato salad ($3.50) and a dish of homemade ice cream ($1), saving your appetite for worthier culinary adventures at dinner. Hot entrees like prime rib and beef Stroganoff are in the $2.75 to $4.25 range. Wine and beer are available. Open 10 a.m. to 3:30 p.m. on weekdays and Saturday, noon to 6 p.m. on Sunday. It does get immensely crowded around lunchtime; however, even if the line is very long, don't despair—it moves quickly.

If your museum-weary feet can't handle even a fast-moving cafeteria line by the time lunchtime arrives, plop yourself down at a table in the adjoining **Cascade Café,** which offers the best waterfall views and waiter service. Here for $6.10 you might enjoy a selection of cheeses, fresh fruits, country pâté, a bread basket, and a glass of wine; a hot-fudge sundae ($2.50) will complete your restoration. Similarly classy fare is offered at two other National Gallery eateries, the **Terrace Café,** overlooking the Mall in the East Building, and the **Garden Café** in the West Building, the latter centered around a fountain under a skylight. Hours of operation are slightly different at each of these; inquire at the information desk. The three restaurants take major credit cards; the cafeteria is on a cash-only basis.

HIRSHHORN AL FRESCO: My favorite Smithsonian eatery is the lovely **Full Circle at the Hirshhorn,** a plaza café outside the museum accessible from Independence Avenue. Not having to trudge through a museum to get to it is a plus. Open daily 11 a.m. to 4 p.m. from Memorial Day to Labor Day, it changes annually but is always charming. Glass-topped white enamel tables, shaded by white canvas Oriental umbrellas and adorned with pots of flowers (gardenias on our last visit) overlook sculptures around a fountain on one side, the Smithsonian "castle" on the other. It's a serene respite from the hustle bustle of the Mall, and service is quick and friendly. Items in the $5 to $7 range might include pasta salads, cheese/fruit/cold cut platters, and pita or croissant sandwiches (e.g. stuffed with tuna, cashews, and sprouts). And I've often stopped by for refreshing iced coffee and desserts like cheesecake with Mandarin oranges or fresh strawberries and whipped cream. Wine and beer are available.

OTHER MALL CAFETERIAS: If you don't want to make a big deal out of eating, some other Mall museums also have cafeterias. The **National Museum of Natural History** offers one of the more attractive settings, with carpeted floors and dozens of flourishing hanging plants (they're maintained by the horticulture department) under four skylights. At **Air and Space** and the **National Museum of American History** you can snatch food off a revolving carousel—fun for kids. The latter scores with a nonsmoking section. All of the above offer inexpensive, if uninspired cafeteria food, fine for a quick bite to shore you up for further sightseeing. And in the works at this writing is the **Crystal Palace** on the first floor of **Air and Space.** It will feature a fast food area, a dining room with waiter service, and outdoor seating.

OTHER MALLS: A wide selection of dining facilities can be found at both the **Pavilion at the Old Post Office,** 1100 Pennsylvania Ave. NW (tel. 289-4224), and the **Shops at National Place,** 1331 Pennsylvania Ave. NW (tel. 783-9090). Details in Chapter VII.

C'EST LA VIE: Vie de France, with several D.C. locations noted in this chapter, has a convenient-to-the-Mall location at 600 Maryland Ave. SW (tel. 554-7870) in the Capitol Gallery Building at the L'Enfant Plaza Metro. For an office building eatery, it's quite charming, with wicker-seated chairs and upholstered blue booths at sturdy oak tables, hushed lighting emanating from wall sconces, many hanging plants, and a cozy blue-tiled bar nestling in one corner. There are additional seats in the atrium café under a skylight, enclosed by potted plants and small trees, and at umbrella tables on a large outdoor patio. And a third eating area has a garden decor and French art posters on the wall. At breakfast, a fresh-from-the-oven butter, almond, or chocolate croissant is 85¢, $2.50 with a glass of fresh-squeezed orange juice and tea or coffee. At lunch or dinner you might order chicken salad with walnuts, raisins, and fresh fruits; a *petit repas* of pâté with brie and fruit; or a hamburger with melted brie and toasted almonds served with coleslaw—all of these priced under $5. All entrees and sandwiches come with or on freshly baked french bread. There's a fancy dessert tray, but you could just hop next door to the adjoining **Fast & Fresh,** under the same ownership, for a fresh-baked chocolate-chip cookie or two. Here the ambience is less elegant but the aroma of the on-premises bakery is extremely enticing. Fast & Fresh is also less expensive, doubly so since its cafeteria service means no tipping is required. There's much more you can enjoy at these adjoining eateries than I've described thus far—gourmet omelets, Belgian waffles, traditional French onion soup, a classic salad Niçoise, marvelous sandwiches on French bread or croissant, palmiers, brioches, etc. This is a great place to pick up picnic fare.

Vie de France is open weekdays from 7:30 a.m. to 9:30 p.m., Saturdays till 4 p.m.; Fast & Fresh, Monday to Friday 7:30 a.m. to 7 p.m., Saturdays 9 a.m. to 4 p.m.

A NEW YORK DELI: Outside of the Big Apple, every pastrami pusher claims to be "just like a New York deli." Ironically, the Washington fare closest to Gotham authenticity is found at the **Dutch Mill Deli,** 639 Indiana Ave. NW, between 6th and 7th Sts. (tel. 347-3665), originally Dutch owned (perhaps they were from a lost tribe) and now run by a nice Jewish boy, Richard Singer, who duplicates their successful formula. He bakes fresh desserts, makes delicious homemade soups, and turns out classic overstuffed deli sandwiches like pastrami, roast beef, corned beef, and fresh roast turkey on rye (all under $5), thick french fries à la Nathan's and homemade potato salad, and cheese blintzes with sour cream like momma used to make. Recently Richard added fresh seafood items like crabcakes, softshell crab, scallops, and fried clams—all served with those homemade fries and all under $6—to his offerings. Not kosher, but delicious. A raw bar is in the works. And at breakfast, of course, you could opt for a bagel with cream cheese and nova, not to mention eggs, pancakes, and Belgian waffles with real whipped cream and fresh strawberries. There's a full bar. The inside dining area has silver-foil-covered and mirrored walls hung with photos of Holland, Dutch art, and wooden shoes. Out front is a lovely awninged patio with white garden furnishings and a border of geranium planters. Service is cafeteria style, so there's no tipping. A great choice. Open weekdays from 6:30 a.m. to 8:30 p.m., 8:30 a.m. to 4 p.m. on Saturday. No credit cards. The National Archives Building is diagonally across the street.

4. Downtown

HOME-COOKING AT ITS BEST: There's no place like **Reeves,** 1209 F St. NW (tel. 347-3781), a Washington institution since 1886. Many of the employees have been here three or four decades, and until a 1984 fire, the decor was largely unchanged from its inception. The renovation has been very tastefully done, however, retaining something of the vintage ambience. Comfortable plush leather booths are lit by turn-of-the-century-style sconces, the exposed brick walls have new oak wainscotting, and the counter still has its original stools. Reeves is about 200 feet long, fronted by a bakery counter filled with scrumptious pies and cakes (one exultant reviewer compared the strawberry pie to desserts at Maxim's in Paris). The owners, brothers Henry and George Abraham, do things the old-fashioned way. Everything is homemade with top-quality ingredients—the turkeys, chickens, salads, coleslaw, potato salad, breads, desserts, even the mayonnaise. At breakfast, you can't beat Reeves' buffet ($3.95 on weekdays, $4.90 on Saturday and holidays, $3.50 and $3.95 respectively, for children eight and under). It includes all you can eat of scrambled eggs, bacon, sausage, home fries, french toast, pancakes, creamed chipped beef, compote, biscuits, grits, corned beef hash, an array of fresh fruits, and homemade doughnuts. At lunch, try a chicken salad sandwich on fresh-baked bread, perhaps with an order of homemade coleslaw or potato salad. There are many hot entrees such as homemade chili and beans, lasagne served with grated cheese and homemade garlic bread, and country-fried chicken (three pieces) with mashed potatoes, gravy, coleslaw, and a roll. This is one place to forget your diet and order dessert—some of Washington's best. The strawberry pie, pecan pie, and strawberry shortcake are all renowned locally. None of the above will break your budget—a soup-to-nuts meal here is easily managed for under $10. A meal at Reeves is like a meal at grandma's house. Open Monday to Saturday from 7 a.m. to 6 p.m. No credit cards.

LOW-PRICED CAFETERIA FARE: Patent Pending, off the courtyard connecting the National Portrait Gallery and the National Museum of American Art, with entrances on 8th and F and 8th and G Streets NW, offers low-priced cafeteria fare in arty surroundings. The interior is pristine and tasteful, with white marble floors and framed art posters adorning white walls, but the courtyard with its shade-providing elms, sculptures, and splashing fountains is definitely the more desirable location. Come for breakfast (croissant and coffee is $1.75; two eggs, $1; bacon, 25¢ a strip) or luncheon fare like ham and swiss on croissant, homemade chili, or tomato stuffed with egg salad and chickpeas, all of those items under $3.75. A carafe of chablis with your meal is $2.25. Open weekdays for breakfast from 10 to 10:30 a.m., lunch from 11 a.m. to 3:30 p.m., on weekends and holidays to 4 p.m. No credit cards.

5. K Street Restaurant Row

BUDGET BEST: Many Washingtonians swear by **Sholl's Colonial Cafeteria,** 1990 K St. NW, in the Esplanade Mall (tel. 296-3065), regarding it as a kind of home away from home. And rather homey it is, as cafeterias go, with red and green carpeting, soft lighting from brass chandeliers, and a few decorative pieces of furniture. The walls are hung with gilt-framed oil paintings, Lion's Club honors, restaurant awards, and prayers (the latter are also on the tables—a different one each day; founder Evan Sholl was a religious man, and his nephews, now running the place, keep up this practice). You'll also get mottoes (usually puritanical ones) with your meals; for example, on a notice for the week's special of oven-baked ham with peach half ($3.25) are the sentiments "He who chops his own wood gets warmed twice" and "I am a great believer in work; I find that the harder I work the more I have of it." And then there's Sholl's own motto: "Live well for less money with quality food at more reasonable prices." Not exactly deathless prose, but it gets the idea across. Sholl's does offer "quality food"—fresh-baked breads and desserts, hamburger meat ground on the premises, fresh vegetables, and home-cooked fare made with fine ingredients. As for the "reasonable prices," they're more than that. Where else could you get a full dinner of roast beef, mashed potatoes, broccoli, a big slab of coconut cream pie, and coffee for $3.50 these days? Or a breakfast of two eggs, bacon, home fries, orange juice, coffee, and homemade biscuits for under $3. Sholl's is open Monday to Saturday from 7 to 10:30 a.m. for breakfast, 11 a.m. to 2:30 p.m. for lunch, and 4 to 8 p.m. for dinner.

FRENCH: Vie de France, 1990 K St. NW, on the second floor of the Esplanade Mall (tel. 659-0055), is owned by a French firm called Grands Moulin de Paris. They specialize in authentic French breads made with American flours carefully blended to match the French equivalents, use French brick and stainless-steel ovens, and employ bakers lured away, say they, from small Paris and Marseilles boulangeries. Light and spacious, it's a pleasant trendy-modern setting with oak floors and tables, hanging plants and halaphane lamps overhead, and a changing exhibit of quality art (it's for sale) on the walls. The taped music is always well chosen; I've often enjoyed Vivaldi and Bach over breakfast, pop and jazz at other times.

Vie de France is a great choice for *petit déjeuner*—a fresh-baked butter, almond, chocolate, fruit, or raisin croissant, with coffee, tea, or milk, and a sizable glass of orange juice is $2.50, $1 more if you select a ham and cheese croissant. The croissants—about a dozen varieties—are also available à la carte, as are brioches, puff pastries, and muffins. Breakfast is cafeteria service. At lunch and dinner there are waiters and waitresses to bring you such fare as sandwiches, like ham and swiss cheese with Dijon mustard or chicken, walnuts, and raisins on baguette, rye, sourdough bread, or croissant; salads, like pasta and broccoli in herb-vinaigrette dressing; soups, such as the traditional French onion gratinée; burgers, for example, with brie and toasted almonds on baguette served with caraway coleslaw; and *les petits repas* such as quiche de jour and salad. All of these items listed are in the $4.50 to $5.50 range. In addition there are dinner specials such as poulet Dijon served with wild rice and vegetable for $7.25, that price including soup du jour, a salad, and freshly baked french bread. There's a full bar, and of course the pâtisseries for dessert are excellent.

Open 7:30 a.m. to 9:30 p.m. Monday to Friday.

There's another, smaller Vie de France at 1723 K St. NW (tel. 775-9193), offering a similar croissant/soup/salad/sandwich menu (no full dinners here), plus beer and wine. Cafeteria service only. Prices are a bit lower. It's open Monday to Friday from 7:30 a.m. to 7:30 p.m., on Saturday from 7:30 a.m. till 4:30 p.m. A third, at 1615 M St. NW (tel. 659-0992) has the same hours.

DELI PLUS: At Ziggy's Deli, 1015 18th St. NW, between K and L Sts. (tel. 331-0860), you can count on big portions of healthy, home-cooked fare. Everything is lovingly prepared and beautifully presented, including fresh-cooked deli meats (corned beef, ham, chicken, pastrami, and turkey) and Ziggy's own salad dressings. The atmosphere is pleasant and cheerful, with orange banquettes, striped wallpaper, and hanging plants overhead. At breakfast, an order of two eggs with hash browns, bacon, toast, and coffee is $2.45; a croissant or fresh-squeezed orange juice, 95¢. At lunch or dinner, you might order lasagne, eggplant parmesan, a scrumptious crab salad with big chunks of crabmeat, fresh chicken salad on a croissant, or a pita sandwich stuffed to bursting with swiss cheese, avocado, cucumber, tomato, and sprouts. All of those items are under $5. A big wedge of carrot cake for dessert is $1.50. Service is cafeteria style, so there's no tipping. Open Monday to Friday from 6 a.m. to 4:30 p.m.; closed Christmas week.

INTERNATIONAL SQUARE: International Square, also known as Farragut West Metro Market, at 19th and K Streets NW, is an eclectic assortment of eateries under a 12-story skylight. Seating is provided for about 300 around a large waterfall/fountain amid lush plantings.

There's Billy's Pit Beef for "belly-busting" barbecue meals (like beef BBQ with french fries and coleslaw for $3.80).

Bagels Etc. offers about a dozen varieties of fresh-baked bagels with sandwich fillings ranging from chopped liver ($3) to a toasted Reuben bagel with swiss cheese and corned beef ($4).

Moussaka and Greek salad are featured at **Stoupsy's of Athens.**

Crescents specializes in fresh-baked croissants, french breads, and gourmet continental fare. A breakfast of fresh-baked croissant, fresh-squeezed orange juice, and coffee is $2.30. Other choices here include a terrific salad bar, deep-dish quiche, and Dove bars.

For chicken meals, head to **Wingmaster's,** where a platter of breastmeat, french fries, a biscuit, and coleslaw is $3.60, a breast of chicken sandwich with ham and cheese on a Kaiser roll costs $3.35, an order of ten wings runs $3.50, and a side of batter-fried onion rings, $1.25. You can request your chicken mild, medium, or spicy, and wing orders come with complimentary celery sticks and homemade bleu cheese.

Pizza is available at **Chef Paolino** ($6.95 for a small pie)—also calzone ($2.80), sausage subs ($3.90), lasagne ($4.60), and many other Italian specialties, most of them served with fresh garlic bread.

Chow mein, an egg roll, and fried rice will set you back $3.95 at **Chow Chow Cup,** a typical Chinese fast-food outlet.

Or perhaps you'd prefer the fresh fried oysters ($3.50) and crabmeat salad ($6.25) at **The Fishery.**

The **French Baker** has desserts like strawberry mousse and mocha eclairs to tempt you.

Finally, there's **Yummy Yogurt,** specializing in various flavors of 100% natural frozen yogurt—chocolate, vanilla, raspberry, carob chip, strawberry, banana, peach, you name it—with toppings like wet walnuts, strawberries, blueberries, and hot fudge. The yogurt is just part of a menu including sandwiches (like cream cheese, avocado, and sprouts on pita for $3.25), assorted salads (try taco chips in a bed of lettuce and tomato covered with chili and sharp cheese for $3.75), plus homemade soups and chili. There are about half a dozen other D.C. locations (check your phonebook).

Most International Square eateries are open daily from about 7 a.m. to 7 p.m.

CONNECTICUT CONNECTION: A similar venture nearby is the Connecticut Connection, Connecticut Avenue and L Street NW at the Farragut North Metro station—a mini-shopping mall with about ten low-priced food outlets. The Connection's gastronomic offerings include a **McDonald's;** cold sesame noodles and sweet-and-sour pork from **Hunan Express; Valentino's** pizza, calzone, and subs; buffalo wings and such from **The Chicken Place;** chili dogs from **Park Avenue Dogs & Chili;** sandwiches, salads, and fresh-baked pastries from **Gourmet Bar Express;** and **Chez Chocolat's** homemade fudge. A **Yummy Yogurt** (see above) and a **Dunkin' Donuts** are additional lures.

Eateries are open Monday to Saturday from 10 a.m. to 6 p.m. There's a pleasant brick-floored dining area with gray Formica tables and seasonal decorations—for example, in spring, sprigs of white cloth cherry blossoms overhead.

6. Dupont Circle Area

CONTINENTAL: Le Souperb/la Salade, 1221 Connecticut Ave. NW, between M and N Sts. (tel. 347-7600), is truly "superb." It's a large and cheerful modernistic-looking place, walls hung with framed art and theater posters and David Levine caricatures of everyone from Colette to LBJ (showing his scar).

Overhead are hanging plants and white enamel lamps, also exposed pipes painted bright red, white, and yellow. Vases of fresh flowers grace every table. Chef Jose Gonzales prepares the hearty soups and stews (he has about 75 in his repertoire); onion soup and chili are always offered, along with additional soups (perhaps cream of broccoli with cheddar cheese, vegetarian cream of mushroom, and navy bean à la Congress—congressmen have told Jose it's better than the Capitol's) and stews (perhaps pot au feu with a matzo ball, fettuccine seafood, chicken cacciatore, or Vietnamese jade fish stew with oysters, clams, shrimp, fish, and Chinese noodles. Soup or stew costs $2.40 for a small bowl, $3.50 for a large, and includes unlimited hot bread and butter (all the fresh-baked bagels, cornbread, rye, sourdough, pumpernickel, etc., you can eat). Le Souperb also has a great salad bar laden with about 35 items; it's priced at $2.75 a pound. There are also hefty deli sandwiches—pastrami, turkey, roast beef, chicken salad, ham and swiss; all made with meats fresh-cooked on the premises —all under $4; potato subs, baked potatoes stuffed with fillings like pork sausage and apples; and homemade desserts like apple strudel or strawberry pie. The latter items can be topped with Inside Scoop ice cream. Wine and beer are available. In addition, Le Souperb features a full breakfast menu (through 11 a.m.) of items like two eggs, sausage, and a fresh-baked bagel for $2.25, fresh-squeezed orange juice for $1.25, and coffee with homemade danish or doughnuts. And weekdays from 5 to 9 p.m. there's an unbeatable nightly special for $4.95—an entree (like baked lasagne, sirloin steak, or shrimp scampi) with a cup of soup, salad bar offerings, and all the above-mentioned breads. Open weekdays from 6:30 a.m. to 8 p.m., Saturday 7:30 a.m. to 3 p.m. No credit cards. Highest recommendation.

The *Washington Post* described the food at **Dupont Villa,** 1345 Connecticut Ave. NW, between N St. and Dupont Circle (tel. 785-2333), as "4H—hefty, hot, hearty, and humbly priced." As to the last, it's one of the few restaurants in town offering lunch prices the entire day. A cozy decor features pecky-pine walls hung with oil paintings, art posters, and photos of Switzerland, comfortable booth seating, and art nouveau-shaded *Casablanca* fan chandeliers and wall sconces. It's basically a more-charming-than-average neighborhood coffeehouse/bar.

Entrees, mostly in the $4.50 to $7 range, run to Italian fare like rigatoni with meatballs and veal parmigiana with spaghetti. But you can also order shish kebab with rice pilaf, all of the above including a salad and a cup of tasty home-made soup. There's pizza too, $4.95 for a small one, with $1 for each extra topping, and sandwiches run the gamut from fried filet of sole served with french fries and coleslaw to a Greek souvlaki—tenderloin beef, feta cheese, lettuce, tomatoes, and onions on pita bread—served with french fries. A large bowl of chef salad or Greek salad is $4.50, and for dessert there's homemade rice pudding and baklava. All bar drinks are available. Open Sunday to Thursday from 11 a.m. to 2 a.m., on Friday and Saturday until 3 a.m.

MIDDLE EASTERN: Offering the most alluring setting for D.C. dining al fresco is the **Iron Gate Inn,** 1734 N St. NW (tel. 737-1370). It's the winner of *Washingtonian* magazine's "most romantic restaurant" award, and the *Washington Post* has praised the establishment for scoring "equally well on food, environment, service, and value." Its outdoor tables, covered in red-and-white checkered cloths, are under the shade of a wisteria vine, a grape arbor (in August you can snack on the grapes until your order comes), and a magnolia tree. Somehow it's cool out here even on the hottest days, and at night with candlelight and colored lamps it's magical. More tables line the covered cobblestone carriageway. In winter, the interior—a converted stable dating to the Spanish and Indian War, complete with the original hay racks, feed boxes, and harness hooks—is marvelously cozy. There are secluded booths in the actual old horse stalls, their walls lined with equestrian prints. And amber lighting creates a romantic atmosphere, enhanced by a blaze in the big brick fireplace. There's an additional dining room upstairs.

Owner John Saah's mother does all the cooking. She's an expert chef whose credits include catering White House functions. Lunch entrees offer Middle Eastern specialties in the $7 to $8 range, such as lamb and vegetable couscous and grape leaves stuffed with lamb and rice, plus fare as American as a chicken salad sandwich—albeit on pita bread if you prefer. For a light meal, consider sharing several hors d'oeuvres with pita bread, perhaps orders of hummus, baba ghanouj, and stuffed grape leaves, along with a half liter of wine, all of which will cost about $7 per person. Finish up with mom's unbelievably scrumptious baklava and Arabic coffee. Dinner entrees are in the $8 to $10 bracket for the most part. Open daily, 11:30 a.m. to 10 p.m. Reservations are advisable at dinner, and it's a good idea to arrive early at lunch if you want to sit outdoors. The Iron Gate Inn is incredibly popular.

THE STEAK SUPREME: A reasonably priced steak dinner is hard to come by, but at **Annie's Paramount Steak House,** 1609 17th St. NW (tel. 232-0395), there's beef for the budget-minded. The Katinas family has been running this fine eatery since 1948—paterfamilias George J. along with four sisters (one of them is named Annie), a few cousins, a brother, two sons, and a daughter. They serve only USDA choice and prime certified Angus beef, butchered and aged (three to four weeks) on the premises. Fresh fish and seafood is another specialty. At lunch, you can't beat the six-ounce sirloin, served with a choice of two fresh vegetables (perhaps mashed potatoes and carrots) for just $5.95. Also in the $4 to $6 range are a Greek salad, a delicious crabcake sandwich served with fries and coleslaw, an eight-ounce cheeseburger served with grilled onions and fries, and stir-fried sirloin tips with salad and Spanish rice. Many dinner entrees are in the $7 to $9 range. And a weekend brunch insert offers a three-egg omelet filled with feta cheese, green peppers, and onions, served with home fries, toast, and coffee for $6.25, among other entrees. Drinks like Bloody Marys and mimosas are just $1.95 at brunch. Good creamy cheesecake here, too.

Though the Katinas dynasty is old, the 17th Street location is brand new and spiffy looking. It's fronted by a sunny glassed-in café area—with windows wide open when the weather warrants—handsomely decorated with cocoa walls, and black leather banquette seating. The interior, entered via a lofty archway, has sienna walls decorated with beer keg covers and black and white checkerboard floors. Seating is in black leather-upholstered booths, and lots of daylight streams in through big plant-filled windows. There's an additional dining area upstairs on the balcony level, and bars are located both upstairs and down. Great food, well chosen background music, and a simpático decor make Annie's low prices a spectacular bargain. Open Monday to Thursday 11:30 a.m. to 11:30 p.m., Friday 11:30 a.m. to 1 a.m., Saturday 10:30 a.m. to 1 a.m., Sunday 10:30 a.m. to 11:30 p.m.

BOOKS AND BRIE: Kramerbooks & afterwords, A Café, 1517 Connecticut Ave. NW, between Dupont Circle and Q St. (tel. 387-1462), is the kind of congenial place you go for a cappuccino at 11 p.m. after the movies, for an intense personal discussion about your love life over a plate of fettuccine, or to linger over a good book and a cognac (both of which can be purchased here) on a sunny afternoon. There's indoor seating at butcher-block tables with wrought-iron chairs under a low, beamed ceiling—a light and pleasant café atmosphere

—additional seating in the upstairs balcony overlooking the bookstore, at the bar, in a glass-enclosed solarium hung with colorful banners, and best of all outside at street café tables. From about 9 p.m. to midnight Friday and Saturday live entertainment—folk music, jazz, blues, or classical—is provided.

The café is open for breakfast, which might range from a croissant ($1.35) to a splurgy smoked salmon platter served with fresh-squeezed orange juice, a bagel, cream cheese, and coffee ($6.25). The rest of the day there are sandwiches like six ounces of turkey breast with fresh dill mayonnaise on french bread for $5.25. Heartier entrees such as quiche of the day; garlicky linguine with scampi, sun-dried tomatoes, mushrooms, and sweet yellow peppers in a parmesan/cream sauce; or baked breast of chicken in mustard/soy marinade over steamed spinach and sesame noodles, are in the $6 to $9 range. And there are also munchies ($5 to $7) such as soup and salad served with bread and butter or barbecued beef quesadillas topped with guacamole and sour cream.

Do save room for rich, sensual desserts like chocolate truffle cake. Ice-cream drinks (for example, two scoops of Sedutto coffee with Amaretto and Crème de Cacao, hot coffee drinks (such as with Irish cream, Irish whiskey, and whipped cream), and frozen fruit daiquiris are also big here, and a large selection of vodkas are served cold. Something for everyone. Very simpático. Open Monday to Thursday from 8 a.m. to 1 a.m., and continuously from Friday at 8 a.m. through Sunday at 1 a.m.

LOW-COST GREEK: Catering to students and other segments of the population who, however financially strapped, never consider forgoing restaurant meals, is the **Astor,** 1813 M St. NW (tel. 331-7994), dishing out hefty portions of Greek fare at very low prices. At this location since 1939, it's a cozy place, with bright Mediterranean-blue tufted leather banquettes and chairs, gilt-framed oil paintings of Greece on the walls, and stained-glass lighting fixtures. There's additional seating upstairs, an area that becomes a nightclub—the Bouzouki Room—every evening at 8:30 p.m. featuring belly dancers. At lunch, $4.95 will buy baked moussaka, stuffed grape leaves, a Greek cheese omelet, or baked eggplant, all served with a vegetable (perhaps chickpea salad or spinach and rice). The same items cost a dollar more at dinner; add another dollar and you have a complete meal with soup, coffee or tea, and homemade rice pudding. That's just a small sampling of the Astor's offerings; the menu's quite extensive, and there's full bar service. The homemade baklava here is delicious. Open Sunday to Thursday from 11 a.m. to 2 a.m., on Friday and Saturday till 3 a.m.

A PUBBY SPORTS BAR AND EATERY: Timberlake's, 1726 Connecticut Ave. NW, between R and S Sts. (tel. 483-2266), is a lively scene with a good juke box and an ambience that ranges from cheerful to raucous—the latter when local sporting events are aired on the TV over the bar to enthusiastic commentary from the clientele. The main dining room is a pubby setting—dimly lit, with bare oak floors, exposed brick walls hung with antique Coke and Pepsi signs, and fans suspended from a pressed-copper ceiling. A boar's head trophy wearing a Redskins cap is mounted on a brick pillar. Never the cave-dwelling type, I prefer the sunshiny skylit back room with garden furnishings and pots of philodendrons overhead. The food here is very good. There are hearty, over-stuffed sandwiches like a Monte Cristo—turkey, ham, swiss cheese, and onions grilled in egg batter and served with vegetables ($6). Burgers (5½ ounces) come with toppings running the gamut from blue cheese to artichoke hearts in béarnaise sauce and are served with onion rings or fries ($5 to $6). Delicious salads and omelets are in the same price range; more serious entrees (such as a filet mignon béarnaise on an English muffin with a baked potato and vegetable) are offered at dinner from $7.50; and any time there are great desserts such as pecan pie à la mode with Ben & Jerry's ice cream. A special brunch menu—very reasonably priced—featuring pancakes, waffles, eggs Benedict, etc., is offered Saturday and Sunday till 3 p.m. Timberlake's fare is all freshly cooked using top-quality ingredients, including fresh-squeezed juices in your drinks, real vegetables, and 100% Vermont maple syrup on your pancakes.

Open Monday to Thursday from 11:30 a.m. to 2 a.m., Friday and Saturday 10:30 a.m. to 3 a.m., Sunday 10:30 a.m. to 2 a.m. Food is served till two hours before closing.

FOOD LIKE MOM'S: Trio Restaurant, 17th and Q Sts. NW (tel. 232-6305), is a real find. Its comfortably roomy burgundy leather booths (the kind with coathooks) are filled each morning with local folk checking out the *Washington Post* over big platters of bacon and eggs ($2.95 with home fries, toast, and coffee). The fare's like mama's home-cooking, served up by appropriately motherly waitresses. Multipaned windows are hung with plants, there are fresh flowers on every table, and in good weather, the awninged outdoor café is always packed. The Trio's been around for 3½ decades—originally Pete and Helen Mallios' mom-and-pop business, now run by son George—and it's on its way to becoming a Washington legend.

The food is fresh, and you can't beat the prices. At lunch, entrees such as crabmeat cakes with buttered green peas and baked macaroni au gratin; turkey (the Trio roasts up four a day) with cornbread dressing, cranberry sauce, homemade candied sweets, and greens; or baked meatloaf with mashed potatoes and green beans are in the $4 to $6 range, those prices including tea or coffee. At dinner, similar specials cost $1 additional but include soup and dessert as well. In addition, you can order all day from an à la carte menu featuring sandwiches like turkey salad and fried fish (all under $3), salads, steaks, seafood, quiche, and more. There's a full bar, so a glass of wine with your meal is an option. A soda fountain turns out hot fudge sundaes and milkshakes. And that's not all—espresso drinks spiked with liqueurs like Grand Marnier and Frangelica and topped with whipped cream are also available at this eclectic eatery. Open daily from 7:30 a.m. to midnight.

Café Splendide, 1521 Connecticut Ave. NW (tel. 328-1503), is owned by two Austrian brothers, Walter and Max, who turn out some of the best homecooked and fresh-baked fare in town. The decor is appropriately kitschy, with trompe l'oeil gingham curtained windows on the walls, baskets of hanging ferns, and numerous framed prints by Austrian artist Hans Rudolf Richter, the Norman Rockwell of Austria. Vases of cloth flowers adorn the tables. In good weather you can dine outdoors on a patio bordered by geranium planters, but you have to enter it from 19th Street between Q Street and Dupont Circle.

Come by for breakfast and enjoy a fresh-from-the-oven cheese danish or apple strudel made with fresh apples along with your morning coffee. And it's excellent coffee by the way. Or opt for the "Scotch woodcock"—scrambled eggs on a muffin with anchovies and capers ($3.05). At lunch and dinner the menu is the same, except for daily specials. Some entrees are Austrian, such as paprikaschnitzel with onions, green peppers, mushrooms, and pimentos; beef Stroganoff; and a platter of broiled bratwurst and knackwurst with potato salad or sauerkraut. But you can also get a tortellini salad with smoked oysters, clams, and vegetables; French onion soup with bread and butter; ratatouille; or a sandwich (on homemade bread) of ham, salami, tomato, pepperoncini, and sauerkraut.

Full entrees (mostly in the $6 to $7 range) are served with fresh vegetables and a choice of noodles, rice, or home fries. Sandwiches, soups, and salads are a few dollars less. Off hours, come by just for dessert and coffee. The crème brûlée ($2) is heaven, ditto the palatschinken—crêpes with apricot jam and powdered sugar ($3.25). Both French and California wines are offered; other beverages range from fresh-squeezed lemonade to piña coladas and daiquiris—not to mention apéritifs, hot apple cider with rum, and Austro-German beers. The menu here changes seasonally. Don't miss the softshell crab if it's listed when you visit. It's superb.

Open Tuesday to Thursday from 9 a.m. to 11:30 p.m., on Friday to 1:30 a.m., on Saturday from 8 a.m. to 1:30 a.m., and on Sunday from 8 a.m. to 11:30 p.m. Reservations suggested. No credit cards.

The **Kozy Korner Restaurant** is indeed cozy, and it also has a corner location at 1253 20th St. at N. St. (tel. 785-4314). It's a friendly family-run business, a place with a lot of regular customers and glowing reviews on the walls amid photographs of the Lincoln and Jefferson Memorials, and historic prints. Beigelinen-clothed tables, brown carpeting, and Tiffany-style lamps enhance the homey atmosphere. A small bar is tucked in one corner. Everything is homemade—the soups (navy bean, red snapper chowder, lentil, etc.), the salad dressings, the deli meats ($3.25 for a fresh turkey salad sandwich, $3.75 for roast beef), even the potato salad and coleslaw. Low-priced platters ($5 to $6) include barbecued ribs with steakhouse potatoes, coleslaw, and a hard roll; fried chicken with the same trimmings; and a fresh open-face hot turkey sandwich with mashed potatoes, gravy, and cranberry sauce. The Kozy Korner is open from 7 a.m. for breakfast (try the homemade french toast with sausage for $3.10) to 10 p.m. Monday to Friday, till 3 p.m. on Saturday. An adjoining carry-out operation is open weekdays from 6:30 a.m. to 3 p.m.

INDIAN: The food at **Katmandu**, 1800 Connecticut Ave. NW, at the corner of S St. and Florida Ave. (tel. 483-6470), is so good I'd like to work my way through the entire menu and then begin all over again. The setting is suitably exotic, with arched doorways and mirrors, Rajasthani fringed mirrorwork canopies and colorful *chitars* (umbrellas) overhead, cut-brass lighting fixtures with variegated bulbs (a festive touch), and paintings from Jaipur of 12th-century scenes adorning the walls.

The award-winning fare features Nepali and Kashmiri specialties. My favorite dish among the latter is murgh zabunnisa—chicken pieces cooked with fresh tomatoes, almonds, cream, and cashews. Among the Nepali selections it's charcoal-grilled jumbo shrimp with Himalayan herbs. Then too the mutton biryani—boneless mutton pieces marinated in Himalayan herbs and spices and cooked with saffron rice, cashews, peas, and almonds—is memorable. Orders of chapatis—grilled Indian bread—and rich, creamy dall shorba are suggested accompaniments. And sweet Indian desserts such as homemade rice pudding flavored with cardamom and sprinkled with pistachios and crushed almonds are refreshing to the palate. Lunch entrees are $4.50 to $7, dinner entrees $6 to $10. Open for lunch weekdays from 11:30 a.m. to 2:30 p.m., for dinner from 5 to 11 p.m. seven days. Reservations advised at dinner.

ITALIAN: **Luigi's Pizzeria Restaurant,** 1132 19th St. NW, between L and M Sts. (tel. 331-7574), makes "the best pizza in the city," according to the *Washington Post*. It's priced from $6.75 for a plain pie for two people (actually ample for three), with additional items like homemade sausage, pepperoni, fresh mushrooms, and extra cheese (there are 19 choices) $1.60 apiece. Other than pizza, the rest of the dinner menu is too expensive for consideration here, but at lunch homemade pasta entrees like spaghetti with chicken cacciatore sauce, red agnolotti filled with sausage and beef, and fettuccine al pesto are all under $7, as are many veal dishes—scaloppine, marsala, parmigiana, etc.—the latter including spaghetti, a vegetable, and bread and butter. Even less expensive are hearty sandwiches such as calzone alla Luigi for $4.75. The upstairs decor features scenes of Italy in brick archways and, scroll-topped columns. Downstairs, white brick and pine-paneled walls are hung with botanical prints of grape varieties and tables are clothed in red linen. And most pleasant is the awninged patio out front. Luigi's is a well-established D.C. eatery run by the Bruzzo family since 1943. Open Monday to Saturday from 11 a.m. to 2 a.m., on Sunday from noon to midnight.

NATURAL FOODS: Food for Thought, 1738 Connecticut Ave. NW, near S St. (tel. 797-1095), exists in a '60s time warp, complete with a community bulletin board plastered with notices seeking workers on an organic farm, clients for holistic massage, and the like. Art and dance posters line the white walls, rattan-shaded globe lights are suspended from a high ceiling, and there's seating in roomy red vinyl booths or at a long marble-topped counter. At night candles in amber glass holders provide atmosphere. Evenings from 7:30 to 10:30 p.m. (8 p.m. to midnight on Friday and 6 p.m. to 12:30 a.m. on Saturday) classical guitarists, folk singers, jazz pianists, and other assorted musicians (once I happened on a dulcimer player) entertain. In between, taped music (anything from the Beatles to Bach) is usually on.

The orientation here is vaguely toward health food—more like healthy junk food in many cases, such as a six-ounce organic beef burger or a nitrate-free, all-beef hot dog, both served on whole-wheat bun with "natural" potato chips. Of course you can also get a fruit and nut salad with apples, bananas, cashews, raisins, and sunflower seeds in yogurt and honey; a pita stuffed with avocado, mushrooms, sprouts, tomatoes, and homemade lemon-tahini dressing; or a cheese board with apple and crackers. All of the above selections are under $5. Heartier entrees ($5 to $8.50) range from a three-cheese lasagne and salad to a whole brook trout sauteed in butter with salad and brown rice or baked potato. About 35% of Food for Thought's regular customers are vegetarians. Desserts run a wide gamut from homemade banana-nut bread to an ice-cream sundae with whipped cream, nuts, and chocolate sauce. Ditto beverages, ranging from wine and beer to papaya juice. Open Tuesday to Thursday from 11:30 a.m. to midnight, on Friday to 1 a.m., on Saturday from noon to 1 a.m., on Sunday from 5 p.m. to midnight, and on Monday from 11:30 a.m. to 3 p.m. and 5 p.m. to midnight. The upstairs bar stays open an hour later.

BAGEL BRANCH: More low key than its Capitol Hill counterpart (see listing above for details and prices), the Dupont Circle **Chesapeake Bagel Bakery,** 1636 Connecticut Ave. NW, between Q and R Sts. (tel. 328-7985), is suited to its more leisurely neighborhood. The setting—with blue-cushioned bentwood chairs, blue enamel lamps overhead, and framed quality art prints on the walls —is attractive and comfortable. The menu is almost identical to the Capitol Hill Chesapeake's—different kinds of baked-on-the-premises bagels are spread with nova and cream cheese or filled with chopped liver, shrimp salad, tuna salad, and such, plus soups, muffins, and desserts. Open Sunday to Thursday from 7 a.m. to 9 p.m., on Friday and Saturday to 11 p.m. No credit cards.

GRACIOUS GREEK: At **Alekos,** 1732 Connecticut Ave. NW, between R and S Sts. (tel. 667-6211), owner Alekos Marountas has transformed an old neighborhood bar into a charming little eatery with oak-wainscotted white stucco walls, colonnaded archways, charcoal gray carpeting, crystal sconces, and an abundance of plants. During the day, the gray matte tables are adorned with fresh flowers; at night they're dressed up with pale gray linen cloths over burgundy and candles in frosted tulip glasses.

But Alekos is not only pretty. It's a very authentic Greek restaurant serving huge portions of hearty homemade fare. At lunch consider a plate of shared appetizers such as taramosalata (red caviar and potatoes whipped with olive oil and lemon), stuffed grape leaves, and saganaki (Greek cheese lightly fried in butter and lemon). With a big Greek salad for each of you and plenty of pita bread and butter, such a feast can be enjoyed for about $7 apiece. Or for the same price, skip the salads and share an Alekos sampler plate laden with moussaka, pastitsio (a Greek macaroni, beef, and cheese dish), spanakotyropeta (spinach and feta cheese pie), and stuffed grape leaves. Finish up with baklava and rich coffee. Dinner prices, except for salads and shared appetizers, are out of our budget range, with entrees at $8 to $13. Friendly service is a plus here. Open daily 11:30 a.m. to 11:30 p.m.

BOUNTIFUL BUFFETS, ITALIAN STYLE: The Café Pettito, 1724 Connecticut Ave. NW (tel. 462-8771), lures diners with a magnificent window display—an antipasto of some 50 items. There are rice salads, bean salads, creamy egg salads, pasta salads, and homemade potato salads; vinaigrettes of tuna and tomato with chunks of onion; marinated eggplant and fried eggplant; escarole with pancetta; artichoke hearts; cold cuts; cheeses; marinated mushrooms; snow peas; olives; even stuffed grape leaves. And it all tastes as good as it looks. Step inside, and you can sample as much of it as you can heap onto a plate for $6.25. Or for the same price, you can order up a lightly fried doughy pizza for two, the recipe for which, our menu informs us, has been passed down "from generations of Pettitos from the small village of San Giovanni in Fiore, Calabria, Italy." It's fabulous, the basic pie topped with plum tomatoes, mozzarella, and fresh basil, with 31 optional toppings priced from $1.75 to $2.50—hot sausage, smoked mozzarella, eggplant, sun-dried tomatoes, hot banana peppers, capers, mussels, baby clams, prosciutto, you name it. Another specialty ($5 to $6.50) is Italian hoagies—hard rolls stuffed with fillings like grilled chicken breast, marinated tomatoes, basil, and olive oil; they're served with roasted potatoes and green bean salad. If you graze from the buffet, a side order of the café's scrumptious garlic bread is highly recommended; it's baked with mozzarella, fresh marinated tomatoes, basil, and olive oil. Reasonably priced Italian wines are available by the glass. And if you have a little room left, the chocolate amaretto cheesecake is notable.

Café Pettito is the creation of brothers Byron and Roger Pettito, highly acclaimed D.C. restaurateurs. It's an unpretentious but pleasant milieu with bare wood tables, black-and-white checkerboard floors, and wainscotted cream stucco walls hung with numerous photos of the Pettitos' extended family. Open Sunday to Thursday from 11:30 a.m. to midnight, Friday and Saturday to 1 a.m. No reservations. Arrive off hours to avoid long lines at this deservedly popular café.

In the same genre, and just a few doors down, is the red- white- , and green-awninged **Pizza & Pasta,** 1712 Connecticut Ave. NW (tel. 232-4768), a cheerful place wherein icing-pink walls are adorned with posters framed by white columns. Hanging plants and vases of colorful cloth flowers add a pleasant note. P & P is light and sunny during the day; at night the red-linened tables are lit by candles in cut-glass holders. And no small part of this restaurant's allure derives from the lavish buffet displayed, like Pettito's, in the front window. Here your piled-high platter costs $5.95, and there's a wide selection of traditional down-to-earth Italian dishes to choose from. Portions are hefty, and everything is homemade. A small pizza with all the toppings—onions, mushrooms, olives, green peppers, pepperoni, sausage, and meatballs—is $7.95. Pasta dishes like spaghetti with sausages, fettuccine Alfredo, and baked tortellini are in the $5 to $7 range, open-faced sandwiches on garlic bread, e.g. eggplant parmigiana, are under $5. And at lunch there are many specials in the $3.50 to $5.50 bracket. P & P has an additional dining room upstairs to seat overflow crowds. It's open Sunday to Thursday from 11:30 a.m. to midnight, Friday and Saturday till 1:30 a.m.

FROZEN PLEASURES: On the same block as the above, **TCBY** (which stands for "The Country's Best Yogurt"), at 1774 Connecticut Ave. NW (tel. 667-0206), is not a restaurant but a small snackery ideal for light, low-calorie meals. Well, some of them are low-calorie, anyway. This Arkansas-based chain's delicious frozen yogurt, 96% fat free and just 29 to 41 calories an ounce (it depends on the flavor) is smooth and creamy. Four flavors are offered each day, always French vanilla and Dutch chocolate, plus changing selections that might include peanut butter, almond, pecan, eggnog, orange, boysenberry, lemon, pumpkin, or piña colada. You can enjoy these in a cup ($1.50 for seven ounces), in a shake, a waffle cone, a fruit smoothie, wrapped in a crêpe with fruit or hot fudge toppings and whipped cream, sandwiched between gourmet chocolate chip cookies, or atop a homemade Belgian waffle. The latter—with French vanilla yogurt and any three toppings plus whipped cream—is the most expensive item on the menu at $3.35. So everything here is most affordable. One of my favorites is the pecan/praline-filled crêpe smothered in hot fudge. There's a great choice of toppings—raspberries, peaches, pineapple, cherries, strawberries, bananas, shredded coconut, chocolate and butterscotch chips, trail mix, sprinkles, nuts, Raisinets, crumbled Oreos, etc. Decorated with hanging plants, TCBY offers limited seating at about half a dozen tables with wicker-back chairs. It's open Sunday to Thursday from 11 a.m. to 10 p.m., till 11 p.m. Friday and Saturday nights, an hour later across the board in summer.

DUTCH TREAT/CARRY-OUT ONLY: **Dutch Treat I, II, and III,** at 1710 L St. NW (tel. 296-3219), 1901 L St. NW (tel. 223-9421), and 818 15th St. NW (tel. 682-0811), respectively, are pristine Dutch carry-out operations run by Bill Verhoeven, a chef from Holland. They're rather charming, with Delft blue tile-like decorations on white walls and hanging copper pots. Broodjes (Dutch sandwiches on a hard roll) are a specialty, stuffed with items like smoked salmon, crabmeat salad, Dutch liverwurst, and pâté de maison. They cost about $2 to $4, and are also available on regular breads, including croissants. Everything is prepared fresh daily: cold cuts, salads (like Russian salad with potatoes, peas, and carrots or mushroom marinade), and—at 1901 only—hot entrees like roast chicken and lasagne. There are pastries from the well-known Watergate bakery and Häagen-Dazs ice creams. Weekday hours are 7:30 a.m. to 4 p.m. at 1910 L St. and 818 15th St., 7:30 a.m. to 6 p.m. at 1710 L St. The latter two are also open on Saturday from 10:30 a.m. to 3 p.m.

7. The Kennedy Center

Its slightly out-of-the-way location, at the southern end of New Hampshire Avenue, makes the Kennedy Center an unlikely choice for dining unless you're touring the building or attending a performance here. In that case, you should take advantage of its excellent dining facilities (tel. 833-8870). All of them are on the Terrace floor.

MODERATELY PRICED DINING: The **Curtain Call Cafe** is an elegant coffee-shop with red leatherette booths and banquettes, flower-bedecked tables, and framed Kennedy Center show posters lining the walls. Pots of philodendrons are suspended overhead. It's open for dinner only from 5 to 8 p.m., days of operation depending on performances. Entrees, mostly in the $7 to $10 range, might include pork chops with apple/peanut sauce, Mediterranean chicken salad with broccoli, or lasagne pizzaiola. Fresh-baked desserts are temptingly displayed.

Adjoining the Curtain Call, and more in our price range, is the **Encore Cafeteria,** a light and delightful dining room with windows all around, high ceilings hung with striking orange and deep-red banners, and comfortable upholstered chairs. Entrees are very good and very reasonable—about $4 for rigatoni in meat sauce, Spanish paella, or fried chicken. Or you might opt for the salad bar, offering about 35 items and priced by the ounce. A glass of wine with your meal is $2.20, and there are fresh-baked pastries and cakes as well as Sedutto ice creams for dessert. Open daily from 11 a.m. to 8 p.m.

BIG SPLURGES: Above our budget is the extremely ornate **Roof Terrace Restaurant,** with red-velvet Louis XV upholstered chairs, crystal chandeliers, elaborate floral displays, and flocked silk wallpapers. Entree prices are $12 to $18. But don't despair. You can enjoy the same deluxe setting at the adjoining **Hors D'Oeuvrerie.** Even more *intime* and charming than the restaurant, it offers cocktails and gourmet snacks in the $5 to $8 range such as grilled spring lamb chops, Chinese dumplings with Peking red dipping sauce, and pizza topped with chicken and sun-dried tomatoes. It's also nice for desserts and coffee. Chocolate strawberry shortcake or peach/hazelnut cheesecake are $3.50. Open from 5 p.m. until a half hour after the last show.

8. Georgetown

FRENCH: Au Pied de Cochon, 1335 Wisconsin Ave. NW, just below O St. (tel. 333-5440), is as close as any American eatery will ever come to being like an authentic French café/brasserie. It's marvelously unpretentious, especially by Georgetown standards. The interior is dimly lit and cluttery with copper pots hanging over the bar, a cartoon-like Parisian-style mural of a pig doomed to slaughter by chefs on the back wall, another pig on a pole atop a weathervane, and historic photos from World War II displayed over red leather banquettes. I prefer the sunny, glass-enclosed café area with its bentwood chairs and white marble pedestal tables, the perfect place to while away an afternoon reading the paper, sipping espresso, and observing the action outside.

A traditional croissant and café au lait breakfast is $3, though for $3.75 you can have two eggs, bacon, pommes rissolés, and buttered toast. Those croissants, by the way, are fresh from the oven and come in delicious varieties like almond, chocolate cinnamon, and fruit. Among the French café classics here are quiche Lorraine served with pommes-frites and ratatouille, coq au vin with boiled potatoes and ratatouille, and pain bagnat (salade Niçoise on french bread), all in the $5.50 to $8 range. A traditional onion soup au gratin is $4, desserts like crème caramel and chocolate mousse $2.75. There are always daily specials for $10 or less—perhaps roast duck à l'orange or roast leg of lamb au jus. "Zee Foot of Zee Pig" recommends a demi-carafe ($4) or carafe ($7.50) of wine with your meal. Open 24 hours a day except from 2 a.m. to 10:30 a.m. Monday morning.

Just next door, and under the same ownership (the *trés charmant* Yves Courbois), is **Aux Fruits de Mer,** 1329 Wisconsin Ave. NW (tel. 965-2377), a rustic nautical-looking place whimsically decorated by Yves's brother. Over the bar is a scene of men and mermaids, a chariot, cupids, and a frolicking dog—all in the water. Another work of art depicts a pig and a lobster at the beach. Like

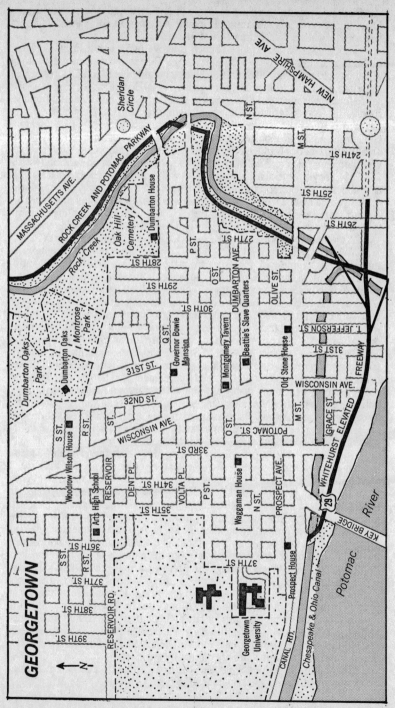

GEORGETOWN

N

Sheridan Circle

NEW HAMPSHIRE AVE.

MASSACHUSETTS AVE.

ROCK CREEK AND POTOMAC PARKWAY

Rock Creek

Oak Hill Cemetery

Dumbarton House

N ST.

M ST.

24TH ST.

25TH ST.

26TH ST.

P ST.

27TH ST.

28TH ST.

29TH ST.

30TH ST.

O ST.

DUMBARTON AVE.

OLIVE ST.

T. JEFFERSON ST.

31ST ST.

WISCONSIN AVE.

M ST.

Dumbarton Oaks Park

Montrose Park

Dumbarton Oaks

Q ST.

Governor Bowie Mansion

Montgomery Tavern

Beattie's Slave Quarters

Old Stone House

31ST ST.

32ND ST.

WISCONSIN AVE.

S ST.

R ST.

ST.

POTOMAC ST.

O ST.

M ST.

GRACE ST.

WHITEHURST ELEVATED FREEWAY

Woodrow Wilson House

Arts High School

RESERVOIR

DENT PL.

34TH ST.

VOLTA PL.

P ST.

33RD ST.

Waggaman House

N ST.

PROSPECT AVE.

Prospect House

KEY BRIDGE

29

Potomac River

S ST.

R ST.

35TH ST.

36TH ST.

S ST.

R ST.

37TH ST.

38TH ST.

39TH ST.

37TH ST.

RESERVOIR RD.

Georgetown University

CANAL RD.

Chesapeake & Ohio Canal

Au Pied de Cochon, the place is dimly lit and cluttered—here with hanging ferns, copper pots, and Tiffany-style lamps. An aquarium of goldfish and portholes in the walls enhance the nautical theme.

Though $12.95 for Sunday brunch is above our budget, Fruits de Mer's buffet is among the most worthy of splurges. Take into consideration that you won't have to eat again all day. It includes a pound of cold Maine lobster, veal Marengo, chicken with mushroom sauce, eggs Benedict, herring in cream sauce, sausage, scrambled eggs, smoked salmon, salads, poached fish, pommes rissolés, croissants, french bread, champagne, and pastries. Dinner too is just a tad above our price range, though some specials like the $13.50 seafood choucroûte with half a lobster, smoked fish, three kinds of fresh fish, sauerkraut and boiled potatoes is indeed a good buy. Ditto the one-pound lobster served with pommes frites and coleslaw for $9.95. At lunch a fried-fish sandwich is $4.75, $4.95 with crabcakes—both served with pommes frites and coleslaw. In addition, there are tempting daily specials in the $6 to $7.50 range like salmon in dill sauce, sea trout Marseillais, and calamaris Provençales. Similar entrees are about $2 more at dinner. Open daily from 11:30 a.m. to 4 p.m. for lunch, from 4 p.m. till 1:30 a.m. (2:30 a.m. on Friday and Saturday nights) for dinner.

Yet a third Courbois enterprise is **Au Croissant Chaud,** close by at 3222 N St. NW just off Wisconsin Ave. (tel. 338-7776). A bakery is on the premises, so the aroma is divine and the fresh-from-the-oven fare scrumptious. Spring through fall there are tables outdoors; in winter it's a takeout operation only—a good place to purchase a picnic lunch. There are about ten varieties of croissant —plain, fruit-filled, almond, chocolate, cinnamon, ham and cheese, sausage, etc.—priced from 60¢ to $1.55, plus a selection of cakes and pastries. More substantial are quiches, pizzas, and croissant sandwiches—all under $3. Open Sunday to Thursday from 6 a.m. to 9 p.m., on Friday and Saturday till 11 p.m.

The Bistro Français, 3124–28 M St. NW (tel. 338-3830), has the feel of a true Montmartre café. Its casual elegance derives from a comfortable clutter of brass and wrought-iron railings, etched-and stained-glass panels, and wainscotted walls hung with ornate mahogany-framed mirrors and 1940s French posters. Tables are covered in white linen, embellished with flower arrangements, and lit by candles in cut-glass holders. Also evocative of Paris is the Bistro's subtle air of excitement, the feeling that romantic trysts and witty conversations are taking place at the tables around you—and, hopefully, at your own.

There are actually two dining rooms here featuring different menus, though food offerings overlap considerably. In either room, for instance, a $12.50 Early Bird Special is offered weekdays from 5 to 7 p.m. and, once again, from 10:30 p.m. to midnight. It includes a glass of house wine; soup du jour, homemade liver mousse, or mussels Niçoise; an entree (perhaps duck with green peppercorns in a brandy cream sauce), and dessert. A similar prix-fixe menu is offered at lunch on weekdays for $8.95. À la carte dinner listings are a bit above our budget—$9.25 to $13—though I often stop in for a light meal such as traditional French onion or fish soup gratinée and a salad, both excellent here; that can be managed, along with bread and butter, a glass of wine, and coffee for about $10. Lunch items—for example, a salad of avocado, artichokes, and hearts of palm; a turkey, bacon, tomato, and mayonnaise sandwich on French bread; a ham and Swiss omelet; and quiche Lorraine—are all $5 or under. This is also a popular spot for late night or afternoon dessert and espresso binges. All the traditional French *pâtisseries* are featured, along with a cheese platter, crème caramel, chocolate mousse, pêche Melba, and other café standards. Finally, premium wines are offered by the glass.

Bistro Français is open Sunday to Thursday from 11 a.m. to 3 a.m., Friday and Saturday till 4 a.m. Reservations suggested.

La Ruche, 1039 31st St. NW, a block below M St. (tel. 965-2684), is as busy as its name ("The Beehive") implies. Everyone comes buzzing round for exquisite desserts—crunchy walnut tortes, creamy cheesecakes, and rich chocolate gâteaux—and the "spéciaux de chef Jean-Claude." At lunch these might include chicken breast sauteed with almonds, grouper with mustard sauce, or boeuf bourguignon—all priced in the $6 to $8 range. Jean-Claude's dinner specials are beyond our budget, but at any time of day the menu features affordable fare ($5 to $6) such as a homemade pâté sandwich on french bread; a traditional croque monsieur (baked french toast sandwich with ham and cheese; ham and cheese quiche with vegetable; and a classic salade Niçoise. This is down-to-earth country French cuisine, and portions are hefty. Everything is cooked, baked, and otherwise prepared on the premises. And speaking of the premises, they're immensely charming, with plants in the windows and suspended from the skylight, French background music (Brassens, Aznavour, etc.), wicker-seated chairs at candlelit tables, flowers in Perrier bottles, and pristine white walls hung with baskets and posters (scenes of Montmartre and the like). In good weather, additional seating is provided in a brick courtyard with a fountain and umbrella tables amid lush plantings. La Ruche is a popular choice for afternoon tea and late-night pastries with cappuccino.

Open from 11:30 a.m. to midnight Monday to Thursday, till 1 or 2 a.m. on Friday and Saturday (depending on the crowd), and till 11 p.m. on Sunday. A fabulous $9.45 prix fixe brunch—a mimosa, eggs Benedict, coffee, and pastry—is served weekends from 10 a.m. to 3 p.m.

TRENDY FARE: The **American Cafe,** 1211 Wisconsin Ave. NW, between M and N Sts. (tel. 337-3600), is the quintessential 1980s restaurant, featuring trendy fare (pesto, pasta, croissant sandwiches, mesquite grilling, and Häagen-Dazs) in equally trendy surroundings—even the flowers on your table are in Perrier bottles. Which is not to put it down—I go there all the time. For one thing, its angular modernistic interior (lots of plants, gallery lights illuminating watercolors on unpainted brick and red tile walls, pink and white perimeter neon lights, terracotta tile floors) is attractive and comfortable. In addition, service is friendly (never any problem about substitutions), and the food is really quite good.

Immense sandwiches served on croissants or double-twist rolls are in the $5.25 to $6.50 range and are served with side dishes such as caraway corn slaw, eggplant salad, or lemon broccoli. These easily comprise a full meal. Some examples: smoked turkey breast with Nantucket cranberry onions, chicken tarragon with water chestnuts and toasted almonds, and hickory/applewood-smoked pork with homemade barbecue sauce. In the same price category are salad plates—for example, a spinach salad tossed with hard-boiled egg, bacon, wild mushrooms, tomatoes, and garlic sourdough croutons in walnut vinaigrette. Ditto cornmeal-crust pizza topped with homemade tomato sauce, red onions, gruyère cheese, pine nuts, basil, and wild mushrooms. Regional American specialties ($7 to $10) are featured at dinner, perhaps mesquite-grilled boneless breast of chicken in herb butter, served with steamed fresh vegetables, rice, and cornbread or a New Orleans crab and shrimp pie with fresh veggies and new potato salad.

Many specialty drinks—like a cooling mix of fresh strawberries, cream, and light and dark rums topped with whipped cream ($3.95)—are featured, as are rich ice-cream desserts such as fudge-nut brownie with a scoop of Häagen-Dazs coffee and fresh whipped cream ($3.25), a concoction to which I personally owe a fair amount of body weight. Everything, including the baked goods, is prepared fresh daily. A full Sunday brunch menu is also offered, including, among other things, a wide choice of fresh-baked croissants, muffins, and danish pastries. Open Monday to Thursday from 11 a.m. to 3 a.m., on Friday and Saturday to 4 a.m., on Sunday from 10:30 a.m. to 1 a.m. A carry-out operation adjoins. There's another American Cafe at 227 Massachusetts Ave. NE (tel. 547-8500), a third at National Place, 1331 Pennsylvania Ave. NW (tel. 626-0770).

HICKORY-SMOKED AND SAVORY: Houston's, 1065 Wisconsin Ave. NW, just below M St. (tel. 338-7760), is part of a chain extending from New Orleans to Chicago. And if the immense popularity of this Georgetown branch is any indication, it will probably be in all 50 states before long. It's easily understandable: Houston's ambience is simpático, and the food served is fresh and first quality.

At lunch order up a hickory-grilled Texas burger (made from fresh-ground choice chuck), topped with chili, grated cheddar, and onion; it's served on a toasted bun with french fries, iron skillet beans, or coleslaw. The same choice of fixings comes with barbecued chicken breast or a club sandwich of ham, turkey, Monterey jack and cheddar cheeses, bacon, lettuce, tomato, and mayo on toasted bread. Portions are huge and everything's delicious. I also love the immense club salad bowl of greens, lightly fried chicken, avocado, bacon, egg, croutons, and tomatoes, served with mustard honey dressing and cheese toast. All of the above are in the $6 range at lunch, $1 or $2 more at dinner. Fresh fish entrees, hickory grilled, are another house specialty, as are Texas standards like barbecued ribs, chili, and steak. There are some marvelous appetizers here, too, for instance creamed spinach and artichoke hearts tossed in parmesan cream sauce and excellent fresh guacamole. Your choice of beverages ranges from premium wines by the glass to an extra-thick chocolate milkshake. And if you don't need to move for the rest of the day you might indulge in a dessert of rich, chewy brownie topped with vanilla ice cream and Kahlúa. The bar serves mixed drinks made with premium liquors, fresh-squeezed juices, and natural spring water.

Houston's is quite an attractive restaurant, with exposed brick walls, flickering gaslight sconces, oak tables lit by shaded lamps, and roomy velvet upholstered booths. The plant-filled rear dining room is under a skylight ceiling, the front room beneath rough-hewn wood rafters. Good music played at a low decibel level enhances the ambience.

Hours are Sunday to Wednesday 11:30 a.m. to 11 p.m., Thursday till midnight, Friday and Saturday to 1 a.m. They don't take reservations; arrive off hours to avoid long lines.

IS IT ITALIAN?: It's name notwithstanding, Charing Cross, 3027 M St. NW (tel. 338-2141), doesn't serve beans on toast or bangers and mash. And though owner Massoud Nadjbadi, who bought the bar in 1975 but left its English pub name intact, is Iranian, he doesn't feature lamb and rice dishes. Charing Cross is an old-fashioned Italian neighborhood restaurant, serving up hefty portions of spaghetti, veal, lasagne, etc., to hungry, budget-minded Washingtonians. And it's so popular that you'll wait in line if you arrive more than half an hour after opening time.

Why the crowd? They come for the tasty homemade fare and the charming Italian bistro setting. Charing Cross has oak floors, candlelit butcher block tables, and wainscotted sienna walls hung with framed artworks. A small back dining area under a beamed ceiling is especially cozy. And the pubby bar is a popular nighttime hangout.

Entrees in the $6 to $11 range, the latter for veal dishes, are served with salad and a big basket of Italian bread and butter. All the traditional specialties are offered—tortellini in cream sauce, cannelloni, manicotti, fettuccine Alfredo, eggplant parmigiana, veal scaloppine, rigatoni and sausage, even spaghetti with meatballs. For dessert you can have a cannoli with your espresso. And, of course, wine with your meal is a must.

Open Sunday to Thursday from 5 to 11:30 p.m., Friday and Saturday till 12:30 a.m.

SIAMESE IF YOU PLEASE: Thai Taste, 2606 Connecticut Ave. NW, just off Calvert St. (tel. 387-8876), offers authentic, individually prepared Thai dishes in congenial surroundings. Seating is in booths along either side—the old-fashioned kind with mirrored walls and coathook posts—and at glossy coral-topped tables adorned with fresh flowers in the center of the room. Each booth is lit by a shell-shaped lamp. Walls are covered in grasspaper and hung with Thai art. It's not a fancy place, but it is pleasant and attractive.

Appetizers are a bit pricey ($3.25 to $6) but very interesting, including crisp spring rolls, jumbo shrimp wrapped in ham and rice paper, pork satay, deep-fried crab balls wrapped in bean curd skin, and deep-fried stuffed chicken, among others. An affordable dim sum–style meal composed of selected appetizers is a good idea here, perhaps supplemented by a nice-sized, tangy chicken salad ($4). Vegetable and noodle/rice dishes—such as mixed sautéed vegetables with hot chili sauce, chicken lo mein, and crabmeat fried rice—are mostly $5 to $6, as are curries and chicken with cashew nuts or basil. Seafood dishes—fresh mussels sautéed with red curry and coconut milk, softshell crab with curry powder and spring onion, or crispy whole fish in a three-flavored sauce—are in the $8 to $10 range. Portions are very large, so consider ordering several appetizers and sharing an entree. Open Monday to Thursday from 11:30 a.m. to 10:30 p.m., Friday and Saturday 11:30 a.m. to 11 p.m., Sunday 5 to 10:30 p.m.

Another branch of this restaurant, featuring the identical menu, is located in Georgetown at 3287½ M St. NW (tel. 965-7988). Hours are Monday to Thursday 11:30 a.m. to 10 p.m., Friday and Saturday till 10:30 p.m., Sunday 5 to 10 p.m.

VIETNAMESE: Georgetown has two adjoining Vietnamese restaurants, both of them meritorious.

Vietnam-Georgetown, 2934 M St. NW (tel. 337-4536), claims to be D.C.'s first Vietnamese restaurant (established in 1972). Its interior is pleasant but not fancy, with wainscotted cream walls hung with oil paintings. Pots of chrysanthemums line the front window, and globe lights painted with Oriental scenes are suspended from above. There's also a charming garden, especially nice on summer nights when you dine at candlelit tables under large trees strung with tiny white Christmas tree lights. All dishes are individually prepared to order (no microwave here), so have a glass of wine and share an appetizer of the scrumptious cha giò—Vietnamese crispy egg rolls, more subtle than the Chinese variety ($4.50)—and prepare for a leisurely dining experience. Vietnamese soups, such as crabmeat and asparagus are in the not-to-be-missed category. Recommended entrees ($6.50 to $8) include beef in lemongrass flavorings grilled on skewers, cinnamon beef with orange, and caramel chicken with ginger. All entrees are served with fried rice and shredded vegetable. At lunch you can order any of the above or select from an abbreviated menu with all entrees under $5.50. For dessert the banana flambé au rum is crisp and sugary, a treat. Open Monday to Thursday from 11 a.m. to 11 p.m., on Friday to midnight, on Saturday from noon to midnight, and on Sunday from noon to 11 p.m. No credit cards.

Viet Huong (it means "Ambrosia"), next door at 2928 M St. NW (tel. 337-5588), is equally cozy. Grasspaper walls are adorned with Vietnamese cut-paper art, baskets, and fans; tables are neatly covered in white linen; and lighting emanates from white paper globe lanterns overhead. I especially favor the spring rolls ($2.75 for an appetizer) at Viet Huong. Good entree choices are grilled lemon chicken on bamboo skewers; steamed filet of haddock with mushrooms, vermicelli, garlic, spring onion, and tomatoes in thick spicy sauce; and Viet Huong noodles—shrimp, chicken, beef, sautéed green vegetables, and garlic, served on crispy golden noodles. And if you'd like to sample a few dishes try the special, a combination platter of shrimp on sugarcane (shrimp paste blended with garlic and Vietnamese fish sauce wrapped around sugar cane and grilled), shrimp toast, sesame-grilled beef, and spring rolls. All entrees include rice. Prices range from $6 to $9. There's a full bar, but to my mind you can't top iced jasmine tea as an accompaniment. Banana fritters for dessert here too. Offered daily: a $4.25 lunch special including rice, spring roll, and a choice of entrees like grilled lemon chicken, grilled sesame beef, and shrimp in Vietnamese sauce. Reservations are suggested at dinner. Open Sunday to Thursday from 11 a.m. to 10:30 p.m., on Friday and Saturday till 11:30 p.m.

PERSIAN: Authentic ethnic restaurants that don't compromise their cuisines by making concessions to an oft-erroneous conception of the "American palate" are all too rare. Such a one, and I consider it a great find, is **Kolbeh,** 1645 Wisconsin Ave. NW, between Reservoir Rd. and Q St. (tel. 342-2000). Not surprisingly, about 60% of the clientele here is Iranian. If you want to experience new taste sensations, begin with a few torshi (pickle) appetizers ($1.25 each) such as pickled garlic or onions (fabulous), mixed vegetables (cauliflower, cabbage, greens, apples, and eggplant in a spicy vinaigrette), or eggplant. Though I had to be talked into pickled garlic the first time, it's now my favorite; do try it. Other excellent appetizer choices ($3.25 to $4.50) are kashk-e bademjan (a mixture of spiced sautéed eggplant, onion, and sour cream, liberally sprinkled with mint leaves), stuffed green pepper, and thick noodle vegetable soup with lentils, spinach, and pinto beans. Among the entrees, I love the braised chicken in piquant pomegranate sauce made with ground walnuts and tomato paste—delicious over rice. Also yummy are subtly seasoned kebabs of marinated grilled chicken, sirloin steak, or ground beef, served with grilled tomato on a heaping platter of buttered rice or wrapped in lavash (a soft flat bread). Best bet: order with rice and get a side of lavash as well. And do ask for sumac powder to sprinkle over your rice. For dessert there are very sweet pretzel-shaped fritters, pastries made of yogurt, and rosewater-flavored homemade Persian ice cream.

Owner Nasr Sateri (whose mom is in charge of the kitchen) has created an attractive dining room here with ornately mirrored white walls, candlelit tables adorned with fresh flower arrangements, and a brass samovar set-up at the entrance. A guitar player entertains during dinner. Open noon to 11 p.m. Sunday to Thursday; on Friday and Saturday till 4 a.m., when for a cover of $5 you can sit upstairs and see a show of Iranian singers and musicians while you dine. The show begins about 10:30 p.m. Reservations are suggested at dinner.

BAGELS AND . . . : The **Georgetown Bagelry,** 3245 M St. NW, between Wisconsin Ave. and 33rd St. (tel. 965-1011), churns out over 10,000 bagels each day under the watchful eye of ex-New Yorker (only New Yorkers can make authentic bagels) Erik Koefoed. It's an immensely popular little place. Locals love to sit by the windows, read the paper (he sells it), and keep an eye on the passing scene. The fresh-baked bagels come in 15 varieties (plain, sesame, rye, pumpernickel/rye marble, oatmeal raisin, onion rye, egg, poppy, onion, garlic, salt, cinnamon and raisin, pumpernickel, honey whole-wheat, and caraway). And there are bialys too. You can get them spread simply with cream cheese or cream cheese and lox, and with less traditional fillings such as homemade chicken salad, hummus and sprouts, and hot pastrami. All bagel sandwiches are under $4. Fresh-squeezed orange juice is $1.19 for eight ounces, a large coffee costs 60¢, and homemade desserts like carrot cupcakes, brownies, and pastries are $1.25 or less. No credit cards. Open Sunday to Thursday from 6:30 a.m. to 9 p.m., on Friday and Saturday until midnight.

9. Adams-Morgan

ETHIOPIAN: There are many Ethiopians among the clientele of the **Red Sea,** 2463 18th St. NW (tel. 483-5000), which speaks well for its authenticity. The jukebox plays Ethiopian tunes, and you'll hear conversations in Amharic. It's a casual and comfortable place with black leatherette chairs and banquettes, red-clothed tables, and an oil painting above the bar depicting the story of King Solomon and the Queen of Sheba. There's additional seating upstairs. Food is served on large metal platters with piles of injera—pancake-like Ethiopian bread made with oats, wheat, buckwheat, and rice flour—which is used in lieu of forks and spoons to scoop up the assorted dishes. (Silverware is available, but do be a bit adventurous.) Most dishes come in two forms, *wat* (hot) and *alecha* (mild); I prefer the former, but you know your own palate. Everything is prepared fresh using homemade spice mixtures.

Very popular are the $7.50 sampler platters, which allow diners to try a number of dishes. Sampler No. 1, for example, offers chicken marinated in lemon, sautéed in butter, and stewed in a hot red pepper sauce flavored with onions, garlic, ginger root, cardamon, and nutmeg; a mild lamb dish cooked in herbed butter and dusted with ginger root, turmeric, and garlic; strips of savory beef in red pepper sauce; and a choice of four vegetables—perhaps bulghur wheat with herbed butter; ground-roasted yellow split peas in red pepper sauce; cabbage sautéed with onions, green peppers, and garlic; and spicy chopped greens. Most à la carte entrees are in the $5.50 to $7 range.

The Red Sea is open daily from 11:30 a.m. to 2 a.m., till 3 a.m. Friday and Saturday nights when there's live Ethiopian music from 9 p.m. to midnight. Reservations suggested at dinner, especially on weekends.

CAJUN COOKIN': Gumbo and jambalaya are all the rage these days, and anything ethnic and trendy is sure to make its way to Adams-Morgan. Hence the **New Orleans Café,** 1790 Columbia Rd. NW, just off 18th St. (tel. 234-5111). Under the culinary auspices of owner/chef Peter Finkhauser, a highly skilled European chef who has worked at many of New Orleans's most famous restaurants, the café offers excellent Créole cuisine from breakfast through late dinner. Start your morning with an order of fresh beignets (New Orleans-style doughnuts), fruit, and chickory-flavored café au lait ($3.50), or opt for pain perdue (New Orleans-style french toast; $4.50), hot biscuits (two for $1.35), or a heartier dish called eggs Créole—two poached eggs on seasoned fried grits with smoked sausage and a spicy sauce ($6.75). This breakfast fare is available at all times. Lunch or dinner, classic Cajun choices include soups like crawfish bisque and gumbo ($3 per bowl), a fried catfish sandwich with spicy mayonnaise on french bread, and the Bourbon Street—rib-eye slivers sautéed with onions, peppers, and mushrooms, and topped with melted cheese on french bread. These and other sandwiches are in the $4.50 to $5.50 range. At dinner a chicken, ham, and sausage jambalaya (something like a paella without the seafood) is $11; you might share one, filling out the meal with a bowl of soup per person to minimize expenditure. Finish things off with a shared dessert of hot bread pudding with whiskey sauce.

The New Orleans Café offers a cheery setting. Its oak-wainscotted, rose-colored walls, are hung with large sepia photos of turn-of-the-century New Orleans gleaned from the National Archives; large plants are suspended from a high pressed-tin ceiling; you can watch the white-capped chef at his work in a large windowed kitchen, the hub of the restaurant; and Dixieland music is played at a low-decibel level—loud enough to enhance the mood but soft enough to allow conversation. Do try this rich and spicy cuisine. I like to go off hours when it's less crowded, since tables are rather close together.

Open Sunday to Thursday from 8:30 a.m. to 10 p.m., on Friday and Saturday till 11 p.m.

LATIN PLUS: One reviewer called **Omega,** 1856 Columbia Rd. NW (tel. 745-9158) "a Cuban restaurant with a Greek-letter name offering Mexican specialties." And if that's not confusing enough, I'll add that owner Salvador Baldo, Jr., is from Barcelona and chicken Créole is one of Omega's most popular dishes. Don't waste time figuring it all out, though. All you need to know is that Washingtonians have been flocking here for over 25 years for hefty home-cooked meals, their quality attested to by a wall lined with restaurant awards. My favorite dish here is that above-mentioned chicken Créole. It's baked in onions and garlic, then marinated in pineapple juice and deep-fried just prior to serving topped with onions boiled in grapefruit juice, oil, garlic, and lemon. Another very tasty dish is chicken cooked Mexican style—shredded in a piquant sauce of tomatoes, jalapeños, onions, bay leaf, and spices and topped with peas and pimentos. Paella Valenciana is a house specialty as is lamb stew in red wine sauce. Other than rice casserole dishes, all entrees come with platters of rice, big bowls of black beans, and baskets of crusty, doughy bread with butter. Extra rice, beans, and bread are on the house. Entrees are $7 to $10.50 at lunch, about $1 more at dinner. They're huge, so you might consider ordering appetizers or salads and sharing a main course. Do get a pitcher of sangría, made from scratch here. And if your appetite holds out try the homemade caramel custard.

Though not fancy, Omega has a certain kitschy charm, with its shuttered windows, stucco walls hung with gilt-framed oil paintings of ships and flowers, and terracotta tile floors. Three dining areas are separated by arched doorways.

Open Sunday to Thursday 11:30 a.m. to 10 p.m., Friday and Saturday till 11 p.m. No reservations are taken. Arrive off hours to avoid a wait for tables.

Chapter IV

D.C. SIGHTS

1. Washington with Children
2. The Major Sights
3. Additional Attractions

SIGHTSEEING IN WASHINGTON is an art. The number of major attractions is mind-boggling, and many of them merit a day in themselves. I've seen hundreds of hapless visitors rushing around town at a frantic pace—often with protesting kids in tow—determinedly dashing in and out of museums and monuments. This popular plunge-in-and-see-it-all plan is the worst possible approach. You end up exhausted, ready for a vacation from your vacation, and your experience is a shallow one to boot.

Resign yourself. You can't see all of Washington's sightseeing attractions (not to mention those that beckon in nearby Virginia) during a week-long or even a month-long visit. I suggest a careful reading of this chapter to find out what most excites your interest. Then plan your sightseeing schedule around those attractions, allowing ample time to experience them properly. No two people will have identical priorities. Art lovers might opt for exploring D.C.'s many art museums in depth and ignoring the rest. Some families will want to spend an entire day at the National Air and Space Museum. Others will prefer to concentrate on the workings of government, sitting in on sessions of Congress and the Supreme Court and touring the White House. And most will probably settle on a more eclectic mix of attractions.

When you've decided what's in your personal not-to-be-missed category, plan out your vacation days, keeping in mind days and hours attractions are open and noting applicable warnings about arriving first thing in the morning to avoid long lines.

As far as possible, conserve time and energy by taking geographic proximity into account—visit places near each other on the same day.

Pace yourself. This is not a job, it's a vacation. Plan a long leisurely lunch, a picnic, or a film at the National Air and Space Museum during the day—anything that allows you to get off your feet and refresh yourself.

Forget about being fashionable. Comfortable shoes and clothing are essential if you're going to last out the day. During Washington's sweltering summers, sneakers or running shoes, shorts, and a T-shirt are the ideal ensemble.

Many museums offer highlight tours, a good way to get a meaningful overview of a vast collection when time is limited. Consider an attraction's tour schedule when you plan your visit.

Spend at least one day away from the Mall. Its immense museums tend to become overwhelming, and you should see some other areas of Washington.

Check out the pandas at the zoo; take a stroll in Dumbarton Oaks' ten-acre formal garden; visit some smaller museums like the Phillips Collection and the Textile Museum; hike the C&O Canal or plan a picnic in Rock Creek Park (see Chapter V); or for a change of scene, leave Washington altogether and spend a day in nearby Alexandria's quaint Old Town.

The good news is that most of the sights listed below are free.

1. Washington with Children

Remember the trip you took to Washington as a kid with your parents or classmates? Visiting the capital is a traditional part of American childhood—the perfect choice for family vacations offering an abundance of activities adults and kids can share. But enjoyable family vacations take a special talent. I've seen kids thrilled with the joy of discovery in Washington, and I've seen them tired, hot, and whiny, trudging disgruntledly after increasingly irate parents. The crucial difference lies in the parents' approach.

A LITTLE HOMEWORK: Kids delight in sights like the **White House,** the **Capitol,** and the **Supreme Court** when they know what they're seeing. They feel proud to understand how our government works. The same thing goes for art, monuments, fossil displays, period rooms, and document viewing. It's up to you to do a little advance homework and enhance the tour guides' patter with child-oriented explanations. Discuss what you're seeing and the kids will stay alert and interested; leave them to their own devices and boredom will soon set in. You don't have to be an expert in government, history, and 100 other areas; just share your perceptions with them.

CAREFUL PLANNING: You want to be flexible—if everyone's ready to drop, skip the final museum on the day's agenda—but a defined itinerary is a good idea. The kids can help in the planning, and you can discuss the night before what you'll be seeing. The more they know, the more meaningful it is.

FAVORITE CHILDREN'S SIGHTS: All the sights listed in this chapter include, where applicable, details on special activities and areas geared to children. Check for special children's events at museum information desks when you enter; better yet, call the day before to find out what's available. The biggest kid-pleasers in town are:

The **National Air and Space Museum**—spectacular IMAX films (don't miss), missiles, rockets, and a walk-through orbital workshop.

The **National Museum of Natural History**—a Discovery Room just for youngsters, an insect zoo, shrunken heads, and dinosaurs.

The **National Museum of American History**—the Foucault Pendulum, locomotives, atom smashers, and an old-fashioned ice-cream parlor.

The **FBI**—gangster memorabilia, crime-solving methods, espionage devices, and a sharp-shooting demonstration. You can't miss.

The **Bureau of Engraving and Printing**—kids like looking at immense piles of money as much as you do.

The **Capital Children's Museum**—all of it's for kids, with sound-and-light shows, hands-on exhibits, and educational computer games.

The **National Zoological Park**—kids always love a zoo, and this is an especially nice one.

Ford's Theatre and Lincoln Museum, and **The House Where Lincoln Died** —Booth's gun and diary, Lincoln's blood-stained pillowcase, the clothes Lincoln was wearing the night he was assassinated; need I say more? Kids adore the whole business.

National Geographic's Explorers Hall—a moon rock, the egg of an extinct "elephant bird" (if it hatched it would weight 1000 pounds), exhibits on primitive man, etc. The magazine comes alive.

Washington Doll's House & Toy Museum—antique dollhouses, dolls, games, and toys, including Lionel train sets.

The **Washington Monument**—easy to get them up there, hard to get them down. If only they could use the steps, they'd be in heaven.

The **Lincoln Memorial**—kids know a lot about Lincoln and enjoy visiting his memorial. A special treat is visiting after dark (same for the Washington Monument and Jefferson Memorial).

The **Arts and Industries Building**—19th-century steam engines, ship models, farm machinery, old clocks, and performances just for children in the Discovery Theater.

The **DAR Museum**—there's a special area on the second floor just for children focusing on a child's life in colonial times.

The **National Archives**—see the original Declaration of Independence, Constitution, and Bill of Rights.

A FEW ADDITIONAL TIPS: As to the rest, plan with your children's ages and interests in mind.

An occasional purchase at a museum shop can quickly revive flagging interest, and most of the museums have wonderful toys and children's books, not to mention items like freeze-dried astronaut ice cream.

The Friday "Weekend" section of the *Washington Post* lists numerous activities (mostly free) for kids: special museum events, children's theater, storytelling programs, puppet shows, video-game competitions, etc.

A hotel with a swimming pool is the best child-refresher known to man; it also means some time alone for adults. Consider this when making reservations; it may be worth a few extra bucks.

Ride the Metro, and let the kids purchase the tickets and insert their own farecards. It will be a high point, especially if they've never been on a subway before.

Take in some of the outdoor attractions listed in Chapter V; go bicycling, rowing, on a guided nature hike, or a Potomac boat ride.

Have fun!

2. The Major Sights

These are Washington's top attractions, though number four, the Smithsonian, brackets all of that astounding institution's components under one heading. A few of those are not really major sights, but for consistency's sake they're included with the others.

(1) THE CAPITOL: Capitol Hill at the east end of the Mall, entrance on East Capitol St. and 1st St. NW (tel. 225-6827). Open from 9 a.m. to 4:30 p.m. (tours till 3:45 p.m.) daily except Thanksgiving, Christmas, and New Year's Days. Between Easter and Labor Day the Rotunda area usually stays open until 10 p.m. Metro: Capitol South.

Its great white dome a Washington Landmark, the Capitol is the focal point of American politics, a worldwide symbol of our nation since 1800 when the government moved here bag and baggage from Philadelphia. For 134 years the building contained not only both houses of Congress but the Supreme Court and the Library of Congress.

Touring the Capitol

Before leaving home (see Chapter I for details), write your congressperson or senator—as far in advance as possible—for tickets to the morning congressional tour specifying the date you wish to visit. Tickets are limited, but it's worth a try. At the same time, request a Visitor's Pass for each member of your party to view a session of the House and/or Senate. Each senator and congressperson seems to have a different policy about distributing these; yours may not send them in the mail. In that case you'll have to pick up a Visitor's Pass at the Capitol. It only takes about ten minutes. Congressional offices—which generally provide passes for both houses—are on the Independence Avenue side of the Capitol. Sometimes visitors get a chance to shake hands with their representative and chat for a while. Passes for both houses are also available at your senator's offices on the Constitution Avenue side of the building. Noncitizens needn't go to any bother; they just have to present their passports at the House galleries or Senate door.

You'll know when the House or Senate is meeting by flags flying over their respective sides of the Capitol. Also check the "Today in Congress" column weekdays in the *Washington Post*. It gives a daily rundown on times and subjects of all House and Senate committee meetings and indicates which are open to the public. If you're not too pressed for time you'll want to pick something that interests you rather than sit in on a hearing about grain elevator bankruptcies. Those interested in a particular bill can call the above-listed number for details.

What to See

If you don't have tickets for the more complete congressional tour, take one of the free 35-minute guided tours that leaves from the Rotunda every 15 minutes (more frequently in summer) between 9 a.m. and 3:45 p.m. On the **East Front** steps where you enter, every president from Andrew Jackson through Jimmy Carter was inaugurated (Reagan changed tradition and was inaugurated on the West Front). At this historic spot Lincoln asked a recently divided nation to forge ahead "with malice toward none, with charity for all. . . ." F.D.R. assured us that "the only thing we have to fear is fear itself." And John F. Kennedy challenged us to "Ask not what your country can do for you—ask what you can do for your country."

The massive bronze doors leading to the **Rotunda** portray events from the life of Columbus. The Rotunda—a huge circular hall some 100 feet across and under the 180-foot dome—is the hub of the Capitol. Nine presidents have lain in state here for public viewing; when Kennedy's casket was displayed, the line of mourners stretched 40 blocks. On the circular walls are eight immense oil paintings of events in American history such as the reading of the Declaration of Independence and the surrender of Cornwallis at Yorktown. In the eye of the dome is an allegorical fresco masterpiece by Constantino Brumidi, *Apotheosis of Washington,* a symbolic portrayal of George Washington surrounded by Greek gods and goddesses watching over the progress of the nation. A trompe l'oeil frieze overhead depicts events in early American history from Columbus through the Wright brothers' flight at Kitty Hawk. There's also a life-size marble statue of Lincoln.

In **National Statuary Hall** you'll experience an unusual acoustical effect—a whisper can be heard clear across the room. In this room the House of Representatives met from 1807 to 1857. Today it contains marble and bronze statues of historically important state figures: California's great missionary, Father Junipero Serra; Vermont's Revolutionary War hero, Ethan Allen; steamboat inventor Robert Fulton from Pennsylvania, and many others.

You'll also visit either the **House** or **Senate** chambers (both on the congressional tour). A reminder if high school was long ago: most bills begin in the House, go to the Senate when approved, then on to the president; a two-thirds vote of the House and Senate can override a presidential veto. After the tour, explore the ornate marble corridors and rooms at your own pace and try to sit in on a legislative session. You should also consider dining with the folks on the Hill; there are many choices, and you'll see a lot of the Capitol just getting to some of them. See Chapter III for a complete rundown.

Finally, get another view of the Capitol at free nighttime band concerts Tuesday, Wednesday, Thursday, and Friday in summer at 8 p.m. on the steps of the West Front.

(2) THE WHITE HOUSE: 1600 Pennsylvania Ave. NW (tel. 456-7041). Entrance at East Gate on East Executive Ave. Open to visitors Tuesday to Saturday from 10 a.m. to noon. Metro: McPherson Square. *Note:* Some days the White House is closed to tourists for official functions; check before leaving your hotel by calling the above 24-hour number.

"I never forget," said Franklin Delano Roosevelt in one of his fireside chats, "that I live in a house owned by all the American people." Not only do Americans own the White House, they're welcome to visit, making it unique among world residences of heads of state.

The White House has been the scene of many great moments in American history. It is the central theater of government, where decisions on national and international policies are made and prominent guests are entertained by the nation's official host and hostess. It has been the setting of foreign invasion, high-fashion weddings, and somber state funerals. And of course it's also the private home of the president and his family, their personal doings and dramas as much a focus of national interest as any happenings in the political arena.

Each administration has its own personal style. John Adams greeted visiting diplomats with almost royal formality while Jefferson once had the butcher in to dinner. The "People's President," Andrew Jackson, invited the public to come in and share a 1400-pound cheese.

Admission to the White House

Until 1902 the public was freely admitted to shake hands and have a few words with the president. So many people took advantage that Lincoln, hounded by the public, once circulated a rumor that he had smallpox to discourage visitors. Today you probably won't see the First Family when you visit (though a glimpse is always possible). Nevertheless, over 1½ million people still line up annually outside the iron fence enclosing the 18-acre estate for a chance to see the sections of the White House that are open to the public. If you can, get tickets in advance from your congressional representative or senator for the VIP tours at 8:15, 8:30, and 8:45 a.m. (details in Chapter I). It's more extensive, and you also get a fully guided tour. On later visits there are guides on hand to answer questions but no actual tour lecture.

If you don't have congressional tour tickets, you can get tickets for the 10 a.m. to noon tours at one of the kiosks on the Ellipse (at 15th Street and Constitution Avenue NW) from 8 a.m. (lines begin forming earlier) on the day of your visit only. Each person must pick up his or her own ticket; it's one to a customer. There's no charge. The time of your tour is stamped on the ticket. Once you've obtained it, you can go out for coffee or sit and wait in the bleachers while glee clubs and bands entertain. Tickets are required from Memorial Day to Labor Day only; the rest of the year you just get on the line.

During spring and summer there are occasional garden tours from 2 to 5 p.m. on weekends. No tickets are required. Call for details.

The best time to visit is in winter when the crowds are lighter. Then you can wander through at your own pace, chatting with the very knowledgeable Secret Service officers who double as guides. Special times to visit are during Christmas season when the decorations are up, and on Easter Monday when children 8 and under can participate in the Easter Egg Roll on the South Lawn.

What to See

Tours begin in the East Wing Lobby. A glass-enclosed colonnade (over-looking the Jacqueline Kennedy Garden) leads to the ground-floor corridor where portraits of First Ladies and selected pieces of White House china are on display. Visitors proceed up the wide marble staircase to see five state rooms, which for all their stage-set appearance are in actual use when not on view.

The gold-and-white **East Room,** where Lynda Bird Johnson was married, John F. Kennedy lay in state, and Nixon delivered his farewell address, is used for presidential press conferences, swearing-in ceremonies for government offi-cials, White House concerts (Beverly Sills sang "Jingle Bells" here at Reagan's request one Christmas season), and discussions on national issues. It's deco-rated in the early 19th-century classical style of the Theodore Roosevelt renova-tion, with parquet Fontainebleau oak floors, and white-painted wood walls with fluted pilasters and relief inserts illustrating Aesop's fables. Here hangs a fa-mous Gilbert Stuart portrait of George Washington.

The **Green Room** (named for a green floor cloth in Jefferson's day, not for its green Rayon watermark silk wall coverings) is used as a sitting room, though Jefferson used it as a dining room. It was completely refurbished in 1971, with furnishings mostly of the early 1800s, many pieces of which are attributed to the famous Scottish-born cabinetmaker Duncan Phyfe. There are many notable paintings in the room, among them Gilbert Stuart's of John Quincy Adams and *The Mosquito Net* by John Singer Sargent.

The oval **Blue Room,** where presidents and First Ladies have officially re-ceived guests since the Adams administration, is today decorated in the French Empire style chosen by James Monroe in 1817. It was, however, Van Buren's decor that began the "blue room" tradition. The walls, on which hang portraits of five presidents (including Rembrandt Peale portrayals of George Washington and Thomas Jefferson, and G.P.A. Healy's of Tyler), are covered in a reproduc-tion of French Directoire paper from 1800, and a settee and seven of the original gilded armchairs Monroe ordered from French cabinetmaker Pierre-Antoine Bellangé remain. Grover Cleveland, the only president ever to wed in the White House, was married in the Blue Room; the Reagans, wearing symbolic yellow, greeted the 53 returned Iranian hostages here; and every year it's the setting for the White House Christmas tree.

The **Red Room,** also a state parlor decorated in the French Empire style, is used for small receptions. An Empire music stand reflects the room's 19th-century use as a music room. The walls are covered in a "Dolley Madison red" twill satin fabric with gold scroll border, the furniture upholstered in the same shade. Among the notable paintings are Albert Bierstadt's *View of the Rocky Mountains* and a Gilbert Stuart portrait of Dolley Madison.

The sparkling gold-accented **State Dining Room** is the last chamber visited on the tour. Scene of many important White House dinners, it has served at various times as a drawing room, office, and Cabinet Room. Andrew Jackson first called it the "State Dining Room." It was originally smaller; a 1902 renovation expanded the room to its current size. Its architecture is modeled after late-18th-century neoclassic English houses. Theodore Roosevelt, a big-game hunter, had a large moose head over the fireplace and other trophies on the walls. Below G.P.A. Healy's portrait of a contemplative Lincoln is an inscription of words written by John Adams on his second night in the White House (F.D.R. had them carved into the mantel): "I Pray Heaven to Bestow The Best of Blessings on THIS HOUSE and on All that shall hereafter Inhabit it. May none but Honest and Wise Men ever rule under This Roof."

Portraits of the past seven presidents hang in the North Entrance, which you'll pass through when leaving the house. In addition to the above, VIP tours visit the Lobby, the Vermeil Room, the China Room, and the Diplomatic Reception Room.

(3) THE SUPREME COURT: 1st St. NE, between East Capitol St. and Maryland Ave. (tel. 479-3030). Open Monday to Friday from 9 a.m. to 4:30 p.m. Metro: Capitol South or Union Station.

In these oft-turbulent times, I find it reassuring to visit the massive Corinthian marble palace that houses the Supreme Court, its serene classical dignity reinforced by the pledge etched in a frieze over the colonnaded entrance: "Equal Justice Under Law." The Court's subtle excitement is well described by Justice Oliver Wendell Holmes, who wrote, "We are very quiet . . . but it is the quiet of a storm center." The highest tribunal in the nation, the Supreme Court is charged with the delicate responsibility of protecting and maintaining a "living Constitution"—with interpreting its enduring principles and applying them to new situations and changing conditions. To do this, the Court has the unique power of "judicial review"—authority to invalidate legislation or executive action in conflict with the Constitution. Issues that come before the Court are often crucial to the nation, by definition turning on principles of law or the Constitution of far-reaching importance. Of some 5000 yearly petitions for hearings, only about 180 cases are accepted. Once the Court rules on an issue, that judgment is final, reversible only by the Court itself.

If you're in Washington at the right time, don't fail to see the Court in session. They meet Monday to Wednesday from 10 a.m. to 3 p.m. (with an hour for lunch between noon and 1 p.m.) from the first Monday in October through late April, alternating, in approximately two-week intervals, between "sittings" to hear cases and deliver opinions and "recesses" for consideration of business before the Court. About 24 cases are argued at a sitting. The Court has a record before it of prior proceedings and relevant briefs, and each side is allowed a 30-minute argument. If your vacation time coincides with a Court session, arrive at least an hour early to line up for seats, even earlier if the case is highly publicized. Only about 150 seats are allotted to the general public. You can find out what cases are on the docket by consulting the *Washington Post*'s "Court Calendar." From mid-May to early July the Court takes the bench every Monday for the issuing of rulings. During this season visitors can attend brief half-hour sessions at 10 a.m.

In some ways as interesting as the issues being decided are the Court's traditions and rituals. At 10 a.m. the entrance of the justices is announced by the marshal. At the sound of the gavel all present rise and remain standing while the justices are seated following the traditional chant: "The Honorable, the Chief Justice and Associate Justices of the Supreme Court of the United States. Oyez! Oyez! Oyez! All persons having business before the Honorable, the Supreme Court of the United States, are admonished to draw near and give their attention, for the Court is now sitting. God save the United States and this Honorable Court!" (Oyez! is "law French" for "Hear ye!") Unseen by the gallery is the "conference handshake"; following a 19th-century tradition symbolizing a "harmony of aims if not views," each Justice shakes hands with each of the other eight when they assemble to go to the bench. On the bench, the Chief Justice sits in the center chair flanked on either side by the most senior justices. You may notice that the chairs are different sizes; each is custom-made for the person who occupies it, and on his or her retirement all of the other justices purchase the chair and present it as a parting gift. The justices wear black robes, but powdered wigs went out early on when Jefferson claimed they made "English judges look like rats peeping through bunches of oakum." A quaint tradition is the use of white quill pens, 20 of which are placed on counsel tables each day the Court sits.

If the Court is not in session during your visit, you can attend a free lecture in the courtroom where Court procedure and details of architect Cass Gilbert's design are discussed. Lectures are given from 9:30 a.m. to 3:30 p.m., every hour on the half hour.

After the talk, explore the Great Hall, its walls lined with busts of former Chief Justices set alternately in niches and on marble pedestals. Double rows of marble columns rise 45 feet to the coffered ceiling. Descend to the ground floor where you can see a 30-minute film on the workings of the Court. Here too are portraits of all former Supreme Court justices and photos of the current nine. The ground floor is a good vantage point to view one of two marble and bronze grand spiral staircases, similar to those at the Paris Opera and the Vatican. The floor is also used for historical exhibits on great Supreme Court justices and the Court itself.

One place you will get justice is at the excellent Supreme Court groundfloor cafeteria. It's quite elegant for a cafeteria, with red leather chairs, red and gold carpeting, and graceful brass chandeliers overhead, but prices are extremely low. For under $5 you can have daily specials like baked stuffed pepper or southern fried chicken with whipped potatoes, a roll and butter, and beverage. Huge sandwiches on croissants are $3.50 and come with potato chips. Homemade pies and cakes are $1.50 or less, and there's an excellent salad bar. In addition to ambience and low prices, a lure of this cafeteria is the possibility of rubbing elbows with some of the justices. It's open for breakfast from 7:30 to 10:30 a.m., for lunch from 11:30 a.m. to 2 p.m. (closed to the public between noon and 12:15 p.m. and 1 and 1:10 p.m.). An adjoining snackbar is open from 10:30 a.m. to 3:30 p.m.

(4) THE SMITHSONIAN INSTITUTION: This awesome complex of museums and facilities came into being in 1846 thanks to the generous bequest of an English scientist named James Smithson. Smithson, who had never visited this country, nevertheless left his entire fortune (over half a million dollars, an impressive sum in those days) to the United States "to found at Washington, under the name of the Smithsonian Institution, an Establishment for the increase and diffusion of knowledge among men." The original bequest has since been many times surpassed by federal funds and private donations.

During its early years, the landmark red sandstone **Smithsonian Institution Building** on the Mall at 1000 Jefferson Dr. SW housed all its operations and collections. Designed by James Renwick (also architect of New York's Grace Church and Saint Patrick's Cathedral, and Washington's Renwick Gallery) in the Norman style with turreted towers, this building, popularly known as "the Castle," today serves as administrative headquarters and contains a Visitor Information Center, exhibits on the institution's history, and James Smithson's tomb. The Smithsonian's mind-boggling collection—over 100 million specimens including everything from George Washington's false teeth to priceless works of art, the legendary Hope diamond, a dinosaur egg, the Apollo II Command Module, and Archie Bunker's chair—has expanded to fill 14 museums and also includes the National Zoo. In addition it is one of the world's major research and educational facilities, focusing on science, history, art, and technology. Its activities and facilities extend far beyond Washington.

You can't "do" the Smithsonian in a day, a week, or even a lifetime, since only about 1% of its vast holdings is on display at any given time. And there's little point to spending an hour scurrying about each museum without absorbing any of what you see. Plan a sightseeing schedule to coincide with your greatest areas of interest. Art lovers might choose to concentrate on the seven art museums; families with kids will want to spend considerable time at the National Air and Space Museum, the museums of Natural History and American History, and the zoo. The descriptive listings below are geared to helping you decide priorities, and you can also write or phone in advance to the **Visitor Information and Associates Reception Center,** Smithsonian Institution, Washington, DC 20560 (tel. 202/357-2700), for general brochures and information on current activities. When in town, call Dial-A-Museum at 357-2020 to find out about concerts, lectures, films, and other Smithsonian events and activities.

All of the museums are closed on Christmas day, but are otherwise open daily. *Note:* Hours given for museum tours are subject to change; call before you go.

The National Air and Space Museum

On the south side of the Mall between 4th and 7th Sts. SW, entrances at 6th St. on Jefferson Dr. or Independence Ave. (tel. 357-2700). Open daily from 10 a.m. to 5:30 p.m.; extended hours in summer determined annually. Metro: L'Enfant Plaza (7th and Maryland exit). Underground pay parking available (entrance on 7th Street).

The Smithsonian's aeronautical collection began in 1876 with a group of Chinese kites. Today it comprises hundreds of historically and technologically significant aircraft, spacecraft, missiles, rockets, airplane engines, and related items, many of them on display here in 23 themed galleries documenting man's conquest of flight. Plan to devote a minimum of three or four hours to this museum. It would take months to explore it in depth.

During tourist season and holiday times especially, arrive just before 10 a.m., and when the doors open, make a beeline for the film ticket line. So popular are the awesome **IMAX** (screen five stories high, seven stories wide) films shown at the Samuel P. Langley Theater that tickets often sell out quickly. At this writing there are three half-hour films. *To Fly,* the most popular, is an aerial scenic tour of America, from an 1800s balloon ascension to a venture in outer space. You'll experience hang gliding and dizzying stunt flights, soar over New York skyscrapers and the Grand Canyon. Equally fascinating is *The Dream Is Alive,* an insider's view of outer space featuring spectacular in-flight footage by 14 astronauts from three space-shuttle missions. And *On the Wing* explores the wonder of flight—from the 65-million-year-old pterosaur to manned aircraft. Tickets cost $2 for adults, $1 for children, students, and senior citizens. Best seats in the house, by the way, are Row J, center.

You'll also want to see (same prices) shows focusing on astronomy at the Albert Einstein Planetarium. So after you've procured your IMAX show tickets, make the Planetarium ticket booth on the second floor your next stop.

Your show schedule settled, you can now begin viewing the exhibits. If time is limited, consider a 1½-hour free highlight tour (daily at 10:15 a.m. or 1 p.m.). There are also recorded tours for rental, narrated by people like Neil Armstrong and Chuck Yeager.

On your own, the logical place to begin is Gallery 100 (**Milestones of Flight**) on the first floor where famous airplanes and spacecraft such as the Wright brothers' 1903 flyer, *Spirit of St. Louis,* the *Apollo 11* Command Module and *Gemini 4* are on display. Here too is the world's only touchable moon rock. In other first-floor galleries you'll learn how a helicopter works, design your own jet plane, study the history of aviation and air transportation, examine sounding rockets and satellites used for scientific purposes, explore astronomy from Stonehenge to the space telescope, and see rockets, lunar exploration vehicles, guided missiles, and manned spacecraft. All the aircraft you see here are the originals.

Second-floor galleries highlight sea-air operations, military aviation, balloons and airships, the solar system, artists' perceptions of space and aviation themes (most unique is Rowland Emett's *SS Pussiewillow II,* a construction that combines elements of a Victorian drawing room with bicycle parts and other hardware to create a fantasy flying saucer with many sound effects), pioneers of flight, and U.S. manned space-flight programs. Kids especially love the walk-through *Skylab* orbital workshop (50 feet high and 23 feet in diameter) where the three-man crews lived and worked for months at a time. Exhibits throughout are enhanced by computer games and slide and video shows. There's even a short film called *Sneaking Through the Sound Barrier,* with Sid Caesar, Imogene Coca, and Carl Reiner. Caesar plays a flying ace with "air in his heart and space in his brain."

Don't miss the large first-floor museum shop of flight-related items—books for adults and children, space games, globes, flight periodicals, model kits, posters, records, and the big favorite, astronaut freeze-dried ice cream and strawberries.

You can also get this ice cream in the museum's third-floor cafeteria. The fare is standard museum fast-food quality (need I say more), but most kids like it, especially since they have to grab their burgers and Cokes off a revolving carousel. Window seats offer a nice view of the Mall. Another choice here is the West End Terrace, with umbrella tables and a trailer selling light fare; in summer Armed Services bands often entertain here during lunch hours. And Crystal Palace, a new first floor restaurant with a fast-food area and a waiter-service dining room will open in the fall of 1988. It, too, will offer al fresco seating in good weather.

The National Museum of American History

On the north side of the Mall between 12th and 14th St., entrances on Constitution Ave. and Madison Dr. (tel. 357-2700). Open daily from 10 a.m. to 5:30 p.m., with extended hours in summer determined annually. Metro: Smithsonian or Federal Triangle.

The National Museum of American History aims "to illuminate, through collections, exhibitions, research, publications, and educational programs, the entire history of the United States, including the external influences that have helped to shape the national character." Here we have a sense of what people mean when they call the Smithsonian "the nation's attic." Exhibits include such wide-ranging items as a pair of Dorothy's ruby slippers from *The Wizard of Oz,* farm machinery, Early American glass, a '30s kitchen, and a Revolutionary War general's tent. It's not surprising that the nucleus of the collection was called the "National Cabinet of Curiosities."

On the first floor, to the left of the Constitution Avenue entrance, is a post office that was located in Headsville, West Virginia, from 1861 to 1971, and was brought lock, stock, and barrel to the museum to serve as a country store-cum-post office (your mail is stamped Smithsonian Station). There's also a turn-of-the-century ice-cream parlor where you can get a 1906 banana split, unfortunately at 1980s prices. Farm machines on this floor range from colonial wooden plows to internal-combustion tractors, harvesters, and combines. The history of transportation is documented in exhibits of antique automobiles, early bicycles, stagecoaches, a 280-ton Pacific-type steam locomotive, an 1888 Seattle cable car, and dozens of ship models, including the *Mayflower*. A section on power machinery demonstrates—with full-size engines and models—their evolution from the age of steam power onward. Other halls trace the development of electricity, phonographs (from one of Edison's first 1877 models), typewriters, and locks. Beautiful weavings, embroideries, and crewelwork are displayed in textiles. Still other exhibit areas concentrate on physical sciences, processes for iron smelting, atom smashers, and medical sciences. Also on this floor—"Engines of Change: the American Industrial Revolution 1790–1860," which tells the story of our transformation from an agricultural to an industrial society, and "The Search for Life: Genetic Technologies in the 20th Century."

At the Mall entrance on the second floor is the original **Star-Spangled Banner,** 30 by 42 feet, that flew over Fort McHenry in 1814 and inspired Francis Scott Key to write a poem that became our national anthem. It is hidden behind a curtain to preserve its tattered fabric, but every hour on the half hour the curtain is withdrawn, and there's a mini sound-and-light show. A major exhibition on this floor is "After the Revolution," which explores the everyday activities of ordinary Americans in the 18th century—their work, family life, and communities. One of the most popular second-floor displays is, of course, the First Ladies' gowns, from Martha Washington's hand-painted silk through Nancy Reagan's lace-overlaid white satin sheath. White House china is also shown here. "A Nation of Nations" (from Walt Whitman's "here is not merely a nation but a teeming Nation of nations . . .") honors the diversity of peoples and cultures that make up our country. But the most thrilling exhibit on this floor, indeed in the entire museum, is the **Foucault Pendulum,** suspended from the ceiling over 70 feet above, that reminds us we live on a rotating planet. The pendulum's vertical plane remains fixed, but as the earth rotates under it, it knocks down, one by one, red markers arranged in a circle.

The third floor contains a vast collection of uniforms, weapons, flags, and ship models illustrating armed forces history, as well as sections on money and medals, news reporting (from early teletype machines to space satellites), printing and graphic arts, stamps and the mails (with over 75,000 rare stamps on display), musical instruments, ceramics (an excellent collection), and glass. Most interesting, perhaps, is the photography section, where early cameras and photographic equipment are enhanced with historic pictures by greats like Lartigue and Eickemeyer. Kids will enjoy creating shadow art at "Lingering Shadows." The most recent installation on this level examines Constitutional guarantees of citizen's rights, juxtaposed with the internment of thousands of Americans of Japanese ancestry during World War II.

Inquire at the information desks about highlight tours (hours vary); demonstrations of printing, spinning and weaving, musical instruments, machine tools, and other museum-related subjects; hands-on programs for children at the first-floor **Electricity Demonstration Center** and the third-floor **Spirit of '76 Demonstration Center.** There's also a full schedule of films, concerts, and lectures, many of them on Saturday. Holidays, when special events often include story-telling, puppet shows, music, games, films, and demonstrations, are exciting times to visit. The major museum shop, on the lower level, is fabulous. It offers toys, books, models of vehicles and ships, crafts items, jewelry, records and tapes, specialty foods from all over the country, and more.

You can grab a quick meal in the cheerful **cafeteria,** where fresh-baked cornbread and croissants are among the offerings, and a nonsmoking area even makes for fresh air.

The National Museum of Natural History

On the north side of the Mall between 9th and 12th Sts. NW, entrances on Madison Dr. and Constitution Ave. (tel. 357-2700). Open daily from 10 a.m. to 5:30 p.m., with extended hours in summer determined annually. Metro: Smithsonian or Federal Triangle.

The National Museum of Natural History contains the nation's largest collection of natural history specimens and artifacts—over 81 million of them. It's one of the world's major centers for the study of animals, plants, fossils, rocks, minerals, and man.

I suggest the **self-guided audio tour,** available in the Rotunda on the first floor. It provides an interesting commentary on the exhibits and enhances your understanding. Adults pay $3, seniors and students $2.50, children under 12, $1.25. Free highlight tours are given daily at 10:30 a.m. and 1:30 p.m.

If you have children, be sure to plan your visit to include some time in the first-floor **Discovery Room,** open Monday to Thursday from noon to 2:30 p.m., on Friday, Saturday, and Sunday from 10:30 a.m. to 3:30 p.m. Filled with creative hands-on exhibits and games designed to encourage a child's natural curiosity, the Discovery Room makes learning fun. Here kids can touch fossil plants and mastodon teeth; play with "discovery boxes" filled with shells, minerals, bones, coral, and other objects; play with American Indian dolls and drums from Kenya; dress in costumes from foreign lands; and peer at specimens under a microscope. One adult must accompany every three kids, and tickets (obtained at the Rotunda information desk) are required on weekends and holidays.

If you've entered on the Mall (having stopped, no doubt, to let the kids climb on "Uncle Beazley," a life-size triceratops dinosaur), you'll find yourself in the Rotunda facing a giant African bush elephant. To your right, in "Fossil Plants and Animals," evolution is traced back billions of years. Exhibits include 400-million-year-old fossil scorpions from New York and a dinosaur egg (70 million years old) from France. A 3½-billion-year-old stromatolite (blue-green algae clump) fossil is one of the earliest direct evidences of life on earth. "Life in the Ancient Seas" documents the dramatic explosion of hard-shelled life at the beginning of the Paleozoic Era, 600 million years ago. "The Conquest of Land" shows how plants and animals made the transition from water to land; here you'll see a fossil of one of the earth's earliest trees. Dinosaurs, of course, loom up next—giant skeletons of creatures that dominated the earth for 140 million years before their extinction about 65 million years ago. A glass-walled lab allows visitors to view museum workers unearthing dinosaur bones and other fossils from ancient rocks. On balconies over Dinosaur Hall are exhibits on ancient birds, including a life-size model of the pterosaur which had a 40-foot wingspan. Also residing above this hall is an ancient shark—or at least the jaw of one, the Carcharodon, that lived in our oceans five million years ago. A monstrous 40-foot-long predator, it had teeth five to six inches long and could have consumed a Volkswagen "bug" in one gulp! "Mammals in the Limelight" focuses on mammalian evolution. Continuing counterclockwise, you'll enter the Ice Age, see a video show about the process of glaciation, and learn about our Neanderthal ancestors. Did you know they buried their dead and believed in an afterlife? Farther along, African, Asian, Pacific, Eskimo, and Indian cultures are explored. You'll hear African musical instruments and song as well as Chinese opera and the music of India and Thailand; see shrunken heads; learn about Samoan rituals, African initiation rites, Laotian Buddhism, Zuni pottery making, and Inca terrace farming. In "Dynamics of Evolution," a push-button exhibit demonstrates the necessity for survival of only the fittest by showing what would happen if all the offspring of any pair of several species survived for eight generations, for example, 628 elephants and an alarming 15,969,850,417,242 cockroaches! (To drive home the latter point, there's a horrifying but riveting tableau of what a kitchen would look like in just three generations if every roach survived.) Less awfully awesome are exhibits on genes and chromosomes and natural selection, and evolution of the modern horse from an animal not much bigger than a house cat. Also on this floor: "The World of Mammals" (a favorite of kids is the exhibit of bat heads; they look like *Star Wars* extras); "Life in the Sea," with an actual living coral reef on display in a 3000-gallon tank, and an adjacent aquarium that simulates the ecosystem of Maine coastal waters; and "Birds"—specimens from all over the world.

Second-floor exhibits include "Minerals and Gems" (you'll see the **Hope Diamond,** the world's largest and finest star ruby, and Marie Antoinette's diamond earrings, as well as a jade boulder from New Zealand and gold crystals of extraordinary size and beauty), "Earth, Moon, and Meteorites" (including actual lunar rocks), "South America: Continent and Culture," "Human Origin and Variation" (life-size murals show how people have altered the human body with tattoos, pierced lower lips, bound feet, etc.), "Western Civilization" (from the end of the Ice Age to about A.D. 500), "Bones" (hundreds of animal, bird, reptile, amphibian, and fish skeletons), and "Reptiles." A highlight—especially for kids—is the Insect Zoo with Plexiglas cages of centipedes, hermit crabs, beetles, immense cockroaches, tarantulas, ants, and other creepy-crawlies.

On the lowest level, or ground floor, is the **Naturalist Center,** an adult Discovery Room where amateur naturalists can examine and study Smithsonian natural history materials. You can bring in specimens for identification, use microscopes and scientific tools, view films and videotapes, and work on projects of special interest. It's open Monday to Saturday from 10:30 a.m. to 4 p.m., on Sunday from noon to 5 p.m. Call 357-2804 for details. This level also houses changing exhibits such as the nature portraits of Robert Bateman.

Inquire at the information desk about the museum's schedule of films, concerts, and lectures.

There's a cafeteria on the first floor. The fare is museum-cafeteria standard, but the setting—with dozens of plants maintained by the horticulture department—is rather nice.

Finally, don't miss the museum shop, also on the first floor, where many interesting fossil reproductions, kits, shells, minerals, books, and educational toys are sold. A special area of this shop focuses only on dinosaurs. There's another museum shop on the Rotunda balcony.

Arts and Industries Building

On the south side of the Mall, Jefferson and 9th Sts. SW (tel. 357-2700). Open daily from 10 a.m. to 5:30 p.m., with extended summer hours determined annually. Metro: Smithsonian.

The second oldest of the Smithsonian museums on the Mall, the red brick and sandstone Arts and Industries Building was completed in 1881—just in time for President Garfield's inaugural ball. It originally housed exhibits from the 1876 United States International Exposition in Philadelphia ("the Centennial"), a grand celebration that marked the nation's coming of age and featured the latest technology. For the Bicentennial in 1976, the Centennial Exhibition was recreated with thousands of objects that were actually shown at the original fair and additional displays relating to the period. And it's still going at this writing. The entrance floor is like a turn-of-the-century mall with display cases of

Victorian furnishings, fashions, clocks, musical instruments, tools, photographic equipment, and medicines. In areas off the magnificent central Rotunda there's machinery that probably evoked oohs and ahs in the 19th century—steam and gas engines, printing presses, corn mills, refrigerator compresses, and tool builders, as well as a considerable display of weaponry and vehicles. Rather impressive is the 45-foot model of the naval cruiser *Antietam,* a steam sloop-of-war. There are also state exhibits highlighting California wines, Kansas corn and wheat, Tennessee lumber, etc., as well as international displays of Turkish carpets, Swiss clocks and watches, and so on. Interspersed are various and sundry displays—French lace, flags, silverware, perfume, and much Victorian decorative frillery and frou-frou.

Upstairs on the balcony level is a horticultural extravaganza complete with period garden furnishings, typical dried-flower arrangements, wire frames for elaborate floral centerpieces, posy holders (nosegays, or small bouquets, were popular 19th-century costume accessories, used to ward off unpleasant street odors and as part of the feminine mystique), ferneries, window gardens, mantelpiece gardens, floral arts and crafts, ornate vases, and a typical Victorian Christmas tree.

There's a charming country-store-like gift shop on the first floor selling jams and jellies, china, candles, needlepoint patterns and samplers, ruffled cushions, fancy soaps, antique reproduction dolls, potpourri, and suchlike.

There are occasional tours (call for details).

Puppeteers, mimes, singers, and dancers perform at **Discovery Theater,** October to June; call 357-1500 for show times and ticket information.

In summer, very much in the Victorian spirit, though unrelated to the museum, there's a carousel across the street.

The National Portrait Gallery

On 8th and F Sts. NW (tel. 357-2700). Open daily from 10 a.m. to 5:30 p.m. Metro: Gallery Place.

The heroes and villains, thinkers and doers, radicals and conservatives, men and women who made "significant contributions to the history, development, and culture of the people of the United States," are here represented in paintings, sculpture, photography, and other art forms of portraiture. The idea for a national portrait gallery officially dates back to 1857 when Congress commissioned G.P.A. Healy to paint a series of presidential portraits for the White House, but American portraiture is as old as the Republic, as evidenced by the Gilbert Stuart and Rembrandt Peale portrayals of George and Martha Washington.

It's great fun to wander the corridors, sometimes putting faces to famous names for the first time. Commentaries accompanying the portraits are both informative and entertaining. Norman Rockwell's Nixon is neatly bracketed as "one of the most cryptic men to occupy the White House. And Henry Clay who, the commentary wryly informs us, said "I'd rather be right than president" only after his last hopes for the office were dashed, is described as "a loveable wit, a serious gambler, a connoisseur of fine horses and good liquor, and a charmer of women," all of which G.P.A. Healy's portrait captures brilliantly.

With the exception of presidents and special exhibitions, no portrait is displayed until ten years after the subject's death.

In addition to the Hall of Presidents on the second floor, notable exhibits include *Time* magazine cover portraits; a portrait of Mary Cassatt by Degas; 19th-century silhouettes by French-born artist August Edouart of people like Henry Clay, John Quincy Adams, and fellow artist Rembrandt Peale; Jo Davidson's sculpture portraits, including a Buddha-like Gertrude Stein; and the C.B.J. Févret de Saint-Mémin miniature engravings. St-Mémin was attached to the elite household guard of Louis XVI, but fled France after the Revolution and settled in New York where he became famous for his copper-plate engravings of prominent people. Alternating centerpieces of the second-floor Rotunda are Gilbert Stuart's famed "Lansdowne" portrait of Washington and "Edgehill" portrait of Jefferson. On the mezzanine, the Civil War is documented in portraiture. Also relating to this era are the classic photographs of the Mathew Brady Studio on the first floor.

In addition to the permanent collection there are temporary exhibits which in the past have included "Hollywood Portrait Photographers" and "The American Portrait: 1700–1776."

Worth a visit for more than just its contents is the Old Patent Office Building, in which the National Portrait Gallery collection (as well as the National Museum of American Art) is housed. Architect Philip Johnson called it "the greatest building in the world." Designed by Robert Mills, whose credits also include the Washington Monument, and Thomas U. Walter, architect of the Capitol dome, this ornate neoclassic mid-19th-century landmark was our first comprehensive "nation's attic" museum displaying such eclectic items and artifacts as the original Declaration of Independence, shrunken heads from expeditions, paintings and sculpture, stuffed birds, and Benjamin Franklin's printing press. Particularly magnificent are the Great Hall and Rotunda on the third floor.

Walk-in tours are given at varying hours on most days between 10 a.m. and 3 p.m. (call 357-2920 for details). The museum shop on the first floor sells items related to exhibits. Do pick up a calendar of events at the information desk when you come in. Perhaps you'll catch a lecture or a musical or dramatic presentation.

In the courtyard/sculpture garden between the Portrait Gallery and the National Museum of American Art you'll find garden furnishings under the shade of ancient elms and overlooking two fountains. It's a marvelous place for a picnic. Bring your own or select items like a bowl of homemade chili, ham and swiss on a croissant, or a tomato stuffed with egg salad and chickpeas from the adjacent Patent Pending restaurant. Any of those items, along with a carafe of chablis, will cost under $6. If the weather is poor, Patent Pending's interior— white walls hung with framed art posters, marble floors—is also simpático.

The National Museum of American Art

On 8th and G Sts. NW (tel. 357-2700). Open daily from 10 a.m. to 5:30 p.m. Metro: Gallery Place.

Sharing the palatial quarters of the Old Patent Office Building with the National Portrait Gallery, the National Museum of American Art owns over 33,000 works representing two centuries of our national art history. A rotating sampling of about 1000 of these works is on display on three gallery floors at any given time, along with special exhibitions highlighting various aspects of American art. These changing shows have ranged from "Modern American Realism" to the photography of Edward Weston.

Twentieth-century art occupies the most exalted setting, the third-floor Lincoln Gallery with vaulted ceilings and marble columns. The name commemorates Lincoln's second inaugural reception which was held here in 1865. Depending on what's showing during your visit, you might see works of Noguchi, Tobey, Hopper, Rauschenberg, Calder, Frankenthaler, Kline, and de Kooning.

A unique work of folk art always on the first floor is James Hampton's visionary religious piece, *Throne of the Third Heaven of the Nations' Millennium General Assembly,* a construction completely covered in aluminum and gold foil. Hampton, a black southerner who worked as a janitor and short-order cook, believed he saw God. He did the piece in the 1950s. The other works on this floor are Early American—by Benjamin West, Ralph Earl, Thomas Sully, Samuel F. B. Morse, Thomas Hart Benton, George Henry Durrie, Charles Willson Peale, and others. An Art of the West Gallery features paintings of John Mix Stanley and Charles Bird King, and George Catlin's Indian portraits from the collection he showed in Paris in the 1840s (the museum owns 445 of them). Additionally, there's a gallery of portrait miniatures on this floor.

Mid- to late-19th-century artists—Thomas Cole, Winslow Homer, Thomas Eakins, Childe Hassam, Mary Cassatt, Albert Pinkham Ryder, and John Singer Sargent—are on the second floor, as is the Hiram Powers Gallery wherein is the contents of the 19th-century classic sculptor's Florence studio.

Recently the museum acquired the $1.4 million Herbert Waide Hemphill, Jr. Folk Art Collection, most of it 19th- and 20th-century works. It will eventually comprise a major exhibit.

Pick up a map at the information desk near the entrance, also a calendar of the museum's schedule of lectures and other events. There are free tours at noon on weekdays and at 1:45 p.m. on Sunday. Also check out the first-floor museum shop of American art books, prints, posters, and gift items. The dining facility here is Patent Pending (details in the National Portrait Gallery listing above).

The National Zoological Park

Located in Rock Creek Park, main entrance in the 3000 block of Connecticut Ave. (tel. 673-4800 or 673-4717). Open daily, weather permitting, May 1 to September 15: grounds open from 8 a.m. to 8 p.m., animal buildings from 9 a.m. to 6 p.m.; rest of the year: grounds from 8 a.m. to 6 p.m., animal buildings from 9 a.m. to 4:30 p.m. Closed Christmas. Metro: Cleveland Park or Woodley Park.

Established in 1889 in response to a growing interest in exotic animals and concern for vanishing species, the National Zoo originally housed a herd of bison threatened with extinction behind the Smithsonian castle. Today it occupies 163 acres and is a world leader in the care, breeding, and exhibition of animals. It's home to over 3000 mammals, birds, reptiles, amphibians, and invertebrates, some of which are endangered in the wild and are being studied and bred as part of a long-term propagation program. The most famous residents since 1972 are Ling-Ling and Hsing-Hsing, two giant pandas that were a gift to the U.S. from the People's Republic of China. There's an ongoing attempt to have the pandas breed in captivity. Best time to view them is at feedings, 11 a.m. or 3 p.m.

When you arrive at the zoo, stop at the **Education Building** near the Connecticut Avenue entrance to pick up a map and a listing of special programs. You can also get these items at information kiosks near the Harvard Street or Beach Drive entrances. If you have children, pick up tickets for **Zoolab** at the Education Building first thing; available on a first-come, first-served basis, they sometimes run out. Zoolab is a learning lab where visitors can handle and examine objects such as hummingbird eggs and elephant tusks, see short films, read books on zoology, and peer at relevant specimens through a microscope. The ticket will specify a time for your visit. Open Tuesday to Sunday from April 1 to October 15, Friday to Sunday the rest of the year; call for hours. Similar in concept is **HERPlab**, a center for the study of reptiles and amphibians, open from noon to 3 p.m. Wednesday to Sunday (free tickets are available at the lab, in the middle of the reptile house). Finally, there's **BIRDlab**, open Friday to Sunday from noon to 3 p.m., with "activity boxes" containing eggs, nests, skulls, and feathers, plus additional avian educative materials; no tickets are required.

There are free films shown in the Education Building Auditorium between 10 a.m. and 4:30 p.m. daily from Memorial Day to Labor Day, weekends only the rest of the year. They include *Zoo* (a behind-the-scenes look at feeding procedures, veterinary care, and laboratory operations, *The Last Chance* (describing activities at the zoo's Conservation and Research Center, and *The Giant Panda*, a film from the People's Republic of China.

Seeing the Zoo: The animals live not in cages, but in sizable open enclosures similar to their natural habitats, along six color-coded trails (3½ miles in all). All trails branch off from a broad red stripe on Olmsted Walk, the zoo's main drag. Along the orange Lion Trail are not only lions, but tigers, panthers, leopards, monkeys, apes, lemurs, reptiles, and small mammals. The invertebrate exhibit on Lion Trail is the only one of its kind in the country. On display are starfish, sponges, anemones, insects, and other spineless creatures. The four largest land mammals—elephants, hippos, rhinos, and giraffes—are on the brown Elephant Trail. Ling-Ling and Hsing-Hsing are bracketed with kangaroos, zebras, and antelopes on the black Zebra Trail. The green Bird Trail contains cranes, cassowaries, condors, flamingos, American bald eagles, and other feathered friends, as well as deer and bongo antelope. Follow the blue Polar Bear Trail for otters, wolves, seals, sea lions, and bears, though none are actually polar bears. More bears (including Smokey of forest-fire fame), big cats, and assorted North American mammals live along the yellow Raccoon Trail.

It's delightful strolling through this beautiful menagerie, its lush landscaping fittingly more untamed than manicured. Especially lovely is a pond of ducks and swans under weeping willows.

On-the-premises facilities include several parking lots, wheelchair- and stroller-rental stations ($3 for the latter plus a $35 deposit or a driver's license), several gift and souvenir shops, and a bookstore. Snackbars and ice-cream kiosks are scattered throughout the park. Most notable is the **Panda Café,** with umbrella tables overlooking the outdoor habitat of the pandas; pizza, hot dogs, burgers, and similar items are offered. Largest facility is the **Mane Restaurant/ Cafeteria,** near the Beach Drive entrance. Its slightly expanded menu includes chili, chicken nuggets, and ham and cheese on rye. Though inexpensive, none of the offerings at these eateries is more than passable. I'd opt for an al fresco lunch at one of the zoo's very nice outdoor picnic areas. Buy fixings across the street at **Primo's Deli Café,** an excellent luncheonette opposite the zoo's main entrance at 3000 Connecticut Ave. NW.

Note: Zoo parking lots tend to fill up quickly in the spring and summer. Arrive early or take the Metro.

Hirshhorn Museum and Sculpture Garden

On the South side of the Mall at Independence Ave. and 8th St. SW (tel. 357-2700). Open daily from 10 a.m. to 5:30 p.m., with extended hours in summer determined annually. Metro: L'Enfant Plaza (7th and Maryland exit).

Latvian-born immigrant Joseph H. Hirshhorn, the 12th of 13 children, came to America in 1905 at the age of 6 with his widowed mother. He dropped out of school at 13, and at the age of 15 got his first Wall Street job, earning $12 a week. In 1916 he invested his savings of $255, became a stock broker, and went on to amass a fortune on the market and in uranium mining. At age 18 he acquired his first works of art—two Dürer etchings, thus beginning a lifelong passion for collecting. Over the years he turned his attention to contemporary painting and sculpture and began building what was to become the most extensive private collection of 20th-century art ever assembled. In 1966 he donated the entire collection—over 4000 drawings and paintings and some 2000 pieces of sculpture—to the United States "as a small repayment for what this nation has done for me and others like me who arrived here as immigrants." Three years later Congress appropriated funds for a building to house it, and in 1974 the Hirshhorn Museum and Sculpture Garden, designed by Gordon Bunshaft, came into being.

Bunshaft's cylindrical concrete and granite aggregate building, 14 feet above the ground to open up a plaza area and provide space for sculpture, is one of the world's best settings for viewing art. Like New York's Guggenheim, the simple circular route makes it easy to see everything on exhibit without getting lost in the honeycomb of galleries that characterizes so many art museums. Unlike the Guggenheim, the Hirshhorn provides ample indoor viewing space for sculpture, and the outdoor sunken sculpture garden is a delight.

A rotating show of about 600 works is on display at all times on the second and third floors. Sculpture is exhibited in the inner galleries where natural light streams in from floor-to-ceiling windows; paintings and drawings are installed in the outer galleries, artificially illuminated to prevent light damage.

Hirshhorn more than doubled the collection after 1974 in bequests before and after his death in 1981, and other gifts have further expanded the museum's holdings. It features just about every prominent 20th-century artist and provides a comprehensive overview of major trends in Western art from the turn of the century to the present. In sculpture, the Hirshhorn has works of Rodin, Arp, Brancusi, Moore, Lipchitz, Nevelson, Picasso, Hepworth, Degas, Matisse, Smith, Noguchi, Epstein, Calder, Cornell, and on and on; think of a modern sculptor—or painter—and his or her work is no doubt part of the collection. There are paintings by Warhol, Pollock, O'Keeffe, Rothko, Rivers, de Kooning, Gorky, Miró, Mondrian, Sargent, Eakins, Tobey, Homer, Davis, and Dali, among many others.

Free docent tours are given Monday to Saturday at 10:30 a.m., noon, and 1:30 p.m., on Sunday at 12:30, 1:30, and 2:30 p.m. Special sculpture garden tours take place daily at noon May 1 to June 15. The museum shop on the plaza level has a good selection of art books, posters, prints, jewelry, and art objects, and the **Plaza Café,** in the Sculpture Garden overlooking the fountain, is a good choice for an al fresco lunch on the Mall.

Pick up an events calendar when you come in to find out about free films (art films, films about art, and animation films), lectures, and concerts.

The Renwick Gallery of the National Museum of American Art

On Pennsylvania Ave. at 17th St. NW (tel. 357-2700). Open daily from 10 a.m. to 5:30 p.m. Metro: Farragut West (Farragut Square exit).

A curatorial department of the National Museum of American Art, the Renwick is a national showcase for American crafts. In the past its changing exhibits have included "American Art Deco" and "Lost and Found Traditions: Native American Art 1965–1985." In conjunction with, and addition to, these exhibits, the Renwick has a comprehensive schedule of events, lectures, concerts, and films. Pick up a schedule at the information desk.

Two special galleries on the second floor are the **Grand Salon,** typifying the Victorian splendor of the 1870s with wainscotted plum walls and a 38-foot skylight ceiling, and the **Octagon Room,** designed originally to show the crowning object of William Corcoran's collection, the female nude *Greek Slave* by Hiram Powers. (The Renwick was originally built as a showplace for the Corcoran collection, which moved at the turn of the century to its present 17th Street location.) Both rooms today are lavishly furnished in 19th-century style, their walls hung with numerous gilt-framed paintings by artists of the 18th and 19th centuries. About 50 works from the permanent collection can be seen in other galleries on this floor.

The building itself, designed in 1859 and constructed of brick with sandstone facings and ornaments and a slate mansard roof, is noteworthy as an example of the French Second Empire style. Today it is named for its architect, James Renwick, who also designed the Smithsonian "castle."

There are no tours. Do check out the museum shop near the entrance specializing in books on crafts, design, and decorative arts, and crafts items, including many things for children.

An additional part of the National Museum of American Art/Renwick Gallery complex is the **Barney Studio House** at 2306 Massachusetts Ave. NW., at Sheridan Circle. Here Alice Pike Barney (Washington's answer to Gertrude Stein) brought culture to the nation's capital in the early 1900s, providing an intimate art center and salon. A wealthy matron and prominent society leader, she was a painter herself and studied with Whistler in Paris, from whence she returned for a one-woman show at the Corcoran Gallery. She filled Studio House with paintings (her own and those of her friends), ornate furniture, Oriental rugs, and objets d'art. According to *Washington Society* magazine, Studio House was the "meeting place for wit and wisdom, genius and talent, which fine material is leavened by fashionable folk, who would like to be a bit Bohemian if they only knew how." Invitations were highly sought after. The house was rented out for 29 years after her death in 1931, then given to the Smithsonian by her daughters, along with many of the original furnishings, photographs, and family records. Today it's open for special events (details available at NMAA) and for tours, October to mid-May by appointment only. Call 357-3111 for reservations.

The Freer Gallery of Art

On the south side of the Mall, at Jefferson Dr. and 12th St. SW (tel. 357-2700). Open daily from 10 a.m. to 5:30 p.m. Metro: Smithsonian (Mall exit). *Note:* During the lifetime of this edition, part or all of the Freer will be closed for construction and expansion. Call before you go. The Freer will eventually connect with the new Sackler Gallery via an underground passage.

In a palatial Florentine Renaissance-style building, the Freer Gallery houses one of the world's finest collections of Asian and Near Eastern art as well as a much smaller number of significant American works from the late 19th and early 20th centuries. Charles Lang Freer, who donated his collection to the nation and left a generous trust fund for additional acquisitions, was a connoisseur of both, hence the unusual combination. A rotating portion of the permanent collection—some 26,000 items—is always on display. Asian/Near Eastern works include Chinese and Japanese sculpture, painting, metalwork, lacquer, and ceramics; Chinese and Korean jades and bronzes; Japanese screens and woodblock prints; Persian manuscripts, metalwork, miniatures, ceramics, and sculpture; Indian sculpture, manuscripts, and painting; early Christian illuminated manuscripts; and Egyptian glass.

American works comprise the largest collection in the U.S. of the works of James McNeill Whistler (1234 pieces), including the famous **Peacock Room,** permanently installed in Gallery XII. This was originally a dining room of a London mansion, for which owner F.R. Leyland purchased a Whistler painting, *Rose and Silver: The Princess from the Land of Porcelain.* Whistler didn't consider the room's decor (the antique Spanish gilded leather and walnut paneling installed at the direction of an architect named Jeckyll) a suitable setting for his work, and painted ornate peacocks all over Jeckyll's meticulously planned interior when Leyland was not at home. Leyland was less than thrilled, and a permanent rift developed between artist and patron. After Leyland's death in 1903, Freer, a close friend of Whistler's, purchased the painting and eventually shipped the entire room here from London. He installed the room in his house in Detroit, and it was sent to his Washington museum after his death. Other American painters in Freer's collection are Childe Hassam, Winslow Homer, Thomas Wilmer Dewing, Albert Pinkham Ryder, John Singer Sargent, and William Tryon.

The Freer is a very pleasant museum with plants and trees adorning its skylit galleries. The main exhibit floor centers on a garden court open to the sky. There's a museum shop on the first floor featuring books relating to the collection and reproductions from it. Fifty-minute tours are given Monday to Saturday at 10:30 a.m. and 1:30 p.m. (afternoons only on Sunday).

A New Museum Complex

A thrilling new $75-million-dollar Smithsonian museum complex opened on the Mall in 1987, comprising two major art museums—the **Arthur M. Sackler Gallery of Art** and the relocated-and-expanded **National Museum of African Art**—plus the **International Center** and the **Enid A. Haupt Garden.** Set on a quadrangle bounded by Independence Avenue, the Freer Gallery, the Smithsonian Castle, and the Arts and Industries Building, its exhibition space is almost completely (96%) underground. Above-ground, and in elegant harmony with neighboring landmark buildings, are two 60-by-90-foot pavilions—one pyramidal in motif, the other utilizing a circular theme of rounded arches—serving as entrances to the subterranean museums. Also visible on the Mall are the garden and a circular kiosk. The design was the inspiration of American architect Jean-Paul Carlhian, who conceived the pavilions as "grand vestibules leading visitors through a sequential series of spaces, down a formal processional stair to the collections below." The domed roofs of the African pavilion reflect the arch motif of the Freer, while the pyramidal silhouette of the Sackler pavilion recalls the roof lines of the Victorian Arts and Industries Building. The former has a light pink granite exterior, the latter dark beige. The pavilions' interior walls are limestone, the floors cream granite from Vermont, the ceilings a series of beams disposed in layers against brilliantly painted backgrounds. And though the bulk of the complex is underground, it is not dark or subterranean in feel. On the lowest level, a monumental three-story skylit concourse—replete with terracotta floors, fountains, seating, circular brick planters and potted palms—serves as a delightful "Main Street" for the complex. Two-hundred-and-eighty-five feet in length, it is highlighted by a vast illusionist mural on the east wall depicting the above-ground Smithsonian structures and garden as seen through ancient stone arches. Construction on the complex began in the summer of 1983, with funds provided by federal appropriations and private donations, the latter including a $1 million gift from the Republic of Korea. Future developments call for a tunnel connecting the Freer to the Sackler Gallery.

The Arthur M. Sackler Gallery: At 1050 Independence Ave. SW (tel. 357-2700). Open daily 10 a.m. to 5:30 p.m. Metro: Smithsonian.

Complementing the adjoining Freer Gallery, this museum of Asian and Near Eastern Art houses close to 1000 rare and valuable objects (the nucleus of its collection) donated by medical researcher, psychiatrist, publisher, and art collector Arthur M. Sackler. In addition to this lavish inaugural gift, Sackler also donated $4 million towards the museum's construction. The Sackler collection includes Chinese bronzes from the Shang (1523–1028 B.C.) through the Han (206 B.C. to A.D. 220) dynasties; 475 Chinese jade figures spanning the millennia from 3000 B.C. to the 20th century; Chinese paintings from the 10th through the 20th centuries; Chinese lacquerware; Near Eastern works in silver, gold, and bronze; ancient Near Eastern objects in ceramics, minerals, ivory, and glass; and stone and bronze sculptures from South and Southeast Asia. The museum's holdings will continue to grow with new donations and purchases. It has already acquired significant collections of Japanese works as well as Persian and Indian paintings, manuscripts, calligraphies, miniatures, and bookbindings. Exhibitions thus far have included "Monsters, Myths, and Minerals"—a survey of animal imagery in Chinese art including a display on the Chinese zodiac; "Pavilions and Immortal Mountains: Chinese Decorative Art and Painting"; and "Chinese Buddhist and Daoist Imagery." Loan exhibitions and major international shows are planned. The Sackler shares curatorial staffs and research facilities with the Freer.

The National Museum of African Art: 950 Independence Ave. SW (tel. 357-1300). Open daily 10 a.m. to 5:30 p.m. Metro: Smithsonian.

Until recently housed in the former home of famed black orator, abolitionist, journalist, and statesman Frederick Douglass, this fine institution—the only museum in the United States devoted solely to the collection, study, and exhibition of African art—has now come to the Mall. And though the Douglass home was in itself interesting, I'm happy to see the NMAA more accessibly located. The museum's collection, numbering some 6,000 art objects from various areas of Africa, focuses on the traditional arts of the vast sub-Saharan region. Most of the collection dates from the 19th and 20th centuries. Works from the western part of the Sudan and the Guinea Coast are particularly well represented. Also among the museum's holdings are the Eliot Elisofon Photographic Archives comprising 150,000 color slides, 70,000 black-and-white photographs, and numerous feature films and other film footage on African arts and culture. Inaugural exhibitions at the new space included "African Art in the Cycle of Life"—works reflecting beliefs and activities surrounding fertility, birth, death, and afterlife in Africa; "Royal Benin Art," featuring works donated by the Hirshhorn Museum; and "Objects of Use," showing African utilitarian objects created by artists. An excellent library is on the premises, and the museum store is especially interesting NMAA's holdings are often supplemented by loans from other museums and collections. Inquire at the desk about workshops (including children's programs), lectures, docent-led tours, films, and demonstrations.

The Enid A. Haupt Garden: A third component of the new complex, this 4½-acre park, though at street level, is actually a rooftop garden, since it sits atop the above-listed subterranean museums. Its main-entrance is the elaborate cast-iron carriage gate flanked by massive red sandstone pillars, made from an 1894 design by "Castle" architect James Renwick. Four other gates punctuate the wrought-iron fence surrounding the garden, which is further sheltered from Independence Avenue activity by rows of trees, including eight 30-foot-tall lindens in front of each museum. Two-hundred-year-old boxwoods and large weeping cherries enhance the "island" garden near the Sackler; Japanese katsura trees line the north side of both museums. In the fall, sour gums, red maples, hawthorns, and Southern magnolias provide a stunning panorama of red foliage. In springtime, saucer magnolias, weeping cherries, wisteria vines, and other plantings are in full pink blossom. Further adorning the garden are 19th-century cast-iron furnishings and lampposts, the latter decorated with lush hanging baskets. And then there are urns overflowing with exotic tropical flowers, topiaries, and vines. Adjacent to each pavilion is a special garden. Near the

Museum of African Art a fountain garden evokes the Andalese or Moorish influence of North Africa featuring terraces, canals, fountains, and a waterfall inspired by the gardens of Shalimar. Near the Sackler Gallery is a garden entered via a moongate, with a circular granite island floating in the midst of a square pool bridged by four sloping granite slabs—a design not unlike that of Beijing's Temple of the Sun. Its benches are backed by English boxwoods under the shade of cherry trees. In the center is a Victorian garden with a parterre of multicolored swags and ribbon beds of flowers. Here 30,000 yellow and blue pansies bloom in spring, summer annuals create a dazzling display, and even in winter, there is brightly colored kale.

This tranquil oasis on the Mall was named for its donor, a noted supporter of horticultural projects. It is open from 7 a.m. to 8 p.m., June 1 through September 30, till 5:45 p.m. the rest of the year.

The International Center: Located on the third or concourse level of the complex (tel. 357-2700), the center sponsors research, scholarly and public symposia, and exhibitions focusing on all the world's cultures. Entered via the circular bronze kiosk near Jefferson Drive, it offers major exhibitions such as the inaugural "Generations" exploring the universality of the birth experience, an event that is marked in every culture with symbolic rituals and imagery. Exhibits range from a Kenyan fertility charm to a Victorian-era porcelain piece showing a baby emerging from a cabbage patch. A show probably still on as you read this examines the world's rapidly disappearing rain forests. Long-term plans call for programs relating to Latin America and the upcoming Columbus quincentenary (1492–1992). Inquire at the desk about lectures, films, and performances.

The Anacostia Neighborhood Museum

Located across Washington's other river, the Anacostia, at 1901 Fort Place SE in Fort Stanton Park (tel. 357-2700). Open daily 10 a.m. to 5 p.m. No Metro here, but the B-4 bus stops at the door.

Created in 1967 as a neighborhood museum concentrating on the history and cultural interests of the predominantly black Anacostia community, this unique Smithsonian bureau has expanded over the years to address every aspect of black history, art, and culture, both American and worldwide. It relocated from a converted movie house to its current address in May, 1987. There is no permanent collection, but through its exhibit design and production laboratory, and its research center, the Anacostia produces a varying number of exhibits each year, often experimenting with new and innovative techniques and formats. Past exhibits have included "Portraits in Black: Outstanding Americans of Negro Origin," "Black Wings: The American Black in Aviation," "The Renaissance: Black Art of the Twenties," and "Climbing Jacob's Ladder: The Rise of Black Churches in Eastern American Cities, 1740–1877."

In addition to exhibits, there's a full schedule of free educational programs and special activities designed to enlarge on exhibit themes. Some examples: a children's concert of the works of Scott Joplin, a print-making demonstration by a black artist, a film on the life of Harriet Tubman (other films have paid tribute to Paul Robeson, Marian Anderson, and other blacks renowned in various fields), black history lessons for children, participatory dance workshops, creative writing workshops, and dramatic events. Pick up an events calendar when you visit, or call ahead for one.

(5) THE NATIONAL GALLERY: On the north side of the Mall between 3rd and 7th Sts. NW, entrances at 6th St. and Constitution Ave. or Madison Dr., also at

4th and 7th Sts. between Madison Dr. and Constitution Ave. (tel. 737-4215). Open Monday to Saturday from 10 a.m. to 5 p.m. on Sunday from noon to 9 p.m. year round, with extended hours in summer determined annually. Metro: Archives or Judiciary Square.

Most people think of the National Gallery as part of the Smithsonian complex. In fact, though it's on the Mall, and it is in some arcane way related to the Smithsonian, it is not actually of it. Hence, this listing apart from the other Mall museums. It houses one of the world's foremost collections of European and American painting, sculpture, and graphic arts from the Middle Ages to the 20th century. It's really like two museums—the original neoclassic, West Building with its domed rotunda and delightful garden courts, and the ultramodern honeycomb triangular East Building designed by I.M. Pei, with great glass walls and tetrahedron skylights. The pink Tennessee marble from which both buildings are constructed was taken from the same quarry; it forms the sole architectural link between the two structures.

About 800 paintings are on display at all times on the main- and ground-floor galleries of the West Building. The former are all decorated to reflect the period and country of the art shown. For example, walls of the Italian galleries are covered in silk brocade, while Dutch galleries are paneled in somber oak. To the right of the Rotunda are 17th-, 18th-, and 19th-century French paintings by Lorrain, Poussin, Watteau, and later, masterpieces of Monet, Renoir, Gauguin, and Degas. Also in this section, below the East Garden Court, are works of American (Homer, Sargent, Cassatt, Stuart) and British (Reynolds, Constable, Turner, Gainsborough) artists. To the left of the Rotunda, surrounding the West Garden Court, are Italian Renaissance paintings, including the only da Vinci outside Europe, *Ginevra De' Benci,* as well as works by Titian, Tintoretto, Fra Angelico, Botticelli, and Raphael. Another gallery features 17th- and 18th-century Italians. The Spanish galleries are highlighted by an entire room of El Grecos, as well as paintings by Goya and Velásquez. German masters include Grunewald, Cranach, Dürer, and Holbein; Flemish masters, in the same section, Jan Van Eyck, Bosch, and Rubens. There's an excellent collection of Rembrandts in the Dutch section.

Rest your museum-weary feet in one of the lovely colonnaded Garden Courts. Under arched skylights, with cherub-statue fountains and comfortable upholstered chairs, the courts are perfect settings in which to contemplate art and life.

Proceed down a level to the ground floor where you'll find American Naïve 18th- and 19th-century paintings (a charming exhibit), 17th- and 18th-century prints, drawings of old masters and moderns, 19th- and 20th-century sculpture (including a marvelous collection of Daumier heads and many pieces by Degas and Renoir), Chinese porcelains, small Renaissance bronzes, 16th-century Flemish tapestries, and extremely ornate decorative arts of the 18th century. Some special exhibitions—such as "American Drawings & Watercolors of the 20th Century," which included Andrew Wyeth's famed Helga pictures—take place on this level. Here too is an immense shop specializing in art books and prints.

Another major museum shop of books, posters, prints, and art objects is located in the Concourse connecting the West and East Buildings by a moving sidewalk. Here as well is the **Café-Buffet,** one of four eateries at the National Gallery (see Chapter III for details on the museum's dining facilities) and an outdoor cobblestone courtyard with a fountain.

The Ground Level of the East Building (up the main stairway from the Concourse) is dominated by an immense Calder mobile under a four-story skylight. The East Wing is used to house temporary exhibits which run the gamut from "Henri Matisse: the Early Years in Nice, 1916–1930" to a Georgia O'Keeffe centennial exhibition. Some shows require free passes available on a first-come, first-served basis. They specify entry times.

At every entrance there's an information desk where you can get a calendar of events and a floor plan of the galleries. The former includes lectures, concerts (every Sunday at 7 p.m., except in summer), and films. You can receive a calendar of events in advance of your visit by writing to the Information Office, National Gallery of Art, Washington, DC 20565.

Free highlight tours of both buildings are given daily; call for exact times. These are excellent and highly recommended. In addition, there are frequent tours focusing on select topics, and audio tours can be rented.

Further explanations of works of art here are offered on information sheets found in many galleries.

(6) THE LINCOLN MEMORIAL: Directly west of the Mall in Potomac Park, at 23rd St. NW, between Constitution and Independence Aves. (tel. 426-6841). Open 24 hours daily, year round, except Christmas. Park staff on duty from 8 a.m. to midnight. Metro: Foggy Bottom.

The Lincoln Memorial attracts some 3½ million visitors annually. It's a beautiful and moving testament to a great American, its marble walls seeming to embody not only the spirit and integrity of Lincoln, but all that has ever been good about America. Visitors are silently awed in its presence.

The monument was a long time in the making. Although it was planned as early as 1867, two years after Lincoln's death, it was not until 1912 that Henry Bacon's design was completed, and the memorial itself was dedicated in 1922.

A beautiful neoclassic temple-like structure, similar in architectural design to the Parthenon in Greece, the memorial has 36 fluted Doric columns representing the states of the Union at the time of Lincoln's death, plus two at the entrance. On the attic parapet are 48 festoons symbolic of the number of states in 1922 when the monument was erected. Hawaii and Alaska are noted in an inscription on the terrace. To the west, the Arlington Memorial Bridge crossing the Potomac recalls the reunion of North and South. To the east is the beautiful Reflecting Pool, lined with American elms and stretching 2000 feet toward the Washington Monument and the Capitol beyond.

The memorial chamber, under 60-foot ceilings, has limestone walls inscribed with the Gettysburg Address and Lincoln's Second Inaugural Address. Two 60-foot murals by Jules Guerin on the north and south walls depict, allegorically, Lincoln's principles and achievements. On the south wall an Angel of Truth freeing a slave is flanked by groups of figures representing Justice and Immortality. The north wall mural depicts the unity of North and South and is flanked by groups of figures symbolizing Fraternity and Charity. Most powerful, however, is Daniel French's 19-foot-high seated statue of Lincoln in deep contemplation in the central chamber. Its effect is best evoked by these words of Walt Whitman: "He was a mountain in grandeur of soul, he was a sea in deep undervoice of mystic loneliness, he was a star in steadfast purity of purpose and service and he abides." It is appropriate to the heritage of Lincoln that on several occasions those who have been oppressed have expressed their plight to America and the world at the steps of his shrine. Most notable was a peaceful demonstration of 200,000 people on August 28, 1963, at which another freedom-loving American, Dr. Martin Luther King, Jr., said "I have a dream."

A totally different view of the Lincoln Memorial—its underside—can be seen on free 40-minute Under the Lincoln Tours given in the spring and fall only. Park rangers lead visitors through caverns with stalagmites and stalactites under the monument's foundation. I've never seen any ghosts down there, but rumor has it the caverns are haunted. These are popular tours, so book far in advance by calling 426-6841.

One further note: There are picnic tables under the trees across the street by the Reflecting Pool—a perfect setting for an al fresco lunch.

(7) THE WASHINGTON MONUMENT: 15th St. and Constitution Ave. NW (tel. 426-6841). Open daily from the first Sunday in April through Labor Day from 8 a.m. to midnight, 9 a.m. to 5 p.m. the rest of the year. Closed Christmas. There's free one-hour parking at the 16th Street Oval. Metro: Smithsonian.

The 555-foot stark marble obelisk that shimmers in the sun and glows under floodlights at night is the city's most visible landmark. It is, like the Eiffel Tower in Paris or London's Big Ben, a symbol of the city.

The idea for a tribute to George Washington first arose 16 years before his death at the Continental Congress of 1783. An equestrian statue was planned, and Washington himself approved the site for it—on the Mall, west of the future Capitol and south of the President's Palace. However, over a century was to elapse before a very different monument was completed. The new nation had more pressing problems, and funds were not readily available. It wasn't until the early 1830s, with the 100th anniversary of Washington's birth approaching, that any action was taken. Then there were several fiascos. A mausoleum was provided for Washington's remains under the Capitol Rotunda, but a grand-nephew, citing Washington's will, refused to allow the body to be moved from Mount Vernon. In 1830 Horatio Greenough was commissioned to create a memorial statue for the Rotunda. He came up with a bare-chested seated Washington, draped in classical Greek garb; a shocked public claimed he looked like he was "entering or leaving a bath," and the statue was relegated to the Smithsonian. Finally in 1833 prominent citizens organized the Washington National Monument Society. Robert Mill's design (which originally contained a circular colonnaded Greek temple base, discarded later for lack of funds) was accepted. The cornerstone was laid on July 4, 1848, and for the next 37 years watching the monument grow—or not grow—was a local pastime. The Civil War and lagging funds brought construction to a halt at an awkward 150 feet. The unsightly stump remained until 1876 when President Grant approved federal monies to complete the project. Rejecting plans for ornate embellishment that ranged from English gothic to Hindu pagoda designs, authorities put the U.S. Army Corps of Engineers to work on the obelisk. Dedicated in 1885, it was opened to the public in 1888.

You can no longer climb the 897 steps, but an elevator whisks visitors to the top in just 70 seconds. The 360-degree views are spectacular. To the east are the Capitol and Smithsonian buildings; to the north, the White House; to the west, the Lincoln and Vietnam Memorials, and Arlington National Cemetery beyond; and to the south, the gleaming-white shrine to Thomas Jefferson and the Potomac River. It's a marvelous orientation to the city.

In tourist season it's a good idea to arrive a little before 8 a.m. Long lines form early on, and the elevator's capacity is limited. Depending on staff availability, one-hour **"Down the Steps" tours** are given on weekends at 10 a.m. and 2 p.m. For details, call before you go or ask the ranger on duty. On this tour you'll gain some insight into how the building was put together and get to see the 190 carved stones inserted into the interior walls. Presented by individuals, societies, cities, states, and foreign nations, these memorial blocks range from a piece of stone from the Parthenon (a gift from Greece) to a plaque presented by the Fire Department of Philadelphia.

There's a snackbar on the grounds where you can get burritos, lemonade, a bagel and cream cheese, and ice cream—not bad fare for a picnic on the grass.

(8) THE JEFFERSON MEMORIAL: Directly south of the Washington Monument on Ohio Dr. at the south shore of the Tidal Basin (tel. 426-6841). Open 24 hours daily, year round, except Christmas. Park staff on duty from 8 a.m. to midnight. Best transportation is via Tourmobile.

President John F. Kennedy, at a 1962 dinner honoring 29 Nobel Prize winners, told his guests they were "the most extraordinary collection of talent, of human knowledge, that has ever been gathered together at the White House, with the possible exception of when Thomas Jefferson dined alone." Jefferson penned the Declaration of Independence, proclaiming "that all Men are created equal, that they are endowed by their Creator with certain unalienable Rights, that among those are Life, Liberty, and the Pursuit of happiness. . . ." He spoke out against slavery. He was George Washington's secretary of state, John Adams's vice-president, and our third president. And he still found time to found the University of Virginia and to pursue wide-ranging interests including architecture, astronomy, anthropology, music, and farming.

Jefferson's circular colonnaded monument with a domed interior is in the neoclassic style that he helped popularize in the U.S. Above the entranceway, sculpture depicts Jefferson before the committee appointed to write the Declaration of Independence. The central focus inside is Rudulph Evan's 19-foot standing statue of Jefferson atop a six-foot black granite pedestal. Engraved on the white marble walls are excerpts from the inspiring writings of America's greatest democratic philosopher—words which expand on Jefferson's core philosophy expressed in the circular frieze quotation, "I have sworn upon the altar of God eternal hostility against every form of tyranny over the mind of man."

From the exterior colonnade walk you can glimpse the Lincoln Memorial, the Capitol, the White House, and the Washington Monument. The Jefferson Memorial is lovely day or night, but it's most beautiful in early April when the surrounding cherry trees are in bloom.

Park staff members give short talks to visitors on request. There's free one-hour parking, and spring through fall a refreshment kiosk at the Tourmobile stop offers snack fare.

(9) THE LIBRARY OF CONGRESS: On 1st St. SE, between Independence Ave. and East Capitol St., lower level (tel. 287-5458). Open weekdays from 8:30 a.m. to 9:30 p.m., on weekends and holidays to 6 p.m. Closed Christmas and New Year's Days. Metro: Capitol South.

The Library of Congress came into being in 1800 when $5000 was provided "for the purchase of such books as may be necessary for the use of Congress—and for putting up a suitable apartment for containing them therein. . . ." It was first housed in the new Capitol and was completely destroyed when British troops burned Washington in 1814. A month later Thomas Jefferson offered his personal library, accumulated over a span of 50 years, as a replacement. His legacy of 6487 books formed the nucleus of what was to become the world's largest library.

Today's Library of Congress contains a mind-boggling 84 million-plus items, with new materials being acquired at the rate of 10 items per minute! Its three buildings house 22 million books and pamphlets in 60 languages; over 36 million manuscripts; the world's largest collection of books printed before 1500; four million maps and atlases, some of them dating to the middle of the 14th century; six million pieces of music, including autograph scores; ten million prints and photographs providing a visual record of life in America and elsewhere; rare Stradivarius instruments; half a million recordings; about a quarter of a million motion pictures; and over three million microfilms. Among its collections are the papers of everyone from Freud to Groucho Marx, sketches by

Alexander Graham Bell, the magic books of Houdini, and the contents of Lincoln's pockets on the night he died.

The library's primary role is still as the research and reference arm of Congress, providing data for complex in-depth studies, summaries of major legislation, and analyses of foreign legislation. To do this it employs a congressional research staff of 850, including political scientists, economists, engineers, oceanographers, and other experts. However, this institution also contains the Copyright Office, affording protection to authors, composers, artists, and filmmakers. Its vast resources are open to scholars, students, and serious researchers in all fields, a service extended across the nation through an interlibrary loan program. Another facet of its operations involves supplying Braille books and magazines, as well as records and cassettes (and equipment to play them on), to the blind and handicapped. The library also maintains the Dewey Decimal System of classification, and finally, it offers a year-round program of concerts, lectures, and poetry readings in the Coolidge Auditorium.

Equal in grandeur to its contents is the ornate Italian Renaissance-style **Thomas Jefferson Building,** designed in 1897 to house the burgeoning collection. Partly intended to make Europe sit up and take notice of America as a viably cultured nation, this magnificent repository required 50 painters and sculptors working for eight years to decorate its interior. Originally projected to hold the fruits of at least 150 years of collecting, it was in fact filled up within 13. It is now supplemented by the **James Madison Memorial Building** and the **John Adams Building.**

Visitors can view an 18-minute introductory slide-sound presentation, *America's Library,* in the **Visitor Services Center** in the west entrance ground-floor lobby. It is shown hourly from 8:45 a.m. to 8:45 p.m. weekdays, till 5:45 p.m. on weekends and holidays. On tours (leaving from just outside the theater every hour on the hour weekdays from 9 a.m. to 4 p.m.), you'll learn about architectural details and see the Great Hall, the viewing gallery of the Main Reading Room (which is under a magnificent 160-foot dome), and permanent exhibits. These include the Gutenberg Bible (one of three perfect surviving examples) and the Giant Bible of Mainz, an illuminated manuscript executed by hand on vellum at about the same time the Gutenberg was printed. There are also changing exhibits from the collection. After the tour you can explore on your own, do research in the reading room, or check out your family tree in the Genealogy Room.

On the way out, pick up a *Calendar of Events* at the ground-floor exit. You might want to bring a picnic lunch; tables out front overlook the Capitol. There are more picnic tables around the corner in front of the James Madison Memorial Building, 101 Independence Ave. SE (tel. 287-5000), which in itself merits a visit. Among other things, it's used to house changing exhibits ranging from "The American Cowboy" (music, paintings, posters, books, and films tracing the cowboy craze from 1870s dime-store novels to today's western fashions) to "The American Solution: Origins of the United States Constitution." In addition, classic, rare, and unusual films are shown in the **Mary Pickford Theater.** The Madison Building cafeteria and buffet dining room on the sixth floor are worthy of consideration whenever you're in the neighborhood (details in Chapter III).

(10) THE FEDERAL BUREAU OF INVESTIGATION: The J. Edgar Hoover FBI Building, E St. between 9th and 10th Sts. NW (tel. 324-3447). Open weekdays only, from 8:45 a.m. to 4:15 p.m.; closed weekends and holidays. Metro: Metro Center or Gallery Place.

Some 4,500 visitors a day learn why crime doesn't pay by touring the FBI's informative exhibits on law enforcement, infamous criminals, and notorious cases. Today the bureau has over 200 fields of jurisdiction. Its major priorities are terrorism, organized crime, white-collar crime, and foreign counterintelligence, but they also keep their hand in kidnapping, extortion, labor racketeering, and illicit narcotics, so don't get any funny ideas.

To take the 1¼-hour tour, arrive early; the line gets extremely long after 9 a.m. One way to beat it is to write to your senator or congressperson—as far in advance as possible—and ask him or her to set up a reservation for a scheduled time.

On the tour, you'll learn about the history of the bureau (it started in 1908) and its past and present activities. Among the highlights are: photos and weapons of big-time gangsters like Dillinger (his death mask, scars and all, is displayed), Bonnie and Clyde, Al Capone, Doc Barker, and "Pretty Boy" Floyd; ingenious espionage devices that have been used to transport microfilm out of the country and an actual surveillance film showing a double agent receiving instructions from the KGB; the current ten most-wanted fugitives (of the 408 fugitives who have made this list since its inception in 1950, 381 have been captured—112 were apprehended through direct citizen cooperation, and two were actually recognized by people on the tour and captured as a result of their identifications); the U.S. Crime Clock, offering a number of startling statistics about life in these United States: a murder every 28 minutes, a rape every six minutes, a burglary every ten seconds; examples of ransom notes kidnappers send and a tape of an actual phoned ransom demand; and 4,500 weapons, many of which have been confiscated from criminals (they're used for reference).

Other displays deal with TV shows and movies about the FBI, white-collar crime, use of fingerprints for positive identification, what you can do to prevent crime, the FBI's telecommunications network, organized crime, agent training, and the FBI's work with the Drug Enforcement Administration. The latter includes a display of drug paraphernalia and substances and a world map detailing routes by which illicit drugs enter the United States. Methods the FBI/DEA uses to combat illicit drugs, via education as well as investigation, are also covered.

You'll observe the serology lab where bloodstains and body fluid stains are examined for evidence; the Document Section, where fraudulent checks, holdup notes, and the like are stored; the ballistics file, where the FBI determines if two bullets were fired from the same weapon; the Instrumental Analysis Unit, where a piece of paint the size of a pinhead can reveal to lab workers the make and model of a car; and the Microscopic Analysis Unit, where hairs and fibers are examined.

The tour ends with a big bang—lots of them in fact—when a sharpshooting agent gives a firearms demonstration in the shooting gallery.

(11) THE JOHN F. KENNEDY CENTER FOR THE PERFORMING ARTS: At

the southern end of New Hampshire Ave. NW at Rock Creek Pkwy. (for general information tel. 254-3600 or nationwide toll free 800/424-8504; for box office information: Opera House, 254-3770; Eisenhower Theater, 254-3670; Concert Hall, 254-3776; Terrace Theater, 254-9895; the instant charge number for credit-card sales is 857-0900). If you'd like to attend performances during your visit, call the toll-free number and request the current issue of *Two on the Aisle,* a free publication that describes all Kennedy Center happenings and prices. You can also charge tickets via this 800 number. Open from 10 a.m. to 9 p.m. Monday to Saturday, from noon to 9 p.m. on Sunday and holidays. Metro: Foggy Bottom. Or take the no. 46 bus down New Hampshire Avenue from Dupont Circle. The no. 81 bus, accessible from downtown hotels, will also get you here.

Plans for a national cultural center began in 1958 when President Eisenhower approved legislation designating 17 acres overlooking the Potomac for the purpose. President Kennedy was very much involved in furthering the project; after his assassination, President Johnson signed another bill authorizing federal matching funds for construction and specifying the current name of the facility. Thus the Kennedy Center, which opened in 1971, serves a dual purpose: as a cultural center for the nation and as a living memorial to John F. Kennedy. Several quotations from Kennedy, such as "the New Frontier for which I campaign in public life can also be a New Frontier for American art," are carved into the center's river facade.

The striking $73-million performing arts center, enhanced by gifts from many nations (Italy provided all the marble—3700 tons of it!), is similar in scope to New York's Lincoln Center. It contains an opera house, a concert hall, two dramatic theaters, and a film theater. The best way to see it, including areas you can't visit on your own, is to take one of the 50-minute guided tours offered Monday through Saturday between 10 a.m. and 1 p.m. Or beat the crowds by writing in advance to your congressperson for tickets for a 9:30 a.m. VIP tour.

First stop is the **Hall of Nations,** where flags of all the countries recognized diplomatically by the United States are displayed. You'll also see the Israeli Lounge, where 40 painted and gilded panels depict musical instruments mentioned in the Bible; the 2,750-seat **Concert Hall,** home of the National Symphony Orchestra; the South Lounge, used for receptions and press conferences; two African rooms, decorated with beautiful tapestries from various African nations; the 500-seat **Terrace Theater,** a Bicentennial gift from Japan; the plush red and gilt **Opera House,** which seats 2,300 and is used for ballet, modern dance, and musical comedy as well as opera; the 1,200-seat **Eisenhower Theater,** mostly used for dramatic productions; the **Hall of States,** where the flags of the 50 states are hung in the order they joined the Union; and the **Grand Foyer,** the size of two football fields and the scene of many free concerts and performances. Your guide will point out many notable works of art along the way, such as a Barbara Hepworth sculpture (gift of England), Henri Matisse tapestries (gift of France), and an alabaster vase from 2600 B.C. found in a pyramid (gift of Egypt). If rehearsals are going on, visits to the theaters are omitted. After the tour, walk around the building's terrace for a panoramic 360-degree view of Washington.

There are three restaurants on the premises (details in Chapter III). See Chapter VI for specifics on theater, concert, and film offerings. There are three parking levels below the Kennedy Center. Daytime charge is $2 for the first hour, $1.50 for each additional hour with a maximum of five hours; nighttime parking is $4 for any length of time.

(12) THE BUREAU OF ENGRAVING AND PRINTING: 14th and C Sts. SW, just a block south of the Mall (tel. 447-9709). Open from 8:30 a.m. to 2:30 p.m., weekdays only. Metro: Smithsonian.

This is where they make the money—every last piece of U.S. currency, amounting to $66 billion annually. A staff of 2,300 works around the clock churning it out at the rate of 22.5 million notes a day. Everyone's eyes pop as they walk past rooms overflowing with money, the kind of rooms that Scrooge McDuck cavorted in. Though money is the big draw, it's not the whole story. The bureau manufactures many different products, including 35 billion postage stamps per year, Treasury bonds, White House invitations, and other miscellanea (700 other items in all). It's the only security printing plant in the world open to the public.

The immensely popular tour (arrive early in tourist season when as many as 5000 people a day line up at the door) begins with a short introductory film.

Then you'll see, through large windows, all the processes that go into the making of real money—the inking, stacking (stacks of currency contain 10,000 sheets, 32 notes to a sheet; a stack of $1 bills thus contains $320,000), cutting, and examination for defects. Exhibits include bills no longer in use, a pair of shears used for cutting notes in the 1880s, an engraver's bench, a display of $2 bills, counterfeit money, and an enlarged photograph of a $100,000 bill designed for official transactions. (Since 1969 the largest denomination printed for general consumption is $100.) Call for details. Upon completion of the tour, leave time to explore the Visitor Center, where the history of money is examined from "pieces of eight" to current currency. There are video displays, money-related electronic games, a display of $1 million, a visitor-operated printing press (for a nominal charge you can produce a piece of paper embossed with the bureau seal), and interesting exhibits on subjects like the evolution of a stamp from the original artwork to finished product and the art of engraving. Here, too, you can buy unique gifts like bags of shredded money and uncut sheets of notes at inflationary prices (like a sheet of four $1 bills for $7.50).

(13) THE NATIONAL ARCHIVES: Constitution Ave. between 7th and 9th Sts. NW (tel. 523-3000 for information on exhibits and films, 523-3220 for research information). The exhibition section is open daily April 1 to Labor Day from 10 a.m. to 9 p.m., the day after Labor Day to March 31 from 10 a.m. to 5:30 p.m. The research side is open Monday to Friday year round from 9 a.m. to 5 p.m. Metro: Archives.

Most famous as a center of genealogical research—Alex Haley began his work on *Roots* here—the National Archives is sometimes called the "nation's memory." This federal institution is charged with sifting through the accumulated papers of a nation's official life—billions of pieces a year—and determining what to save and what to destroy. The Archives' vast accumulation of census figures, military records, naturalization papers, immigrant passenger lists, federal documents, passport applications, ship manifests, maps, charts, photographs, and motion-picture film (and that's not the half of it) spans two centuries. And it's all available for the perusal of anyone 16 or over. All you have to do is get a research card; to apply, enter the building on the Pennsylvania Avenue side at 8th Street and have some photo I.D. on hand (a driver's license, school card, passport, or birth certificate are accepted). If you're casually thinking about tracing your roots, stop in first at Room 400 where a staff member can tell you whether it's worth the effort and how to go about it.

But the National Archives merits a visit even if you have no research project. The neoclassical building itself, designed by John Russell Pope in the 1930s (he was also the architect of the National Gallery and the Jefferson Memorial) is an impressive example of the Beaux Arts style. Seventy-two columns create a Corinthian colonnade on each of the four facades. Great bronze doors herald the Constitution Avenue entrance, and allegorical sculpture centered on *The Recorder of the Archives* adorns the pediment. On either side of the steps are male and female figures symbolizing guardianship and heritage, respectively. Guardians of the Portals at the Pennsylvania Avenue entrance represent the past and the future, and the theme of the pediment is destiny.

Within the building, the public Exhibition Hall Rotunda, under a 75-foot domed ceiling, is equally imposing. Under the dome, permanently displayed here, are the parchment originals of America's three most important documents—the Declaration of Independence, the Constitution, and the Bill of Rights. Immense murals on either side of the exhibit depict Jefferson presenting the Declaration of Independence to John Hancock, and Madison submitting the Constitution to George Washington and the Constitutional Convention. The document displays are enhanced by changing exhibits such as the current "The American Experiment: Creating the Constitution" and, in the Circular Gallery, "The American Experiment: Living With the Constitution."

Free docent tours are offered daily by appointment at 10:15 a.m. and 1:15 p.m. (tel. 523-3183). Pick up a schedule of events when you visit; the National Archives has frequent lectures, films, and genealogy workshops.

(14) THE WASHINGTON NATIONAL CATHEDRAL: Mount St. Alban, Massachusetts and Wisconsin Aves. NW, entrance on Wisconsin Ave. (tel. 537-6200). Open Monday to Saturday from 10 a.m. to 4:30 p.m., on Sunday from 8 a.m. to 5 p.m. Metro: Cleveland Park. Or take any T bus up Massachusetts Avenue from Dupont Circle.

Pierre L'Enfant's 1791 plan for the capital city included "a great church for national purposes," but possibly because of early America's fear of mingling church and state, over a century elapsed before the foundation for the National Cathedral was laid. Its actual name is the Cathedral of Saint Peter and Saint Paul. Though it's Episcopalian in denomination, it has no local congregation and seeks to serve the entire nation as a house of prayer for all people. It has been the setting for every kind of religious observance from Jewish to Serbian Orthodox.

A church of this magnitude (it's the sixth-largest cathedral in the world!) is a long time in the building. Its principal (but not original) architect, Philip Hubert Frohman, worked on the project from 1921 until his death in 1972. Theodore Roosevelt laid the foundation stone (a stone from a field in Bethlehem set into a larger piece of American granite) in 1907, and the Bethlehem Chapel opened for services in 1912. But construction, interrupted by two World Wars and periods of financial difficulty, still goes on today.

Fourteenth-century English Gothic in style (with several distinctly 20th-century innovations, such as a stained-glass window commemorating the flight of *Apollo XI* and containing a piece of moon rock), the cathedral is built in the shape of a cross, complete with flying buttresses. It is, along with the Capitol and the Washington Monument, one of the most dominant structures on the Washington skyline. Its 57-acre landscaped grounds contain two lovely gardens; four schools, including the College of Preachers; an herb garden, a greenhouse, and a shop called Herb Cottage (buy seeds and start your own); the London Brass Rubbing Centre; and a carver's shed where, on weekdays, you can see stonecarvers at work.

Over the years the cathedral has seen much history. Services to celebrate the end of World Wars I and II were held here. It was the scene of President Wilson's funeral (he and his wife are buried here), as well as President Eisenhower's. Helen Keller and her two companions, Anne Sullivan and Polly Thomson, are buried in the cathedral at her request. So is social worker Jane Addams. Martin Luther King, Jr., preached his last sermon here. And during the Iranian crisis a round-the-clock prayer vigil was held in the Holy Spirit Chapel throughout the hostages' captivity. When they were released, the hostages came to a service here, and tears flowed at Col. Thomas Schaefer's poignant greeting, "Good morning, my fellow Americans. You don't know how long I've been waiting to say those words."

The best way to explore the cathedral and see its abundance of art, architectural carvings, and statuary is to take a free 45-minute tour. They leave continually, Monday to Saturday from 10 a.m. to 3:15 p.m., on Sunday at 1 and 2 p.m. Among the highlights are dozens of stained-glass windows with themes ranging from the lives of Civil War Generals Lee and Jackson to the miracles of Christ; three exquisite rose windows; the nave, stretching a tenth of a mile to the high altar; Wilson's tomb; the delightful children's chapel; St. John's chapel, where needlepoint kneelers memorialize great Americans; the Holy Spirit Chapel, painted by Andrew Wyeth's father, N.C. Wyeth; and crypt chambers like the Bethlehem Chapel, first section of the cathedral to be constructed.

Allow time to tour the grounds or "close," and to visit the Observation Gallery where 70 windows provide views of the Washington Monument, the Capitol, and distant vistas of Maryland's Catoctin range and Virginia's Blue Ridge Mountains.

Another view is afforded when you attend services at the cathedral (Monday to Saturday at 7:30 a.m., noon, and 4 p.m.; on Sunday at 8, 9, and 11 a.m., and 4 p.m.). September to June there's a folk guitar Mass on Sunday at 10 a.m.

The cathedral hosts numerous events: organ recitals; choir performances; flower markets; films and slide lectures; workshops in brass rubbing, flower arrangements, needlepoint, calligraphy, and other arts; jazz, folk, and classical concerts. Past performances have ranged from Ravi Shankar playing Indian music at a memorial for Gandhi to a Stravinsky Centennial with Leonard Bernstein conducting. The 53-bell carillon is played on Saturday at 5 p.m. during spring and summer, 12:30 p.m. winter and fall; the ten-bell peal follows the 11 a.m. Sunday service. Organ recitals are usually given on the great organ following Sunday evening services at 5 p.m. The men and boys choir can be heard Sunday mornings at 11 a.m.; the boys alone Monday to Wednesday at 4 p.m. during the school year. There are free concerts every Tuesday at 8 p.m. during July and August.

A large gift shop on the premises (proceeds go toward upkeep and continued construction) sells replicas of cathedral statuary, religious books and art, Christmas cards, and more.

3. Additional Attractions

The following sights are grouped by location so that you can easily fit them into your itinerary.

NEAR THE CAPITOL: The Folger Shakespeare Library, the U.S. Botanic Garden, and the Voice of America are within easy walking distance.

The Folger Shakespeare Library

Located at 201 East Capitol St. SE (tel. 544-7077). Open from 10 a.m. to 4 p.m. Monday to Saturday, daily from April 15 to Labor Day; closed on federal holidays. Metro: Capitol South or Union Station.

"Shakespeare taught us that the little world of the heart is vaster, deeper, and richer than the spaces of astronomy." Those words are part of an essay written by Ralph Waldo Emerson in 1864 on the occasion of the Tercentenary of Shakespeare's birth—an essay that profoundly affected Amherst student Henry Clay Folger when he read it in 1879. Folger purchased an inexpensive set of Shakespeare's plays and went on to amass the world's largest collection of the Bard's printed works, today housed in the Folger Shakespeare Library. By 1930, when Folger, and his wife, Emily (whose literary enthusiasms matched his own), laid the cornerstone of a building to house the collection, it contained 93,000 books, 50,000 prints and engravings, and thousands of manuscripts. The Folgers made it all a gift to the American people.

The building itself is classical in style, its Georgian marble facade decorated with nine bas-relief scenes from Shakespeare's plays. A statue of Puck stands in the west garden, and quotations from the Bard and from contemporaries like Ben Jonson adorn the exterior walls.

The facility, today containing some 250,000 books, 100,000 of which are rare, is an important research center not only for Shakespearean scholars, but for those studying any aspect of 16th- and 17th-century England. And the oak-paneled Exhibition Hall, reminiscent of a Tudor long gallery, is a popular attraction for the general public. It has an intricate plaster ceiling decorated with Shakespeare's coat-of-arms, fleurs-de-lis, and other motifs. On display are rotating exhibits from the permanent collection. You might see portraits and busts of Shakespeare; an artist's conception of the original Globe Playhouse; playbills; promptbooks; first editions; Renaissance musical instruments, paintings, drawings, photographs, and prints of famous Shakespearean scenes; costumes, books, letters, and other Shakespeareana.

At the end of the Exhibition Hall is a theater designed to suggest an Elizabethan innyard theater where Shakespeare's plays can be seen under conditions similar to those for which they were intended. The timber and plaster walls are adorned with painted decorations; the gallery is triple-tiered and supported by oak columns with handcarved satyrs. The best way to see it, of course, is to attend a theatrical production here (details in Chapter VI).

Free walk-in tours of the Exhibition Hall and theater (though the latter cannot be seen if a rehearsal is in progress) are given weekdays between 11:30 a.m. and 1 p.m.

The United States Botanic Garden Conservatory

At 1st St. and Maryland Ave. SW (tel. 225-8333). Open daily from 9 a.m. to 5 p.m., till 9 p.m. June through August; closed Christmas. Metro: Federal Center SW.

Even in the hectic rush of Washington sightseeing you should stop and smell the flowers—particularly when they're so conveniently located in an immense greenhouse right at the foot of the Capitol. The Botanic Garden is like a lush tropical jungle with pools, waterfalls, and fountains, amid orchids, ferns, cacti, Spanish moss, and palm trees. The garden is ablaze with poinsettias around the Christmas season; the Easter show features masses of flowering spring plants (lilies, tulips, narcissi, hyacinths, and trellised nasturtium), and in the fall chrysanthemums dominate. Much appreciated by Washingtonians is the Summer Terrace Display of plants and flower beds with umbrella tables (a perfect picnic spot) overlooking the Capitol's reflecting pool. A self-guided tour map is available at the entrance, as is information on free classes and lectures on subjects like "Cacti and Succulents," and "Growing Begonias and African Violets." Call 225-7099 for an events recording and to find out which flowers are abloom.

The Voice of America

North Building of the Department of Health and Human Services, 330 Independence Ave. SW, entrance on C St. between 3rd and 4th Sts. (tel. 485-6231). Open weekdays with tours, by reservation only, at 8:45, 9:45, and 10:45 a.m., and 1:45 and 2:45 p.m. Metro: Federal Center SW.

The first Voice of America broadcast went on the air on February 24, 1942, 79 days after the attack on Pearl Harbor. In German, it informed listeners that "Daily, at this time, we shall speak to you about America and the war. The news may be good or bad. We shall tell you the truth."

Over 45 years later this is still the aim of VOA. The worldwide radio network of the U.S. Information Agency, it endeavors to promote understanding abroad of the U.S.—its people, culture, and policies. In an average week, over 130 million listeners tune in to its over 1200 hours of news programs, features, editorial roundups, commentaries, interviews, and music shows broadcast in 42 languages from Albanian to Uzbek. Correspondents throughout the world supplement UPI, AP, Reuters, and Agence France Presse bulletins. In its efforts to portray the diversity of American society, VOA has presented interviews with such wide-ranging subjects as blues singer Memphis Slim, Motion Picture Association president Jack Valenti, members of Congress, violinist Isaac Stern, and an Appalachian coal miner.

On a free 30-minute guided tour (call for reservations), you'll get a good overview of operations, learn how VOA deals with Soviet interference or "jamming," see the newsroom, hear actual broadcasting going on, and visit the "Bubble" where phones ring all day as foreign correspondents call in.

NEAR THE WHITE HOUSE: On the day you visit the White House, consider these sights in its general vicinity: the Corcoran Gallery, The National Museum of Women in the Arts, the National Aquarium, the DAR Museum, Decatur House, St. John's Church, the Octagon, and the OAS.

The Corcoran Gallery of Art

At 17th St. between E St. and New York Ave. NW (tel. 638-3211). Open from 10 a.m. to 4:30 p.m. Tuesday to Sunday, with extended hours Thursday evenings until 9 p.m. Closed on Monday, Thanksgiving, Christmas, and New Year's Days. Metro: Farragut West or Farragut North.

The first art museum in Washington, and one of the first in the country, the Corcoran Gallery was housed from 1874 to 1896 in the red brick and brownstone building that is now the Renwick. The collection outgrew its quarters and was transferred in 1897 to its present Beaux Arts building, designed by Ernest Flagg. Classical in style, it features a double atrium with two levels of fluted columns and a grand staircase.

The collection itself—shown in rotating exhibits—focuses chiefly on American art. A prominent Washington banker, William Wilson Corcoran was among the first wealthy American collectors to realize the importance of encouraging and supporting American artists. Enhanced by further gifts and bequests, the collection comprehensively spans American art from 18th-century portraiture to 20th-century moderns like Nevelson, Rothko, and Noland. Nineteenth-century works include Bierstadt's and Remington's imagery of the American West; Hudson River School artists like Cole, Church, and Durand; genre paintings; expatriates like Whistler, Sargent, and Mary Cassatt; and two giants of the late 19th century, Homer and Eakins. Displayed on the second floor is the white marble female nude, *The Greek Slave,* by Hiram Powers, considered so daring in its day that it was shown on alternate days to men and women.

The Corcoran is not, however, an exclusively American art museum. On the first floor is the collection from the estate of Sen. William Andrews Clark—an eclectic grouping of Dutch and Flemish masters, European painters, French impressionists, Barbizon landscapes, Delft porcelains, a Louis XVI salon transported in toto from Paris, and more. Clark's will stated that this diverse collection—which any curator must long to disperse among various museum departments—must be shown as a unit. He left money for a wing to house it which opened in 1928. Other non-American aspects of the collection include a room of exquisite Corot landscapes, another of medieval Renaissance tapestries, and numerous Daumier lithographs donated by Dr. Armand Hammer.

In addition the Corcoran features an ongoing series of special exhibitions. These have included in recent years: "Hispanic Art in the United States: 30 Contemporary Painters and Sculptors"; Richard Avedon's "In the American

West"; "An American Vision: Three Generations of Wyeth Art"; and the renowned Corcoran biennials of American painting. Since the Corcoran School of Art is on the premises, there are also occasional shows of faculty and student work.

Worth checking out are the Corcoran's ongoing series of gallery talks, concerts, art auctions, and other events. Free 30-minute tours are given Tuesday through Sunday at 12:30 p.m. and Thursday night at 7 p.m. The museum shop has a great selection of art cards, reproductions, books, posters, jewelry, and art nouveau glassware. A museum restaurant serving light luncheon fare is in the works at this writing.

The National Museum of Women in the Arts

At 13th St. and New York Ave. NW (tel. 783-5000). Open Tuesday to Saturday 10 a.m. to 5 p.m., Sunday noon to 5 p.m. Admission is free. Metro: Metro Center.

Celebrating "the contribution of women to the history of art," this new museum (opened 1987) is Washington's 72nd but a national first. Founders Wilhelmina and Wallace Holladay, who donated the core of the permanent collection—over 200 works by 115 women spanning the 16th through the 20th centuries—became interested in women's art on a European trip in the 1960s. While abroad, they were intrigued by the work of Clara Peeters, a 17th-century Flemish still-life painter whose works they saw at the Prado. "When I looked her up in the standard art text, H.W. Janson's *History of Art,* I found that not only was she not listed, but no woman was included . . . ," Wilhelmina Holladay recalls. "And there still is no woman listed today in Janson's latest edition." The Holladays began collecting women's art, and the concept of a women's art museum to begin correcting the inequities of underrepresentation soon evolved. (Though women make up close to 40% of working artists in the U.S., over 95% of the works hanging in museums are by men!). Artists in the Holladay collection include the handful-plus of well-known women artists, such as Elaine de Kooning, Rosa Bonheur, Barbara Hepworth, Kathe Kollwitz, Lee Krasner, Nancy Graves, Mary Cassatt, and Georgia O'Keeffe. But most exciting to me is the opportunity NMWA offers to view at long last the overlooked masterpieces of female contemporaries of Rembrandt, Degas, and Leonardo.

At least half of NMWA's 35,000 square feet of exhibition space will be devoted to visiting shows such as "Native American Artists: the Matriarchs" and "Women in the Irish Arts." Negotiations are underway at this writing for an exchange of works by Russian and American women. The inaugural exhibit, "American Women Artists, 1830–1930" focused on 123 works from that 100-year period and was the first major exhibition of American women artists to travel to significant museums around the country. It offered wonderful surprises, such as a very talented sister in the famed Peale family of 19th-century portrait painters, Sarah Miriam Peale.

The landmark building housing the museum is magnificent. Designed in 1907 as a Masonic temple by noted architect Waddy Wood (he also designed Woodrow Wilson's house), it is a lavish, Renaissance-revival, flatiron-shaped edifice fronted by giant columns and pilasters. Visitors enter through the Great Hall, a grandiloquent space with Turkish white marble floors, silk-brocaded walls, gilded moldings, and Belgian crystal chandeliers suspended from an exquisitely detailed ceiling. Two sweeping brass-railed, white marble staircases lead to commodious, high-ceilinged galleries. Also noteworthy is the museum's fine library on women in art, an important resource that currently numbers 2,000 volumes and is growing.

I particularly like the Holladays' rare-in-the-'80s philosophy of collecting.

"We have never bought art for investment," says Wilhelmina Holladay. "We have never sold a painting or upgraded. Anything we've bought we have because art is a spiritual aspect of our lives. It's like music or poetry. You don't own it; you just enjoy it and then it goes on to others. So we decided to give it away."

The National Aquarium

Located in the Department of Commerce Building at 14th and Constitution Aves. NW (tel. 377-2825 or 377-2826). Open daily except Christmas day from 9 a.m. to 5 p.m. You can view shark feeding Monday, Wednesday, and Saturday at 2 p.m., piranha feeding Tuesday, Thursday, and Sunday at 2 p.m. Admission: $1 for adults, 50¢ for children and senior citizens. Metro: Federal Triangle.

Washington's small aquarium is the oldest one in the United States and one of the oldest in the world. Established in 1873 by the Federal Fish Commission, its original purpose was "the artificial propogation of desirable fishes." Today some 1,000 specimens, representing over 200 species of fish, are on public view in 66 display tanks. They range from moray eels to sharks. Other denizens of the deep you'll see here are ornate lionfish, seahorses, colorful reef fish, turtles, alligators, and various invertebrates. There's a touch tank where kids can examine crabs, starfish, sea urchins, and snails. Other exhibits are arranged geographically (for example, African lakes, South American rivers, and Caribbean and Pacific reef life) or thematically (such as a display of stream and pond life). A 15-minute slide presentation about underwater life is shown continuously in the aquarium's Mini-Theater. You'll learn lots of interesting ichthyological facts here. Did you know that some members of the tuna family are capable of exceeding speeds of 50 miles per hour in short bursts? I bet not. A cafeteria, open every day till 2 p.m., is on the premises.

The DAR Museum

Its apt address is 1776 D St. NW (tel. 628-1776). Open weekdays from 9 a.m. to 4 p.m., on Sunday from 1 to 5 p.m. Closed holidays and during the organization's Congress week in April. Metro: Farragut West.

Memorial Continental Hall, a landmark Beaux Arts building, is the National Headquarters of the Daughters of the American Revolution and a museum of American decorative arts from the 17th to mid-19th centuries. It is dedicated to all the recognized heroes of the American Revolution. When ground was broken for the building in 1902 (the cornerstone laid with the same trowel George Washington used in laying the cornerstone of the Capitol) it faced the White House lot where presidential cattle grazed and was one of the few buildings of consequence west of the executive mansion.

Washington has changed, but the past is well preserved here in a stunning collection of early American art and artifacts. Among some 50,000 objects on rotating display are examples of the Chinese export porcelain used in Colonial times, English pottery, quilts and coverlets, needlework samplers, pewterware, period furnishings, glassware and silver, manuscripts, diaries, a flag carried in the Revolutionary War, and many notable paintings, including a Rembrandt Peale portrait of Washington.

Four floors are occupied by 34 rooms (which state chapters purchased to help finance the building of the hall) furnished as rooms in 18th- and 19th-century homes. Touring these is great fun. They range from an opulent Victorian Missouri parlor to the stately New Jersey room, an English Council chamber of the 17th century with woodwork and furnishings created from the British frigate *Augusta* that sank in Redbank in 1777. Other states are represented on these floors by art objects they've donated. Exhibits from the Americana Collection of documents, wills, correspondence, manuscripts, and other period papers are displayed on the second floor. Kids will especially like New Hampshire's "Children's Attic," filled with 19th-century toys, dolls, and children's furnishings. Opposite the Attic is the "Touch of Independence," also geared to kids with hands-on exhibits like Colonial drinking vessels, Early American toys, and the life of a Revolutionary soldier. And the second-floor **Children's American Revolution Museum** features dolls and dollhouse furnishings, tea services, elementary school grammar books, Colonial household objects, children's clothing, weaponry, and displays on skills like candle-making and glass-blowing.

Constitution Hall, an impressive 4000-seat auditorium decorated in federal blue and gold motif, offers some of Washington's best nighttime entertainment, and it's not all highbrow. Even Eddie Murphy and Joan Rivers play here. See Chapter VI for details.

Also on the premises is the DAR's Library of over 75,000 books and pamphlets and some 30,000 manuscripts, mostly on genealogy, open to the public at a daily fee weekdays from 9 a.m. to 4 p.m. Call 879-3228 for details.

The best way to see the museum is to take the free guided tour offered between 10 a.m. and 3 p.m. weekdays, between 1 and 5 p.m. on Sunday. On your own you can't view the state period rooms or the "Touch of Independence." Before you leave, check out the gift shop for handcrafted items like straw dolls, needlework kits, books on decorative arts, and more.

Decatur House

At 748 Jackson Pl., corner of H St. NW on Lafayette Square (tel. 673-4030). Open from 10 a.m. to 2 p.m. Tuesday to Friday, from noon to 4 p.m. weekends and holidays; closed on Monday, Thanksgiving, and Christmas. Admission is $2.50 for adults, $1.25 for students and senior citizens. Metro: Farragut West (17th Street exit) or Farragut North.

This three-story Federal-style brick town house was designed in 1818–1819 by Benjamin Latrobe, one of the most noted architects of the day. His client, the dashing Commodore Stephen Decatur, was a naval hero famous for his victories at sea and in the War of 1812. Decatur delivered a patriotic toast that is still quoted—though more often misquoted—today: "Our country—In her intercourse with foreign nations, may she always be in the right, and always successful, right or wrong." He and his wife, Susan Wheeler, made their new home a glittering social center, but their stay was short. After 14 months Decatur was mortally wounded in a duel, and his distressed wife moved to Georgetown. The house continued to attract distinguished occupants, including the French and Russian legations, Henry Clay, Martin Van Buren, Alexandria hotel proprietor John Gadsby, a vice-president, and five congressmen. In 1871 Gen. Edward Fitzgerald Beale and his wife, Mary, added Victorian sandstone trim to Latrobe's design, work that her daughter-in-law, Mrs. Truxton Beale, later undid, restoring the home to its original appearance.

Today the first floor is furnished in the style of the Decatur's occupancy, with period furnishings and mementoes of his life and naval exploits. The second floor is Victorian in decor, representing the General Beale era. The history of the house and its architecture and interior design are explained on 30-minute tours given throughout the day on the hour and the half hour. For three weeks every December, period Christmas decorations are put up, and in November Decatur House hosts an annual Colonial crafts fair.

St. John's Church

Across from Lafayette Square at 16th and H Sts. NW (tel. 347-8766). Open from 8 a.m. to 4 p.m. daily, with services (or Wednesday organ recitals) at 12:10 p.m. Monday to Friday, at 8, 9, and 11 a.m. on Sunday. Metro: McPherson Square (Vermont Avenue exit).

Every president of the United States since 1816 has worshipped at the Episcopal church across Lafayette Square from the White House. The Madisons were charter members of the congregation. Other presidents who were parishioners include James Monroe, Andrew Jackson, Martin Van Buren, William Henry Harrison, John Tyler, Zachary Taylor, Franklin Pierce, and Chester A. Arthur. The morning after John F. Kennedy's assassination, Lyndon Johnson came here for quiet prayer. And President Ford attended services almost every Sunday when he was in town.

A Greek Revival building with a dome and colonnaded portico entrance, St. John's was designed by Benjamin Latrobe, an architect famous for his work on the Capitol and the White House. In 1883 another famous Washington architect, James Renwick, was engaged to add a Palladian window over the altar (*The Last Supper,* designed by the curator of stained-glass windows at Chartres). Other notable stained-glass windows added in the 1880s include one presented by Chester A. Arthur in memory of his wife, who was a St. John's choir member. The window faces the White House so that Arthur could see it from his office. *The Adoration of the Magi* window commemorates Presidents Madison, Monroe, and Van Buren. On the opposite side of the church, the *Sower's Window* is a memorial to William H. Seward, Lincoln's secretary of state. And the beautiful *Madonna of the Chair* window in the south transept of the balcony is modeled after a painting by Raphael.

The **Parish House** next door, also open to visitors, served as the residence of British Minister Lord Ashburton during U.S.-British negotiations in 1842 to settle the Canadian boundary dispute. Here Secretary of State Daniel Webster and Lord Ashburton smoothed the difficulties of negotiation with sumptuous meals, balls, parties, and receptions. (Ashburton provided expensive wines and desserts prepared by his French chef for these occasions; Webster personally visited markets to select the finest Maine salmon, Maryland crabs, and Chesapeake ducks). The Canadian border was most amicably settled.

There's a guided tour of the church every Sunday after the 11 a.m. service. Organ recitals are given every Wednesday at 12:10 p.m. except during Lent, August, and September; the church has an exceptionally fine organ. There's a service in French every Sunday at 4 p.m.

The Octagon

At 1799 New York Ave. NW, at 18th St., between E and F Sts. (tel. 638-3105). Open Tuesday to Friday from 10 a.m. to 4 p.m.; on Saturday and Sunday from 1 to 4 p.m.; closed on Monday, Thanksgiving, Christmas, and New Year's Days. Suggested admission is $2; children under 12, 50¢. Metro: Farragut West.

One of the first town houses to be built in a still-somewhat-rural Washington, the Octagon was designed in 1798 by Dr. William Thornton for Col. John Tayloe III, a Virginia planter, breeder of racehorses, and friend of George Washington. Thornton, who also designed the Capitol and Woodlawn Plantation (see Chapter VIII), was something of a Renaissance man. Architecture, which it's said he mastered in only two weeks, was just one of his many fields of expertise; others included astronomy, medicine, philosophy, art, language, and finance.

The building is steeped in history. George Washington, who occasionally inspected the construction site, died before the building was completed, but in the early 1800s the Octagon was a prominent social center visited by Adams, Jefferson, Madison, Monroe, Webster, Clay, Lafayette, and Calhoun. And when the White House was destroyed by fire in the War of 1812, James and Dolley Madison moved into the Octagon; it was here that Madison signed the Treaty of Ghent in 1815 establishing peace with Great Britain.

Today this gracious mansion, an excellent example of the Federal period style by one of the capital's most noted architects, is under the auspices of the American Architectural Foundation. In an ongoing project, the house is being returned as nearly as possible to its original state. The portico was recently completed and the door painted in glossy chocolate brown typical of the period.

Off the marble-floored circular entrance hall, with its two original Adamesque coal stoves, are the dining room, its Coadestone mantel flanked by Saint-Mémin portraits of Dr. Thornton and Colonel Tayloe, and the drawing room. Both are furnished in period pieces, some of which belonged to the Tayloes.

Ascending to the second floor up the magnificent oval staircase, you'll come upon the circular Treaty Room (Madison's study) which contains the table on which the Treaty of Ghent was signed and the box in which it was brought over to the U.S. Two additional rooms on this floor are used for changing exhibitions, such as a collection of Japanese prints once owned by, and very inspiring to, Frank Lloyd Wright; a show on Richard Morris Hunt in conjunction with New York's Metropolitan Museum; and "The Architect and the British Country House" in conjunction with the National Gallery. Shows here often complement National Gallery exhibitions, focusing on architectural aspects.

And one flight down from the main floor, via the servants' stairway, is the brick-floored kitchen with its large cooking fireplace and the adjoining wine cellar.

Docents are on duty at all times and are happy to take visitors on a tour. A special tour given every Tuesday, Friday, Saturday, and Sunday at 1 p.m. focuses on the restoration. You're welcome to picnic on the garden lawn.

The Organization of American States

At 17th St. NW and Constitution Ave. (tel. 789-3751). Open from 9:30 a.m. to 5 p.m. Monday to Friday (visits by appointment only). Metro: Farragut West.

Founded on Pan American Day, April 14, 1890, the organization now known as the OAS has three main goals: maintaining international peace among member nations, strengthening the security of the western hemisphere, and promoting economic and social development.

The organization's Washington home belongs to 32 American republics of the western hemisphere, including the United States of America. Set amid verdant lawns and sycamores, it is one of Washington's most beautiful buildings, with many Latin touches like a terracotta-tiled roof, black wrought-iron balconies, palatial staircases, and arched doorways. Especially delightful is the skylit garden patio with palms and tropical plants around a rose-colored fountain. Here stands the Peace Tree (part fig, part rubber) that President Taft planted when the building was dedicated. Throughout the building, architectural embellishments reflect motifs of pre-Columbian and Spanish colonial art.

Flags of all the member nations hang in the stately **Hall of Heroes,** and busts on marble pedestals of heroes of the Americas like José Martí, Simón Bolívar, and George Washington line the walls.

High-ranking dignitaries are received in the neoclassic **Hall of the Americas,** a magnificent room with glittering crystal Tiffany chandeliers and 24 Corinthian columns supporting a 45-foot-high vaulted ceiling. Adjoining is the old **Council Room,** its bronze relief panels depicting the exploits of Cortés, Bolívar, Balboa, and others. No longer large enough for council meetings, it is used for committee meetings. All the chairs and the table in this room are carved from a single mahogany tree—a symbol of unity. Today major OAS decisions are made in the ultramodern Simón Bolívar Room (new Council Room) on the first floor.

You can see all of the above on a free 45-minute guided tour; if you're interested, you must call for reservations. Before you leave, be sure to see the art exhibit on the first floor and stroll through the formal **Aztec Garden** out back where Xochipilli, the Aztec god of flowers, watches over a blue-tiled lily pond.

Museum of Modern Art of Latin America

After visiting the OAS, proceed to the nearby Spanish colonial-style building at 201 18th St. NW, at Virginia Ave. (tel. 789-6016), where works of contemporary artists from the Caribbean and countries south of the Rio Grande are shown. There's a rotating permanent collection, with about 200 works on display at any given time. Most major Latin American artists are represented. The museum was a Bicentennial gift to the United States from OAS member countries. It's open from 10 a.m. to 5 p.m. Tuesday to Saturday.

NEAR THE LINCOLN MEMORIAL: The Vietnam Memorial is actually right next to Lincoln's shrine. You don't have to go out of your way to combine the two sights.

The Vietnam Veterans Memorial

Just across from the Lincoln Memorial, east of Henry Bacon Dr. between 21st and 22nd Sts. NW (tel. 426-6841). Open 24 hours. Metro: Foggy Bottom.

To my mind, the saddest sight in Washington is the Vietnam Veterans Memorial—two long, black granite walls inscribed with the names of the men and women who gave their lives, or remain missing, in the longest war in our nation's history. Even if no one close to you died in Vietnam, it's emotionally wrenching watching visitors grimly studying the directories at either end to find out where their husbands, sons, and loved ones are listed. The slow walk along the 492-foot wall of names—close to 60,000 people, many of whom died very young—is a powerful evocation of the tragedy of all wars. And whatever your views on the war, it's also affecting to see how much the monument means to Vietnam vets who visit it. Because of the raging conflict over U.S. involvement in Vietnam, its veterans had received virtually no prior recognition of their service.

The memorial was conceived by Jan Scruggs, a former infantry corporal. He founded the Vietnam Veteran's Memorial Fund, a nonprofit organization that raised $7 million entirely through private contributions; no federal funds were appropriated. VVMF requested and was granted a site of two acres in Constitution Gardens to erect a memorial that would make no political statement about the war and would harmonize with neighboring memorials. By separating the issue of the wartime service of individuals from the issue of U.S. policy in Vietnam, VVMF hoped to begin a process of national reconciliation. Yale senior Maya Ying Lin's design was chosen in a national competition open to all citizens over 18 years of age. It consists of two walls in a quiet, protected park setting, angled at 125 degrees to point to the Washington Monument and the Lincoln Memorial. The walls' mirror-like surface reflects surrounding trees, lawn, and monuments. Names are inscribed in chronological order, documenting an epoch in American history as a series of individual sacrifices from the date of the first casualty in 1959 to the date of the last death in 1975. A flag flies from a tall staff, the base of which contains emblems of the five services. A statue of young soldiers by Frederick Hart was unveiled on November 9, 1984, at the site;

two days later, on Veteran's Day, the memorial became the property of the U.S. government.

Like the war it commemorates, the memorial, though nonpolitical in intent, is still a scene of controversy and demonstrations at this writing. It was dedicated November 13, 1982. Since Christmas Eve of that year, a group of veterans and concerned citizens called the National League of POW/MIA Families has stood a 24-hour vigil at the monument with petitions to make the release of POWs and MIAs (Missing in Action) a national priority. They claim that close to 2500 Americans are still POWs or MIAs in Vietnam.

GEORGETOWN: The Old Stone House is right in the center of Georgetown's shopping and restaurant scene. Dumbarton Oaks is a short walk out of the way, but well worth it.

The Old Stone House

At 3051 M St. NW (tel. 426-6851). Open from 9:30 a.m. to 5 p.m. Wednesday to Sunday. Closed on all major holidays. No Metro; take any no. 30 to no. 38 bus from Pennsylvania Avenue.

Believed to be the only surviving pre-Revolutionary building in historic Georgetown, the Old Stone House dates from 1765. It was a private residence in the days when Georgetown was one of the most significant tobacco markets on the Atlantic seaboard. The first owner, cabinetmaker Christopher Layman, used the ground floor as a workshop. After his death the house was acquired by Cassandra Chew, a prosperous businesswoman and leading socialite, who raised two daughters here. The house remained in the Chew family through the early 1880s, when the eldest daughter, Mary, lived here as a widow with two sons and four daughters.

Today the rooms are furnished in late-18th-century period pieces. Park rangers in Colonial garb provide information about the house and sometimes demonstrate 18th-century homemaking skills like cooking on an open fireplace, spinning, and making candles and pomander balls. The grounds, once used for a kitchen garden and stable, now enclose an exceptionally pretty 18th-century English flower garden with fruit trees.

The Old Stone House is an interesting contrast to the grand historic estates usually open for view, providing an insight into how the average middle-class person lived in Colonial times.

Dumbarton Oaks

At 1703 32nd St. NW; entrance to the collections on 32nd St., between R and S Sts., garden entrance at 31st and R Sts. (tel. 338-8278 or 342-3200). Collections open from 2 to 5 p.m. Tuesday to Sunday; the garden, 2 to 5 p.m. daily, weather permitting (till 6 p.m. April 1 to October 31). Both are closed on national holidays and Christmas. Admission to the garden is $2 for adults, $1 for children under 12 and senior citizens.

Dumbarton Oaks, a 19th-century Georgetown mansion at the crest of a wooded valley, was the intermittent home (in between assignments) of career diplomat Robert Woods Bliss and his wife, Mildred. Both independently wealthy, the Blisses pursued three major interests: Byzantine art, pre-Columbian art, and landscape architecture. In 1940 they turned over their palatial home, art collection, comprehensive libraries (on all three subjects), and ten acres of exquisite formal gardens to Mr. Bliss's alma mater, Harvard University, and provided endowment funds for continuing research in these areas.

During the limited hours noted above, you can visit the house and tour its galleries. The Byzantine collection—one of the finest in the world—includes glittering mosaics, illuminated manuscripts, ivory carvings, metalwork, sixth-century ecclesiastical silver, gold jewelry, and a fourth-century sarcophagus. It's housed in rooms and corridors surrounding an open courtyard pool. Pre-Columbian works are displayed in eight exquisite circular marble- and oak-floored glass pavilions designed by noted architect Philip Johnson in 1963. Arranged chronologically, the collection features sculptures of Aztec gods and goddesses, stone masks from the Classic period (A.D. 300–600), Olmec jade and serpentine figures, Mayan relief panels, gold necklaces done by the lost-wax process, jade pendants, Mochica and Nazca funerary pottery, and textiles from 900 B.C. to the Spanish Conquest. Another wing, also added in 1963, houses the Garden Library.

Subscription concerts are held in the historic **Music Room,** scene in 1944 of the Dumbarton Oaks Conversations where the principles later incorporated into the charter of the United Nations were established. Furnished in French, Italian, and Spanish antiques, the elaborate Music Room has an 18th-century parquet floor, a beamed ceiling in the 16th-century French style, and an immense 16th-century stone fireplace. Its sculpture, paintings, and tapestries include some important works, among them El Greco's *The Visitation.*

The ten acres of **formal gardens** are of course a delightful highlight of visits to Dumbarton Oaks. Flagstone paths meander around the Orangery (dating from 1810), the Rose Garden (final resting place of the Blisses amid 1000 rose bushes), tranquil pools and fountain terraces, wisteria-covered arbors, herbacious borders, groves of cherry trees and fragrant magnolias. This enchanting landscape, enhanced by garden statuary, was designed for the Blisses by Beatrix Farrand. **Dumbarton Oaks Park,** consisting of 27 acres once belonging to the estate, borders the gardens to the north. Consider a picnic in the park, an activity *verboten* in the garden.

NEAR THE FBI: You're right near the scene of a century-old crime—the shooting of Lincoln. Kids will especially enjoy combining these two sights.

Ford's Theatre and Lincoln Museum

At 511 10th St. NW, between E and F Sts. (tel. 347-4833 for box office information, 426-6927 for the museum). Open daily from 9 a.m. to 5 p.m. Metro: Metro Center.

On April 14, 1865, President Lincoln was in the audience of Ford's Theatre, one of the most popular playhouses in Washington. Everyone was laughing at a funny line from Tom Taylor's celebrated comedy, *Our American Cousin,* when actor John Wilkes Booth grabbed center stage by shooting the president. Doctors carried the mortally wounded Lincoln to William Petersen's house across the street, and the president died there the next morning.

That tragic episode rang down the curtain on Ford's Theatre (public opinion forced him to close down operations permanently) until a century later when the 88th Congress allocated over $2 million for the purpose of restoring the property to its 1865 appearance. (In the interim the building had served as office and warehouse space, but it did house a Lincoln Museum from 1932.) Today the theater is furnished as it was during the final performance, the interior recreated according to detailed research.

Except when rehearsals or matinees are in progress (call before you go), visitors can examine the theater and trace Booth's movements from the Dress Circle to the passageway behind the Presidential Box where he waited to strike. After shooting Lincoln, Booth leapt dramatically to the stage, breaking a leg but nevertheless escaping out the back of the theater. Fifteen-minute talks on the history of the theater and the story of the assassination are given daily at 10 minutes after the hour and 35 minutes after the hour between 9:10 a.m. and 4:35 p.m. Admission is $1 per person, $3 per family, free for those under 12 or over 62.

Downstairs is a museum of Lincoln memorabilia and exhibits on his life. On display are pieces of White House china from his administration, correspondence, books, furnishings, the shaving mug he used before growing a beard (pictures show him without the beard, midway, and with full beard), and his model for a new wagon-making principle. Echoing what you see above are exhibits of the clothes Lincoln was wearing on the night he was assassinated, the Derringer pistol from which Booth fired the fatal bullet, and Booth's confidential diary outlining his rationalization for the act.

Performances at the theater are scheduled throughout the year (details in Chapter VI).

The House Where Lincoln Died

After touring the theater and museum, cross the street to 516 10th St. NW (tel. 426-6830) to see the Petersen House, where Lincoln was carried after the assassination. Furnished with authentic period pieces, including a rocking chair that actually came from Lincoln's Springfield, Illinois, home, it looks much like it did on that fateful April night. You'll see the front parlor where an anguished Mary Todd Lincoln spent the night with her son, Robert. Her emotional state was such that she was banned from the bedroom because she was creating havoc. In the back parlor Secretary of War Edwin M. Stanton questioned witnesses. The room where Lincoln died contains a bed of the same design as the original, complete with a real bloodstained pillow on which he rested. This is the room from which Stanton emerged at 7:22 a.m. on April 15, 1865, to announce, "Now he belongs to the ages."

The Petersen House, its rooms documented for self-guided touring, is open for viewing from 9 a.m. to 5 p.m. daily except Christmas. Admission is free.

UNION STATION: The Capital Children's Museum is not really near any other attraction, though you might want to take a look at Union Station, a noble neoclassic building with a portico modeled after the Arch of Constantine leading into a waiting room inspired by the Baths of Diocletian. It's a monument to the great age of rail travel.

Capital Children's Museum

At 800 3rd St. NE, at H St. (tel. 543-8600). Open daily from 10 a.m. to 5 p.m. Closed Christmas, New Year's, Easter, and Thanksgiving. Admission: $4 per person, $1 for senior citizens. Metro: Union Station.

It's not on the Mall, and it's not part of the Smithsonian, but for your kids the Capital Children's Museum might just be the highlight of a Washington vacation. Its fascinating child-size hands-on exhibits reflect the museum's old Chinese proverb motto, "I see and I forget, I hear and I remember, I do and I understand."

Communication is the theme of many activities. A replica of a 30,000-year-old cave—complete with sound effects of dripping water and wolves howling in the distance—illustrates the use of cave drawings and rituals as Ice Age means of communication. Youngsters send messages by a Greek torch system that dates to A.D. 300, by Morse Code using naval lamps, and by African drums. In the photography section they explore a giant camera from the inside, view a hologram, make slides and film shows, and create shadow art on a wall. They play metric shopkeeper and measure each other's feet for shoes in Metricville, work an old-fashioned switchboard and talk on telephones of the future in a telecommunications area. Other fun activities include baking tortillas from scratch and playing with "Rosie" the goat in "Mexico," and climbing through a manhole to an underground street in the City Room. Of course there are numerous computer learning games too. The second and third floors are connected by a talking (in 22 languages) Tower of Babel staircase.

Inquire about ongoing workshops for children in computers, arts and crafts, music, and many other areas. There are also frequent films, theater performances, puppet shows, magicians, storytellers, and so on. Call or write ahead (zip code is 20002) for a schedule of events during your stay.

NEAR DUPONT CIRCLE: Do try to get over to the Dupont Circle area while you're in Washington. It's one of the most vital parts of town. The Explorers Hall and B'nai B'rith Museum are a few blocks southeast of Dupont Circle; the Textile Museum, Woodrow Wilson House, Phillips Collection, and Fondo del Sol, a few blocks northwest. This grouping of sights makes for an interesting day's itinerary, and at some point you'll have to cross Dupont Circle, making it easy to plan a midday lunch at one of the area's many fine restaurants.

A walking-tour brochure detailing Dupont Circle-area museums is available. Write (enclosing a self-addressed, stamped envelope) to Dupont-Kalorama Museum Walk, c/o the Phillips Collection, 1600 21st St. NW, Washington, DC 20009-1090.

National Geographic's Explorers Hall

At 17th and M Sts. NW (tel. 857-7588 on weekdays, 857-7000 on weekends). Open from 9 a.m. to 5 p.m. Monday to Saturday, and 10 a.m. to 5 p.m. on Sunday. Closed Christmas Day. Metro: Farragut North (Connecticut Avenue and L Street exit).

Utilizing video presentations and other innovative exhibit enhancements, National Geographic's Explorers Hall, like the magazine, explores in a fascinating manner the earth's deserts, jungles, and mountain peaks, goes beneath the sea, and looks out at the moon and stars. All the exhibits are on one floor; pick up an orientation map at the 17th Street entrance. It's a great place to take children.

At the entrance, you'll see a videotaped introduction to the society. Man's prehistory is explored in a multimedia presentation called "The Human Odyssey: Journey Through Time." A tableau of the Southwest cliff dwellers, who vanished mysteriously about the year 1290, shows men in an underground room or kiva (the primitive away-from-the-women answer to today's den). The flag and dog sledge of Robert E. Peary, first man to reach the North Pole, is on display (his 1909 expedition was funded by the National Geographic Society). The pride of Explorers Hall is the world's largest free-standing globe, 34 feet around the equator with a scale of one inch for 60 miles. Henry, a talking macaw and major museum attraction, watches over a replica of an Olmec head, a huge stone sculpture dating to 32 B.C. (The Olmec civilization precedes ancient Mayan and Aztec cultures.) A model of Jacques Cousteau's diving saucer that brought fish-like freedom to man at 25,000-foot depths is shown, along with some of Cousteau's underwater photographs. National Geographic's leadership in color photography is further attested to in 12-foot color transparencies called "Windows of the World." There's also a 3.9-billion-year-old moon rock brought back to earth on *Apollo 12* and an egg of the extinct flightless *Aepyornis maximus*—an "elephant bird" over ten feet high weighing 1000 pounds.

In addition, special exhibits have included artifacts from Spanish galleon shipwrecks, a pageant of toy soldiers, Fabergé creations, and holographs. The publications desk sells all National Geographic publications, maps, globes, records, videotapes of TV specials, and books for adults and children. *Note:* In celebration of the Society's Centennial in 1988, there will be many special exhibits during the course of this edition.

B'nai B'rith International Center and Klutznick Museum

At 17th St. and Rhode Island Ave. NW (tel. 857-6583). Open Sunday to Friday from 10 a.m. to 5 p.m.; closed on Saturday, and Jewish and legal holidays. Suggested donation: $2 for adults, $1 for children under 12. Metro: Farragut North.

Located at the international headquarters of B'nai B'rith, the Klutznick Museum documents Jewish history in displays of ceremonial and folk art objects spanning 20 centuries. Permanent exhibits include modern and ancient Hannukah lamps, Passover plates, Kiddush cups, candlesticks, coins, Torahs, prayer shawls, religious books, and marriage contracts from all over the world. There's a small sculpture garden, and changing exhibitions highlight Jewish artists or Jewish themes (for instance, the art of the Jewish wedding, Yiddish Theater in America, and Judaica from the Smithsonian). Of American historical significance is a letter from George Washington to a Hebrew congregation in Newport, Rhode Island (". . . the Government of the United States . . . gives to bigotry no sanction, to persecution no assistance . . ."), one of several pieces of correspondence between presidents and Jewish groups. There are occasional films, lectures, and concerts (call for details). The museum and bookstore offer a range of modern Jewish crafts and antiquities, Jewish books, and ceremonial items for the home.

The Textile Museum

At 2320 S St. NW (tel. 667-0441). Open Tuesday to Saturday from 10 a.m. to 5 p.m. and on Sunday from 1 to 5 p.m. Suggested donation: $2 for adults, 50¢ for children. Metro: Dupont Circle.

In 1896 George Hewitt Myers (as in Bristol-Myers) bought an Oriental rug for his dorm room at Yale, the first acquisition in what would become one of the world's greatest collections of rugs and textiles. His wide-ranging collection, specializing in hand-woven rather than industrially produced pieces, includes Islamic, Tibetan, Chinese, Caucasian, Turkish, and Navajo rugs. Among the textiles are Peruvian tunics, Chinese silks, Mexican serapes, Navajo blankets, and Egyptian tapestries. The collection of 11,000 textiles and 1200 rugs spans a time period from 3500 B.C. to the present. The museum is housed in two distinguished red brick Georgian buildings—Myer's former home, designed in 1913 by John Russell Pope of National Gallery fame, and an adjoining 1908 residence designed by Waddy Wood who was also the architect of Woodrow Wilson's home (details below).

Lectures, seminars, and workshops complement exhibits which run the gamut from "Song of the Loom: New Traditions in Navajo Weaving" to "Persian Textiles from the 16th to the 19th Centuries." Walk-in tours are conducted on Sunday from 2 to 4 p.m. September to June only, but you don't really need a guide to appreciate this artistically exciting collection. On the premises is the Arthur D. Jenkins Library of 9,000 books and periodicals relating to textile arts (open to the public from 10 a.m. to 5 p.m. Wednesday to Friday, to 1 p.m. on Saturday).

The Textile Museum also contains one of Washington's most exciting gift shops, offering an extensive selection of books on carpets and textiles, as well as Indian silk scarves, Bolivian ruanas, Kilim pillows, Bokhara crêpe silk ties, Tibetan rug squares, and much more. Craftspeople will flip over items like Turkish silk embroidery patterns from the 16th century, patchwork patterns, and suchlike. Contemporary fiber art is displayed in a gallery adjacent to the shop.

The museum has a lovely garden with a fountain and lawn furnishings where you're welcome to enjoy a picnic lunch.

The Woodrow Wilson House

At 2340 S St. NW (tel. 387-4062). Open from 10 a.m. to 4 p.m. Tuesday to Sunday. Closed the month of January, weekdays in February, Thanksgiving, and Christmas. Admission: $3.50 for adults, $2 for students and senior citizens, free for children under 7. Metro: Dupont Circle.

Woodrow Wilson is the only former president ever to make his home in Washington, D.C. The city was home to his second wife, Edith (he courted and married her while in the White House), and Wilson wanted to be near the Library of Congress for research purposes. The Georgian Revival town house on S Street, designed by Waddy Wood in 1915, appealed to Mrs. Wilson as "an unpretentious, comfortable, dignified house, suited to the needs of a gentleman's home." The retired president, broken in health and spirit after years of futile efforts to establish a League of Nations, lived here for only three years before his death in 1924. He spent those years receiving prominent visitors like David Lloyd George, Bernard Baruch, and Clemenceau; reading (his personal library contained over 8,000 volumes); motoring with Mrs. Wilson in nearby Rock Creek Park; and attending many theatrical performances. After Wilson's death, his widow carefully preserved their home, its furnishings and memorabilia. In her will, she bequeathed the house and its contents to the National Trust for Historic Preservation.

On 45-minute tours given continuously throughout the day, you'll see three floors of the house as they looked in Wilson's day. In the library are the books he wrote and his movie projector; he was a film fan, and local theaters often loaned him movies for private viewing. The drawing room decorations include a mosaic of St. Peter given to Wilson at the Vatican and a Gobelin tapestry that was a wedding gift from the people of France; photographs of English royalty adorn the room. The typical 1920s kitchen has a coal and gas stove and oven, an oak ice box, and one of the first electric refrigerators. And the office (his family called it "the dugout") contains a Wilson memento from an army-navy baseball game the president attended with King George V of England (Wilson got to keep the ball, and the king autographed it).

Wilson is buried nearby in the Washington National Cathedral.

The Phillips Collection

At 1600–1612 21st St. NW, corner of Q St. (tel. 387-2151). Open from 10 a.m. to 5 p.m. Tuesday to Saturday, on Sunday from 2 to 7 p.m. Closed on Monday, July 4, Thanksgiving, and Christmas. Admission, charged weekends only, is $3 for adults, $2 for students and senior citizens. Anyone under 18 is admitted free. Metro: Dupont Circle.

Displaying an eclectic but exquisite collection launched by Duncan Phillips in 1918, this is the oldest museum of modern art in the country. It is housed in the elegant 1890s brownstone of avid collectors and proselytizers of modernism Duncan and Marjorie Phillips, and is one of Washington's most intimate museums. Carpeted rooms with leaded- and stained-glass windows, oak paneling, carved plaster ceilings, plush chairs and sofas, and frequently, fireplaces, create a comfortable, homelike setting for viewing art.

Conceived as "a museum of modern art and its sources," the collection of over 2500 works includes paintings by forerunners of modernism like Delacroix, Ingres, Constable, El Greco, Goya, Corot, Courbet, Chardin, Manet, and Giorgione. Among the highlights are superb collections of Daumier, Dove, and Bonnard paintings; five Cézannes (including his famous self-portrait), some splendid small Vuillards, five works by Georgia O'Keeffe, three Van Goghs, and Renoir's magnificent *Luncheon of the Boating Party*. Rothko, Marin, Avery, Klee, Picasso, Roualt, Degas, Ryder, Matisse, and Kokoschka are also represented, along with many other notables.

The Phillipses began showing their collection in 1921 in three rooms of their home. By 1930, when the collection had grown to 600 paintings, the family moved out of the house and had it renovated as a museum. Today the collection occupies two floors of the old building and three floors of a wing added in 1960.

An ongoing series of temporary shows, often supplemented by works from other museums and private collections, is presented here, along with a rotating portion of the permanent collection. Past shows have focused on the works of Cézanne, Marin, Bonnard, Howard Hodgkin, Georges Braque's late paintings (1940–1963), Morris Graves, Dove, and the color abstractions of Franz Kline. Other shows have highlighted the collection itself or a particular school such as impressionism.

Free tours are given on Wednesday and Saturday at 2 p.m. There's also a full schedule of events. Free concerts in the ornate music room (September to May, every Sunday at 5 p.m., except Easter) are very popular; early arrival is advised. Additional activities include films, lectures, and gallery talks, the latter given the first and third Thursdays of every month at 12:30 p.m.

Fondo del Sol Visual Art and Media Center

At 2112 R St. NW (tel. 483-2777). Open Tuesday to Saturday from 12:30 to 5:30 p.m. Metro: Dupont Circle.

A nonprofit organization run by artists and community people, Fondo del Sol (it means "center of the sun"), established in 1973, is interested in "presenting, promoting, and preserving the cultures of the Americas." Housed in a Victorian town house, with five rooms used as galleries, it features changing exhibitions of contemporary arts and crafts, video programs, films, poetry readings, performance art, and music programs. Also under the organization's auspices is the **Caribbeana Arts Festival** every July or September, with exhibitions of the works of Caribbean artists; reggae, steel drum, and salsa; ethnic foods; and rum punch. Call the above number for exact date and location.

UPPER WISCONSIN AVENUE: This one's off by itself at the D.C./Maryland border. You might want to do some shopping up here though; see Chapter VII for suggestions.

Washington Dolls' House and Toy Museum

At 5236 44th St. NW, one block west of Wisconsin Ave., between Jenifer and Harrison Streets (tel. 244-0024). Open Tuesday to Saturday from 10 a.m. to 5 p.m., on Sunday from noon to 5 p.m. Admission: $2 for adults, $1 for children under 14. Metro: Friendship Heights.

Flora Gill Jacobs's fine collection of antique dollhouses, toys, dolls, and games, most of them Victorian, is a delight—worth the trip north to the D.C./Maryland border. Her treasure trove of toys is shown in rotating exhibits that are particularly wonderful at Christmas and other holiday seasons. Some of my favorites: a tin tea party from Germany in which three ladies raise their cups while a fourth plays the piano; a miniature mansion from Mexico complete with aviary, motorized elevator, wrought-iron balustrades, and a chapel with full ecclesiastical furnishings; a mid-19th-century Noah's ark with over 150 paired animals (one of several such sets); a Lionel train set from the 1930s with all signals, accoutrements, and sound effects; and a street of Victorian gingerbread houses.

Mrs. Jacobs, an internationally recognized expert on dollhouses and author of several authoritative works on the subject, can answer all your questions about collecting. Don't miss the two museum gift shops. One offers miniature pieces of furniture, lamps, fireplace fenders, Oriental rugs, you name it; the other carries dollhouse building and wiring supplies, kits, and books. Of course you can also buy a dollhouse here.

Chapter V

THE GREAT OUTDOORS

LIKE MOST CITIES, Washington has manicured pockets of green amid its high-rise office buildings and superhighways. Unlike most cities it is also extensively endowed with vast natural areas—thousands of parkland acres, two rivers, a 185-mile-long tree-lined canalside trail, an untamed wilderness area, and a few thousand cherry trees—all centrally located within the District. And there's much more just a stone's throw away. This chapter explores D.C.'s wealth of sporting and outdoor facilities. Also refer to Chapter IV for details on three other natural sights—Dumbarton Oaks, the National Zoological Park, and the U.S. Botanic Garden.

1. The Sporting Life

SPECTATOR SPORTS: The Washington Bullets (NBA) and the Washington Capitals (NHL) play home games at **Capital Centre,** Exit 15A or 17A off the Capital Beltway in Landover, Maryland (tel. 301/350-3400). The 20,000-seat stadium is also used for Georgetown University basketball games, Harlem Globetrotter games, wrestling, and annual events like the Washington International Horse Show, the Ice Capades, and the World Professional Figure Skating Championships. Also big-name concerts. Call 202/432-0200 for ticket information.

The 55,000-seat **Robert F. Kennedy Memorial Stadium** and the 10,000-seat **D.C. Armory complex,** East Capitol St. between 19th and 20th Sts. SE (tel. 547-9077), is the D.C. home of the **Washington Redskins** (NFL). Events here also include wrestling, nationally televised boxing, roller derby, the circus, rodeos, and *Disney on Ice.* Call 202/432-0200 for ticket information.

The Patriot Center, 4400 University Dr. in Fairfax, Virginia (tel. 703/323-

2672), opened in late 1985 on the campus of George Mason University. A 10,000-seat facility, it is used for college basketball games, Virginia Slims Tennis at the end of March, gymnastic competitions, horse shows, and other events. To get here take the Wilson Bridge to Braddock Rd. W. (Rte. 623) and proceed for about eight miles to University Drive. For ticket information call 202/432-0200.

BOATING: Thompson's Boat Center, Virginia Ave. at Rock Creek Pkwy. NW (tel. 333-4861), rents canoes, sailboats, windsurfers, rowing shells, and rowboats. ID and a $10 deposit are required. They're open late March to the end of November from 7 a.m. to dusk. A similar operation is **Fletcher's Boat House,** Reservoir and Canal Rds. (tel. 244-0461), offering canoes and rowboats. It's open the same season as Thompson's from 9 a.m. to dusk. Fletcher's includes a snack bar and also sells fishing bait and tackle. Rest rooms and picnic tables with barbecue grills are nearby.

CYCLING: Both of the above boat-rental houses also rent bicycles, as does **Big Wheel Bikes,** 1034 33rd St. NW, just below M St. (tel. 337-0254), open 11 a.m. to 7 p.m. weekdays, 10 a.m. to 6 p.m. weekends. A deposit of $10 or $20 and ID is required to rent bicycles.

If you'd like some pedaling partners, contact **Potomac Pedalers Touring Club,** P.O. Box 23601, Washington, DC 20026 (tel. 363-TOUR). They organize at least a dozen free guided bike rides every weekend year round, ranging from leisurely family rides on neighborhood trails to fast-paced all-day excursions. Their trips are rated from A (the most strenuous) to D (the easiest). Most bike-rental stores keep a copy of the club's monthly newsletter, *Pedal Patter,* on hand; it details trips.

FISHING: The Potomac River around Washington provides an abundant variety of fish—some 40 species, all perfectly safe to eat. Good fishing is possible from late February to November, but mid-March through June (spawning season) is peak. Perch and catfish are the most common catch, but during bass season a haul of 20 to 40 is not unusual. The Washington Channel offers good bass and carp fishing year round. No fishing license is required in the District.

GOLF: There are dozens of public courses within easy driving distance of the D.C. area, but in the District itself **East Potomac Park and Rock Creek Park** (details below) contain the only public courses.

HIKING PLUS: Many hiking suggestions are detailed further on in this chapter. If you prefer group hikes, the **Sierra Club** (tel. 547-2326) organizes guided hikes of varying length and ruggedness just about every weekend of the year. These include backpack trips to local wilderness areas, day hikes to nearby national parks and forests, also bike trips and whitewater and flatwater canoe trips. There's an optional charge of 50¢ for each hiking trip, and people sharing rides chip in for gas. A calendar of events is available for $4 a year; call the above phone number for information or write to Sierra Club, 1863 Kalorama Rd. NW, Apt. 1B, Washington, DC 20009.

ICE SKATING: My favorite place for winter skating is on the **C&O Canal,** its banks always dotted with cozy fires at which one can warm frozen extremities. You might find it inspiring to skate on the **Reflecting Pool** between the Lincoln Memorial and the Washington Monument, especially by night when it's dramatically lit. Guest Services, Inc., operates the **National Sculpture Garden Ice Rink** across the Mall from the Hirshhorn Museum (tel. 347-9042), the **Pershing Park**

outdoor rink at 14th St. and Pennsylvania Ave. NW (tel. 737-6938), and a huge hockey-size indoor facility, the **Fort Dupont Ice Arena,** at 3779 Ely Pl. SE, at Minnesota Ave. in the park (tel. 581-0199). All three offer skate rentals. There's an admission fee ($3.50 for two hours for adults, $2.25 for children 12. and under) at the arena; it's open from Labor Day weekend to the middle of April.

RIDING: Rock Creek Park has 14 miles of wooded trails to explore and a stable (tel. 362-0117) offering horses for trail rides and instruction (details below).

SWIMMING: There are 44 swimming pools in the District run by the D.C. Department of Recreation Aquatic Program (tel. 576-6436). Among the nicest are the **Capitol East Natatorium,** an indoor/outdoor pool with sundeck and adjoining baby pool at 635 North Carolina Ave. SE (tel. 724-4495 or 724-4496); the outdoor pool in **East Potomac Park** (tel. 576-6436); and the **Georgetown** outdoor pool at 34th St. and Volta Pl. NW (tel. 576-6436). Indoor pools are open year round, outdoor pools from Memorial Day to Labor Day. Call for hours and details on other locations.

Some hotels allow visitors to use their pools on a fee basis. At this writing an attractive and centrally located hotel pool open to the public is at the **Gramercy Hotel,** 1616 Rhode Island Ave. NW (tel. 347-9550), for $5 per person. It's open from 10 a.m. to 9 p.m. from Memorial Day to Labor Day. Hotels tend to change these policies without much notice, so call before you go.

If you have a car, your absolute best bet is the **Providence Recreation Center,** 7525 Marc Dr. in Falls Church, Virginia (tel. 703/698-1350). To get there, take the Beltway to Exit 8E (Route 50), make a right on Jaguar Trail, another right on Marc Drive. This is a terrific suburban recreation center with a near-Olympic-size indoor pool, a large sundeck, weight rooms, Ping-Pong, dressing rooms, racquetball courts, and saunas. It's open daily year round, and the fee for using all facilities (except racquetball courts, which are extra) is just $3.50 for adults, $2.50 for children under 15 and senior citizens.

TENNIS: There are 144 outdoor courts in the District (60 of them lighted for night play) at 45 locations. To play, you need a free permit, obtainable by sending a stamped, self-addressed envelope with your request to the **D.C. Department of Recreation,** Permit Section, 3149 16th St. NW, Washington, DC 20010 (tel. 673-7646). They'll send it by return mail. If you'd rather not wait, stop by in person between 8:30 a.m. and 12:30 p.m. or 1:30 and 4:30 p.m. Monday to Friday. Court locations are listed on the permit. Most courts are open year round, weather permitting. In addition, there are 22 courts in **Rock Creek Park** (tel. 723-2669) and 24 in **East Potomac Park** (tel. 554-5962) available on a fee basis. Details are in the Rock Creek Park listing, below.

2. Rock Creek Park

Created in 1890, Rock Creek Park was purchased by Congress for its "pleasant valleys and ravines, primeval forests and open fields, its running waters, its rocks clothed with rich ferns and mosses, its repose and tranquility, its light and shade, its ever-varying shrubbery, its beautiful and extensive views." An 1800-acre valley within the District of Columbia, extending 12 miles from the Potomac to the Maryland border (another 2700 acres along the same valley stream in Maryland are known as Rock Creek Regional Park), it's one of the biggest and finest city parks in the nation. Parts of it are still wild; its not unusual to see a deer scurrying through the woods in more remote sections. There are numerous park activities and facilities, some of which are detailed below. The

Carter Barron Amphitheatre and the **Zoo** are described in Chapters VI and IV, respectively. For full information, visit the **Rock Creek Nature Center** (see below), a focal point for park programs, or—on weekdays only from 7:45 a.m. to 4:15 p.m.—contact Park Headquarters, 5000 Glover Rd. (tel. 426-6832). Though the park is most easily reached by car, the E2, E3, E4, and E5 buses stop at Military Road and Oregon Avenue, right in the center of things. There's convenient free parking throughout the park.

THE ROCK CREEK NATURE CENTER: Located at 5200 Glover Rd. NW (tel. 426-6829), the Nature Center sponsors outdoor park activities and educational programs for adults and children. On weekends the schedule usually includes planetarium shows for adults and children, nature films followed by live animal demonstrations, and guided nature walks. Throughout the year this basic program is augmented by a daily mix of lectures, films, musical events, puppet shows, and other activities. A calendar is available upon request. There are always guided nature walks and ecology programs, and self-guided nature trails begin here. Just about all activities are free, but sometimes you need to pick up tickets a half hour in advance. Inside, in the Main Exhibit Hall, are displays on birds, rocks, plants, and insects, including a working beehive. The center is open from 9 a.m. to 5 p.m. Tuesday to Sunday; closed Monday and holidays.

PIERCE MILL: Tilden St. and Beach Dr. (tel. 426-6908). Built by Isaac Pierce in 1820, Pierce Mill harnessed power from Rock Creek to grind grain into flour for local farmers. It operated through the turn of the century when it was superseded by more efficient steam-powered mills. Today it's once again a working operation, grinding corn and wheat between great stone slabs and selling the resultant products to visitors. Open from 8 a.m. to 4:30 p.m. Wednesday to Sunday; closed holidays. Pierce's old carriage house is today the **Art Barn** (tel. 426-6719), used for exhibits of local artists. It's open the same days as the Mill from 10 a.m. to 5 p.m.

PICNICKING: There are some 30 picnic areas—some with fireplaces—scattered throughout the park. Call 673-7646 or 673-7647 for group reservations. A brochure available at Park Headquarters or the Nature Center details locations.

TENNIS: At 16th and Kennedy Sts. NW are 17 soft-surface and five hardsurface courts. To use them April through mid-November you must make a reservation in person at Guest Services (tel. 723-2669) on the premises. There's a fee of $6.50 an hour to use clay courts and $4 an hour for hard courts on weekends, holidays, and after 4 p.m. weekdays; $4 for clay and $2.55 for hard courts on weekdays from 7 a.m. to 4 p.m. The rest of the year the five hard-surfaced courts are available free on a first-come, first-served basis. There are six additional soft-surface courts off Park Road just east of Pierce Mill (tel. 429-0661). They're open May to September daily. Rates are $4 an hour from 7 a.m. to 4 p.m., $6 an hour from 4 p.m. to dark. Reservations must be made in person on the premises.

JOAQUIN MILLER CABIN: Poetry readings and workshops are held at the one-time residence of High Sierra poet (he wrote *Song of the Sierras*) Joaquin Miller, Beach Dr. north of Military Rd. Call 426-6832 for information.

GOLF: The 18-hole **Rock Creek Golf Course** and clubhouse, at 16th and

Rittenhouse Sts. NW (tel. 723-9832), are open to the public daily year round (except Christmas) from dawn to dusk. A snackbar and lockers are on the premises, and clubs and carts can be rented. A fee is charged.

RIDING: The **Rock Creek Park Horse Center,** near the Nature Center on Glover Rd. NW (tel. 362-0117), offers rental horses for trail rides and riding instruction. There are 14 miles of woodland bridle paths to explore. Several trail rides ($9 per person) are offered Tuesday to Friday between 1:30 p.m. and dusk, on Saturday and Sunday between noon and dusk. No riding experience is required. Lessons are $18 for a half hour.

CYCLING: You can't, unfortunately, rent bikes in the park, (rent at Thompson's Boat Center; see below), but there is a marvelous 11-mile bike route from the Lincoln Memorial through the park into Maryland, much of it on a separate paved pathway. It's especially pleasant on holidays and weekends (7 a.m. Saturday to 7 p.m. Sunday) when a long stretch of road is closed to vehicular traffic.

JOGGING: A **Parcourse Jogging path,** a gift from Perrier, opened here in 1978. Its 1½-mile oval route, beginning near the intersection of Cathedral Ave. and Rock Creek Pkwy., includes 18 calisthenic stations with instructions on prescribed exercises. There's another Perrier Parcourse, this one with only four stations, at 16th and Kennedy Sts. NW.

HIKING AND BACKPACKING: There are no campgrounds in Rock Creek Park, so only day-long hikes are permitted. Fifteen miles of beautiful wooded trails—from easy to strenuous—traverse the park. You can go out on your own or participate in guided hikes. Details and maps are at Park Headquarters or the Nature Center.

BOATING: **Thompson's Boat Center,** at the southern end of the park right on the Potomac, Rock Creek Pkwy. and Virginia Ave. NW (tel. 333-4861), rents bikes, canoes, and sailboats. Open daily, late March to the end of November from 7 a.m. to dusk.

3. The Chesapeake & Ohio Canal National Historic Park

One of the great joys of living in Washington is the C&O Canal and its unspoiled 184½-mile towpath. One leaves urban cares and stresses behind while hiking, strolling, jogging, cycling, or boating in this lush, natural setting of ancient oaks and red maples, giant sycamores, willows, and wildflowers. I've never walked the canal without making an exciting discovery—a proud mother duck with a new family in tow; a glimpse through the trees of the Potomac; raspberries suddenly abundantly in season; a brilliant flowering tree amid the greenery; a quaint canalside home; a sudden appreciation of light shimmering on the water and reflections of trees and foliage. The canal is a happy place. People who frequent it tend to smile when they pass each other, as if sharing some delicious secret. It wasn't always just a leisure spot for city people, however.

CANAL HISTORY: In the 1800s water transportation was considered vastly superior to road travel. George Washington first envisioned a water route through the Potomac Valley to the west, but actual construction didn't begin until 1828 when Pres. John Quincy Adams turned the first ceremonial spadeful of earth. From the first, the building was beset by problems. Labor was scarce, and indentured workers from Europe had to be brought in; money ran out periodically; disease swept the labor camps; there was fighting among different nationalities; and most significant, the Baltimore and Ohio Railroad going up at the same time on the same route (its now-defunct tracks still parallel the canal) competed for property rights and land titles. It wasn't until 1850—eight years after the B&O had reached the same point and beyond—that the entire canal route linking Georgetown to Cumberland, Maryland, was completed. By that time the faster, less expensive railroad had rendered the canal obsolete, and plans to extend it as far westward as Pittsburgh were dropped. It never did achieve a great measure of economic success, though it was used as a leisurely means of transporting lumber, coal, flour, and grain to Washington through 1924. Today the canal is greatly valued by Washingtonians as a prime recreation area.

ACTIVITIES ON THE CANAL: Headquarters for canal activities is the **Office of the Superintendent,** C&O Canal National Historical Park, P.O. Box 4, Sharpsburg, MD 21782 (tel. 301/739-4200); closer by—a local call—is a **National Park Service** office at Great Falls Tavern (tel. 301/299-3613). Contact either of the above offices for maps and information.

Hiking

There's hiking along the entire towpath, with occasional more rugged paths branching off the main route. Picnicking is permitted anywhere along the canal, but there are frequent designated areas with tables and grills. Coming from Georgetown, the first picnic area is at Fletcher's Boathouse, about a 2½-mile walk.

Boating and Biking

About 2½ miles from Georgetown, at the intersection of Reservoir and Canal Roads, **Fletcher's Boat House** (tel. 244-0461) rents out bicycles (one-speed only) for use on the towpath, as well as canoes and rowboats. They also sell bait and tackle. You don't have to walk to Fletcher's; it's accessible by car and has plenty of free parking. A snackbar is part of the complex, and there's a picnic area with tables overlooking the Potomac. Open daily from 9 a.m. to dusk from the end of March through November, weather permitting. You can also rent bikes from **Big Wheel Bikes,** 1034 33rd St. NW, just below M St. (tel. 337-0254).

Rock Climbing

The 100-foot cliffs just below Great Falls in the **Carderock Recreation Area** are ideal for rock climbing.

Boat Trips

The least strenuous way to enjoy the canal is from the comfort of a muledrawn boat. Park Service personnel in period dress lead mule teams along the towpath guiding 19th-century boats. They regale passengers with canal legend and lore, and sing river songs. Tickets are sold in Georgetown below M St. at 1055 Thomas Jefferson St. NW (tel. 472-6885) and at Great Falls Tavern (tel. 299-3614). Fare is $4 for adults, $2.50 for children under 12 and senior citizens. There are departures Wednesday to Sunday from mid-April to mid-October between 10:30 a.m. and 5 p.m.; call for exact times.

Camping

Approximately every five miles along the 170-mile section from Swain's Lock to Cumberland, there are walk-in camping areas with toilets, picnic tables, fire grills, and usually, water. Only one site—Antietam Creek—has adjacent parking. Use is on a first-come, first-served basis. Campgrounds are open mid-April to mid-October.

And More

Hundreds of Washingtonians don skates and glide the frozen surface in winter. . . . There's extraordinary birdwatching—great blue heron, scarlet tanager, black-billed cuckoo, and many other species. . . . Fish for carp, catfish, and bass on the canal between Georgetown and Chain Bridge.

4. Theodore Roosevelt Island

A serene 88-acre wilderness preserve located on the Potomac just below Georgetown, Theodore Roosevelt Island is a memorial to our 26th president in recognition of his contributions to conservation. An outdoor enthusiast and expert field naturalist, Roosevelt once threw away a prepared speech and roared, "I hate a man who would skin the land!" During his administration the U.S. Forest Service created 150 national forests, 18 national monuments, five national parks, 51 bird refuges, and four game refuges. Forty-one states created their own conservation agencies to carry on the work begun by the national government during his term.

A 17-foot statue of Roosevelt stands in the northern center of the island overlooking an oval terrace encircled by a water-filled moat. In summer there are lovely splashing fountains. From the terrace rise four 21-foot granite tablets inscribed with quotations from Roosevelt on Nature, Manhood, Youth, and the State, for example, "There is a delight in the hardy life of the open. There are no words that can tell the hidden spirit of the wilderness—that can reveal its mystery, its melancholy, and its charm."

The island preserve of swamp, marsh, and upland forest is a haven for rabbits, chipmunks, great owls, red and gray fox, muskrat, turtles, and groundhogs. Cattails, arrowarum, and pickerelweed grow in the marshes, creating a hospitable habitat for red-winged blackbirds, marsh wrens, and kingfishers. Woodpeckers, chickadees, and wood thrushes share the deep upland forest treetops with squirrels and rabbits. You can explore this complex ecosystem by hiking the island's 2½ miles of foot trails. There's fishing for bass, crappie, carp, and catfish (no license necessary), and picnicking is permitted on the grounds near the memorial.

To get to the island, take the George Washington Memorial Parkway exit north from the Theodore Roosevelt Bridge. Or paddle over in a canoe from **Thompson's Boat Center** at Rock Creek Pkwy. and Virginia Ave. NW (tel. 333-4861). The parking area is accessible from the northbound lane of the George Washington Memorial Parkway in Virginia, and a pedestrian bridge connects the island with the Virginia shore. A footbridge from Roslyn Circle to the island is in the works for the future.

For further details, contact the superintendent, Theodore Roosevelt Island, George Washington Memorial Pkwy., c/o Turkey Run Park, McLean, VA 22101 (tel. 703/285-2598).

5. Potomac Park: The Cherry Blossoms

Comprising 720 riverside acres and separated by the Tidal Basin, East and West Potomac Parks contain numerous outdoor attractions.

WEST POTOMAC PARK: River views; Constitution Gardens with over 2,000 trees, the Vietnam and Signers of the Declaration of Independence Memorials, a 7½-acre lake, with a small island that is home to ducks and turtles; the Lincoln and Jefferson Memorials; and the Reflecting Pool are all part of West Potomac

Park. But its crowning glory is the ring of 1,300 cherry trees bordering the Tidal Basin—90% of them of the Yoshino variety with great profusions of white cloud-like blossoms, the remainder Akebonos, adding a delicate tint of pink to the display.

The Cherry Blossom Festival

The unofficial beginning of spring in the capital is marked by the yearly blooming of the cherry trees. Hundreds of thousands of tourists descend on Washington in hopes of catching the stunning floral display and accompanying festivities. Unfortunately, there's no predicting from year to year when they'll bloom. They've come out as early as March 20 and as late as April 17, with the average date being April 5. Since they're gone in under two weeks, timing your visit with their appearance is a question of luck or flexibility. The trees were a gesture of friendship from Japan in 1912, an annually recurring gift that is newly appreciated each year. Twelve varieties—3,000 trees in all—were shipped on board the S.S. *Awa Maru;* Mrs. Taft planted the first Yoshino tree, and the wife of the Japanese ambassador planted the second. Workmen did the rest, planting the remaining Yoshino trees and the other 11 varieties in East Potomac Park.

The annual week-long festivities officially commence with the lighting of the 300-year-old, 8½-foot-high **Japanese Stone Lantern** presented to the city of Washington by the governor of Tokyo in 1954. The Lantern, located at West Basin Dr. and Independence Ave. near Kutz Bridge, commemorates Commodore Perry's historic mission to Japan. **A Cherry Blossom Parade** (tel. 293-0482), with floats, bands, clowns, and Clydesdale horses, travels the route along Constitution Avenue from 7th to 17th Streets NW. Waving from the floats are the **Cherry Blossom Princesses,** one from each state and U.S. territory. Band competitions, sporting events, concerts, tea dances, entertainers, fashion shows, and a gala black-tie ball with celebrity guests are also part of the fun. Check the *Washington Post,* call the National Parks Service (tel. 485-9666), or visit the Washington, D.C., Visitor Information Center, between 14th and 15th Sts. on Pennsylvania Ave. NW (tel. 789-7000), to obtain details on events and activities. Some events—like the ball and parade bleacher seats—require advance tickets.

EAST POTOMAC PARK: Though not the scene of major celebrations, East Potomac Park actually has more cherry trees (1,800 of them) and more varieties (11). The deep-pink Kwanzan trees are especially lovely and can often be enjoyed a week or two after the Tidal Basin blossoms have fallen. East Potomac Park also offers beautiful weeping willows, picnic grounds, 14 hard-surface (nine outdoor, five indoor) and 10 soft-surface tennis courts (tel. 554-5962), a regulation 18-hole golf course and a short nine-hole course (tel. 893-9007), a large swimming pool (tel. 724-4369), and waterside paths for hiking, jogging, and biking. At Hains Point, at the southern tip of the park, is the famous statue of *The Awakening* by J. Seward Johnson.

The two parks are connected just below the Thomas Jefferson Memorial on the Potomac. Spring through fall, bicycles can be rented from **Thompson's Boat Center,** Rock Creek Pkwy. and Virginia Ave. (tel. 333-4861). Tidal Basin pedal boats can be rented from **Guest Services, Inc.,** 15th St. and Maine Ave. SW (tel. 484-3475). For further information on East and West Potomac Parks, call 485-9666 weekdays, 485-PARK weekends and holidays.

6. The U.S. National Arboretum

Administered by the U.S. Department of Agriculture as a research center focusing on trees and shrubs, the National Arboretum, 3501 New York Ave.

NE (tel. 475-4815), occupies 444 acres of rolling hills. On display are rhododendrons, 70,000 azaleas (the most extensive plantings in the nation), day lilies, hollies, boxwoods, maples, cherry trees, aquatic plants, dogwoods, and dwarf conifers. The **Herbarium** contains 500,000 dried plants for reference purposes; there are trees and shrubs given to the U.S. by Khrushchev in 1960; and along **Fern Valley Trail** is the Franklin Tree—a species now extinct in the wild—discovered in 1765 by a botanist friend of Benjamin Franklin. A Japanese garden leads to the pavilion housing the exquisite **National Bonsai Collection**—a $4.5-million Bicentennial gift of 53 miniature trees, some of them over three centuries old; it can be seen daily between 10 a.m. and 2:30 p.m. Don't miss it! **The Herb Garden,** another highlight, includes a historic rose garden (120 old-fashioned fragrant varieties), a contemporary interpretation of a 16th-century English-style "knot" garden, and ten specialty gardens—a dye garden, a medicinal garden, a fragrance garden, a culinary garden, etc.

In spring the Arboretum is awash in color. Magnolias and daffodils bloom late March through early April; dogwoods, wildflowers, azaleas, and rhododendrons from late April to mid-May. The autumn foliage is also spectacular.

There are 9½ miles of roadways and paths to explore by car or on foot. A map is available at the Information Center where you enter. Frequent lectures, films, and slide presentations are offered on subjects like "Herb Gardens Around the World." Parking is free. Open daily (except Christmas) weekdays from 8 a.m. to 5 p.m., weekends and holidays from 10 a.m. to 5 p.m. If you don't have a car, take the Metro to Stadium-Armory, and from there catch a B2, B4, or B5 bus.

7. River Cruises

A riverside city should be seen by boat, and **Spirit of Washington,** Pier 4 at 6th and Water Sts. SW (tel. 554-8000), makes it possible. From late March through mid-November they offer a variety of daily river cruises departing from Pier 4. Make reservations in advance.

Afternoon Lunch Cruises—weekday lunch aboard a 500-passenger paddlewheeler—are sun-dappled hour-long cruises on the Washington Channel. The meal consists of a soup and salad bar, a deli sandwich, dessert, and tea or coffee; alcoholic beverages are available at extra cost. The fare, including the meal, is $12.95. Departures are Tuesday to Friday.

Sunday Brunch Cruises, including a meal and live entertainment along with narrated sightseeing, cost $13.95.

A popular half-day excursion takes in D.C. sights en route to **Mount Vernon** plantation, George Washington's beautifully situated Potomac estate. The trip is about 1½ hours each way. One-way fare is $7.75 for adults, $5.50 for children 2 to 11; round trip, $10.75 for adults, $6.25 for children.

Late March through June **Moonlight Dance Cruises** are offered for adults with live bands and cash bars on board Tuesday and Friday evenings. Music is 1940s to top 40s, geared to adults, not teens. The boats head toward Alexandria. Cost for this 2½-hour cruise is $9.

Call for departure times.

8. The Mount Vernon Trail

A joy to hikers, bikers, and joggers is the 17-mile Mount Vernon Trail, paralleling the beautiful George Washington Memorial Parkway along the Potomac from the Lincoln Memorial to Mount Vernon. There's an unobstructed view of the Washington skyline from **Lyndon Baines Johnson Memorial Grove in Lady Bird Johnson Park.** Dedicated to Lady Bird's efforts to beautify America, the park is particularly gorgeous in spring when a profusion of a million daffodils bloom. The trail also passes through Old Town Alexandria, abandoned forts, parks, picnic areas, woodlands, and wildflower-blanketed meadows. A side path takes you to **Dyke Marsh,** a 240-acre wetland area where hundreds of species of birds can be sighted.

Maps and information are available from the superintendent, George Washington Memorial Pkwy., c/o Turkey Run Park, McLean, VA 22101 (tel. 703/285-2601).

Chapter VI

WASHINGTON AFTER DARK

1. Theater
2. The Performing Arts and Big-Name Entertainers
3. What's Free (or Almost Free)
4. Hitting the Clubs
5. The Bar Scene
6. Dancing
7. Films

TO THOSE HEARTY SOULS who after a long day's trudging around museums and monuments still have the energy to consider nightlife—my congratulations. Your stamina will be rewarded, for Washington really swings at night. At this writing the week's offerings (which are typical) include major productions of *My Gene* starring Colleen Dewhurst, *Cats, Nunsense* starring Peggy Cass, *Sherlock's Last Case* starring Frank Langella, and Arthur Miller's *The Crucible;* a production of *Tosca* by the New York City Opera; a Mostly Mozart Festival at Kennedy Center; concerts by Madonna, Kris Kristofferson, the Gatlin Brothers, Chuck Mangione, Dizzy Gillespie, Nancy Wilson, Sun Ra, and Stan Getz; and the San Francisco Ballet. Joan Rivers is performing in town too. That's not to mention the numerous discos and singles bars that are packed nightly, comedy clubs, big-band ballrooms, free concerts, and cabaret theaters.

For a complete rundown of nighttime events during your stay, pick up Friday's *Washington Post;* the "Weekend" section tells all. You might also call *Ticketron* (tel. 659-2601) and listen to their recording, or stop by their office at 1101 17th St. NW at L St. Call 789-6552 for additional Ticketron locations. To charge tickets call 432-0200 or toll free 800/223-0120.

There are two only-in-Washington nighttime options I particularly recommend. One is Stephen Wade's one-man, five-banjo folkloric show at the Arena Stage's Old Vat Room, one of the most enchanting and pleasurable entertainments I've ever attended (and several times at that). To quote one of many raves, Wade "is an impassioned banjoist, a nimbly authoritative clog dancer, a soulful singer of folk music and an enthralling tall-tale raconteur. He gyrates to the pipes of Pan." It's Washington's longest-running show, and it's a must-see.

My other favorite is the cabaret show at Chez Artiste, detailed later in this chapter.

1. Theater

Washington can't compete with New York, but it does offer a wider spectrum of first-rate theatrical productions than any other American city. Proximity to the Great White Way makes D.C. a major tryout city for Broadway-bound shows, and numerous post-Broadway hits with star casts come to town. There are several nationally acclaimed repertory companies and theaters here, and of course the **Kennedy Center** (see below) is of vital importance to the scene.

Tickets are generally less expensive than New York equivalents, especially if you purchase them at **TICKETplace,** a service of the Cultural Alliance of Greater Washington. At their outlet on F Street Plaza, between 12th and 13th Sts. NW (tel. T-I-C-K-E-T-S), you can pick up half-price tickets—on the day of performance only—to productions at every major Washington-area theater: Kennedy Center, Warner's Folger, Arena Stage, Ford's, National, Wolftrap, and many more. The reduced-price tickets are not just for dramatic productions, but for opera, ballet, headliner entertainers, and other events. You must pay in cash, and there's usually a minimal service charge. If you're trying to get tickets to a very popular show, the earlier you arrive the better your chances. Full-price tickets for advance performances are also sold here; these can be paid for by credit card. **TICKET-**place is open Monday from noon to 2 p.m. and Tuesday to Saturday from 11 a.m. to 5 p.m.; tickets for Sunday shows are sold on Saturday.

Note: Consider combining your ticket quest with breakfast or lunch at nearby **Reeve's Bakery** (details in Chapter III).

The luxurious, Federal-style **National Theater,** 1321 Pennsylvania Ave. NW (tel. 628-6161), renovated to the tune of $6.5 million in 1983, is the oldest continuously operating theater in Washington (since 1835) and the third-oldest in the nation. It's exciting just to see this stage on which Sarah Bernhardt, John Barrymore, Helen Hayes, and so many other venerables have performed. The National is called "the theater of the presidents," because every president since McKinley has attended a performance here. Reagan made a speech at the National's 1984 inaugural. It's also the closest thing Washington has to a Broadway-style playhouse. Managed by New York's Shubert Organization, the National presents star-studded hits—often pre- or post-Broadway—such as *Social Security, Cats, I'm Not Rappaport* starring Judd Hirsch, *Broadway Bound* with Linda Lavin, and *Ian McKellen Acting Shakespeare.* Tickets range from about $20 to $40, with discounts, subject to availability, for students with I.D., senior citizens, military personnel, and the handicapped.

The National also offers free public-service programs: Saturday-morning children's theater (puppets, clowns, magicians, dancers, and singers), free summer films, and Monday-night showcases of local groups and performers. Call 783-3370 for details.

The **Shakespeare Theater at the Folger,** 201 East Capitol St. SE (tel. 546-4000), modeled after an Elizabethan innyard, is one of the few places in the world where you can see Shakespearean productions in the kind of setting for which they were intended. An excellent professional classical ensemble company puts on four or five productions during the October to June season, at least two of which are Shakespearean. Others might include *The Cherry Orchard* or Molière's *The Miser.* Occasionally the season extends through the summer. The 1987 season featured productions of *The Winter's Tale, Romeo and Juliet, Love's Labour's Lost,* and *Mandragola,* a play by Machiavelli. Tickets are in the $10 to $30 range, with standing room available for less.

Another house group, the **Folger Consort,** an early music ensemble (three players with guest artists), performs on six weekends during the season. Their lute duos, Gregorian chants, folk tunes, court ensembles, and troubadour songs are a delight. Tickets are about $12 to $15.

If tickets are available an hour before show time, students and seniors can get them for half price.

Other offerings at the Folger include free **Midday Muse** entertainment—concerts, poetry readings, mimes, jugglers, bell choirs, etc.—at 12:15 p.m. on selected Thursdays. There are also free evening lectures, usually on Monday at 8 p.m., on scholarly subjects like "Attitudes toward Socrates in Erasmus, Rabelais, and Montaigne." On other evenings you might attend a poetry reading or poetry seminar conducted by a well-known poet; the former is usually $5, the latter free. The Folger also administers the PEN/Faulkner Award for fiction and presents a series of benefits each year to help support the award. These performances feature readings by authors such as John Irving, Nadine Gordimer, and Eudora Welty. Call to find out if one is on during your stay.

The Folger's artistic director, Michael Kahn, is one of the most respected classical directors in the country.

At the **Arena Stage,** 6th St. and Maine Ave. SW (tel. 488-3300), one of American's finest repertory companies presents eight annual "art theater" productions (as opposed to fluff) ranging from searing drama to comedy. The theater has three stages: the **Arena,** a theater-in-the-round; the smaller, fanshaped **Kreeger;** and the **Old Vat Room,** a cabaret space where a one-man, five-banjo American folklore show called *Banjo Dancing* has been playing for years to great critical acclaim. Don't miss it! The Arena's September to June seasons (sometimes extended into the summer) is a delight to serious theatergoers. A recent season included George Bernard Shaw's *Heartbreak House,* Arthur Miller's *The Crucible, Crime and Punishment, Measure for Measure,* and works by Sam Shepard, Christopher Durang, and Anne Devlin. Arena Stage's theater company was the first outside of New York City to win a Tony award. They also represented American theater on a 1977 State Department tour of Russia and performed at the renowned International Arts Festival in Hong Kong in 1978. Several of the company's graduates have gone on to commercial stardom, Ned Beatty, Robert Prosky, James Earl Jones, Jane Alexander, and George Grizzard among them. Ticket prices range from about $14 to $25, with discounts available for students and senior citizens.

Ford's Theatre, 511 10th St. NW, between E and F Sts. (tel. 347-4833), the theater where Lincoln was shot, has been restored to its 1865 appearance and is once again one of Washington's major playhouses. Ford's season is usually year round (summers are sometimes slow), and productions are first rate. In the past they've presented Peggy Cass in *Nunsense, All My Children* starring Richard Kiley, *Greater Tuna,* a revival of *Godspell,* and the New Vic Theatre of London's adaptation of *The Canterbury Tales.* A big event here is the annual star-studded fundraising gala, usually televised nationwide; a recent one was an all-star salute hosted by Richard Chamberlain and Jaclyn Smith featuring David Copperfield, Tommy Tune, Sandy Duncan, Paul Anka, and many luminous others. The Reagans attended. Ticket prices range from $17 to $22. To order by phone, call 432-0200 or toll free 800/468-3540. Discounts are available for senior citizens and students with I.D.

The **Source Theater Company** (tel. 462-1073) is Washington's largest theater-producing organization, offering a year-round schedule of plays on its own two stages and utilizing other facilities around town as well. The Source presents the city's best local artists in well-chosen dramatic and comedic productions. Its largest space, **Warehouse Rep,** is at 1835 14th St. NW, between S and T Sts. Productions here have included *Equus* (a long run) and Viveca Lindfors in a one-woman show called *Anna.* The Rep also presents a midnight series featuring works like *The Hitchhiker's Guide to the Universe* and *Sexual Perversity in Chicago. For Colored Girls* . . . , *The Glass Menagerie,* and Ionesco's *The Bald Soprano* and *The Lesson* are among the plays that have shown at the medium-sized **Source Main Stage,** 1809 14th St. NW, between S and T Sts. Annual events include an open-air production in August or September for which the Source sponsors foreign troupes like the Berlin Players in Goethe's *Faust.* And during summer the Source's Washington Theatre Festival showcases—in readings workshops, and full productions—over 60 new and rarely seen plays at the Main Stage, the Warehouse, and Theatre Alley, the latter an outdoor summer theater.

Source tickets are in the $11 to $15 range, $5 for midnight shows.

The **New Playwrights' Theater,** 1742 Church St. NW, between 17th and 18th Sts., just above P St. (tel. 232-1122), plays an important role both locally and nationally. Since 1972, this fully professional theater has been involved in promoting the creation, development, and production of new works by American playwrights. Between October and June each year they première five to seven plays, many of which go on to further productions in New York and other parts of the country. Sometimes New Playwrights' also provides a second stage for contemporary plays. For example, Elizabeth Swados's *The Beautiful Lady* went from a production here to the Mark Taper Forum in Los Angeles. Show times are Tuesday to Sunday at 8 p.m. and Saturday at 2 p.m. Tickets are $14 to $17. Also very interesting are the theater's Monday-night rehearsed readings of new works and works in progress, followed by audience discussion. Admission is by donation ($5 is recommended).

Hartke Theatre, Harewood Rd. NE, at 4th St. and Michigan Ave. (tel. 635-5367), is the theater of the prestigious Drama Department of the Catholic University whose gifted graduates include Susan Sarandon, Jon Voight, Ed McMahon, Henry Gibson, and Laurence Luckinbill. The school's highly professional performances have garnered raves locally, bringing many Washingtonians to campus productions, and some efforts have been enhanced by guest stars like Helen Hayes, Cyril Ritchard, and Mercedes McCambridge performing with the students. About five plays are presented annually between October and April. They range from classical productions (Shakespeare, Molière, Euripides) to experimental works and musicals like *High Button Shoes* and Sondheim's *Merrily We Roll Along.* Tickets are $7.50, $6 for senior citizens, $4 for students with I.D. There's a Metro station, Brookland-CUA, right on campus.

The very centrally located **Studio Theater,** a few blocks from Dupont Circle at 1401 Church St. NW (tel. 265-7412), established in 1978, has maintained a strong commitment to the nurturing of talent and the development of a community of artists in the D.C. area. Under the artistic direction of Joy Zinoman, the theater has received numerous Helen Hayes awards for outstanding achievement. And it has recently opened an additional 200-seat stage nearby at 1501 14th St. NW (tel. 265-7412). Productions are very professional, and the wide-ranging material worthwhile. In past seasons, Studio plays have included Carson McCullers's *The Member of the Wedding,* Clifford Odets's *Waiting for Lefty,* Brendan Behan's *The Hostage,* Thurber's *Many Moons,* Tennessee Williams's *Camino Real,* William Hoffman's *As Is,* Pinter's *The Birthday Party,* and Arthur Miller's *Playing for Time.* They've also done some Shakespeare. The season runs from September to July. Ticket prices are in the $12 to $17 range, with discounts available for students and seniors. Parking across the street is free.

Though it's a longish drive—about 30 to 40 minutes from Dupont Circle, depending on traffic—you might consider an evening at the **Harlequin Dinner**

Theatre, 1330 E. Gude Dr. in Rockville, Maryland (tel. 301/340-8515). Even on weeknights the Harlequin is usually packed, because dinner theater is fun, these productions are much superior to the usual offerings of the genre, and the lavish buffets are delicious. To quote Richard Coe, critic emeritus of the *Washington Post:* "The Harlequin is unusual, strikingly professional, affectionately regarded and happily successful . . . Harlequin standards are high." The productions are musicals with a full orchestra. Over the past decade they've included *A Chorus Line, Best Little Whorehouse in Texas, Godspell, My Fair Lady, Pippin,* and *South Pacific.* As for that bountiful buffet, it proffers a wide choice of entrees—on my last visit, Polynesian chicken, fish parmesan, enchilada casserole, and top round of beef—plus fresh stringbeans with mushrooms, spinach soufflé, stuffed potato skins, stir-fried vegetables, a full salad bar (about 20 items), a fruit and cheese bar, and a dessert bar. It's an all-you-can-eat affair. Coffee and beverages (there's a full bar) are extra. The Harlequin season is year round. There are performances Tuesday to Sunday nights and Wednesday and Sunday matinees, with additional matinees on selected Saturdays. Ticket prices for show and dinner are $27 to $30. To get to the Harlequin, simply take Wisconsin Avenue north (it will become Rockville Pike to Rte. 28 and turn right, and make a left at E. Gude Drive. The theater is also accessible via Metro. Take the Red Line to Rockville Station and from there a taxi (call 301/984-1900 from the station) to the theater, about 1½ miles away.

2. The Performing Arts and Big-Name Entertainers

Read this section carefully. These hard-to-classify establishments offer some of the top entertainment options in and around town, including opera, ballet, jazz, theater, films, concerts, comedy, and headliners.

THE KENNEDY CENTER: At the southern end of New Hampshire Ave. NW and Rock Creek Pkwy., the **John F. Kennedy Center for the Performing Arts** offers an exciting choice of first-rate performances in its five facilities—an opera house, two theaters, a concert hall, and a film theater. In itself, it can provide a vacationer with ample entertainment options every night of the week. You can find out what will be on during your stay before leaving home (and charge tickets) by calling a toll-free number, 800/424-8504. In town, call 254-3600 for information about current productions, 857-0900 to charge tickets on any major credit card. Half-price tickets are available for full-time students, senior citizens, enlisted military personnel, and the handicapped; call 254-3774 for details. There's parking underground ($4 all evening). Call either the toll-free number before you leave home, or the local number after you arrive, and ask for a copy of *Two on the Aisle,* a free publication that lists all Kennedy Center events and productions.

At the **Opera House** (tel. 254-3770), the lineup comprises ballet, modern dance, and musical comedy as well as opera, with occasional star-studded honors galas and events like the tapings of Bob Hope's 80th birthday (the Reagans attended, and Loretta Lynn, Flip Wilson, Tom Selleck, Dudley Moore, Brooke Shields, and Lucille Ball were among the guest performers). More typical, though, are performances by visiting companies such as the American Ballet Theater, the Joffrey Ballet, and the New York City Ballet. The Peking Opera has appeared here, and theatrical offerings have run the gamut from *Les Misérables* to *Carousel.*

The crystal-chandeliered, gold-and-white **Concert Hall** (tel. 254-3776) is home to the **National Symphony Orchestra** under the inspired direction of Mstislav Rostropovich. During the winter season (September to June), the orchestra presents several series of concerts, evening and matinee, available by subscription and single sales; some are free. Offerings have ranged from an all-Copland program (with Leonard Bernstein, Rostropovich, and Copland conducting) in honor of Aaron Copland's 80th birthday, to Young People's Concerts. But that's not all that goes on in the Concert Hall. Orchestras, chamber music societies, and choral groups from all over the world have performed here; there have been programs of Indian music, jazz, and gospel; and numerous headliners have included Johnny Mathis, Emmylou Harris, Charles Aznavour, and Frank Sinatra. Even Jim Henson and the Muppets have taken the Concert Hall stage. Every Christmas season there's a free concert, the very popular *Messiah* Sing-Along.

The pretty 500-seat **Terrace Theater** (tel. 254-9895), decorated in shades of violet, mauve, and rose, presents a potpourri of small chamber works, opera, theater, choral recitals, musical and comedy revues, modern dance, etc. It opened in 1970 with the *Grand Kabuki* of Japan (the theater was a Bicentennial gift from Japan to the U.S.), and has since presented such diverse entertainments as *Some Enchanted Evening* (a cabaret of songs by Rogers and Hammerstein), the National Black Music Colloquium, the Maria Benitez Spanish Dance Company, and *Orchards,* a show based on seven Chekhov plays. The annual American College Theater Festival is held here every spring; about six finalist productions from colleges all over the country are presented. Tickets for these are free and distributed in advance on a first-come, first-served basis.

Concentrating on dramatic productions, the elegant **Eisenhower Theater** (tel. 254-3670) premiered with Claire Bloom in *A Doll's House.* Subsequent productions have included several Shakespearean plays, Genet's *The Blacks,* Thornton Wilder's *The Skin of Our Teeth* starring Elizabeth Ashley, the Comédie Française, *Citizen Tom Paine* starring Richard Thomas, *Arsenic and Old Lace* with Jean Stapleton and Marion Ross, and Anne Jackson and Eli Wallach in *Opéra Comique.* Tickets are in the $18 to $40 range.

The **American Film Institute** (tel. 785-4600 or 785-4601) showcases current and classic American and foreign films, animation works, and video events in a 224-seat theater designed to offer the highest standard of projection, picture, and sound quality. There's something showing almost every night (and weekend afternoon) of the year except Christmas. A typical AFI preview calendar offers such gems as *Pride and Prejudice, My Sister Eileen, Sunset Boulevard, The Importance of Being Earnest,* and my all-time favorite, *The Man Who Came to Dinner.* Tickets are $4.50, less for members ($24 a year for one, $32 for two) who also receive many other privileges. There are discounts for students with I.D. and senior citizens. In addition to films, AFI sometimes brings in major film directors (like Scorcese) and stars (like Liv Ullman, Alan Arkin, Cicely Tyson, Ellen Burstyn, Sissy Spacek, and Donald Sutherland) for audience-participation discussions.

The good news is that many events and performances are free. The National Symphony gives free **Family Concerts** a few times each year. The **Theater Lab** mounts a full schedule of free performances for children such as a musical production of Kipling's *The Jungle Book* and a show called *Tales and Music of World Cultures.* Other gratis offerings might include clowns and jugglers, dance troupes, improvisational theater, storytelling, concerts, and films. Call 254-3600 for details, or check listings in the *Washington Post.* Christmas and Easter are especially event-filled times.

Whenever you're attending a performance at the Kennedy Center, consider a meal in one of the restaurants on the Terrace Level (details in Chapter III).

WOLF TRAP: Just a 20-minute drive from downtown Washington, **Wolf Trap Farm Park for the Performing Arts,** 1551 Trap Rd., Vienna, Virginia, is the nation's only national park devoted to the performing arts. It offers an incredible wealth of eclectic year-round entertainment. During the **Summer Festival Season** (June through the beginning of September), performances might include the American Ballet Theater, Alvin Ailey Dance Company, the National Symphony Orchestra, the New York City Opera, or Wolf Trap's resident opera company; headliners like Ella Fitzgerald, Johnny Cash, the Statler Brothers, Judy Collins, the Smothers Brothers, and Arlo Guthrie; visiting symphony orchestras; and major star-studded theatrical productions like *South Pacific* starring Robert Goulet. Summer performances are held in the 7,000-seat Filene Center, about half of which offers seating under the sky. You can also buy cheaper lawn seats on the hill—in some ways the nicest way to go. Everyone brings a picnic dinner. Lawn seats are $10 to $14, and it's a good idea to arrive early to line up for the best spots (the lawn opens an hour before the performance). Inside tickets range from $14 to $40.

During the **Barn Season** (October to May), varied productions are offered in the 350-seat German Barn, a converted pre-Revolutionary structure. The lineup usually includes folk and country music, chamber music, jazz and pop artists, children's shows, modern dance, small ensemble plays, Gershwin nights, even barn dances.

For information on Filene Center performances, or to charge tickets, call 255-1860 (938-2404 for the Barn). Tickets are available at Ticket Center locations (1801 K St. NW and Hecht's Department Stores). To get to Wolf Trap take Route 66 W to exit 20. Bear right on Route 267 (a toll road); the second exit after the 50¢ toll is the Wolf Trap parking lot. The gate opens two hours prior to performances.

CONSTITUTION HALL: You'll be surprised at the headliners appearing at **Constitution Hall,** 1776 D St. NW (tel. 628-4780), the magnificent 4,000-seat Federal-motif auditorium at the National Headquarters of the Daughters of the American Revolution. Past performers have included Joan Rivers, Julian Lennon, Ricky Skaggs, B.B. King, Eddie Murphy, and Luciano Pavarotti. Ticket prices vary widely with the performer. The tricky part is—where do you get the tickets? Since each concert is handled by a different promoter, distribution policies also vary. Check the papers for details. Many times, of course, tickets are obtainable from Ticketron outlets (tel. 659-2601 for locations, 800/223-0120 to charge tickets).

MERRIWEATHER POST PAVILION: Just off Route 29 in Columbia, Maryland (tel. 301/982-1800), the Merriweather Post Pavilion presents big-name entertainers almost nightly from late May to mid-September—people like Whitney Houston, Huey Lewis, Kenny Rogers, Neil Diamond, Barry Manilow, Liza Minnelli, and the Oak Ridge Boys. You can sit in the open-air pavilion (conveniently roofed in case of rain) or on the lawn (no refunds for rain; you get soaked). Pavilion tickets range from $16.50 to $25; lawn tickets, $11 to $14. Purchase pavilion seats as far in advance as possible since the first buyers get the best seats. You can charge tickets at the above number or purchase them through any Ticketron outlet. The Merriweather Post Pavilion is about a 45-minute drive from downtown D.C.; admission includes parking.

CAPITAL CENTRE: Even closer to town than the above, the Capital Centre, Exit 15 or 17A off the Capital Beltway in Landover, Maryland (tel. 301/350-3400), hosts a variety of concerts and headliner entertainment in between sporting events. Some of the big names that have played this 20,000-seat theater are the Rolling Stones, Billy Joel, Prince, Bruce Springsteen, Diana Ross, Paul

McCartney, Frank Sinatra, and Bob Dylan. Ticket prices depend on the performer. Call 432-0200 for ticket information.

THE WARNER THEATER: This 2,000-seat facility at 513 13th St. NW, between E and F Sts. (tel. 626-1050), is a former vaudeville house. Today it offers a format of pre- and post-Broadway shows alternating with headliner entertainment. Among the former: Yul Brynner in *The King and I, Sugar Babies* with Mickey Rooney and Ann Miller, *Doonesbury, Fiddler on the Roof* with Herschel Bernardi, and *Lena Horne—The Lady and Her Music.* And headliners here have included the Talking Heads, David Allan Coe, Nina Simone, B.B. King, Phillip Glass, Ray Charles, Nancy Wilson, the Rolling Stones, Prince, and Whitney Houston. Show times vary with the entertainment. Tickets for plays are in the $15 to $40 range, $12.50 to $17.50 for most concerts. They're available at the box office, at Ticketron and Ticket Center outlets (Hecht's Department Stores).

THE PATRIOT CENTER: This 10,000-seat facility of George Mason University, 4400 University Dr. in Fairfax, VA (tel. 703/323-2672), opened in 1985 and has already hosted some major headliners. Conway Twitty, Hank Williams, Jr., Frankie Laine and Kay Starr, Chicago, the Beach Boys, Billy Idol, and Kenny Rogers have all played here. To get to the Patriot Center take the Wilson Bridge to Braddock Road W. (Route 623) and continue for about eight miles to University Drive. For ticket information and to charge tickets call 202/432-0200.

THE ROBERT F. KENNEDY MEMORIAL STADIUM: This 50,000-seat facility at East Capitol St., between 19th and 20th Streets SE (tel. 547-9077), is where the biggest names pack 'em in—Michael Jackson, Bruce Springsteen, Bob Dylan, Madonna, and other superstars who can fill the immense stadium. Call 432-0200 for ticket information.

3. What's Free (or Almost Free)

Before you read further, one note of caution. All of the hours and locations for concerts listed below were correct at press time, but they are subject to change. Call before you go.

Thousands of Washingtonians make the scene at **Concerts on the Canal,** 30th and Thomas Jefferson Streets (tel. 862-1336). Sponsored by Mobil Corporation, these free outdoor afternoon concerts, right on the C&O Canal in Georgetown, feature jazz, folk, Dixieland, blues, classical, flamenco, Irish, bluegrass, and country artists. They take place every other Sunday afternoon (1:30 to 4:30 p.m.) from early June to mid-September.

The **U.S. Army Band, "Pershing's Own"** (tel. 696-3718), presents free outdoor summer concerts June through August with music ranging from Bach to blues (also including country, choral music, jazz, pop, and show tunes). There are outdoor performances at 8 p.m. every Friday on the steps of the West Terrace of the Capitol and every Tuesday at the Sylvan Theater on the lawn south of the Washington Monument. On Wednesday at 7 p.m. the band joins forces with the Third U.S. Infantry to present *Twilight Tattoo,* a military parade and pageant at the Ellipse. The program includes intricate drills with bayonet-tipped rifles, and a musical salute to America's military heritage. Come early to get good seats, and pack a picnic dinner. "Pershing's Own" and the Third Infantry also join forces every June to present *The Spirit of America,* a pageant tracing key events and personalities of American history from the Revolution to the present. It takes place at the Capital Centre in Landover, Maryland (see above). For free tickets, write in advance to Spirit of America, Fort McNair,

Washington, DC 20319. The highlight of the summer season is an August performance of Tchaikovsky's *1812 Overture* complete with the roaring cannons of the Third U.S. Infantry. In winter (October through April) the U.S. Army Band concerts move indoors, with alternating solo recitals and concerts on Tuesday and Thursday nights at 8 p.m. in Brucker Hall, Fort Myer, Arlington, Virginia.

Anheuser-Busch, along with the National Parks Service, sponsors two marvelous outdoor summer concert series. **Fort Dupont Summer Theatre,** Randle Circle and Minnesota Ave. SE, in Fort Dupont Park (tel. 426-7723), presents free jazz concerts on the lawn every Friday and Saturday night at 8:30 p.m. from late May or June to the end of August (bring a picnic dinner and blanket; arrive by 6 p.m. to stake out a good spot). Major jazz artists are featured—people like Betty Carter, Stanley Turrentine, Joe Williams, Art Blakey, Jimmy Witherspoon, Ahmad Jamal, Carmen McRae, and Roy Ayers. At the 4500-seat **Carter Barron Amphitheater,** Colorado Ave. and 16th St. NW in Rock Creek Park (tel. 829-3200), the above-mentioned sponsors present top jazz, classical, Latin, rock, and avant-garde artists from mid-June to the end of August on Saturday and Sunday nights at 8:30 p.m. Offerings for a recent season included Phoebe Snow, B.B. King, Roberta Flack, Nancy Wilson, Melba Moore, and notable others. Tickets at both facilities are amazingly low priced (about $7.50). They go on sale at Ticketron outlets (call 789-6552 to find one near your hotel) about a week in advance and sell out fast. Seating is on a first-come, first-served basis, so arrive good and early.

Concerts at the Capitol, An American Festival (tel. 485-9660), is a series of four free summer concerts with the National Symphony Orchestra on the west side of the Capitol. Sponsored by the National Parks Service and Congress, they take place at 8 p.m. on Memorial Day, July 4, Labor Day, and a fourth summer evening determined annually. Once again, seating is on the lawn and picnics are in order. The music ranges from classical to show tunes of the Gershwin, Rodgers and Hammerstein, Leonard Bernstein genre. Major guest stars like Leontyne Price, Peter Ustinov (a narrator and host), and Morton Gould participate.

The **U.S. Navy Band, "The World's Finest"** (tel. 433-2525), offers a similar concert series. June through August they perform alternately at 8 p.m. on Monday at the Capitol West Terrace and at 8 p.m. on Thursday at the Sylvan Theater. Their big August bash, usually the third Thursday, is the Children's Lollipop Concert, with elaborate sets and costumes, balloons, clowns, and free lollipops for all. Lollipop Concert themes are child-oriented (like "A Salute to Disney" or "Rainbow Magic"—songs about rainbows).

The **U.S. Marine Band, "The President's Own"** (tel. 433-4011), is at the Capitol West Terrace June through August on Wednesday at 8 p.m., at the Sylvan Theater on Sunday at 8 p.m. During January and February they give concerts and recitals on Sunday at 3 p.m. in the Coolidge Auditorium of the Library of Congress, and at the same day and time March through May in the John Philip Sousa Band Hall at the Marine Barracks on 8th and I Sts. SE. And Friday evenings, beginning at 8:20 p.m., they present a military parade and concert at the Marine Barracks that President Reagan called "the best show in town." Call 433-6060 to reserve seats.

The **U.S. Air Force Band and Singing Sergeants,** "America's International Musical Ambassadors" (tel. 767-5658), also performs June through August—on Tuesday at 8 p.m. at the Capitol West Terrace, on Friday at 8 p.m. at the Sylvan Theater. The summer series includes jazz and rock bands, choral groups, full symphonies, and some years, a Broadway show or musical. And the Friday closest to August 25 is set aside for "Christmas in August" (a cooling concert of carols and other Christmas music). In February and March, check out the band's guest artist series on Sunday at 3 p.m. at Constitution Hall in the DAR Building. Past guests have included Freddy Fender, Toni Tenille, Larry Gatlin, Fred Waring, Dizzy Gillespie, William Conrad, and Mr. Rogers—an eclectic grouping if ever I've heard one.

The National Parks Service and the Corporate Community Family are among the sponsors of free Wednesday-night **Big Band Concerts** June through August at the Sylvan Theater on the lawn south of the Washington Monument (tel. 485-9660). There's a dance floor in front of the stage. Concerts begin at 8 p.m.; arrive by 7 p.m. to get a good seat. Everyone brings a picnic dinner.

The **Spanish Ballroom at Glen Echo Park,** MacArthur Blvd. and Goldsboro Rd. (tel. 492-6282, office hours only), is the scene of Friday-, Saturday-, and Sunday-night dances from April to October. Friday and Sunday nights are set aside for square and folk dances (anything from English country to Bavarian) and Saturday nights you can trip the light fantastic to big-band sounds. Folk and square dances begin at 8 or 8:30 p.m., ballroom dancing at 9 p.m. Call before you go, because there are occasional gaps in the schedule. Admission is $4 to $7.

Finally, check out **The Pavilion at the Old Post Office,** 1100 Pennsylvania Ave. NW (tel. 289-4224). It offers many free performing arts events.

4. Hitting the Clubs

NIGHTSPOTS: Perhaps the most avant garde nightspot in uppercase, D.C., **d.c. (district creative) space,** 443 7th St. NW at E St. (tel. 347-1445 or 347-4960), opened in 1978 to promote the performance arts. Its exciting mix of jazz, art theater, rock, films, poetry readings, comedy, and musical cabaret entertainment attracts hip Washingtonians and in-the-know New Yorkers. Sam Rivers, Don Cherry, David Murray, Ken McIntyre, Chico Freeman, Wynton Marsalis, Julius Hemphill, Abbey Lincoln, Jackie McClean, Air, Sun Ra, Oliver Lake, Mal Waldron, and Don Pullen are among the well-known jazz artists who've played d.c. space. Art performer Laurie Anderson made her first appearance here. And musical revues have included *The Fantastiks,* several Jacques Brel shows, and *Side by Side by Sondheim.* In formal Washington, d.c. space's comfortable, unpretentious interior (an eclectic assortment of tables and chairs including old movie-theater seats) and casual atmosphere are a refreshing change. Walls function as an art gallery space for changing exhibits by local artists. And there's entertainment almost every night. Ticket prices are in the $3 to $9 range, depending on the entertainment. Occasionally there's also a food or drink minimum, but in any event dinner here is a good idea. Quality American fare, all fresh and homemade—burgers, pasta dishes, fresh veggies, and delicious desserts—is featured, and prices are moderate.

The Bayou, 3135 K St. NW, on the Georgetown waterfront under the Whitehurst Freeway at Wisconsin Ave. (tel. 333-2897 or 333-2898), is a lively nightclub featuring local bands playing dance music (mostly rock) on Friday and Saturday nights, a mix of entertainment—rock, rhythm and blues, and C&W—the rest of the eek. Sometimes really big names play the Bayou—people like Kris Kristofferson, Southside Johnny, and Iggy Pop. And there are occasional well-known comics such as *Monty Python's* Graham Chapman and Harry Anderson of *Night Court* fame. The cover charge ranges from $3 to $13, depending on the entertainer. There's no minimum, but drinks and light fare are available. Shows usually begin between 8 and 9 p.m. Minimum age for admission: 21.

JAZZ: You'll find **Blues Alley** (known as "Blues in the Mews") nestled in an alley behind M St. at 1073 Wisconsin Ave. NW (tel. 337-4141). Housed in a converted red brick stable that dates to Colonial times, it's one of the nation's top jazz showcases, featuring major artists like Tony Bennett, Sarah Vaughan, Ramsey Lewis, Chick Corea, Phyllis Hyman, Betty Carter, Dizzy Gillespie, Stan Getz, and Carmen McRae. Great acoustics further enhance your listening pleasure. There are two shows a night Sunday to Thursday, three on Friday and Saturday. Reservations are essential, and since seating is on a first-come, first-served basis you'll get the best seats by arriving at 7:30 p.m. for dinner. An evening at Blues Alley doesn't come cheap. Cover price is $10 to $28, and there's a $2 food or drink minimum. Entrees on the à la carte steak and seafood dinner menu (Créole specialties are highlighted) are in the $11 to $16 range, though snacks, burgers, and sandwiches are much less; drinks are $3 to $5.

There are also frequent jazz performances at the **Fort Dupont Summer Theater** and the **Carter Barron Amphitheater** (see "What's Free") and at d.c. space (see above).

SOME ENCHANTED EVENING: Romantic settings don't abound in D.C., which makes the cabaret show at **Chez Artiste,** 1201 Pennsylvania Ave. NW (tel. 737-7772), a particularly cherished find. Every Thursday, Friday, and Saturday night a marvelously talented company here called Cabaret Américain—headed up by a pianist at a gorgeous $40,000 Lucite grand piano—takes the audience on a musical journey from the Andrews Sisters to the Supremes, all with appropriate staging and costumes. They do everyone's old favorites from the pop charts and Broadway, from "Inka-Dinka-Doo" to "Going to the Chapel." The shows are utterly delightful, as is the setting, an elegant country French restaurant offering candlelit tables, plush velvet seating, and the drama of flambé specialties prepared tableside. If you come for dinner, the cover charge is waived and you can enjoy such scrumptious fare as breast of duckling with honey, raisins, Armagnac, and wild rice or fresh trout stuffed with crabmeat and caviar. Entrees are in the $15 to $20 range, not so bad for dinner and a fabulous evening of entertainment. If you don't want dinner, pay a $5 cover and have drinks or dessert with espresso during the show. Shows begin at 8:30 p.m.

MORE CABARET: Over at the Omni Shoreham, 2500 Calvert St. NW, at Connecticut Ave. (tel. 234-0700), the **Marquee Cabaret,** a plush art deco nightclub, is the setting for first-rate entertainment. For many years the showcase for political satirist Mark Russell, the Marquee has, in the recent past, offered *Forbidden Broadway,* Garry Trudeau's *Rap Master Ronnie,* and other politically themed satrical revues such as *Capitol Steps* (the performers are actually a talented group of young government bureaucrats and staffers) and *Mrs. Foggybottom and Friends.* The Marquee is an elegant setting with Louis XV-style rose velvet chairs and moss-green banquettes and Lalique-like frosted lamps flickering on marble tables. Drinks and light fare are available. There's one show a night Tuesday through Friday, two shows Friday and Saturday. Admission is $15 on weeknights, $18 weekends.

COMEDY: All over the nation comedy clubs are opening. It seems to be the vogue of the '80s. And to serve these clubs, a large cadre of professional traveling comedians has developed. These are the guys you see on Johnny Carson's *Tonight Show, Star Search,* and *Late Night With David Letterman,* and they're considerably funnier at the clubs than they are on TV. A comedy club provides a great evening's entertainment. Washington has three.

The **Comedy Café,** 1520 K St. NW (tel. 638-JOKE), offers two shows every Friday night (8:30 and 10:30 p.m.) and three every Saturday night (7:30, 9:30, and 11:30 p.m.), each show featuring three comedians. The quality of these acts is very high. Jay Leno, Shirley Hemphill, and Larry "Bud" Melman have all been headliners here. Admission is $7, and there's no food or drink minimum. Reservations are recommended, and it's a good idea to arrive early to secure a good seat. Since it's no fun sitting and waiting for a show to begin, you might as well opt for the dinner/show package—$14.95 for entrees like deep-fried butter-fly shrimp with potatoes and coleslaw. Or pay the regular admission and order light fare such as nachos, buffalo wings, or potato skins with cheddar cheese, $3.50 for any of these. The Comedy Café is on the second floor. Below, under the same ownership, is **Jonathan's** a dance club where waitresses are dressed in '50s garb and a DJ plays only oldies. Plan to go down and dance after the show.

Garvin's, sharing quarters with a posh restaurant called Maxime, 1825 I St. (tel. 726-1334), is Washington's oldest comedy club—and its most peripatetic. "If you can find us," jokes owner Harry Monocrusos, "you can find Jimmy Hoffa." Garvin's has moved every year since I've been writing about D.C. Lets hope this new home is permanent, but do call before you go. The current location is the best so far. Maxime is a lovely French restaurant down a flight of stairs from street level. It has candlelit flower-bedecked tables clothed in peach and beige linen and walls hung with gilt-framed oil paintings in the Impressionist style. Lots of big names have played Garvin's—people like Charley Barnett, Marcia Warfield *(Night Court),* Emo Phillips, Joe Piscopo, and Yakov Smirnoff —and occasionally major stars of comedy have been known to drop in and take the stage for awhile. Among those who've dropped in to date are Eddie Murphy, Rodney Dangerfield, and Redd Foxx. Actually, this drop-in phenomenon might happen at any of the clubs here listed. Garvin's features two shows nightly (8:30 and 10:30 p.m.) on Friday and Saturday nights. Cover charge is $7, and there's no minimum. Drinks average $3.25 to $4. Continental entrees like veal Cordon Bleu and poached salmon in dill sauce are in the $10 to $16 range. And there is a light fare menu featuring items like toasted brie with almonds for $5.50. If you don't find Garvin's here, just check the local paper; it's sure to be somewhere.

The newest entry in the field is the **Georgetown Comedy Stop,** 34th and M Sts. NW (tel. 342-7775), and it offers the most ambitious entertainment schedule. Open seven nights, the Comedy Stop features open-mike nights on Monday and Tuesday nights (that means anyone who signs up (within reason) can step up to the stage and do a shtick. Monday nights open mike is usually limited to a particular profession, such as funniest lawyer, congressman, bartender, etc., in Washington. Wednesday, Thursday, and Sunday nights there's one show a night featuring three comics, at least one of whom is a nationally acclaimed headliner, at 9 p.m.; Friday and Saturday there are two shows per night at 9 and 11:15 p.m. Open-mike nights also begin at 9 p.m. Admission is $6 to $10, depending on who's performing. Sunday to Thursday a dinner/show ticket is $12.95, Friday and Saturday $16.95. Food options here range from gourmet fare such as breast of chicken in white sauce with oysters, served with herbed rice and vegetable du jour to burgers, salads, and smoked baby back ribs. Though new in D.C., Comedy Stop is a well-established enterprise with a sister club in Atlantic City. It draws big names. I recently saw Robert Townsend *(Hollywood Shuffle)* here.

5. The Bar Scene

The Washington bars where singles mingle tend to fit a basic format: they usually have cafés out front, serve a full restaurant menu, and provide a D.J. or live music for dancing. The following, all of which offer all or most of the above, are currently the favored stops on the nightly pub crawl.

Rumors, 1900 M St. NW (tel. 466-7378), has been named D.C.'s no. 1 singles bar for several years in a row by *Washingtonian* magazine and one of the nation's top ten by *Playboy*. Fronted by an open-air café under a striped tent top, it offers a plush California-style neo-Victorian setting complete with dozens of hanging plants, brass rails, and *Casablanca* fans. A D.J. from Lyric, Washington's most popular record-spinning company, plays contemporary dance tunes. Food is served nightly till midnight—a choice of light fare like eight-ounce burgers with cottage fries ($5.95) or more substantial entrees like fresh fish, baked potato, and vegetable ($8.95). Sometimes there are live bands here, and there are occasional promotional events and celebrations—like the Irish coffee contest in March (many other local bars and restaurants participate) and *Putting on the Hits* auditions (contestants lip-synch to hit records, imitating pop stars). There's no cover or minimum. The average drink is $3. You must be 21 to get in. Open Sunday to Thursday until 2 a.m., on Friday and Saturday until 3 a.m.

No need to go pub-hopping. Just start the evening at **Déjà Vu,** 2119 M St. NW (tel. 452-1966), and when you feel the need for a change of scene wander into another of its eight rooms. On the premises are three dance floors, six bars, and **Blackie's House of Beef,** a full restaurant serving beef and seafood entrees in the $11 to $16 range till 10:30 p.m. nightly. Blackie's also contains a small museum, the highlight of which is a stunning collection of antique cash registers. The decor throughout is turn-of-the-century New Orleans. You'll enter via the Parlor, furnished with plush burgundy velvet couches and armchairs. It contains a dance floor and a massive carved-oak fireplace, ablaze in winter. A larger dance floor is in the Main Room, which also boasts a fireplace as well as a high skylight ceiling and much lush foliage. The upstairs Gallery, its walls hung with many paintings, is used only when Déjà Vu is mobbed, but it's always open if you want to slip away for a quiet conversation. Perhaps the prettiest room is the Garden, another skylight chamber with fountains, garden furnishings, and a veritable jungle of greenery. There's also a western-themed Boot Hill Room, a Gallery Bar (under the Gallery Room), an outdoor café, and a Mardi Gras Room. The Victorian setting is enhanced throughout by beautiful antiques, stained-glass panels, and gilt-framed oil paintings.

Dance music, provided by a D.J., is about 60% oldies from the '50s, '60s, and '70s (the place is named Déjà Vu for a reason), 10% top-40 tunes, and the rest a mix of big band and jitterbug. No cover or minimum; no one under 21 is admitted. Every Thursday night Déjà Vu sponsors a jitterbug contest (first prize is $50), and there are frequent promotion parties—Christmas in July, New Year's in August, the real Christmas and New Year's, Halloween, special dance contests, etc. Do consider a dinner-and-dance evening at Blackie's. A menu special offers aged U.S. prime rib with a big baked potato, bleu cheese and crackers, and a basket of breads and butter for just $10.50. Open Sunday to Thursday until 2 a.m., on Friday and Saturday to 3 a.m.

Champions, 1206 Wisconsin Ave. NW, down an alley just north of M St. (tel. 965-4005), is, according to *Playboy,* Washington's best singles bar. It's also the city's main sports bar, a hangout for the Redskins and the Capitals, along with visiting jocks and other celebs. Everyone from the Beach Boys to Darryl Hannah has stopped in. The place is choc-a-bloc with autographed sports photos, posters, and artifacts—Sugar Ray Leonard's boxing gloves, Mitch Kupchak's uniform, Phil Chenier's basketball jersey, Moses Malone's sneakers, etc. *Sports Collectors Digest* described the decor as "20th-century jock . . ." and a sports "hall of fame . . . with a liquor license." Champion's occupies two floors, with the heaviest boy-meets-girl action at the first-floor bar; the upstairs bar and glassed-in deck are a mellower scene. Sunday through Thursday there are promotions almost every night—Princess Di look-alike contests, aerobics contests, auctions of sporting paraphernalia, etc. And VIP parties take place with some frequency. A DJ plays top-40s tunes for dancing nightly on the main floor, and sports events from all over the world are broadcast on two satellite TVs. Light fare is available—nachos, burgers, chili, and the like—assuming you can snag a table. The place is always packed wall to wall. If you ever make your way through the mob to the glass-topped, 18th-century German bar, you'll see that it's pasted over with $15,000 worth of baseball cards. Champions is open Sunday to Thursday till 2 a.m., Friday and Saturday till 3 a.m.

Flaps Rickenbacker's, 1207 19th St. NW, between M and N Sts. (tel. 223-3617), is a congenial hangout housed in a white-shuttered brick town house that once belonged to Teddy Roosevelt's chief justice. The bar's upstairs, and though there's no dance floor a D.J. plays oldies and Motown tunes from 9 p.m. till closing Wednesday through Sunday. People just dance wherever—it's part of Flaps informality. Both levels are cozy and bistro-like, and in keeping with the Flaps theme there are airplane propellers overhead and historic aviation photos and paintings lining the stairwell walls. Flaps' Happy Hour (weekdays, 4 to 8 p.m.) offers beer at greatly reduced prices. Then there are various nighttime promotions such as half-priced burgers on Tuesdays, outdoor barbecues on Sundays, and Thursday's $1.50 Michelobs and door prizes. The basement bar specializes in draught beer. The big event here is the Bahama Mama Party every May, a private beach party with a 15-piece steel band, tropical decorations, limbo contests, sand on the floor, and goombay punch served in pineapples. Flaps has an extensive, reasonably priced menu with items like chef's salad or a sliced New York strip steak sandwich in the $7 range. Food is served till 10:30 p.m. Sunday to Thursday, to midnight on Friday and Saturday. The most simpático place to eat is the street café with umbrella tables. There's no cover or minimum. Flaps stays open till 2 a.m. Sunday to Thursday, to 3 a.m. on Friday and Saturday.

The **Bottom Line,** 1716 I St. NW (tel. 298-8488), is a popular sports bar partly owned by Dick Heidenberger, who plays for the Sud Americano rugby team. Consequently, lots of ruggers and other athletes hang out here. Monday nights sporting events are televised at the bar, and free hot dogs are given out to customers. Tuesday to Saturday there's dancing to music provided by a D.J. from 9 p.m. to closing (1:30 a.m. weeknights, 2:30 a.m. on Friday and Saturday). Some people describe the Bottom Line as a place to come and go nuts. There is a definite anything-goes attitude, enhanced by frequent zany promotions. On Unknown Customer Night everyone who came in had a bag with eyeholes and a funny face placed over their heads; there were also numbers on the bags called out during the evening for prizes. One night anyone who could sit on a block of ice for an hour had $100 donated to a charity of his or her choice—plus unlimited free drinks while ice-sitting. And, of course, there's a big holiday bash on Christmas, New Year's, Valentine's Day, St. Patrick's Day, etc.; let's just say the party never stops. There's no cover or minimum. The average drink is $2.50. A reasonably priced menu—salads, omelets, pita sandwiches, deli sandwiches, and burgers, mostly under $5—is offered till 11 p.m. Closed Sunday.

Clyde's, 3236 M St. NW (tel. 333-0294), is Washington's answer to P.J. Clarke's—a classy oak-paneled New York-style saloon with white tile floors, bentwood chairs, checkered cloths on the tables, and gaslight wall sconces. Frequented by a mix of old-line Washingtonians, college students, political types, and Yuppies, Clyde's is where the action is at night and Sunday brunch. Both the front room and railroad bars (the latter utilizes some railroad photos and memorabilia in its decor) are mobbed most evenings, but if you want a romantic setting, head for the skylight patio, a candlelit haven amid a veritable jungle of plants with brightly colored papier-mâché toucans and parrots perched overhead enhancing the effect. Also popular is the famous Omelette Room with its copper-canopied open kitchen. Food is served until 1 a.m. nightly; the bar stays open until 2 a.m. Sunday to Thursday, to 3 a.m. on Friday and Saturday. There's a choice of fairly pricey entrees like beer-batter shrimp with orange mustard sauce, coleslaw, and fried potatoes ($11.95), or lighter fare such as a hamburger with fried potatoes ($5.25). The average drink is about $2.50. Clyde's cocktail hour "Afternoon Delights" menu of appetizers—like 12 rock shrimp broiled in garlic butter and served with french bread ($2.95)—inspired the Starland Vocal Band's hit of the same name; their gold record hangs on the wall.

F. Scott's, 1232 36th St. NW, between N and Prospect Sts. (tel. 342-0009), recreates Fitzgerald's era right down to the well-dressed and well-heeled clientele. This is Ivy League country, the Washington haunt of Muffy and Binky. The bar—so mobbed it's a feat to walk across the room—is on the upper level; the dance floor, where taped music of the '20s to the '80s is played (eras progress as the night goes on), a few steps down. Period art posters, *Vanity Fair* covers (the original), Peter Arno cartoons, and such adorn the walls. There's no cover or minimum, but drinks are a pricey $4 and up. A full dinner menu features haute cuisine entrees like grilled Dover sole with lemon butter and sautéed tournedos with green peppercorns and brandy in the $12 to $17 range. There's also lighter fare such as eggs Benedict ($6.50), gourmet pizzas (from $4.50), and pasta dishes ($9 to $11). Food is served until 11:30 p.m. Sunday to Thursday, to 1 a.m. on Friday and Saturday, with closing times at 2 and 3 a.m., respectively. Minimum age is 21, and jackets are required for gentlemen.

6. Dancing

In addition to the listings below, the already-covered Spanish Ballroom (see "What's Free"), **The Bayou** and **Bronco Billy's** (see "Hitting the Clubs"), and **Rumors, Pierce Street Annex, Déjà Vu, Flaps Rickenbacker's,** and **F. Scott's** (see "The Bar Scene") also have live or recorded music to dance to.

If you want to get down and boogie—not just socialize at the bar—**Mirage,** 1330 19th St. NW, between N St. and Dupont Circle (tel. 463-8888), is the place. It attracts about 1000 people on weekend nights with a huge dance floor and two ten-foot video screens playing the latest video clips. Wednesday nights Mirage presents fashion shows featuring styles from Washington's leading boutiques. There are some comfy couches where you can sit out a dance or two and enjoy the video show, and if you do want to socialize at the bar you have a choice of three of them (average drink is $3.75). You can even sit outside on a brick patio with umbrella tables and carry on a quiet conversation. Admission is free weeknights, $5 on Friday and Saturday. Mirage opens at 9 p.m., and the action picks up around 10:30 p.m.; it's open until 2 a.m. Wednesday and Thursday, to 3 a.m. on Friday and Saturday, closed Monday and Tuesday. Minimum age is 18½. Light fare—fried zucchini, fried chicken, etc.—is served all night.

7. Films

With the advent of VCRs, classic film theaters are nearly extinct. Only one remains in Washington. Also check museum listings for interesting films, and don't forget the above-mentioned **American Film Institute** at the Kennedy Center.

The **Biograph,** 2819 M St. NW (tel. 333-2696), specializes in themed film festivals—comedy, new wave, great ladies of the silver screen, French movies, Hitchcock films, etc. You can also catch relatively recent releases you may have missed the first time around, for instance, a double bill like *Blue Velvet* and *Stop*

Making Sense or *My Beautiful Laundrette* and *Letter to Brezhnev*. Then again, they could be showing *The Festival of Claymation* or *Krishnamurti*. Admission is $4, and most shows are double features. A discount ticket book good for ten admissions Monday to Thursday evenings and at all matinee and midnight shows is $17.50. Stop by and pick up a calendar if you're going to be in town for a while.

Chapter VII

THE WASHINGTON SHOPPING SCENE

1. A Georgetown Ramble
2. All Around the Town

D.C. DOESN'T HAVE any large concentration of budget shops—nothing to compare to New York's Lower East Side or Miami's "Schmatte Alley." It's also a little short on variety. Washingtonians are the nation's most conservative dressers, and the clothing stores cater to them. This is the only place I've ever had a saleswoman comment on a dress I was considering that "it would be perfect for fundraisers."

What D.C. does offer is a delightful shopping area, historic Georgetown, with hundreds of boutiques, antique shops, and a neo-Victorian mall providing excellent browsing. This chapter begins with a walking tour of Georgetown's main streets, highlighting its most intriguing offerings. The second section deals with the most interesting and/or budget-oriented shops throughout the District, the suburban malls, and the major department stores.

Nearby Alexandria has even more quaint and varied shops to explore than Georgetown (see Chapter VIII).

And don't forget the shops mentioned in Chapter IV. There are marvelous high-quality selections at all the Smithsonian museum shops—unique toys, craft items, educational games for children, posters and art reproductions, books, jewelry, etc.—and at many other museums and attractions as well.

1. A Georgetown Ramble

Georgetown is Washington's "in" neighborhood—the area with the trendiest cafés and restaurants, the liveliest nighttime scene, and the most seductive shopping. Day or night, cruising Georgetown's main streets is an activity in itself.

The action centers on two perpendicular streets—Wisconsin Avenue NW from just below M Street to about Reservoir Road, and along M Street between 28th and 35th Streets. In addition to shops, you'll encounter numerous street vendors hawking T-shirts and handmade jewelry.

If you drive into Georgetown—definitely not advised because parking is almost impossible—check out the side streets off Wisconsin Avenue above M Street for possible spots. Lots abound, but rates are ruinous. There's plenty of public transportation to Georgetown, and even a cab would probably be cheaper than a few hours of parking.

Georgetown Park (tel. 342-8190), at the junction of Wisconsin Ave. NW and M St., is a good place to begin exploring the shopping scene. A multi-million-dollar "neo-Victorian" extravaganza with four shopping levels and a marble fountain under a glass skylight, this mall wins points with me for playing classical music instead of Muzak. With 150 shops and restaurants, most of them on the posh side, it's Washington's most exclusive mall. It contains an elegant department store/boutique, **Garfinckel's,** and other classy emporia like **Conran's, F. A. O. Schwarz, Godiva Chocolatier, Georgetown Zoo** (a zoo's worth of stuffed animals), **Abercrombie and Fitch, Uzzolo** (quilts and linens), and **Crabtree and Evelyn.** Restaurants include the **Japanese Steakhouse, Vittorio's** for Italian fare, **Clyde's and Houlihan's** for American fare, and a French café. The mall is open from 10 a.m. to 9 p.m. Monday to Friday, from 10 a.m. to 7 p.m. on Saturday, from noon to 6 p.m. on Sunday. Georgetown Park will send you a gratis package of coupons and premiums if you write to Susan Hastings, Georgetown Park, 3222 M St. NW, Washington, DC 20007.

Along M Street, beginning at 28th Street, some highlights follow:

The **American Needlework Center,** 2803 M St. (tel. 337-1534), carries its own needlepoint designs as well as cross-stitch and knitting patterns and supplies for all three crafts. If you're a novice the friendly staff will help you get started. Open weekdays from 10 a.m. to 4 p.m.; closed in August.

Estate Book Sales, 2824 Pennsylvania Ave. NW (which merges with M St. here; tel. 965-4274), buys up estate libraries. It has everything from first editions and rare collector's items to low-priced paperbacks. There are three floors chock-a-block with books. Open Monday to Saturday 11 a.m. to 9 p.m., Sunday to 7 p.m.

Jameson & Hawkins, 2910 M St. NW (tel. 965-6911), has everything you need for the romantic look of yesteryear—frilly camisoles, nightgowns, and pantaloons; high-necked Victorian and Edwardian white gowns (including wedding dresses); beaded dresses from the '20s; evening wear from 1915 to 1955; and great costume jewelry to go with it all. Open daily from 10 a.m. to 6 p.m.

The **Junior League Shop of Washington,** 3037 M St. NW (tel. 337-6120), is a secondhand clothing shop selling goods donated or consigned by some very upper-crust Washingtonians. You can pick up designer gowns, furs, formal wear, preppy wear, and good costume jewelry for a song. Children's clothes too. The proceeds all go to charities like the Children's Hospital Center and Recording for the Blind. Hours are limited so call for specifics; closed in July and open only sporadically in August.

Crown Books, 3131 M St. NW (tel. 333-4493), is great. Their motto: "If you paid full price you didn't buy it at Crown Books." There's a minimum 10% discount on any book, but you get 25% off on *New York Times* fiction and non-fiction paperback bestsellers, 35% on hardbacks. Even the magazines (a vast selection) are discounted. Remaindered books here too. Crown Books stays open from 11 a.m. to 11 p.m. Monday to Thursday, till midnight on Friday and Saturday, and till 8 p.m. on Sunday.

Laura Ashley, 3213 M St. NW (tel. 338-5481). Her romantic-look natural fiber clothing, lingerie, floral-design fabrics, and wallpapers are adored by many women, myself included. Her clothes are not only beautiful, they're well made and long lasting. Open Monday to Saturday from 10 a.m. to 6 p.m. (Thursday nights until 8 p.m.), on Sunday from noon to 5 p.m.

Scandia Down, 3303 M St. NW (tel. 342-2245), has everything to entice you never to get out of bed—exquisite imported and domestic linens, plush down comforters and pillows, and attractive decorative cushions. They also carry brass beds and accessories like soaps and sachets. Open from 10 a.m. to 6 p.m. Monday to Saturday, Sunday noon to 5 p.m.

Pier 1 Imports, 3307 M St. NW (tel. 337-5522), is a nationwide chain selling international imports: Indian rugs, straw mats from the People's Republic of China, bamboo furnishings from Thailand, African carvings, cane-seated chairs from Italy, and much more, including toys, glassware, kitchenware, baskets, matchstick blinds, posters, picture frames, folding director's chairs, planters, and clothing. Even the plants adorning the store are for sale. Best of all, you can park free in the adjoining lot while you shop here. Hours: 10 a.m. to 9 p.m. Monday to Saturday, noon to 6 p.m. on Sunday.

Now along Wisconsin Avenue, begin at the bottom just above the canal:

The Red Balloon, 1073 Wisconsin Ave. NW (tel. 965-1200), is a store both parents and kids will adore. It's filled with the kind of inexpensive but irresistible little items that bring back your childhood allowance-spending days: little tops, sparkler twirls, Mexican jumping beans, finger traps, tin tea sets, squirt guns, and suchlike. In fact, there are 683 items priced under $4. The Red Balloon also has very nice painted pull toys and children's clothing. I once spent a half hour browsing when I had much else to do. Open daily year round; hours vary seasonally.

Off the Cuff Limited Additions, 1077 Wisconsin Ave. NW (tel. 337-2666), is a clothing store where you can create original get-ups with beaded gloves, feather masks, glitzy jewelry, and lacy blouses. It shares the premises with **Vanity Flair** (tel. 338-8224), an antique clothing shop that carries 1850s to 1950s fashions, including many beaded dresses from the '20s. The latter has both men's and women's clothing, including tuxedos, prom and other gowns, felt poodle skirts, taffeta dresses, and crinolines. Both stores are open Monday to Saturday from 11 a.m. to 7 p.m., on Sunday from noon to 6 p.m.

Olsson's Books & Records, 1239 Wisconsin Ave. NW, between M and N Sts. (tel. 338-6712 for records, 338-9544 for books), discounts records and tapes 10% to 20% and offers 30% off on *Washington Post* hardback bestsellers and 25% off on special sale books. Though the book selection is eclectic, a strong political/military/historical section makes for a sizable government worker clientele. Open Monday to Thursday from 10 a.m. to 10 p.m., on Friday and Saturday to midnight, on Sunday from noon to 6 p.m., with extended hours in summer.

La Strega III, 1323 Wisconsin Ave. NW (tel. 338-2255), is among the most interesting of the dozens of clothing boutiques on this street. The look is high-style and elegant but not uptight, and the staff knows fashion; they can help you put together a smashing outfit for any occasion. Open weekdays from 10:30 a.m. to 8 p.m., on Saturday to 7 p.m., on Sunday from noon to 6 p.m.

Georgetown Coffee, Tea & Spice, 1330 Wisconsin Ave. NW, between N and O Sts. (tel. 338-3801), stocks about 50 varieties of coffee—everything from flavors like hazelnut and coconut to exotic Haitian Port-au-Prince and Ethiopian Harrar. Also sold here—gourmet teas such as Assam Manjushere, Chinese gunpowder, and Kenyan broken-leaf orange pekoe; Lindt and other fancy chocolates, spices, cookware, porcelains, and homemade salad dressings. Open Monday to Friday 10 a.m. to 6 p.m., Saturday till 7 p.m., Sunday till 5 p.m.

Appalachian Spring, 1415 Wisconsin Ave. NW at P St. (tel. 337-5780), specializes in American-made craft items—stuffed animals and dolls, candles, rag rugs, ceramic pieces, patchwork quilts, hammered pewter, wood cookware, and jewelry. Open Monday to Saturday from 10 a.m. to 6 p.m., on Sunday from 1 to 6 p.m. Closed Sundays in winter.

Little Caledonia, 1419 Wisconsin Ave. NW (tel. 333-4700), is a rabbit warren of tiny rooms (I counted at least seven) filled with indoor and outdoor furnishings (18th- and 19th-century mahogany reproductions are featured), dolls,

Beatrix Potter ceramic figures, stuffed animals, children's books and toys, exquisite fabrics, housewares (copperware, cookbooks, cookie jars, baking molds, etc.), candles, fancy gift wrappings, Indian durrie rugs, tablecloths, wallpapers, lamps, and much much more. A delight. Open Monday to Saturday from 10 a.m. to 6 p.m.

Proceeds of items bought at the **Christ Child Opportunity Shop,** 1427 Wisconsin Ave. NW (tel. 333-6635), go to various children's charities. Among the first-floor items (donations all), I saw a wicker trunk for $5 and the usual thrift-shop jumble of jewelry, clothes, shoes, hats, and odds and ends. Upstairs, higher quality merchandise is left on a consignment basis; it's considerably more expensive, but if you know antiques you might find bargains in jewelry, silver, china, quilts, paintings, and other items. Good browsing. Open Monday to Saturday from 10 a.m. to 3:45 p.m.; closed the entire month of August.

Secondhand Rose, 1516 Wisconsin Ave. NW (tel. 337-3378), is a fancy consignment shop specializing in designer merchandise. Creations by Norma Kamali, Armani, Donna Karan, Perry Ellis, Calvin Klein, Yves St. Laurent, Ungaro, Ralph Lauren, etc., are sold at about a third of the original value. Everything is in style, in season, and in excellent condition. On a recent visit I saw a three-piece Nina Ricci silk suit, easily worth $700-800 new, for $185, Yves St. Laurent pumps in perfect condition for $45. Secondhand Rose is also a great place to shop for gorgeous furs, designer shoes and bags, and costume jewelry. Open Monday to Friday 10 a.m. to 6 p.m., Saturday to 5 p.m.

The **French Market,** 1630-32 Wisconsin Ave. NW, between Q St. and Reservoir Rd. (tel. 338-4828), has been supplying Washingtonians with fancy French fare for over 35 years—long before most Americans knew pâtés from potatoes. Run with élan by three French brothers, Georges, Robert, and Jean Jacob, the French Market contains a *boucherie* carrying game (pheasant, quail, partridge, guinea hens, and mallards) in addition to European-cut meats. Other departments include a charcuterie (homemade pâtés en croûte and in loaf, superb salads, escargots, etc.); a *boulangerie* for baguettes, croissants, and pastries; and a *fromagerie* offering over 50 French cheeses. You can also get imported oils and vinegars, soups, mustards, crème de marrons, canned pâtés, and other fine French groceries here as well as wines, champagnes, and French-roast coffees. *C'est merveilleux!* Open Monday to Saturday from 8:30 a.m. to 6 p.m., except on Wednesday when it closes at 1:30 p.m.

Yes! Bookshop, 1035 31st St. NW, just below M St. (tel. 338-7874), is the personal expression of Peace Corps veteran Ollie Popenoe and his wife Cris. The Popenoe's publish a free quarterly newspaper called *Pathways*—"a journal and resource guide to personal and social transformation in the Washington/Baltimore area," and their bookshop offers reading material in a similar vein. You'll find books on Jewish mysticism, channeling, Jungian philosophy, sacred geomentry, spiritual healing, Tibetan Buddhism, you name it. And, in another realm, the Popenoe's carry the largest selection of travel books, traveler's tales, travel literature, and phrase books (cassettes, too) in the Washington area. Part of the store is a video club, specializing in quality tapes on the arts, travel, etc. Adjoining the Yes! Bookshop is **Yes! Natural Gourmet** at 1015 Wisconsin Ave. NW (tel. 338-1700 or 338-0883), where you can purchase health-food items in bulk at reduced prices—Asian/macrobiotic foods, natural vitamins, beans, nuts, grains, organic produce, imported honeys, nonalcoholic beers, quality imported cosmetics, and much more.

Bookstore hours are Monday to Saturday 10 a.m. to 10 p.m. and Sunday noon to 6 p.m. Yes! Natural Gourmet stays open from 10 a.m. to 7 p.m. Monday to Saturday, till 9 p.m. Thursday, Sunday noon to 6 p.m.

2. All Around the Town

BOOKS: **Crown Books** offers 25% off *New York Times* fiction and nonfiction paperback bestsellers, 35% off hardcovers. Other books, which range widely in subject matter—art, cooking, history, gardening, religion, philosophy, business, nature, children's books, sports, psychology, and more—are also discounted a minimum of 10%. Even magazines are reduced. There are six D.C. locations: 3131 M St. NW (tel. 333-4493); 1710 G St. NW (tel. 789-2277); 1275 K St. NW (tel. 289-7170); 1200 New Hampshire Ave. at M St. NW (tel. 822-8331); 4400 Jenifer St. NW, adjacent to Mazza Gallerie (tel. 966-8784); and 2020 K St. NW (tel. 659-2030). All are open seven days a week (except 1710 G St., which is open Monday to Saturday). Some stores also carry discounted computer software. Call for hours.

A good place for low-priced reading material is **Too Many Books,** 3301 M St. NW (tel. 337-9502). They sell publishers' closeouts, overstock, and remaindered books at 35% to 90% discounts. It's an ever-changing selection; you never know what you'll find here. Open Monday to Thursday from 10 a.m. to 10 p.m., on Friday and Saturday until midnight, on Sunday from 11 a.m. to 8 p.m.

Olsson's Books, mentioned above in Georgetown and featuring 30% off on *Washington Post* bestsellers, has another location at 1307 19th St. NW, between N St. and Dupont Circle (tel. 785-1133). Open Monday to Saturday from 10 a.m. to 9 p.m., on Sunday from noon to 6 p.m.

The **Government Printing Office** is the world's largest printer, with close to 16,000 titles (books and pamphlets). Every conceivable area is covered, from *How to Buy Fruits and Vegetables* to *Starting and Managing a Small Business on Your Own* to *The British Redcoat, 1755-1788 to the Everglades Wildguide.* If you're probing any new hobby, interest, or activity; writing a term paper; trying to understand a medical problem; looking for a new career; or considering a major purchase, you'll probably find some helpful literature here. The collection makes for fascinating browsing. The GPO also sells books of photographs (like *A Century of Photographs: 1846-1946,* selections from the Library of Congress) and sets of actual photographs (like a set of seven photos portraying marines in combat situations, suitable for framing); also prints, lithographs, and posters. Locations: 710 North Capitol St. NW, between G and H Sts. (tel. 275-2091); 14th St. and Pennsylvania Ave. NW (tel. 377-3527); and 1717 H St. NW (tel. 653-5075). Call for days and hours.

CAMERAS AND PHOTOGRAPHIC EQUIPMENT: **Penn Camera,** 915 E St. NW (tel. 347-5777), offers discounts of up to 30% on all major brand-name equipment—Konika, Canon, Minolta, Pentax, Leica, Vivitar, Nikon, etc. The staff is very knowledgeable, the inventory wide ranging. Many professional Washington photographers shop at Penn. All of the merchandise is brand new and comes with a U.S. warranty. Check the Friday *Washington Post* for announcements of special sales. Open Monday to Saturday from 9 a.m. to 6 p.m., summer Saturdays till 3 p.m. only.

CLOTHING (FOR MEN, WOMEN, AND CHILDREN): **T. H. Mandy,** 1118 19th St. NW, between L and M Sts. (tel. 659-0024), sells top-designer and brand-name women's clothing, mostly better sportswear, at prices 20% to 50% below retail. There's a roomy dressing area with individual booths (no curtains), and sales help is excellent for a discount operation. Their motto is: "T.H. Mandy, how do you do it?" Open weekdays from 9 a.m. to 7 p.m., on

Saturday from 10 a.m. to 6 p.m., on Thursday till 8 p.m., on Sunday from noon to 5 p.m.

There's a branch of **Lane Bryant** at 10th and F Sts. NW (tel. 347-1500) carrying large sizes (14 to 28) in women's clothing. Hours are Monday to Friday 10 a.m. to 7 p.m., Saturday 10 a.m. to 6 p.m.

Outfit the kids for school or camp at **7th Heaven,** 1110 F St. NW (tel. 638-5263), where the best names in children's fashions—Gitano, Oshkosh, Levis, Lee, Jet Set, Izod, Jordache, Wrangler, Billy the Kid, etc.—are 20% to 40% less than retail. There are 100 racks of merchandise—sportswear, underwear, sleepwear, outerwear, belts, even diaper bags. For girls and boys they carry newborn to size 18. Discounts are even better during special sales. Open Monday to Saturday from 10:30 a.m. to 6 p.m.

Few women want to spend a fortune on maternity clothes. Hopefully, one regains one's figure and they became obsolete. **Linn's Maternity,** 513 11th St. NW, between E and F Sts. (tel. 737-0132), sells current styles in major brand and designer maternity wear at 30% to 40% below retail. Labels are cut out of the garments, so you'll have to comparison shop or simply opt for what looks like quality. Private dressing rooms here. Open Monday to Saturday from 9:30 a.m. to 5:30 p.m.

If you favor the M*A*S*H look, **Sunny's Surplus,** 14th and H Sts. NW (tel. 347-2774), is the place. They carry a full line of military surplus (mostly new, some used), including sweat shirts, T-shirts, work shoes and clothing, insulated underwear, heavy thermal socks, rainwear and winter garments, pea coats, camouflage fatigues, army blankets, navy wool insignia middy blouses, all camping accessories (tents, sleeping bags, mess kits, canteens, etc.), even World War I Snoopy helmets. These are the styles that inspired surplus chic. Other locations at 9th and E Sts. NW (tel. 737-2032), and 3342 M St. NW (tel. 333-8550). All are open Monday to Saturday. Call for hours.

Best bet for men's clothing is **Dash's Designer,** 1111 19th St. NW, at L St. (tel. 296-4470). They buy up current major designer styles in suits, slacks, topcoats, blazers, rainwear, ties, shirts, and accessories in large quantities and sell them at 30% to 50% below retail. There are even bigger bargains during special sales in the early fall, early spring, and August. You'll find labels like Oleg Cassini, Givenchy, and Adolfo. Dash's carries extra-large sizes, and alterations are reasonably priced. Other locations at 1309 F St. NW (tel. 737-6008) and 3229 M St. NW (tel. 338-4050). Call for days and hours.

CRAFTS—DOING WELL BY DOING GOOD: Save the Children, a marvelous 55-year-old organization committed to helping needy children throughout the world, runs **The Craft Shop,** 1341 Connecticut Ave. NW (tel. 822-8426). Money you spend here is like a double contribution: it not only helps put food in the mouths of hungry children in depressed areas ranging from Appalachia to Ethiopia, but allows the adults in those communities to supplement their meager incomes by selling the crafts they produce. The organization's far-reaching programs also include day-care centers, health care, schools, and other much-needed facilities. By stressing community projects that encourage self-sufficiency, they provide a means by which parents can break the cycle of suffering and poverty and establish a more meaningful life for their children.

At the shop, you'll discover an exquisite collection of folk arts and handicrafts—most of it from Save the Children project areas. There's something here for everyone on your gift list, and since prices are reasonable, you can even stock up on future gifts and help this very worthy cause at the same time. The festive array of merchandise is ever changing. On my last visit there were colorful mola pillows from Panama, Ecuadorian wall hangings, gilt and lacquer wooden boxes from Thailand, lovely hand-embroidered cotton dresses from Mexico and El Salvador for women and children, Peruvian and Zambian dolls, Haitian primitive art paintings, Navaho and Indonesian jewelry, Nepalese jackets and puppets, Mexican pottery, hand-painted boxes and wooden toys from Haiti, adorable stuffed mouse dolls from Sri Lanka, quilts from Appalachia, and papier-mâché boxes from India. That's just a small sampling—there's much more. Everything you buy is wrapped in brightly colored tissue paper. And there's something for every budget: prices begin at just a few dollars for delightful little bone animals from Kenya. Major credit cards are accepted. Open Monday to Friday from 10 a.m. to 6 p.m., Saturday till 5 p.m., Sunday noon to 5 p.m.

DEPARTMENT STORES: Garfinckel's, at 14th and F Sts. NW (tel. 628-7730), in the Georgetown Park Mall (tel. 628-8107), and at 4820 Massachusetts Ave. NW (tel. 363-7700), is the poshest of the local department store chains—something like Bergdorf Goodman in New York. It caters to the carriage trade, specializing in women's designer clothing (Krizia, Rykiel, Ungaro, Carolyn Roehm, Gloria Sachs, Armani, Chanel), men's designer clothing (Jaeger, Aquascutum, Burberry, Perry Ellis, Polo, Armani, Andrew Fezza), silver, china, crystal, and jewelry. The store at 14th and F is the largest branch, with seven floors of merchandise. Georgetown Park has no men's department. Call for days and hours at the various locations.

Woodward & Lothrop, 11th and F Sts. NW (tel. 347-5300), known locally as Woodie's, has been serving Washingtonians for over a century. It's an archetypal full-service, ten-story department store with an extensive line of home furnishings; full clothing and shoe departments for men, women, and children; designer showrooms (such as Fendi, Calvin Klein, Oscar de la Renta, Ralph Lauren, and Byblos); three restaurants; a large bridal department; gourmet food; gourmet housewares; appliances, etc. Promotions at Woodies include frequent celebrity appearances—e.g. Debbie Reynolds for Leslie Fay, Liz Claiborne, and intimate apparel designer Bill Tice. Open Monday and Thursday from 10 a.m. to 9 p.m., till 7 p.m. on Tuesday, Wednesday, Friday, and Saturday. There are 15 other locations in the area; check your phonebook.

Hecht's, 12th and G Sts. NW at Metro Center, like Woodie's, has been in Washington for about a century. However, this branch is brand new. With five floors, it's a full-service moderate- to higher-priced store carrying home furnishings, china, brand names in clothing and footwear for men, women, and children, and all else you'd expect to find in a major department store. One thing that makes Hecht's fun is its many promotions and events. These include frequent fashion shows, clothing consultants, in-store personality appearances (everyone from Richard Simmons to the cast of *42nd Street),* contests (drawings for cars, trips, etc.), and demonstrations of housewares, cosmetics, exercise equipment, and so on. Hours at most Hecht stores are 10 a.m. to 7 p.m. daily, till 8 p.m. Thursday and Friday, and noon to 5 p.m. Sunday. There are about a dozen Hecht's stores in the D.C. area. Each of them houses a **Ticket Center** outlet selling tickets to major shows, sports events, and concerts around town. You get the best available seats for the price at the time you buy.

Three stores that require no description (they're known nationwide) are **Neiman-Marcus,** in the Mazza Gallerie at Wisconsin and Western Aves. NW (tel. 966-9700), open Monday to Friday from 10 a.m. to 8 p.m., on Saturday till 6 p.m. . . . **Lord & Taylor,** just behind Mazza Gallerie at 5255 Western Ave. NW between Wisconsin Ave. and River Rd. (tel. 362-9600), open weekdays from 10 a.m. to 9:30 p.m., on Saturday to 6 p.m., and on Sunday from noon to 5 p.m. . . . and **Sears Roebuck & Co.,** 4500 Wisconsin Ave. NW at Albemarle

St. (tel. 364-1299), and at 2845 Alabama Ave. SE, between 30th St. and Naylor Rd. (tel. 575-5500), both stores are open seven days a week; hours vary seasonally.

DRUGSTORES: Two major drugstore chains, both carrying diversified merchandise that ranges from frozen foods to charcoal briquettes to appliances, are **Drug Fair** (with 7 stores in D.C.) and **Peoples** (with about 40 stores). Check your phone book for the most convenient locations. There's a 24-hour Drug Fair (pharmacy section open only from 8 a.m. to 10 p.m. weekdays, on Saturday from 9 a.m. to 9 p.m., and on Sunday from 9 a.m. to 7 p.m.) at 1815 Connecticut Ave. NW at the junction of Florida Ave. and S St. (tel. 332-1718). There are 24-hour Peoples at 14th St. and Thomas Circle NW off Vermont Ave. (tel. 628-0720) and Dupont Circle (tel. 785-1466), both with round-the-clock pharmacies.

EYEGLASSES: Hefty discounts on single-vision glasses (with frame, lens, tint, and photo-gray extra), designer frames (Pierre Cardin, Elizabeth Arden, Gloria Vanderbilt, Givenchy, Dior, etc.), and designer sunglasses (Bausch & Lomb and others) are offered at **For Eyes Opticals'** three locations: 2021 L St. NW (tel. 659-0077), 1725 K St. NW (tel. 463-8860), and 1624 Wisconsin Ave. NW (tel. 333-1120). All three stores are open Monday to Friday from 9:30 a.m. to 6 p.m., Saturday 10 a.m. to 5 p.m.

FISH: The best home-cooked meal I ever had in Washington was fresh-caught red snapper from the **Southwest Waterfront Fish Market,** between 11th and 12th Sts. SW along Maine Ave. Here, about half a dozen merchants sell a wide selection of just-off-the-boat fish and seafood—shrimp, softshell crabs, crabmeat, lobster, red snapper, bluefish, and whatever else the day's catch brings. It's a picturesque outdoor market, and there's usually a boat selling produce as well. Most of the stalls are open from 8 a.m. to 9 p.m. daily.

HAIR: The Hair Cuttery, with six Washington locations—1645 Connecticut Ave. between R St. and Dupont Circle (tel. 232-9685) and 2400 Wisconsin Ave. (tel. 333-9745), among them—is an inexpensive unisex hair salon offering trendy cuts and styling on a walk-in, no-appointment-necessary basis. A shampoo, cut, and blow-dry styling is $9.50 to $10.50 (slightly more for long hair); perms begin at $30, including shampoo, cut, and blow-dry or set; and it's just $5 for a shampoo and cut for children under 6. The Hair Cuttery also does hair coloring, frostings, and reconditioning. The two above, and most other locations, are open seven days; call for hours.

LIQUOR: Central Liquor, 516–518 9th St. NW between E and F Sts. (tel. 737-2800), comprises two buildings worth of bottled booze with some 35,000 items on display, including thousands of wines ranging from the 99¢-a-bottle variety to Château Mouton Rothschild. It's all discounted 10% to 25% with special sales on loss leaders at all times. Check Monday's *Washington Post* for details on special sales. Good deals are also offered when you buy by the case. Open Monday to Saturday from 10 a.m. to 7 p.m.

If you want to comparison-shop, also check the prices at **Calvert Woodley,** another major discount wine and liquor store at 4339 Connecticut Ave. NW (tel. 966-4400). In addition to an immense selection (66 feet of wines alone), Calvert Woodley has a complete gourmet food store offering hundreds of cheeses, charcuterie meats and pâtés, smoked salmon and whitefish, fresh halvah, an extensive selection of fine coffees (beans are ground to order), pastries and breads, caviars, salads, etc. Open Monday to Saturday from 10 a.m. to 8:30 p.m.

MALLS: There are several shopping malls in the D.C. area, including the above-mentioned **Georgetown Park,** at the hub of the Georgetown shopping scene.

Mazza Gallerie

Right at the D.C./Maryland border is the swank **Mazza Gallerie,** 5300 Wisconsin Ave. between Western Ave. and Jenifer St., with 58 stores including a branch of **Neiman-Marcus** (a **Lord & Taylor,** though not part of the mall, adjoins it); Raleigh's, a smaller chick department store specializing in top-quality men's and women's clothing; posh shops like **Ted Lapidus, Pierre Deux** for antiques, **F.A.O. Schwarz, Williams/Sonoma** (gourmet cookware), **Kron Chocolatier,** and numerous other clothing and shoe stores, eateries and snackeries, gourmet food shops, bookstores, gift boutiques, home furnishings stores, a beauty salon, a **KB-Cinema** movie theater, jewelers, etc. Open Monday to Friday from 10 a.m. to 8 p.m., on Saturday to 6 p.m.; about half the stores are also open on Sunday from noon to 5 p.m. There's two-hour free indoor parking.

Springfield Mall

Springfield Mall (tel. 971-3600) about ten miles from downtown D.C. in Springfield, Virginia (take I-95 south to the Franconia exit and stay in the righthand lane), is the area's largest shopping mall with over 200 shops, 25 restaurants, and 10 movie theaters. There's free parking for about 6,000 cars. Major stores include branches of **Garfinckel's, J.C. Penney, Raleigh's, Lane Bryant, Herman's Sporting Goods, W. Bell,** and **Montgomery Ward.** There are over a dozen shoe stores, and numerous shops and boutiques selling clothing, gourmet food, health food, bridal wear, furniture, toys, books, carpets, gifts, cosmetics, maternity wear, records, tobacco—you name it. That's not to mention a dentist, a pet center, an optician, a bank, several hair salons, and a video-game arcade to keep the kids amused while you shop. A major new department store will soon be added. Open Monday to Saturday from 10 a.m. to 9:30 p.m., on Sunday from noon to 5 p.m.

Tyson's Corner

Tyson's Corner (tel. 893-9400), about 30 minutes away in McLean, Virginia (take the Beltway, I-495, to Exit 10B or 11B), has over 120 shops, 18 restaurants, and 12 movie theaters. Here you'll find branches of such well-known emporia as **Bloomingdale's, Woodward & Lothrop, Hecht's, Garfinckel's, Brooks Brothers, Woolworth's, The Gap, Raleigh's, Hoffritz for Cutlery, Lane Bryant, Radio Shack, Crabtree & Evelyn, Waldenbooks, Ann Taylor, Williams/ Sonoma,** and **F.A.O. Schwarz.** Once again there are about a dozen shoe stores, and services include several banks, a finishing school, hair salons, and a U.S. post office. Computer terminals throughout the mall provide up-to-the-minute information about special sales. Free parking is provided for 6,500 cars. About 100 new stores will open here in the fall of 1988. Open Monday to Saturday from 10 a.m. to 9:30 p.m., on Sunday from noon to 5 p.m.

The Pavilion at the Old Post Office

Billing itself as a "festival mall," the Pavilion at the Old Post Office, 1100 Pennsylvania Ave. NW (tel. 289-4224), is as much of a tourist attraction as a retail complex. Certainly no mall offers a more exquisite setting. Opened in

1983 in the capital's oldest federal building—an actual 1899 government postal department—it is a vital part of the renovation of the entire Pennsylvania Avenue area. The tallest structure in the city, after the Washington Monument, its ten floors soar 196 feet to a skylight ceiling and are crowned by a 315-foot clock tower. The atrium is lined with balconied corridors reminiscent of an Italian palazzo, the arched galleries of the upper floors overlook a magnificent inner court 99 feet wide and 184 feet long, and the exterior stonework, turrets, and massive arches were inspired by the Romanesque cathedrals of 12th-century France. It's worth viewing from an architectural standpoint alone. In the tower are ten great bells, a Bicentennial gift to Congress from the British. While you're here, do take the glass elevator to the tower observation deck for a thrilling 360-degree panoramic view from lofty, open-air arched windows. You can descend several flights of stairs and see the bells themselves. And if you'd like to hear them, bellringers practice on Thursday evening between 7 and 9 p.m. Otherwise, they're only played for State occasions. The listening is best in the 12th Street courtyard of the Federal Building.

But I digress. This is a shopping chapter. The Old Post Office complex contains about 50 establishments—restaurants and shops—the latter for the most part of a somewhat frivolous variety. Though there are elegant men's and women's clothing stores, a fine cutlery shop, a women's shoe store, and a while-you-wait shoe repair shop, most merchants carry such wares as puppets and marionettes, an array of heart-motif items, rubber stamps with wiseacre sayings (none of them funny enough to quote here), Christmas-all-year-round accessories, papier-mâché vegetables, and holography jewelry and paperweights. It makes for fun browsing.

The restaurants, however, include several serious dining possibilities. There's a much-acclaimed Chinese restaurant, **House of Hunan; Blossoms,** featuring a gorgeous brick-terraced café and immense salads, among other American/continental entrees; the brass-railed Enrico's Trattoria; and the British fox hunt-themed **Fitch, Fox, & Brown** for sophisticated nouvelle American fare—though they do offer that all-American kid's favorite, a peanut butter and jelly sandwich with milk and toll house cookies. These are all plush eateries, quite pricey at dinner but fairly reasonable at lunch. Some have outdoor cafés. In addition there are over a dozen fast-food kiosks on the Stage Level purveying pastrami on rye, chili dogs, fried chicken, blintzes, sweet-and-sour pork, pizza, shrimp baskets, barbecue, stuffed potatoes, vegetable biryani, salad bar fixings, and homemade ice cream with waffles. You can take these victuals to café tables overlooking the stage, where there's frequent free entertainment throughout the day—dancers, singers, musicians, jugglers, puppeteers, clowns, jazz ensembles, etc. On Saturday much of the entertainment is geared to children.

Pavilion hours are Monday to Saturday from 10 a.m. to 9:30 p.m., on Sunday from noon to 6 p.m. Restaurants stay open later, and some eateries open earlier for breakfast.

The Shops at National Place

Marking the final stage of the revitalization of Pennsylvania Avenue—a project that includes not only the Old Post Office, but the refurbished National Theater and a flagship J.W. Marriott hotel—are the Shops at National Place, 1331 Pennsylvania Ave. NW (tel. 783-9090). Opened in April 1985, this is yet another of those ubiquitous Rouse Company projects (South Street Seaport, Harborplace, Faneuil Hall, etc.). The four-tiered, 125,000-square-foot retail complex houses over 85 stores and eating places in the renovated National Press Building, home of the National Press Club and a very large concentration of national and international news organizations. From this site, newspaper readers, television viewers, and radio listeners are served with a steady outpouring of worldwide media coverage. This is a stunning retail complex—a terracotta-floored, multitiered, balconied, colonnaded, fountained mall in the best American tradition.

You can do some serious shopping here. Among the better known emporia are **B. Dalton, Naturalizer** and **Red Cross** shoes, **Benetton, The Sharper Image** (toys for the executive), **Hudson Trail Outfitters, Pappagallo,** and **Melart Jewelers.** You can also purchase liquor, fashions for the entire family, records and tapes, exquisite leather goods, lascivious lingerie, and, of course, gifts of every description at various shops.

The Food Hall, on the top level, is a fast-food cornucopia with outlets offering chili, diner fare, subs, beef lo mein, pizza, stuffed potatoes, salads, yogurt, hot dogs, and Häagen-Dazs. There are numerous tables and chairs for dining. Other choices for hungry shoppers include a **Bagel Place** (anything from tuna melt to cream cheese and nova on a fresh-baked bagel, plus a salad bar), **Le Café** (sandwiches on fresh-baked croissants and french bread, plus homemade desserts), and the **Boston Seafood Company** which features a raw bar as well as traditional seafood entrees and sandwiches. All three are among the Colonnade Shops, just off Marriott's posh chandeliered lobby. They all offer corridor café seating. Also in the complex is the **American Café,** at the corner of 13th and F Sts. NW (tel. 737-5153), serving breakfast, lunch, and dinner daily. It follows the format of the American Café (see my descriptions under "Capitol Hill" and "Georgetown" in Chapter III), and it even offers a children's menu with Yuppie-in-training items like peanut butter and jelly on a croissant.

The Shops at National Place are open Monday to Saturday from 10 a.m. to 7 p.m. (on Thursday till 8 p.m.), on Sunday from noon to 5 p.m. Cafés open earlier for breakfast, and restaurants stay open later.

NEWSPAPERS AND MAGAZINES: Periodicals, 3109 M St. NW (tel. 333-6115), boasts "the largest selection of periodicals in the U.S." Whether you're seeking the St. Louis Post, Soviet Life, or the Sunday London Times, you'll find it here, along with at least a dozen magazines on subjects like needlework and a similar number about woodworking, photography, fishing, boating, muscle building, and food and wine. There are magazines in Arabic, Italian, French, German, and just about every other language; comic books; a magazine for skateboard enthusiasts called Thrasher; another for people who like knives called Blade. I could go on and on. It makes great browsing. And you can even pick up such mundane publications as Newsweek and People while you're here. Open daily from 8 a.m. to 10 p.m. There's another location at International Square, 1825 I St. NW at the Farragut West Metro (tel. 223-2526). It's open weekdays from 7 a.m. to 7 p.m., on weekends from 10 a.m. to 5 p.m.

RECORDS AND TAPES: Melody Record Shop, 1529 Connecticut Ave. NW at Q St. (tel. 232-4002), discounts all records and tapes 10% to 20% and sells new albums at 20% to 40% off. They carry a wide selection of rock, classical, jazz, pop, show music, new wave, folk, and international records. This is also a good place to shop for discounted cassette and CD players, and blank tapes and cassettes. Open Monday to Saturday from 10 a.m. to 9 p.m., on Sunday from noon to 5 p.m.

Olsson's Records, mentioned above at its Georgetown location, 1239 Wisconsin Ave. NW, between M and N Sts. (tel. 338-6712), has an equally complete selection and offers similar discounts. Other locations are at 1307 19th St. NW at N St. (tel. 785-2662) and 19th and L Sts. NW (tel. 785-5037). Call for days and hours.

The biggest selection of records, tapes, cassettes, and CDs in town is at **Tower Records,** 2000 Pennsylvania Ave. NW at the corner of 21st and I Sts. (tel. 331-2400). In fact, this 18,000-square-foot store is, the company claims, the third-largest record store in the country (the other two are Tower Records emporia in New York). There are large departments for jazz, rock, classical, and any other type of music you might favor. And a quintessentially '80s ambience is created by flashing lights, ultramodern decor, and about 20 monitors showing rock videos, cartoons, and movies like *The Road Warrior.* Everything is sold for at least $1 below list, less for sale items. Ongoing contests—drawings for trips to reggae festivals in Jamaica, stereo equipment, concert tickets, etc.— add to the fun. Open daily from 9 a.m. to midnight.

RESALE AND THRIFT SHOPS: Big families are no longer in fashion, but children still outgrow clothes at the alarming rate they did in hand-me-down days. That's why a store like **Kid's Stuff,** 5615 39th St. NW, between McKinley and Northampton Sts. just off Connecticut Ave. (tel. 244-2221), is such a find. This is no junk shop. The owners take on consignment only quality merchandise in excellent condition, and they display it attractively. You'll always find major brand and designer name clothing—Oshkosh, Florence Eisman, Levis, Gloria Vanderbilt, Polly Flinders, Ruth of Carolina, etc.—as well as toys, children's furniture, strollers, and even maternity clothes. Open Monday to Saturday from 10 a.m. to 5 p.m.; closed Saturday during July and August.

Another excellent resale shop where everything is screened, cleaned, and in mint condition, is **Once Is Not Enough,** 4830 MacArthur Blvd. NW near Reservoir Rd. (tel. 337-3072). Consignors are mostly upper-crust Washingtonians, many of whom think once—or at most a few times—is enough to wear their fancy duds. Hence, finds like a cream-colored delustered satin Galanos gown with lace and seed pearls worn by a prominent Washington lady to receive visiting royalty, originally over $1,000, sold here for $150. Or a barely worn, perfectcondition Ralph Lauren cotton blouse retailing for $125, here $10. No wonder that many locals are practically addicted to this shop. In addition to women's designer clothing, you'll find an excellent selection of exclusive children's clothes, jewelry, furs, men's formal wear, and occasionally toys. There's an ongoing sale rack. Open Monday to Saturday from 10 a.m. to 4:30 p.m., till 8 p.m. on Thursday.

If the above is all too fancy, and you'd like to wade through the usual thrift-shop jumble, try **Better Buys,** 4435 Wisconsin Ave. NW at Albemarle St. (tel. 363-4165). Here the pickings always include men's, women's, and children's clothing (some of it designer labels), toys, and jewelry, but you also might come across a pair of ski boots, a set of barbells, an African sculpture, glassware, China, a toaster oven, or a Persian rug. Better Buys is run by the National Council of Jewish Women and Pioneer Women, and profits go to various charities they support. Open Monday to Saturday from 10 a.m. to 5 p.m.

Chapter VIII

EXCURSIONS FROM THE CAPITAL

1. Arlington
2. Alexandria
3. Potomac Plantations
4. Fredericksburg

GRANTED, THERE'S PLENTY to keep the ardent sightseer occupied for well over a month without ever leaving the District. But within a day's drive of the capital are attractions so fascinating—and so relevant to your Washington experience—that they easily merit wearing out another pair of shoes. Read this chapter carefully and consider planning a few days of your vacation away from the Mall time-traveling through the nation's history.

1. Arlington

ARLINGTON NATIONAL CEMETERY: The Arlington Memorial Bridge at the base of the Lincoln Memorial symbolizes the reunion of North and South after the Civil War. On the Virginia side, in Arlington National Cemetery, is the restored mansion of Confederate leader Robert E. Lee.

For over a century Arlington National Cemetery has been a cherished American shrine commemorating the lives of members of the United States armed forces, but these grounds have always figured prominently in American history. In 1778 the "Arlington estate" was purchased by John Parke Custis, son of Martha Washington by her first marriage. Custis died during the siege of Yorktown, and his son, George Washington Parke Custis, inherited the estate and continued to develop it. He erected the Greek Revival Custis-Lee mansion (his daughter married Robert E. Lee), today known as **Arlington House.** The house and grounds were in Mrs. Lee's possession when the Civil War broke out, and the property was seized by the U.S. government. It was many years after the war, following lengthy litigation, that the Supreme Court ruled Robert E. Lee's son, George Washington Custis Lee (it does get confusing; why couldn't they have called an occasional kid Larry or Steve?), to be the rightful owner. In 1883 Lee sold the Arlington estate to the U.S. government for $150,000.

Arlington National Cemetery is open to visitors April through September from 8 a.m. to 7 p.m., until 5 p.m. the rest of the year. Its seemingly endless graves mark the mortal remains of the honored dead, the known and unknown, who served in the Revolutionary War, the War of 1812, the Mexican War, the Civil War, the Indian Campaigns, the Spanish-American War, the Philippine Insurrection, World Wars I and II, the Korean War, Vietnam, and Grenada. Two presidents, William Howard Taft and John F. Kennedy, are interred here, as are Robert F. Kennedy, capital architect Pierre Charles L'Enfant, Rear Admiral Robert E. Peary, John Foster Dulles, two *Challenger* crew members, and many other notables. A more complete list is provided on a free map distributed at the Visitor Center. Call 692-0931 for details.

Getting There and Getting Around

You can either drive over the bridge and park in the huge lots (you're not allowed to drive around the cemetery) or take the Metro to the Arlington Cemetery stop on the Blue Line. Once arrived, unless you're a hiking enthusiast, head for the **Visitor Center** and purchase a $2.25 **Tourmobile** ticket ($1 for children 3 to 11) that allows you to stop at all major sights and reboard when you're ready. Service is continuous, and the narrated commentary is interesting. On the other hand, walking makes for a more contemplative experience. Riding the Tourmobile with crowds of sightseeing tourists (usually in a holiday mood) makes me feel like I'm at Universal Studios. A good compromise is to walk some and ride some. On hot and humid summer days, walking requires an almost Spartan determination.

John F. Kennedy and Robert F. Kennedy Gravesites

Just south of Arlington House, the gravesite monument to Pres. John F. Kennedy is marked by an eternal flame. It's rendered additionally poignant by the presence of the small graves of two infants who predeceased their father—a son, Patrick Bouvier Kennedy (August 7–9, 1963) and an unnamed daughter (born and died August 23, 1956)—and the nearby grave, marked by a simple white cross, of the president's brother, Sen. Robert F. Kennedy. It's a place for quiet contemplation, best achieved if you arrive as close as possible to 8 a.m. before the hordes of tourists and "classroomfuls" of youngsters descend. Looking north there's a spectacular view of the capital city across the river (during his presidency Kennedy once remarked of this spot, "I could stay here forever"). A few steps below the gravesite is a wall inscribed with JFK quotations, including the one he's most remembered for, "And so my fellow Americans, ask not what your country can do for you, ask what you can do for your country. My fellow citizens of the world, ask not what America will do for you, but what together we can do for the freedom of man."

The Tomb of the Unknown Soldier

Watched over by America's most distinguished honor guard (specially chosen members of the First Battalion of the Third U.S. Infantry), the Tomb of the Unknown Soldier is a tribute to all soldiers who have given their lives for their country in war. The 50-ton white marble tomb rests above the remains of unidentified soldiers slain during World War I, World War II, Korean War, and Vietnam unknowns are in the crypts on the plaza in front of it. Plan your visit to coincide with the changing of the guard ceremony—an impressive ritual of rifle maneuvers, heel clickings, and military salutes. It takes place every hour on the hour October through March, every half hour the rest of the year. Adjoining the tomb is the Greek Revival outdoor Memorial Amphitheater, used for special Easter Sunrise, Memorial Day, and Veteran's Day services. Free Tourmobile transportation from the Visitor Center parking lot is provided on these occasions.

Arlington House

After it was acquired by the U.S. government in 1883, Arlington House was used for several decades as office space and living quarters for cemetery staff. In 1925, however, Congress empowered the secretary of war to restore the house to its pre-Civil War appearance and furnish it with original pieces (insofar as possible) and replicas. Since 1933 the house has been under the auspices of the U.S. Department of the Interior, and in 1955 Congress designated it a permanent memorial to Robert E. Lee. It was from this house that Lee received word of the dissolution of the Union and Virginia's secession. He left the next morning to offer his services to his state and never returned to the house.

There's a self-guided tour, and volunteers in period dress are on hand to give an introductory talk, hand out brochures, and answer questions. Actually, it's nice being able to tour at your own pace. Entrance is via the greenhouse. You'll see Custis's painting studio, later used by Mrs. Lee as a morning room; 1838 portraits of the Lees over the mantels in the White Parlor; the center hall, where the family welcomed Lee home after the Mexican War; the family parlor in which the Lees were married; the dining room where a portrait of G. W. P. Custis, builder of Arlington House, hangs over the fireplace; the upstairs bedrooms and playroom; the pantry with its original walnut cupboard; the schoolroom/sewing room; the Custises' bedroom; a guest room; the winter kitchen with its huge fireplace; and the wine cellar. About 30% of the furnishings are original. Servants' quarters and a small museum adjoin. Admission is free. Open daily from 9:30 a.m. to 4:30 p.m. October to March, till 6 p.m. April through September (closed Christmas and New Year's Days).

THE IWO JIMA STATUE: On the northern periphery of Arlington National Cemetery, just off Route 50, is the U.S. Marine Corps War Memorial, a symbol of the nation's esteem for the honored dead of the U.S. Marine Corps. The tribute is the Iwo Jima statue, recalling the marine invasion of Iwo Jima in February 1945 and the placing of a flag atop the island's extinct 550-foot-high volcano, Mount Suribachi. Newsphotographer Joe Rosenthal won a Pulitzer Prize for his photo of the flag-raising, and sculptor Felix W. de Weldon, then on duty, was moved to create a sculpture based on the scene Rosenthal had captured. Three survivors of the flag-raising posed for the work (the other participants had been killed during later phases of the Iwo Jima battle, but Weldon used photographs and other data in modeling their faces). The figures, 32 feet high, are shown erecting a 60-foot bronze flagpole from which an actual flag flies 24 hours a day. On the base of the memorial are the names and dates of every principal Marine Corps engagement since the founding of the corps; the inscription, "In honor and in memory of the men of the United States Marine Corps who have given their lives to their country since November 10, 1775"; and the tribute of Fleet Admiral Chester W. Nimitz to the fighting men of Iwo Jima: "Uncommon valor was a common virtue."

The grounds are used for military concerts/parades on Tuesday from 7 to 8:30 p.m. in summer, and at all times many visitors picnic on the grass.

THE NETHERLANDS CARILLON: Close to the Iwo Jima statue is the Netherlands Carillon, a gift from the people of Holland, with 49 bells, each carrying an emblem signifying a segment of Dutch society. For instance, the smallest bells represent Dutch youth. Verses cast on each bell were composed by poet Ben van Eysselsteijn. The carillon was officially dedicated on May 5, 1960, the 15th anniversary of the liberation of the Netherlands from the Nazis. The 127-foot-high open steel tower housing it stands on a plaza with steps guarded by two bronze lions. Over 15,000 tulip bulbs are planted on the surrounding grounds, a beautiful display in spring. Carillon concerts are presented from 2 to 4 p.m. on Saturday and national holidays from April through September. Visitors are permitted into the tower after the carillonneur performs to enjoy spectacular views of Washington.

THE PENTAGON: Hawk or dove, you'll find it interesting to tour the Pentagon (tel. 695-1776), the immense five-sided headquarters of the American military establishment. Built during the early years of World War II, it's the world's largest office building, housing 24,000 employees. For their convenience, it contains a complete indoor shopping mall (not the kind with fountains and skylights; the ambience is more like a bomb shelter), complete with a bank, post office, Amtrak ticket office, beauty salon, dry cleaner, vision clinic, shoe repair shop, clothing boutiques, a jeweler, a florist, and more. It's a self-contained world. There are many mind-boggling statistics to underscore the vastness of the Pentagon—for example, the building contains enough phone cable to run halfway to the moon!

For almost 30 years the Pentagon was probably the only military ministry in the world completely open to the general public. However, Vietnam-era demonstrations and an actual bomb explosion in a fourth-floor washroom in 1972 changed all that. You can, however, take a free tour of certain areas. The tour takes an hour and 20 minutes, and no reservation is necessary. Departure is from the Concourse area; the line forms near the Metro exit. In tourist season avoid a long wait on line by arriving at 8:30 a.m.; you can shop for souvenirs while you wait. Tours leave every half hour on the half hour between 9:30 a.m. and 3:30 p.m. May 1 to September 30; the rest of the year is the same except the 10:30 a.m. and 1:30 and 3 p.m. tours are eliminated.

The best way to get to the Pentagon is via Metrorail's Blue or Yellow Lines right into the Concourse area. If you drive, take I-395 to Boundary Channel Drive North Parking Exit, and park in the E-1 lot on the left-hand side. It costs 20¢ an hour to park and shuttle buses make frequent runs between the lot and the Concourse.

The tour begins with a short introductory film about the development of the Pentagon. Then a crew-cut military guide, walking backward to ensure that tour participants don't wander into security areas, takes you around. You'll first visit the **Commander-in-Chief Corridor,** lined with portraits of all past presidents (here you'll learn a bit of presidential trivia; for instance, that William Harrison gave the longest inauguration speech on the coldest day of the year, causing him to catch pneumonia and die so that he also served the shortest term). You'll also see:

The **Air Force Art Collection,** which holds works commemorating historical events for the U.S. Air Force, including cartoons done by Walt Disney when he was an ambulance driver during World War I.

The **POW Alcove,** hung with artist conceptions of life in POW camps like the "Hanoi Hilton."

The **Air Force Executive Corridor,** where, as you might have guessed, air force heads have their offices. It's lined with models of past and present air force craft.

The **General Daniel James Alcove,** commemorating the first black man to achieve the rank of four-star general. He's buried in Arlington National Cemetery.

The **POW-MIA Corridor** where the over-2,400 men who are still missing in action are honored with a flame that will burn until they are all accounted for.

A fascinating display of **recruitment posters** dating back as far as the 18th century.

The **Marine Corps Alcove,** a small display, because the marines are actually headquartered in the Navy Annex a quarter of a mile away. Did you know the reason the marines are called "leathernecks" is that they used to wear leather collars to protect their necks from fatal sword blows?

The **Navy Executive Corridor,** lined with British artist John Hamilton's paintings of World War II navy battle scenes; doors in this corridor are modeled after ship doors.

The **Army Executive Corridor,** or Marshall Corridor, named for Gen. George C. Marshall, the only military man ever to receive a Nobel Peace Prize (for the Marshall Plan used to reconstruct Europe after World War II). Displayed here are army command and divisional flags and 168 army campaign streamers dating from 1775 through Grenada.

The best art (most military art is not likely to end up at the National Gallery) is in the **Time/Life Art Collection Corridor.** During World War II *Time/Life* hired civilian artists to paint battle scenes at the front line. Most affecting is *Two-thousand Yard Stare,* showing a soldier suffering from battle fatigue due to lack of food, sleep, and water.

Gen. Douglas MacArthur is honored in the **MacArthur Corridor;** his career spanned 52 years during which he served in three wars under nine presidents.

The **Hall of Heroes** is where Medal of Honor recipients are commemorated. The medal is given out only during wartime and usually posthumously. The most highly decorated World War II soldier to receive a Medal of Honor was Audie Murphy.

The role of women throughout our armed service history is documented in **Women in the Military.**

State and territorial flags, from the first Union Jack to the 50-star flag of today, are displayed in the **Flag Corridor** where the tour concludes.

Note: You'll have to go through a metal detector and have your bags searched before the tour, so leave your guns, knives, and loose joints at the hotel.

2. Alexandria

Founded by a group of Scottish tobacco merchants, the seaport town of Alexandria came into being on a sunny day in July 1749 when a 60-acre tract of land was auctioned off in half-acre lots. Colonists came from miles around, in ramshackle wagons and stately carriages, in sloops, brigantines, and lesser craft, to bid on land that would be "commodious for trade and navigation and tend greatly to the ease and advantage of the frontier inhabitants. . . ." The auction took place in **Market Square** (still intact today), and the surveyor's assistant was a capable lad of 17 named George Washington.

Today the original 60 acres of lots in George Washington's hometown (also Robert E. Lee's) are the heart of **Old Town,** a multi-million-dollar urbanrenewal historic district. As you stroll Old Town's brick sidewalks and cobblestone streets, you'll see over 2,000 18th- and 19th-century buildings. You'll visit **Gadsby's Tavern,** where two centuries ago the men who created this nation discussed politics, freedom, and revolution over tankards of ale. You'll stand in the tavern's doorway where Washington reviewed his troops for the last time (he trained them in Market Square), visit Lee's boyhood home, and sit in the pews of **Christ Church** where both men worshipped.

Many Alexandria streets still bear original colonial names (King, Queen, Prince, Princess, Royal—you get the drift), while others like Jefferson, Franklin, Lee, Patrick, and Henry are obviously post-Revolutionary.

In this "mother lode of Americana" the past is being ever-increasingly restored in an ongoing archeological and historical research program. And though the present is manifested by an abundance of quaint shops, boutiques, art galleries, and restaurants capitalizing on the volume of tourism, it's still easy to imagine yourself in Colonial times—to smell the fragrant tobacco; hear the rumbling of horse-drawn vehicles over cobblestone; envision the oxcarts piled with crates of chickens, country-cured ham, and casks of cheese and butter; and picture the bustling waterfront where fishermen brought in the daily catch and foreign vessels unloaded exotic cargo as well as necessities of life.

GETTING THERE: It's about a seven-mile trip. If you're driving, take the Arlington Memorial or 14th Street Bridge to the scenic George Washington Memorial Parkway, which will take you right into King Street, Alexandria's main thoroughfare. Parking permits are available (details below).

But the easiest way to do the trip is via **Metro.** And the sights of Old Town are so compact, you won't need your car once you arrive. Take the Yellow Line to the King Street station. From the station, board a DASH bus (60¢) to King and Fairfax—right to the door of the Visitors Center. Take a transfer, and you can board any DASH bus for three hours. It's a short ride from the station; in fact you could walk it, but better to save your feet for sightseeing. *Note:* Many Alexandria attractions are closed on Monday, so that's not the best day to come.

FIRST STOP IN ALEXANDRIA: Before you do anything else, visit the **Ramsay House Visitors Center,** 221 King St. at Fairfax St. (tel. 703/549-0205), which is open daily from 9 a.m. to 5 p.m. (closed Thanksgiving, Christmas, and New Year's Days). Here you can pick up a map/self-guided walking tour, DASH bus schedule, and brochures about the area; find out about special events that might be taking place during your visit; and get answers to any questions you might have about accommodations, restaurants, sights, shopping, and whatever else.

If you came by car, get a free three-day parking permit here for gratis parking at any two-hour meter for as many hours as you like.

Also available at Ramsay House: a block ticket for admission to four historic Alexandria properties: Gadsby's Tavern, Lee's Boyhood Home, the Carlyle House, and the Lee-Fendall House, all major sights. The ticket, which can also be purchased at any of the four buildings, costs $5 for adults, a $3 saving over purchasing the tickets separately. Children 6 to 17 pay $3; under 6, free.

You'll find the staff friendly and knowledgeable; they'll even be happy to book your hotel room or make restaurant reservations.

By the way, you've already begun your historic tour by visiting Ramsay House, a reconstruction of the first house in Alexandria.

GETTING AROUND: As a glance at your walking-tour map will indicate, Old Town is pretty compact. Park your car for the day, don comfortable shoes, and start walking—it's the easiest way. It's helpful to know, when looking for addresses, that Alexandria is laid out in a simple grid system. Union to Lee Street is the 100 block, Lee to Fairfax the 200 block, and so on up. The cross streets (more or less going north and south) are divided north and south by King Street. King to Cameron is the 100 block north, Cameron to Queen the 200 block north, and so on. King to Prince is the 100 block south, etc., etc., etc.

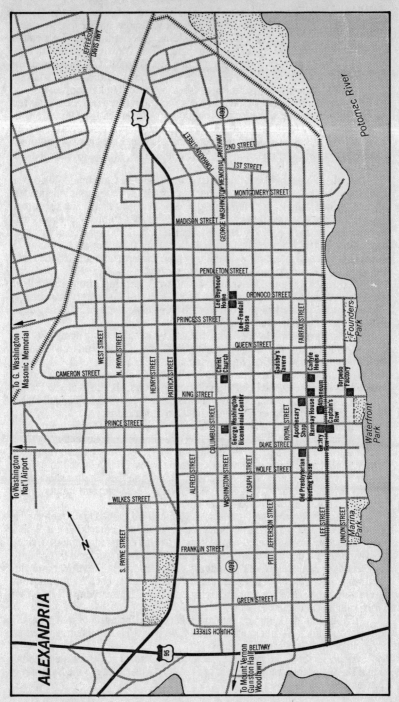

ALEXANDRIA

ANNUAL EVENTS: February is a big month here for obvious reasons: **George Washington's Birthday** honors the town's most famous native son. A recent year's celebration included a Colonial costume banquet followed by a ball at Gadsby's, a Revolutionary War encampment at Fort Ward, complete with British and Colonial uniformed troops engaging in a skirmish, Colonial games for children, strolling musicians, a period fashion show, and the nation's largest George Washington's Day parade attracting 75,000 to 100,000 people.

Several events center on Alexandria's Scottish roots. The fourth weekend in July each year is set aside for the traditional **Virginia Scottish Games,** a two-day Celtic festival featuring professional and amateur athletic events (ever seen a caber toss?); bagpipe, fiddling, harp, and Highland dancing competitions; sheep dog demonstrations; Scottish foods and goods, genealogy exhibits; and more.

Another Scottish celebration is the **Annual Scottish Christmas Walk** on the first Saturday in December, just a debut of Alexandria's numerous yuletide festivities. Kilted bagpipers, Highland dancers, Scottish clans, Scottish breed horses and dogs parade through the streets, and many holiday events center around the parade—cooking demonstrations, fashion shows, music, storytelling, films, hanging of wreaths and holly; caroling (with bagpipe accompaniment); puppet and magic shows; a military reenactment; hot mulled punch; and on a less frivolous note, a Scottish worship service.

And while we're in December (second week), there's also the **Old Town Christmas Candlelight Tour** at historic homes and an 18th-century tavern. Traditional music, carolers singing on street corners, Colonial dancing, string quartets, and refreshments are part of the fun.

Not to be outdone by the Scots, the city's Irish stage a big annual **St. Patrick's Day Parade** on the second Saturday in March; it's followed by a "hooley" in Market Square with Irish entertainment.

And though definitely outdone by Washington festivities, Alexandria's other famous citizens, the Lees' (Revolutionary War Col. "Light Horse Harry" Lee and his son, Robert E.) joint birthdays are feted at the Lee-Fendall House and Lee's boyhood home on the fourth Sunday each January.

Chiliheads (that's what aficionados of "bowls of red" call themselves) won't want to miss the annual **War Between the States Chili Cookoff** in October at Waterfront Park. There are contestants from almost every U.S. state and territory, and you can taste all the entries (each contestant is required to prepare about 25 gallons) if you pay a few dollars' admission fee. The proceeds go to charity. Fiddlers contests, jalapeño pepper–eating contests, and country music add to the fun. Call 703/683-5340 for details.

On **August Tavern Days** (determined annually) Colonial life is recreated at Gadsby's with 18th- and 19th-century music, food, and entertainment. This is your chance to sample biscuits and switchel, (a drink containing molasses, cider, and vinegar!). There are also events for children. On a weekend in mid-July, authentically equipped Civil War military units demonstrate Civil War camp life and stage a **Reenactment of the Battle of Fort Stevens** at Fort Ward Park complete with mock casualties and smoking muskets. The everyday life of a Civil War soldier is highlighted.

Throughout the summer, **Sundays at Fort Ward** include different programs on selected Sundays—demonstrations of Civil War drills and firearms, lectures, musical performances, and suchlike.

Again in the military mode, Colonial regiments recreate **Washington's Final Review of the Troops** in front of Gadsby's Tavern the second Saturday in November.

As part of the annual **Historic Garden Week in Virginia,** the fourth Saturday in April is highlighted by tours of privately owned homes and gardens in Alexandria. April is also time for the month-long **Sculpture Festival,** an indoor/outdoor show of contemporary art by regional artists.

Every spring and fall there's a **Lyceum Lunchtime Lecture Series** with free programs at 12:30 p.m. every Friday at the Bicentennial Center. Participants bring lunch (coffee and tea are provided), listen to lectures, and see demonstrations on a historic topic (like "Those Inventive Victorians").

Finally, there's the **Red Cross Waterfront Festival** on an annually selected weekend in June, celebrating Alexandria's historic importance as a seaport with historic ships, boat races, ship tours, entertainment, food booths, historic walking tours of the waterfront, nautical art exhibits, children's games, films, balloon ascents, fireworks, regattas, concerts, and other exciting happenings; this is a biggie.

Those are only the *major* events. If you're planning to participate in any of them, book your accommodations far ahead and contact the Visitors Center for details and necessary advance tickets.

Whenever you come, you're sure to run into some activity or other—a jazz festival, tea garden or tavern gambol, quilt exhibit, wine tasting, or organ recital. It's all part of Alexandria's *ceād mile failte* (100,000 welcomes) to visitors.

WHAT TO SEE: Your walking tour brochure lists 17 attractions. The following, beginning with the four on the block ticket, are in the not-to-be-missed category.

About Admissions: Chances are you'll have purchased the money-saving block ticket described above. If you purchase tickets separately to these first four attractions, adult admission is $2 and children pay $1.

Note: Many attractions are closed on Monday.

Gadsby's Tavern Museum

Alexandria was at the crossroads of Colonial America, and the center of life in Alexandria was Gadsby's Tavern, 134 North Royal St. at Cameron St. (tel. 703/838-4242). Consisting of two buildings, the 1770 City Tavern and the 1792 City Hotel, it's named today for a memorable owner, Englishman John Gadsby, who combined the hostelries in 1796 transforming a simple "ordinary" into a "gentleman's tavern" renowned for elegance and comfort. The rooms are restored to their 18th-century appearance with the help of modern excavations and colonial inventories that included such minutiae as lime squeezers.

It was at Gadsby's that itinerant merchants sold their wares, the latest hats from London were shown, and traveling doctors and dentists practiced on hapless patients. There were elegant entertainments, lottery drawings, theatrical performances, Jockey Club and town meetings. The second-floor ballroom with its musicians' gallery was the scene of Alexandria's most lavish parties, and since 1797 George Washington's annual birthday ball and banquet has been a tradition here.

On the 30-minute tour, you'll get a good look at the Tap Room, Game Room (where tobacco was sometimes used as currency), the Assembly Room, the second floor ballroom, typical bedrooms, and the underground ice house, which was filled each winter from the icy river.

Gadsby's is open Tuesday to Saturday from 10 a.m. to 5 p.m., on Sunday from 1 to 5 p.m. Tours depart at 15 minutes before and after the hour, with the final tour at 4:15 p.m.

To cap off the experience, you can dine at a Colonial-style restaurant in three tavern rooms (about which more later).

The Boyhood Home of Robert E. Lee

Revolutionary cavalry hero Gen. "Light Horse Harry" Lee brought his wife, Ann Hill Carter, and five children to the early Federal-style mansion at 607 Oronoco St. (tel. 703/548-8454) in 1812 when Robert, destined to become the Confederate military leader, was just five years old. A tour of the house, built in 1795, provides a glimpse into the gracious lifestyle of Alexandria's gentry. George Washington was an occasional guest of earlier occupants, Col. and Mrs. William Fitzhugh. In 1804 the Fitzhughs' daughter, Mary Lee, married Martha Washington's grandson, George Washington Parke Custis, in the drawing room. And the Custises' daughter married Robert E. Lee. It's a little complicated; suffice it to say that just about everyone was related.

Light Horse Harry died in 1818, but his widow, Anne Hill Carter, stayed on till 1825. In 1824 General Lafayette paid her a formal visit at the house as a tribute to his old comrade. The drawing room today is called the Lafayette Room to commemorate that visit.

On a fascinating tour, you'll see the nursery with its little canopied bed and toy box; Mrs. Lee's room (she was ill a great deal but had a magnificent setting in which to lie abed); the Lafayette Room, furnished in period antiques with the tea table set up for use; the morning room, where *The Iliad* translated into Latin reposes on a gaming table (both Light Horse Harry and Robert E. Lee were classics scholars), and the winter kitchen. Tours depart from 10 a.m. to 4 p.m. Monday to Saturday, from noon to 4 p.m. on Sunday.

The Lee-Fendall House

The handsome Greek Revival-style house at 614 Oronoco St., corner of Washington St. (tel. 703/548-1789), is a veritable Lee family museum of furniture, heirlooms, and documents. Light Horse Harry Lee never actually lived here, though he was a frequent visitor, as was his good friend, George Washington. He did own the original lot, but sold it to Philip Richard Fendall (himself a Lee on his mother's side), who built the house in 1785.

However, 37 Lees did occupy the house over a period of 118 years, and it was from this house that Harry wrote Alexandria's farewell address to Washington, delivered when he passed through the town on his way to assume the presidency. (Harry also wrote and delivered, but not at this house, the famous funeral oration to Washington that contained the immortal words: "First in war, first in peace, and first in the hearts of his countrymen.")

Fendall was not only a Lee, but he married three Lee wives, including Harry's first mother-in-law, and later, Harry's sister.

Of special interest on the 30-minute tour are the marvelous antique dollhouse collection on the third floor and the Colonial garden with its magnolia and chestnut trees, roses, and boxwood-lined paths. Much of the interior woodwork and glass is original.

Open from 10 a.m. to 4 p.m. Tuesday to Saturday, from noon to 4 p.m. on Sunday.

The Carlyle House

Not only is Carlyle House, 121 North Fairfax St. (tel. 703/549-2997), regarded as one of Virginia's most architecturally impressive 18th-century houses, it also figured prominently in American history. In 1752, Scottish merchant John Carlyle built the mansion for his bride, Sara Fairfax of Belvoir, who hailed from one of Virginia's most prominent families. It was patterned after a Scottish manor house, and furnished lavishly. Carlyle, a successful merchant, was able to import the best furnishings and appointments available abroad to his new Alexandria home.

When it was built, Carlyle House was a waterfront property with its own wharf. A social and political center, the house was visited by numerous great men of the time, George Washington among them. But its most important moment in history occurred in April 1755 when Maj. Gen. Edward Braddock, commander-in-chief of His Majesty's forces in North America, met with five colonial governors here and asked them to tax colonists to finance a campaign against the French and Indians. Colonial legislatures refused to comply, one of the first instances of serious friction between America and Britain. Nevertheless, Braddock made Carlyle House his headquarters during the campaign, and Carlyle was less than impressed with him. He called the general "a man of weak understanding . . . very indolent . . . a slave to his passions, women and wine, . . . as great an Epicure as could be in his eating, tho a brave man." Possibly these were the reasons his unfinanced campaign met with disaster. Braddock received, as Carlyle described it, "a most remarkable drubbing."

A tour of Carlyle House takes about 40 minutes. Two of the original rooms —the large parlor and the adjacent study—have survived intact; the former, where Braddock met the governors, has its original fine woodwork, paneling, and pediments. The house is furnished in period pieces; only a few of Carlyle's possessions remain. An upstairs room houses an exhibit called "A Workman's View," that explains 18th-century construction methods with hand-hewn beams and hand-wrought nails.

Tours are given every half hour on the hour and half hour between 10 a.m. and 4:30 p.m. Carlyle House is open Tuesday to Saturday from 10 a.m. to 5 o.m., on Sunday from noon to 5 p.m.

Christ Church

This sturdy red brick English-style church at 118 North Washington St., corner of Cameron St. (tel. 703/549-1450), would be an important national landmark even if its two most distinguished members were not Washington and Lee. It's been in continuous use since Colonial times (1773 to be exact).

There have, of course, been many changes since Washington's day. The bell tower, church bell, galleries, and organ were added by the early 1800s, the "wineglass" pulpit in 1890. But much of what was changed later has since been unchanged. The pristine white interior with wood moldings and gold trim is colonially correct, though modern heating has obviated the need for charcoal braziers and hot bricks. And for the most part, the original structure remains, including the hand-blown glass in the windows that the first worshippers gazed through when their minds wandered from the service. The town has grown up around the building that was first called "The Church in the Woods" because of its rural setting.

Christ Church has had its historic moments. Washington and other early church members discussed revolution in the churchyard, and Robert E. Lee met here with Richmond representatives who offered him command of the military forces of Virginia at the beginning of the Civil War. You can sit in the pew where George and Martha sat with her two Custis grandchildren, or in the Robert E. Lee family pew.

It's a tradition for U.S. presidents to attend a service here on a Sunday close to Washington's birthday and sit in his pew. One of the most memorable of these visits took place shortly after Pearl Harbor when Franklin Delano Roosevelt attended services with Winston Churchill on the World Day of Prayer. Ronald Reagan attended a service on February 21, 1982.

Visitors are welcome Monday to Saturday from 9:30 a.m. to 4:30 p.m., on Sunday from 2 to 5 p.m. (4:30 p.m. in winter), and of course you're invited to attend a service. There's no admission, but donations are appreciated. A docent gives brief lectures to visitors, but there's no formal tour. In 1987, the Old Parish Hall was completely restored to its original appearance; it now houses a gift shop. Do walk out in the weathered graveyard after you see the church. Alexandria's first and only burial ground until 1815, its oldest marked grave is that of Issac Pearce who died in 1771. The remains of 34 Confederate soldiers are also interred here.

The Stabler-Leadbeater Apothecary

When it closed its doors in 1933, this landmark drugstore at 105–107 South Fairfax St. (tel. 703/836-3713) was the second oldest in continuous operation in America. Run for five generations by the same family (beginning in 1792), its famous early patrons of course included Robert E. Lee (he purchased the paint for Arlington House here) and George Washington. Gothic Revival decorative elements and Victorian-style doors were added in the 1860s.

Today the apothecary looks much like it did in Colonial times, its shelves lined with about 900 of the original hand-blown gold-leaf-labeled bottles (the most valuable collection of antique medicinal bottles in the U.S., actually), old scales stamped with the royal crown, patent medicines, and equipment for blood letting. The clock on the rear wall and the porcelain-handled mahogany drawers are from about 1790, as are two mortars and pestles. Note the globes of colored water in the window. An apothecary tradition (many modern drugstores still have them), they're supposed to have warned the illiterate of epidemics like plague and cholera. Among the shop's documentary records are such as this 1802 epistle from Mount Vernon: "Mrs. Washington desires Mr. Stabler to send by the bearer a quart bottle of his best Castor Oil and the bill for it."

The Stabler-Leadbeater Apothecary is open Monday to Saturday from 10 a.m. to 4 p.m. except around lunchtime. There's no tour, but a ten-minute recording guides you around the displays. Admission is free; the adjoining antique shop, however, uses its proceeds to maintain the apothecary.

The Old Presbyterian Meeting House

Presbyterian congregations have worshipped in Virginia since Jamestown days when the Rev. Alexander Whittaker converted Pocahontas. The brick church at 321 South Fairfax St. (tel. 703/549-6670) was built by Scots-Irish pioneers in 1774. Though it wasn't George Washington's church, the Meeting House bell tolled continuously for four days after his death in December 1799, and memorial services were preached from the pulpit here by Presbyterian, Episcopal, and Methodist ministers. According to the Alexandria paper of the day, "The walking being bad to the Episcopal church the funeral sermon of George Washington will be preached at the Presbyterian Meeting House. . . ." Two months later on Washington's birthday Alexandria citizens marched from Market Square to the church to pay respects to his memory.

Many famous Alexandrians are buried in the church graveyard—John and Sara Carlyle, Dr. James Craik (the surgeon who treated, some say killed, Washington, dressed Lafayette's wounds at Brandywine, and ministered to the dying Braddock at Monongahela), and William Hunter, Jr., founder of the St. Andrew's Society of Scottish descendants (bagpipers pay homage to his grave the first Saturday of each December). It is also the site of a Tomb of an Unknown Revolutionary Soldier, and Dr. James Muir, whose distinguished ministry spanned the years 1789–1820, is buried beneath the pulpit in his gown and bands.

The original Meeting House was gutted by a lightning fire in 1835 but restored to its simple Colonial beauty in just a few years. The present bell, said to be recast from the metal of the old one, was hung in a newly constructed belfry in 1843, and a new organ was installed in 1849.

The Meeting House closed its doors in 1889 and for 60 years it was virtually abandoned. Older Alexandrians recall playing hide and seek in the graveyard. But in 1949 it was reborn as a living church, and today the old Meeting House looks much as it did following the restoration after the fire. The original parsonage, or manse, is still intact.

The church is open to visitors Monday to Friday from 9 a.m. to 4 p.m., and on most Sundays from noon to 4 p.m. Services are on Sunday at 11 a.m. There's no admission fee and no guided tour, but there are recorded narratives in the church and graveyard.

The Athenaeum

A handsome Greek Revival building with a classic tetrastyle portico and unfluted Doric columns, the Athenaeum, 201 Prince St., at Lee St. (tel. 703/548-0035), is home to the Northern Virginia Fine Arts Association. Their widely varying art exhibits run the gamut from Matisse lithographs to shows of East Coast artists to state-of-the-art contemporary architecture in the Washington area. Many important juried shows take place here. The building itself dates to 1851, and originally contained the Bank of the Old Dominion. The bank's operations were interrupted by the Civil War when Alexandria was occupied by Union forces and Yankee troops turned the building into a commissary. Later, Edward Leadbeater of the famed apothecary used it to store pharmaceuticals, and still later it had an incarnation as a Free Methodist church.

Open Tuesday to Saturday from 10 a.m. to 4 p.m., on Sunday from 1 to 4 p.m. Gallery shows take place September to June. The building is always closed in August and sometimes in July as well. Admission is free; donations are appreciated.

The Lyceum

Alexandria's other Greek Revival building, the Lyceum, 201 South Washington St. (tel. 703/838-4994), is a museum focusing on Alexandria's history from colonial times through the 20th century. It features changing exhibits (they range from decorative art shows to an exploration of the participation of Alexandria citizens in creating the Constitution), and an ongoing series of lectures, concerts, and films. An adjoining nonprofit shop carries 18th-century reproductions, candles, needlepoint patterns, and such.

In addition, the Lyceum serves as an information center for all Virginia state attractions, highlighting Alexandria attractions in particular. Here you can pick up maps and brochures, and a knowledgeable staff will be happy to answer your questions.

But even without its manifold offerings, the brick and stucco Lyceum itself merits a visit. Built in 1839, it was designed in the Doric temple style (with imposing white columns) to serve as a lecture, meeting, and concert hall. The first floor originally contained the Alexandria Library and various natural science and historical exhibits. It was an important center of Alexandria's cultural life until the Civil War when Union forces took it over for use as a hospital. After the war it became a private residence, and still later it was subdivided for office space. In 1969, however, it was only the City Council's use of eminent domain that prevented the Lyceum's demolition for the proverbial parking lot.

The Lyceum is open seven days a week from 10 a.m. to 5 p.m., there's no admission charge. There are facilities for the handicapped.

Fort Ward Museum and Park

A short drive from Old Town, at 4301 West Braddock Rd. (tel. 703/838-4848), is a 45-acre museum, park, and historic site that takes you for a leap forward in Alexandria history to the Civil War. The action here centers, as it did in the early 1860s, on an actual Union fort which Lincoln ordered erected to defend Washington, D.C. It was part of a system of Civil War forts surrounding Washington. The Northwest Bastion has been restored, and six mounted guns (there were originally 36) face south waiting for trouble that in fact never came; the fort was not attacked.

Visitors can explore the fort and replicas of the Ceremonial Entrance Gate and an officer's hut. Markers throughout the area provide informative commentary. There's a museum on the premises where you can view Civil War weaponry, armor, correspondence, and exhibits on medical care and the feeding of troops. In addition, there are changing exhibits on subjects such as the Civil War navy, period artillery, and Lincoln memorabilia. And tours of the fort are given by guides in Union soldier costumes on selected Sundays.

On a more peaceful note is the **Annual Heirloom Care Series** in October and November, featuring advice on home care of antiques and collectibles.

There are picnic areas with barbecue grills in the woods surrounding the fort, and concerts are presented on Thursday evenings June through mid-September in the outdoor amphitheater. The park is open daily from 9 a.m. to sunset; the museum, from 9 a.m. to 5 p.m. Tuesday to Saturday, from noon to 5 p.m. on Sunday. To get here from Old Town, follow King Street west, make a right on Kenwood Avenue, then a left on West Braddock Road. Continue for three-quarters of a mile to the entrance, on your right.

The Torpedo Factory

Studio space for some 200 professional artists and craftspeople who create and sell their own works on the premises is contained in this block-long, three-story building at 105 North Union St. (tel. 703/838-4565). Here you can see artists at work—potters, painters, print-makers, photographers, sculptors, and jewelers, as well as those engaged in making stained-glass windows, wall hangings, quilts, even violins.

In addition, on permanent display are exhibits on Alexandria history provided by **Alexandria Archaeology** (tel. 838-4399), also headquartered here and engaged in extensive city research. Their special exhibit area and lab are open to the public on Friday and Saturday from 11 a.m. to 5 p.m. with a docent or staff member on hand to answer questions. Changing exhibits here have included "Artifacts, Advertisements, and Archaeology," featuring artifacts excavated from merchant sites during urban-renewal projects on King Street in the 1960s and 1970s. Another was "Archaeologists at work: Excavations at the Stabler-Leadbeater Apothecary Shop."

And this being Alexandria, the building itself is of course of historic interest. It's a converted torpedo shell-case factory built by the U.S. Navy in 1918 and operated as such through the early 1950s. Later, the Smithsonian used it to store various and sundry, including dinosaur bones.

The Torpedo Factory is open seven days a week from 10 a.m. to 5 p.m. Admission is free.

The George Washington Masonic National Memorial

American Masons will of course want to make a pilgrimage to their world mecca at King St. and Callahan Dr. (tel. 703/683-2007), a memorial to their most illustrious member and the first Worshipful Master of Alexandria Lodge No. 22, George Washington. And though it wouldn't be first on my list of sights for non-Masons, if you're here for a while, do visit.

The imposing neoclassical shrine on 36 acres of land atop Shooter's Hill was dedicated in 1932 with President Hoover assisting in the rites. And both Taft and Coolidge spoke at the cornerstone laying in 1923.

On a thorough 45-minute guided tour of the building, elucidated by recorded narratives and slide presentations, you'll see the ornate Great Hall, wherein a 17-foot bronze statue of George Washington is the focal point; Memorial Hall, in which murals and stained-glass windows depict significant episodes and people in Washington's life; a replica of the original Lodge No. 22 containing Washington memorabilia (both his and Lafayette's Masonic aprons, the trowel he used to lay the cornerstone of the Capitol, and on a more grisly note, bleeding instruments used during his last illness and his bedroom clock stopped at 10:20 p.m., the time he died); museum objects ranging from a key to the Bastille (presented to the lodge by Lafayette) to pottery recovered in Alexandria digs, to Washington's family bible; the world's largest Persian rug, worth over $1 million; and such mystically titled chambers as the Royal Arch Chapel Room, the Cryptic Room, the Knight's Templar Chapel, and the Grotto Archives Room. On the ninth floor is an observatory parapet where the 360-degree panoramic view takes in the Potomac, Mount Vernon, the Capitol, and the Maryland shore. And back on the ground floor is a miniature mechanical Shriner's parade that marches round and round a large table to recorded music.

The Masonic Memorial is open from 9 a.m. to 5 p.m. daily (except Christmas, New Year's, and Thanksgiving) with free tours available every 45 minutes between 9:15 a.m. and 4 p.m.

The Schooner Alexandria

The Alexandria Seaport Foundation, an organization devoted to maritime heritage, acquired the Scandinavian schooner *Alexandria* (formerly the *Lindø*) in 1983, and when she's in port (sometimes she's elsewhere participating in tall-ship festivals) she's docked at Waterfront Park and open to the public weekends from noon to 5 p.m. A red-sailed Baltic trader vessel built in 1929 (she carried coal, dynamite, and other goods), the ship was remodeled for passenger use in the 1970s. You can tour above and below deck, see one stateroom (the others are used by the crew), and visit the rather elegant Main Salon downstairs. Call 703/549-7078 for details. The tour is free, but donations are appreciated.

Tours

Though it's easy to see Alexandria on your own, putting yourself in the hands of guides at the various attractions, you may find your experience enhanced by a comprehensive walking tour. Offered by several companies, these usually leave from Ramsay House, so you can get information on tour options there. Some have guides in Colonial dress.

SHOPPING AND BROWSING IN ALEXANDRIA: Old Town has hundreds of charming boutiques, antique stores, and gift shops selling everything from souvenir T-shirts to 18th-century reproductions. Some of the most interesting are at sightseeing attractions (like the Museum Shop at the Lyceum), but most are clustered on King and Cameron Streets and their connecting cross streets. Plan to spend a fair amount of time browsing in between visits to historic sites. A guide to antique stores is available at the Visitor Center. And here are some suggestions to get you started.

On King Street

The Tiny Dwelling, 1510 King St. (tel. 703/548-1223), is filled with charming dollhouses, furnishings, and accessories. There are little framed paintings, wallpapers, floor tiles, Oriental rugs, tiny electrical supplies, beautiful porcelain sinks and tubs, and a selection of every kind of furniture, including wicker.

Angie's Doll Boutique, 1114 King St. (tel. 703/683-2807), sells new and antique dolls of all races and nationalities, handcrafted dolls, modern collectibles, clothing, and clothing patterns.

Just upstairs in the same building is **Bachelor II Antiques** (tel. 703/836-0866), the delightful abode of hundreds of dolls and stuffed bears from all over the world. There are dolls that walk and sing, personality dolls (Elvis, Shirley Temple, et al.), and expensive collectibles like turn-of-the-century German bisques. As for bears, they range from tiny Paddingtons to the over-$500 Steiff 1980 papa (a collector's bear), "Bearilyn" Monroe, and "Cub Canabearal" in astronaut garb. Great browsing here.

The Small Mall, 118 King St., is a little warren of shops (about 11 of them), the most intriguing of which is **Serendipity** (tel. 703/683-3555), featuring traditional American craft items (much stenciling equipment), porcelain dolls, folk art and suchlike.

On Cameron Street

There are two charming toy stores your kids will enjoy. **John Davy Toys** at no. 301 (tel. 703/683-0079) has a lovely selection of dolls, books, games, building things, and puppets. And just next door at no. 303, **Granny's Place** (tel. 703/549-0119) specializes in imported and domestic children's clothing (up to size 14 for boys and girls) and wooden toys. Many excellent gifts for toddlers can be found here.

La Cuisine, 323 Cameron St. (tel. 703/836-4435), will delight those who can pore endlessly over copperware, cookbooks, terrines, and cooking implements.

Gossypia, 325 Cameron St. (tel. 703/836-6969), carries an exquisite line of Mexican and South American wedding dresses, Guatemalan and Mexican masks, and beautiful clothing and jewelry from India, Central America, and Thailand.

On South Union Street

At **The Christmas Attic,** 125 South Union St. (tel. 548-2829) it's always the holiday season. Christmas decorations and gifts are sold year round. Accoutrements of other holidays are sold in their proper months.

Caswell Massey, 203 South Union St. (tel. 703/548-5533), is most appropriately located in this historic town. Established in 1752 (the first store was in Rhode Island), it still offers the men's cologne (no. 6) that was used by George Washington, and presumably by Lafayette (Washington gave him some as a gift). Other intriguing products here include carrot soap, dwarf pine-scented bubble bath, beeswax moisturizer, porous plasters, Dolley Madison's white rose cologne, and lettuce-leaf-based hand cream—among hundreds of fascinating others.

The **Carriage House,** 215 South Union St., contains about six shops. Do check out **Rocky Road to Kansas** (tel. 703/683-0116), where over 100 traditional, new, and antique quilts are on display along with country accessories. Also notable here: reproductions of old wooden signs, quilting supplies, and handcrafted items (jewelry, rugs, pottery, hand-blown glass, etc.) at **Gadfly** (tel. 703/548-0218); the aromatic **Olde Town Coffee, Tea & Spice** (tel. 703/683-0856), which in addition to about 40 kinds of coffee and 60 kinds of tea has gourmet imports like German cornichons, Swiss vegetable pâté, and cordial balls with various liqueurs in the center; and **Laura of Olde Towne** and the adjoining **Laura Too** (tel. 703/548-1372) for an exquisite selection of dried flower arrangements and wreaths, handmade baskets, Paper White heirloom handmade white linen and cotton clothing for women and children, embroidered and lacy petticoats and pillows, distinctive handcrafted jewelry from the Texas hill country, and more.

On North Lee Street

Crilley Warehouse Mall, 218 North Lee St., houses about eight shops on two levels in a turn-of-the-century bakery. In later years the building served as a storehouse, hence the name. Among the most interesting of its shops are **Monday's Child** (tel. 703/548-3505) featuring gorgeous clothing for children; **Slightly Laced** (tel. 703/836-2666) for French brassieres, satin remarqué loungewear (it can be belted and double as fancy evening wear), hand-embroidered petticoats from Madeira, and many other lovely underthings; and **Great Gatsby** (tel. 703/683-0094) for '20s-look and romantic styles in women's clothing, including a great selection of costume jewelry.

On Prince Street

Olde Towne Gemstones, 6 Prince St. (tel. 703/836-1377), is owned by rock and fossil enthusiasts Pat, Mike, and Marvin Young. Some of the fossils you can buy here are 500-million-year-old specimens. There's also a wide-ranging collection of minerals, gemstones, petrified wood, and objets d'art and jewelry made from them. Banded agate clocks are a big item.

There's oodles more—unfortunately, more than space allows and much of it noteworthy—which you'll discover on your rambles around town.

WHERE TO EAT: After hours of trudging around Old Town shopping and sightseeing, you've earned your lunch. Alexandria offers numerous and diverse high-quality eateries. In fact, Washingtonians often drive down to Old Town just for a meal.

Absolutely great is the **Hard Times Cafe,** 1404 King St., near South West St. (tel. 703/683-5340), which caters to a diverse clientele including cowboys, cab drivers, and the Capitol Hill crowd. They all come for the top-secret-recipe homemade chilis (Cincinnati or Texas style; I prefer the later) and fresh-from-the-oven cornbread and pies. Not to mention the old-fashioned Texas chili parlor ambience, complete with southern flags and historic Old West photos on the walls, a longhorn steer hide on the ceiling, comfortable roomy oak booths, great country music on the jukebox, and a laid-back young staff in jeans and T-shirts. Lunch or dinner, a big bowl of Texas, Cincinnati (cooked with sweeter spices, including cinnamon), or vegetarian (soy protein) chili with or without beans is $3.55 and includes a big chunk of cornbread. Available extras for a quarter or less are cheese (parmesan or cheddar) and chopped onions. An order of homemade steak fries cooked with the skins is $1.45; deep-fried onion rings or a bottle of Lone Star beer to wash it all down, $1.75. For dessert there's homemade pecan walnut or apple crumb pie ($1.95).

Hard Times is open Monday to Thursday from 11:30 a.m. to 10 p.m., Friday and Saturday from 11:30 a.m. to 11 p.m., and on Sunday from 4 to 10 p.m. They don't take reservations, so arrive early or late and beat the hungry mob.

Why not a picnic, either combined with a visit to Fort Ward Park (described above), or right in Old Town at Founders Park, bordering the Potomac at the foot of Queen Street? It doesn't have picnic tables, but there are benches and there's plenty of grass to sit on. Market Square is another possibility.

Buy the fixings at **The Deli on the Strand,** 211 The Strand, entrance on

South Union St. between Duke and Prince Sts. (tel. 703/548-7222). They bake breads on the premises, so the aroma here is divine, and you can get reasonably priced cold-cut sandwiches on fresh-baked rye and wheat bread, as well as crois-sants, muffins, and on weekends, bagels. Also available are luscious homemade salads like seafood/pasta, about 75 varieties of cheeses, yummy desserts, beer, wine, and champagne. There are a few picnic tables outside.

Open 8 a.m. to 8 p.m. Monday to Thursday, till 9 p.m. on Friday and Satur-day, till 7 p.m. on Sunday.

Even fancier picnic fare (also a bit more expensive) is sold at a gourmet-to-go shop called **Bittersweet,** 103 North Alfred St. (tel. 703/549-2708). Here the offerings might include tarragon chicken with artichokes ($3 for a third of a pound), pasta with olive oil and fresh basil ($1.50 per serving), green beans in raspberry vinaigrette ($1.50 a serving), or chicken breast stuffed with spinach and ricotta ($3.40). For dessert a fresh-baked coffee blondie or chocolate cream cheese brownie is $1.

Open Monday to Friday from 11 a.m. to 5 p.m., Saturday 11 a.m. to 4 p.m.

So popular is the **Fish Market,** King and Union Sts. (tel. 703/836-5676), that even its original seven dining rooms were not ample to contain potential patrons. So it expanded to include another 3,000 square feet in the building next door. The original corner location is an over-200-year-old warehouse used to store cargo in the days when Alexandria was a major eastern seaport. Owner Ray Giovannoni renovated the entire building to its appearance, "during its mercantile heydey of the 19th century." Lots of ambience here—oak-plank flooring, beamed ceilings, exposed brick and stucco walls adorned with authen-tic nautical antiques (many of them retrieved from sunken ships), copper pots and pans suspended over a fireplace, copper-topped bars, saloon doors, and a breakfront used to display pewterware all contribute to the various dining rooms' cozy comfort. The newer Sunquest Room, named for a company sail-boat that went down in Hurricane Kate in 1985, is bright and sunny, with light streaming in through floor-to-ceiling cathedral windows. Its white walls are hung with antique musical instruments. You can dine on fresh seafood here for surprisingly little. At lunch a crab cake sandwich is $3.95, a hearty bowl of sea-food stew runs $2.95, and a platter of fried oysters costs $6.75, the latter served with fries, hush puppies, and coleslaw. Dinner entrees are just $1 or $2 higher. Wine, beer (a 32-ounce schooner is just $2), and all bar drinks are available; fresh fruit daiquiris are a house specialty. Only fresh-squeezed juices are used at the bar. At the entrance is a carry-out operation offering really good buys like an immense roast beef sandwich for $2.95 or eight ounces of chowder for $1.75. And finally, there's live entertainment—ragtime piano and sing-along—every night in the downstairs piano bar, the upstairs Main Dining Room, and the Sunquest Room.

Open daily from 11:15 a.m. to 2 a.m.

Named, in case you didn't know, for a character in *The Hobbit,* **Bilbo Baggins,** 208 Queen St. (tel. 703/683-0300), is a charming two-story restaurant offering scrumptious fresh and homemade fare. Both levels have lots of plants flourishing in the sunlight. The downstairs area is rustic looking, with wood-plank floors, wood-paneled walls, oak tables, and a working brick oven; up-stairs there's another dining room with stained-glass windows and seating on old church pews. It adjoins a lovely skylit wine bar with windows overlooking Queen Street treetops. Candlelit throughout at night, it becomes an even cozier setting. Bilbo described it long ago as "a perfect house, whether you like food or drink or storytelling or singing or just sitting and thinking best, or a pleasant mixture of them all. Merely to be there was a cure for weariness, fear or sad-ness."

Unless you plan to just sit and think, dinner is beyond our price range, but at lunch you might enjoy entrees for $5 to $7 such as quiche Lorraine, tortellini pesto, a turkey, avocado, and swiss sandwich on fresh-from-the-oven bread, or one of chef Michael Armellino's daily specials, perhaps fresh filet of salmon in sour cream/cucumber/lime sauce. There's also a Bilbo Baggins brunch featuring a choice of omelets like bacon, mushrooms and gruyère for $5.25. An extensive wine list is available (32 boutique wines are offered by the glass), as are all bar drinks and out-of-this-world homemade desserts such as steamed dark chocolate bread pudding topped with fresh sliced bananas.

Open for lunch Tuesday to Friday 11:30 a.m. to 2:30 p.m., Saturday from 11:30 a.m. to 3 p.m., for brunch on Sunday from 11 a.m. to 2:30 p.m. No reservations. Dinner entrees are in the $10 to $15 range, but affordable light fare is served between lunch and dinner.

One of the few places for an early breakfast in Alexandria is **Bread and Chocolate,** 611 King St. (tel. 703/548-0992), which like a Swiss *konditerei* has a bakery counter up front displaying a tempting array of fresh-baked breads, croissants, napoleons, chocolate truffle cakes, Grand Marnier cakes, Bavarian fruit tarts, and other goodies. The interior is modern, bright, and cheerful, with folk art prints on white walls lit by gallery lights and decorator bulbs.

At breakfast, a café mocha and an almond, chocolate, or nut-filled croissant will run you $2.80; fresh-squeezed orange juice is $1.45, and a three-minute egg with a selection of cheeses and a basket of bread goes for $4. The rest of the day, entrees such as quiche Lorraine, baker's salad (like a chef salad), and a fresh fruit plate with brie are all priced under $6 and served with a basket of fresh-baked breads. And after your meal, a trip to the bakery counter is, of course, irresistible.

Open Monday to Saturday from 7 a.m. to 7 p.m., on Sunday from 8 a.m. to 5 p.m. No reservations.

For a change of pace (how much quiche and homemade bread can you eat?), there's very good Greek fare at **Athenian Corner,** 801 King St. (tel. 703/836-0148), and though once again dinners are above our range, at lunch you get a lot of elegance for the price. The Flame's interior is most attractive: brick and stucco walls with pretty oil scenes of Greece painted in alcoves, seating in burgundy leather armchairs at tables draped with blue-and-white cloths, arched windows, lots of plants, and graceful chandeliers overhead. A combination appetizer—taramosalata, stuffed grapevine leaves, baby octopus in lemon/oil sauce, feta cheese, olives, and anchovies ($5.25 for two)—served with bread and butter, makes a decent light meal in itself. More substantial entrees like moussaka, pastitsio (baked macaroni with ground sirloin, topped with cheese, egg, and béchamel sauce), and souvlaki—all served with vegetables, potatoes, and bread and butter—are under $5. Homemade Greek pastries for dessert are delicious.

Lunch is served daily from 11 a.m. to 3 p.m.

In the spirit of history, pass through the portals where Washington reviewed his troops for the last time and lunch at the famous **Gadsby's Tavern,** Royal and Cameron Sts. (tel. 703/548-1288). Here the period furnishings, wood-plank floors, fireplace, and gaslight-style lamps recreate an authentic Colonial atmosphere. You dine off the same kind of pewter and china plates our forefathers used, and waiters and waitresses are appropriately costumed. The coachyard serves as an outdoor dining area.

All the fare is homemade, including the sweet Sally Lunn bread baked on the premises daily. You might start off with soup from the stockpot served with homemade brittlebread ($1.50), continue with an entree of baked ham and cheese pye (a sort of Early American quiche) or hot roasted turkey with bread/

sage stuffing and giblet gravy on Sally Lunn bread. Entrees at lunch are in the $6 range. For dessert try the creamy buttermilk custard pye with a hint of lemon or English trifle. Colonial "coolers" are also available—scuppernong, wench's punch, and such. The menu changes a bit for Sunday brunch, when you might order thick slices of toast dipped in a batter of rum and spices, with sausage, hash browns, and hot cinnamon syrup ($5.95). Half-priced children's portions are available. Dinner is very pricey.

Open for lunch Monday to Saturday from 11:30 a.m. to 3 p.m., for brunch on Sunday from 11 a.m. to 3 p.m.

A special offering at Gadsby's is the "Publick Table," a bountiful 18th-century feast on "the seasons best meats, fishes, fowl, vegetables, Sally Lunn bread, relishes, and a fine dessert. Two entrees, an appetizer, coffee, and a glass of port or Madeira are included in the price of $17, half for children, plus gratuity. That's far above the usual listings in this book, but this is more than just a meal. It's a feast with period entertainment. A serving wench entertains with toasts, songs, news, and humor. Publick Table takes place Sunday and Monday evenings at 6:30 p.m. and Sunday afternoons at 3:30 p.m. Reservations are essential.

Terlitzky's, 1324 King St., at South West St. (tel. 703/836-7885), is a Jewish, New York-style deli, or at least an Alexandria interpretation thereof. Unpretentious in decor, it has brown leather booths, Formica tables, and walls lined with photos of actors, many of them of proud owners' Sam and Mitzy Terlitzky's son, Stephen Fenning (a stage name), who played Linus in New York's production of *Snoopy.* Another son, Jerry, runs the deli with mom and dad. Nicest place to sit is upstairs on the screened-in garden patio. And if the setting is funky, the food is good, fresh, and authentic, which is why Terlitzky's is often packed.

Lunch or dinner, $5 or less will buy pastrami or corned beef on rye, a combination of homemade chopped liver and pastrami, potato pancakes with sour cream or apple sauce, or blueberry blintzes with sour cream. The correct beverage is Dr. Brown's cream soda, though you might also opt for an egg cream, or less traditionally, a glass of wine (just $1.35). For dessert there's a wide selection including deli favorites like cheesecake, apple strudel, and halvah, as well as hot-fudge ice-cream cake. Terlitzky's is a good breakfast choice, by the way, for eggs, bagels, pancakes, waffles, you name it.

Open downstairs Monday to Saturday from 7 a.m. to 5 p.m. The candlelit upstairs room and garden patio stay open till midnight Tuesday to Saturday. No credit cards.

Murphy's, 713 King St. (tel. 703/548-1717), is a self-described "grand Irish restaurant and pub," and it couldn't be more cozy and fun-loving. Exposed brick walls are hung with Irish flags. The bar serves up Irish liqueurs and whiskeys (Bailey's Irish cream is highly recommended), Irish coffee and hot buttered rum, and has Guinness stout on tap. Fireplaces are ablaze on both floors during the winter, and Irish bands entertain nightly. The jukebox alternates Irish tunes with mellow rock. This is the kind of bar where you can take the whole family; the kids will love it.

The food is fresh and tasty. For $4.50 you can have the plowman's lunch—two kinds of cheese, pickle, french bread and butter, and a pint of beer or glass of wine; same price for a crabcake sandwich served with cottage fries (they're great), $4.95 for a hearty Irish stew. There's a low-priced children's menu with all items under $3.50, and desserts include chocolate-fudge cake with Häagen-Dazs ice cream. At Sunday brunch Murphy's offers champagne with a choice of entrees—perhaps bacon, eggs, sausage, homefries, homemade biscuit, and jelly—for $5.95.

Open daily from 11 a.m. to 2 a.m.

The last two listings offer good food at especially low prices.

Happy to say, there's now a **Chesapeake Bagel Bakery** in Old Town at 601 King St. (tel. 703/684-3777). Like its D.C. counterparts (see Chapter III), it offers fresh-baked New York quality bagels (nine varieties) with fillings like chopped liver; cream cheese, walnuts, raisins, and carrots; and hummus and sprouts—all at under $3. There's also homemade soup, and desserts like brownies, blondies, and carrot cake. The setting is pleasant and unpretentious. One wall is used for a large community bulletin board, the others are charcoal gray and hung with a changing exhibit of photographs and Chinese kites. Seating is in bentwood chairs at navy blue Formica tables. The corner location makes for lots of sunlight.

Open seven days a week from 7 a.m. to 7 p.m. No credit cards.

The **Cameron St. Cafe,** 407 Cameron St. (tel. 703/548-9002), is pleasantly pristine in appearance with wainscotted stucco walls, brass chandeliers and sconces, and seating in church pew banquettes. The café menu is very reasonably priced, and everything is homemade. A barbecued pork sandwich on sesame seed bun, served with potato chips and pickle, is $3.25; a bowl of homemade soup and all you can eat from the salad bar is $3.55; and there are daily specials like chicken cacciatore served with vegetables, pasta, a small salad, and roll and butter ($3.75). In addition to the above, there's a sizable breakfast menu. Two eggs with ham, bacon, or sausage, homemade hash browns, and toast costs $3.45; substitute pancakes for the eggs and toast (you still get the potatoes) and it runs just $2.85. Homemade desserts here like pumpkin pie and chocolate-chip cheesecake are $1.50 to $2.

Open Monday to Friday 7:30 a.m. to 3 p.m., Saturday from 8:30 a.m. to 3 p.m., on Sunday from 9 a.m. to 1 p.m. No credit cards.

WHERE TO STAY: Though most visitors make Alexandria a day trip from Washington, D.C., there are ample attractions here for you to consider staying a few nights. If you do, make your reservations as early as possible, especially during major events and festivals (see above). April, September, and October are the busiest months.

Just a few blocks from the center of Old Town activity is an **Econo Lodge,** at 700 North Washington St., between Wythe and Madison Sts., Alexandria, VA 22314 (tel. 703/836-5100 or toll free 800/446-6900). Part of a well-run budget chain whose motto is "spend a night, not a fortune," it offers standard American motel facilities with all amenities—color TV, direct-dial phone, air conditioning, and full bath. The rooms are paneled in pine or freshly painted in white, nicely furnished, and of goodly size, and because there are no frills, rates are low: $52 a night single, $57 double, $61 for a double-double, with children under 12 free in a room with their parents. An extra person pays $5, another $5 if a rollaway bed is required. Parking is free.

Finally, the **Bed & Breakfast League** has several low-priced accommodations in Alexandria. See the Washington, D.C., hotel listings (Chapter II) for details. In the same chapter, you'll also find **Alexandria Lodgings,** an excellent low priced guesthouse in easy walking distance of the King Street Metro.

3. Potomac Plantations

Though the riverside plantations described below date from Colonial rather than Civil War times, they are the vast white-columned mansions with shady tree-lined drives you've always imagined. It's easy to picture Scarlett saying "fiddle-dee-dee" to Rhett Butler on the spacious lawns of Mount Vernon or Gunston Hall. These are the homes of the men who shaped the government and its institutions that you've been perusing in Washington. To visit them is an education in early American thought, politics, sociology, art, architecture, fashion, and the decorative arts—something, in fact, for everyone.

Happily, in the last decade or so there's been a movement in Virginia toward a meticulous concern for historical accuracy. Using data from excavations, old documents, and books of the period, those involved in estate restoration have attempted to recreate the settings in which men like George Washington lived and worked.

MOUNT VERNON: In 1784 George Washington wrote the Marquis de Lafayette, "At length my Dear Marquis I am become a private citizen on the banks of the Potomac, and under the shadow of my own Vine and my own Fig-tree, free from the bustle of a camp and the busy scenes of public life, I am solacing myself with those tranquil enjoyments, of which the Soldier who is ever in pursuit of fame, the Statesman whose watchful days and sleepless nights are spent in devising schemes to promote the welfare of his own, perhaps the ruin of other countries, as if this globe was insufficient for us all . . . can have very little conception. I am not only retired from all public employments, but I am retiring within myself; and shall be able to view the solitary walk, and tread the paths of private life with heartfelt satisfaction . . ."

Alas, Washington's announcement of retirement to his beloved ancestral plantation home (the estate's title dates from a 1674 land grant to his great-grandfather) was premature. In 1787 he once again heeded the call to duty, presiding over the Constitutional Convention in Philadelphia. In 1789 he became the first president of the United States, and managed to visit Mount Vernon only once or twice a year during his eight-year term. It wasn't until 1797, two years before his death, that Washington was finally able to devote himself fully to the "tranquil enjoyments" of Mount Vernon.

The home and final resting place of George and Martha Washington has been one of America's most visited shrines since the mid-19th century when tourists arrived by the boatload (you still can) via the Potomac. Today over a million visitors tour Mount Vernon annually. Since 1858 the house and grounds have been under the auspices of the Mount Vernon Ladies' Association, a nonprofit organization chartered by the Commonwealth of Virginia and charged with the preservation and restoration of George Washington's former home. For over a century this organization has been involved in an ongoing effort to locate and return the estate's scattered contents and memorabilia, thus enhancing its authentic appearance circa 1799.

A visit to Mount Vernon provides a unique glimpse into 18th-century plantation life. Washington's original estate contained five independent farms (he was among the first to realize the importance of crop rotation and soil conservation) on which over 300 slaves toiled. It was Washington's custom when in residence to ride daily about these farms, directing operations and planning for the future. These outlying farms no longer exist (Washington's will, which also freed his slaves, divided the land), but you will see the mansion and surrounding grounds—a New World version of an English country gentleman's estate. The bowling green entrance still contains some of the trees originally planted by Washington.

There's no formal tour of Mount Vernon, but attendants stationed throughout the house and grounds provide explanatory commentary.

The house itself—an outstanding example of Georgian architecture—is constructed of beveled pine painted to look like stone. You'll enter by way of the "large dining room" (the last addition to the house), which contains the original chairs, Hepplewhite mahogany sideboards, and paintings. The 18-foot plaster ceiling has an agricultural motif. Before proceeding to other rooms, step outside and enjoy the view that prompted Washington to declare, "No estate in United America is more pleasantly situated than this."

In the passage, or central hall (the social center of the house in Washington's day), hangs a key to the Bastille which Lafayette presented to Washington in 1790 via messenger Thomas Paine. Four adjoining rooms can be seen from the passage. The "little parlor" contains the English harpsichord of Martha Washington's granddaughter, Nelly Custis (music and dancing were major recreations during this period, and the unmusical Washington regretted that he could "neither sing one of the songs, nor raise a single note on any instrument"). In the "west parlor" you'll see a portrait of Martha at 25 and her china tea service laid out on the table. In the "small dining room" a sweetmeat course set up on the original mahogany dining table—nuts, raisins, candied fruits, and port and madeira wines—is based on a description of an actual Mount Vernon dinner in 1799. The fourth room on view from the passage is the "downstairs bedroom," used to accommodate the many overnight guests Washington mentions in his diary.

Continuing upstairs, you'll view five additional bedchambers, including the "Lafayette room" named for its most distinguished occupant, and George and Martha's bedroom, the room in which Washington died. The latter contains the original four-poster.

Downstairs again, Washington's study contains its original globe, desk, and dressing table. Washington often rose to work at 4 or 5 a.m.; he'd light his own fire and dress in the study. It was from this room that Washington managed his estate and penned numerous letters of historic import.

The kitchen is in a separate building (a common feature of Colonial architecture because of the risk of fire). It's one of several outbuildings, or "dependencies," on view, the others including servants' quarters (see how the other half lived), slave quarters with squirrels strung up for dinner, a storeroom, paint cellar, smokehouse, washhouse, coachhouses, overseer's quarters, and stables. A museum on the property contains many interesting exhibits—a Houdon bust of Washington, his swords, military sashes (one of these is said to have been presented to him by General Braddock as he lay mortally wounded), books, and family documents; Martha's needlework, satin wedding slippers, china sets, ivory fan, and bathing dress of blue and gray homespun; also Revolutionary War and other memorabilia. A special exhibition, on view through 1989, focuses on Washington and the Constitution. Details of the restoration of Mount Vernon are explained in the museum annex. There's a gift shop on the premises.

You'll want to have plenty of time to tour the grounds, see the wharf, the slave burial ground, the tomb containing George and Martha Washington's sarcophagi, the lawns, gardens, and greenhouse. Allow at least two hours for the entire house and grounds tour.

The house and grounds are open to the public 365 days a year from 9 a.m. The entrance gate closes at 5 p.m. March 1 to October 31, at 4 p.m. the rest of the year. Admission is $5 for adults, $4 for senior citizens, $2 for children 6 to 11, free for those under 6. A detailed map is provided at the entrance.

Getting There

There are several ways to get to Mount Vernon. You can take Tourmobile (see Chapter I for details).

By car it's a pleasant drive (the estate is 16 miles south of Washington) via the George Washington Parkway/Mount Vernon Memorial Highway.

You can also take either the Blue or Yellow Metro line to Huntington and there catch the 11P bus to the entrance gate to Mount Vernon. Call 637-2437 for departure times.

Or travel up the Potomac by boat. From late March through October there are three sailings a day departing from Pier 4 at 6th and Water Sts. SW (tel. 554-8000 for exact times). Fare for the 1½-hour trip is $7.75 for adults, $5.50 for children 2 to 11; the round trip is $10.75 and $6.25, respectively.

Best time to visit Mount Vernon is off-season when the crowds are sparser. If you must visit in summer, avoid weekends and holidays or resign yourself to very long lines. On Washington's Birthday by the way (the federal holiday, not the actual date), admission is free and a wreath-laying ceremony is held at his tomb. For further details, phone 703/780-2000.

Where to Eat

There are several dining options open to Mount Vernon visitors. At the entrance is a snackbar serving light fare (burgers, hot dogs, fries, soda, etc.). It's open daily from 9:30 a.m. to 5:30 p.m., and there are picnic tables outside.

However, much nicer is the **Mount Vernon Inn** (tel. 703/780-0011), a quaintly charming Colonial-style restaurant complete with period furnishings and working fireplaces. Lunch here is very reasonable. Be sure to begin with an order of homemade peanut and chestnut soup. Entrees range from Colonial pye (a crock of meat or fowl and garden vegetables with a puffed pastry top; $5.20) to a 20th-century burger and fries ($4). There's a full bar, and premium wines are offered by the glass. At dinner, tablecloths, candlelight, and entrees in the $12 to $16 range makes this a much plusher choice. There is, however, an early dinner served Monday to Saturday from 5 to 6:45 p.m. It's a prix fixe at $9.95 to $10.95 that includes soup or salad, entree, homemade breads, dessert, and beverage. Such a dinner might consist of broccoli cheddar soup, Maryland crabcakes, and cherry-filled crêpes.

The Inn is open for lunch Monday to Saturday from 11:30 a.m. to 3:30 p.m., Sunday till 4 p.m. Dinner is served Monday to Saturday from 5 to 9:30 p.m.

If you pack your own picnic, consider driving about a mile north on the George Washington Memorial Parkway to **Riverside Park,** where picnic tables are situated in a lovely area overlooking the Potomac.

WOODLAWN PLANTATION: Depending on your enthusiasm for plantation sightseeing, while in the area you might also want to visit Woodlawn Plantation (tel. 703/557-7881), just three miles west of Mount Vernon on Route 1. Originally a 2000-acre part of the Mount Vernon estate (today some 130 acres remain), Woodlawn was a wedding gift from George Washington to his adopted daughter (and Martha's actual granddaughter), the beautiful Eleanor "Nelly" Parke Custis, and his nephew, Maj. Lawrence Lewis. The Lewises married in 1799 and moved into the house—designed by William Thornton, first architect of the Capitol—in 1802 (by that time with two children in tow). They furnished it primarily with pieces from Mount Vernon, and had trees cut away to afford views of that estate and the Potomac. The views today are still spectacular. Under the auspices of the National Trust for Historic Preservation, the restored mansion and its elegant formal gardens reflect many periods of history. Post-Lewis occupants included antislavery Quaker and Baptist settlers from the North (1846–1889); New York City playwright Paul Kester (1901–1905), who lived here with his mother, his brother, and 60 cats; and Elizabeth Sharpe of Pennsylvania (1905–1925), who commissioned Waddy Wood (architect of the Woodrow Wilson house in D.C.) to restore the house to a semblance of its original appearance, spending $100,000 on this project during her tenure. Finally, Sen. Oscar Underwood of Alabama and his wife, Bertha, retired here after his failure to obtain the Democratic nomination for the presidency in 1924 (outspoken opposition to the Ku Klux Klan defeated him). The Underwood family occupied the house through 1948, retaining Waddy Wood to continue Miss Sharpe's restoration.

The estate is open daily (except Christmas, Thanksgiving, and New Year's Days) from 9:30 a.m. to 4:30 p.m. Thirty-minute tours are given on the half hour. Admission is $4 for adults, $3 for students (kindergarten through 12th grade) and seniors, under 5 free; it may be higher during special events. In the gift shop/bookstore you can purchase needlework and quilting instructions, a cookbook of Martha Washington's recipes, and other quaint items.

Allow at least an hour to see the house and grounds. Among the rooms on view is the bedroom of the Lewises' son, Lorenzo, an amateur taxidermist whose stuffed birds are displayed here; it's said he looked like a bird as well, and a portrait in the parlor bears this out. You'll also see the Lewises' dining room. A New York congressman visiting Woodlawn in 1817 wrote to his wife describing the typically sumptuous repast enjoyed in this room: "the first course consisted of beef, mutton, oysters, soup, etc. The first cloth was removed with the viands and the clean one below was then covered with pies, puddings, torts, jellies, whips, floating island, sweetmeats, etc., and after these we came to the plain table. Clean glasses were brought on and a lighter kind of wine with fruit, raisins and almonds. . . ."

Like Mount Vernon, Woodlawn has a regal "Lafayette bedroom" named for its most famous guest. It contains a French New Orleans-style bed with gold-fringed canopy. You'll also see the "white bedroom," another principal guest chamber; a child's room; the master bedroom with its original peaked crown canopy bed; the music room (where a recording of Nelly's music is played), and the "Underwood room," another dining facility.

The grounds, with nature trails designed by the National Audubon Society, are representative of many periods in the estate's history, and the gardens include the largest collection on the East Coast of 19th-century species of roses.

Also on the premises, though not open to the public at this writing, is **Grand View,** a house built about 100 yards from the mansion in 1858. The **Pope-Leighey House,** designed by Frank Lloyd Wright in 1940 for the Loren Pope family of Falls Church, is open to the public, by appointment on weekends only, March through December from 9:30 a.m. to 4:30 p.m. In the path of highway construction, it was rescued from demolition and brought to the Woodlawn grounds in 1964. The house, built of cypress, brick, and glass, was created as a prototype of well-designed architectural space for middle-income people. "The house of moderate cost," said Wright in 1938, "is not only America's major architectural problem but the problem most difficult for her major architects. As for me, I would rather solve it with satisfaction to myself and Usonia, than build anything I can think of. . . ." Usonia was utopianist Samuel Butler's name for the United States, and Wright used the term for his "houses of moderate cost." In 1946 the house was purchased by a Mr. and Mrs. Robert A. Leighey, hence the double name. After living in the house for 17 years, the Leigheys donated to the National Trust both the house and the money to dismantle and move it. Admission is the same as for Woodlawn, but a reduced-price combination ticket to both attractions is available.

THE GRIST MILL: Mount Vernon (the part of it that later became Woodlawn) contained a grist mill which neighboring farmers used for grinding corn and wheat (they paid a toll of one-eighth the volume). In 1932 the Virginia Conservation Commission purchased part of the property known as Dogue Run Farm on which the mill and other buildings had been located. The site was excavated, and part of the original water wheel, the bearings for the wheel, part of the trundlehead, complete wheel buckets, and other articles were found. Old books and documents from Mount Vernon were also used in the reconstruction of Washington's 1770 mill.

Three miles west of Mount Vernon on Route 235, what is now called **George Washington's Grist Mill Historic State Park** is open to the public daily from 10 a.m. to 6 p.m. Memorial Day through Labor Day. Admission is $1 for adults, 75¢ for children 6 to 12 (under 6, free). Guided tours, given throughout the day, will tell you everything you ever wanted to know about milling grain. For further information call 703/339-7265.

POHICK CHURCH: Travel farther south along Route 1 for about 4½ miles, and you'll come to the pre-Revolutionary Pohick Church (on your left), built in the 1770s from plans drawn up by George Washington. The interior was designed by George Mason, owner of Gunston Hall (see below), with box pews like those prevalent in England at the time. During the Civil War, Union troops stabled their horses in the church and stripped the interior. The east wall was used for target practice. Today the church is restored to its original appearance and has an active Episcopal congregation. It's open daily from 8:30 a.m. to 4 p.m. No admission is charged. Call 703/339-6572 for details.

GUNSTON HALL: Yet another 18th-century plantation awaits exploration if you continue south on Route 1 to Route 242, also known as Gunston Road. It's the magnificent estate (originally 5000 acres; today, 550 remain) of George Mason (1725–1792), a statesman and political thinker who, while shunning public office, played an important behind-the-scenes role in founding our nation. Jefferson called him "the wisest man of his generation." Mason drafted the Virginia Declaration of Rights, model for the Bill of Rights and for constitutions of subsequent emerging democracies throughout the world. The most famous sentence of the Declaration of Independence is based on Mason's statement, "That all men are by nature equally free and independent and have certain inherent rights . . . namely, the enjoyment of life and liberty, with the means of acquiring and possessing property, and pursuing and obtaining happiness and safety. . . ." A little editing, and *voilà!* A staunch believer in human rights, Mason refused to sign the Constitution (which he helped write) because it didn't abolish slavery or, initially, contain a Bill of Rights (Mason did live to see the Bill of Rights added in 1791).

Gunston Hall, a 1½-story brick Georgian mansion, today belongs to the Commonwealth of Virginia and is administered by the National Society of the Colonial Dames of America. Following excavations and painstaking research, it has been restored to its appearance in the days when Washington and Jefferson visited. It's open from 9:30 a.m. to 5 p.m. daily (except Christmas) for self-guided tours. Admission is $3 for adults, $1 for children 6 through 15 (under 6, free). For details call 703/550-9220.

The entrance is at a reception center/gift shop where a 15-minute film introduces visitors to the estate. En route to the house you'll pass a small museum of Mason family memorabilia—bibles, portraits, clothing, books, snuff boxes, etc. Inside the house a guide is on hand to answer questions and show you around.

A highlight is the Palladium Room, the chef d'oeuvre of Gunston Hall's brilliant young creator, an indentured English craftsman in his early 20s named William Buckland who worked here from 1755 to 1759. The room's intricately carved woodwork was inspired by 16th-century Italian architect Andrea Palladio.

Also worth noting is a room with Chinoiserie interior, the latest London range in the mid-18th century. This is the first example of Chinese-influenced decorative trim in America. The table here is often set up with a typically lavish dessert course of fruits, wines, tarts, marzipans, cakes, and nuts.

You'll also view the room that served as Mason's library and study, in which his son, John, recalled "he absented himself as it were from his family sometimes for weeks together, and often until very late at night during the Revolutionary War. . . ." The writing table on which Mason penned the Virginia Declaration of Rights is among the many surviving family furnishings you'll see here; the rest are in the style of the period.

The center hallway was, as per colonial tradition, the most popular room in the house. Our forefathers liked to hang out in the hallway where doors at either end allowed a breeze from the Potomac to sweep through—a blessing in Virginia's hot and humid summers. Balls were held here with musicians on the balcony providing guitar, flute, and harpsichord tunes for minuets, reels, and country dances.

The upstairs bedrooms, domain of the nine young Masons and an English governess, evoke the lively atmosphere of games and laughter that must surely have existed in this house.

After touring the house, proceed to the outbuildings—a kitchen, smokehouse, dairy, schoolhouse, well, and laundry. You'll also want to tour the grounds where Mason "would several times a day pass out of his study and walk for a considerable time wrapped in meditation." Hog Island sheep, an 18th-century breed, graze in pastures adjacent to the lawn. The formal gardens, restored by the Garden Club of Virginia, focus on the 12-foot-high English boxwood allee planted by Mason over 200 years ago and contain only plants found in Colonial days. A nature trail leads down the Potomac past the deer park and woodland area. Also on the premises is the family graveyard where George and Ann Mason are buried.

POHICK BAY REGIONAL PARK: Close to Gunston Hall, also on Route 242, is a 1000-acre park focusing on water-oriented recreations. In fact "Pohick" is an Algonquin word for "the water place." The park occupies a spectacular bayside setting on the historic 100,000-acre Mason Neck peninsula. It offers the largest swimming pool on the East Coast, boat access to the Potomac (sailboat and paddleboat rentals are available), 200 campsites available on a first-come, first-served basis, a four-mile bridle path, scenic nature trails, an 18-hole golf course and pro shop, miniature golf, and sheltered picnic areas with tables and grills. It's the perfect place to refresh yourself after a morning spent traipsing around old plantations.

The park is open all year from 7 a.m. to dark, the pool from Memorial Day to Labor Day. Admission is $4 per car. Use of the pool is $2.50 for children 2 to 11 and senior citizens, $3 for adults. For further details call 703/339-6100.

4. Fredericksburg

Fifty miles south of Washington, D.C., the tranquil southern town of Fredericksburg came into being in 1728 as a frontier settlement of 50 acres on the banks of the Rappahannock River. Like other early Virginia towns it is steeped in American history. Though George Washington always called Alexandria his hometown, he spent his formative years in the Fredericksburg area at Ferry Farm (that's where he chopped down the cherry tree with his little hatchet). His mother later lived in a house he bought her on Charles Street, and she is buried on the former Kenmore estate.

Despite the fact that Fredericksburg is named for Frederick, Prince of Wales, the son of George II, and its streets for members of the royal family, the town was a hotbed of revolutionary zeal in the 1770s. Troops drilled on the courthouse green on Princess Anne Street, and even the ladies were involved in making lead bullets at the Gunnery.

It was in Fredericksburg that Thomas Jefferson, George Mason, and other founding fathers met in 1777 to draft what later became the Virginia Statute of Religious Freedoms and the basis for the First Amendment guaranteeing religious freedom and separation of church and state. Jefferson included this statute as one of the three major achievements he wanted listed in his epitaph.

James Monroe began his law career in Fredericksburg in 1786.

During the Civil War, its strategic location—equidistant from two rival capitals, Richmond and Washington—made Fredericksburg a fierce battlefield, scene of one of the war's bloodiest conflicts. The combined Union and Confederate casualties in the four battles that took place in the Fredericksburg area were over 100,000. Clara Barton nursed wounded Federal soldiers in the still-extant Presbyterian church. Cannonballs embedded in the walls of some prominent buildings and the 17,000 Civil War soldiers buried in the town's cemeteries are grim reminders of that era.

In the 40-block National Historic District there are over 350 structures built prior to 1870. In imagining early local color, take into consideration that hogs and goats running wild through the streets remained a major problem through the 1760s!

Fredericksburg is about an hour's drive from Washington, D.C. Go south on 14th Street NW to I-395, which leads you to I-95. Exit at Route 3 East, which becomes William Street and takes you to the heart of town. Fredericksburg is also accessible by bus (Trailways or Greyhound) and Amtrak. Make your first stop in town (just follow the signs) the **Fredericksburg Visitor Center** at 706 Caroline St. (tel. 703/373-1776), itself housed in a historic 1817 house. Here you can see a 12-minute slide presentation on Fredericksburg's Colonial history; pick up maps and brochures on hotels, restaurants, and sights; obtain a pass for free parking anywhere in the city (including the lot across the street); and purchase a block ticket for six main attractions. The latter costs $8, a saving of $6 over individual admissions, and includes the Hugh Mercer Apothecary, the Rising Sun Tavern, the James Monroe Museum, the Mary Washington House, Belmont, and Kenmore. Children 13 and under are admitted free when accompanied by an adult. The ticket can also be purchased at any of these attractions. The center is open daily from 9 a.m. to 5 p.m., except Christmas and New Year's Days.

THE SIGHTS: There's ample to occupy you for a day or two in Fredericksburg, hence some hotel choices later on in this section. The block ticket is certainly advised. If you haven't time to explore the town in depth (for instance, if you're stopping for an hour or two en route to Richmond), you might consider **Confederate Tours'** (tel. 703/371-6131) 45-minute guided minibus tours departing every half hour on the hour and half hour between 9:30 a.m. and 3:30 p.m. from in front of the Visitor Center. They're very comprehensive. Cost is $9 for adults (children under 8, free). However, if you have the day to spend, everything is easily reachable on foot, and the Visitor Center walking-tour map shows you where all the historic attractions are located. The center even has a brochure detailing buildings said to be haunted by ghosts! *Note:* The six block-ticket attractions listed below are closed December 24, 25, and 31, Thanksgiving and January 1.

Kenmore

A book called *The 100 Most Beautiful Rooms in America* includes a room from Kenmore, 1201 Washington Ave., between Lewis and Fauquier Sts. (tel. 703/373-3381). This mid-18th-century brick Georgian mansion was built for

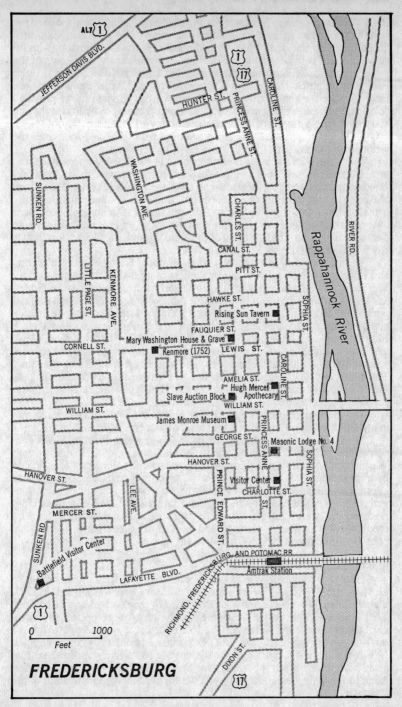

ALT 1

JEFFERSON DAVIS BLVD.

1
17

HUNTER ST.

CAROLINE ST.

PRINCESS ANNE ST.

WASHINGTON AVE.

SUNKEN RD.

CHARLES ST.

CANAL ST.

PITT ST.

LITTLE PAGE ST.

KENMORE AVE.

HAWKE ST.

SOPHIA ST.

Rising Sun Tavern

FAUQUIER ST.

Mary Washington House & Grave

CORNELL ST.

Kenmore (1752)

LEWIS ST.

CAROLINE ST.

AMELIA ST.

Hugh Mercer
Slave Auction Block   Apothecary

WILLIAM ST.

WILLIAM ST.

James Monroe Museum

PRINCESS ANNE ST.

GEORGE ST.

Masonic Lodge No. 4

HANOVER ST.

SOPHIA ST.

HANOVER ST.

PRINCE EDWARD ST.

Visitor Center

LEE AVE.

CHARLOTTE ST.

MERCER ST.

SUNKEN RD.

Battlefield Visitor Center

RICHMOND, FREDERICKSBURG, AND POTOMAC R.R.

Amtrak Station

LAFAYETTE BLVD.

1

0   1000
Feet

DIXON ST.

17

Rappahannock River

RIVER RD.

FREDERICKSBURG

Betty Washington (George's sister) by her husband, Fielding Lewis, one of the wealthiest planters in Fredericksburg. The original 861-acre plantation produced tobacco, grains, and flax. In addition to George Washington (who involved himself considerably in the building, decoration, and furnishing of the estate), Kenmore's illustrious guests included Lafayette, Rochambeau, John Paul Jones, Patrick Henry, and Thomas Jefferson. During the Revolution, Lewis financed a gun factory, built vessels for the Virginia navy, provided "clothing and necessaries" to the troops, and accepted responsibility for the sick and wounded. As a result of his large expenditures in the cause of patriotism, he eventually had to sell Kenmore to liquidate his debts. He died soon after the victory at Yorktown.

Today the house is meticulously restored to its Colonial appearance, the original exquisitely molded plaster ceilings and cornices comprising its most outstanding feature. Most of the floors and all of the woodwork and paneling are also original, and the authentic 18th-century English and American furnishings contain several Lewis family pieces. You can take a 20-minute guided house tour given on the hour and half hour between 9 a.m. and 5 p.m. April through October, 10 a.m. to 4 p.m. the rest of the year. Without the block ticket, adults pay $4; children under 18, $2; under 6, free.

The tour begins with a short recorded talk about Fredericksburg in general and Kenmore in particular, with visual effects provided by a diorama exhibit. The dining room has a ceiling with a sun-themed portrait in the center (historians aren't sure if it is meant to represent Apollo or Louis XIV), and original portraits of Mr. and Mrs. Lewis hang over a Chippendale-Hepplewhite mahogany hunt board. The drawing room has one of the most elegant ceilings in the country, with a central tobacco-leaf motif. Also note the drawing room's Irish lead-crystal chandelier of exceptional quality. During the Civil War Kenmore was used as a hospital, and operations were performed in this stunning setting. The master bed chamber on the first floor also has a beautiful carved ceiling (its theme is the four seasons) and mantel fresco. Here a table is set for tea, always served immediately upon a weary guest's arrival.

The children's room (the Lewises had 11, but five died in infancy) is charming, with scaled-down furnishings and carved wooden soldiers on the mantel.

You'll also see guest bedrooms; the office in which Fielding Lewis conducted his widespread business affairs (he was, among other things, George Washington's agent in many important transactions); the Mary Washington bedroom where, though her own house was practically next door, Betty's mother often stayed; and finally, the kitchen where cold spiced tea and delicious gingerbread (Mary Washington's recipe, the same she served to Lafayette in 1784) is served—a lovely treat. After touring the house, take a walk through the famous boxwood gardens, restored and maintained according to the original plans by the Garden Club of Virginia. A gift shop is also on the premises.

Mary Washington House

George Washington purchased the house at 1200 Charles St., corner of Lewis St. (tel. 703/373-1569), for his mother, Mary Ball Washington, in 1772. She was then 64 years old and had been living at the nearby Ferry Farm since 1739. Here Lafayette visited during the Revolution to pay respects to the mother of the greatest living American. And Washington, who once said "All that I am I owe to my mother," came in 1789 to receive her blessing before going to New York for his inauguration. He did not see her again; she died later that year. Mary Washington is buried near "Meditation Rock"—a place she often came to meditate, read, and pray—on the former Kenmore plantation of her daughter.

The house is open daily from 9 a.m. to 5 p.m. Thirty-minute tours are given by hostesses in Colonial garb throughout the day. Admission without the block ticket is $2 for adults, 50¢ for children.

Mary Ball Washington never posed for a portrait, but in the parlor is an artist's conception of her at 75 (remove the bonnet and you've got George).

The engravings on the wall of her bedroom were among her most prized possessions. In this room you can also check yourself out in her "best dressing glass." The hand-painted, quilted bedspread is an exact replica of the original. Note the needlepoint English fire screens which you'll see in most Colonial homes; ladies of the day wore makeup with a wax base, and if they sat unprotected near the fire the results were a little gruesome.

Other typically Colonial items are the corner chair (designed to allow a sword-carrying soldier to sit comfortably) and a needlework frame (Mary was a great needlewoman), both in the dining room.

Upstairs, a copy of her will in which she disposes of "my negro man, Tom, and all his decendants," among other possessions, makes interesting reading. There's also a letter to George expressing typically motherly sentiments; her writing sheds some light on how poorly women were educated in her day.

The gardens carefully tended by Mary Washington contain her own sun dial and some of the original boxwood hedge she planted. An avid gardener, she is said to have greeted Lafayette while working in the garden wearing an apron. A brick path connected her garden with Kenmore, and the grandchildren ran across it to visit just about every day.

You'll also see the kitchen (the original, one of the few from this time that never burned down), the bedroom where George slept when visiting, and the room of Mary's companion, Polly Skelton. There are exquisite rugs throughout the house, including an Austrian Savonnerie and an antique silk Samarkand from Central Asia.

James Monroe Law Office—Museum and Memorial Library

The low brick building at 908 Charles St., between William and George Sts. (tel. 703/373-8426), was James Monroe's first law office. He came here in 1786, practiced for three years, and went on to hold a number of high public offices—U.S. senator; American minister to France, England, and Spain; governor of Virginia; secretary of state; secretary of war; and fifth president of the United States. His shingle still hangs outside, and within, all of the furnishings are from the Monroes' White House years or their retirement home. It is believed that some pieces were bought in France at a public auction of Marie Antoinette's effects while she was incarcerated. Among these is the Louis XVI desk on which the Monroe Doctrine was signed. Its secret compartments were not discovered until 75 years after the president's death.

The law office/museum is open daily from 9 a.m. to 5 p.m. Thirty-minute tours are given by hostesses in Colonial dress throughout the day. These are enhanced by recorded information in each room.

In Monroe's cozy office you can peruse correspondence from Thomas Jefferson (a letter partially in code), James Madison, George Washington, Lafayette, and Benjamin Franklin. Here too is the gun and canteen Monroe used in the American Revolution. Other than Washington, he was the only president to actually fight in the war for independence. He shared the grim winter at Valley Forge.

In the museum, cases are filled with china and silver the Monroes used in the White House. Also on display are a number of portraits, including a Rembrandt Peale of Monroe; the outfits (among others) that the Monroes wore at the court of Napoleon (hers is an Empire velvet gown with topaz jewelry); silhouettes of the Monroe's by Charles Willson Peale; her teensy wedding slippers; his dueling pistols; and other memorabilia.

The library of some 10,000 books is a reconstruction of Monroe's own personal collection; in addition it contains many books about Monroe and his era.

A gift shop on the premises specializes in Virginia-made craft items. Without the block ticket, admission is $2 for adults, 50¢ for children.

The Rising Sun Tavern

Fredericksburg's "living history" tours with hosts and hostesses in period dress enacting the roles of their Colonial counterparts are among the best in Virginia. At the Rising Sun Tavern, 1306 Caroline St., just off Fauquier St. (tel. 703/371-1494), you'll be shown around by a tavern wench—an indentured servant sentenced to seven years for stealing a loaf of bread in England. "My only hope," she confides, "is that a wealthy farmer might buy me from the tavern keeper for a wife."

The Rising Sun was originally a residence, built in 1760 by Charles Washington, George's youngest brother, but it served as a tavern for some 50 years, beginning in the early 1780s. The building is preserved, not reconstructed, and though the 17th- and 18th-century furnishings are not all originals they are typical of what would have been here.

The 30-minute tour provides many insights into Colonial life. The Rising Sun was a proper high-class tavern—not for riffraff like tinkers and razor grinders. Men were required to take off their boots and spurs in bed, and only five were allowed per bed! (People slept sitting up across the bed rather than lengthwise.) Not exactly the Holiday Inn. If you're tall, watch out for low doorways: the average man in the 18th century was 5'6", the average woman between 4'6" and 4'11".

In the Great Room the gentry congregated over madeira and cards (an actual deck from the period is displayed). The ladies didn't hang out here, however. They were consigned to the Ladies Retiring Room where they would spend the entire day gossiping, doing needlework, and reading the Bible (novel reading was *verboten*). Their meals were served here, and they didn't even leave to use the little girl's room; there was none, just a chamber pot or "necessary." At bedtime (5:30 p.m.) a serving wench would show them to their bedchambers by candlelight.

Meanwhile the menfolk were having a rollicking good time in the Taproom (the tavernkeeper's son will serve you wassail—a delicious spiced drink—here during the tour), over multicourse meals and numerous tankards of ale. In the taproom you'll learn the origin of expressions like "two bits" (they actually used to make change by cutting coins into bits) and "mind your Ps and Qs" (pints and quarts).

You'll see the bedrooms, including a room where Lafayette once stayed, after which it was named for him, of course; the tavernkeeper's storeroom for quilts, linens, towels, candle molds, a hip bath (it was used only during summer months; our forebears feared pneumonia too much to bathe in winter), and spinning wheels; and the office, where items of interest include a spit box (men would make bets about being able to hit it from across the room) and an English boot jack for removing shoes and boots. Guests' boots and shoes were left in the office overnight as insurance they'd pay before leaving. A night's stay, by the way, was about $1.06 for bed space, food, and horse boarding, more than it sounds actually when you consider that the average annual income was only $200 to $300 a year.

In the downstairs hall the tavern's original license is displayed, along with a standing desk designed by Thomas Jefferson (he had back problems and preferred to work standing up).

Also on the premises are a gift shop, garden, and dovecote, the latter used to trap birds destined for the kitchen. Open daily from 9 a.m. to 5 p.m. March through November, 10 a.m. to 4 p.m. the rest of the year. Admission without the block ticket is $2 for adults, 50¢ for children.

Hugh Mercer Apothecary Shop

You've only to visit this Colonial apothecary at 1020 Caroline St., corner of Amelia St. (tel. 703/373-3362), to realize the ghastliness of getting sick in the 18th century. Dr. Hugh Mercer practiced medicine and operated the shop from 1761 to 1776 before giving his life as a Revolutionary War brigadier-general at the Battle of Princeton. Gen. George S. Patton was his great-great-great-grandson. Mercer was a much-admired patriot and scholar—a close friend of George Washington—but I can't help feeling, though he suffered a violent death, that Mercer gave as good as he got.

For openers, the waiting room at this little shop of horrors doubled as an operating room, since those waiting for treatment often had to hold down the wretch under the knife. Opium, the only known anesthesia, was too expensive and too difficult to obtain; the best Mercer could do was to keep pouring rum into a patient until he became unconscious. On display are Mercer's various instruments of torture—bleeding devices, a heated cup for removing boils and carbuncles, a knife to cut out cataracts, an ominous-looking tooth key (most conveniently, dental needs were also seen here), and a saw (hence the early name "sawbones" for doctors).

At this one-stop shop you could also get your wig powdered, if you could divert your thoughts to vanity in such a setting.

Downstairs in the apothecary are the drugs commonly dispensed in the 18th century, such as snake root (to make you sweat), senna (for a laxative), and ipecac (to make you vomit). Come in with a simple case of the flu and after being bled with leeches you'd be administered all three! Colored water in the jars in the window (the kind of jars pharmacies still use today for decorative purposes) indicated health warnings—like red for smallpox. If you'd never had it, you might consider leaving town for a while. Many people couldn't read, but they knew what the colors meant.

Open 9 a.m. to 5 p.m. March through November, 10 a.m. to 4 p.m. the rest of the year. A hostess in Colonial dress gives a fascinating tour. Admission without the block ticket is $2 for adults, 50¢ for children.

Belmont

Situated on 27 hillside acres overlooking the falls of the Rappahannock River, Belmont, on Virginia Route 1001 just off Route 17 (tel. 703/373-3634), began as an 18th-century farmhouse (the central eight rooms of the house date to the 1790s) and was enlarged to a 22-room estate by a later owner. The house is furnished with the art treasures, family heirlooms, and European antiques of famed American artist Gari Melchers, who lived here from 1916 until his death in 1932. His wife, Corinne, gave Belmont to the Commonwealth of Virginia in 1955.

Not a great deal is known about Belmont's early owners. The first to make significant changes was Joseph Burwell Ficklen, who completely remodeled the house in the early 1840s for his new bride, Ella McGee, adding the present drawing room, an enclosed kitchen, two bedrooms, porches, and the North wing. Unfortunately, Ella died within two years; she and her infant daughter are buried on the grounds. Ficklen remarried in 1847 to Ann Eliza FitzHugh, and the couple had six children. During the Civil War Belmont's lawn was used for cannon emplacements in defense of Union positions north of the river. Happily, attack never came, and Belmont was preserved. Three generations of Ficklens made Belmont their home.

The Melcherses were the next occupants. They added the stone studio (today a small museum where the artist's works and correspondence are on display), built a gazebo overlooking the river, and increased the acreage. With the help of a caretaker Melchers operated Belmont as a farm. In addition to Melcher's own works there are many wonderful paintings in the house—a watercolor sketch by Jan Brueghel; 19th-century paintings by Morisot, Rodin, and Childe Hassam among others; and in the dining room, an enormous work by the 17th-century Flemish master Frans Snyders. Also noteworthy is the Savonnerie carpet in the large drawing room, woven by the supplier to Louis XV.

Belmont is open daily year round. Hours April 1 to the end of September are 10 a.m. to 5 p.m. Monday to Saturday and 1 to 5 p.m. on Sunday; the rest of the year hours are 10 a.m. to 4 p.m. Monday to Saturday and 1 to 4 p.m. Sunday. Admission is $2 for adults, 50¢ for youngsters 6 to 18 (under 6, free). Tours (about an hour long) are given throughout the day.

Masonic Lodge No. 4

Not only is the lodge at the corner of Princess Anne and Hanover Sts. (tel. 703/373-5885) the mother lodge of the father of our country, it's also one of the oldest Masonic lodges in America, established, it is believed, around 1735. Though the original building was down the street, Masons have been meeting at this address since 1812. On display are all kinds of Masonic paraphernalia and memorabilia—the Masonic punchbowl used to serve Lafayette, an honorary member of the Fredericksburg Lodge and himself a *francmaçon;* a Gilbert Stuart portrait of Washington in its original gilt Federalist frame; two chairs that belonged to Mary Ball Washington; a Civil War altar and Bible; a copy of the Houdon bust of Washington; a piece of the cornerstone of the Capitol; early charters for the lodge and other historic documents; and the 1668 Bible on which Washington took his Masonic obligation (oath).

Lodge No. 4 is open year round (except Christmas and New Year's Days) from 9 a.m. to 4 p.m. Monday to Saturday, from 1 to 4 p.m. on Sunday. Admission is $2 for adults, 50¢ for college students, 45¢ for children under 13. Tours are given throughout the day.

Touring Civil War Battlefields

Fredericksburg has never forgotten its Civil War victories and defeats. In **Fredericksburg and Spotsylvania National Military Park** you can take a self-guided auto tour of 16 important sites relating to four major battles. The entire battlefield trail is 75 miles long, but of course you needn't do the whole thing.

Starting point is the **Fredericksburg Battlefield Visitor Center,** 1013 Lafayette Blvd., at Sunken Rd. (tel. 703/373-6122), where you can get detailed tour brochures and rent 2½-hour-long auto tapes ($2.50 per battlefield for cassette player and tape). I definitely recommend the tapes; they enhance the experience. The center offers a 12-minute slide-show orientation and related exhibits. Visitors can purchase books and pamphlets ranging from serious historical studies to collections of Confederate recipes (both culinary and medicinal). Inquire here too about "living history" programs in the park. Open daily from 9 a.m. to 5 p.m., with extended hours in summer determined annually.

The Battle of Fredericksburg took place on December 11–13, 1862, when the Union army, commanded by Gen. Ambrose E. Burnside, attempted to occupy the town with a strength of 110,000 men and push on toward Richmond. However, the northern army took a drubbing at the hands of Lee's smaller (75,000 men) but better organized force. You can stand on the hill from which Lee directed the victorious Confederate defense, see the remains of fortifications, and visit sites like Pontoon Crossing, where the Union army crossed the Rappahannock by means of boat bridges called "pontoons." The Georgian mansion, Chatham (details below), is on the auto tape tour; during the war it became frontline headquarters for Union generals.

The first leg takes you as far as Chancellorsville (about ten miles), site of another important battle. Stop at the **Chancellorsville Visitor Center** (tel. 703/786-2880) to see another 12-minute audio-visual orientation and related exhibits. During summer there are often special historical programs here. Once again an auto tour tape is available.

The Battle of Chancellorsville was fought May 1–4, 1863. After the disastrous Federal defeat in December 1862, both armies had wintered around Fredericksburg. Union commander Gen. Joseph Hooker led about 80,000 men in a flanking maneuver up the north side of the Rappahannock, leaving another 25,000 in Fredericksburg to hold Lee in position. Gen. T.J. "Stonewall" Jackson moved toward Chancellorsville, and General Hooker retreated under Jackson's pressure. Although this battle too resulted in a Confederate victory, it was a costly one in which Jackson was accidentally shot by his own men. The house in which he died (22 miles from Chancellorsville) is still standing, and signs and a recording on the grounds tell of Jackson's final days. Other sites on the tour include the bivouac where Lee and Jackson met for the last time on the night of May 1 and planned the Battle of Chancellorsville; Catharine Furnace, a Confederate munitions manufactory and scene of an artillery duel; and Hazel Grove, the battlefield's most important military position. You might also want to make a stop at Old Salem Church, six miles east of Chancellorsville, around which battle swirled on May 3–4, 1863, in conjunction with the Chancellorsville campaign.

From Chancellorsville, enthusiasts can continue farther to the Wilderness and Spotsylvania Battlefields, while the battle-weary return to Fredericksburg.

The battlefield outing makes a pleasant family excursion. Even if Civil War sites don't excite you, the drive is scenic, there's lots of walking through woods and meadows involved, and many picnic spots are provided along the way.

If you'd like to do a little advance planning, write to the superintendent, Fredericksburg and Spotsylvania National Military Park, P.O. Box 679, Fredericksburg, VA 22404, for information.

Chatham

This pre-Revolutionary mansion built between 1768 and 1771 by wealthy planter William Fitzhugh has figured prominently in American history. In the 18th century it was a center of southern hospitality, often visited by George Washington (you'll see the room where he spent many nights). Fitzhugh was by this time already a fourth-generation American, who supported the Revolution both politically and financially.

During the Civil War the house, now belonging to J. Horace Lacy, served as headquarters for Federal commanders and as a Union field hospital. Lincoln visited the house twice, and Clara Barton and Walt Whitman nursed the wounded here. Exhibits on the premises tell about the families who've owned Chatham and detail the role the estate played during the war. Plaques on the grounds identify battle landmarks, and in summer there's a "living history" program.

The house is open daily from 9 a.m. to 5 p.m. Five rooms and the grounds can be viewed on a free self-guided tour, with National Parks Service employees on hand to answer questions. A picnic area is on the premises. If you're taking the above-described battlefield tour, visit Chatham en route. Otherwise, take Route 3 (William Street) east across the river and follow the signs. For details, call 703/373-4461.

The Old Stone Warehouse

Originally used to house tobacco, the warehouse at 923 Sophia St., corner of William St. (no phone), is Fredericksburg's oldest building. Built prior to 1760 (the exact date is unknown) of sandstone blocks and massive wooden beams, its walls were 18 to 25 inches thick to provide ample protection for the valuable contents housed within. In Colonial times a tobacco warehouse was like a bank and tobacco a viable form of currency. The building has four stories with the lower level accessible to the river for cargo loading. The old street level is now underground, and the basement's brick floor is covered by a few feet of hardened river mud.

From 1900 to 1936 the building was used as a salted herring factory, and the salt from those years preserved the wood while the building stood vacant for the next 45 years. In the last decade, major repairs have been made and an ongoing excavation and restoration are still in progress. The warehouse now contains a museum of Colonial and Civil War artifacts, some of which were found on the premises (such as a cannonball). The collection is a fascinating jumble of crocks, bottles, Spanish silver, clay pipes, buckles, medicinal vials, peach seeds, buttons, weapons, and more. Most interesting, however, is the ongoing archeological dig in the basement. Excavated souvenirs are among the items on sale in the gift shop.

Open Sunday only from 1 to 4 p.m. Admission is free.

St. George's Episcopal Church

Martha Washington's father and John Paul Jones's brother are buried in the graveyard of this church on Princess Anne St., between George and William Sts. (tel. 703/373-4133), and members of the first parish congregation included Mary Washington and Revolutionary War generals Hugh Mercer and George Weedon. The original church on this site was built in 1732, the current Romanesque structure in 1849. The town clock in the church tower was installed in 1850. During the Battle of Fredericksburg the church was hit at least 25 times, and in 1863 it was used by General Lee's troops for religious revival meetings. In 1864, when wounded Union soldiers filled every available building in town, it served as a hospital. The church has three signed Tiffany windows.

Open weekdays 9 a.m. to 5 p.m. and the same hours on Saturday unless a wedding is taking place. Sunday services are at 8 and 11 a.m.

The Presbyterian Church

Located on the corner of George and Princess Anne Sts., (tel. 703/373-7057), the Presbyterian church dates to the early 1800s, though the present Greek Revival building was completed in 1855—just in time to be shelled during the Civil War, and like St. George's to serve as a hospital where Clara Barton nursed Union forces. There is a plaque to her memory in the churchyard. Cannonballs in the front left pillar and scars on the walls of the loft and belfry remain to this day. The present church bell replaces one that was given to the Confederacy to be melted down for making cannons. After the war, various people in the north provided funds to restore the devastated church, and the first postwar service was held in 1866.

~Open weekdays from 8:30 a.m. to 3 p.m. Sunday service is at 11 a.m.

The Courthouse

Those of you interested in architecture should be sure to look at the Courthouse, Princess Anne and George Sts., built in 1853 in the Gothic Revival style. Its architect was James Renwick, who also designed New York's St. Patrick's Cathedral, the original Smithsonian building ("the castle"), and the Renwick Gallery. A former building on this site, erected in 1733, was the previous Fredericksburg courthouse, and the present structure is used for the same purpose. Exhibits in the lobby include originals of the will of Mary Ball Washington and George Washington's address to the city council in 1784. There's also a reproduction of a "Plan for the Town of Fredericksburg" from 1721.

Washington Avenue

Washington Avenue, between Lewis and Pitt Streets, just above Kenmore, a quiet residential area of Victorian homes, is the site of several notable monuments. At **Meditation Rock,** a spot where Mary Washington often came to pray and meditate, the mother of the father of our country is buried, and there's a monument in her honor. It is a very peaceful place. Just across the way is the **Thomas Jefferson Religious Freedom Monument,** commemorating Jefferson's Fredericksburg meeting with George Mason, Edmond Pendleton, George Wythe, and Thomas Ludwell Lee in 1777 to draft the Virginia Statute of Religious Freedom, later to become the First Amendment of the Bill of Rights. The **Hugh Mercer Monument,** off Fauquier St., honors the doctor and Civil War general about whom more above (see "Hugh Mercer Apothecary Shop").

Scheduled to open about six months after this book goes to the press, the **Fredericksburg Area Museum and Cultural Center,** 900 Princess Anne St. at William St. (tel. 703/371-5668), will occupy a Town Hall that dates to 1816 and is located in a Market Square that has existed since the middle of the 18th century. Market Square was, for over a century, the center of trade and commerce in Fredericksburg, Town Hall the city's social and legal center. Lafayette was entertained at Town Hall in 1824 with lavish parties and balls, and the building continued in its original function through 1984. Now it is being restored and preserved both for its own historical importance and to serve as a serious museum of regional history.

The first level, which opens on the cobblestoned market square (to be used for special events, concerts, and outdoor markets) will serve as a changing exhibit area and house the museum shop. The opening exhibit will be "From Market House to Town Hall: Fredericksburg in the Constitutional Era," which will focus on life here from 1766 to 1816. The second floor will house permanent exhibits on: Indian settlements and pre-English explorers (the earliest years); colonial settlement, including the reconstructed interior of an early 18th-century cabinetmaker's shop; the Revolution and Federal Fredericksburg, including architectural and decorative aspects of the period; the antebellum period (1825 to 1861), focusing on the development of canals, early industry, railroads, and the cholera epidemic of 1833; the Civil War and its aftermath, graphically depicting the reality of the war as experienced by the local citizenry; Fredericksburg's evolution from town to city, 1890 to 1920; and, finally, 20th-century Fredericksburg. Exhibits will be enhanced by audiovisual presentations and crafts demonstrations. On the third floor, the Hall's 19th-century Council Chamber is being restored.

The Town Hall itself, which a museum spokesperson describes as "municipal neoclassic" in style, will retain its original exterior, and interesting interior architectural aspects within (such as stone walls and archways) will be preserved. For the most part, however, the interior is being redone as a functional modern museum space. The museum will be open seven days a week; hours and admission policy have not yet been decided.

ANNUAL EVENTS: Pick up a calendar of events at the Fredericksburg Visitor Center. There's almost always something in the works.

A **Christmas Candlelight Weekend** in early December is highlighted by a nighttime walking tour to historic homes—all seasonally decorated—led by guides in Colonial costume. Strolling carolers and musicians, horse-drawn carriage rides, concerts (ballet excerpts from *The Nutcracker,* performances of Handel's *Messiah,* etc.), children's parties and puppet shows, and traditional refreshments are part of the fun. Fredericksburg also celebrates Christmas with a parade, a tree-trimming ceremony, and special events at various attractions.

February is a big month for celebrations honoring **George Washington's Birthday.**

The annual **Doll Show** in April features new and antique dolls on exhibition and for sale. April also brings **Historic Garden Week** (a statewide affair) with open house at 18th- and 19th-century homes.

In May Fredericksburg celebrates **Mother's Day** with a reenactment of Washington's farewell visit to his mother at the Mary Washington House. And in mid-month there's the traditional **Market Square Fair,** an annual event since 1738. Cobblestoned Market Square is filled with crafts booths and food stalls; musicians, clog dancers, and other entertainers perform.

The **Annual Fredericksburg Art Festival,** an outdoor show of works of professional and amateur artists, takes place in June, as does the **Great Rappahannock River Whitewater Canoe Race.**

On July 4th weekend there's a three-day celebration of the town's Colonial, Revolutionary, and Civil War roots—the **Fredericksburg Heritage Festival**—with walking tours, races, a riverside carnival, fireworks, arts and crafts shows, treasure hunts, battle reenactments, musical entertainment, food, and games. A recent year's events included a puppet show, a tug-of-war, a Huck Finn raft race, storytelling, and a karate exhibition as well. Fredericksburg is a great place to spend Independence Day.

If patchwork quilts are among your passions, be sure to catch the **Annual Quilt and Loom Show** in mid-September, with demonstrations, lectures, and quilts (both old and new) on exhibition and up for sale. Major museums loan quilts from their collections, some dating back to the early 1800s.

Those are the major events, but at any time you're likely to happen on an antique show, a needlework exhibition, an agricultural fair, a music festival, or a wine tasting.

SHOPPING: Like Alexandria, Fredericksburg caters to tourists with dozens of quaint "shoppes." Pick up a guide called *Antique Shops* at the Visitor Center for details on stores featuring collectibles, country furniture, hand-dipped candles, Amish quilts, hooked rugs, needlework supplies, and the like.

A few additional shops are worth seeking out:

Ben Franklin, 925 Caroline St., at William St. (tel. 703/373-0550), sells materials for every conceivable crafts activity—wreath making, duck decoy painting, stenciling, quilting, doll making, woodburning, pillow making, basketmaking, and all needlecrafts, among others. Many terrific kits for kids here too.

At **Galvanized Yankee,** 725 Caroline St., at Hanover St. (tel. 703/373-1886), merchandise runs the gamut from Civil War artifacts found in the area to

Civil War uniforms and pistols to T-shirts proclaiming "Save Your Confederate Money . . . the South Will Rise Again." The shop also features memorobilia from World Wars I and II and Vietnam.

At **Fredericksburg Pewter,** 309 Princess Elizabeth St., between Princess Anne and Charles Sts. (tel. 703/371-0585), craftsman Pelham L. Felder III creates exquisite pewter pieces—bowls, baby cups, goblets, spoons, plates, etc.—while you watch. It's quite interesting, and Felder's reasonably priced items make great gifts.

In a similar vein, **The Copper Shop,** 701 Sophia St., at Charlotte St. (tel. 703/371-4455), is the domain of coppersmiths Allen H. Green II and his son Allen III. They create handcrafted lamps, weathervanes, family crests, and other designed-to-order pieces.

WHERE TO EAT: Though generally I avoid restaurant chains, you can't beat **Shoney's Family Restaurant,** 2203 Plank Rd. at I-95 and Route 3 (tel. 703/371-5400), for breakfast. At all of its 80 locations, this southern chain offers an all-you-can-eat buffet of eggs, bacon, homefries, sausage, chipped beef, sauteed apples, pancakes, grits, fresh-baked buttermilk biscuits, country gravy, blueberry muffins, fruit, grated cheddar cheese, sliced tomatoes, and coffee for $3.79 on weekdays, $4.29 on weekends and holidays. Children under 12 pay $1.99 at any time. Kids can keep busy with free activities books while adults linger over the feast. Shoney's has a comfortable coffeeshop atmosphere with seating in roomy leather booths and a large glass-enclosed café area under a striped awning. It's open Sunday to Thursday from 6 a.m. to 11 p.m., on Friday and Saturday from 6 a.m. to midnight. No credit cards.

Sammy T's, 801 Caroline St. at Hanover St. (tel. 703/371-2008), is an inexpensive and simpático eatery offering a tasteful setting, good music, and a vaguely health-food orientation. It has a western feel, with large overhead fans suspended from a high pressed-tin ceiling, roomy knotty-pine booths, a long oak bar, and painted barnwood walls adorned with framed art posters. Sporting events are aired on a widescreen TV. Everything here is made from scratch. You might begin your meal with one of the hearty homemade soups, perhaps a Brunswick stew of chicken, tomatoes, potatoes, okra, lima beans, and corn ($1.10 a cup, $2.10 a bowl). Entree selections in the $3.50 to $6 range (mostly the former) include vegetarian lasagne; a baked potato stuffed with mushrooms, tomatoes, walnuts, sunflower seeds, three cheeses, and sprouts, topped with sour cream and served with soup; a whole-wheat pita stuffed with lightly sauteed vegetables and herbs topped with cheddar sauce and melted mozzarella; a cook's special salad of three cheeses, green peppers, mushrooms, tomatoes, ham, turkey, greens, and sprouts; and rare roast beef on a kaiser roll. Among the beverage choices are a good selection of beers, a French house wine, and gourmet teas and coffees. For dessert try fresh-baked creamy cheesecake with graham cracker crust ($1.75). Open Monday to Saturday from 11 a.m. to midnight, on Sunday to 9 p.m.

Arbuckle's, 1101 Sophia St. at Amelia St. (tel. 703/371-0775), is right on the Rappahannock River, and a long wall of riverside windows allows for superb views of the water and lush woods beyond. The outdoor scene grabs your attention, but the rest of the decor is tasteful—butcher-block tables, Breuer chairs, fans overhead, green carpeting, and hanging plants. An attractive bar/lounge adjoins. Though there are pricey dinner entrees, including many fresh seafood entrees, the entire menu is offered all day. At any hour you can order the quiche de jour with dinner salad, chef salad, a crabcake sandwich, and eight-ounce char-broiled burgers with toppings like sauteed mushrooms, fried onions, bacon, cheeses, etc. All of those are under $5. Arbuckle's is open on Sunday from 10 a.m. to midnight, Monday to Friday from 11:30 a.m. to midnight, and on Saturday to 1 a.m.

The delightful **La Petite Auberge,** 311 William St., between Princess Anne and Charles Sts. (tel. 703/371-2727), is designed to look like a garden, an effect enhanced by a back wall with windows and a door that seems like the rear of a house, white latticework, and garden furnishings. Unpainted brick walls are hung with copper pots and cheerful oil paintings, and candlelit white-clothed tables are adorned with fresh flowers. A cozy lounge adjoins.

The menu changes daily. On a recent lunchtime visit it included a salade Niçoise, tortellini in cream sauce, poulet aux champignons, avocado stuffed with curried chicken salad, and fresh country sausage baked with tomatoes, onions, and green peppers—all in the $4.50 to $6.50 range. A great bargain here is the Early Bird dinner, a prix fixe in the $9 to $11 range served Monday to Thursday from 5:30 to 7 p.m. It begins with a soup (perhaps lobster bisque) and salad, goes on to a choice of about ten entrees (like bluefish amandine, chicken with Amoretto, pasta stuffed with ground veal in cream sauce, or eggs Benedict), and finishes with a dish of ice cream. Later dinners are *très cher.* Open weekdays for lunch from 11:30 a.m. to 2:30 p.m., for dinner Monday to Saturday from 5:30 to 10 p.m. Reservations suggested at dinner. Saturday nights owner/chef Christian Renault's trio plays jazz in the lounge, and local musicians come to jam.

There's more Colonial ambience over at **Chimneys Tavern,** 623 Caroline St., at Charlotte St. (tel. 703/371-9229), a restaurant housed in a handsome Georgian building that dates back to 1769. The original wide-plank flooring can still be seen in the drawing room and bar; the building has sash windows, beaded weatherboards, and end chimneys, all very typical of the period; and in the tap room a section of the original brickwork is exposed. The dining rooms are lovely, especially the drawing room with its ornately trimmed ceiling. Throughout, paneling and wainscotting are painted in traditional Williamsburg colors. Pewter sconces and chandeliers, classical music, fresh flowers on every table, working fireplaces, and at night, hurricane-lamp lighting all combine to create a charming setting. Dinner here is out of our league, with entrees in the $10 to $16 range, but at lunch, items like a baked brie and chicken breast sandwich, a smoked trout platter, an avocado and duck breast sandwich, deep-dish quiche, and brook trout amandine are in the $4 to $6 range. For dessert there's a very good fresh-baked pecan pie, and six to eight premium wines are featured by the glass each day. Chimneys recently opened a Back Porch café and patio. Open daily from 11:30 a.m. to 12:30 a.m., this al fresco area offers a light-fare menu with items in the $3.50 to $8 range. Live music is planned. Chimneys Tavern is open daily for lunch/Sunday brunch from 11:30 a.m. to 3 p.m. Reservations suggested.

Fredericksburg boasts a very good—and very reasonably priced—Italian eatery called **Ristorante Renato,** 422 William St. at Prince Edward St. (tel. 703/ 371-8228). Its decor is homey—candlelit (at night) white-linened tables adorned with fresh flowers, ceramic candelabra chandeliers overhead, oil paintings of Italy lining the walls, and a working fireplace. A room off to the side with polished pine floors, wainscotted walls, lace-curtained windows, and just six booths, is especially cozy. And the ambience throughout is enhanced by Italian opera played as background music.

In addition to a regular menu, Renato features a complete luncheon Monday to Friday for just $5.95. It includes salad, bread and butter, and a choice of entrees like eggplant parmigiana, fettuccine Alfredo, steamed mussels in white sauce, and pollo alla zingara—chicken breast with spring onions and mushrooms in brandy sauce. A similar Early Bird dinner, served from 4:30 to 7 p.m.

weekdays only, features salad, bread, choice of entree, dessert, coffee, and a glass of wine for $9.95, $18.95 per couple with a demi-carafe of wine. À la carte entrees run the gamut from baked lasagne ($4.95) to shrimp scampi ($8.95). For dessert try a Sicilian cannoli. Ristorante Renato is open weekdays for lunch from 11:30 a.m. to 2 p.m., nightly for dinner from 4:30 to 10:30 p.m.

Over at the quaintly charming **Smythe's Cottage,** 303 Fauquier St., at Princess Anne St. (tel. 703/373-1645), you can dine on traditional Virginia fare on the site of a blacksmith's stable operated by George Washington's brother. The current building is a later converted blacksmith's stable dating from 1840. The original owner hailed from an old Virginia family, hence the photograph of General Grant upside down next to a photo of her great-great-grandfather who was hung by the Union army in the Civil War. The low-ceilinged interior is extremely cozy with Colonial-style furnishings, old oil portraits and family memorabilia on the walls, white-curtained multipaned windows, and oak tables (candlelight at night) adorned with Federalist blue napkins wound in the drinking glasses. In winter the restaurant is warmed by a wood-burning stove; in summer there's al fresco dining in a flower-bordered garden. Waiters and waitresses are attired in a facsimile of Colonial garb. The inn-like ambience is enhanced by a menu featuring lunch items like peanut soup (the best I've ever had; $1.75), a hearty beef stew in ginger sauce ($6.50), and delicious chicken pot pie with carrots, onions, and mushrooms (also $6.50). The latter entrees are served with a basket of homemade biscuits and cornbread, a salad, and a buffet of vegetables that included bourbon sweet potatoes, peas, stringbeans, and hot cinnamon applesauce on my last visit. After all that, you won't really have room for the homemade desserts, but you might just manage to split an order of apple cobbler or blueberry crisp. Dinner entrees are mostly in the $9 to $11 range. "Sherman on the Run," made from gin, white wine, lemon juice, cherry brandy, and grenadine, is the house specialty drink. Open daily except Tuesday from 11 a.m. to 9 p.m. Reservations suggested on weekends. Even Yankees are welcome.

WHERE TO STAY: Instead of rushing about madly trying to see everything in a day, why not spend a night or two in this charming town? There are some very special accommodations to choose from, beginning with a quaint country inn.

A stay at the **Fredericksburg Colonial Inn,** 1707 Princess Anne St. (between Ford and Herndon Sts.), Fredericksburg, VA 22401 (tel. 703/371-5666), can only enhance the Fredericksburg journey-into-history experience. Among other things, it happens to be a hub for Civil War buffs, and people participating in local Civil War reenactments often drop by; don't be surprised to see musket-toting Blues and Grays in the lobby. In the Conference Room there's a display of Civil War weaponry and Confederate dollars, as well as literature on the era. And each of the 30 rooms (10 of them are actually two-room suites with full parlors) is named for a period notable such as Robert E. Lee or Jefferson Davis; if you're a Yankee, ask for the Lincoln room. They're all exquisitely furnished with antiques (owner Alton Echols, Jr., is an avid collector). Perhaps you'll draw a marble-topped walnut dresser, rag rug, canopied bed, bowl and pitcher, Victorian sofa, or a bed that belonged to George Mason's son. Floors are glossy pine, and walls are adorned with beautiful works of art and antique mirrors. Even the hallways are lined with English hunting prints and fine paintings. All rooms have marble-topped sinks and such modern amenities as private bath, air conditioning, a small refrigerator, cable color TV, and clock radio (no phones, but the desk takes messages on incoming calls, and there's a public phone in the lobby). Speaking of the lobby, it's comfortably furnished with wicker rocking chairs, magazines and books are provided, and there's a player piano on which you can listen to oldies like "I'll Be with You in Apple Blossom Time." Guest sing-alongs are a frequent evening activity. A single is $40; a double, $45; a suite, $55 for two; a two-room family unit, $65 for four; $5 for each additional person. Rates include complimentary coffee and doughnuts in the morning, and there's no charge for children 6 and under. One final plus: a laundry room where guests can use washers and dryers free of charge. This delightful inn is extremely popular. Reserve far in advance. Highest recommendation.

Equally quaint is the lovely **McGrath House,** 225 Princess Anne St. (just off Elizabeth St.), Fredericksburg, VA 22401 (tel. 703/371-4363), offering bed-and-breakfast accommodations in a restored early-19th-century home on a quiet tree-lined street. Charming hostess Sylvia McGrath invites guests to share a drink by the fire or watch the color TV in her parlor. She serves up breakfast (fresh fruit or fresh-squeezed juice, homemade biscuits or muffins, homemade jams, and tea or coffee) at an old oak table in a country kitchen with brick floors, hand-hewn beams, and gingham-curtained windows. Her three rented rooms are charmingly furnished with antiques but offer 20th-century comforts like air conditioning and clock radios. They don't have phones, but messages are taken on incoming calls. There's a picnic table in the garden. Rates, including breakfast, are $35 single, $40 double. Guests share an immaculate redwood-paneled bathroom down the hall. McGrath House is a gem. Once again, reserve far in advance.

Moving into the 20th century, there's a 48-room **Econo Lodge** conveniently located at the junction of I-95 and Route 3 (tel. 703/786-8374 or toll free 800/446-6900). Here you have your standard modern American motel room with direct-dial phone, color TV, and tub/shower bath. Rates are $27 to $29 for one person in a room with one double bed, $32 to $34 for two in a room with one double bed, $37 to $39 for two in a room with two double beds. An extra person pays $4; children under 12 stay free.

If the above is filled, or you'd like a motel with a swimming pool, there's another **Econo Lodge** (this one with 175 rooms) a few miles south just above the intersection of I-95 and U.S. 1 (tel. 703/898-5440 or toll free 800/446-6900). Rates here are just a tad higher, especially in summer, I suppose because of the pool and a Scotty's Pancake House on the premises.

Both Econo Lodges offer a seventh night free if you stay for six nights.

One final choice is the spanking-new **Hampton Inn,** 2310 Plank Rd. at the Intersection of I-95 and Route 3 East, Fredericksburg, VA 22401 (tel. 703/371-0330 or toll free 800/HAMPTON). Built in July, 1986, it is part of a new affordable-accommodations chain operated by Holiday Inn. Hampton Inn hotels have no on-premises restaurants or lounges but are located near such facilities. In this case Shoney's (see above) is just across the street, and a Chesapeake Bay Seafood House plus inexpensive Mexican and Polynesian restaurants are very close by. The hotel itself is a five-minute drive from the Historic District of Fredericksburg. The Inn's 166 rooms are nicely decorated in forest green/sienna/ecru color schemes and furnished with attractive oak pieces. All offer direct-dial phone, color TV with HBO, and modern bath. On premises facilities include a nice-sized outdoor pool and courtyard and a washer/dryer for guest use. Parking is free, as are local calls and a continental breakfast (juice, doughnuts, and coffee) served in the lobby each morning.

Rates are $45 single, $55 double April through October, about $5 less across the board the rest of the year. There's no charge for an additional person of any age. Under the same ownership are two nearby properties offering similar facilities and rates. So if the Hampton Inn is fully booked, ask to be placed at one of these.

Chapter IX

FARTHER AFIELD

1. **Charlottesville**
2. **Richmond**
3. **Williamsburg**
4. **Jamestown**
5. **Yorktown**
6. **Annapolis**
7. **Baltimore: The Inner Harbor**

IF YOU HAVE MORE TIME at your disposal, you'll certainly want to explore the history-rich areas farther away from Washington. From Williamsburg and Jamestown in the east to Charlottesville in the west to a jaunt to Annapolis and Baltimore, Maryland. Any of these destinations, each well worth a trip in its own right, can provide a memorable addition to your Washington visit.

1. Charlottesville

In the foothills of the Blue Ridge Mountains—an arcadian setting of scenic rolling hills and pastureland—Charlottesville is "Mr. Jefferson's Country." One of America's most passionate believers in freedom and human rights, Thomas Jefferson was born four miles east of Charlottesville. Here he built his famous mountaintop home, Monticello; selected the site for and helped plan Ash Lawn, home of James Monroe; designed his "academical village," the still-extant University of Virginia; and died on July 4, 1826, at home—"All my wishes end where I hope my days will end . . . at Monticello." (An eerie note: Three out of our first five presidents, the others being Adams and Monroe, died on July 4th).

Established in 1762 as the county seat for Albermarle, the town was named for England's Queen Charlotte, the young wife of George III. The original town consisted of 50 acres centered on Court Square, its Court House complete with a jail, whipping post, pillory, and stocks to keep fractious citizens in line. In the early days the Court House doubled as a church, with rotating services for different denominations and everyone attending them all. Jefferson called it the "Common Temple." It also served as a marketplace. Elections were held in Court Square followed by raucous political celebrations. The taverns across the street were well patronized. Today the historic square is a quiet place, and the action centers on a very up-to-date pedestrian mall of shops and restaurants adjacent to it.

Jefferson and Monroe were not Charlottesville's only famous early citi-

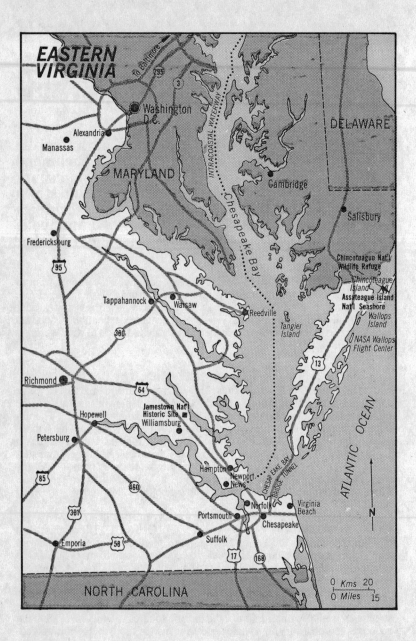

EASTERN VIRGINIA

zens. James Madison also lived close by. The trio (our third, fourth, and fifth presidents) was instrumental in developing the emerging nation. Jefferson was our first great democrat, advocating freedom of religion, public education, and abolition of slavery. He wrote the Declaration of Independence. Madison was involved in the development of our Constitution and Bill of Rights. And Monroe was one of the two American presidents to actually fight in the Revolution. More of Monroe's achievements are detailed in the description of Ash Lawn, below.

On the 200th anniversary of Charlottesville in 1962, another great American, John Fitzgerald Kennedy, commented, "Both the natural beauty of the surrounding countryside and the man-made beauty of Charlottesville combine to weave a tapestry of American history which few other towns or cities can boast."

Though today's Charlottesville is a cosmopolitan center, it is still sufficiently unchanged and pastoral for visitors to imagine themselves back in Colonial times when Jefferson would ride two miles on horseback to visit his friend, Monroe. The sights include not only the above-mentioned Monticello, Ash Lawn, and the University of Virginia, but a restored 18th-century tavern that welcomed many a famous guest.

To get there, take the Theodore Roosevelt Memorial Bridge (Route 66) to U.S. 29 South. It's a 120-mile drive.

FIRST STOP: Make your first stop in town the **Thomas Jefferson Visitors Bureau** (tel. 804/977-1783), on Route 20 just off I-64 (you'll see signs as you approach from Washington). The center provides maps and literature about local and state attractions, makes hotel/motel reservations, and answers any questions; in short, it offers all visitor services.

In addition to welcoming visitors, the Bureau maintains a marvelous permanent exhibit called "Thomas Jefferson at Monticello," a collection of some 400 objects and artifacts, family memorabilia, architectural models, audiovisual presentations, and explanatory postings that allow the visitor to trace the evolution of Monticello from wooded mountaintop to full working plantation. Perusing it will very much enhance your visit to Jefferson's home. Among the exhibits are Jefferson's preliminary drawings for the house with his candlestick and quill pen alongside; his books and writings; his calling card to the court of Louis XVI; a letter written by Jefferson with his left hand after he dislocated his right wrist in a fall; tools and implements from his blacksmith shop and nailery; a full-scale model of the plough he invented; slave artifacts; a copy of the deed of manumission freeing Robert Hemings, a slave on Jefferson's plantation; detailed farm journals kept by Jefferson: recipes; and much more. Jefferson's private life, both at Monticello and elsewhere is explored in depth. Many of the objects on display here have only recently been uncovered during archaeological excavations on the Monticello grounds. The exhibit is arranged chronologically in ten sections beginning with the design and construction of the house based on ancient Roman architecture and the creation of orchards, vineyards, flower and vegetable gardens. Gardening was Jefferson's lifelong passion. After the death of his wife in 1782, Jefferson wrote, "The state of my mind concurred in recommending the change of scene," and he embarked on a European tour, serving for some years as Minister to France. Greatly influenced by European culture, he returned to America with exciting plans for Monticello and immediately began to restore his depleted farmlands and create additional sources of income for the plantation. By 1796, the hub of Monticello activity was Mulberry Row, where numerous artisan shops, a stable, and storage sheds were located. The next period explored is Jefferson's retirement to Monticello in 1809 after a term as vice president and two as president. His domestic pursuits from this time through his death in 1826 are examined here. Jefferson wrote of the disciplined regimen he followed in retirement: "My mornings are devoted to correspondence. From breakfast to dinner, I am in my shops, my garden, or on horseback among my farms. From dinner to dark, I give to society and recreation with my neighbors and friends. From candle light to early bedtime I read." The creation of the University of Virginia occupied a great deal of these final years. The last section of the exhibit deals with Monticello after Jefferson (1826 to the present).

After viewing the exhibition, purchase the **Presidents' Pass,** a combined discount ticket for admission to Monticello, Michie Tavern, and Ash Lawn. Cost is $12, a savings of about 20%. Don't buy it for children under 12; they pay just $1 at each attraction anyway. The center is open daily from 9 a.m. to 5 p.m., till 5:30 p.m. March through October. A gift shop is on the premises. If you'd like to receive information before you arrive, write to the Thomas Jefferson Visitors Center, P.O. Box 161, Charlottesville, VA 22902.

SIGHTSEEING IN "MR. JEFFERSON'S COUNTRY": There's so much to see and do in Charlottesville that although it's only a 2½-hour drive from D.C., I recommend staying over a night or two. Three major sights are conveniently grouped near each other on Virginia Route 53. The first of these is:

Monticello

The phrase "Renaissance man" might have been coined to describe Thomas Jefferson. Perhaps our most important founding father, he was also a lawyer, architect, scientist, musician, writer, educator, and horticulturist. Monticello (pronounced "Montichello"), the home he built over a 40-year period (1769—1809) on the "little mountain" where he played as a boy, is considered an architectural masterpiece. It's often remarked that no other home in America so well reflects the personality of its owner. Monticello was the first Virginia plantation to sit atop a mountain (great houses were usually by rivers), and Jefferson rejected the Georgian architecture that characterized his time, opting instead for the 16th-century Italian style of Andrea Palladio whose works he knew largely from books. Jefferson was later influenced by the houses of noblemen at the court of Louis XVI that he observed during his five-year term as minister to France. Upon his return in 1789 he enlarged his house, doubling it in size and incorporating features of the Hôtel de Salm in Paris, a building he greatly admired. He explained this occupation to a visitor thusly: "architecture is my delight, and putting up and pulling down one of my favorite amusements."

Work on the dome, based on that of the ancient temple of Vesta in Rome, began in 1800. The friezes at Monticello are also adapted from Roman buildings.

In addition to innovative architecture, Jefferson introduced some newfangled gadgetry into his home—a dumbwaiter, a seven-day clock, and a revolving door with shelves so that servants could send food into the dining room without being present themselves (the first Automat).

Today the house is restored as closely as possible to its appearance during Jefferson's retirement years. Nearly all of the furniture and other household objects were owned by Jefferson or his family. The garden has been extended to its original 1000-foot length, and the Mulberry Row dependencies—a joinery, smokehouse, dairy, nailery (Jefferson's nail factory supplied much of central Virginia), blacksmith shop, weaver's cottage, slave and servants' quarters, etc. —have been excavated. You can view their foundations.

Twenty-minute guided tours of the house (tel. 804/295-8181 or 295-2657 for details) are given from 8 a.m. to 5 p.m. March through October, 9 a.m. to 4:30

p.m. the rest of the year. Admission is $6, $1 for children 6 to 11. It's best to avoid weekends when tourist traffic is heaviest, and during summer the first tour at 8 a.m. is advised. Allow at least another half hour to explore the grounds (you'll be given a map at the end of the house tour). There are lovely wooded picnic areas with tables and grills on the premises. In summer box lunches can be purchased.

In Jefferson's day the Entrance Hall was a museum. The antlers and moosehead here displayed were brought back from Lewis and Clark's famed expedition, and the mastodon fossils are close to 10,000 years old. (Jefferson also displayed American Indian artifacts here.) Busts of Turgot, Voltaire, Jefferson, and Hamilton, and a statue of Ariadne, are as Jefferson placed them. This room also contains the seven-day calendar clock, which still works.

Just off the Entrance Hall is Jefferson's high-ceilinged bedroom, which features a skylight overhead. Jefferson died in this room at the age of 83.

Opposite the bedroom is his Book Room, which contained over 6,000 books, later sold to the government and forming the nucleus of the Library of Congress. A revolving chair, revolving table, and chaise-lounge-like Windsor couch allowed him to work in a recumbent position, a necessity in later years when he was troubled with rheumatism. On the desk is a polygraph, not a lie detector but an 18th-century duplicating device; writing with one pen automatically operates a second, creating an exact replica. One of his telescopes (he was also an amateur astronomer) sits in the south window.

In the adjacent "South Square Room," used as a sitting room, is a portrait of Jefferson's oldest daughter, Martha, painted by Thomas Sully in 1836 when she was 64. Martha inherited the home along with sizable debts, and within five years sold it for a mere $7,000.

The Parlor, a semi-octagonal room with a Jefferson-designed parquet cherry floor of ten-inch squares bordered in beechwood (unique in its day), was the scene of family musicales (Jefferson played violin; his wife, Martha, the harpsichord), marriages, and christenings. Many of the furnishings were Paris purchases, including the large pier mirrors and the gilt and marble clock. Busts of Alexander V and Napoleon flank the doors to the lawn, and the walls are hung with many of Jefferson's finest paintings.

The Parlor opens into the Dining Room, where the family would assemble for the evening meal at 3:30 p.m. Here you'll see the dumbwaiters which allowed wine to be sent up from the cellar, and the revolving serving door. Jefferson liked to dine *en famille* without servants listening in on the conversation. He kept books by the table, so he could read while waiting for the family to assemble. The busts of Benjamin Franklin, John Paul Jones, George Washington, John Adams, and Lafayette in the connecting Tea Room are copies of Houdon originals that once graced this room.

Across the passage is the octagonal Madison Room, its wallpaper of the lattice and treillage pattern Jefferson saw and admired in Paris. An unusual feature for the 18th century was a built-in closet, though even Jefferson didn't think of hangers. Cupboards and linen presses were the order of the day.

Second- and third-floor rooms are not open to visitors. On the grounds you'll see the "dependencies," including the kitchen, wine room, rum cellar, and "cyder room." There's an orchard with about ten varieties of fruit, a vineyard, a vegetable garden, and a beautiful English garden with groupings of ornamental trees and flower beds. Mulberry Row (described above) was named for the mulberries Jefferson planted there; stop in at the nearby gift shop. At the end of the south terrace is the "Honeymoon Cottage," to which Jefferson brought his bride on a cold, snowy night in 1772. Because of deep snow they had to abandon their horse-drawn carriage and proceed the last few miles of rough mountain terrain on horseback. Criss-crossing the grounds are farm roads, roundabouts, serpentine walks, and wooded pathways. Jefferson's grave is in the family burial ground (still in use), inscribed according to his instructions with his own words "and not a word more"—"Here was buried Thomas Jefferson/Author of the Declaration of Independence/Of the Statute of Virginia for religious freedom/And Father of the University of Virginia."

After visiting the graveyard, you can take a shuttle bus back to the visitor parking lot or walk through the woods via a delightful path.

Historic Michie Tavern

Unless you're picnicking at Monticello, plan your visit to Michie Tavern (pronounced "Mickey"), down the road a stretch on Route 53 (tel. 804/977-1234), to coincide with lunchtime. In the "Ordinary," a converted log cabin with original hand-hewn walls and beamed ceilings, hot meals are still served to weary travelers for reasonable pence. You can sample traditional southern cuisine—fried chicken, black-eyed peas, corn, homemade coleslaw, fresh-baked biscuits and cornbread, potato salad, stewed tomatoes, and green-bean salad. It's served in an all-you-can-eat buffet priced at $7.35 for adults, $2.75 for children ages 6 to 11, under 6 free. You'll dine off pewter plates at rustic oak tavern tables, in winter before a blazing fire. The meal is served from 11:30 a.m. to 3 p.m. daily. (*Note:* There is no smoking in this historically precious dining room.)

In 1746 Scotsman John Michie (known as "Scotch John") purchased 1152 acres of land from Patrick Henry's father, and in 1784 Michie's son, William, built this historic tavern on a well-traveled stagecoach route. It was moved in 1927 to its present location but is otherwise unchanged. There are many colorful stories about Scotch John. Ousted from Scotland in 1716 following the Jacobite uprising in which he took part, it's said that he and his friend, James Watson, were among a group of prisoners sentenced randomly to death or deportation. The prisoners lined up to draw beans from a bag. A white bean meant deportation, a black bean death. Michie reached in and drew a white bean. His friend, Watson, a "poltroon," was shaking so much he could not raise his arm to draw one. So Michie handed him his white bean and promptly drew another, also white—and those were the only white beans drawn that day! Probably 95% legend, but a good yarn.

In addition to running the inn, the Michies also farmed the land, did some blacksmithing, and ran a general store in which women could purchase a ribbon or pair of shoes and men could buy gunpowder, boots, nails, and wagon wheels. There was slave help, of course, though the superstitious slaves refused to tend the tomato crop. Many people still believed tomatoes were poisonous in Colonial times; they were often called "the devil's apples."

Like the Rising Sun Tavern described above in Fredericksburg, Michie's had rules: no more than five to a bed, no boots to be worn in bed, no dogs allowed upstairs, organ grinders to sleep in the wash house, and no razor grinders or tinkers taken in.

William Michie was an ardent patriot who later served in the militia. After the war, he returned to run the inn. Michie descendants owned the property through 1910.

The tavern contains an excellent collection of pre–Revolutionary War furniture and artifacts. William Michie's rifle hangs over the mantel in the Keeping Hall (where food was kept warm en route from kitchen to dining room) and an 18th-century still stands in the wine cellar.

You can take a self-guided tour, enhanced by recorded narratives in each room, daily between 9 a.m. and 5 p.m. (except Christmas and New Year's days). Admission is $3.50 for adults, $1 for children 6 to 11. An introduction is given by hostesses in Colonial dress when you enter.

In the Ladies' Parlor you'll see 18th-century women's boots and a skirt hoop. The Ballroom was the social center of the whole countryside, where fiddlers played tunes like "Lumps of Pudding" and "The Sow in the Sack," and lively Virginia reels and minuets were danced. The ballroom was also the scene of weddings, and like the Court House, sometimes served as a place of worship. Items like a cheese press, curd breaker, and corn shucker can be seen in the Eating Hall.

Behind the tavern are reproductions of the "dependencies"—an old log kitchen; a "necessary" (note the corncobs, not exactly squeezably soft); the dairy, which in Michie's time was filled with crocks of butter, milk, cream, eggs, and cheeses; the smokehouse, where deer, rabbit, and other game was cured; the ice house; and the root cellar, in which apples, corn, and wheat were stored.

The general store is recreated, along with an excellent crafts shop and Virginia wine exhibit on the floor above. Behind the store is a grist mill which has operated continuously since 1797. There's a corn sheller and wheat cleaner to examine here too.

Ash Lawn–Highland

James Monroe played a sizable role in early American history. He fought in the Revolution and was wounded in Trenton, recovered, and went on to hold more offices than any other president, including several foreign ministries, four-time governor of Virginia, U.S. senator, secretary of state, and secretary of war. He was president for eight years (1817 to 1825, known as "The Era of Good Feelings"), negotiated the Louisiana Purchase with Napoleon's representatives, and, via the Monroe Doctrine, warned European rulers that this hemisphere was henceforth off-limits.

Monroe's close friendship with Thomas Jefferson brought him to Charlottesville, where Jefferson wished to create "a society to our taste." In 1793 he purchased 3500 acres 2½ miles south of Monticello and built an estate he called Highland, perhaps because of his Scottish ancestry. (The name Ash Lawn dates to 1838 and a later owner, John Massey; Massey also built the two-story addition with Victorian portico entrance in 1930 which today makes the house seem more imposing than it was in Monroe's time.) Before Monroe had a chance to settle in, Washington named him minister to France and sent him off to Europe for five years. During his absence, Jefferson sent gardeners over to start orchards, and the Madisons also made agricultural contributions. By the time Monroe returned from France in 1799 and moved into Highland with his wife, Elizabeth, he was already in financial difficulties (a situation which would last to the end of his life), and his "cabin castle" developed along more modest lines than originally intended. When he retired in 1825 his debts totaled $75,000, and he was forced to sell the beloved farm where he had hoped to spend his last days.

Since 1974 Ash Lawn and 550 surrounding acres have been under the auspices of the College of William and Mary (Monroe's alma mater), and restoration/excavation/historical research has been an ongoing process. On a 40-minute house tour you'll see some of the estate's original furnishings (the rest are appropriate period pieces) and artifacts, and learn a great deal about our fifth president. Many special events (concerts, festivals, etc.) take place here (details below), there are crafts demonstrations (weaving, spinning, Colonial cooking, etc.) in the old kitchen, horses and cattle graze in the fields, and about two dozen peacocks roam the boxwood gardens wherein is a statue of Monroe.

Five of the original rooms remain today, along with the basement kitchen (where you can see a Colonial waffle iron—Monroe loved waffles—and a cook-

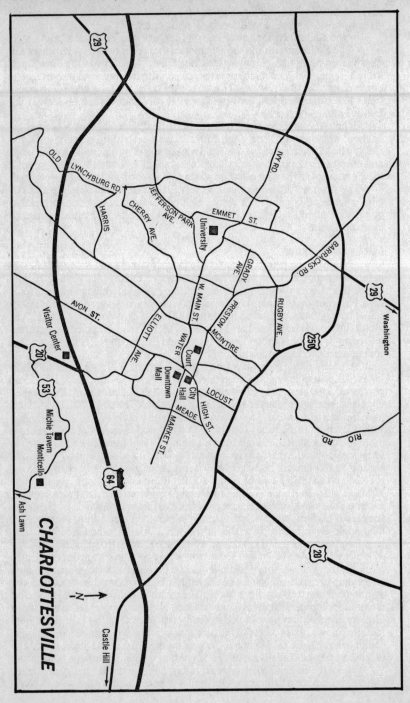

ie press with a picture of George Washington), the overseer's cottage (Monroe owned about 30 slaves), restored slave quarters, and the old smokehouse. Of special interest are the French hunting-motif wallpaper—a reproduction of an 1831 design—in the sitting room (the Monroes were very Frenchified in their taste); the pine floor in the study, once a porch, made with nails from Jefferson's foundry; the many original Monroe pieces in the dining room, a Hepplewhite mahogany table and White House chairs among them; and the 18th-century dolls and original crib and cradle in the children's room. On the grounds are a gift shop and picnic tables.

Ash Lawn is open for viewing daily from 9 a.m. to 6 p.m. March 1 through October 31, from 10 a.m. to 5 p.m. the rest of the year. Adults pay $4; children 6 to 11, $1. For further details, call 804/293-9539.

The University of Virginia

Charlottesville is a lively university town centered on Jefferson's "academical village," the University of Virginia, on University Ave. (tel. 804/924-7969), with its spacious lawns, serpentine-walled gardens, colonnaded pavilions, and classical rotunda inspired by the Pantheon in Rome. Jefferson regarded its creation (all the more remarkable when you consider it was begun in his 75th year) as one of his three greatest achievements.

He was in every sense the "father" of this institution. He conceived it, wrote the charter, raised money for its construction, drew the plans (thousands of drawings accounting for every minute detail), selected the site, laid the cornerstone in 1817, supervised construction, served as the first rector, selected the faculty, and created the curriculum. His good friends, Monroe and Madison, sat with him on the first board, and Madison succeeded him as rector, serving for eight years.

Jefferson described his design as follows: "The plan of the building is not to erect one single magnificent building to contain everybody and everything, but to make of it an academical village in which every professor should have his separate house, containing his lecturing room with two, three or four rooms for his own accommodation according as he may have a family or no family . . . distinct dormitories for the students, not more than two to a room; and separated boarding houses for dieting them by private housekeepers."

Focal point of the university and starting point for tours is the Rotunda (at Rugby Road). Except for two weeks around Christmas, there are free half-hour tours daily at 10 and 11 a.m., and 2, 3, and 4 p.m.

Some 600 feet of tree-dotted lawn extends from the south portico of the Rotunda to what is now Cabell Hall, a building designed at the turn of the century by Stanford White. Originally there was a view of the mountains that Jefferson loved. On either side of the lawn are pavilions designed and still used for faculty housing (by having faculty living on campus, Jefferson hoped to encourage student-faculty fraternization), each of a different architectural style (though harmonious) "to serve as specimens for the Architectural lecturer." Behind each pavilion is a large garden, originally functional in use (faculty members grew vegetables and kept livestock), but today kept up as decorative landscaping by the Garden Club of Virginia. Behind the gardens are the original student dormitories, used—and greatly coveted—by graduate and honor students today. Though centrally heated, they still have working fireplaces. The room Edgar Allan Poe occupied when he was a student here (no. 13, wouldn't you know it?) is authentically furnished as it would have been in 1826 and on view to visitors.

Lest you think colleges were serene havens of learning in Jefferson's day, it may interest you to know that the first year of the University of Virginia's existence (1825) was marked by student rioting and a consequent faculty resignation. Strict rules followed, and students rioted again (over wearing uniforms) in 1831 and publicly horsewhipped the chairman of the faculty in 1839. A year later a professor was actually shot and mortally wounded by a rowdy student. After that, things settled down a bit—at least until the 1960s.

The Rotunda has gone through many changes over the years, and was ruined in a fire in 1895. Happily for us, it is today restored as Jefferson designed it. On the tour you'll see the oval-shaped chemistry room; the Rotunda bell, originally hung on the south portico and used to wake students at dawn (no wonder they rioted); classrooms; the library; and the magnificent colonnaded Dome Room. The Alexander Galt statue on the second floor (originally the main entry level) is said to be an excellent likeness; there's another statue of Jefferson, by Sir Moses Ezekiel, on the esplanade north of the Rotunda.

While exploring the grounds and gardens, do take a peek in the lovely chapel built in 1890.

Montpelier

The home of James Madison, Montpelier was opened to the public by the National Trust in 1987 after decades as a private residence belonging to the du Pont family. Located in beautiful Virginia hunt country, the 2,700-acre estate overlooking the Blue Ridge mountains was home to three generations of the Madison family.

Born in 1751, James Madison rose to prominence early in life. At the 1776 Constitutional Convention in Williamsburg, he insured the guarantee of religious freedom in the Virginia Declaration of Rights. He remained a strong advocate of the separation of church and state throughout his life. From 1780 to 1783, he represented Virginia at the Continental Congress in Philadelphia, and later, elected to the House of Representatives of the new nation, he worked for passage of the Bill of Rights and for the creation of the executive departments. These efforts earned him the title "Father of the Constitution." After four terms in Congress, Madison retired to his father's modest two-story, red-brick Georgian residence, and with advice from his good friend Jefferson, began expanding its proportions. He married the widow Dolley Payne Todd in 1794; Aaron Burr introduced them. In 1801, Madison became secretary of state under Jefferson and in 1809 succeeded Jefferson as president, leading the fledgling nation during the War of 1812. After his term, Madison (Jefferson called him "the best farmer in the world") returned to his Montpelier plantation. Like Jefferson he pioneered agricultural improvements and struggled with the moral dilemma posed by slavery. He proposed a plan for gradual emancipation and the transportation of freed slaves to Liberia, however, for economic reasons he was never able to free his own slaves. Madison's final years, once again like Jefferson, were much taken up with the University of Virginia where he served as rector. After his death, Dolley, in poor health and spirits, spent vast sums paying off debts incurred by the ne'er-do-well son of her first marriage, John Payne Todd, an alcoholic and gambler. She sold Montpelier in 1848 to continue supporting him and died a year later.

The estate changed hands many times between 1844 and 1901, when it was purchased by William du Pont, Sr. He enlarged the mansion and added barns, staff houses, a saw mill, blacksmith shop, train station, dairy, and greenhouses. His wife created a 2½-acre formal garden. And when daughter Marion du Pont Scott inherited the property she had a steeplechase course built on it and initiated the Montpelier Hunt Races which are still held here every November. The National Trust acquired the property following her death in 1984.

To date, little has been done to restore the sparsely furnished 55-room house. However, it still makes for an interesting tour. Visitors enter via Dolley Madison's drawing room, which in her day was hung with Gilbert Stuart portraits. Highlights include the ornate Adam Room with its silk damask wallpaper, wedgewood fireplace, and intricate gilded ceiling; the art deco Red Room, its walls covered with photographs of Mrs. Scott's racehorses; the du Pont dining room, wherein a film about Madison is shown; and Dolley's dining room, which the du Ponts used as a billiard room. For some reason, most of the rooms are papered or painted in yellow. Do leave time after the tour to explore the gardens. On the way out, you'll see the family cemetery where James and Dolley are buried.

To get to Montpelier take Route 29 north to Route 33 east at Ruckersville. At Barboursville, turn left onto Route 20 north. Admission price—$5 for adults, $4 for seniors, $1 for children 6 to 11, under 6 free—includes a 10-minute slide show adjacent to the admissions booth, a bus tour of the grounds, and the house tour. A gift shop on the premises sells country store items—dried flowers, patchwork place mats, needlepoint kits, and such. Tours depart every half hour between 10 a.m. and 4 p.m.

Once again, keep in mind that this is no Monticello. Years of research into architecture and social history will be necessary before Montpelier takes its place alongside similar Virginia restorations.

WINERY TOURS: Charlottesville is not only horse country and Jefferson country, it's wine country. There have been vineyards here since the 18th century, and Jefferson hoped to someday produce quality wines in Virginia. Today his dream is a reality, and area wineries offer tours and tastings. Pick up a brochure at the Visitors Bureau.

The Albemarle County Court House

The center of village activity in Colonial days, today the Court House has a facade and portico dating from the Civil War. There's no guided or self-guided tour here, but you can take a glance at Jefferson's will in the County Office Building. Pick up a brochure called *A Guide to Historic Downtown Charlottesville* for a walking tour detailing this and other historic downtown sights.

The Mall

Stroll into the 20th century along a charming pedestrian brick mall extending for about eight blocks on downtown Main Street. You can park free for two hours with merchant validation in the lot at 505 East Market St. or on any of the lots along Water Street. In addition to shops and restaurants (several with outdoor cafés), the mall has a movie theater that charges only $1.50 for tickets to major features. It's enhanced by fountains, benches under shade trees, and big pots of flowers. Call 804/296-8548 to find out about events on the mall during your stay. They might include art shows, musical performances, plays, etc.

A few blocks off the mall at 201 2nd St. NW, between Market and Jefferson Sts. (tel. 804/295-7973), take a look at the works displayed at the **McGuffey Art Center.** Local artists and craftspeople—painters, potters, quiltmakers, sculptors, photographers, etc.—have studios on the premises and exhibit and sell their creations. The Second Street Gallery, showing contemporary art from all over the U.S., is also located here. Open Tuesday to Saturday from 10 a.m. to 5 p.m., on Sunday from 1 to 5 p.m.

WHAT'S HAPPENING IN CHARLOTTESVILLE: Be sure to pick up an events calendar at the Visitor Center when you arrive in town. There's always something exciting happening, from race meets (this is Virginia horse country) to

old-fashioned balloon rides (inquire at the Boar's Head Inn; tel. 804/296-2181). Many events take place at Ash Lawn; phone 804/293-9539 for details on these. Among the major annual events are:

Historic Garden Week, late in April, is part of a statewide festivity with house and garden tours, and luncheons at selected historic estates and magnificent homes in the area (tel. 804/977-1783).

James Monroe's Birthday, April 28, is of course celebrated at Ash Lawn with a featured speaker and special house and grounds tours. For information call 804/293-9539.

Also in April—the **Champagne and Candlelight Tour** at Ash Lawn (the driveway and gardens are lined with about 1000 luminaria, the house is candlelit, there's 18th-century music, and champagne is served); the **Annual Dogwood Festival** featuring a track meet, barbecue, concert, rides, fashion show, and parade (tel. 804/978-7200); and the **Spring Running of the Foxfield Races** (another takes place in the fall), the Foxfield International Cup Steeple Chase (tel. 804/293-9501).

May brings **Annual Kite Day** at Ash Lawn, a celebration of spring. Awards are given for the best design and the best flight. The coming of summer is also heralded at Ash Lawn on **Midsummer's Eve** with a buffet supper, bonfire, and live entertainment. Reservations are required.

July 4th weekend is **Colonial Crafts Weekend** at Ash Lawn; you'll learn papermaking, cordwaining, pewter making, soap making, silhouette cutting, gunsmithing, lacemaking, spoon carving, and the uses of herbs, among other quaint skills; dance to 18th-century music; enjoy period storytellers and balladeers; and play period games. Also at Ash Lawn, a costumed 18th-century regiment reenacts camp life during the Revolutionary War with tents, campfires, and camp followers. It's a weekend event that provides a fascinating insight into life during this struggle. In addition, Independence Day is uniquely celebrated in Charlottesville with **Naturalization Ceremonies** of about 75 Virginia residents at Monticello each year to a fife and drum accompaniment. And of course there are the usual Independence Day concerts, games, and fireworks.

Particularly marvelous is the **Ash Lawn Opera Festival,** running from the end of June through mid-August with entertainments in the boxwood gardens every night except Monday and Friday, summer. A recent season included operas by Mozart, Rossini, and Donizetti. Company members are very professional. The operas are performed outdoors in English. Contact Ash Lawn for tickets. The operas are part of the **Ash Lawn Summer Festival,** which also includes Shakespearean productions, chamber music concerts, lectures, art exhibits, and shows for children.

The **Albemarle County Fair** in August or September (tel. 804/973-1371 or 973-5393) is the traditional kind, with cooking, handicrafts, and livestock competitions.

Charlottesville is wine country (inquire about winery tours at the Visitor Bureau), and the **Albemarle Harvest Wine Festival** (tel. 804/296-4188) takes place at the Boar's Head Inn mid-October.

The Boar's Head Inn is also the focal point of a lavish **Thanksgiving** feast. The Blessing of the Hounds Service and the Thanksgiving Foxhunt, however, take place at Grace Episcopal Church.

Equally traditional (traditional in these parts; you may not fox hunt in your neck of the woods) is Charlottesville's **Yuletide Traditions**—cut your own tree at Ash Lawn; watch local residents adorn Monroe's home with pine boughs, magnolia leaves, holly, and fruit; take a Christmas homes tour; participate in an ornament workshop; enjoy a Candlelight Christmas open house at Monticello with music in the parlor. Also caroling by the piano, tree trimming, lighting of the Yule log, and sipping spiced cider by the fire at Ash Lawn. Lavish banquets are served at the Ordinary at Michie Tavern. There's much more, including concerts, crafts shows, and "Merrie Ole England" festivals. Call 804/293-6789 for details.

Fireworks at midnight usher in the New Year on December 31 and culminate **First Night Virginia** celebrations, which include concerts, dramatic presentations, and children's entertainment. A $3 lapel pin allows admission to all activities. Call 804/296-8548 to purchase one.

In addition to all the above, every kind of sports activity is offered— swimming, canoeing, hiking, boating, riding, fishing, polo, you name it.

WHERE TO STAY: There's so much to do and see, you'll likely want to settle in for as many days as you can spare.

Best bet is the brand-new **Hampton Inn,** P.O. Box 8260, Seminole Square on Route 29N between U.S. 250 and Rio Rd., Charlottesville, VA 22906 (tel. 804/978-7888 or toll free 800/HAMPTON). Though a budget property, it's one of the best-run hotels I've ever encountered. I was immediately impressed by the rooms, furnished in handsome oak pieces and attractively decorated in blue or tan color schemes, the walls hung with Gauguin and Cézanne prints. Real art—what a boon! All of the rooms have sofas which can double as extra beds; color TVs with free Showtime and pay movie stations, not to mention the luxury of bedside remote control; AM/FM digital alarm clock radios; and, in many cases, desks and/or armchairs with hassocks. The bath is equipped with a three-way mirror, a real closet is equipped with ample hangers, and bedside lamps have 100-watt bulbs to provide good reading light. These little things add up to comfort, as does the iron and full-sized board delivered to your room on request (so many hotels provide miniature boards that make ironing hell). Facilities include free parking, a nice-sized outdoor pool (ample for lap swimmers) and sundeck, ice/soda machines on every floor, and cigarette/sundry/snack machines on the main floor. A gratis continental breakfast of fresh fruit, doughnuts, juice, tea, and coffee is served each morning in the sunny lobby, a pleasant setting decorated in teal, rust, and apricot with comfortable armchairs and sofas as well as tables. Free transportation is offered to and from the airport. Local calls are free. And both handicapped and non-smoking rooms are available. Finally, many restaurants are within walking distance, and a shopping center surrounds the property.

Rates are $34 for one person in a room with two double beds, $38 for one person in a king, $42 for two people in either accommodation. An extra person of any age can stay free in your room. The Hampton Inn is highly recommended.

Bed-and-breakfast accommodations in elegant homes and/or private estate cottages are handled by **Guesthouses Reservation Service, Inc.,** P.O. Box 5737, Charlottesville, VA 22905 (tel. 804/979-7264 or 979-8327). You can write for a brochure, but reservations must be made by phone. All of this organization's hospitable hosts are carefully screened. Rates range from about $40 and up for singles, $46 and up for doubles. For the best choice and lowest prices, reserve a few weeks in advance; lower rates are offered on stays of two nights or more. You might draw an architect-designed contemporary home, an English country house, a 150-year-old log cabin nestled in the woods, or an antique-filled room with fireplace in an 18th-century home. When making reservations through this or any other B&B service, be sure to get details about bath facilities (private or shared, etc.), type of breakfast served, use of TV, phone, etc. GRS takes some credit cards. The office is open weekdays from noon to 5 p.m.

There are two **Econo Lodges** in town. A 60-room branch of this chain, at

400 Emmet St. (at Massie Rd.), Charlottesville, VA 22903 (tel. 804/296-2104 or toll free 800/446-6900), offers a Shoney's just down the block and a nice-size swimming pool. The University of Virginia is adjacent. It's under new management and looking very spiffy. They've completely redecorated the rooms in a handsome light-brown and navy-blue color scheme and installed attractive new oak furnishings—a bureau, desk/telephone table, headboard and upholstered chairs. The Econo offers all modern amenities—cable color TV, full bath, and direct-dial phone (local calls are free). Rates are $35 single, $39 for two in a room with one double bed, $43 for two with two double beds. An extra person pays $4; children under 12 stay free.

The other is the 48-room **Econo Lodge** at 2014 Holiday Dr. (off the 29-250 Bypass near the Holiday Inn), Charlottesville, VA 22901 (tel. 804/295-3185 or toll free 800/446-6900). There's no pool, but rooms are cheerful and attractive. They contain all the above amenities plus in-room coffee makers. Rates are about $2 less across the board, and children under 14 stay free.

Finally, there's the 22-room **Cardinal Motel**, 1807 Emmet St. (on U.S. 29 at the U.S. 250 Bypass), Charlottesville, VA 22901 (tel. 804/293-6188), offering motel rooms with all the above-mentioned amenities and an on-premises Pancake House. A bonus here is a swimming pool with chaise longues and umbrella tables. A long, pristine-white building with a sloped roof and cheerful red doors and shutters, the Cardinal has a bit of old-fashioned charm. The white-walled rooms, hung with framed travel posters, are rather nice, and the view from the pool sundeck is of the lush greenery of woods behind the property. May 1 through early October, one or two people pay $32 to $44 for a room with one double bed, $38 to $48 for a room with two double beds. The rest of the year rates are $35 to $40 for one double, $34 to $38 for two. Year round, an extra person pays just $2. Exceptions to the above rates occur during university-related events—football weekends, graduation, etc.—when it's hard to get a room anywhere in town and rates tend to go up a bit everywhere.

WHERE TO EAT: Like most student towns, Charlottesville offers an abundance of good, low-priced restaurants. And don't forget picnic areas at Ash Lawn, and Monticello, plus the Ordinary at Michie's, detailed above.

Across the street from the university is a restaurant called **Martha's,** 11 Elliewood Ave. off Main St. (tel. 804/971-7530), which, though it seems to change its name and owner with considerable regularity, has been a standby for many years offering innovative, tasteful, and reasonably priced fare. The reason for its consistency is that Martha was the original owner, and the subsequent owners have usually been people who worked for her—or later disciples—and run things on similar lines. Those lines include making everything from scratch, using the finest and freshest ingredients. At both lunch and dinner (menus change daily; they're posted on a blackboard), all entrees are served with a salad and a fresh-baked muffin or bread. Most lunch entrees are in the $4 to $5 range, dinner entrees $4 to $8. Culinary offerings might include stir-fried shrimp, pasta with scallops and cream sauce, a bean and cheese enchilada, pasta with artichoke hearts and red wine sauce, or boneless breast of chicken with champagne cream sauce. And there are fabulous homemade desserts, also changing daily, like chocolate walnut pie. For Saturday and Sunday brunch, items like eggs sardou and blueberry pancakes with sausage are added to the menu. Wine and beer are available. Martha's is a cozy little place warmed in winter by a working fireplace. There are curtained windows, bookshelves, shaded wall lamps, pedestal tables—each adorned with a few fresh flowers, and over the mantel, a whimsical touch, a large ink rendition of the Mad Hatter's tea party. Classical music, usually chamber music, elevates the tone. In good weather most diners opt for the brick terrace under the shade of two ancient elms. Open for lunch weekdays from 11:30 a.m. to 2 p.m., for dinner Monday to Saturday from 5:30 to 8 p.m., for Sunday brunch from 11:30 a.m. to 2:30 p.m. No credit cards.

Also in the university area is **The Virginian,** 1521 W. Main St., near Elliewood Ave. (tel. 804/293-2606). A congenial student hangout with seating in roomy oak booths and at an always well-populated bar, it's a simpático setting. Good jazz or rock is played at a low decibel level, pine-paneled walls are hung with a changing exhibit of works by local photographers, shaded wall sconces provide subdued lighting, and major sporting events are aired on a TV over the bar. Most important, all the fare is homemade, including yummy fresh-baked breads, and portions are large enough to satisfy the most voracious of students. There's a menu posted on the walls of each booth, and additional specials are listed on blackboards overhead. Most items are under $5, though a few dinner entrees are $6 to $8. At lunch or dinner you can't go wrong with a heaping bowl of linguine marinara with fresh mushrooms and mozzarella or a burger with homemade french fries on a fresh-baked kaiser roll. A typical lunch special is homemade chicken with walnuts and chutney served with bread and butter plus soup or salad. Fresh seafood, fileted in the kitchen, is featured at dinner in entrees like bluefish in lime sauce with almond-studded stringbeans and sauteed potatoes. The oven-fresh desserts also change daily. I had a scrumptious genoise filled with blueberries and lemon curd. The Virginian is open weekdays from 9 a.m. to 2 a.m., on weekends from 10 a.m. to 2 a.m.

Though its greasy-spoon facade, complete with faded Pepsi sign, might make you hesitate, don't be deterred. The **C&O Restaurant,** 515 Water St., a block off the mall (tel. 804/971-7044), has received kudos from Craig Claiborne, Phyllis Richman *(Washington Post), Travel & Leisure, Bon Appétit,* and other food mavens. Raved a *Food & Wine* reviewer: "I can assure you that not since Jefferson was serving imported vegetables and the first ice cream at Monticello has there been more innovative cooking in these parts. . . ." And should you need further reassurance, the entrance, warmed by a wood-burning fireplace, is most welcoming. Upstairs is a very elegant restaurant serving dinner entrees in the $20-and-up range. But if you head downstairs to the extremely rustic bar area, you can dine on the C&O's nouvelle American cuisine at plausible prices. Menus change daily. At lunch your choices might include homemade spinach and egg fettuccine with fresh mussels and cream sauce or calf liver with Pommery mustard cream sauce and creamy/garlicky/cheesy C&O potatoes. Both include salad and a loaf of fresh-baked bread. Dinner is a little pricey for this book, but a worthy splurge. You might happen upon pan-fried swordfish with Cajun spices served with fresh asparagus and C&O potatoes or game hen stuffed with quails. Lunch entrees are $4.50 to $7.50, dinner entrees mostly $6 to $10. At either meal you can get premium wines by the glass, and the fresh-baked desserts will include irresistibles like a layered hazelnut and chocolate genoise with espresso butter cream filling; it's brushed with Frangelico, a hazelnut liqueur.

The setting is a mix of exposed brick and rough-hewn barnwood, subdued lighting, and walls hung with an array of prints and photos, some of them of the old Chesapeake Ohio Railroad (its defunct station is across the street). A bit of charm is added by white-clothed tables adorned with pretty flower arrangements. Reservations suggested. Thursday through Saturday nights the C&O offers live music (jazz, blues, and bluegrass) in an adjoining club. Admission is $3 to $4, and light fare is available.

The bar area is open weekdays for lunch from 11:30 a.m. to 3 p.m., for dinner nightly from 5:30 to 10:30 p.m.

Another good choice is **eastern standard,** paradoxically the last building on

the western end of the mall (tel. 804/295-8668). Its airy and elegant contemporary decor is lovely. The downstairs dining room has pale-peach walls hung with
arty photographs taken by owner Ken Mori; beautifully arranged flowers, both
on bar and tables, the latter lit by small shaded lamps; and a high cream-colored,
pressed-tin ceiling. The upstairs dining rooms are similar but a bit homier in
feel, with bare oak floors, Japanese prints on the peach walls, and big arched
windows overlooking the mall. There's also a delightful graveled patio out back
enclosed by a white fence; a small tree grows out here, and there are potted
ferns. The cuisine is as sophisticated as the setting, and extremely eclectic.
Menus change frequently, but lunch entrees (in the $4.25 to $6 range) might
include chicken breast stuffed with sauteed brie and pears; linguine with shrimp,
garlic, onions, and sweet red peppers; a sausage and ricotta torte; lamb and artichokes with couscous; and curried chicken with apples, coconut, currants, and
red and green bell peppers over rice. There are also soups and salads. Fresh-
from-the-oven desserts are likely to include such delectables as a moist and rich
Egyptian orange cake topped with chocolate icing and English trifle. Dinner upstairs is an elegant affair, beyond our budget with entrees in the $15 range. But
eastern standard also offers a downstairs dinner menu with entrees priced as
they are at lunch. I recently enjoyed a dinner of salad, pasta puttamesca (baked
in a sauce of sliced tomatoes, garlic, basil, black olives, olive oil, and anchovies),
and a glass of wine for under $10.

Open for lunch weekdays 11:30 a.m. to 2:30 p.m., for dinner downstairs
nightly from 6 to 11 p.m. or midnight. The bar stays open until 2 a.m. and is a
nighttime hangout for a sophisticated local crowd.

A terrific new addition to the Mall is **The Coffee Exchange**, 120 E. Main St.
(tel. 804/295-0975), a pristinely charming setting in which to enjoy your morning
coffee and croissant. The coffee will be fresh-ground and fresh-roasted, the
croissant straight from the oven and scrumptious. They come in at least seven
varieties—plain, almond, strawberry, cheese, cinnamon, blueberry, and
chocolate—and there are also freshly baked sticky buns and muffins to tempt
you. Other breakfast choices are eggs Benedict baked in a croissant ($2.95) or a
Belgian waffle topped with fresh fruit ($3.50). Later in the day, try the Exchange
for sandwiches like chicken salad, turkey and swiss, and roast beef made from
meats cooked on the premises ($4 to $5); a salad of lettuce, tomatoes, carrots,
radishes, cucumber, almonds, and raisins topped with homemade dressings
(such as creamy parmesan, lemon-basil, and honey mustard); or a stuffed baked
potato. Everything here is made from scratch using first-rate ingredients. And
since the bakery operation is excellent this is the perfect place for afternoon tea
(or espresso) with white chocolate cheesecake or homemade cookies.

The Coffee Exchange is a comfortable restaurant, with delicate shell-pink
walls and tablecloths, a high Wedgwood-blue ceiling, art posters and shelves of
coffee makers and mugs lining the walls, and a long bakery display case and row
of bins filled with coffee beans. Columned archways create a center aisle sepa-
rating the seating area from the counter. The aroma of fresh-baked breads and
roasting coffee is ambrosial.

Hours are Monday to Saturday 9 a.m. to 6 p.m., Sunday 10 a.m. to 6 p.m.,
with extended hours Thursday through Saturday in summer.

And a final choice in the mall is the simpático **Miller's**, 109 West Main St.
(tel. 804/971-8511), a converted old-fashioned pharmacy with the original white
tile floor, schoolroom-style lights suspended from a cream-colored pressed-tin
ceiling, mahogany soda fountain back bar, and cherry woodwork and shelving.
The walls are hung with historic photographs of old Charlottesville drugstores.
Out front on the mall, tree-shaded tables overlooking a fountain are enclosed by
planters of geraniums, marigolds, and other window-box flowers. The food is all

fresh and homemade. Roast beef and turkey are roasted and carved on the premises and served on fresh-baked french bread ($3.35 for either, lunch or dinner). At lunch you might opt for the daily special—perhaps four-cheese pasta served with salad and an oven-fresh muffin ($2.95). Dinner entrees (served with french bread, vegetable, and rice or potato) include jambalaya (shrimp, chicken, bacon, and tomatoes with New Orleans seasonings over rice) and beef bourguignon, as well as quiche and spinach lasagne. Few items are over $5.50. Wine, beer, and mixed drinks are available; desserts are homemade. Lunch is served weekdays from 11:30 a.m. to 2 p.m., dinner from 5:30 to 9:30 p.m. Monday to Thursday, on Friday and Saturday from 5:30 to 10:30 p.m. After dinner a limited à la carte menu is available through midnight, and drinks are served till 2 a.m. There's nighttime entertainment—jazz, classical, pop, folk, or blues—and on weekends there's a nominal cover after 9:30 p.m. It's good listening music. Reservations suggested at dinner.

And last but not least, there's a **Shoney's** at Emmet St. and Arlington Blvd. (tel. 804/295-4196), offering their unbeatable buffets. See details in Fredericksburg listings, above.

2. Richmond

Ninety miles from Washington via I-95, Richmond has been the capital of Virginia since 1780 when it supplanted the more militarily vulnerable Williamsburg. But Richmond's history dates back to 1609 when John Smith sailed up the James River looking for a short route to the Pacific. It was the site of the first Thanksgiving in 1619, though the settlers were not much later besieged by Indian attacks; a 1622 massacre resulted in death by tomahawk of a third of the population. It was in Richmond's St. John's Church that Patrick Henry concluded his address to the second Virginia Convention with the stirring words "Give me liberty or give me death." The traitorous Benedict Arnold led British troops down what is now Main Street in 1781 and set fire to many buildings, including tobacco warehouses, in those days the equivalent of banks; he used St. John's as barracks for his troops. Cornwallis briefly occupied the town, and Lafayette came to the rescue.

All this Colonial history notwithstanding, Richmond is more famous for its role in the Civil War. For four years the capital of the Confederacy, it was surrounded by battling troops while hospitals filled to overflowing with the wounded and converted tobacco warehouses filled with Union prisoners. Here Jefferson Davis presided over the Confederate Congress and Robert E. Lee accepted command of Virginia's armed forces. The Treasury of the Confederate States of America was housed in what is today the post office building.

Richmond visitors can explore old battlefield sites around the city and peruse war-related exhibits and artifacts at the Museum of the Confederacy and the Valentine Museum. Imposing statues of Lee, Davis, J.E.B. Stuart, Stonewall Jackson, and other Civil War heroes line Monument Avenue, and at Hollywood Cemetery other monuments, stones, and epitaphs mark the graves of Davis, Stuart, and 18,000 Confederate soldiers. On a lighter note, you can stop by the restored Jefferson Hotel at Franklin and Adams Streets and see its sweeping lobby staircase, reputedly the model for the one in *Gone With the Wind*. Or take a horse-and-buggy ride down the quaint cobblestone streets of Shockoe Slip, the old tobacco warehouse district.

A visit to Richmond will enhance your understanding of the Civil War era in the same way that Colonial Williamsburg, Fredericksburg, Alexandria, and Charlottesville shed light on America's earliest days. The attractions here are well worth a few days' vacation time. Richmond is just an hour's drive from either Charlottesville or Williamsburg. *Note:* Two of the below-listed sights,

Berkeley and Shirley Plantations, are about midway between Richmond and Williamsburg. Consider visiting them en route in either direction.

GETTING YOUR BEARINGS: It's helpful to know that Foushee Street divides the city east and west, while Main Street divides it north and south. Broad Street is the major east-west thoroughfare (it actually extends, becoming highway of course, from Charlottesville to Williamsburg), and it's one of the few downtown streets with two-way traffic.

For orientation and information, make your first stop the **Metro Richmond Visitors Center** at 1700 Robin Hood Rd., Boulevard Exit 14 from I-95/64 (tel. 804/358-5511). They provide a host of services: brochures, maps, a ten-minute ongoing video orientation, and assistance with dining and lodging (they'll be happy to make reservations for either). If you have kids, send them out back to play with an old plane, train, and fire engine on the premises while you peruse pertinent literature within. If your time is limited, inquire about the center's **Certified Tour Guide** service (a guide accompanies you in your car for $55 for two hours of sightseeing, $75 if a rental car is required. You can reserve in advance by calling 804/782-2777. **Gray Line** (tel. 804/644-2901) also has tours of Richmond and other historic Virginia cities via sightseeing coach. And there are walking tours, both guided and self-guided. The center is open daily from 9 a.m. to 5 p.m., with extended hours in summer. There's a small picnic area just outside.

ANNUAL EVENTS: Be sure to pick up a seasonal calendar at the Visitors Center, because in addition to the below-listed once-every-year happenings there are always numerous special activities in town. Where no phone number is provided, for details call 804/780-6021.

January highlights are geared to special-interest groups—the mid-month **Race Car Auction,** and end-of-month **Virginia Kennel Club Show, Bassarama** (everything related to bass fishing from boats to gear; tel. 804/329-4437), and the **Camping and RV Show.**

In February the **Ringling Bros. and Barnum & Bailey Circus** comes to town (tel. 804/780-4956), and major Arena and State Fairgrounds events include the **Doll Collectors Show** (tel. 804/329-4437), the **Richmond Boat Show,** and the **Miller Highlife 400 Winston Cup Series Auto Races** (tel. 804/329-6796).

March brings a major **St. Patrick's Day Parade** down Broad Street.

Easter is celebrated with a festival on Monument Avenue—music, magicians, jugglers, rides, food, an art show, hot-air balloons, and strollers in their Easter finery. You can catch the opening season game of the **Richmond Braves** at the Diamond Stadium (tel. 804/359-4444). And **Historic Virginia Garden Week,** late in April, is the time to tour private homes and gardens.

May visitors will catch the **Westover Azalea Festival and Parade** (tel. 804/233-4351), not to mention the **May Fest** at Point of Rocks Park, which features such folksy events as a greased pig chase, tobacco-spitting contest, and a buffalo chip toss (tel. 804/748-1623). Another outdoor activity—and a more elevated endeavor—is **Arts in the Park** at the Carillon Mall in Byrd Park; about 400 craftspeople and artists display their works (tel. 804/353-8198).

There's a **Horse Show** and a **Dairy Goat Show** at the Fairgrounds in June (tel. 804/329-4437).

The next month's celebrations, of course, focus on the **Fourth of July,** with fireworks, music, hay rides, Living History shows, clogging, sack races, and much more; get a full rundown at the Visitors Center.

In August are the **Virginia Food Festival** at the Fairgrounds (tel. 804/643-3555); the **Carytown Watermelon Festival** with watermelon-eating contests, games, entertainment (tel. 804/353-3887).

In September, don't miss the **Richmond Jazz Festival** (major artists perform; tel. 804/644-1434 or 780-1768) or the **State Fair of Virginia** (tel. 804/329-4437).

Celebrate rural life in October at the **Meadow Farm Harvest Fest** (tel. 804/649-0566).

See details below for Berkeley Plantation, where an annual **Virginia First Thanksgiving Cruise and Celebration** takes place the first Sunday of November.

And there are dozens of **Christmas/New Year's** activities each year—special planetarium shows, 18th- and 19th-century celebrations, house and plantation tours, productions of Handel's *Messiah*, walking tours, madrigal singers, and so on. The winter calendar of events tells all.

THE MAJOR SIGHTS: They're many and varied, from James River plantations and Confederate battlegrounds to a major amusement park, an Edgar Allan Poe Museum, a modern tobacco factory, and excellent museums of science and art.

Richmond National Battlefield Park

April 3, 1865: "As the sun rose on Richmond, such a spectacle was presented as can never be forgotten by those who witnessed it. . . . All of the horrors of the final conflagration, when the earth shall be wrapped in flames and melt with fervent heat, were, it seemed to us, prefigured in our capital. . . ."

Thus did an observer recall the coming of the Yankees and the disastrous final hours of the war that had raged for four bitter and bloody years around the Confederate capital of Richmond. As the political, medical, and manufacturing center of the South—the primary supply depot for troops operating on the Confederacy's northeastern frontier—Richmond was a prime military target. Seven major drives were launched against the city between 1861 and 1865.

A 100-mile tour of battlefields in the park begins at the **Chimborazo Visitor Center,** 3215 East Broad St. (tel. 804/226-1981). A 12-minute slide show about the Civil War is shown throughout the day (it's open from 9 a.m. to 5 p.m. daily except Christmas and New Year's days), and you can rent a three-hour auto tape tour with cassette player that covers the major 55-mile portion of the battlefield route. You can also view a 25-minute film here called *Richmond Remembers;* it documents the social and economic impact of the Civil War on the Confederate capital. Park rangers are on hand to answer all questions.

There are smaller visitor centers at Fort Harrison, about eight miles southeast, and at Cold Harbor, about eight miles northeast. The latter was the scene of a particularly bloody encounter in 1864 during which 7,000 of Grant's men were killed or injured in just 30 minutes. "Living History" programs—costumed Union and Confederate soldiers reenacting life in the Civil War era—take place at Fort Harrison daily during the summer (inquire at Chimborazo). The Cold Harbor center is unstaffed (there are brochures, a bulletin board, and interpretive exhibits). Fort Harrison is staffed in summer only.

The Chimborazo Visitor Center occupies one of the Confederacy's largest hospitals: 76,000 patients were treated here during the war. It's convenient to combine visits to Shirley and Berkeley plantations with a battlefield tour; they're just slightly off the route. Not only are battlefield tours historically interesting, they're scenic drives that involve a considerable amount of leaving the car and walking through fields and woods. There are always interpretive facilities, sometimes including audio stations, and picnic areas can be found along the way.

The Museum of the Confederacy

In case you missed the Civil War, you can find out all about it at 1201 East Clay St., at 12th St. (tel. 804/649-1861). The museum was founded in 1890 for the purpose of "collecting, preserving, exhibiting, and interpreting artifact and manuscript materials relating to the Civil War period." It houses the largest Confederate collection in the country, much of it contributed by veterans (in the early days they often served as guides) and their descendants. All the war's major events and campaigns are documented, and exhibits include period clothing and uniforms, a replica of Lee's headquarters, Victorian furnishings, the role of blacks in the Civil War, Confederate memorabilia, weapons, and art. You'll see the sword and elegant gold-braided uniform Lee wore at Appomattox; a pictorial record of the war in the oil paintings of Confederate Sgt. Conrad Wise Chapman and the watercolors of William Ludwell Sheppard; tattered battle flags carried on the fields of Gettysburg; and the suit worn by Jefferson Davis the morning he was captured. A library on the premises contains a wide selection of books, manuscripts, personal papers, maps, photographs, navy logs, and other materials documenting the war.

Next door is the **White House of the Confederacy,** official residence of Jefferson Davis from 1861 to 1865. A neoclassic, early 19th-century town house, it's currently undergoing restoration to its wartime appearance as an official and family residence, and will probably be open to the public by the time you read this. You'll be able to take a guided tour of the house and see orientation exhibits and a slide show on its architecture, the period, and the Davis family. The rooms are spacious, with 16-foot ceilings, some of them with exquisite plaster moldings. And many of the furnishings are original Davis pieces.

Many books on the Civil War, along with Confederate flags, dolls, and souvenirs, are on sale in the museum gift shop. The museum is open Monday to Saturday from 10 a.m. to 5 p.m., on Sunday from 1 to 5 p.m. Admission is $2.50 for adults, $1 for children 7 to 12, $2 for senior citizens. There's free parking. When the White House is open, an additional fee will be charged.

The Valentine Museum

Named for Mann S. Valentine II, a 19th-century businessman and patron of the arts, this museum at 1015 East Clay St. (tel. 804/649-0711) documents the history of Richmond from prehistoric times through the 20th century. It includes the elegant Federal-style Wickham-Valentine House, built in 1812 by John Wickham, and its formal gardens. At the time, Wickham was Richmond's wealthiest citizen. Guided house tours, included in the price of admission to the museum, are given every hour on the hour. The house is restored to reflect a century of changing styles and furnishings—from a field desk that belonged to British army General Braddock during the Revolution to ornate Victoriana. Highlights are the Oval Parlor with its neoclassic frescoes, designated as "one of the hundred most beautiful rooms in America," and the circular Palette Staircase ending in a landing shaped like an artist's palette. Restoration work is still underway, so many exciting new aspects will be revealed in coming years.

The museum itself has been open since 1898. In the last few years, it has broadened its scope from a museum of local lore to encompass all of American urban history focusing on the experience of Richmond. The upstairs space is devoted to changing exhibits such as "Free to Profess: The First Century of

Richmond Jewry, 1786–1886," which explored the life of Richmond's early Jewish community and commemorated the 1986 bicentennial of the Virginia Statute of Religious Freedom. Another focused on Jackson Ward, one of Richmond's oldest black neighborhoods. The Valentine's extensive costume and textile collection is also regularly featured in exhibits here. Such as "Elegant Attire, Genteel Entertainments: Leisure and the Elite, 1787–1830." Downstairs are two permanent exhibits. In the Children's Gallery kids will enjoy seeing a replica of a one-room schoolhouse complete with rows of wooden desks and a pot-bellied stove, along with exhibits of historic dolls, toys, games, and photos of children. An exhibit called "Richmond Revisited" chronicles the city's past. Displays include: ancient fossils and petrified wood; trade beads from the 1600s; an Indian canoe; historical documents, books, and prints; comments of visitors Dickens and Thackeray on slavery; old newspapers; and much more. A 25-minute film called *Richmond Remembers 200 Years* plays throughout the day. Open Monday to Saturday from 10 a.m. to 5 p.m. and on Sunday from 1 to 5 p.m., the Valentine Museum is a good place to begin your sightseeing as it provides a comprehensive introduction to Richmond. Admission is $2.50, with families charged a maximum of $6; children under 6 are admitted free. There are many events and activities for children; call for details.

Berkeley

On December 4, 1619, 38 English settlers (all men; the first women came a year later) brought here by the Berkeley Company put ashore after a three-month voyage. They named their riverfront Virginia home Berkeley Plantation and Hundred, and fell on their knees in a prayer of Thanksgiving—the first such official ceremony in the New World.

In 1691 Berkeley was acquired by the Harrisons, already a James River family for three generations and members in good standing of Virginia's aristocratic ruling class. Benjamin Harrison (III) made Berkeley into a prosperous commercial center including the nation's first shipyard and a tobacco warehouse. In 1726 his son, Benjamin Harrison (IV)—a leader in colonial affairs—built the three-story Georgian mansion still extant today and heralded as a "beau ideal" of the baronial dwellings that graced Virginia's "Golden Age." Benjamin Harrison (V) was a signer of the Declaration of Independence and thrice governor of Virginia. Politics notwithstanding, these were the days of fox hunts and fancy-dress balls. George Washington was a frequent guest, and indeed, every president through Buchanan enjoyed Berkeley's gracious hospitality (Lincoln was next, in case you've forgotten, and was definitely persona non grata). The next generation produced William Henry Harrison (they finally thought of a new name), the great Indian fighter of the Northwest Territory called "Old Tippecanoe." Misrepresenting himself to the country as a humble frontiersman, he became our ninth president and wrote his inaugural address at Berkeley in the room in which he was born. Forty-seven years later his grandson, another Benjamin Harrison, would serve as the nation's 23rd president.

A few years after William Henry's death, Berkeley went out of the Harrison family, its owners by this time plagued by insurmountable debts. Several new owners tried and failed to keep it up, but the establishment was so grand that it needed to be run on a magnificent scale, and the tobacco-exhausted land was not what it had been. Like many other Richmond plantations, Berkeley was deserted (its owners having temporarily relocated to safer areas) by the time the Union army under General McClellan marched in with 140,000 soldiers and turned the manorial center of a dynasty into an army base and temporary hospital. The gardens and grounds were trampled, all but three trees were axed for campfire fuel, the elegant furnishings were also chopped up for firewood, and the rich carpeting was "completely covered with mud and soaked with human gore." Lincoln actually did visit Berkeley during this time to discuss the war with the general. It was also during the Yankee occupancy that Gen. Dan Butterfield composed "Taps."

The Civil War occupation of Berkeley was not its first. During the Revolution the Harrisons also wisely fled to safer quarters, before the British army under Benedict Arnold occupied their home, burned their family portraits (Arnold knew what would most hurt a Virginia aristocrat), practiced target shooting on their cows, and went off with 40 of their slaves.

Returning to the Civil War—after it was over, most owners (including those of Berkeley) did not return to their slaveless, and therefore impossible-to-run, plantations. A considerably lower class of Yankee farmers took them over and ran them into further ruin. The gracious days of the Old South seemed gone forever. In 1907 John Jamieson, a New Yorker of Scottish birth who had served as a drummer boy in McClellan's army 50 years earlier, purchased the disfigured manor house and 1400 acres. It was left, in 1927, to its present owner, his son, Malcolm, who along with his wife, Grace, is responsible for the complete restoration of the house and grounds to the glorious appearance of the early days of the Harrisons. The floors, window frames, pediment roof, and masonry are all original, while the furnishings and household effects have been meticulously chosen as representative of the period. Berkeley today is a working plantation, raising sheep and producing grains, soybeans and other crops.

A 30-minute drive from downtown Richmond (take Route 5 south), Berkeley is open to the public daily (except Christmas) from 8 a.m. to 5 p.m. Twenty-minute guided tours of the house are given throughout the day by guides in Colonial dress following a ten-minute slide presentation. Allow at least another half hour to explore the magnificent grounds and gardens. Lunch is served in a quaint restaurant on the grounds called the **Coach House Tavern** (tel. 804/829-6003), daily from 11 a.m. to 4 p.m. In summer it's lovely to sit out on the covered veranda overlooking the gardens. Lunch fare includes homemade soups, salads, and sandwiches, as well as heartier entrees. Prices are moderate. There are also picnic grounds on the premises. Admission to Berkeley is $6 for adults, $3 for children 6 to 12; under 6, free. For further information, call 804/829-6018.

If you should be in town on the first Sunday of November you can participate in the annual Thanksgiving celebration at Berkeley. Except for the change in date, this is in accordance with the orders in the charter of the first Berkeley settlers who came over on the *Margaret:* "Wee ordained that the day of our ships arivall at the place assigned for plantacon in the land of Virginia shall be yearly and perpetually keept holy as a day of thanksgiving to Almighty God." Celebrations include a house tour, a historic reenactment of the landing of the *Margaret,* Indian dances, speeches by dignitaries (sometimes including descendants of the *Margaret's* captain, John Woodlief), and of course a feast. A James River cruise (tel. 804/226-1238) is offered in conjunction with this event.

Shirley

Another historic James River plantation along Route 5, Shirley (tel. 804/795-2385) was founded in 1613 and has been in the same family for ten generations since 1660. The present mansion, built by Edward Hill (III) or his son-in-law, John Carter (historians are not sure), dates to 1723. Since that time the Hills and the Carters—two very distinguished Virginia families—have married each other so often that they are as one.

Because of this continuous ownership, many original furnishings and family possessions, portraits, and memorabilia remain at the estate, making it one of the most interesting plantations open to public view. The staircase, rising three stories with no visible means of support, is world famous, an interesting departure from traditional 20th-century architecture. The house survived the Revolution, the Civil War, and Reconstruction, as did the dependencies—an 18th-century laundry room (later used as a schoolroom, where Robert E. Lee had lessons as a boy), a two-story kitchen, smokehouse, dovecote, stable, and barns. And of equal interest are the stories of Shirley's occupants and their roles in history over the centuries.

John Carter, who married Elizabeth, the daughter of Edward Hill (III), was the son of "King Carter," considered the wealthiest man in Colonial America with his 300,000 acres of prime land, 1,000 slaves, 2,000 head of cattle, and 100 horses. John and Elizabeth had three residences: Shirley, a house in Williamsburg, and a Carter home on the Rappahannock River; their household was practically a gypsy caravan, though on a very magnificent scale.

Their son, Charles Carter, inherited in 1771, just before the Revolution. Though his leanings had always been Loyalist, when the Revolution came his allegiance was to the land of his birth. Shirley served as a supply center for the Continental Army and Carter as a member of the militia. After the war Shirley prospered under his management, and he owned more slaves and cattle than any other man in Virginia. He didn't stint on children either—he had 23, though several died in infancy. His daughter, Anne, married Revolutionary War hero Light Horse Harry Lee at Shirley in 1793 (they were Robert E. Lee's parents).

The next heir, Charles's son, Robert, was serious, shy, and socially conscious. Unable to relish a way of life that depended on slavery, he decided to become a doctor in his late 20s. In this he was much influenced by the eminent Quaker physician from Philadelphia, Benjamin Rush. Rush's antislavery and temperance views were in line with his own and formed a bond. However, Carter's medical career never got off the ground; he died of a violent fever contracted in Paris in 1805.

Shirley then passed to his son, ten-year-old Hill Carter, under the guardianship of two uncles until he came of age. Under this somewhat disinterested guardianship the estate and its fortunes dwindled until Hill Carter turned 21 in 1816. In fact some of the uncles' transactions—selling furniture and lead stripped from the roof—were most dubious. As a feisty 16-year-old midshipman aboard the war sloop *Peacock,* Hill was noted for bravery during the War of 1812. A year after returning to Shirley he married Mary Braxton Randolph, a direct descendant of Pocahontas. With the drive and determination he had exhibited in war, Hill began vigorously tackling the plantation's problems. Though no Simon Legree, he was not plagued by the qualms that troubled his father. He planted tobacco-depleted fields with wheat, experimented with fertilizers and peat mosses, and initiated crops that would allow him to use his slaves year round. In winter months he engaged them in repairs, fence-mending, spinning, and weaving. Life was not all work and no play for "massa," however. The Carters entertained lavishly in the gracious style of the Old South. It is to Hill Carter's diplomacy and stamina that the survival of Shirley through and after the Civil War must be credited. Though they lost a son at the Battle of Chancellorsville, the merciful Carters nursed and fed wounded Union soldiers on their lawn. A grateful McClellan gave them safe-conduct passes and other signs of appreciation during the days of occupation.

Robert Randolph Carter was next to inherit Shirley, in 1866, and with it the problems of running a plantation without slave labor. He died in 1888 and left his very competent daughter, Alice Carter Bransford, a widow of 39, in charge. She gained a reputation as "the best farmer on the river," but in the absence of slave labor, claimed she worked like a slave herself. She died of cancer in 1925 and left the house to her sister, Marion. Their second cousin, Hill Carter, Jr., is Shirley's present owner.

The house is open daily (except Christmas) from 9 a.m. to 5 p.m. with 35-minute tours given throughout the day. Last tour departs at 4:30 p.m. Allow at least another 30 minutes to explore the grounds and dependencies. Charge for adults is $5, $4 for students, $2.50 for children 6 to 12; under 6 free.

The Virginia State Capitol

The first of many public buildings in the New World created in the classical revival style of architecture, and the second-oldest working capitol in the U.S. (in continuous use since 1788; before its completion the Virginia General Assembly met in a tobacco warehouse on 14th and Cary Streets), the Virginia State Capitol was designed by Thomas Jefferson. French architect Charles-Louis Clérisseau helped him draw up the plans. Jefferson was minister to France when he was commissioned to work on the Capitol, and greatly admired the Maison Carrée, a Roman temple built in Nîmes during the first century. The Capitol is closely patterned after it, though Jefferson changed its Corinthian order to Ionic, added windows, and used brick and stucco instead of stone. His plaster model is displayed in the entrance hall. Set on a hill, the building was designed to overlook the James, but tall buildings nowadays obscure that Olympian view. The colonnaded wings on either side were added between 1904 and 1906.

The central portion of the Capitol is the magnificent Rotunda, its domed skylight ceiling (not visible from the exterior) ornamented in Renaissance style. The room's dramatic focal point is Houdon's life-size portrait of George Washington, said to be a perfect likeness. "That is the man, himself," said Lafayette. "I can almost realize he is going to move." A Carrara marble bust by Houdon of Lafayette also graces the Rotunda, as do busts of the seven other Virginia-born presidents (Jefferson, Madison, Monroe, William Henry Harrison, Tyler, Taylor, and Wilson). Though one's attention is drawn upward to the dome, look down as well and you'll see 450-million-year-old fossils of giant snail shells in the limestone floor.

Resembling an open courtyard, the old Hall of the House of Delegates is now a museum. The Virginia House of Delegates met in this room, the largest in the Capitol, from 1788 to 1906. Here, in 1807, Aaron Burr was tried for treason (and acquitted) by John Marshall while Washington Irving took notes. The room was also a meeting place of the Confederate Congress (the building served as the Capitol of the Confederacy during the Civil War and, luckily, escaped damage). Museum artifacts include an Edwardian-style gold-washed silver mace, statues of Henry Clay and Robert E. Lee, and busts of great Virginians—Patrick Henry, George Mason, George Wythe, and Richard Henry Lee—and Confederate notables like J.E.B. Stuart, Stonewall Jackson, and Jefferson Davis.

The former Senate chamber, now used for occasional committee meetings, contains historically themed paintings such as Griffith Bailey Coale's depiction of the three ships (the *Susan Constant,* the *Godspeed,* and the *Discovery)* that brought the first settlers to Virginia in 1607. In this room Stonewall Jackson's body lay in state after his death in 1863.

Free 30-minute tours are given daily from 9 a.m. to 5 p.m. (December through March the building opens at 1 p.m. on Sunday) throughout the day.

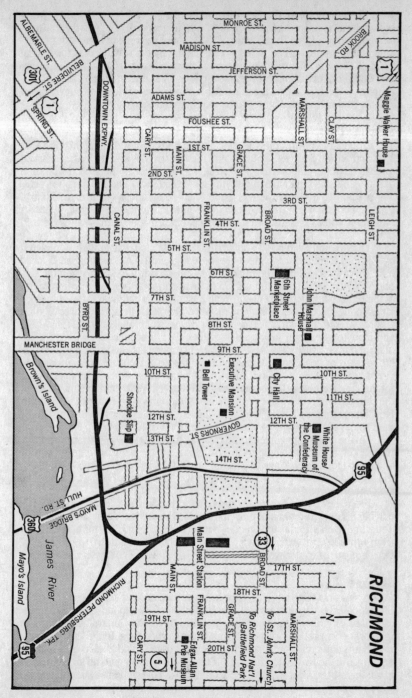

RICHMOND

N →

After the tour, explore the Capitol grounds. To the east is the **Executive Mansion,** official residence of governors of Virginia since 1813. Another historic building is the old **Bell Tower,** built in 1824, often the scene of lunch-hour entertainment in summer. The Bell Tower building, by the way, houses the official **Virginia Division of Tourism's Welcome Center,** where you can obtain information and literature about all state attractions. A statue of Edgar Allan Poe is nearby. You can picnic on the grass. Most impressive is the equestrian statue of Washington surrounded by seven famous Virginians.

St. John's Church

Originally known simply as the "church on Richmond Hill," St. John's, at 25th and Broad Sts. (tel. 804/648-5015), dates to 1741 and the oldest marked tombstone in the graveyard to 1751. Edgar Allan Poe's mother and Declaration of Independence signer George Wythe are buried here. The congregation actually predates the church; it was established at Henricus (named for Henry, Prince of Wales) in 1611, and Alexander Whitaker was the first rector. Whitaker ministered to the Indians, instructed Pocahontas in Christianity, and baptized her.

The original Richmond Hill white frame building was fittingly completed by Richard Randolph, the great-great-great-grandson of Pocahontas. It faced east, toward Jerusalem. The building was enlarged in 1772, and when the second Virginia Convention met in 1775 to discuss the rights of American subjects of the English king (the first was in Williamsburg), the church was the only place large enough to contain it. Attending were Thomas Jefferson, George Wythe, George Mason, Benjamin Harrison, George Washington, Richard Henry Lee, and many other major historic personages. They introduced a bill for assembling and training a militia, and Patrick Henry made his famous declaration: "Is life so dear, or peace so sweet, as to be purchased at the price of chains or slavery? Forbid it, Almighty God! I know not what course others may take, but as for me, give me liberty or give me death." Later that year another convention at the church planned Virginia's defense and a temporary government. American-British antagonisms having long since healed, St. John's was visited in 1860 by the Prince of Wales, later to become Edward VII of England.

On the 20-minute guided tour you'll see the original 1741 entrance and pulpit; the Church of England prayerbook, printed in the reign of King William III and bound for Queen Anne (a Bicentennial gift from King George VI in 1941); the exquisite stained-glass windows; the pew where Patrick Henry sat during the convention.

From the last Sunday in May through the first Sunday in September, there's a living history program at 2 p.m. re-creating the second Virginia Convention. Tours are given Monday to Saturday between 10 a.m. and 3:30 p.m., on Sunday from 1 to 3:30 p.m. Admission is $1 for adults, 50¢ for children 6 to 18; under 6, free. You are of course welcome at the 8:30 or 11 a.m. Sunday service.

Shockoe Slip

A historic district of century-old warehouses and cobblestone streets, Shockoe Slip is the hub around which the city of Richmond grew. When the capital of Virginia was moved to Richmond in 1780, the General Assembly met in Shockoe Slip at the corner of 14th and East Cary Streets. In the 1800s tobacco merchants and grain shippers traded their goods here and loaded merchandise on barges in the Kanawha Canal. In 1865, when the city could no longer defend itself against the Union army, the Confederate government ordered Shockoe warehouses ignited to keep their valuable contents out of enemy hands, and the business district was destroyed. Following the war the current buildings were constructed and the city's commercial activity centered here once more. However, the coming of the railroad reduced the importance of Shockoe's waterfront location, and the area faded in significance.

In the mid-1970s a major revitalization was begun, somewhat along the lines of San Francisco's Fisherman's Wharf. Numerous restaurants and shops have emerged, there are organized walking tours of the area, and old factory buildings, mills, banks, and warehouses have been renovated (though kept intact for historic ambience, of course) to house additional shops, eateries, and trendy nightspots. The two major buildings, both at 13th and Cary, are Commercial Block, a converted 1870s barrel factory, and Columbian Block, the former grain and commodities exchange. The district in question is bordered on the south by the James River, on the north by Main St., and on the east and west by I-95 and 12th St., respectively. It's the scene of frequent events and festivals themed around jazz, art, holidays (including an annual Great Pumpkin Party at Halloween), food, and historic events. A nonprofit organization called **Richmond on the James,** at 1805 E. Broad St. in Shockoe Bottom (tel. 804/780-0107), functions as an information office for area attractions and distributes maps, brochures, and information on walking tours (guided and self-guided) in the area. It's open daily from 9 a.m. to 5 p.m.

Shockoe Bottom, by the way, where the office is located, is an area that predates even Shockoe Slip. Just to the east of the Slip, it, too, offers trendy restaurants and art galleries, as well as a farmer's market that operates daily on the corner of 17th and Main Sts., occupying a site that has been used for this purpose for over two centuries.

The Virginia Museum of Fine Arts

This is an art museum of which any city would be proud. It houses impressive collections of art nouveau, art deco, 19th- and 20th-century French paintings, contemporary American art, and the art of India, Nepal, and Tibet. In fact it documents the history of creative achievement from the ancient world to the latest innovations of the 20th century. But even with none of the above, it would be well worth visiting to see the largest public Fabergé collection in the free world—over 300 objets d'art from the workshop of master jeweler Peter Carl Fabergé, created just before the turn of the century for Czars Alexander III and Nicholas II. The Imperial jewel-encrusted Easter eggs evoke what art historian Parker Lesley calls the "dazzling, idolatrous realm of the last Czars." They also evoke awe at the amounts of money members of the Romanoff family spent on bibelots for one another at Eastertime. But most important, they're exquisitely beautiful works of art. One of the most spectacular in the museum's collection was presented to the czarina by Nicholas II in 1896. Ten inches high, it is a rock-crystal hollow globe, encircled by a diamond band and crowned by a 26-carat Siberian cabochon emerald. Its pedestal is made of gold and rock crystal, and inside the egg are miniature paintings of Russian royal residences. The emerald, when pressed, engages a tiny hook which revolves the paintings. In addition to the Imperial eggs, there are smaller eggs, miniature bejeweled flowers and animals, and ornate photograph frames.

Other highlights include the Goya protrait *General Nicholas Guye,* a rare life-size marble statue of Caligula, Monet's *Iris by the Pond,* and six magnificent Gobelin *Don Quixote* tapestries. And that's not to mention works of de Kooning, Gauguin, Van Gogh, Delacroix, Matisse, Degas, Picasso, Gainsborough, and others, or antiquities from China, Japan, Egypt, Greece, Byzantium, Africa, and South America.

In 1986 the museum celebrated its 50th anniversary with the opening of an impressive new 90,000-square-foot West Wing to house the superb collections donated by two generous couples, Sydney and Frances Lewis and Mr. and Ms. Paul Mellon. Centered on a large rosy Verona/marble court, the two-level West Wing has large, well-lit galleries and a wraparound terrace used to display sculpture. The exterior is constructed of buff-colored Indiana limestone. The Mellon collections consist of 18th- through 20th-century British, French, and American paintings, drawings, prints, and sculpture, as well as exquisite jewelry and objets d'art by Jean Schlumberger. Many of the works are in the genre of sporting art, usually equestrian themed. Among the artists represented on the upper level are Picasso, Boudin, Léger, Dufy, Gericault, Delacroix, Seurat, Van Gogh, Cézanne, Lautrec, Monet, and Renoir—what a list: On the lower level, English and American works are featured, including a marvelous collection of George Catlin's mid-19th-century paintings of American Indians and South America. Here, too, are works by Homer, Eakins, and Bierstadt; an extensive collection of English hunt prints; and Herbert Haseltine's sculptures of British champion animals. On this same floor is the Lewises collection of contemporary American painting and sculpture. Represented are such artists as Rothko, Gottlieb, de Kooning, Jack Beal, Duane Hanson, Roy Lichtenstein, Julian Schnabel, and Tom Wesselmann, among others. My favorite part of the Lewis gift, however, is on the upper level—a decorative arts collection that includes Tiffany lamps, vases, and stained-glass windows; Lalique jewelry; Emile Gallé, Frank Lloyd Wright, and Hector Guimard furnishings; Alphonse Mucha lithographs, and other masterpieces of art nouveau, art deco, and modernism done between 1885 and 1935.

The museum also contains the 500-seat **Theatre Virginia** (tel. 804/257-0831), where professional productions range from Broadway hits to *Macbeth*. The season runs from October through April. There is also an ongoing program of lectures (topics run the gamut from "The England of Jane Austen" to "Hatshepsut: A Reinterpretation of Some Egyptian Sacred Cows"), classic films (like *Casablanca* and *Singin' in the Rain)*, special events, and seminars.

The Virginia Museum of Fine Arts is located at The Boulevard and Grove Ave. (tel. 804/257-0844). It's open Tuesday to Saturday from 11 a.m. to 5 p.m., on Sunday from 1 to 5 p.m., Thursday till 10 p.m. Suggested donation is $2 for adults; no fee is asked for children under 16 or senior citizens. A low-priced cafeteria on the premises offers quite decent food and seating in the lovely sculpture garden overlooking a waterfall that cascades into a pool with a Maillol fountain. Parking is free.

The Science Museum of Virginia/Ethyl UNIVERSE Theater

In addition to a distinguished art museum, Richmond boasts a worthy museum of science complete with state-of-the-art planetarium. There are few "Do Not Touch" signs in this museum's galleries; hands-on exhibits are the norm, making it an ideal attraction for youngsters. In fact, there are often so many youngsters about that near mayhem results. During the school year they arrive by the classroomful every morning; put off your visit till the afternoon and you'll find that things have quieted down a bit.

Five large crystalline-shaped structures on the rotunda floor create the setting for "Crystal World." Here you can venture inside a crystal, step into the center of a diamond, and see a crystal split a laser beam. Of course kids go wild in the "Computer Works" area, where the hows and whys of computer technology are explored in considerable depth. Visitors create programs, discuss their problems with a computer shrink, view the tiny world of integrated circuits through a microscope, and play "shill" for a computer magician.

Elsewhere, you'll learn about optical illusions inside a giant kaleidoscope, try to get your bearings in a full-size distorted room, make your own animated film, poke your head into a fishtank, arrange 13-million-year-old whale bones, and crawl into a space capsule.

Not to be missed, of course, are the shows at the 300-seat **Ethyl UNIVERSE Planetarium/Space Theater** (tel. 804/25-STARS for show times and ticket prices). It contains an Omnimax 70-millimeter motion-picture projector for showing those spectacular you're-in-the-picture Omnimax films (I never tire of them) as well as the most sophisticated special-effect projection systems for multimedia planetarium shows.

Even without all these exciting exhibits, the building itself merits attention. The Science Museum is housed in the former Broad Street Station, designed in 1919 by John Russell Pope (architect of the Jefferson Memorial, the National Archives, and the National Gallery of Art in Washington). In the Beaux Arts tradition, with a soaring rotunda, classical columns, vaults, and arches, it was created to evoke a sense of wonder—very fitting for a museum of science.

The museum, at 2500 West Broad St., three blocks east of The Boulevard (tel. 804/257-6797), is open seven days a week, but hours vary seasonally in a manner too complicated to report here; call ahead. Admission is $2.50 for adults, $2 for children 17 and under and senior citizens. Omnimax or planetarium shows are $1.50 additional. However, you can get a ticket for admission to the museum and both shows for $4.50 adults, $4 for all others.

The Edgar Allan Poe Museum

The Poe Museum consists of five buildings (enclosing an "Enchanted Garden") at 1914–1916 East Main St. (tel. 804/648-5523), wherein the poet's rather sad life is documented in assiduous detail and his years in Richmond highlighted. The museum centers on the Old Stone House, the oldest building in Richmond, dating to about 1736. Poe's connection with this building is dubious; when Lafayette visited Richmond and was entertained here in 1824, the young Poe (age 15) was part of the Junior Volunteer Honor Guard. Today it is furnished in mid-18th-century style and contains a small but interesting museum shop where Poe's works, as well as biographies and commentaries, are sold. A diorama in the admissions building shows Richmond in Poe's time. The other four buildings were added to house the growing collection which began in 1921.

Though Poe spent his 6th to 12th years in England, he then came to Richmond with his adoptive parents (his real parents died when he was 2), John and Frances Valentine Allan. The adoption was not legal, and only his middle name was Allan. Poe's real parents were married in Richmond. His mother, an actress named Elizabeth Arnold Poe who died of tuberculosis at the age of 24, is honored in one of the museum's buildings.

As a young man Poe worked as a journalist in Richmond at the *Southern Literary Messenger*. A desk and chair such as he used at the *Messenger* are among the effects on display here, along with photographs, portraits, and documents; his wife's trinket box (she also died at the age of 24 from tuberculosis); a copy of a pastel by Whistler of Annabel Lee, along with the original manuscript; and furnishings from Moldavia, the Allan mansion on 5th and Main Streets. One room is furnished with Poe's childhood bed, its original quilted cover, and period antiques. Most fascinating is the Raven Room, in which artist James Carling's 43 marvelously evocative illustrations of *The Raven* are displayed. Poe received only $15 for this famous work, and though he became well known in his time, he died penniless at the age of 40. The "Enchanted Garden" contains a bust of the poet and is planted with flowers mentioned in his works.

The museum is open Tuesday to Saturday from 10 a.m. to 4 p.m., on Sunday and Monday from 1:30 to 4 p.m. Admission is $3 for adults, $1 for students of any age; under 6, free. Forty-minute tours are given throughout the day, and there's a 12-minute slide show about Poe's life. Free parking on the premises.

The Philip Morris Manufacturing Center

Though as an ex-smoker I loathe and disdain cigarettes, I did enjoy a tour of the Philip Morris factory in southern Richmond; take Exit 8 off I-95 (tel. 804/274-3342 or 274-3329). A $200-million showcase of state-of-the-art manufacturing technology, it's one of the largest and most modern facility of its kind in the world. Here 5000 employees turn out over 500 million cigarettes a day to be distributed worldwide.

The streamlined tour operation is also state of the art. Visitors are welcomed and directed to a tobacco museum where they can browse until tour time. It contains numerous fascinating smoking-related artifacts—antique lighters and match boxes; African, American Indian, and Eskimo pipes; opium and hashish pipes from the Orient; decorative pipes; exquisite cigarette and snuff boxes; and old tobacco advertisements. The display is enhanced by a narration via earphones.

Earphones are also donned during the 20-minute tram ride through the manufacturing area (it's the length of three football fields and then some) where workers are kept busy producing 6000 cigarettes per minute. There's also an exhibit area where you'll learn about growing, harvesting, and curing tobacco, and see some TV commercials for cigarettes. At the tour's end you'll get a free pack of your favorite brand (assuming it's in the Philip Morris family) and a souvenir pen.

Open weekdays from 9 a.m. to 4 p.m., except July 4th, Christmas, New Year's, and a few other odd holidays like the Friday before the Kentucky Derby. Call before you go. The tour is free and aromatic.

The 6th Street Marketplace

Downtown Richmond has been the scene of a major urban-renewal effort in recent years, and its most notable manifestation is the $24-million 6th Street Marketplace (tel. 804/648-6600). Opened in September 1985, it is one of James W. Rouse's Enterprise Company projects (Rouse being of Harborplace and Faneuil Hall fame). The Marketplace focuses on a stunning glass-enclosed elevated pedestrian bridge spanning Broad Street between a Marriott hotel and two major department stores. It is bordered south and north by Grace Street and the Coliseum, by 5th and 7th Streets west and east. Park your car at the lot on 5th and Marshall (rates are very low) and enter on 6th Street off Broad where you can pick up a brochure at the information kiosk. It lists shops and eateries and details daily events. The 93-foot-high Crystal Palace and the connecting Blues Armory (used to house Confederate troops during the Civil War) contain some 100 retail stores, vendors, and pushcarts under striped awnings. There are three restaurants, plus specialty-food shops like The Fudgery, where the preparers entertain with fudge-making songs. You can enjoy a picnic lunch in the large park area at the north end of the complex. And inside and out of the Crystal Palace, musicians perform on a regular basis. Open Monday to Saturday from 10 a.m. to 9:30 p.m., on Sunday from noon to 6 p.m.

Main Street Station

Along similarly grandiose lines, this second marketplace (also opened in September of 1985) is located near the intersection of three Interstate highways

(I-95, I-64, and I-195) at Main and 15th Sts. (tel. 804/225-1301). Housed in a renovated turn-of-the-century Beaux Arts railroad station, topped by an historic clock tower, the complex offers 142,000 square feet of skylit shopping space festively decorated with banners, colorful awnings, and railroad memorabilia. Numerous outlets of regional and national manufacturers feature discounted merchandise of every description—clothing, luggage, golfwear, brass, jewelry, shoes, toys, books, pottery, etc. There's adjacent free parking for over 900 cars. Eating facilities include a food court with over a dozen vendors and a luxury restaurant called the Palm Court (details later in this chapter). Open Monday to Saturday from 10 a.m. to 9 p.m., on Sunday from noon to 6 p.m.

Agecroft Hall

Richmond's attractions are nothing if not diverse. Agecroft Hall, at 4305 Sulgrave Rd. (tel. 804/353-4241), is an authentic late-15th-century Tudor manor house built in Lancashire, England. In the 1920s the house was threatened with destruction, and Virginians Mr. and Mrs. T. C. Williams, Jr., decided to save it. They bought the house, had it carefully taken down, every beam and stone numbered, and shipped it to Richmond for reconstruction in an elegant neighborhood overlooking the James. Williams unfortunately died a year after the rebuilding was completed, but today Agecroft serves as a museum portraying the architecture, interior decor, and lifestyle of a wealthy English family of the late Tudor and early Stuart eras. Typical of its period, the house has ornate plaster ceilings, massive fireplaces, rich oak paneling, leaded- and stained-glass windows, and a two-story Great Hall with a mullioned window 25 feet long. The furnishings, such as an Elizabethan oak four-poster bed from a castle in Hertfordshire, authentically represent the period as well. Adjoining the mansion are a formal sunken garden, rectangular in shape and resembling one at Hampton Court Palace, and a formal flower garden, Elizabethan knot garden, and herb garden.

Agecroft is open Tuesday to Friday from 10 a.m. to 4 p.m., on Saturday and Sunday from 2 to 5 p.m. Visitors see a 12-minute slide show about the estate followed by a half-hour house tour. Plan time to explore the gardens as well. Admission is $2 for adults, $1 for students, $1.50 for senior citizens.

Kings Dominion

If running real rapids scares you silly, head over to Kings Dominion, 20 miles north in Doswell, Virginia (tel. 804/876-5000), a 400-acre major theme park where a star attraction is **White Water Canyon.** This $3-million wet-and-wild ride simulates whitewater rafting, offering the thrills and excitement without the danger of falling into the water and getting dragged away by a swirling current. You will, however, get soaking, sopping wet on this 1800-foot manmade river which is enhanced by geysers spraying water 20 feet into the air, waterfalls, and turbulent whitecaps created by wave-makers.

Other thrill rides here include roller coasters—Shock Wave (it has a 360° loop and you ride it standing up!), the Grizzly (an immense wooden coaster), and Scooby Doo, a children's coaster, among others. Racing Rivers is a trio of water slides—Riptide, a speeding sled that drops three stories in three seconds; Splashdown, a shoot-the-chute two-person raft experience; and Torpedo, a wild plunge through an enclosed tube. Another wet experience awaits you at Diamond Falls, a water ride with a 50-foot waterfall drop to a deserted mine. Less hair-raising is a Wild Animal Safari area with over 100 free-roaming animals; it's viewed from a monorail.

In addition to 45 rides, Kings Dominion offers nine live shows throughout the day (get a schedule when you come in). There's a lavish musical extravaganza each year, usually an oldies-but-goodies show, a country music show, a bird show, a 180° cinema, a dolphin show, and a costume character show. The latter features Hanna-Barbera creations like Yogi Bear and Scooby Doo, not to mention the Smurfs. Costumed characters also roam the park, as do mimes and magicians. But the most spectacular entertainment is offered at the park's outdoor amphitheater, the Showplace, featuring headliners like Jimmy Buffett, Patti LaBelle, Conway Twitty, and New Edition.

Kings Dominion is on I-95 (take the Route 30 exit). It's open weekends only from mid-March through the end of May, daily from June through the end of August, and weekends again from September through early October. The one-price admission entitling visitors to unlimited rides and attractions is $16.95; children 2 and under, free. Headliner shows are $4 to $7 extra.

Maymont

In 1886, Major James Henry Dooley, a 25-year-old self-made millionaire who made his fortune in real estate, purchased a 100-acre dairy farm in Richmond on which to build a 33-room mansion surrounded by beautifully landscaped grounds. Now, over a century later, his opulent estate, Maymont House, is open to tourists, and the grounds comprise a park that any city might envy. Maymont, by the way, was the maiden name of Dooley's wife, Sallie. The mansion is in the neo-Romanesque style popular at the turn of the century, complete with colonnaded sandstone facade, turrets, and towers. The architectural details of the formal rooms reflect various periods, most notably 18th-century French as exemplified by the drawing rooms. The ladies drawing room is plushly pink, with an elaborately decorated plaster ceiling, gilded chandelier and fireplace, and marble sculptures. Stained-glass transoms, woodwork (each room is done in a different wood, with connecting doors veneered to match on either side), ceilings, and mantels vary in design from room to room. The dining room has a stunning coffered rosewood ceiling, the library a stenciled strapwork ceiling. A grand stairway leads to a landing from which rise two-story-high stained-glass windows. And the house is elaborately furnished with pieces from many periods chosen by the Dooleys—Oriental carpets, an art nouveau swan-shaped bed, marble and bronze sculpture, porcelains, tapestries, Tiffany vases, and bibelots from England, France, Italy, and Germany. Maymont is, inside and out, a monument to the Victorian era.

The same care that was lavished on the house was also given to the grounds. The Dooleys placed gazebos wherever the best views were to be enjoyed, they laid out Italian and Japanese gardens, and planted horticultural specimens and exotic trees culled from the world over. At Mrs. Dooley's death in 1925, the property and grounds became Maymont Park. The hay barn today is the **Parsons Nature Center,** with outdoor animal habitats on the grounds for birds, bison, beaver, deer, elk, and bear. Exhibits here explore interdependent ecological systems. At the **Children's Farm,** youngsters can mingle with and feed chickens, piglets, goats, peacocks, cows, donkeys, and sheep. Also in the park is the **Carriage House,** wherein a collection of late 19th- and early 20th-century horse-drawn carriages—surreys, phaetons, hunting vehicles, etc.—is on display. Carriage rides in the park are also a weekend afternoon option April through mid-December.

Maymont grounds, including the Children's Farm, are open daily 10 a.m. to 7 p.m. April 1 to October 31, 10 a.m. to 5 p.m. the rest of the year. Admission is free. Guided tours of the house are given continuously between noon and 4:30 p.m. Tuesday through Sunday. Admission is free, donations accepted. For information on carriage rides, call 804/358-7167. The park is located just north of the James River between Route 161 and Meadow St. There's a parking lot off Spottswood Road, another at Hampton St. and Pennsylvania Avenue. For information about all Maymont attractions and facilities call 804/358-7166.

Hollywood Cemetery

Perched on the bluffs overlooking the James River, Hollywood Cemetery, 412 S. Cherry at Albemarle St. (tel. 804/648-8501) is no Forest Lawn but the serenely beautiful resting place of 18,000 Confederate soldiers, two American presidents (James Monroe and John Tyler), six Virginia governors, Confederate President Jefferson Davis, and Confederate General J.E.B. Stuart, the latter one of 22 Confederate generals interred here. Designed in 1848, it was conceived as a place where nature was accentuated and, as much as possible, undisturbed. Its winding scenic roads, ornamental shrubs and flowering trees, stone-bridged creeks, and ponds remain largely intact today. Monroe was the first person to be buried at Hollywood, in 1858, and when the War Between the States broke out a few years later, the struggle's first casualty was laid to rest here. Eventually, Hollywood would contain the graves of more Confederate notables than any other cemetery in the country. It was here that Memorial Day, now a national holiday, began as a local tradition. And over the years, many notables have been buried here, including novelists Ellen Glasgow and James Branch Cabell. However, the cemetery is most visited by Civil War buffs. The section in which the Confederates are buried is marked by a 90-foot granite pyramid, a monument constructed in 1869.

Hollywood Cemetery is open daily from 8 a.m. to 5 p.m.

WHERE TO STAY: The **Massad House Hotel,** 11 North 4th St. (between Main and East Franklin Sts.), Richmond, VA 23219 (tel. 804/648-2893), is too good to be true. Its 64 rooms are housed in a four-story Tudor-style brick building that looks as if it belongs in an English village. Inside it's homey and immaculate, from the cheerful lobby to the freshly painted hallways hung with prints, to the comfortable rooms. The latter have colonial-style maple furnishings, along with some modern pieces, and white stucco walls hung with paintings. Amenities include air conditioning, color TV with movie stations, direct-dial phone, and private bath. There's free parking on the premises, and an inexpensive restaurant is right next door. As for the location, it couldn't be more central. Rates are $32 for singles, $40 for doubles, $5 per extra person, $50 for a suite accommodating four. Reserve far in advance. A Budget Rent-A-Car agency is on the premises.

In summer Massad House offers horse-drawn carriage tours to historical points of interest around town—or custom tours if you so desire. Rates are $15 per half hour, $25 per hour. Call 804/780-0647 for details.

Carefully chosen bed-and-breakfast accommodations are offered by **Bensonhouse of Richmond,** P.O. Box 15131, Richmond, VA 23227 (tel. 804/648-7560). Administrator Lyn Benson was inspired to develop her service after spending a night on a business trip at a guest house in Savannah, Georgia. Exhausted after a long day's work, she returned to her room to find the bed turned back, a mint on her pillow, and a glass of brandy on the nightstand. When, back in Richmond, she found there were no comparable lodgings, she set to work finding hospitable hosts and attractive private residences. To date she has 18 listings, all within ten minutes of major attractions. All her hosts are knowledgeable about the city, and they provide brochures on major sights in guest rooms. Rates range from about $38 to $48 single, $45 to $60 double, continental breakfast included. Many hosts even prepare a full breakfast. At the lower end of the scale you're generally sharing a bath. The choices range from an 1870 Victorian home to a Duncan Lee 1915 mansion once owned by a leading tobacco merchant who entertained Charles Lindbergh and Lady Astor, among other notables. Reserve far in advance for the best rates and widest choices.

Conveniently down the street from the Visitors Center is an **Econo Lodge** at 1501 Robin Hood Rd., Richmond, VA 23220 (tel. 804/359-4011 or toll free 800/446-6900), with 156 nicely decorated standard motel rooms offering all the expected amenities—direct-dial phone, air conditioning, private bath, AM/FM clock radio, and color TV with HBO movies. On the premises is an Italian restaurant with wrought-iron candelabra chandeliers and stained-glass windows. There's also a pool and sundeck. Rates are $30 to $35 single, $33 to $43 double or twin, $5 for an extra person or a rollaway bed. There's no charge for children under 12 sharing a room with their parents. Parking is free. A good choice.

And, happy to say, your Richmond budget accommodation options include a **Motel 6**, 5704 Williamsburg Rd. (Route 60) near Airport Dr., Sandston, VA 23150 (tel. 804/222-7600). It's just across the street from the Richmond Airport. If you have a car, you're just seven miles from downtown. The 137 air-conditioned rooms have one or two double beds, shower bath, and color TV. And there's a swimming pool on the premises. Rates are $23.95 single, $28.95 for two, $32.95 for three, $36.95 for four. A restaurant next door at the Best Western Motor Lodge serves all meals.

RICHMOND RESTAURANTS: Whenever you start your dining day, do it at **Aunt Sarah's Pancake House**, 4205 West Broad St., between Antrim St. and Sauer Ave. (tel. 804/358-8812), a 24-hour eatery offering hearty down-home breakfast fare at reasonable prices. For $3.20 you can order old-fashioned buttermilk pancakes with whipped butter and a choice of syrups, two eggs, fresh-squeezed orange juice, and endless cups of steaming hot coffee. The pancakes come in all varieties, of course—banana nut, stoneground buckwheat, blueberry, apple, southern pecan, etc.—and there are corncakes, waffles and Irish potato pancakes (don't call them latkes) as well. Aunt Sarah's is a good place for inexpensive family lunches and dinners too. A Chesapeake Bay crabcake sandwich on roll with tomato, lettuce, and french fries is $3.10; a half-pound burger served with coleslaw and fries runs $3.45. And three big pieces of Uncle John's honey-dipped chicken with Aunt Sarah's pancakes or french fries is $3.95. For children under 10 a spaghetti-and-meatballs dinner with milk or soda is $2.40, one of several kiddie-priced meals. For everyone there's deep-dish apple pie à la mode for dessert. Aunt Sarah's is a cozy place, with seating at oak tables in big, comfortable leather-upholstered booths. Rough-hewn woodpaneled walls are hung with farm implements, old posters, World War I and II newspaper clippings, and historic documents. Waitresses are attired in gingham aprons and caps.

Grace Place, 826 West Grace St., between Schaeffer and Laurel Sts. (tel. 804/353-3680), is an absolutely delightful vegetarian restaurant occupying the second floor of a classic Victorian home. It has pine plank floors, white and unpainted brick walls hung with paintings by local artists, a fireplace, pots of geraniums in lace-curtained windows, and flower-bedecked oak tables. Standing lamps add a homey touch. Grace Place is sunny and cheerful by day, charming at night by candlelight. Low-key, low-decibel recorded background music (classical or folk) helps set the tone; occasionally there's even a guitarist on hand. You can also dine al fresco on the outdoor patio under shade trees.

As for the food, it's fresh, homemade, and healthful. Head chef Michael King follows a macrobiotic diet. Throughout the day, you can order big salads in the $2.50 to $4.25 range, perhaps a canteloupe stuffed with fresh fruit and topped with yogurt, honey, and nuts; an Indonesian salad of brown rice, sesame seeds, vegetables, pineapple, and cashews in a sweet/sour dressing; or a traditional tabbouli salad. There are sandwiches in the same price range such as falafel; avocado melt with Muenster cheese, shredded carrots, sprouts, and sliced tomatoes on homemade bread; and pizza in a pita. More serious lunch entrees, all under $5, include a farmer's platter of fried brown rice, sauteed vegetables, beans du jour, and raw vegetable garnish with fresh-baked bread— delicious, though I'd like to meet the farmer whose diet consists thereof. Evening specials ($5.50 to $6.50) include pastas, burritos, and other substantial items. Wine, beer, and coffee are available for those who can only go so far with this kind of thing; for purists there's a wide selection of herbal teas and specialty drinks like fresh-squeezed organic carrot juice and smoothies—icy fruit and yogurt shakes. Homemade desserts also provide a choice ranging from the sugarless (apple crisp) to the sinful (cheesecake). Open Monday to Saturday from 11:30 a.m. to 3 p.m. for lunch, from 5:30 to 9 p.m. for dinner. No credit cards.

The **Commercial Café**, 111 North Robinson St., between Floyd and Grove Aves. (tel. 804/355-8206), is hip and simpático—the kind of place with a good atmosphere, good food, and good music. You've seen it before in other cities: fans, lush hanging plants, and globe lights with rattan shades suspended from a pressed-tin ceiling; red-and-white checkered tablecloths; gallery lights over the bar; and barnwood walls hung with news clippings of major events like "Nixon Resigns." But the fact that it's familiar doesn't make it any the less likable, especially since the food is excellent. Hickory-smoked meats (from "plump, pampered, peanut-fed pigs") are the house specialty: try a smoked-pork barbecue or western beef sandwich ($5.50) served with delicious fresh-cut fried potatoes and barbecued beans. Or split a huge platter of nine ribs and fried potatoes ($13.75). Omelets, barbecued chicken, burgers, and salads are also offered, as is chocolate cheesecake for dessert. There's additional seating upstairs in the bar area, a cozy pine-paneled room with three windows overlooking the street. Open on Monday from 5 to 11 p.m., Tuesday to Friday from 11:30 a.m. to 2:30 p.m. and 5 to 11 p.m., on Saturday and Sunday from 11:30 a.m. to 11 p.m. Another branch of the Commercial Café is located in the Sixth Street Marketplace.

Very popular with locals—and it won't take you long to figure out why—is the **Strawberry Street Café**, 421 North Strawberry St., between Park and Stuart Aves. (tel. 804/353-6860). It's decorated in more-or-less turn-of-the-century style, with a beautiful oak bar at one end of the room, Casablanca fan chandeliers with art nouveau shades overhead, white walls decorated with many mirrors, and a plant-filled café-curtained window facing the street. Red-and-white striped tablecloths on candlelit (at night), flower-bedecked tables add a cheerful note. The salad bar, under an art nouveau stained-glass creation, is the focal point of the room and an excellent reason for eating here. For $4.25 at lunch, $5 at dinner, you can help yourself to unlimited quantities of greens, cottage cheese, sprouts, pepperoni, tomatoes, olives, fresh fruits, pasta salads, carrots, croutons, peaches, and more—plus fresh-baked bread and butter. At lunch or dinner it's $2.50 additional when you order a broccoli and cheddar quiche ($3.99) or a six-ounce burger made of prime ground beef served on an English muffin with fries ($3.50). At dinner, entrees like chicken in lemon butter sauce or beef liver with onions include not only salad bar (all you can eat) but a baked potato, fries, wild rice, or vegetables. There's strawberry shortcake for dessert. In short, it's easy to stuff yourself here at dinner for $10, dessert included, and to reach the same point of oversatiation even less expensively at lunch.

Strawberry Street is open Monday to Thursday from 11:30 a.m. to 11 p.m., Friday 11:30 a.m. to midnight, Saturday 11 a.m. to midnight, Sunday 10 a.m. to 11 p.m. A special brunch menu is offered through 3 p.m. on weekends. Weekdays, no food is served between 2:30 and 5 p.m.

The **Texas–Wisconsin Border Cafe,** 1501 W. Main St., at Plum St. (tel. 804/355-2907), is exactly what its name evokes—a rustic/western/hip eatery offering the kind of cookoff-winning chili—and chili parlor ambience—seldom found outside the Lone Star State. The two owners, one from Texas, one from Wisconsin, met as art students at Virginia Commonwealth University, and after graduation they created a restaurant. The setting: a longhorn steer horn over the door, fans suspended from a dark green pressed-tin ceiling, pine-wainscoted cream walls hung with boar and elk heads, photos of everyone from Pancho Villa to LBJ (showing his scar), and works of local artists. The music is mellow rock, blues, or country. Sporting events are aired on the TV over the bar—a bar that serves 25 bottled beers plus four on tap. The food: all fresh and homemade, highlighting, from Texas, widow-maker chili; a baked potato filled with fajitas and drenched in chili con queso; and red beans and rice. From Wisconsin there's a quarter-pound Milwaukee hot dog topped with melted swiss and sauerkraut; Welsh rarebit (what could be more Wisconsin than a dish made with cheddar cheese and beer); and potato pancakes (don't ask me, I've never been in Wisconsin). In addition, you can order terrific salads, omelets served with thick slabs of Texas toast and homemade fries, and sandwiches stuffed with everything from bratwurst (served with hot German potato salad) to Southern-fried chicken. Everything on the menu is under $5. Homemade desserts like bread pudding and rich chocolate cake round things (and people) out. Open daily from 11 a.m. to 2 a.m.

Everyone told me I had to visit the **Curles Neck Place,** 1600 Roseneath Rd. at W. Moore St. (tel. 804/355-1745), because they had the best milkshakes in the world. I did, and they did. Curles Neck makes homemade ice cream with milk from their own dairy farm in over a dozen flavors, and it's great, whether you order it by the scoop, smothered in hot fudge, or in a thick, totally satisfying milkshake. In fact, everything you order here is good—all of it made from scratch with fresh ingredients. Stop by for breakfast—e.g., two eggs with sausage, hash browns, biscuits, fresh-squeezed orange juice, and coffee ($3.35). At lunch or dinner, sandwiches like ham, swiss cheese, and sliced egg; barbecued beef; or sliced chicken are under $2.50. Or you might opt for the $3.25 daily special such as Wednesday's country-style steak with mashed potatoes, gravy, pinto beans, and rolls or Saturday's corned beef and cabbage with boiled parsley potatoes and corn bread. This is a great place for hearty, yummy, low-priced family meals that end in an orgy of ice cream. Curles is a Richmond tradition since 1946, and until recently it was appropriately old-fashioned and funky. In 1986, I'm sorry to say they renovated and now it's almost antiseptically cheerful with yellow and green leather booths and a modernistic blue enamel lighting fixture. Nevertheless, it's nice and sunny (there's a wall of window), and the food's as good as ever. Curles Neck is open Monday to Thursday from 7 a.m. to 4:30 p.m., Friday and Saturday 7 a.m. to 9:30 p.m., Sunday 8 a.m. to 3:30 p.m.

Another very popular Richmond establishment is **Baker's Treat,** 2904 W. Cary St., just off Colonial (tel. 804/358-0449). It's a great place for continental breakfasts and afternoon teas. The specialty here is fresh-from-the-oven croissants—plain, almond, fruit, chocolate, cheese, and combinations thereof. Brioches and apple turnovers are also featured, along with gourmet teas and coffees. The place itself is nothing much to look at—a dozen or so pedestal tables with ice cream parlor chairs under rattan-shaded lamps, a few additional tables outdoors. Weekend mornings it's especially hectic. Consider stocking up and heading over to nearby Maymont Park for breakfast al fresco. Open Monday to Friday 7:30 a.m. to 6 p.m., Saturday 9 a.m. to 5 p.m., Sunday 9 a.m. to 2 p.m.

And speaking of picnic fare, **Coppola's Delicatessen** right next door at 2900

W. Cary St. (tel. 804/359-NYNY), is one of the best places to obtain it. Owner Joe Coppola is an Italian guy from Brooklyn and he says of his store, "it's not like New York, it *is* New York." The aromatic clutter of cheeses, sausage, olives, pickles, and things marinated evokes Little Italy, and Joe enhances the setting by playing classical and Italian music. It's great. Behind-the-counter temptations include pasta salads, antipastos, stromboli (sesame bread stuffed with very thinly sliced salami, ham, pepperoni, cheeses, and sweet peppers), cannolis, Italian rum cake, even knishes from Brooklyn. Prices are low; this is a down-to-earth deli, not a pretentious gourmet emporium, though Joe's fare is as good as any of the latter offer. Joe, like Baker's Treat, has some tables (ten of them) inside and two out on the street. Open daily from 9 a.m. to 8:30 p.m.

Much plusher than any of the above, but still surprisingly affordable at lunch, is the **Peking Pavilion,** 1302 East Cary St. (tel. 804/649-8888), an excellent Shockoe Slip choice. Its three spacious high-ceilinged dining rooms are very elegant, beautifully decorated in cream and pale pink set off by flattering rosy lighting and a burgundy carpet. The exquisite woodcarvings and tapestries on the walls, as well as the dragon-motif-backed chairs, are all from mainland China. Yet for all its elegance, Peking Pavilion offers luncheon platters like spicy Tai Chien chicken, Szechuan beef chicken with cashew nuts, and sweet-and-sour pork for $5, all served with soup, eggroll, and fried rice. And most dinner entrees—among them Hunan beef in hot sauce with Chinese mushrooms, broccoli, and bamboo shoots; Mongolian-style lamb; and moo shu pork—are in the very moderate $7 to $9 range. Open Sunday to Thursday from 11:30 a.m. to 10 p.m., on Friday till 11 p.m., on Saturday for dinner only from 5 to 11 p.m.

RICHMOND AT NIGHT: Richmond is a major city, and there's usually quite a bit going on at night. Pick up a free copy of a magazine called *Style* at the Visitors Center. It provides details on theater, concerts, dance performances, and all other happenings.

3. Williamsburg

"I know of no way of judging the future," said Patrick Henry, "but by the past." That particular quotation couldn't be more apt as an introduction to Williamsburg. For one thing, Patrick Henry played a very important role here when, as a 29-year-old backcountry lawyer, he spoke out against the Stamp Act in the House of Burgesses in 1765. Many considered him an upstart and called the speech traitorous; others were inspired to revolution.

Another reason the quote is so apt—if you *can* judge the future by the past, you'll never have a better opportunity of doing so. Williamsburg is unique even in history-revering Virginia. It's gone beyond restoring and recreating important sites of the past. It's a completely reconstructed 18th-century town where women wear long dresses and ruffled caps, men don powdered wigs, Colonial fare is served in restaurants, blacksmiths' and saddlemakers' shops line cobblestone streets, and the local militia drills on the village green. Most of the year (except May 15 to July 4) a British flag flies over the Capitol.

A LITTLE HISTORY: To understand how it all came about, we must travel back almost 300 years to 1699. In that year, following the destruction of the State House by fire (the fourth one to burn down), and following a century of famine, fevers, and Indian battles, the beleaguered Virginia Colony abandoned the mosquito-infested swamp that was Jamestown for a planned model colonial city six miles inland. They named it Williamsburg for the reigning British monarch, King William of Orange. (Previously the town had been sparsely settled as a stockaded outpost against Indian attack and was known as Middle Plantation;

by 1699 there were a handful of houses, two mills, a small brick church, and a few shops.) The royal governor, Francis Nicholson, laid out the capital with a 99-foot-wide central thoroughfare (previously a horse trail) forming the principal east-west artery, the Duke of Gloucester St. It stretched a mile from the Capitol to the College of William and Mary, the latter dating to a 1693 royal charter granted for a college to be named in honor of the British sovereigns. Evidently not one to hide his light under a bushel, Nicholson named the other two major streets Francis St. and Nicholson St. He also planned public greens and allotted every house on the main street a half acre of land. Most of the houses were wood frame (trees being abundant) and painted white; kitchens were outside because of the risk of fire and the heat they generated in summer. People used their land allotment for growing vegetables and raising livestock; most kept a few chickens, perhaps a cow and a horse or a team of oxen. Cities were much more rural in the 18th century.

A residence for the royal governor was completed in 1720. The town prospered and soon became the major cultural and political center of the colonies. The government met here twice annually (April and October, conveniently comfortable months weather-wise), and during these "Publick Times" rich planters and politicos (one and the same in most cases) converged on Williamsburg and the population, normally about 1800, doubled. Shops displayed their finest imported wares, and there were balls, horse races, fairs, and auctions. In the years from 1699 to 1781 (when the offices of the new Commonwealth were moved to Richmond to be safer from enemy attack), Williamsburg played a major role in early American history, first as a seat of royal government and later as a hotbed of revolution. Here occurred many of the incitive events leading up to Richard Henry Lee's proposal in Philadelphia that Congress declare the colonies "absolved from all allegiance to the British Crown," and following close upon that, the Declaration of Independence. Thomas Jefferson and James Monroe studied at the College of William and Mary. Jefferson was also the second and last occupant of the Governor's Palace before the capital moved to Richmond. Patrick Henry was the first. During the Revolution, Williamsburg served as the wartime capital for four years and was variously the headquarters of Generals Washington (he planned the siege of Yorktown in George Wythe's house), Rochambeau, and Cornwallis.

A REVEREND AND A ROCKEFELLER: After 1780 Williamsburg was no longer an important political center, and the town retreated to the back pages of American history. For close to 150 years it was a quaintly charming Virginia town, unique only in that it changed so little. As late as 1926 the Colonial town plan was virtually intact, including numerous original 18th-century buildings. The Rev. W. A. R. Goodwin, former rector of Bruton Parish Church, saw the significance of Williamsburg's enduring heritage and envisioned a restoration of the entire town to its Colonial appearance. He inspired John D. Rockefeller, Jr., with his dream of creating a tangible symbol of our early history. As the work progressed, Rockefeller expressed his enthusiasm for the project: "The restoration of Williamsburg . . . offered an opportunity to restore a complete area and free it entirely from alien or inharmonious surroundings as well as to preserve the beauty and charm of the old buildings and gardens of the city and its historic significance. . . . I have come to feel that perhaps an even greater value is the lesson that it teaches of the patriotism, high purpose, and unselfish devotion of our forefathers to the common good."

During his lifetime Rockefeller contributed some $68 million to the project, and set up an endowment to help provide for the permanence of the restoration and its educational programs.

WILLIAMSBURG REBORN: Today the Historic Area covers 173 acres of the original 220-acre town. A mile long, it encompasses 88 preserved and restored houses, shops, taverns, public buildings, and dependencies which survived to the 20th century. An additional 50 buildings and many smaller structures have been rebuilt on their original sites after extensive archeological, architectural, and historical research. The Capitol, the Governor's Palace, and the Raleigh Tavern were among the latter.

Williamsburg set a very high standard for other Virginia restorations. Researchers investigated international archives, libraries, and museums; sought out old wills, diaries, court records, inventories, letters, and other documents; carefully studied 18th-century architecture, detailing its every aspect from paint chemistry to brickwork; and recovered thousands of artifacts at archeological digs while excavating 18th-century building sites to reveal original foundations.

The Historic Area includes 90 acres of gardens and greens, and 2300 surrounding acres serve as a "greenbelt" protective measure against commercial encroachment. Income from visitor purchases—including admissions—provides about 75% of the cost of exhibiting, interpreting, and maintaining Colonial Williamsburg and carrying forward its educational programs, so just by visiting you're helping support the project. Income from the three hotels, three Colonial taverns, and merchandising operations—along with the Rockefeller endowment—provides the rest of the needed funds.

FIRST STOP: The entire operation is overseen by the Colonial Williamsburg Foundation, a nonprofit, educational organization whose activities include an ever-ongoing restoration. To serve the annual one million visitors, they've created the **Colonial Williamsburg Visitor Center** off U.S. 60 (tel. 804/229-1000). You can't miss it. Bright green signs point the way from all access roads to Williamsburg. Stopping here is a must. Open 365 days a year from 8:30 a.m. to 5 p.m. in January and February, till 8 p.m. the rest of the year, the center offers maps and guidebooks, tours, and information on lodgings, dining, and evening activities. Since cars are not allowed—except in a limited way—into the Historic Area between 8 a.m. and 6 p.m. daily (Memorial Day to Labor Day till 9 p.m.), drivers must park at the center and proceed via a special bus that makes ten convenient stops at historic sites. There's a marvelous bookstore specializing in American history books on the premises, and a 35-minute orientation film, *Williamsburg—The Story of a Patriot,* is shown continuously throughout the day.

Most important, the center is where you buy your tickets for the dozens of attractions that make up Colonial Williamsburg. These include historic buildings and homes furnished with antiques and household goods of the period, craft shops where colonially costumed artisans employ 18th-century tools and methods, the old windmill, gaol, guardhouse, etc.

There are three types of general admission tickets available. All entitle you to see the orientation film at the Visitor Center and use the Historic Area bus service. A **Basic Admission Ticket** (providing admission to your choice of any 12 attractions) costs $14.50 for adults, $7.25 for children 6 to 12 (children under 6 are admitted free). The Governor's Palace requires an additional ticket, as do Carter's Grove, Bassett Hall, the Abby Aldrich Rockefeller Folk Art Center, and the DeWitt Wallace Decorative Arts Gallery. The **Royal Governor's Pass** ($19.50 for adults, $9.75 for children) includes all Historic Area attractions, except Carter's Grove, Bassett Hall, and the Folk Art Center. My advice is to shell out the $24.50 ($12.25 for children) for the **Patriot's Pass,** good for one year of unlimited free admissions at all Colonial Williamsburg attractions, *including* the Governor's Palace, Carter's Grove, Bassett Hall, the Folk Art Center, and the

Decorative Arts Gallery—plus a one-hour guided walking tour. There's so much to see and do that you don't want to have to pick and choose, probably omitting some attractions that interest you in the process. And the attractions that charge supplements with the Basic Admissions Ticket are must-sees, so you'd probably be paying the same amount anyway. You've come all this way; you may as well see it all.

If you're traveling with children, inquire about special tours and activities geared to various age levels and featuring music, games, storytelling, puppet shows, and an opportunity to practice 18th-century crafts.

Bus service from the Visitor Center begins at 8:50 a.m. (earlier in summer to transport visitors to special programs) and serves the Historic Area with departures every five minutes through 5:30 p.m., every 15 minutes from 5:30 to 10 p.m.

If you'd like to peruse informative brochures prior to arrival, call the number listed above or request them by mail; write to the Colonial Williamsburg Information Center, P.O. Box B, Williamsburg, VA 23187. They'll be happy to send brochures and maps. It's also a good idea (in summer, it's essential) to call ahead and make restaurant reservations at one of the Colonial taverns (details below) if you so desire.

GETTING THERE: Williamsburg is 150 miles south of Washington, D.C., via I-95 and I-64. Patrick Henry Airport is 14 miles from Williamsburg, and limousine service is available. Flights to the area also come into Norfolk Airport, about 45 miles from town. There's also bus service via Greyhound and Trailways, and rail transport via Amtrak. Don't worry about coming without a car; the Historic Area is compact.

GETTING THE PROPER ATMOSPHERE: How authentic is Colonial Williamsburg? Would Patrick Henry and Thomas Jefferson feel right at home? In some ways yes; in others, thank goodness, no! We of the 20th century are not quite ready to immerse ourselves totally in 18th-century conditions. Modern sanitary facilities such as toilets and sewers have been installed to comply with modern health department regulations as well as comfort. Our forebears used the chamber pot and the necessary house—a smelly and uncomfortable business. Air conditioning is a blessing in hot Virginia summers, but it also protects the valuable antique furnishings in the display houses. All of these modern conveniences are concealed so as not to jar. Jefferson and Henry would also find the town considerably tidier in the 20th century—minus the saddle and draft horses, the ubiquitous livestock in the streets, the dust, flies, mosquitoes, and the odors of backyard outhouses, animal manure, and a population not overly given to bathing (they thought it unhealthy). Sociologically, keep in mind that the average man had little education, the average woman less. Boys were apprenticed to trades at 14 years or younger, and much of the population consisted of slaves and indentured servants. Lectures, exhibits, and films attempt to evoke this missing background.

SIGHTS IN AND AROUND THE HISTORIC AREA: Williamsburg and its environs have ample attractions to keep the average family busy for at least a week, and at least two days are required to experience its offerings. If you have only a few hours to see the town, take a two-hour walking tour that provides an overview and visits about three attractions. Days and hours of operation for each sight are listed on a Visitor Center brochure you'll get with your ticket. Titled *This Week in Colonial Williamsburg,* it also lists special events taking place during your stay.

The Capitol

Virginia legislators met in the H-shaped, Renaissance-style Capitol at the eastern end of Duke of Gloucester St. throughout most of the 18th century (1704–1780). America's first representational assembly, it was modeled on an English bicameral legislature with an upper house (His Majesty's Council of State consisted of 12 members appointed by the royal governor) and a lower house (the House of Burgesses, elected by the freeholders of each county; by 1776 there were 128). All civil and criminal cases (the latter punishable by mutilation or death) were tried in the General Court, and since juries were sent to deliberate in a third-floor room without heat, light, or food, there were very few hung juries. Blackbeard's pirate crew faced trial here, and 13 of them were sentenced to hang for their crimes. The General Assembly met when called by the governor, with sessions lasting anywhere from a few days to several months, depending on the amount of business at hand. The burgesses represented the people of Virginia and considered petitions from their electors and royal orders. They initiated legislation and bills, then sent them to the Council for approval or rejection. As 1776 approached there were increasing petitions and resolutions against acts of Parliament considered infringements on the rights of self-government. The House of Burgesses became a training ground for patriots and future governors such as George Washington, Thomas Jefferson, Richard Henry Lee, and Patrick Henry. On a table in the Hall of Burgesses you'll see Patrick Henry's resolutions against the Stamp Act. The basis of his argument—no taxation without representation—became the motto of the Revolution. In other historic moments at the Capitol, George Washington was praised for his role in the French and Indian War and George Mason's Virginia Declaration of Rights (the prototype for the Bill of Rights) was passed. History was made here once again in May 1983 when the Summit Conference of Industrialized Nations convened in the House of Burgesses and President Reagan met with leaders from France, Great Britain, Canada, Italy, West Germany, Japan, and the EEC.

On 25-minute tours offered continuously throughout the day you'll see the plush Council Chamber, a suitable venue for royal representatives; the Joint Conference Room, where burgesses and councillors met for morning prayer and held meetings to resolve differences (herein are original Gilbert Stuart portraits of Washington, Jefferson, and Madison); the Secretary of the Colony's Office (he was second in importance to the royal governor, and enjoyed a lifetime appointment; note the Charles Willson Peale portrait of Washington); the Hall of Burgesses; and the General Courtroom. "What a temptation," mused John D. Rockefeller, "to sit in silence and let the past speak to us of those great patriots whose voices once resounded in these halls." The original Capitol burned down in 1747, was rebuilt in 1753, and succumbed to fire again in 1832. The reconstruction is of the 1704 building, complete with Queen Anne's coat-of-arms adorning the tower and the Union Jack flying overhead.

The Governor's Palace

Another complete reconstruction, this stately Georgian mansion, residence and official headquarters of royal governors, is today meticulously furnished in authentic Colonial pieces and staffed much as it was for several decades prior to the Revolution. A few years ago fresh scholarly data led to the complete revamping of the building (originally opened in 1934). Most important was information gleaned from a vital document—the inventory of Royal Governor Lord Botetourt, who died in office at the palace in 1770. It itemized over 16,500 objects contained in the 61-room complex, and shed light on the staff and facilities needed to maintain such an elaborate household. As at other

Williamsburg sites, where authentic period pieces were not available reproductions have been crafted to exacting standards by artisans thoroughly schooled in 18th-century methods. The final 15 years of British rule is the period portrayed. Though the sumptuous surroundings, nobly proportioned halls and rooms, ten acres of formal Renaissance gardens and greens, and vast wine cellars all evoke the splendor of the official residence of the king's foremost representative, research has indicated that by the 1760s the royal governor was a functionary of great prestige but limited power. He was more apt to behave like a diplomat in a foreign land than an autocratic colonial ruler.

The palace's residents included seven royal governors—from Alexander Spotswood, who supervised construction and moved in in 1714, to the Earl of Dunsmore who fled the premises in the face of armed resistance to royal authority just before dawn on June 8, 1775, thus ending British rule in Virginia. After independence, the state's first elected governors, Patrick Henry and Thomas Jefferson, lived here.

The palace is open daily, and tours are given continuously throughout the day. Admission for Basic Ticket holders is $10.50.

The tour offers substantial sociological insights and interesting tidbits; for instance, did you know that wig size in Colonial times connotated status? The larger the wig, the greater the status of the wearer—hence the term bigwig. And speaking of wigs, a service room off the back hall was a men's "powder room" used for powdering wigs. The massive display of weaponry in the hall and on the staircase was intended to impress visitors with the power of the British crown. It includes a circle of bayonets on the ceiling and walls hung with pistols, swords, and muskets. Upstairs, the Roman Catholic paintings are loot from Spanish ships taken by English pirates. In various chambers you'll see walls covered with hand-tooled gilded leather over two centuries old, rococo mirrors, and fireplaces lined with English Delft tiles. The palace was the glittering center of Virginia's high society prior to the Revolution. In the candlelit ballroom the governor entertained the colony's elite at large dinners, elegant balls, and concerts of baroque and classical compositions. The tour winds up in the gardens, where you can explore at your leisure the elaborate geometric parterres, topiary work, bowling green, pleached allées, gardens, fish pond, and a holly maze patterned after the one at Hampton Court. Plan at least 20 minutes to wander these stunning grounds. A map is available. During excavations the unmarked graves of 156 Revolutionary veterans were discovered. Today a simple stone under the shade of a weeping willow marks their sacrifice.

The Raleigh Tavern

Reconstructed on its original site in 1932 using data from old insurance policies, engravings, inventories of past proprietors (after the death of 1770 owner Anthony Hay, every article in the tavern was listed), and information gleaned from archeological excavations, the Raleigh occupies a fittingly central location on the north side of Duke of Gloucester St. After the Governor's Palace, it was the social and political hub of the town, especially during Publick Times when Williamsburg turned into a thronging metropolis. Colonists gathered here in 1769 to draw up a boycott of British goods—one of many meetings where grievances against the crown were aired—and regular clients included some of our most esteemed forefathers. George Washington frequently noted in his diary that he "dined at the Raleigh." A public reception here honored Peyton Randolph, first president of the Continental Congress, upon his return from Philadelphia in 1775. Thomas Jefferson wrote ruefully in a letter the morning after the night before, "Last night, as merry as agreeable company and dancing with Belinda in the Apollo [the Raleigh's ballroom] could make me, I never could have thought the succeeding Sun would have seen me so wretched." However, he was often here on less frivolous business, such as a meeting in 1773 with Patrick Henry, Richard Henry Lee, and Francis Lightfoot Lee to discuss revolution. Patrick Henry's troops gave their esteemed commander a farewell dinner at the Raleigh in 1776. And when the Revolution was a success, the triumph was also celebrated here. In 1824 Lafayette was feted at an Apollo banquet. In 1859 the tavern was destroyed by fire.

This most famous of Williamsburg taverns was named for Sir Walter Raleigh, who was instrumental in Britain's efforts to colonize the New World (note the bust of him over the main doorway). Its facilities include two dining rooms (George Washington often rented the smaller one for private dinners); the famed Apollo ballroom, scene of elegant entertainments; a club room which could be rented for private meetings, be they political conclaves or card games; a billiards room; and a bar where ale and hot rum punch were the favored drinks. The bedrooms upstairs offered nothing in the way of privacy. In fact it is believed that the expression "politics makes strange bedfellows," originated in the custom of renting bed space, especially during Publick Times when a smelly pig farmer might sleep next to a wealthy planter.

Eighteenth-century taverns like the Raleigh served as postal and news centers. Travelers brought news from diverse areas and took letters addressed to their ongoing destinations. They were also commercial centers where traveling salesmen displayed their wares and land and slaves were auctioned.

In the tavern bakery you can buy 18th-century confections like gingerbread, Shrewsbury cake, and apple pastry, and cider to wash it down.

Comprehensive tours are given.

One final note: The honor fraternity, Phi Beta Kappa, was founded at the Raleigh Tavern in 1776.

Wetherburn's Tavern

Though less important than the Raleigh, Wetherburn's also played an important role in Colonial Williamsburg. George Washington occasionally favored the tavern with his patronage, and Peter Jefferson (father of Thomas) closed a land deal here with William Randolph over "Henry Wetherburn's biggest bowl of Arrack Punch," the house specialty.

Like the Raleigh, it was mobbed during Publick Times and frequently served as a center of sedition and a rendezvous of Revolutionary patriots. Unlike the Raleigh, it's a restoration. The building, dating from 1715, first served as a private house for a prominent Virginia family. Henry Wetherburn ran it as a tavern from 1738 until his death in 1760, after which his heirs leased the property to other innkeepers. And in subsequent years it was reincarnated as a school for young ladies, a boardinghouse, and a store. The heart of yellow pine floors are original, so you can actually walk in Washington's footsteps; windows, trim, and weatherboarding are a mixture of old and new; and the outbuildings, except for the dairy, are reconstructions. A long, detailed inventory from Wetherburn's day listing the contents of the tavern room by room provided an excellent blueprint for furnishings. In addition, excavations on the site turned up an astounding 192,000 artifacts, including porcelain, pottery, clay tobacco pipes, and 42 unbroken bottles that had contained brandied cherries. Further information came from letters, diaries, gazettes, and records offices.

Wetherburn was a prosperous innkeeper. He ran not only this tavern, but also the Raleigh and other establishments at various times. When his first wife died in 1751, a captious town diarist wrote, "he has found her hoard." Wetherburn, seemingly immune to public scorn, remarried a week later the widow of another successful innkeeper, Mrs. Anne Marot Ingles Shields, thus assuming control of three additional taverns. It is perhaps an interesting coincidence that his first wife had also been an innkeeper's widow with several properties. Mr. Wetherburn's romances were profitable, but a trifle suspect. Keep in mind, in the 18th century, a woman's property automatically became her husband's when she wed.

Scene of auctions, balls, business dealings, and political meetings, the Wetherburn lodged 38 or more men in its 19 ropespring beds for 7½ pence a night (extra for horse bedding). A dozen slaves served guests and saw to the cooking, gardening, cleaning, and horse grooming. Gambling and drinking went on all night, not just in the gaming room but in the dining rooms and bedrooms—this in spite of licensing regulations condemning both activities.

Twenty-five-minute tours are given.

George Wythe House

On the west side of the Palace Green is the elegant restored brick home of George Wythe (pronounced "With")—foremost classics scholar in 18th-century Virginia, noted lawyer and teacher (his illustrious students included Thomas Jefferson, James Monroe, Henry Clay, and future Chief Justice John Marshall), and member of the House of Burgesses. A close friend of Royal Governors Fauquier and Botetourt, Wythe nevertheless sided with the patriots during the Revolution; he was the first Virginia signer of the Declaration of Independence. (On principle, Wythe did not sign the Constitution, because it did not contain the bill of rights or antislavery provisions he had fought for.) In 1777 he was elected Speaker of the House of Delegates, in 1778 one of the three judges of Virginia's High Court of Chancery, and in 1779 he became the first professor of law at an American college—William and Mary. During a 1782 case he helped establish the concept of judicial review with these words: "If the whole legislature . . . should attempt to overleap the bounds . . . I, in administering the public justice of the country, will meet the united powers at my seat in this tribunal; and pointing to the Constitution, will say to them, Here is the limit of your authority; and hither shall you go but no further."

Thomas Jefferson called Wythe "my faithful and beloved Mentor in youth, and my most affectionate friend through life."

Despite a distinguished career spanning over half a century, Wythe came to a sticky end in 1806. His grandnephew, George Sweeney, finding himself in dire financial straits, poisoned the 80-year-old Wythe in hopes of hastening his inheritance. The plot backfired; Wythe survived the attempt—though in agony —for two weeks, long enough to change his will and disinherit Sweeney. Sweeney did, however, get off, since the major evidence against him was that of a slave who witnessed the act, and a slave's testimony was not admissible in court. Wythe's will also freed his slaves; like many wealthy Virginians he had kept slaves while abhoring the practice in principle. He is buried in St. John's Churchyard in Richmond.

The house, in which he lived with his second wife, Elizabeth Taliaferro (her father designed and built it), was Washington's headquarters prior to the siege of Yorktown and Rochambeau's after the surrender of Cornwallis. Domestic crafts typical of the time—spinning, basketmaking, weaving, chairmaking, open-hearth cooking, etc.—are demonstrated by artisans in the Wythe House outbuildings. These include a kitchen, smokehouse, laundry, dovecote, fowl house, and stable. A topiary garden leads to a pleached arbor.

Shops and Crafts

The 18th-century crafts practiced on the grounds of Wythe House are among numerous similar exhibits throughout the Historic Area. Such goings-on were of course a facet of everyday life in this preindustrial era. Several dozen crafts are practiced in cluttered shops by over 100 master craftspeople. They're an extremely skilled group, many having served up to seven-year apprenticeships both here and abroad. When Queen Elizabeth visited Williamsburg in 1954 she was presented with a handcrafted silver tea service and cribbage board made by the town's artisans; Winston Churchill received a silver town crier's bell and a leather-covered case in 1955; President Kennedy netted silver reproductions of Paul Revere's lanterns; and all presidents since have received articles made by Williamsburg silversmiths.

The program is part of Williamsburg's efforts to present an accurate picture of Colonial society, portraying the average man and woman as well as more illustrious citizens. There are books available on Colonial crafts at the Visitor Center, and several films shown in the evenings provide further elucidation. Products from the shops are sold at stores in the Historic Area to help defray operating costs. Craft displays are open five to seven days a week from 9 a.m. to 5 p.m., with evening tours available (visitors carry lanterns) in the spring and fall, and extended hours in summer. Crafts seminars are held on Saturday in winter. Some examples:

At **Anthony Hay's cabinetmaking shop,** fine furnishings are produced of cherry, walnut, and mahogany using foot- and hand-powered tools. Thomas Jefferson was among the patrons of the original **Hay.**

Next door, **musical instruments** are fashioned—harpsichords, English guitars, and others.

A **music teacher** instructs students in these and other period instruments— cello, flute, oboe, violin, viola, recorder, etc., at his shop; you can always enjoy a concert of period music here, his students being most accomplished.

The **wigmaker** operates out of the **King's Arms Barber Shop.** Here you'll see the cone-shaped mask which men donned in order to breathe while their wigs were powdered with pulverized starch and plaster.

James Geddy's silversmith shop adjoined his house (details below) and was right across from the master bedroom so that he could hear any hankypanky going on at night (silver items are valuable).

A **jeweler and engraver** share headquarters in which 18th-century clocks, fine cutlery, jewelry, and other antiques are displayed, including a silver tobacco box made in 1723.

Also in cahoots are the **printer and bookbinder,** together turning out 18th-century books of children's tales. They operate out of a working **post office** where your letters receive a hand-stamped postmark patterned after one used here in 1771. On these premises printer William Parks (a colleague of Benjamin Franklin) published the first issue of the *Virginia Gazette* in 1736. Parks was also the colony's first postmaster. During excavations at this site, several hundred pieces of type, bookbinder's ornaments, and lead border ornaments used in printing paper money during the French and Indian War were unearthed.

Tubs, buckets, barrels, kegs, and other containers made of staves are produced at the **cooper's shop.**

The workshop of colonial **coachmaker** Elkanah Deane is today utilized by a maker of saddles and harnesses. He shares the premises with a blacksmith who turns out toasting forks, hinges, wagon tires, and many other wrought-iron objects both decorative and functional.

In addition to boots, the **bootmaker** creates drinking mugs, dice cups, belts, hornbooks, fire buckets, and other leather items. Shoe and boot styles varied, but right and left shoes did not; that was a later innovation. In a 12-hour day, an 18th-century shoemaker could turn out two pairs. The shop is on the site of a 1773 shoemaking establishment.

Exact replicas of weapons carried by Colonial Virginians—English flint-lock muskets, rifles, and fowling pieces used to shoot ducks and geese—are fashioned by a skilled **gunsmith** at Ayscough House.

The **milliner** (in the 18th century carrying all fashion wear, not just hats) explains the styles of the day for men, women, and children. For example, you'll learn that women didn't carry handbags, because pockets in their gowns went through to sacks in their farthingales (skirt extenders or—give me a break—hip wideners). A fashionable gown in our forefathers' day cost more than a roundtrip sail to England! No one, by the way, wore underwear.

At the Raleigh Tavern bakery, a **baker** in Colonial garb slaves all day over two hot brick dome-shaped ovens rebuilt from documents, drawings, and actual remains. You can purchase his wares.

The **textile dyer** utilizes roots, nuts, barks, leaves, even bugs in the making of colors.

Candlemaking is always fun to watch, and the smell of bayberry wax is alluring. Tallow and beeswax were also used, as was oil from the head of sperm whales. (The latter is not used today for ecological reasons, since great sperm whales are threatened with extinction.)

A **shinglemaker** demonstrates his ancient craft using cypress and cedar. Most Williamsburg houses were covered with wood shingles secured by wooden pegs.

And always interesting in a morbid way is the **apothecary shop,** where sore feet were treated with leeches between the toes, a headache with leeches across the forehead, and a sore throat with leeches on the neck—often in addition to elixirs, ointments, and herbs. Eighteenth-century doctors had no concept of germ theory or sterilization; those who washed or cleaned their instruments before an operation were regarded as eccentric. In the surgery are gruesomelooking tools, including amputation instruments. A herb garden out back was used to grow medicinal plants.

These crafts exhibits are among the most fascinating in Colonial Williamsburg. Sometimes the artisans go into detail about what they're doing, sometimes they work in silence while you watch. In the latter case, ply them with questions.

The James Anderson House

Originally owned by the secretary to Royal Governor Dinwiddie, William Wither, from 1755 to 1760, this historic building was later a tavern operated by Mrs. Christiana Campbell, and George Washington frequently stayed the night. Blacksmith James Anderson acquired the property in 1770 and set up shop. Prior to and during the Revolution he was Virginia's official armorer, and he worked here until 1798.

Today the building is used for exhibits excavated in Williamsburg archeological digs and found in Colonial wells (it was the custom in the 18th century to toss unwanted objects into abandoned wells). A display of 88 objects removed from the earth is shown in conjunction with an adjoining bedroom which was reconstructed using these objects as guidelines. They include fragments of scissors, candlesticks, coins, medicine bottles, tobacco pipes, turkey bones and oyster shells (clues to meals), Delftware, shoes, and a sword hilt. Other exhibits focus on ceramics—British Delftware, English brown stoneware, German gray stoneware, English slipware, British white salt-glazed stoneware, Chinese export porcelain, etc.—brass and copper, and glass bottles. Also on display is a map of Williamsburg drawn up by a French cartographer in 1782. Taped lectures explain what you're seeing. This is a must-see.

Behind the house is a reconstruction of Anderson's blacksmith shop where a corps of workmen at seven forges turn out nails, farm tools, and tradesmen's tools. Costumed interpreters explain the various processes of blacksmithing to visitors. Since horseshoes are made here as well, there's a pole for playing horseshoes, a pastime even kids nurtured on video games enjoy immensely. The shop itself was constructed by local artisans using 18th-century tools and methods. They even felled the trees used for lumber in nearby forests. If James Anderson could stop by today, he'd surely recognize his old place of business.

The Publick Gaol

They didn't coddle criminals in the 18th century. Punishments included not only public ridicule (the barbarous stocks and pillories), but also lashing, branding, mutilation, and hanging, the latter evoked even for such lightweight crimes as burglary, forgery, and horse stealing. A prisoner sentenced to death was given a few weeks to make his peace with God and was taken by the gaoler to Bruton's Parish Church every Sunday to do so. Those who escaped more severe punishments and were sentenced to prison found it no picnic. In winter the dreary cells were bitterly cold, in summer stifling. Beds were rudimentary piles of straw; leg irons, shackles, and chains were used frequently; and the daily diet consisted of "salt beef damaged, and Indian meal." Prisoners with shillings to spare had meals and liquor sent in from nearby taverns.

In its early days (before the construction of a "Lunatick Hospital") the gaol doubled as a madhouse, and during the Revolution redcoats, spies, traitors, and deserters swelled the prison population. A famous Revolutionary prisoner was Henry Hamilton, governor of the Northwest Territory (he was known as "Hair Buyer," because he paid Indians for American scalps).

The gaol opened in 1704 (frontier colonies couldn't go long without one; of course, neither could we); debtors cells were added in 1711 (though the imprisoning of debtors was virtually eliminated after a 1772 law made creditors responsible for their upkeep), and keeper's quarters were added in 1722. The thick-walled red brick building served as the Williamsburg city jail through 1910. The building today is restored to its 1720s appearance.

The Peyton Randolph House

The Randolphs were one of the most prominent—and wealthy—families in Colonial Virginia, and Peyton Randolph was one of its most distinguished members. His father, Sir John Randolph, was a highly respected lawyer and Speaker of the House of Burgesses. He was Virginia's representative to London and the only native Virginian ever to be knighted by George II. When he died he left his library to a 16-year-old Peyton, "hoping he will betake himself to the study of law." When Peyton Randolph died in 1775 he left his collection of books to his cousin, Thomas Jefferson; they eventually became the nucleus of the Library of Congress. Peyton Randolph did follow in his father's footsteps, studying law in London after graduating from the College of William and Mary. He served in the House of Burgesses from 1744 to 1775, the last nine years as Speaker of the House. He was unanimously elected president of the First Continental Congress in Philadelphia in 1774, and though he was a believer in nonviolence who hoped the colonies could amicably settle their differences with England, he was a firm patriot. He was known as the great mediator. After his death his widow, Betty Harrison Randolph of Berkeley, continued to live at the house through 1783, though she did relinquish the premises to the Comte de Rochambeau while he prepared the siege of Yorktown. In 1824 another famous Frenchman, the Marquis de Lafayette, was a guest at his home during his visit to Williamsburg.

The house (actually, two connected homes) dates to 1715 and is today restored to that period; note the exquisite original red oak paneling. It's open to the public for self-guided tours.

Robertson's Windmill, in back of the house, is a post mill of a type popular in the 18th century. Today it's an operating craft shop.

The Brush-Everard House

One of the oldest still-extant buildings in Williamsburg, the Brush-Everard House was occupied without interruption from the time armorer, gunsmith, and keeper of the Powder Magazine John Brush built it as a residence-cum-shop in 1717 through 1946. Charged not only with maintaining and repairing weaponry, Brush also had to take part in various ceremonies requiring gun salutes, such as royal birthdays. At one of these he wounded himself slightly and applied—without success—to the House of Burgesses for damages. Little else is known about him. He died in 1726. The next owner of whom information comes down to us was William Dering, an artist and dancing teacher (at the College of William and Mary) who acquired the property in 1742. But the most distinguished owner was Thomas Everard, clerk of York County from 1745 to 1771 and two-time mayor of Williamsburg. Though not as wealthy as Wythe and Randolph, he was in their elite circle. He enlarged the house, adding the two wings that give it a U-shape. Today the home is restored and furnished to its Everard era appearance.

An introductory talk is given to visitors in the library, its shelves lined with 300 books recommended by Thomas Jefferson for the guidance of a young planter. (They cover many topics and include the classics, drama, history, philosophy, science, religion, and law, as well as works of fiction which Jefferson deemed "useful as well as pleasant.") Following that you can tour on your own. Most notable is the elaborate central stairway with richly ornamented carvings. The library and the northeast bedroom contain wallpapers reproduced from design fragments. The smokehouse and kitchen out back are originals, and candlemaking is demonstrated in the latter. The oldest surviving box hedges in Virginia, now grown to twisted trees, can be seen in the garden.

The James Geddy House and Silversmith Shop

This two-story L-shaped 1750 home and attached shops and dependencies have been constructed on their original sites with the intention of showing how a comfortably situated middle-class family lived in the 18th century. Unlike the fancier abodes you'll visit, the Geddy House has no wallpaper, no oil paintings, and no elaborate paneling; a clock, mirror, and spinet from England, however, indicate relative affluence. The spinet was much used by a granddaughter of James Geddy, Sr., who inspired a secret admirer to publish a poem in the *Virginia Gazette* of December 20, 1768, in her honor:

> When Nancy on the spinet plays
> I fondly on the virgin gaze,
> And wish that she was mine;
> Her air, her voice, her lovely face,
> Unite with such excessive grace,
> That nymph appears divine!

It was rather easy to get into print in Colonial Williamsburg.

The Geddy dynasty begins with James Sr., an accomplished gunsmith and brass founder who advertised in the *Virginia Gazette* of July 8, 1737, that he had "a great Choice of Guns and Fowling Pieces, of several Sorts and Sizes, true bored, which he will warrant to be good; and will sell them as cheap as they are usually sold in *England.*" He also informed the public of his willingness to make "several Sorts of wrought Brasswork," and to cast "small bells." He died in 1744, leaving his widow with eight children and little money.

His enterprising oldest and third sons, David and William, took over, offering their services as "Gunsmiths, Cutlers, and Founders," and on the side they did a little blacksmithing and engraving and sold a "Vermifuge . . . which safely and effectually destroys all Kinds of Worms in Horses" as well as cures for "all Diseases incident to Horses." A younger son, James Jr., became the town's foremost silversmith. Archeological digs have unearthed thousands of artifacts from all of these trades on the property.

James Jr. worried that his shop was too far from the Capitol (perhaps our forefathers weren't as hardy as we imagine). In a notice in the *Virginia Gazette* he expressed the hope that "the reasonableness of his prices would remove that Objection of his Shop's being too high up Town . . . and the Walk may be thought rather an Amusement than a Fatigue." George Washington was one of his customers. Geddy rented out shop space to a "watch finisher" from London and to his brother-in-law, William Waddill, an engraver. Waddill's engraved nameplate for Governor Botetourt's coffin is displayed in the shop, where craftspeople will show you how silver items are made from ingot to finished product. To round out his many activities, Geddy imported and sold jewelry and was a member of the city's Common Council involved in furthering the patriot cause.

The Magazine and Guardhouse

The magazine is a sturdy octagonal brick building designed by the first royal governor, Alexander Spotswood, and constructed in 1715 to house ammunition and arms for the defense of the British colony. It has survived intact to the present day. In Colonial Williamsburg every able-bodied freeman belonged to the militia from the ages of 21 to 60, and did his part in protecting hearth and home from Indian attack, riots, slave uprisings, and pirate raids.

The high wall and guardhouse were built during the French and Indian War to protect the magazine's 60,000 pounds of gunpowder (they were later torn down, but have been reconstructed with the aid of archeological findings and artist's renderings). As the Revolution approached and news of Boston rebellion reached Williamsburg, Lord Dunmore decided to steal the gunpowder from the magazine lest it fall into patriot hands. He informed London of his planned action in response to "The series of dangerous measures pursued by the people of this Colony against Government," and upon receiving permission, ordered British marines to remove the gunpowder at night. However, word leaked out to the colonists, and Patrick Henry led a band of armed men to the capital demanding the return of the powder or payment for it. Payment was duly made and the rebels dispersed, Dunmore providing the lame explanation that he had removed the powder upon hearing of "an intended insurrection of the slaves" and that he "certainly rather deserved the thanks of the country than their reproaches." Nobody bought it.

The magazine was again used for storing gunpowder during the Civil War; it has also served as a dancing school, Baptist meeting house, and livery stable over the years.

Today the building is stocked with 18th-century equipment—British-made flintlock muskets, powderhorns (for carrying gunpowder), cartridge boxes, cannons and cannonballs, barrels of powder, bayonets, and drums, the latter for communication purposes. Drum calls told soldiers when to go to bed, attack, retreat, etc.; there were 83 calls.

Guards on breaks from sentry duty warmed themselves by the fire in the guardhouse. There's usually a guard present to talk to visitors. Note the squirrel tails—souvenirs of meals!

A 20-minute horse-drawn carriage ride around the Historic Area departs from a horse post to the left of the guardhouse, at a cost of $3 per person. There's a free oxcart ride for children age 9 and under.

Carter's Grove

To my mind, Carter's Grove—a magnificent plantation home that has been continuously occupied since 1753 on a site that was settled over 3½ centuries ago—is one of the most intriguing historical attractions in Virginia. Even getting here is a thrill. The estate is reached via a stunningly scenic one-way, seven-mile wilderness road traversing streams, marshes, meadow, woodlands, and ravines. A recreation of a Colonial carriage pathway, the road is dotted with markers indicating old graveyards, Indian encampments, plantation sites, and other points of interest.

The history of Carter's Grove takes us back to the earliest days of the colonies. Searching for traces of lost plantation outbuildings on the banks of the James, archeologists have discovered here the "lost" 17th-century village of Wolstenholme Towne, site of a 20,000-acre tract settled in 1619 by 220 colonists who called themselves the Society of Martin's Hundred. Named for Sir John Wolstenholme, one of the society's most influential shareholders, the early town was short-lived. The great Indian uprising of March 22, 1622, destroyed most of the settlement and left only about 30 or 40 living inhabitants, who fled to Jamestown. At least half of the original town has been lost to us through erosion by the James River, but archeologists have found the remnants of a fortified compound and lookout tower, dwellings, a corral for penning livestock, graves, and other structures. A 1624 census of Martin's Hundred's military capability listed a single cannon "with all things thereto belonging." The cannon has not been found, but a cannonball has been discovered that would indicate it was a big gun with a range up to 2,000 yards.

Over a century after the abandonment of Wolstenholme Towne, Robert "King" Carter (Virginia's wealthiest planter) purchased the property for his daughter, Elizabeth, widow of Nathaniel Burwell. In his will he specified that the plantation should pass to Elizabeth's son, Carter Burwell, and "in all times to come be called and go by the name of Carter's Grove." Today 790 acres remain of the original 1,400-acre tract purchased by King Carter.

Between 1750 and 1753 Carter Burwell built the 2½-story, 200-foot-long mansion that has been called "the most beautiful house in America" and considered "the final phase of the evolution of the Georgian mansion." The Burwells were an extremely prominent Virginia family. Carter Burwell was a member of the House of Burgesses, and his son, Nathaniel, was a member of the Virginia Convention that ratified the Constitution of the United States. The most elite members of Virginia society were frequent guests at Carter's Grove. The West Drawing Room—with its exquisite fireplace mantel of white and Sienna marble and carved frieze panel—is often called the "Refusal Room"; legend has it that southern belle Mary Cary refused George Washington's proposal of marriage in this room and Rebecca Burwell said "no" to Thomas Jefferson (Jefferson called her "fair Belinda"; see his comment, above, in the Raleigh Tavern listing). In 1781 British cavalryman Banastre Tarleton headquartered at Carter's Grove and is said to have ascended the magnificent carved stairway on his warhorse while hacking at the balustrade with his saber.

Despite Tarleton's abuse, Carter's Grove remains one of the best preserved old houses in America. The Burwells occupied it through 1838, after which there were several owners. One did desecrate the exquisite paneling of the great hall in honor of the 1881 Yorktown Centennial by painting it red, white, and blue. Fortunately, in 1927 the property was acquired by Mr. and Mrs. Archibald M. McCrea (she was a direct descendant of Williamsburg's first royal governor, Alexander Spotswood; his portrait hangs in the office). The McCreas, who entertained Franklin Delano Roosevelt here in 1936, hired renowned architect Duncan Lee to restore the property. When Mrs. McCrea died in 1960, she willed the estate and its grounds to be preserved and displayed to the public. Rockefeller interests acquired the property in 1963, and since 1969 it has been owned and administered by the Colonial Williamsburg Foundation.

It is still in an ongoing stage of development as a showcase of plantation life from the early 17th century through the 1930s. Reconstructions are under way of portions of Wolstenholme Towne. There are tobacco, apple, corn, and grain crops, and related crafts demonstrations such as rail splitting, scything, sickling, and coopering. Sometimes visitors can ride in a horse-drawn wagon to a tobacco field where living history actors—planters, fieldhands, and foremen—explain the role of tobacco in the Colonial Virginia economy. A tobacco barn, where harvested leaves will be cured, is under construction. Orchards and gardens are also being restored.

There's so much to see and do here—sites along the country road, a house tour, an archeology tour, etc.—that you should allow at least two hours for your visit. A new 10,000-square-foot reception center, housed in a red cedar building, serves as an orientation area. Visitors view a 14-minute slide presentation on Carter's Grove and an exhibit area where archaeological artifacts, historic photographs, and documents tell the story of the land at Carter's Grove and its people. A gift shop is on the premises. Upon leaving the reception center, you'll cross a foot bridge that spans a 100-foot-deep ravine en route to the house. The house is open daily March to November and during Christmas season from 9 a.m. to 5 p.m.; the country road (take South England Street and follow the signs to get on it) is open from 8:30 a.m. to 4:30 p.m.; it only goes one way, so you must return to Williamsburg via Route 60. Admission for Basic Ticket holders is $6.50.

Bassett Hall

This is your chance to find out how the Rockefellers really live. Though colonial in origin (built between 1753 and 1766 by Col. Philip Johnson), Bassett Hall was the residence of Mr. and Mrs. John D. Rockefeller, Jr., in the mid-1930s, and it is restored and furnished to reflect their era. The mansion's name, however, derives from the ownership of Burwell Bassett, a nephew of Martha Washington who lived here from 1800 to 1839.

The Rockefellers purchased the 585-acre property in the late 1920s and moved into the restored two-story dwelling in 1936, having added various and sundry embellishments such as a new service wing. In spite of changes they made, much of the interior is original, including woodwork, paneling, mantels, and yellow-pine flooring. During their years here the Rockefellers entertained such royal notables as Britain's Queen Elizabeth, King Paul and Queen Frederika of Greece, and Emperor Hirohito of Japan. Bequeathed to the Colonial Williamsburg Foundation along with its furnishings in 1979, the house is, however, cozy and warm, not in the least formal or forbidding. The *New York Times* once characterized the rooms where the Rockefellers ate, slept, and entertained as "downright homey and full of the sort of exuberant mix of furnishings that curators abhor but people adore." Which is not to say it isn't full of treasures. Much of the furniture is 18th- and 19th-century American in the Chippendale, Federal, and Empire styles. There are beautifully executed needlework rugs in the hallways, three of them made by Mrs. Rockefeller herself. Six early-19th-century prayer rugs adorn the morning room, while French Aubusson carpets and Bessarabian rugs enhance the parlor and dining room. Hundreds of examples of ceramics and china are on display (the 164-piece Chinese porcelain dinner service is to die for), as are collections of 18th- and 19th-century American and English glass, Canton Enamelware, and folk art (125 pieces comprising weather vanes, stencil paintings, mourning embroideries, Pennsylvania chalkware, children's portraits, and schoolgirl samplers; there's much more, of course, at the Abby Aldrich Rockefeller Folk Art Center, about which more later). Mr. Rockefeller's bedroom reflects his patriotic zeal; it has carved eagles and walls decorated with three versions of Edward Savage's painting *George Washington and His Family*. John D. Rockefeller 3rd and his wife, Blanchette, who inherited the house in 1960, scarcely changed the furnishings.

The grounds were laid out in the 1930s by Arthur A. Shurcliff, the first landscape architect to be associated with Colonial Williamsburg. The "homestead" area, based on sketches of original sites, consists of 18 acres surrounding the hall and includes the impressive oak-framed access road. Turf panels to the south and west of the rear wings are bordered by dwarf boxwood, and an oak allée culminates in a vista cut through the woodlands to tidal estuaries of the James.

Forty-minute tours of the house are given between 10 a.m. and 5 p.m. daily by reservation only (tel. 804/229-1000, extension 4119; or write to Bassett Hall Reservation Office, P.O. Box C, Williamsburg, VA 23187). Visitors are greeted by a guide in the adjacent reception building and taken to the front entrance where a brief history of the property is given. The tour visits the morning room, parlor, master and guest bedrooms, bathrooms, the service wing, and its three bedrooms, caretaker's living room, kitchen, pantry, and dining room. It ends in the garden, which you can explore at your leisure. Here you'll see—in addition to the above—the great oak tree where in 1926 Dr. W. A. R. Goodwin and Rockefeller first discussed the restoration of Williamsburg, and two original 18th-century outbuildings (a smokehouse and dairy). Admission for Basic Ticket holders is $5.50.

The Abby Aldrich Rockefeller Folk Art Center

The works of folk art displayed at Bassett Hall are just a small sampling of enthusiast Abby Aldrich Rockefeller's extensive collection of South England St. This delightful museum contains over 2,000 folk art paintings, sculptures, and art objects. Mrs. Rockefeller was a pioneer in this branch of collecting in the 1920s; other collectors of the day looked upon American Folk art as merely curious or quaint, and ignored its artistic appeal. A gallery guide described a folk artists as one who, "unfamiliar with the academic solutions . . . for rendering correct linear perspective, anatomy, color balance, or the proper use of light and shadow . . . somehow solves the technical difficulties he encounters in his work and intuitively produces a satisfying picture, carving, or household furnishing." Also known as naïve, primitive, provincial, and nonacademic art, folk art is of interest not only aesthetically but as visual history; since Colonial times untutored artists have creatively recorded everyday life. It's also, for the most part, rather charming.

The Abby Aldrich Rockefeller collection includes household ornaments and useful wares (hand-stenciled bed covers, butter molds, pottery, utensils, painted furniture, boxes, etc.), mourning pictures (memorial embroideries honoring departed relatives and national heroes, usually with gravestones under weeping willow trees), family and individual portraits, shop signs, carvings, whittled toys, calligraphic drawings, weavings, and paintings of scenes from daily life (see in particular *The Quilting Party,* a lovely depiction of a mid-19th-century quilting bee done in oil on board, and *The Old Plantation,* a watercolor from about 1,800 showing dancing slaves).

The Public Hospital

Built in 1771–1773, the "Public Hospital for Persons of Insane and Disordered Minds" was America's first lunatic asylum. Previous to its advent, the mentally ill were often thrown in jail or confined to the poorhouse, where they were perhaps better off. From 1773 to about 1820, treatment—or one might say mistreatment—of mental patients involved restraint, solitary confinement, and a grisly course of action designed to "encourage" patients to "choose" rationality over insanity and restore the physical balance of body and brain. It was commonly assumed that patients willfully and mistakenly chose a life of insanity. So-called therapeutic techniques included the use of powerful drugs to exhaust or stimulate, frequent evacuation of the bowels (though sometimes, conversely, constipation was induced), submersion in cold water for extended periods, bleeding, blistering salves, and an array of torture-chamber-like restraining devices. There was even an electrostatic generator—the forerunner of electroshock therapy—used to shock patients with sparks. On a self-guided tour you'll see a 1773 cell, with its filthy straw-filled mattress on the floor, ragged blanket, manacles, and chamber pot. This 11-foot-square room became the patient's isolated world except for rare exercise in the yard. Patients were totally idle and without distraction of any kind—a condition that might drive anyone crazy.

During what is called the Moral Management Period (1820–1865), a great change was manifest in society's view of the mentally ill. Patients were seen to have an emotional disorder and were treated with kindness and dignity. Occupational therapy and social interaction were stressed, and the use of restraints and strong drugs deemphasized. Many changes were introduced to diversify the monotony of daily life, and dining—at least for convalescents—became a group activity. The high point of the Moral Management Period was the compassionate and innovative administration of John Minson Galt II, from mid-1841 to his death in 1862. (Members of the Galt family had operated the institution since its inception.) Galt, a deeply committed man (no pun intended), endeavored to understand the roots of insanity and effect a cure. He hoped that by engaging patients in a wide range of interesting and fulfilling activities, the sick mind would be "silently withdrawn from its illusions." He created a carpentry shop, a shoemaking shop, a game room, and sewing, spinning, and weaving rooms. He also conducted reading and music classes, having purchased violins and flutes for patients, and organized evening lectures, concerts, and social gatherings. Idleness and isolation, he opined, only encouraged the withdrawal to which mental patients were already prone. Patients' dress and environment were also improved. An 1845 cell seen on the tour has a comfortable bed with a patchwork quilt, a rug, table and chair, and a real door instead of the earlier board-and-batten type. Exterior sashes have replaced window bars. Galt also experimented with hypnosis. However, for all his good intentions, Galt admitted that "practice invariably falls short of theory." His rate of cure was not notable, and some patients even found hospital life so pleasant they had no desire to leave.

After Galt's death, a tragedy that coincided with the ravages of the Civil War, conditions at the hospital deteriorated markedly. Between 1865 and 1885 (when the asylum was destroyed by fire) the hospital was administered by nine different superintendents—a factor mitigating against any real continuity in treatment. Confidence in reform and government intervention on behalf of the unfortunate diminished in this age of Social Darwinism. Survival of the fittest was the new ethic (or lack thereof). Though some of the improvements initiated during the Moral Management Period were extended (there were picnics, excursions, games, and fishing expeditions, and a farm on which patients worked and blacksmith-harness shop were added), restraining devices once more came into vogue. One of the most horrible—on view in an exhibit area—is a cage-like protection bed with a screened cover and sides. This final period, when patients were essentially warehoused with little hope of cure, is known as the Custodial Care Period.

The tour shows the evolution of health care throughout the hospital's existence, and sets one thinking about our often equally ineffective methods of treating the mentally ill today. The Public Hospital is open daily. It's located on Francis St. between Nassau and Henry.

The DeWitt Wallace Decorative Arts Gallery

Adjoining the Public Hospital is the most recent attraction to open its doors in Colonial Williamsburg—a 62,000-square-foot museum designed by Kevin Roche and housing some 8,000 English and American decorative art objects from the late 17th, 18th, and 19th centuries. In its galleries you'll see period furnishings, ceramics, textiles, paintings, prints, silver, pewter, clocks, scientific instruments, mechanical devices, and weapons. The collection is one of the most important of its kind in the world.

The $14 million in funding for this project, provided by the late DeWitt Wallace (who, with his wife, Lila Acheson Wallace, founded the *Reader's Digest),* represents the largest gift in the history of Colonial Williamsburg, apart from the support of John D. Rockefeller, Jr., and his family. The monies were also used for the reconstruction of the Public Hospital, described above. The introductory gallery serves both as an underground passage between the hospital and gallery and as a prelude to the museum. It contains a period dining room vignette, a craft shop, and a sampling of the antiques in other exhibit areas. Having viewed 18th-century furnishings and artifacts in their utilitarian guise throughout the Historic Area, visitors are here encouraged to see them as individual works of art. In the masterworks gallery, rising along a tiered stone staircase to a second level through a colonnaded skylit atrium, an 18th-century governor's chair is flanked by a coronation portrait of King George III of England and a Charles Willson Peale study of George Washington. Surrounding the atrium are some 150 objects representing the highest achievement of American and English artisans from the 1640s to 1800—furniture, textiles, silver, ceramics, and prints. And off the masterworks gallery are a series of individual study galleries highlighting the above-mentioned areas.

At the east end of the museum is a 6,000-square-foot area with four galleries around a skylit courtyard. They're used for changing exhibits such as "Patron and Tradesman: Forces that Fashioned Objects, 1660–1800" and a display of colonial maps. On the first level you'll see small exhibits of musical instruments, objects related to European conquest and expansion in the New World, and 18th-century dining items. A small café here offers light fare, beverages, and a limited luncheon menu. And a museum shop in the lower-level entry foyer offers a comprehensive selection of books about the decorative arts.

A delightful aspect of the museum is the Lila Acheson Wallace Garden located on the upper level. A contemporary English-style garden, designed by renowned British landscape artist Sir Peter Shepheard, it centers on a pond with two fountains, a trellis-shaded seating area at one end, a six-foot gilded bronze statue of *Diana* by Augustus Saint-Gaudens at the other. The garden is surrounded by a 19-foot-high, plum-colored brick wall embellished with flowering vines—Carolina yellow jessamine, climbing hydrangea, coral honeysuckle, Virginia creeper, and trumpet vine. The western end of the garden encompasses a neatly clipped Yaupon holly hedge, and the north and south borders display a colorful array of iris, phlox, day lilies, asters, and daisies. Surrounding the *Diana* statue are potted verbena, coleus, and bulbs. The garden's beautiful terracotta pots with relief decoration depicting birds and iris leaves, and the bronze furnishings with similar motifs, were created by French artists Claude and François-Xavier LaLanne.

Admission for Basic Ticket holders is $5, though a combination ticket for the DeWitt, Abby Aldrich Rockefeller Folk Art Center, and Bassett Hall is $8.

The Old Country/Busch Gardens

At some point you'll need a break from early American history, especially if you have kids in tow. That's the time to head over to Busch Gardens, a 360-acre family amusement park just three miles east of Colonial Williamsburg. True, it too is historically themed, with attractions in eight authentically detailed 17th-century European hamlets, but no mental effort is required to enjoy the rides, shows, and festivities. Any educational overtones are obscured by a pure pursuit of fun.

One of the most popular rides is the terrifying Big Bad Wolf, a suspended roller coaster that travels, seemingly out of control, through wooded ravines; it culminates in an 80-foot plunge into the "Rhine River." Another "scream machine," the serpentine Loch Ness Monster, is a roller coaster with two interlocking 360-degree loops and a 130-foot drop; it's one of the fastest coasters in America. The curves, drops, and spins on several other coasters in the park are almost as scary. There are more dizzying thrill rides that spin or plummet you into a state of delicious terror in the Oktoberfest area. Not to be missed is The Enchanted Laboratory, a fascinating production utilizing computer-animated special effects in recounting the misadventures of a wizard's apprentice. It's in the Hastings section of the park. And a 40-foot plunge plus a hair-raising trip through a dark sawmill highlight Le Scoot, a wet-and-wild flume ride in New France; you'll get soaked. Relax from all the excitement on a 20-minute "Rhine River" cruise aboard a steam launch.

Many rides and attractions—including an entire kiddie area called Grimm's Hollow in the German-themed Oktoberfest area—are geared to younger visitors. There's a ball crawl, a cloud bounce, and a punching bag forest, and tots can try "hang gliding" on L'alliante Piccolo, an adaptation of one of Da Vinci's inventions. Kids also love the Anheuser-Busch Clydesdale horses in Scotland, and Le Mans Racetrack with manually steered, gasoline-powered 1913 Stutz Bearcat cars they can "drive" through the French countryside.

Your one-price admission entitles you not only to unlimited rides but to a variety of top-quality shows presented several times each day in various hamlets. They change each year, but they generally include, among others, a lavish Las Vegas–style musical extravaganza (sans nudity—this is a family park), a country music revue, an Olympic-style ice revue, and a bird show starring performing macaws and cockatoos. Get a show schedule when you come in. Strolling bands and costumed street characters—like a "Barbers of Seville" barbershop quartet—entertain at various locations, as do jesters, jugglers, and storytellers. You can dine on canneloni and sip Italian wines while enjoying a medley of folk songs, arias, and contemporary Italian tunes performed on an open-air stage in Italy (the food's pretty good). A similar set-up in Germany is the 2,000-seat festival hall, "Das Festhäus." Here an oompah band and Rhineland folk dancers perform on a two-tiered stage while the audience tucks away bratwurst, German potato salad, and Bavarian pastries. And the Smokehouse in New France specializes in barbecued chicken and ribs. I might mention that there are over 40 restaurants/food stands as well as a picnic area on the premises; you won't go hungry.

Getting back to entertainment, worth the price of entry alone are the headliner shows at the 5,200-seat Royal Palace Theater in France, featuring artists like Crystal Gayle, Wilson Pickett, James Brown, John Schneider, and the Oak Ridge Boys.

In Threadneedle Faire you can try your skill at medieval games like crossbows, antler ringtoss, and sling shots. Another offering is a program of visiting artisans demonstrating their skills. A potter shows how to mix clay, throw on the wheel, fire, and glaze; other craftspeople include an Italian porcelain artist, a glass engraver, a glassblower, a blacksmith, and an artist from Goebel, maker of Hummel figurines.

Skyrides, monorails, and railroads get you from one village to another without too much wear and tear on the feet. They also provide scenic vistas. The 7,150-foot-long Eagle One monorail takes visitors to the Anheuser-Busch Hospitality Center for a brewery tour and complimentary beer.

Busch Gardens is open weekends form early April to mid-May, daily from mid-May to early September, and weekends again through the end of October. Hours are 10 a.m. to 7 p.m., except in summer when the park is open evenings. A single-price admission of about $17 entitles visitors to unlimited rides, shows, and attractions. A nominal price is charged for headliner concert tickets. Children 2 and under are admitted free. Two-day tickets are available, and discount nighttime tickets are offered during the summer. Parking is $2 in the 6,500-car lot. For further details, call 804/253-3350.

Water Country U.S.A.

In June of 1984, with Governor Robb officiating, Virginia's first water theme park—40 acres of wet-and-wild attractions—opened its floodgates. The 1½ million gallons of water used in its activities would fill 600,000 bathtubs! A highlight is Surfer's Bay, a man-made wave pool the size of five Olympic swimming pools that produces a perfect 3½-foot wave every four seconds. An immense amount of sundeck surrounds this attraction, allowing visitors to rest up and work on their tans. The Jet Stream, a water flume, propels you down a 450-foot slide at up to 25 miles an hour toward the splashdown pool. You can experience the thrills of white-water tubing on the Run-a-Way Rapids or "surfboggan" at the Rampage. Of course there's a high-diving show. Also a sea lion show. And the younger set (under 12) can frolic safely at Polliwog Pond, either under a giant red mushroom-shaped fountain or in cheerful bright-yellow tunnels.

At Polliwog Port, a dry area, younger kids can also scramble about in a ball crawl, climb netting, and bounce off Boppety Bags. Elsewhere, the L-shaped, 10,000-square-foot Activity Pool, offers a fountain at its entrance and a center island accessible by swimming, an inner tube walk, a bridge, and overhead rings. This pool also has an area for serious lap swimmers, and pool slides, along with hydrochutes and flumes geared to various levels of thrill seeking, are located at the deep end. Finally, there's Rambling River, 800 feet long with scenic views of lush woodlands and a lake, along which visitors can float lazily on rafts or inner tubes.

Lifeguards, by the way, are much in evidence. On the premises are the Sun Deck Café and a picnic area, and there are snack stands located throughout the park. There's also a shop, should you need to purchase swimwear, and the use of a bathhouse with complete changing facilities is included in your admission price. Water Country U.S.A. is located at Route 199 where it intersects I-64. Just follow the signs. Admission, including parking, is $12.50, $9.50 after 4 p.m., $6.50 after 6 p.m., $4.95 for a spectator ticket for those who don't plan to get wet. Children under 4 are admitted free. All-day locker rental is $2.50. The park is open late May to June 14 from 10 a.m. to 6 p.m., June 15 to Labor Day till 8 p.m. For further information, call 804/229-9300.

ANNUAL EVENTS/SPECIAL EVENTS: Whenever you visit Williamsburg you'll find numerous events enhancing the regular attractions day and night. Your ticket will list special activities for the week of your visit. The last time I was there these included a slide lecture on English silver; 18th-century gambols at a local tavern; several militia reviews with soldiers drilling to tunes played by the Fife and Drum Corps; nightly films on subjects ranging from Colonial basket-making to Christmas traditions in 18th-century Williamsburg; a harpsichord performance in the Ballroom of the Governor's Palace, and an orchestral concert; an 18th-century ballad opera; a recital at the College of William and Mary; a candlelight tour of Bruton Church, including a bell and choir concert; a Colonial comedy called *The Sham Doctor;* and a candlelight visit to the Capitol with living history debates in the House of Burgesses, trials in the General Court, and period music in the committee rooms.

It's a good idea to write or call the Colonial Williamsburg Visitor Center in advance of your trip to find out what will be happening during your stay. Some activities require registration or tickets. (Address and phone are listed above.)

Christmas season each year gets off to a brilliant start with the Grand Illumination about ten days prior to December 25. That night the entire Historic Area is decorated, the buildings are lit by thousands of candles, there's a Fife and Drum Corps parade and a fireworks display, and the 20,000-or-so people participating join in caroling. Other Noël festivities include special entertainments like magic shows and parties; Colonial games, music, and dancing on the Governor's Palace lawn; art exhibits; caroling at the Courthouse of 1770 around bonfires; tavern nights; the beating of holiday drums; a tree-lighting ceremony on Market Square on Christmas Eve; Christmas decoration workshops; recitals of Handel's *Messiah;* and several big New Year's Eve bashes.

The **Annual Williamsburg Antiques Forum** takes place in early February. Each year it focuses on a specific theme, like "Arts of the Early South, 1750–1810," with lectures by experts and scholars in the field, film presentations, craft demonstrations, banquets, teas, receptions, and special exhibits. Later in the months there's a **Learning Weekend Program** at the Abby Aldrich Rockefeller Folk Art Center. Participants learn about American folk art from expert lecturers and crafts specialists and try to get their hands at such traditional folk art techniques as silhouette portraiture and stenciling. Exhibits, dinners, and demonstrations are part of the fun. There are also **Colonial Weekends** in February and March such as "Taste of the Past" featuring culinary demonstrations in Colonial kitchens. You'll learn to make 18th-century treats like lemony Savoy cake and collared beef (a spicy rolled meat dish), listen to talks on Colonial cooking and dining customs (manners were a bit crude; it was well after 1800 that forks were in common usage), and attend dinners and receptions.

A week in mid-March, designated as **Canada Time,** means discounts at hotels, shops, and restaurants, plus many special events, for our neighbors to the north.

April gets under way with an **Easter Sunday Sunrise Service** in nearby Jamestown and continues with the annual **Garden Symposium.** The latter program features lectures by leading horticulturists on subjects like "Orchids Are for Everyone," flower-arranging demonstrations, woodland and garden tours, birdwatching walks, and seminars on tree pruning, care of boxwood, etc. (Garden enthusiasts, by the way, can avail themselves of a special Gardener's Tour of Colonial Williamsburg at any time of the year.)

Early July through mid-August, the William and Mary College **Shakespeare Festival** is on. For information about productions, write to the Virginia Shakespeare Festival, College of William and Mary, Williamsburg, VA 23185, or call 804/253-4377.

Independence Day festivities begin with the **Prelude of Independence** on May 15 (the date in 1776 when Virginia legislators pledged their lives to full freedom from England) and continue through July 25, the anniversary of the day news of the Declaration of Independence reached Williamsburg. The period is highlighted by the raising of the Stars and Stripes over the Capitol, gun salutes, parades, historical reenactments, concerts, and of course, fireworks on the Fourth. On July 25, following musketry and marching, the famous document is read aloud on the Courthouse steps by an actor dressed as an 18th-century dignitary.

The entire month of September is **Senior Time,** which means those over 55 are eligible for reduced ticket prices for attractions, discounts at restaurants and shops, and reductions on admissions to special events and nighttime entertainments. Greens fees at a local golf course are also reduced. If you're in the right age group, get a brochure at the Visitor Center detailing benefits. Fifes and drums herald the September 3 celebration each year on the **Anniversary of the Treaty of Paris,** signed by John Adams, Benjamin Franklin, and John Jay in 1783. The treaty ended hostilities between the newborn United States of America and Great Britain. Historical reenactments of the news reaching Williamsburg and soldiers erecting a drum altar at Bruton Parish Church are followed by singing of the national anthem, a parade, a reading of the proclamation, and a gun salute.

The **Colonial Fair** takes place in October, offering visitors an unparalleled view of 18th-century Williamsburg during Publick Times. Hundreds of costumed military units and camp followers erect tents in Market Square and the Courthouse Green area. Selected crafts are demonstrated near the Courthouse, 18th-century market booths are set up, peddlers hawk additional items, and an auctioneer elicits bids for his merchandise. Puppeteers, jugglers, magicians, musical ensembles, boisterous 18th-century comedies, fiddling contests, and games are also part of the fun. Another October festival, the annual **Occasion for the Arts** on the first Sunday of the month, features performing arts, fine arts, and crafts in Merchant's Square.

And of course November is marked by **Thanksgiving**-related activities—a feast, concerts, magic shows, recitals, a parade, and 18th-century theater productions.

WILLIAMSBURG WITH CHILDREN: Williamsburg provides an unexampled opportunity for kids to slip ahead of their grade-school peers by actually gleaning an understanding of what American history is all about. As with Washington sights, the more interpretation parents can provide of what's being seen, the more enthusiastic children generally are. Colonial Williamsburg offers a helping hand to the parent who is not a history whiz in the form of several tours geared specifically to youngsters. Tickets to all children's programs cost $4 and are available at the Information Center or the Courthouse of 1770.

Once Upon a Town, a program for 4-, 5-, and 6-year-olds, lets tiny tots see Williamsburg at their own pace with activities and explanations geared to their level of understanding. Departing daily at 1:30 p.m., the two-hour tour includes music, games, storytelling, a puppet show, a chance to feed chickens and pet sheep, and meetings with Colonial characters.

Boys and girls 8 to 14 can take part in a hands-on program called **The Townsteaders.** Participants get a chance to try 18th-century crafts like spinning, weaving, candle dipping, and Colonial cooking. The two-hour program is offered daily at 10 a.m.

The 7- to 12-year-old set is eligible for **The Tricorn Hat Tour,** a 2¼-hour walk through the Historic Area with a Colonial-costumed guide. Activities include locking each other in the stocks at the Public Gaol, a musket-firing demonstration, a game of bowls on the green at Market Square, an 18th-century baking demonstration followed by gingerbread cookies at the Raleigh, and of course an introduction to Colonial life and times. The youngsters are given souvenir tricornered hats. Departures daily at 2 p.m.

Outside of the Historic Area, remember **Busch Gardens** and **Water Country U.S.A.,** both described above.

SHOPPING IN COLONIAL WILLIAMSBURG: Few other American towns have streets lined with shops selling 18th-century merchandise. It's great fun to browse and buy in Colonial Williamsburg.

Duke of Gloucester St. is the center for 18th-century wares created by local craftspeople plying the trades of our forefathers. The goods offered include hand-wrought silver jewelry (engraving available on the premises) from the **Sign of the Golden Ball;** pewterware from the **James Geddy** shop; promanders to ward off the plague from **McKenzie's Apothecary;** hand-woven linens from **Prentis Store;** handmade paper, books bound in leather, and hand-printed newspapers from the **post office;** Shrewsbury, oatmeal, and gingerbread cakes from the **Raleigh Tavern Bake Shop;** and everything from foodstuffs to fishhooks from **Tarpley's,** a general store.

Not to be missed is **Craft House,** like the above run by the Colonial Williamsburg Foundation. There are two locations, one in Merchants Square, the other near the Abby Aldrich Rockefeller Folk Art Center. Featured at Craft House are exquisite works by master craftspeople—silver, pottery, pewter, glassware, brass, and authentic reproductions of Colonial furnishings. Needlework enthusiasts will be thrilled with the authentic 18th-century samplers, some of the most beautiful embroidery patterns available anywhere; they come complete with stitching instructions and the correct thread colors for the period. There are also reproduction wallpapers, china, toys, games, maps, books, prints, and souvenirs aplenty.

One of these Craft Houses is, as mentioned, in **Merchants Square,** an 18th-century-style complex of about 50 shops at the end of town near William and Mary College between Boundary and Henry Streets west and east and Prince George and Francis Streets north and south. Merchants Square "shoppes" offer a wide range of merchandise: antique furnishings, antiquarian books and prints, 18th-century floral arrangements, homemade ice cream and candy, hand-crafted pewter and silver items, needlework supplies, and Oriental rugs. It's not all of the "ye olde" variety, however; you can also find a Baskin Robbins ice cream parlor, a branch of Scribner's, a drugstore that offers Excedrin in lieu of leeches, a camera shop, clothing stores, and other fully up-to-date emporia.

Shopping in the Historic Area is fun, but the biggest merchandising draw in town is out on **Richmond Road** (Route 60W) where the famed Williamsburg Pottery Factory and numerous factory outlet shops are located. A good way to tackle it all—a project that can easily occupy a day—is to head out on Richmond Road, stopping first at the **Williamsburg Pottery Factory** (tel. 804/564-3326), five miles west of Williamsburg (you can't miss it). Open daily from 8 a.m. to 8 p.m. in summer, till 6:30 p.m. in spring and fall, and from 9 a.m. to 5 p.m. in January and February, this is a 200-acre shopping complex with over 31 buildings selling merchandise from all over the world. It's all bought in large volume and sold at competitive prices. Pick up a shopping cart and a map in the parking lot and charge in.

It would be easier to describe what you can't buy here than what you can. Shops on the premises sell Christmas decorations, garden furnishings, lamps, art prints (a good selection; you can have them framed while you're browsing and pick them up later in the day), dried and silk flowers, luggage, linens, Mexican baskets, hardware, glassware, bridal wear, cookware, candles, toys, crafts, clothing, food, jewelry, grandfather clocks, plants (there's a large greenhouse nursery), you name it. There's plenty of quality and plenty of kitsch. And of course, you can buy pottery here. This vast operation began as a small pottery in 1938 where James E. Maloney made 18th-century saltglaze items at his own wheel. He was successful and added china and glassware to his offerings. Continuing to expand, over the next five decades he eventually wound up with the immense extravaganza that exists today and draws over four million annual visitors. There's parking for 8,000 cars. Everything is discounted year round, but in January and February, called Skid Row, prices are rock bottom. Frankly, I find the maze of cinderblock and steel shops here almost overwhelming. It makes an Arab souk seem as orderly as Bloomingdale's. But it's just the beginning.

Continue a bit farther along Route 60 and you'll come to the **Pottery Factory Outlets**—the discount offerings of 20 major manufacturers under one roof. They include Black & Decker, Van Heusen, Cannon, Manhattan, and Cabin Creek Furniture. At Ann Michele Originals, you can buy designer fashions (Calvin Klein and others). Offerings at other shops range from brass beds to shoes for the entire family, from peanuts and pecans to knitting and needlework supplies.

Proceed farther along Route 60 until you see signs for the **Williamsburg Soap & Candle Company** (tel. 804/564-3354) across the road, your first stop en route back to town. It's open from 9 a.m. to 5 p.m. daily, with extended hours in summer. Here you can see a narrated slide presentation on candle making while watching the process through viewing windows that look out on the factory. Some 12 million candles are produced here every year, and an infinite variety are sold. You can buy them scented, unscented, tapered, or shaped like a mouse. There's also an incredible array of soaps for sale. And as you browse through the row of shops you'll encounter glassware, Cannon sheets and towels at white-sale prices, homemade fudge, imported goods, housewares, gifts, toys, needlecraft supplies, and everything for Christmas. A cozy, country-style restaurant is on the premises.

Continuing toward town, especially if you have little girls in your party, the next stop is the **Williamsburg Doll Factory** (tel. 804/564-9703). Limited-edition porcelain collector's dolls made here include Prince Charles, Diana, Prince William and Henry, and Sarah Ferguson. You can observe the dollmaking process and even buy equipment to make your own. Other items sold here are stuffed animals, dollhouse furnishings, clowns, books on dolls, and dolls, dolls, and more dolls. Open daily from 9 a.m. to 5:30 p.m.

Finally, if you still have the money and stamina, you can peruse the wares at dozens of factory-owned stores and outlets under a cross-shaped roof at **Outlets Ltd. Mall** (tel. 804/565-3378), a little farther east on Route 60. It's all here—designer-label clothing, jewelry, books, home furnishings, luggage and handbags, footwear, kitchenware, sporting goods, and so on—all at discounts of 20% to 70%. Winter hours are 9 a.m. to 9 p.m. Monday to Saturday, 11 a.m. to

6 p.m. on Sunday; the rest of the year the mall is open from 9 a.m. to 9 p.m. daily. There are no fountains or skylights at this mall, but it is a pleasant shopping environment.

The above are the Route 60 highlights; there's actually quite a bit more, which you'll see as you drive along.

WHERE TO STAY: In a town where the major industry is tourism it's not unusual for local innkeepers to put the screws, shilling-wise, to the hapless visitor. Such is the case in Williamsburg. Expect to pay a little more for accommodations here than in other areas explored in this book, especially during the crowded summer season. A compensating factor is that in line with the general atmosphere of Colonial charm, your room will probably be of a slightly higher standard than usual. And no matter how tourist-filled the town, you would be asked to share bed space with total strangers as you would have in the 18th century.

To be sure of getting a room, reserve in advance. The **Williamsburg Hotel/ Motel Association** (tel. 804/220-3330 or toll free 800/446-9244) will make reservations for you in any price range. It's a free service. Their listings include most of the accommodations mentioned below.

A boon to budget travelers is the **Williamsburg Hotel Group,** 1408 Richmond Rd., Williamsburg, VA 23185 (tel. 800/446-8930). Under their auspices are ten centrally located hotels, (most of them low-priced, a few moderate), so one call to the above toll free number puts you in line for over 1,100 rooms. And guests at any of the Group's hotels can use the facilities at any of the others. That means, no matter where you stay, you have access to Jacuzzis, complete health clubs, indoor and outdoor pools, (some near Olympic size), etc. Five of the properties, **Econo Lodge No. 1,** 1413 Richmond Rd. (tel. 804/229-8551), **Econo Lodge No. II,** 1408 Richmond Rd. (tel. 804/229-2981), **Williamsburg TraveLodge,** 1408 Richmond Rd. (tel. 804/220-2367), **The New Minuet Manor,** 1408 Richmond Rd. (tel. 804/220-9304), and **Carolyn Court,** 1446 Richmond Rd. (tel. 804/229-6666) are adjacent to one another in a compound about a mile from the Historic Area. On-premises facilities include one outdoor and four indoor pools, a picnic area, complete fitness center, game room, wading pool, children's playground, three restaurants—the nautically themed Lobster House, the Prime Rib House, and the rather charming Southern Pancake House—Rumor's cocktail lounge, and many attractively landscaped acres. Other Williamsburg Hotel Group properties range from an **Econo Lodge East** at 505 York St. (tel. 804/220-3100), just 2½ blocks from the Historic Area, to the **Ramada Inn West** (tel. 804/565-2000) which is closer to the Pottery shopping area. There's something for everyone—whether you want a room with a double, two doubles, or a king; an executive suite; accommodations with a completely equipped kitchen; or a family-size unit. Just discuss your needs with the reservationist. All rooms in the complex provide the expected amenities—cable color TV, full bath, direct-dial phone, air conditioning, and there's always plenty of free parking.

Rates at these properties are mostly in the $34 to $41 single, $36 to $43 double range November 1 to the end of March, about $10 to $20 higher across the board April 1 to mid-June and September/October, reaching a peak of $48 to $71 single, $50 to $73 double mid-June through the first week in September. Lowest rates are at the **Pocahontas Motel,** 800 Capitol Landing Rd. (tel. 804/ 229-2374), a slightly less luxurious but still very adequate accommodation.

Another budget chain, **Thr-rift Inns,** is also represented in Williamsburg with a property at 304 2nd St., Williamsburg, VA 23185 (tel. 804/229-0500 or toll free 800/336-0500). About a mile from the Historic Area, it offers 107 rooms—

all of the standard modern motel genre with direct-dial phone, air conditioing, color TV and full tub/shower bath. A swimming pool/sundeck is on the premises. Rates, once again, are seasonal. In high season, May 1 through August 31, singles pay $43, doubles $48 to $53. Low season, November 1 through April 30, rates are $30 for one person, $33 for two. And September 1 through October 31 they're $35 for one, $40 for two. A third person in a room pays $5, children under 12 stay free. It's possible to rent a room with two double beds and a pull-out double-bed sofa for $57 in high season, $38 to $40 the rest of the year; these accommodate up to six people—a good buy for sizable families. Also available are 12 completely equipped kitchenette rooms with two double beds.

Homier than either of the above, no doubt because it is privately owned and not part of a nationwide chain, is the **White Lion Motel,** at 912 Capitol Landing Rd., Williamsburg, VA 23185 (tel. 804/229-3931 or toll free 800/368-1055). About a half mile from the Historic Area, it offers 38 rooms including 18 efficiencies.

The rooms housed in white wood cottages with shuttered windows, have pretty maple furnishings and contain two double beds, a king-size, or a double and a single. The cottages themselves are bordered by holly hedges with pots of geraniums out front. Rates are $52 for one or two people from June through the end of August, about $36 the rest of the year. Some years the hotel is closed December and January.

The efficiency units accommodate up to six people (there are two double beds and a pullout double-bed sofa). Large and comfortable (the sofa is supplemented by an armchair and coffee table), they come with full kitchens (stoves, sinks, and refrigerators), though you do have to supply your own dishes, pots, and utensils. Rates are $56 for two in high season, $40 the rest of the year. An extra person in any accommodation pays $4. All rooms offer air conditioning, tub and/or shower bath, and cable color TV, but no phone. On-premises facilities include a picnic table by the woods, a swimming pool, and free ice. An excellent choice.

Under the same ownership is the **Motel Rochambeau,** just across the street at 929 Capitol Landing Rd., Williamsburg, VA 23185 (tel. 804/229-2851 or toll free 800/368-1055). The Rochambeau nestles in the woods (you'll wake each morning to the chirping of hundreds of birds) and is further adorned by well-tended flower beds, a water wheel, and hanging pots of geraniums. The 22 rooms are cozy, with curtained windows, floral-print bedspreads, and carpeted floors. They offer a double and a single, a king-size, or two double beds, color TV with movie channels, air conditioning, and full bath, but no phone; guests are invited to use the swimming pool across the street. Rates for one or two people are $46 June 1 through the end of August, $34 the rest of the year. An additional person is charged $4, and another $4 if a rollaway or crib is required. The Rochambeau is closed December and January.

Absolutely the best budget bet in town is a **Motel 6** at 3030 Richmond Rd., Williamsburg, VA 23185 (tel. 804/565-3433). The only catch is that to snag one of their 169 low-priced rooms you usually have to reserve far in advance—a good idea anyway, especially during the busy summer months. Rooms are immaculate, with white walls and carpeted floors, two double beds, air conditioning, phones, (local calls are free), color TVs, and showers. A nice swimming pool and sundeck are out back. A woodsy location is yet another plus. The rates: $24.95 for one person, $29.95 for two, $33.95 for three, $37.95 for four.

In the same area as the above, **Days Inn,** 5437 Richmond Rd., Williamsburg, VA 23185 (tel. 804/565-2700 or toll free 800/325-2525), offers 122 air-conditioned rooms—all with two double beds, color TV, direct-dial phone, and tub/shower bath. Both it and the Motel 6 are about two miles from the Historic Area. Rates here are seasonal, and there are at least five seasons; suffice it to say that they range from about $28 to $52 single or double, $4 for each additional person, $3 for children under 18 sharing a room with their parents, $3 for a rollaway. A swimming pool and reasonably priced Tasty World Restaurant are on the premises.

The Cedars is a charming seven-room guesthouse within walking distance of the Historic Area at 616 Jamestown Rd., Williamsburg, VA 23185 (tel. 804/229-3591). Though this three-story Georgian-style house is only 70 years old, it seems of an earlier period because it's built of 200-year-old bricks from an old plantation. All the rooms are air-conditioned and attractively furnished, some with canopied or four-poster beds. They're painted in Williamsburg colors or papered in pretty floral prints. They don't have phones or TVs, but there is a public phone in the sitting room. For $95 a night you can rent a cozy cottage with a fully equipped kitchen; it accommodates up to six. Or you might opt for an upstairs bedroom with dormer windows and a sloped roof. Fronted by a garden under the shade of an ancient elm and situated between two churches, the Cedars offers a suitably tranquil setting for your Williamsburg stay. Hostess Marianna Woodruff is a delightful person and very knowledgeable about local attractions and restaurants. Excepting the above-quoted, rates are $40 for one or two people in a room with shared bath, $45 to $50 with private bath, $5 for an additional person. Adjoining rooms with a connecting bath are available for families. Rates include a daily continental breakfast—doughnuts, juice, and coffee—served in the sitting room.

Finally, there's **The Elms,** a guesthouse at 708 Richmond Rd., Williamsburg, VA 23185 (tel. 804/229-1551), just seven blocks from the Historic Area and convenient to numerous restaurants. The four air-conditioned rooms are homey and comfortable, and the price is right. A twin-bedded room with private bath is $25 a night, a room with a single bed and shared bath is $13, and two rooms with double beds and semiprivate baths are $20. Mr. and Mrs. E. J. Stinnett are your host and hostess.

WHERE TO DINE: Williamsburg abounds with restaurants catering to the tourist horde. Particularly popular are three reconstructed Colonial taverns where George Washington (among others) broke bread in days of yore. All three do offer delightful 18th-century ambience, but they're also overpriced and the food is so-so. Nonetheless, hardly anyone, myself included, can resist their lure at least once, so descriptions will follow. They are all under the auspices of the Colonial Williamsburg Foundation, so the splurge is in a good cause.

Should you have just one dinner out in Williamsburg, do resist the lemming-like drift to the Colonial taverns and head instead to the **Trellis Café, Restaurant & Grill,** on Duke of Gloucester St. in Merchants Square (tel. 804/229-8610). The *New York Times* calls it "the best restaurant in this part of Virginia." Evocative of California's delightful wine-country restaurants in both decor and exciting, contemporary cuisine, it is entered via a grapevine-covered trellis. A largish space, it's divided into intimate dining areas with varying ambiences—something to suit most any dining mood.

The Garden Room is the plushest setting, with apricot velvet furnishings, a forest-green English Wilton carpet, a painted Venetian glass chandelier, and Venetian gilt-framed mirror. There are big bouquets of flowers here and there, more flowers adorning the tables, and pots of flowering plants and a ficus tree flourishing in sunlight streaming in through multipaned windows. The Trellis Room is country-contemporary in feel—very woody with forest-green upholstered pine furnishings, floors of century-old pine, a trellised ceiling, and walls minimally adorned with vineyard baskets full of dried flowers and antique French farm implements. In the Grill Room, rust-colored velvet furnishings go nicely with more of the forest-green carpeting. Here you can watch food being prepared over an open-hearth grill using Texas mesquite wood. Very cozy is the Vault Room, with tables under an arched ceiling of narrow heart-of-pine beams. And in the Café Bar an authentic Mexican terracotta tile floor provides a harmonious contrast to glazed green Italian tiles, and walls are hung with antique wine-motif prints. Finally, if the weather is fine, you might dine al fresco on the planter-bordered brick terrace overlooking Merchants Square.

Owners Marcel Desaulniers (he's an award-winning chef, on the *Food and Wine* magazine "Honor Roll of American Chefs" and one of 23 chefs honored in the *Who's Who of Cooking in America),* John Curtis, and Tom Power sum up the Trellis's approach thusly: "We have always tried to avoid menu clichés and gimmicks. . . . Imagination and excitement have been added through our selection and unexpected combinations of seasonal and regional ingredients." I couldn't have explained it better.

By now you're probably thinking that a meal at the Trellis is going to cost a bundle. Wrong. The extensive and varied menu offers diners choices at several price levels. Selections change seasonally. On my last visit luncheon entrees included a sandwich of lemon-marinated chicken breast seared over mesquite wood served on hot, crusty french bread ($4.75); another delicious sandwich of tuna tossed with mayo, seedless grapes, and chopped walnuts on whole wheat ($3.95); and fresh fish grilled over flaming mesquite wood served with freshly baked bread and a green salad ($7.25).

At dinner the light menu served in the Café Bar and outdoor terrace features items like a hearty serving of Chesapeake chowder ($4.50) and Trellis quiche—all that quiche was ever meant to be, a classic ($7.50); both are served with freshly baked breads and salad. Delicious sandwiches too. Menus in the other dining areas list dinner entrees in the $12 to $17 range, but you can dine in style and spend much less: the Trellis offers a complete prix-fixe dinner for $14.95. There's a well-chosen wine list, and in addition to the house wine, at least two premium wines are always offered by the glass. The Trellis, by the way, is no place to pass up desserts; the chocolate temptation, for instance, is not to be believed.

Open Monday to Saturday from 11:30 a.m. to 9:30 p.m., on Sunday (with a special brunch menu) to 3 p.m. Reservations are advised at dinner. Highest recommendation.

Old Chickahominy House, 1211 Jamestown Rd. at Route 199 (tel. 804/229-4689), though not part of the Colonial Williamsburg complex, is a reconstructed 18th-century house with mantels from old Gloucester homes and wainscotting from Carter's Grove. Floors are bare oak; walls are painted in traditional Colonial colors (like James Geddy tan) and hung with gilt-framed 17th- and 18th-century oil paintings. Since three large rooms and the basement house an adjoining antique/gift shop crammed with beautiful Early American and other period furnishings, you can be sure many fine pieces also adorn the several dining rooms. The entire effect is extremely cozy and charming, from the rocking chairs on the front porch to the blazing fireplaces within.

Authentic southern fare is featured at breakfast and lunch. The house specialty in the morning is the plantation breakfast—real Virginia ham with two eggs, biscuits, cured country bacon and sausage, grits, and tea or coffee ($5.25). If your appetite's not quite that hearty, you might opt for Miss Melinda's fruit pancakes ($2.75). At lunch Miss Melinda's special is a cup of Brunswick stew with Virginia ham on hot biscuits, fruit salad, homemade pie, and tea or coffee ($4.75, $3.75 without the stew). Maxine Henderson is the genial hostess. The Old Chickahominy House is not a slick tourist spot—it's an authentic down-home restaurant and very popular with locals. After dining it's fun to roam through the warren of antique-filled rooms. And if you've further appetite for browsing, you can check out the handcrafted pewterware at **Shirley Pewter Shop** next door.

Open daily from 8:30 a.m. to 3 p.m.

It's hard to beat breakfast at the Old Chickahominy, but there is one drawback—it doesn't open till 8:30 a.m. If you need an earlier start, head up Richmond Road where over a dozen pancake houses beckon from shortly after cockcrow. One of the nicest is **Nick's Pewter Plate,** 1329 Richmond Rd. (tel. 804/229-4309), where two eggs or pancakes with ham and orange juice costs $4.75, including a large pot of coffee left on your table when you order. Nick's has comfortable booths and bamboo garden chairs, there are lots of hanging plants, a fountain is bordered by trees and potted plants, and a glass case used to display pewter doubles as a room divider. This is also a great choice for lunch. Sandwiches like lump backfin crabmeat with avocado and tomato slices; lemon-marinated charbroiled chicken breast; and tuna mixed with creamy mayonnaise and chopped walnuts are in the $3.50 to $4 range. Open daily from 6:30 a.m. to 2:30 p.m. No credit cards.

Continue down the road apiece and you'll come to a **Shoney's** at 1611 Richmond Rd. (tel. 804/229-2170), where an immense all-you-can-eat buffet breakfast is just $3.29 weekdays and $3.99 for adults, $1.99 for children 6 to 12, free for under-5s. Those prices allow you unlimited amounts of scrambled eggs, grits, home fries, biscuits, chipped beef, sausages, sausage patties, bacon, ham, fresh fruit, grated cheddar, french toast, pancakes, spiced apples, and tomatoes. And equally good values are offered at lunch and dinner. You can't go wrong. Shoney's is a pleasant place with terracotta tile floors, orange vinyl booths, shuttered windows, and many hanging plants. It's open from 6:30 a.m. to 11 p.m., till midnight on Friday and Saturday. No credit cards.

Also out along Richmond Road is an excellent place for lunch or early dinner, the **Black Forest Café & Bakery,** 151 Monticello Ave. (it's just off Richmond Rd. behind the Williamsburg Shopping Center; tel. 804/229-2692). Delicious sandwiches on fresh-baked breads such as smoked turkey breast and pastrami, or chef salad (cheddar, ham, salami, boiled eggs, and dressing), served with potato chips and sliced pickles, are $3 or less.

And a big bowl of homemade soup—perhaps fisherman's stew, onion, or cream of broccoli—is $2.25 with a fresh-baked roll and butter. A glass of wine is $1.50. After your entree, check out the bakery counter up front for fresh-from-the-oven desserts like Boston cream pie. The Black Forest's not a fancy place—it has yellow walls, Formica tables, Breuer chairs, and big windows overlooking the parking lot—but it is light and sunny. Open Monday to Saturday from 10 a.m. to 8 p.m. No credit cards.

A less likely find in a shopping center—or in a budget book—is the exquisitely elegant **Le Yaca,** on Route 60 East in the quaint Village Shops at Kingsmill (tel. 804/220-3616). The complex is directly across from the Hilton. Centered on a large open hearth on which a leg of lamb is often roasting, creating a tantalizing aroma, Le Yaca is charmingly provincial with glossy oak floors, rough-hewn beams overhead, and romantic soft lighting from oil candles and shaded lamps. The pale-cream walls are hung with lovely prints of Paris scenes. It looks like a meal here would cost a fortune—and it can. But there are also some very economical menu options. At lunch a create-your-own-salad table is just $4.50 for all you desire of 15 scrumptious French salads—cucumber with fresh cream and escargots, potato salad with lamb, carrots rapé, salad du riz, and tomato vinaigrette, among them; fresh-baked bread and butter is included. Or you might choose an entree like marinated breast of chicken in lemon and ginger sauce, served with soup and rice for $5.95, $1 extra if you include the *table des salades*. Dinner entrees are indeed pricey, but Monday to Thursday nights you can enjoy a full prix-fixe meal for just $13. I recently did so and dined on the following: a heavenly cream of onion soup, an entree of fresh sea scallops in tangy chablis butter, an array of fresh vegetables, salad, and for dessert, ice cream in a marbleized raspberry cream sauce. Do treat yourself to a meal at Le Yaca. Open Monday to Saturday for lunch from 11:30 a.m. to 2 p.m., for dinner Monday to Thursday from 6 to 9:30 p.m., on Friday and Saturday till 10:30 p.m. Reservations suggested.

At this writing Le Yaca is about to open a moderately priced gourmet restaurant in Merchant's Square in the Historic Area. Called **Le Clos des Marchands** it will feature crêpes, salads, and pasta dishes. Look for it.

And now for those three Colonial taverns. If you're planning on dinner at one of these restaurants, make your reservations first thing in the morning—if not a day or two before—by calling the Information Center (tel. 804/229-1000). In the spring-to-fall season it's a good idea to reserve even prior to arrival (you can do so up to 60 days in advance). Especially during this busy tourist season they are mobbed nightly. All three are reconstructed 18th-century "ordinaries" or taverns, and aim at authenticity in fare, ambience, and costuming of the staff. Modern conveniences are concealed from view. In addition to the interiors described below, all offer al fresco dining in good weather on brick patios under grape arbors.

Kings Arms Tavern is on the site of a 1772 establishment on the south side of Duke of Gloucester St., directly across from the Raleigh. It is actually a recreation of the tavern and an adjoining home, that of *Virginia Gazette* publisher Alexander Purdie. The enlargement was to provide more space for diners. Outbuildings—including stables, a barbershop, laundry, smokehouse, and kitchen—have also been reconstructed.

The original proprietress, Mrs. Jane Vobe, was famous for her fine cooking. She named the tavern Kings Arms and entertained notables like George Washington and Revolutionary War Major-General Baron von Steuben, the latter running up a bill of £288 for food, drink, and lodging in 1781—quite a sum in those days. Proximity to the Capitol made Mrs. Vobe's establishment a natural meeting place during Publick Times. After her death in 1788, a Mr. Philip Moody bought the place and in the spirit of Independence changed the name to the Eagle Tavern.

Today the 11 dining rooms (eight with fireplaces) are all painted and furnished following authentic early Virginia precedent. The Queen Anne and Chippendale pieces are typical appointments of this class of tavern, candle stands used for lighting are antique reproductions, and the prints, maps, engravings, aquatints, and mezzotints lining the walls are genuine examples of Colonial interior decorations. Balladeers wander the rooms during dinner and entertain.

Though the atmosphere is quainter by candlelight, prices are lower at lunch. Midday fare includes items in the $4.50 to $5 range like Smithfield ham and Old English cheddar cheese on manchet (wheat) bread with Dijon mustard and dill pickle garnish and meat pie baked in a casserole with Yorkshire pudding and served with salad. At dinner there's a $15 prix fixe—a nut soup to nut pie meal beginning with Virginia peanut soup and continuing with an entree of pan fried boneless breast of chicken and Smithfield ham in grape sauce, vegetables, salad, Sally Lunn bread and Indian corn muffins, and pecan pie. Before dinner you might try typical Colonial drinks like punch made of fresh lemons and sugar spiked with rum, scotch, bourbon, Irish whiskey, or brandy ($2.75); same price for grog, a rum toddy, or sangaree (an 18th-century version of sangria). Lunch or dinner, try the delicious cream of peanut soup. And do note that children's menus are available on request.

Open daily for lunch from 11:30 a.m. to 2:30 p.m., for dinner (with three nightly seatings) from 5:15 to 9:30 p.m.

Chowning's Tavern, also on Duke of Gloucester St. (adjoining the Courthouse of 1770 in Market Square), dates to 1766 when Josiah Chowning announced the opening of a tavern "where all who please to favour me with their custom may depend upon the best of entertainment for themselves, servants, and horses, and good pasturage." Smaller (four dining rooms, three downstairs and one upstairs) and less elegant than the Kings Arms, Chowning's catered to a less genteel clientele. It is nevertheless very charming today, with low beamed ceilings, raw pine floors, and sturdy country-made furnishings. Sporting prints and 18th-century cartoons decorate the walls, there are two working fireplaces, and at night one dines by candlelight.

Chowning's features nightly gambols from 9 p.m. to 1 a.m. with 18th-century games, ballads, and musicians. There's no cover or minimum, and light, inexpensive fare is offered, e.g., a hot ham-and-cheddar cheese sandwich on homemade bread served with dill pickle wedge and a pint of draft ale. At lunch there's Welsh rarebit—melted cheddar cheese blended with beer and seasonings on homemade toast ($4.75), perhaps followed by buttered apple pie (made with apples from the Shenandoah Valley) à la mode. Like the Kings Arms, Chowning's has, in addition to à la carte entrees, a prix-fixe dinner—plantation vegetable soup, salad with chutney dressing, sauteed backfin crabmeat and ham topped with butter and laced with sherry, vegetable, baked potato, homemade bread, and deep-dish apple pie with cheddar cheese—all for $16.50. Here, too, children's menus are available on request.

Open daily for lunch from 11:30 a.m. to 3:30 p.m., for dinner (three seatings nightly) from 5 to 8:30 p.m., and for gambols until 1 a.m.

Christiana Campbell's Tavern, close to the Capitol on Waller St., is "where all the best people resorted" circa 1765. These elite citizens included Royal Governor Fauquier, who was dining here one night when an angry mob surrounded Col. George Mercer (distributor of stamps at a time when Virginians were enraged by the Stamp Tax) and chivied him to the porch of the tavern. Fauquier linked arms with Mercer and walked him safely through the disgruntled crowd to the Palace. George Washington was also a regular (in 1772 he recorded in his diary that he dined here ten times over a two-month period). As for Mrs. Campbell, she was evidently no beauty. She was described in 1783 by a young Scottish merchant as "a little old Woman, about four feet high, and equally thick," with "a little turn Pug nose." After the capital moved to Richmond, business declined and operations eventually ceased. In its heyday, however, the tavern was famous for seafood, and today that is once again the specialty.

Like the above-mentioned establishments, Campbell's is an authentic reproduction with 18th-century furnishings, blazing fireplaces, and waiters and waitresses in Colonial dress. Flutists and balladeers entertain diners.

Between 10 a.m. and 2:30 p.m. daily brunch (definitely not an 18th-century concept) is served here. The choices include a traditional southern breakfast—mulled apple cider, Virginia ham, fried chicken, scrambled eggs, spiced apples, and coffee for $6.50—a lot to spend for breakfast, but it should keep you going until dinner. Other possibilities in the $5.25 to $6.50 range are chicken croquettes with mornay sauce and pecan waffles with country sausage and warm maple syrup. At dinner, served from 5:30 to 9:30 p.m. nightly, a full meal for $13.95 includes clam chowder, southern-fried chicken, Virginia ham, vegetables, and pumpkin fritters. The seafood specialties are à la carte, though backfin crab is included in a $17 prix fixe. Children's menus are available.

Another eatery operated by the Colonial Williamsburg Foundation is **A Good Place to Eat,** at 410 Duke of Gloucester St. in Merchants Square. This is an especially good place for inexpensive family meals. The food is high quality for a cafeteria operation—burger meat is prepared from the best cuts of chuck and round, breads and cakes are baked fresh on the premises, and ice cream is homemade. Though one eats off paper plates rather than 18th-century china, and with plastic utensils, the setting is rather attractive. There's a big indoor dining room with terracotta tile floors, imitation-oak Formica tables, and many hanging plants. Better yet is the outdoor seating at umbrella tables on a geranium-bordered brick patio overlooking the square.

Here a breakfast of scrambled eggs and ham with homemade biscuits is $2.25; a croissant or sweet-potato muffin, 90¢; coffee, 65¢. At lunch or dinner a turkey sandwich, a hamburger, or a chef's salad are all priced under $3. Leave room for a sundae with homemade ice cream and fresh whipped cream.

Open daily from 7:30 a.m. to 8 p.m., till 10 p.m. mid-June to the end of August. No credit cards.

In good weather, a picnic should definitely be considered. There are benches throughout the restored area (lots of grass too), and if you have a car you can drive to nearby scenic picnic areas off Colonial Parkway. The **Cheese Shop,** 424 Prince George St. in Merchants Square, between North Boundary and North Henry Sts. (tel. 804/220-0298), is a good place to purchase the fixings. They carry over 100 cheeses, wines in small and large bottles, croissants, salamis, prosciutto, pâté, fresh-baked breads, seafood salad, cheesecake, Godiva chocolates, and many more goodies. Open Monday to Saturday from 10 a.m. to 6 p.m.

4. Jamestown

Beginning in Washington, we've been traveling backward through the years to historic Virginia towns that figured prominently in the Civil War and the Revolution. Now we come to the place it all began. The James River is the Euphrates of the New World, and Jamestown the cradle of American civilization.

ARRIVAL IN THE NEW WORLD: The first permanent English settlers in America—104 men and boys—arrived at Cape Henry on the Virginia coast on April 26, 1607, after a voyage of four months aboard three small ships, the *Susan Constant,* the *Godspeed,* and the *Discovery.* Their expedition—an attempt to compete with profitable Spanish and Portuguese encroachments in the New World—was sponsored by the Virginia Company of London and supported by King James I.

The travelers were lured by promises of wealth. Upon arrival they were heartened to find, if not streets paved with gold, "faire meddows and goodly tall trees . . . freshwaters running through the woods . . . fine beautiful strawberries," and an abundance of fish and game. The group raised a cross in the sand dunes and thanked God for their safe arrival, and Capt. Christopher Newport read out the names of the crown-appointed officals and reminded the colonists that "the way to prosper and achieve success is to make yourselves all of one mind . . . and to serve and fear God." His suggestion was no doubt a response to the dissension and feuds that had marked the journey and which, advice notwithstanding, would plague the first years of the settlement.

The settlers' optimism was short-lived. The very day of their arrival they were attacked by Indians and some of their number wounded by arrows. They left Cape Henry and continued searching for another two weeks for a site that offered greater protection from the Spanish and the Indians.

On May 13 the band of English adventurers moored their ships at Jamestown in "six fathom water" and the next day "set to worke about the fortification." A small fort, a chapel, a storehouse, and thatched huts within the stockade were the first order of business.

A MODEST BEGINNING: Over a third of the group was composed of English gentlemen who watched as laborers and sailors cleared the land, planted wheat, and began building James Fort—a huge triangle, 420 feet on its river side, 300 feet on each of its other sides. Until the church was completed a board between trees with a canvas awning served as a pulpit. Captain Newport led an expedition up the James to the fall line to discover the nature of the new land and to search, in vain, for gold. Upon his return, Chaplain Robert Hunt administered the first "communyon" in America; the next day on June 22, 1607, Newport and his crew set sail back to England for additional supplies.

The problem of the group's lack of qualifications for the tasks before them would soon emerge. The gentlemen were unaccustomed to work of any kind and had little inclination or aptitude for it. Most of the others were city dwellers. Some were ne'er-do-wells. None was a farmer. None was equipped for survival in a primeval wilderness. By 1608 John Smith would admit, "Though there be Fish in the Sea, Foules in the ayre, and Beasts in the woods, their bounds are so large, they so wilde, and we so weake and ignorant, we cannot much trouble them."

THE BITTER YEARS: It was not an easy life for the settlers. As one on-the-scene chronicler described it, "a world of miseries ensewed." Food in the new storehouse "contained as many worms as grains," and a high mortality rate due to an unhealthy climate, contaminated water, famine, disease, and Indian attacks had a damping effect. And there were no women. Discord and fighting among the settlers continued. The men were "night and day groaning in every corner of the Fort most pittiful to hear," and by autumn only 50 remained alive. The only boon was that the Spanish found the new colony too insignificant and pathetic to pose any threat and therefore ignored it.

The Tidewater Indians were ambivalent to the new arrivals. Without their gifts of corn and agricultural advice the settlement couldn't have survived at all. But the settlers often thanked them for their troubles by grabbing land and supplies. "What will it availe you," asked Chief Powhatan, "to take [by] force [that which] you may quietly have with love, or to destroy them that provide you with food?"

By the end of the first year the Indians were hostile and suspicious. When Capt. John Smith (who governed the new settlement after several others had already been deposed) tried to barter for corn and grain in December 1607, the Indians took him prisoner and carried him to Powhatan at Werowocomoco. They would have killed him, but Powhatan's daughter, 11-year-old Pocahontas, interceded and saved his life. Though grateful to her, Smith was not much of a diplomat in dealing with natives, and he helped sow seeds of dissension that would result in centuries of hostility between the Indians and the white man.

Newport returned in January of 1608 with food, supplies, and 120 new settlers, who arrived just in time to see their new home burn to the ground along with desperately needed provisions and ammunition. Spring planting was delayed while rebuilding proceeded. Reconstruction was well under way when the second supply fleet arrived in October with another 70 settlers, this time including two women, a Mrs. Forrest and her maid, Ann Burras. Ann Burras might have been a beauty or she might have been ugly as sin; she was instantly snatched up as a bride by one of the settlers, and their marriage was the first in the new colony. Their child, born the next year, was named Virginia.

But soon after, the effects of the late planting began to manifest themselves. Exacerbating matters, rats got into what corn had been stored for the winter and ate almost all of it. Smith scattered the settlers, sending some to eat at the oyster banks; this unbalanced diet caused "their skin to peel off from head to foot." The arrival of another shipload of 400 hopefuls in August of 1609—400 additional mouths to feed—placed an unbearable burden on the colony. And the Indians, fully aware of the plight of the settlers, increased hostilities to the point where it became dangerous to wander outside the fort, making it even more difficult to obtain food. In the autumn of 1609, the colony suffered another loss. John Smith, who by force of character had held the little group together through these grueling times, was injured by gunpowder and forced to return to England for medical treatment. During the ensuing "Starving Time," as the settlers called it, the population shrank from over 500 to about 60. After the storehouse edibles were exhausted, they were reduced to eating horses, then "dogges, Catts, Ratts, and myce."

ALMOST ABANDONED: Sir Thomas Gates, the governor, arrived in May 1610, having been long delayed due to a shipwreck on the Bermuda coast. He took one look at the fort and its wretched occupants and decided it was hopeless. Ruin and desolation reigned. He described Jamestown "raither as the ruins of some auntient fortification, then that any people living might now inhabit it. . . . We found the pallisadoes torne downe, the portes open, the gates from off the hinges, empty howses (which the owners' death had taken from them) rent up and burnt, rather than the dwellers would step in to the woods as stones cast off from them to fetch other firewood, and it is true, the Indian killed as fast without, if our men stirred but beyond the bounds of their block-house as famine and pestilence did within."

Gates distributed what provisions he had, introduced martial law, and decided to abandon the settlement. On June 7, 1610, the remaining settlers boarded his ship and started down the James. But the next morning word reached them that Lord de la Warre had arrived with 150 settlers and very ample supplies. The group hastened back to Jamestown. It was like the coming of the cavalry in one of those old movies. Jamestown was saved!

A NEW BEGINNING: Under Gates and his lieutenant-governor, Sir Thomas Dale, between 1611 and 1615 Jamestown's budding industries—which had come to a screeching halt during the great famine—began to pick up. Blacksmiths, coopers, shipbuilders, and others got to work and began exporting their products in ships returning to England.

In 1613 John Rolfe (the father of the Virginia tobacco trade) introduced a new aromatic tobacco which proved popular in England. In 1615–1616, 2,300 pounds were exported; the next year demand had so risen that 20,000 pounds were sent, and by 1619 over 40,000 pounds were required. The settlers had discovered not the glittery gold they had expected, but the "golden weed" that would be the foundation of Virginia's fortunes.

The year 1619 was marked by several other important happenings: the Virginia Company sent a shipload of 90 women ("Maides young and uncorrupt to make wives to the Inhabitants . . . to make the men there more settled and lesse moveable") to suitors who paid their transportation costs; 22 burgesses were elected to set up the first legislative body in the New World; and 20 Negroes arrived in a Dutch warship to work as indentured servants, a precursor of slavery.

THE SAD TALE OF POCAHONTAS: While on a trading expedition in 1613 Capt. Samuel Argall (a notable pioneer who was adept at shipbuilding, an adventurous explorer, and a fearless soldier) captured Pocahontas and brought her to Jamestown as hostage in an attempt to deal with her father. Powhatan refused to pay her ransom, and Pocahontas came to prefer English life and declined to return to her native village. She was instructed in the Christian faith and eventually baptized.

In April 1614 John Rolfe married Pocahontas, not for "carnall affection; but for the good of this plantation, for the honour of our countrie." According to some accounts, she was in love with John Smith, but had been told he was dead. The marriage improved relations between natives and settlers for some years, but imagine Pocahontas's astonishment when she sailed to England with Rolfe in 1616 and encountered a living Smith. Upon meeting him she was overcome with emotion, about which the hard-hearted Smith reported, "After a modest salutation, without any word, she turned about, obscured her face, as not seeming well contented; and in that humour . . . we all left her two or three houres, repenting my selfe to have writ she could speake English. But not long after, she began to talke, and remembered mee well what courtesies shee had done." Finally, she recovered herself sufficiently to explain her condition— "They did tell us alwaies you were dead, and I knew no other till I came to Plimoth . . . because your Countriemen will lie much." She died in 1617 and never returned to Virginia.

THE INDIAN WARS: The early 1620s saw the expansion of the Virginia colony with new settlements dotting the James River. In 1622 Powhatan's successor, Opechancanough, reversed this development somewhat by planning a brilliant surprise attack. For many months prior to the attack the Indians had been so friendly to the colonists that the settlers had come to trust them inside the gates and take their presence for granted. Then one day the Indians simultaneously rose up and attacked the unsuspecting settlers, killing over 500 of them. Jamestown was the only river settlement saved, because, according to legend, Chanco, an Indian youth who had been treated particularly well by settlers, warned them. The remaining colonists retaliated fiercely, killing so many Indians in the process that relative peace reigned for the next 22 years. An aged Opechancanough made another attempt to wipe out the settlers in a 1644 massacre and 300 colonists were killed. Opechancanough was himself murdered in 1646.

RUMBLINGS OF REVOLT: There was strife not only with the Indians. Over a century prior to the Revolution, Virginia colonists were already beginning to chafe under British authority. A representative of the crown investigating the London Company in 1624 had his ears cut off for giving the king's commissioners certain official papers. A string of agents were sent from Virginia to London over the years to negotiate with the crown. In 1635 the unpopular royal governor Sir John Harvey was deposed in a peaceful revolution.

The tyrannical rule of Royal Governor Sir William Berkeley sparked what came to be known as Bacon's Rebellion. Nathaniel Bacon, Oxford-educated scion of a distinguished family, arrived at Jamestown in 1674. He was immediately made a member of the Governor's Council. In 1675 Berkeley enraged colonists by refusing their pleas for commanders to lead them in defense of their "lives and estates" during a massive (and, one might add, well-deserved) attack of the Susquehannock and allied tribes, and forbade further requests for help "under great penalty." Bacon assumed leadership and sent messengers to the governor asking for a commission. Berkeley responded by calling Bacon "the greatest rebel that ever was in Virginia," but he was a hero to fellow settlers who flocked to join his ranks. Ignoring Berkeley, Bacon organized a successful attack against the Indians, then brought his rebels to Jamestown to confront the governor and eventually force him to sign the desired commission. Berkeley raised troops and fled to the eastern shore, and Bacon for a time headed up the government. The latter mobilized a majority of the colonists into signing an oath pledging themselves to aid in the Indian wars; to oppose the royal governor ("For having . . . raised unjust Taxes . . . For assuming the monopoly of the Beaver Trade . . . For having protected, favoured, and emboldened the Indians . . . Wee accuse Sir William Berkeley, as guilty"); and to resist British suppression until the king was made aware of colonial grievances.

Bacon was one of the first colonists to envision an American Republic independent of British rule. He sent out a ship to capture Berkeley, but in this attempt he was foiled by a British captain who delivered the ship to the governor. Bacon burned down the town to prevent its reoccupation by Berkeley, and issued a proclamation declaring that if the English supported Berkeley, Virginians ought to defend their freedom or abandon the colony. Bacon, however, soon died of a fever, and without his leadership the revolt collapsed. Berkeley retaliated by hanging 20 men and confiscating the property of many others. Charles II was not pleased with this behavior and recalled the governor to England, where he also died. Berkeley was succeeded by other harsh royalist governors who sought to destroy popular government in Virginia.

Another revolt in 1682, against the refusal of the British to do anything about the low cost of tobacco, resulted in a night ride in which planters destroyed thousands of plants to create a scarcity and drive up prices. Six of them were executed in reprisal.

Actual revolution was still almost a century away, but the series of rebellions were an omen of things to come.

In 1698, the capital succumbing to flames once again—this time by accident rather than design—a move to Williamsburg was indicated. By 1772 Jamestown was a ghost town—"an abundance of bricks and rubbish with three or four inhabited houses."

RECENT HISTORY: Jamestown figured in history again during the Civil War. In 1861 Confederate troops built a fort near the site of the first Jamestown fort, and a year later the island was occupied by Union troops.

The first efforts at preserving the site came in 1893 when the Association for the Preservation of Virginia Antiquities (a nonprofit organization dedicated to the acquisition, preservation, and restoration of "ancient historic grounds") purchased 22½ acres of the original town site. They protected the area and began restoration work, including construction of a seawall to halt erosion of the grounds. In 1940 the federal government joined the APVA in a unified program of development and administration of 1,559½ acres designated as Jamestown National Historic Site. The site is part of the larger Colonial National Historic Park, which also includes the Yorktown Battlefield and the scenic 23-mile Colonial Parkway linking Williamsburg, Jamestown, and Yorktown.

The last four decades have yielded an increasingly clear picture of life in 17th-century Virginia. Over 100 building frames have been excavated, and archeologists have uncovered evidences of manufacturing ventures (pottery, winemaking, brickmaking, glassblowing, etc.), early wells and old roads, as well as millions of artifacts of everyday life—tools, utensils, ceramic dishes, armor, keys, and the like. Research is an ongoing process.

VISITING JAMESTOWN: Jamestown is just nine miles south of Williamsburg via the Colonial Parkway. Allow a full day for your visit, and consider packing a picnic lunch. Other than a cafeteria at Jamestown Festival Park, there are no restaurants, but there are scenic picnic areas along the parkway (the nicest is called Great Neck).

Jamestown Festival Park

This year-round exhibit, open daily (except Christmas and New Year's Days) from 9 a.m. to 5 p.m., 7 p.m. June 15 through August 15, tells the story of our beginnings in America through exhibits and reconstructions. Admission is $5 for adults, $2.50 for children 6 to 12 (under 6, free). If you're also planning to visit the **Yorktown Victory Center** (it doesn't have to be the same day), purchase a money-saving combination ticket to both attractions at $8 for adults, $4 for children. A large gift shop is on the premises and parking is free. For information, call 804/229-1607.

Visitors are welcomed in the **Information Center.** Here you can obtain tickets and brochures, and find out about special programs and tours. Self-guided tours are enhanced by costumed historic interpreters in the reconstructed areas. Allow about two hours for this attraction.

From the Information Center, visitors proceed to the **Old World Pavilion** where tableaux of wax figures depict three generations of Tudor monarchs, the development of British sea power, and the beginnings of colonization. The story begins with John Cabot's petitioning Henry VII to support an expedition to North America in 1496, and moves to the infamous Henry VIII, who in addition to marrying many times, forged the British navy into the finest maritime force in Europe. Later Queen Elizabeth I meets with Sir Francis Drake, men are lured to Virginia with promises of wealth (gold) in the New World, and finally, three ships sail to Jamestown in 1606. Other exhibits include royal seals, reproductions of crown jewels, royal succession, and engravings by Theodor de Bry relating to the settlement of Virginia; they date to 1590.

The **New World Pavilion** begins with the story of Jamestown. Exhibits depict Indian life, the successful cultivation of tobacco, the marketplace at Jamestown, the seven Virginia presidents (busts), and the role of Virginia in American history.

Note: Some of this may be closed when you visit, while a new museum complex, doubling the amount of exhibit space, is under construction.

Following the pavilions is an outdoor exhibit area. An Indian village modeled after the town of Secota (as documented in the watercolors of John White) focuses on Native American life around 1600. There are several structures—a chief's house, a pottery, a temple, and family dwellings—and Native American crafts such as pottery, basket weaving, hide tanning, and flint knapping are demonstrated.

Especially evocative is a replica of **James Fort,** with 18 reconstructed buildings, including a storehouse, church, guardhouse (where armor, helmets, and cannonballs are stored), and a number of rudimentary wattle-and-daub thatch-roofed houses with dirt floors and straw beds. Demonstrations of 17th-century carpentry, agriculture, food preparation, and armoring are given in this area.

Next come full-scale replicas of the *Discovery,* the *Godspeed* (when in port), and the *Susan Constant*—the three ships that carried 104 men and boys to Virginia in 1607. You can board one of the vessels and explore the cramped quarters in which the settlers lived for four months.

When you leave Festival Park, go back to the Colonial Parkway and turn right. You'll soon come to the Ranger Station entrance gate where a $5-per-car admission is charged to visit Jamestown Island. The gate is open from 8:30 a.m. to 4:30 p.m. in winter, with extended hours spring through fall. If any of the occupants of your car is a senior citizen—62 or over—the car is admitted free.

Jamestown National Historic Site

Exploration of the actual site of the first permanent English settlement in America begins at the **Visitor Center** here (tel. 804/229-1733) under the auspices of the National Park Service. Open daily except Christmas (from 9 a.m. to 5 p.m. in winter, once again, with extended hours spring through fall) it contains an information desk, a gift shop, an exhibit area, and a theater in which a 12-minute orientation film is shown every half hour. Allow at least two hours for this attraction.

Exhibits document the 92 years when Jamestown was capital of Virginia. An area focusing on possessions brought from England features artifacts of the home (the kind of chest in which a colonist brought his meager possessions, a Bible predating 1611, written in Latin—possibly Lord de la Warre's, etc.). Frontier life exhibits include defensive equipment (examples of typical muskets, armor, helmets, gun rests, etc.) and artifacts such as a pair of earrings believed to have belonged to Pocahontas. There are models of the three ships that brought the settlers to Jamestown, Indian artifacts (beads, pipes, weapons, pottery), Spanish coins and pottery, a model of a colonist's home (a chair represented real luxury), a replica of James Fort, a 17th-century pile driver, and displays on animals in the colony, on food preparation, on health and religion (intimately related because the high mortality rate made funerals the most frequently performed religious service), on shaping the land, on shelter, and on prosperity (the last showing the more luxurious state of affairs after tobacco had made Jamestown a viable economic enterprise). An excellent gift shop is on the premises.

From the Visitor Center, a footpath leads through the actual site of **"James Cittie,"** where reconstructed rubbly brick foundations of 17th-century homes, taverns, shops, and statehouses with artists' renderings and recorded narratives aid visualization of the past. Spring through fall there are frequent rangerguided half-hour tours of the site, in summer enhanced by living history programs. Most complete are the remains of the tower of one of the first brick churches built in Virginia (1639). The first timber church went up in 1608 and burned to the ground a few weeks later. Other wood-frame churches—settings of historic moments like the wedding of Pocahontas and John Rolfe and the meeting of the first legislative assembly in the New World—met the same fiery fate. Today you can see the remains of the 46-foot-high tower with its three-foot brick walls laid in English bond; it is the only 17th-century structure standing above ground in Jamestown. Directly behind the tower is the Memorial Church, a 1907 gift of the

Colonial Dames of America. It houses remnants of early Jamestown churches; a 17th-century tomb, possibly containing the remains of Sir George Yeardley, an early royal governor; and the tomb of the Rev. John Clough, an early minister.

The footpath continues to the seawall, the site of the original James Fort, and the May 13, 1607, landing site. There are many monuments and memorials throughout James Cittie: the Tercentenary Monument, a 103-foot-shaft erected in 1907 to commemorate the 300th anniversary of the Jamestown settlement; statues of John Smith and Pocahontas; a shrine dedicated to Robert Hunt, the colony's first Anglican minister; and a memorial cross marking some 300 shallow graves of colonists who died during the "Starving Time," the winter of 1609–1610.

At **Dale House,** near the statehouse ruins, there are demonstrations of pottery making using 17th-century designs discovered in excavations and the same type of clay. You can buy the works created here.

The Island Drive

A fascinating five-mile loop drive (beginning at the Visitor Center parking lot) winds through 1,500 wilderness acres of woodland and marsh that has been allowed to return to its natural state in order to approximate the landscape as 17th-century settlers found it. Markers and large paintings interpret aspects of the daily activities of the colonists—tobacco growing, lumbering, silk production, pottery making, farming, etc. There is an optional three-mile loop if your time is limited.

The Glasshouse

Before leaving Jamestown, stop at the remains of America's first factory, a 1608 glassworks on the shore of the James where settlers attempted to make glass of coarse river sand. Nearby is a thatch-roofed reproduction of the original building with a working 17th-century–style furnace. Inside, costumed craftspeople trained in Colonial glassblowing techniques create simple glass objects which can be purchased by visitors. The Glasshouse is open from 8:30 a.m. to 5 p.m. in winter, to 5:30 p.m. in spring and fall, to 6 p.m. in summer.

5. Yorktown

At the eastern end of the Colonial Parkway, 14 miles from Williamsburg, Yorktown was the setting for the last major battle of the American Revolution. Here, on October 19, 1781, George Washington wrote to the president of the Continental Congress, "I have the Honor to inform Congress, that a Reduction of the British Army under the Command of Lord Cornwallis, is most happily effected." Though it would be two years before a peace treaty was signed, and sporadic fighting would continue, the Revolution, for all intents and purposes had been won. America had demonstrated to the world her ability to defend the independence declared five years earlier.

Though tourist attention focuses to a large degree on the town's role as the final Revolutionary battlefield, Yorktown is also of interest as one of America's earliest Colonial towns.

BEFORE THE REVOLUTION: Though a number of settlers lived and farmed in the area by the 1630s, Yorktown's history really dates to 1691 when the General Assembly at Jamestown (Virginia's capital until 1699) passed the Port Act creating a new town on the site. It was one of the assembly's many attempts to encourage development of towns in rural tidewater country. For the purpose, 50 acres were purchased from Benjamin Read for 10,000 pounds of "merchantable sweet scented tobacco and cask." York County supervisor Lawrence Smith laid out the town and divided it into 85 half-acre lots, each to be offered for sale at the price of 180 pounds of tobacco. Buyers were required to improve and develop their land within six months or forfeit ownership. Within a year 61 lots had been sold, 36 of them on the first sale date. A town was under way.

By the end of the century two important institutions—Grace Episcopal Church (built with the help of Royal Governor Francis Nicholson, who would later design Williamsburg) and the York County Courthouse—were built, and Yorktown was on the way to becoming a principal mid-Atlantic port and a center of tobacco trade.

Small by today's standards, in the 18th century Yorktown was a thriving metropolis with a population of several thousand planters, innkeepers, seamen, merchants, craftsmen, indentured servants, and slaves. After the waterfront officially became part of the town in 1738, Water Street, paralleling the river, was lined with shops, inns, and loading docks. Foreign ships brought in cargoes of fashionable European clothing, wines and liquors, silver plate, weaponry, books, jewelry, furniture, and slaves. A picture of the town emerges from the following description by an English visitor in 1738:

"You perceive a great Air of Opulence amongst the Inhabitants, who have some of them built themselves Houses, equal in Magnificence to many of our superb ones at St. James's. . . . Almost every considerable Man keeps an Equipage. . . . The Taverns are many here and much frequented. . . . the Court house is the only considerable publick Building, and is no unhandsome structure. . . . The most considerable Houses are of Brick, some handsome ones of Wood, all built in the modern Tasts. . . . There are some very pretty Garden spots in the Town; and the Avenues leading to Williamsburg, Norfolk &c., are prodigiously agreeable."

Yorktown flourished through the 1770s with prosperity peaking in the 1750s. Then a combination of circumstances brought its downfall. Rivers ceased to be the principal arteries of trade, the soil which had been planted with tobacco year after year for over a century was sadly depleted, and the blockade of ports by British troops further diminished the town's affluence. Though it is doubtful that Yorktown would have recovered from the destruction and waste that accompanied the Siege of 1781, it received the coup de grâce in the "Great Fire" of 1814. It declined steadily over the years, becoming a quiet rural village. In fact, like Williamsburg, it changed so little that many of the picturesque old streets, buildings, and battle sites have survived intact to this day.

THE WORLD TURNED UPSIDE DOWN: The Revolutionary War was a bloody seven-year conflict, marked with many staggering defeats for the patriots. Historians believe that it was only the superb leadership and pertinacity of Gen. George Washington that inspired the Continental Army (a ragtag group of farmers, laborers, backwoodsmen, and merchants) to continue so long in the face of overwhelming odds.

But in March of 1781 a turning point came. A British "victory" at Guilford Courthouse in North Carolina was accompanied by such severe losses that Cornwallis decided to leave the Carolinas and march northward into Virginia to rest and recoup. By August he had established a base at the York River, moved his army there, and begun to fortify the town and nearby Gloucester Point. Cornwallis viewed Yorktown as a strategic naval station, with the river location providing an access route for reinforcements or withdrawal as needed.

Two weeks after Cornwallis settled into Yorktown for the winter, General Washington, whose army was camped outside British-occupied New York City, received word from French Admiral Compte de Grasse that he was taking his squadron, with troops and artillery aboard, to the Chesapeake, and that his men and ships were at Washington's disposal through October 15 (after that he had prior military commitments). "I shall be greatly obliged to you," wrote de Grasse, "if you will employ me promptly and effectually during that time."

After conferring with the Compte de Rochambeau, commander of the French troops in America, Washington decided to march 450 miles to Virginia with the objective of engaging and defeating Cornwallis. Leaving a small force to defend the Hudson Highlands, he departed with great secrecy (he was in Philadelphia by the time the British noted his absence) taking the majority of the American army and Rochambeau's troops.

Meanwhile, on September 5, 1781, a fleet of 19 British ships under Admiral Thomas Graves appeared at the entrance to Chesapeake Bay with the aim of reinforcing Cornwallis's Yorktown entrenchment. They were met by 24 French ships under de Grasse. Though the battle ended in a stalemate, Graves was forced to return to New York to repair his ships. The French remained to block further reinforcements or the possibility of escape by water. And the French and American armies under Washington neared Yorktown to block aid or escape by land.

Cornwallis had never envisioned having to defend his position from the landward side. His troops hastily constructed an inner defense line of earthworks, redoubts (small square forts secured by sharp, pointed logs), and batteries.

The siege began on September 28 when 17,000 men under Washington occupied a line encircling the town within a mile of the British outworks. The allied army, spread out in camps extending six miles, dug siege lines and bombarded the redcoats with heaving cannonfire. British defeat was inevitable.

Cornwallis compounded his tactical errors by evacuating almost all outworks except for Redoubts 9 and 10 in order to concentrate his troops closer to town and better defend it. Washington was now able to move his men within 1,000 yards of British lines. Highly trained French engineers and artillerymen busied themselves in constructing the siege line. By October 9 the allies were ready to respond to British artillery.

They didn't wait to respond. The French were the first to fire. Two hours later George Washington personally fired the first American round. By October 10 the British were nearly silenced. On October 11 the allies moved up about another 500 yards.

On October 14 the French stormed Redoubt 9 while the Continentals made short work of Redoubt 10. Both columns began their assaults at 8 p.m. The Americans were through by 8:10 p.m.; the French, whose target was stronger, by 8:30. The signal for the Americans to attack had been the word "Rochambeau," which sounded to them like "rush on boys."

On October 16, following a last-ditch and fruitless attempt to launch an attack on the allies, a desperate Cornwallis tried to escape with his troops across the York River to Gloucester Point, but his efforts were doomed by a violent storm that scattered his ships.

On October 17 at 10 a.m. a British drummer appeared on the rampart. He beat out a signal indicating a desire to discuss terms with the enemy. A cease-fire was called, and a British officer was led to American lines where he requested an armistice.

On October 18 commissioners met at the house of Augustus Moore (about which more below) and worked out the terms of surrender.

On October 19, 1781, at 2 p.m. the French and Continental armies lined Surrender Road, each stretching for over a mile on either side. The French were resplendent in immaculate white uniforms, their officers plumed and decorated; the Americans were in rags and tatters. The British army (about 5,000 British soldiers and seamen), clad in new uniforms, marched between them out of Yorktown to a band playing a tune called "The World Turned Upside Down." Gen. Charles O'Hara of the British Guards represented Cornwallis who, pleading illness, did not surrender in person.

The battle marked the end of British rule in America and made a permanent place for Yorktown in the annals of American history.

AFTER THE REVOLUTION: A fire destroyed much of Yorktown in 1814. In 1861 Confederate soldiers landed at the wharf that had once received Cornwallis's fleet. They used an abandoned waterfront warehouse as a hospital and renewed the extensive 80-year-old British earthworks as barriers against Union troops.

Today most of Yorktown—including the surrounding battlefield areas—is part of the 9,300-acre Colonial National Historical Park. The region came under the auspices of the National Park Service in 1931. Grace Episcopal Church (gutted by fire and rebuilt in 1848) is still in use, and there are about 300 local residents.

YORKTOWN VICTORY CENTER: Like Jamestown, Yorktown merits a full day of sightseeing. First stop is the Yorktown Victory Center (tel. 804/887-1776), open daily except Christmas and New Year's from 9 a.m. to 5 p.m., till 7 p.m. mid-June to mid-August. Set on 21 acres overlooking part of the battlefield of 1781, the center offers an excellent orientation to Yorktown attractions, including a film and multimedia museum exhibits. Admission is $5 for adults, $2.50 for children 6 to 12 (under 6, free); or you can purchase a combination ticket for this and Jamestown Festival Park at $8 for adults, $4 for children.

Visitors can take a "nighttime" stroll down **Liberty Street,** a full-size reproduction of an 18th-century Tidewater Virginia village (lit by gaslight-style streetlamps) with animated tableaux à la Disneyland. The era is evoked by sound effects—a horse and carriage departing, harpsichord music emanating from one of the houses, sounds of merrymaking from within the Black Swan Tavern, etc. Mr. Shepherd, editor of an imaginary newspaper called the *Tidewater Gazette,* is reading over the proofs for the paper of December 12, 1773. He tells a young typesetter that the colonies will not tolerate any more of King George III's "blasted taxes" and that he expects trouble from those tea ships in Boston. "It's time to take action!" he declares. The next scene is a reenactment of the Boston Tea Party. Other exhibits include a full-scale model of Washington's campaign tent; a multimedia presentation about the battles from Concord to Yorktown; a light-show mural foretelling the political consequences of the Revolution, both in America and abroad; a 12-foot-high copy of the Declaration of Independence; and a multimedia presentation explaining why Yorktown was the setting for the conclusive battle of the war.

In the **Gallery of the Revolution** there are changing exhibits relating to the period, such as a show of hand-hooked tapestries depicting landmark scenes in American history.

The Road to Yorktown, a 28-minute documentary film produced by David Wolper (of *Roots* fame), follows the movements of Generals Washington and Rochambeau and documents the final grueling days of the Revolution. The film covers the 450-mile march from New York to Virginia, Washington's Williamsburg headquarters at Wythe House and Rochambeau's at the Peyton-Randolph House (details above), the allied armies' entry into Yorktown, the blocking of the British escape route by de Grasse at the mouth of the Chesapeake Bay, the battle, the surrender, and the exit of the British on Surrender Road. It's a very evocative orientation.

And since the American Revolution brought not only independence from Great Britain but a new and free nation in which people from all over the world found an opportunity to prosper, another exhibit, called "An American Dream," explores this aspect. It is based on the life of Nick Mathews, a Greek immigrant who founded a famous Yorktown restaurant called Nick's Seafood Pavilion. Displays on his career and family portray an American dream achieved.

Finally, there's a Continental Army encampment where talks and demonstrations focus on subjects like how battle wounds were treated, army camp cooking, musket firing, etc. The encampment contains nearly 20 tents and is laid out according to Baron von Steuben's *Regulations for the Order and Discipline of the Troops of the U.S.* published in 1779.

A large picnic area under the trees, a gift shop, and a parking lot are on the premises. Allow at least 1½ to 2 hours for the Victory Center.

Sometime during the day you might consider an al fresco lunch at the above-mentioned area or at a waterfront picnic area with tables and grills at the foot of Comte de Grasse Street near the cofferdam. There's another gorgeous picnic area called **Ringfield,** seven miles from Williamsburg on the Colonial Parkway. If the weather is wrong for picnicking, try the **Duke of York Motor Hotel** dining room on Water and Ballard Sts. (tel. 804/893-3232), overlooking the river and offering low-priced luncheon specials.

YORKTOWN BATTLEFIELD VISITOR CENTER: After you've seen the Yorktown Victory Center, head over to National Park Service Visitor Center (tel. 804/898-3400), starting point for self-guided auto tours of the battlefield and a full-service information center.

Here too there's an orientation film. A 12-minute documentary called *Victory at Yorktown,* it's about the formal surrender of the British and their German mercenary allies. William Conrad narrates.

Museum displays include Washington's actual military headquarters tent; a replica (which you can board and explore) of the quarterdeck of the H.M.S. *Charon;* additional objects recovered from the York River in the excavations, including several intact garrison guns; battlefield artifacts (bayonets, uniform buttons, flintlock muskets, artillery, and musket balls); exhibits about Cornwallis's surrender and the events leading up to it; and dioramas detailing the siege. Upstairs, an on-the-scene account of the battle of Yorktown is given by a 13-year-old soldier in the Revolutionary army named John Whitney; his taped narrative is accompanied by a sound-and-light show.

The Siege Line Overlook on the roof provides a panoramic view of strategic points on the battlefield.

National Park Service rangers are on hand to answer questions and help plan your visit. On spring and fall weekends, and daily in summer, they give free tours of the British inner defense line. The center is open daily except Christmas from 9 a.m. to 5 p.m., with extended hours spring through fall.

An excellent gift shop on the premises sells Yorktown-related items and many books on the Revolution for both adults and children.

The Battlefield Tour

The National Park Service Visitor Center is the starting point for the 7.7-mile Red Arrow route and the 10.2-mile Yellow Arrow route auto tours of the battlefield. You'll be given a map indicating both routes and detailing major sites; don't worry about getting lost—signs clearly mark the way. At each stop there are explanatory historical markers (sometimes taped narratives as well), but for the most interesting experience, rent a cassette player and tape at the Visitor Center for $2.08. Narrated by British and American colonels whose polite hostilities to each other are most amusing, the taped commentary further elucidates the battlefield sites. You won't stay in your car the whole time; it's frequently necessary to park, get out, and walk to redoubts and earthworks. A lot of the drive is very scenic, winding through woods and fields abundant with birdlife; the Yellow route is especially beautiful. If you purchase the cassette, listen to the introduction in the parking lot; it will tell you when to depart. Auto tour highlights include:

The **Grand French Battery:** This was a large artillery area in the French section of the first siege line. Here French soldiers manning cannons, mortars, and howitzers fired on British and German mercenary troops.

Moore House: When Lord Cornwallis realized the inevitability of his defeat, he sent a message to General Washington: "Sir, I propose a cessation of hostilities for twenty-four hours, and that two officers may be appointed by each side, to meet at Mr. Moore's house, to settle terms for the surrender of the posts of York and Gloucester." General Washington granted Cornwallis just two hours to submit general terms. On the afternoon of October 18, 1781, two British commissioners, Col. Thomas Dundas and Maj. Alexander Ross, met in "Mr. Moore's house" with American Col. John Laurens and French representative the Viscount de Noailles. Negotiation went on late into the evening, the British protesting terms of Article III which required them to march out of Yorktown "with shouldered arms, colors cased [that means flags furled], and drums beating a British or German march." They finally agreed to the humiliating exit, and negotiations would up just before midnight. Washington made a few adjustments, the Articles of Capitulation were signed by Cornwallis and his senior naval officer, and the document was delivered back to Washington at Redoubt 10.

Moore House has a long history. The land it is on originally belonged to Royal Governor Sir John Harvey, one of the first men to own property along the river south of Yorktown. When Harvey was deposed in 1735 and forced to leave Virginia, his 752-acre York Plantation was acquired by a George Ludlow, and over the years passed to a series of related owners. In the early 1700s Lawrence Smith constructed the two-story white frame building that would become Moore House when the property went to his daughter, Lucy, and her husband, Augustine Moore. The Moores, who added 500 acres to the estate, lived in the house from 1768 until their respective deaths in 1788 (his) and 1797 (hers). Moore left the estate to his good friend, Gen. Thomas Nelson (see below). Though surviving the battle of Yorktown unscathed, Moore House suffered considerable damage during military action in the Civil War. Shellfire destruction was aggravated by soldiers stripping away siding and other usable wood for fuel. The house was pretty much abandoned (sometimes even used as a cow barn) until John D. Rockefeller, Jr., purchased it in 1931 and the Park Service restored it to its Colonial appearance. It is today furnished with appropriate period pieces, some of which are believed to have been in the house during the surrender negotiations.

Moore House is open spring and fall weekends from 10 a.m. to 5 p.m., daily in summer to 6 p.m. Twenty-minute living-history tours are given throughout the day.

Surrender Field: Here your imagination, stoked by visions from orientation films, can evoke the British march out of Yorktown. William Conrad narrates the story of the surrender scene from a pavilion overlooking the field. Surrender cannons encircle the pavilion below.

Along the Yellow Arrow route you'll come to the sites of Washington's and Rochambeau's headquarters, a French cemetery and Artillery Park, and allied encampment sites.

TOURING THE TOWN: Self-guided walking tours of old Yorktown—including some places of interest not related to the famed battle—are available at the **Battlefield Visitor Center.** Begin your ramble close to the center at—

The **Victory Monument:** News of the allied victory at Yorktown reached Philadelphia on October 24, 1781. On October 29 Congress resolved "that the United States . . . will cause to be erected at York, in Virginia, a marble column, adorned with emblems of the alliance between the United States and his Most Christian Majesty; and inscribed with a succinct narrative of the surrender of Earl Cornwallis to his excellency General Washington, Commander in Chief of the combined forces of America and France; to his excellency the Count de Rochambeau, commanding the auxiliary troops of his Most Christian Majesty in America, and his excellency the Count de Grasse, commanding in chief the naval army of France in the Chesapeake."

All very well in theory, but due to financial difficulties—Congress couldn't even pay the Revolutionary soldiers, so monuments seemed rather in the nature of frills—no action was taken for a century. As the centennial approached, pressure was brought to bear on Congress to come across as promised. Finally, on October 18, 1881, the cornerstone for the monument was laid by Masons as an appropriate opening to the Yorktown Centennial Celebration. The highly symbolic 98-foot marble shaft overlooking the York River was completed in 1884. The podium is adorned with 13 female figures hand in hand in a solemn dance to denote the unity of the 13 colonies; beneath their feet is the inscription "One country, one constitution, one destiny," a moving post-Civil War sentiment. The column itself symbolizes the greatness and prosperity of the nation, and its stars represent the "constellation" of states in the Union in 1881. Atop the shaft is the figure of Liberty.

The Cornwallis Cave

According to legend, Cornwallis lived here in two tiny "rooms" during the final days of the siege when he hoped to withdraw to the river and escape overland to New York. The two rooms were carved out by various occupants of the cave—which may at one time have included the pirate Blackbeard—and Confederate soldiers later enlarged the shelter and added a roof. A taped narrative at the entrance tells the story. The cave is at the foot of Great Valley, right on the river.

The Dudley Digges House

You can only view the restored 18th-century white weatherboard house on Main and Smith Sts. from the outside; it's a private residence, not open to the public. Its dormer windows set in the roofline and surrounding outbuildings—a kitchen, granary, smokehouse, well, and stable—are all typical of Virginia architecture in the mid-1700s. Owner Dudley Digges was a Revolutionary patriot who served with Patrick Henry, Benjamin Harrison, and Thomas Jefferson on the Committee of Correspondence. After the war he was rector of the College of William and Mary.

Nelson House

Scottish merchant Thomas Nelson (known as "Scotch Tom") made three voyages between Great Britain and Virginia before deciding to settle in Yorktown in 1705. A go-getter of the first order, he proceeded to sire a dynasty.

By 1707 he had acquired two lots, along with a number of slaves, and built himself a house at Main and Nelson Streets. Between 1711 and 1723 he obtained title to several other lots and became co-operator of a ferry, charter member of a trading company, builder of the Swan Tavern, trustee of York's port land, and a large-scale planter. By 1728 he had added 600 acres, a private warehouse and wharf, and a mill to his holdings. In 1743 "Scotch Tom" retired and let his very capable sons run the business. He died in 1745 leaving a large estate.

His son, William (married in 1728 to Elizabeth Carter Burwell, daughter of another Virginia aristocrat), soon began adding to his father's empire, at the same time building a distinguished political career. In 1742 he was elected to the House of Burgesses. In 1746 he was appointed to the Council, a body of 12 men who were advisors to the royal governor. His younger brother, Thomas, a promising lawyer who had been deputy secretary of the colony (acting for the secretary who remained in England) was appointed to take William's place in the House of Burgesses. Like their father, both Thomas and William also served as county judges.

In 1761 William's son, also called Thomas (for clarity I'll call him Thomas II) was elected to the House of Burgesses and made a county court judge. He married Lucy Grymes, daughter of a member of the Council, and the newlyweds moved into "Scotch Tom's" Yorktown mansion. In the following years crops flourished, land was added to the property, a family was raised (they had 11 children), and strife between England and the colonies increased. Thomas II was among the 68 signers (along with Patrick Henry, Thomas Jefferson, and George Washington) in 1769 of a pact refusing to import any English product taxed for revenue purposes. In 1772 William died, and his sons, Thomas II and Hugh, promoted longtime employee Augustine Moore, granting him a partnership in their far-reaching business enterprises. Thomas II was elected to the Continental Congress in Philadelphia and signed the Declaration of Independence as a member of the Virginia delegation. Though becoming quite ill shortly afterward, he helped raise militia forces and pledged his personal property to obtain money for the Revolution. He became governor of Virginia in 1781, and happily saw his mansion, though damaged (cannonballs remain embedded in the brickwork), survive the battle of Yorktown. (Cornwallis seized the house for a command post during part of his occupation.) After the war the state was unable to pay him the moneys for which he had pledged his property and he was forced to sell various holdings, but not the mansion itself. He died in 1789, and his descendants continued to occupy the house through 1907. The National Park Service acquired the Nelson House in 1968 and restored it to its original appearance.

Nelson House is open daily in summer, and on weekends in spring and fall, for elaborate living-history tours (check at the Visitor Center for a schedule). You're greeted by a costumed 18th-century character, and vignettes depicting the lives of various occupants during different eras are acted out in each room. Perhaps you'll tour the house as a guest of Thomas Nelson and meet some of Revolutionary-era York's leading citizens. Tours take 30 to 45 minutes.

The Sessions House

Just across from Nelson House, this is the oldest house in Yorktown, built in 1692 by Thomas Sessions. At least five U.S. presidents have visited the house, today a private residence off-limits to the public. You may, however, stare at it.

The Customhouse

At the corner of Main and Read Sts., and dating to 1721, this sturdy brick building was originally the private storehouse of Richard Ambler, collector of ports. It became Gen. J.B. Magruder's headquarters during the Civil War. Today it is maintained by the Daughters of the American Revolution as a museum, open on weekends only. Call 804/898-4788 for exact hours.

Grace Episcopal Church

At Church St. near the river, and an active house of worship since the 17th century, Grace Church originally dates to 1697. Its first rector, the Rev. Anthony Panton, was dismissed for calling the secretary of the colony a jackanapes. Gunpowder and ammo were stored in the church during the siege of Yorktown. The building was badly damaged in the 1814 fire but was restored in 1848. And during the Civil War it served as a hospital. It's open to visitors daily from 9 a.m. to 5 p.m. The original communion silver, made in England in 1649, is still in use. Thomas Nelson (II) is buried in the adjacent graveyard.

The Swan Tavern

For over a century the Swan Tavern, at the corner of Main and Ballard Sts. (tel. 804/898-3033), was Yorktown's leading hostelry. Originally owned by Thomas Nelson ("Scotch Tom"), it was in operation 20 years before Williamsburg's famous Raleigh. The Swan was demolished in 1863 by an ammunition explosion at the courthouse across the street, rebuilt, and destroyed again by fire in 1915. Today it is reconstructed as per archeological, architectural, and historical research, and the premises house a fine antique shop. Call for hours.

BIG DAY AT YORKTOWN: One final note: If you can manage to time your visit to Yorktown for October 19, you'll get in on a major annual celebration with noted speakers, wreath-laying ceremonies, band concerts, a parade, and a Brunswick stew luncheon. Call 804/898-3400 for details.

6. Annapolis

The Annapolis area was first settled in 1649 by Puritans who lived on the north side of the Severn River. A year later, the first lot was surveyed on the south side of the river, present site of the town. It was named Annapolis in honor of Britain's Princess Anne (later Queen Anne) in 1694, and at the same time became the capital of Lord Baltimore's province of Maryland. Annapolis prospered throughout the 1700s due to a flourishing tobacco trade, and from 1750 to 1780 it was Maryland's commercial, political, and social center, home of the colony's first library and theater. During the 18th century many prominent residences were built, several of which are intact and on view today (details below). In 1769 Maryland—like the other colonies chafing against British rule —began moving toward independence with a nonimportation agreement forbidding import of any goods taxed by England. On May 24, 1774, Annapolis adopted resolutions of sympathy with Boston (in response to the Tea Party) and appointed an Annapolis Committee of Correspondence to support other colonies in their struggles against the crown. The town also emulated Boston in its "Peggy Stewart Tea Party" of 1774. The brig Peggy Stewart sailed into the harbor with 2320 pounds of tea ordered by Annapolis merchants Williams & Co., and owner Anthony Stewart aroused public protest by paying duty on the tea at the custom house. He was forced by irate citizens to burn the Peggy Stewart with full sails set and the tea still on board.

Annapolis was the capital of the United States from November 26, 1783, to August 13, 1784, and its State House was the scene of several historic monuments including the ratification of the Treaty of Paris by Congress, officially ending the Revolution.

Today Annapolis is many things—a lively college and naval town, home of the United States Naval Academy; a state capital; a bustling yacht and fishing harbor; a marketplace for handcrafted sailboats and pleasure craft; and a quaintly charming town with brick streets and, thanks to a group called Historic Annapolis, Inc., a well-preserved historic district. There's plenty to occupy a tourist for a day or two.

Annapolis is easily reached by car; it's 30 miles from Washington via U.S. 50, an extension of New York Avenue. Bus transport is also available via **Dillon's Bus Service** (tel. 301/647-2321) which picks up passengers at the Foggy Bottom Metro and other District locations. It lets you off in Annapolis at the Naval Stadium parking area or on West Calvert St. One-way fare is $5. Call for departure times.

SEEING THE SIGHTS: First stop in Annapolis should be the **Visitor Information Center** at the City Dock (tel. 301/268-TOUR), a full information service offering maps and brochures as well as help with accommodations, sightseeing, etc. It's open from 10 a.m. to 5 p.m. daily April through October. The rest of the year the same services are offered at the **State House Visitor Center,** inside the State House at State Circle (tel. 301/269-3400), open from 9 a.m. to 5 p.m. daily.

Since the historic district sights are so compact, your best bet is to park your car for the day and proceed on foot. Otherwise you'll find yourself constantly feeding meters which at best have a two-hour duration. You can park free at the **Navy Marine Corps Stadium,** just off Rowe Blvd. at Taylor Ave. From there, a 60¢ shuttle bus takes you into the historic district, making several stops en route. It runs every 15 minutes in both directions between 6:30 a.m. and 7 p.m., weekdays and Saturday only.

A money-saving **Ring Ticket** to five attractions—the William Paca House, the William Paca Garden, the Victualling Warehouse, the Tobacco Prise House, and the Barracks—is available at $4.50 for adults, $4.25 for senior citizens, $2 for students 6 to 18. It can be purchased from Historic Annapolis headquarters at the Old Treasury Building in State Circle or the Victualling Warehouse. A three-sight Ring Ticket is also offered.

The United States Naval Academy

The U.S. Naval Academy is our navy's undergraduate professional college. Their mission: "To prepare midshipmen [and women] morally, mentally, and physically to be professional officers in the naval service." Tourists—about a million a year—are greeted with a hospitable "Welcome Aboard" Monday to Saturday from 9 a.m. to 5 p.m. (or sunset, whichever is later), on Sunday from 11 a.m. to sunset. Park your car in the visitor lots adjacent to Halsey Field House and trot over to the **Visitors Information Center** in Rickets Hall at the end of King George St. (tel. 301/263-6933). Guided one-hour tours leave the center on the hour between 10 a.m. and 3 p.m. March 1 through the end of May, on the half hour between 9:30 a.m. and 4 p.m. June 1 through Labor Day weekend, and on the hour between 10 a.m. and 3 p.m. Labor Day weekend through Thanksgiving weekend. Their cost is $2 per adult, $1 for children under 12. The rest of the year there are tours by appointment only; a comprehensive walking tour brochure is, however, available. While waiting for your tour to depart you can watch a half-hour film on the life of a midshipman and examine a scale model of the entire 300-acre academy grounds. A souvenir shop and cafeteria are also on the premises.

Your tour begins, after a brief orientation prior to departure, at **Lejeune Hall,** a physical education center. Lejeune houses an immense swimming pool (all midshipmen have four years of swimming and must be able to dive from a 17-foot board for abandon-ship drill) and five wrestling rings with spectator seating for 620. On display here are all the sports trophies representing victories over Army.

En route to Bancroft Hall, you'll pass the **Captain's Homes** on Porter Road. Built in 1902, these lovely homes with screened and awninged patios house heads of academic divisions (senior officers all). Across the street is **Ward Hall,** a computer center that also houses coaches' offices; it's not open to the visiting public. You'll also note **Dahlgren Hall,** which contains the ice-skating rink; it too is closed to the public. And your guide is sure to point out **Tecumseh,** the bronze Indian known as the "God of Passing Grades." During exam weeks students toss pennies at Tecumseh; if the penny falls into his quiver, a passing grade is indicated. Tecumseh is actually a bronze replica of a wooden figurehead from the *Delaware III,* a 74-gun ship launched in Norfolk in 1820. Though students named him Tecumseh, he's really Tamanend, a Delaware chief.

Bancroft Hall is an imposing eight-winged building consisting of a Beaux Arts–style central portion built in 1901 and later additions. The world's largest dormitory, it accommodates 4,300 midshipmen under one roof and contains a dining hall that can feed them all at one sitting. The galley can cook 4,500 burgers, roast 240 turkeys, or prepare a ton of french fries at one go. A barber, shoe repair, and naval uniform shops, medical and dental facilities, a post office, and recreation areas are also to be found here. There are 4½ miles of corridor space. It's all very grand, with rotundas, columns, and expanses of marble. You can examine a typical dorm room—not at all bad as such accommodations go. Of course, the mids have to keep their rooms in apple-pie order.

Outside, a plaque in front of the stairs marks the spot where Commander Franklin Buchanan stood on October 10, 1845, when he officially opened the school. The building's name honors the secretary of the navy at that time, George Bancroft. To the left of the plaque is the 15th-century Japanese bell brought back from Okinawa by Commodore Perry. To the right of the plaque is the bell from the U.S.S. *Enterprise,* a World War II fighting ship. The four bronze guns flanking the steps were also Commodore Perry's.

Inside, a room called **Memorial Hall** is dedicated to all Annapolis graduates who lost their lives in conflicts from the Civil War through El Salvador. Historic paintings, flags, murals, and memorabilia are worth noting here; in an adjoining alcove are plaques erected in memory of deceased graduates by friends and relatives. Four exquisite Czechoslovakian hand-cut and polished lead-crystal chandeliers hang from the ceiling: the two largest are 16 feet tall, contain 20,000 crystals, and weigh over two tons apiece; the others are half that size. Commodore Oliver Hazard Perry's flag from the War of 1812, bearing the legend "Don't Give Up the Ship," is displayed. Memorial Hall is used as a sitting room for midshipmen in which they can entertain family and friends (bringing guests to rooms is *verboten).* Dances, ceremonies, and social functions also take place here. From the balcony there's a great view of the Chesapeake Bay and the eastern shore of Maryland.

On the way to the chapel you'll see the circular, colonnaded **bandstand** and **Herndon Monument,** a granite obelisk that is a memorial to Commander William L. Herndon. First to explore the Amazon to its headwaters, Herndon went down with his ship, the *Central America,* in a hurricane off Cape Hatteras in 1857 after first rescuing 152 passengers and crewmen. During Plebe Recognition Ceremony in May, the monument is greased, and plebes are required to climb it and remove a midshipman's cap that is glued to the top. According to tradition, the plebe removing the cap will become the class's first admiral.

Enormous anchors flank the steps of the **chapel;** they are from the armored cruiser *New York* that was in service during the Spanish-American War. The building itself was erected between 1904 and 1908. It is entered via massive bronze doors decorated with figures symbolizing Patriotism, Peace, Invention, and Prosperity, and bearing the motto "Non Sibi Sed Patriae" ("not for self but for country"). The tallest building in the yard, it measures 210 feet from floor to dome top, creating an impressive interior space. Many "mids" get married here after graduation. There are notable stained-glass windows, including an arch-framed Tiffany above the altar showing Christ walking on the waters. The *Commission Invisible* window depicts a recently graduated ensign reading his commission with the figure of Christ and an American flag in the background to remind future naval officers that they hold two commissions—one to God and one to country. A 5,000-pipe organ is located behind the right-hand pulpit. Suspended from the balcony is a 12-foot votive ship, a copy of a 15th-century Flemish merchant vessel; it symbolizes "man's faith in a supreme being who respects the vows and hears the prayers of those in peril on the sea." A candle burns in memory of prisoners of war and the missing in action in Vietnam. The chapel is nondenominational.

Under the church is the crypt of John Paul Jones, "Father of the American Navy," who first sailed from Scotland to Virginia as an adventurous lad of 12. In 1776 he received a captain's commission from the president of Congress. He fought during the American Revolution and in 1779 uttered the immortal words "I have not yet begun to fight." He died in Paris in 1792 and was buried there. In 1899 United States ambassador to France Gen. Horace Porter launched an intensive search for the grave of his naval hero. It took six years and cost him $35,000. An apartment building had gone up over the burial ground where Jones's grave was located. Pres. Theodore Roosevelt ordered a squadron of eight naval ships to convoy Jones's remains back to America in 1905. The crypt was completed and the coffin lowered into the black and white marble sarcophagus in 1913. The walls of the crypt are lined with important mementoes, paintings, and historic treasures such as Jones's career sword, a sword presented to him by Louis XVI, and naval decorations.

Last stop is the **Naval Academy Museum** in Preble Hall. Documenting early and modern naval history, its collections of over 50,000 items include: models of sailing ships from the mid-17th to the mid-19th centuries, graphic prints depicting major naval engagements from the 1500s to 1873, commemorative coin medals dating from 254 B.C. to 1936, historic American flags and captured foreign banners augmented by books on the subject, nautically themed oil paintings and sculptures, nautical artifacts, and weaponry. Your guide will leave you here to browse at leisure and find your way back on your own.

About the Academy: The U.S. Navy was created in 1794, and in 1800 Pres. John Adams proposed to Congress that a training school be started. In 1821 (things moved slowly in the early 19th century) such a school was established aboard the U.S. frigate *Guerrière,* docked in New York, a second school was formed the same year aboard the *Java* in Norfolk, and a third opened at the Boston Navy Yard in 1833. In 1839 Secretary of the Navy James Paulding opened a naval school in Philadelphia in what had previously been a home and hospital for navy and Marine Corps veterans. It was so successful that the New

York, Norfolk, and Boston schools were closed. Unfortunately, the building was limited in size, and in 1845 it was decided to move the operation to Fort Severn in Annapolis, the present site. The first class contained only 50 students and the faculty consisted of seven men. During the Civil War the property was used by Union forces as a camping ground and military hospital. Except for that interruption, it has served continuously as a naval academy.

Today's students, numbering about 4,500 (including several hundred women), engage in a four-year program. Nine months of the year are devoted to academic work toward a Bachelor of Science degree. There are over 18 possible majors, all of the serious genre, such as chemistry, naval architecture, mathematics, oceanography, and aerospace (this is not the kind of college where you can major in basket-weaving). And it's possible to proceed to advanced studies in areas like surface warfare training and nuclear power. Summer months are spent acquiring professional training in all aspects of navy and Marine Corps life. Athletics are stressed, with unexampled facilities including an indoor ice-skating rink (used for hockey, not for perfecting figure-eights), a golf course, a football stadium, an all-weather outdoor track, a baseball park, tennis and squash courts, and three indoor swimming pools—and that's not the half of it.

Upon graduation, five years on active duty as a commissioned officer are required.

The State House

The oldest state capitol building in continuous use in America, the State House, on State Circle (tel. 301/974-3400), also has the unique distinction of having served for ten months as the nation's first peacetime capitol. The governor's office is in the building, and his residence, **Government House,** is across the street, enabling him to walk to work.

The building is open daily from 9 a.m. to 5 p.m. (except Christmas, Thanksgiving, and New Year's), and free tours are offered. Visitors can enter into a small theater to view a ten-minute videotape about the history of Maryland, concentrating on the role of Annapolis and the State House. It's shown, on request, on the half hour between 9:30 a.m. and 4:30 p.m.

Tours (departing at 10 and 11 a.m., noon, and 2, 3, and 4 p.m.) begin in the lobby and proceed to the **Old Senate Chamber.** In this room Gen. George Washington resigned his commission as commander-in-chief of the Continental Army on December 23, 1783. A bronze plaque marks the spot where he stood to deliver his farewell speech. On January 14, 1784, the Treaty of Paris officially ending the Revolutionary War (it having pleased both parties "to forget all past Misunderstandings and Difficulties that have unhappily interrupted the good Correspondence and Friendship which they mutually wish to restore") was ratified in this same room. And on May 7, 1784, Thomas Jefferson was here appointed our first minister plenipotentiary (ambassador) to all of Europe. Eight pieces of the original furniture remain, and a Charles Willson Peale painting, *Washington at Yorktown,* hangs over the fireplace. Above the room is a Ladies Gallery bordered with handcarved tobacco-leaf motif. Like Virginia, Maryland's early economy revolved around tobacco.)

The Maryland General Assembly meets for 90 days every winter in the **House of Delegates.** The larger of the two legislative chambers, the House has 141 members. There's an electronic voting board connected to buttons on each desk which register "yea" and "nay" votes. Note the Tiffany skylight above, one of several Tiffany windows in the building.

The **New Senate Chamber** also meets every winter for 90 days. The walls are hung with paintings of Maryland's four signers of the Declaration of Independence. This room also boasts an electronic voting board and a Tiffany skylight.

The State House is easy to find: it's the highest point in Annapolis.

The Hammond-Harwood House

Just off State Circle at 19 Maryland Ave., the Hammond-Harwood House (tel. 301/269-1714) was built in 1774 by 26-year-old Matthias Hammond as a residence for his future bride. A staunch patriot and colleague of Declaration of Independence signers William Paca and Charles Carroll, Hammond published his opinions in the *Maryland Gazette* and served as quarter-master of the county militia. As legend has it, his fiancée became disenchanted with him—some say she was put off by his obsession with details of design—and broke the engagement. In 1776 the embittered Hammond resigned his elected office, and abandoning future political ambitions, retired to the country, leaving his "elegant and commodious dwelling" unoccupied for eight years. He died unmarried at the age of 38 in 1786.

Though Hammond's interest in the house flagged, it was not before he had managed beforehand to underwrite one of America's greatest examples of Georgian architecture. To create his mansion he had hired famed architect William Buckland, who already had Gunston Hall to his credit by 1774. The house Buckland built is in the Palladian tradition, with a main house and two flanking wings connected by enclosed passages called "hyphens." The beautifully carved front door—a prelude to the elaborate interior—is framed by columns and topped with an exquisite banded-leaf frieze and pediment. Two 18th-century visitors, Thomas Jefferson and Charles Willson Peale, were so impressed with the mansion's understated dignity and pure proportions that they included sketches of it in their diaries.

Over the years the house passed through a series of renters and owners. At one time, just before the Civil War, William Harwood, great-grandson of William Buckland, lived here. The last occupant was Harwood's youngest daughter, Hester Ann, a spinster who became a recluse as the years went by. She died in 1924 leaving no will (she had made and destroyed many), and in 1925 the house and its contents were put up for public auction. The furnishings were sold, and the house was purchased by St. John's College which used it as a museum of decorative arts. The depression forced the college to close the museum, and for five years the house stood empty. Finally, in 1940 a nonprofit organization called the Hammond-Harwood House Association bought the landmark property. They have kept it open to visitors ever since.

Today the rooms are arranged and furnished to reflect Hammond's era, including five signed pieces by famed cabinetmaker John Shaw and many items recovered from the 1925 auction. You can peruse them on 45-minute tours given throughout the day Tuesday to Saturday from 10 a.m. to 5 p.m. and on Sundays from 2 to 5 p.m. April 1 through October 31; the rest of the year from 10 a.m. to 4 p.m. Tuesday to Saturday and 1 to 4 p.m. on Sunday. Adults pay $3; students 6 to 18, $2; under, 6 free.

The first room you'll see is the reception hall, in its compact size a departure from traditional Georgian architecture, though it does have the usual symmetry and balance of that school. The large brass lock on the front door is the original, as are many of the interior locks and door handles. Furnishings include one of the oldest objects in the house, a birdcage clock dating to about 1660 (still in working condition). The Maryland hunt board is one of the Shaw pieces; upon it is an unusual piece of Chinese export porcelain decorated with scenes copied by Chinese artists from English 18th-century hunting prints.

The gentleman's library (designed as a retreat for the gentleman of the house) contains only about 30 books, the typical number for this time. The card table, secretary, and bookcases are Shaw pieces, and there are portraits by both Charles Willson Peale and his son, Rembrandt, the latter of George Washington on horseback.

Directly across is the ladies parlor with its dainty moldings and carvings, lacy cornice, and delicate Hepplewhite and Federal furnishings. It is arranged for tea, with a fragile china porcelain service on the table.

The dining room (off the reception hall) was the focal point of the house. The carved-wood ornaments and plaster cornice of this exquisite room are still as crisp and clear as when first created. Griffin heads and leafy arabesques adorn the doors, windows, and fireplace. The room contains some Shaw pieces and portraits by Charles Willson Peale of William Buckland, Buckland's daughter, Sarah (holding her daughter Anne), and of two other children. Off the dining room is the withdrawing room, where the women went after dinner, leaving the men to their pipes and port.

The kitchen, here part of the house (most 18th-century kitchens were outbuildings), is protected from fire by a brick floor and a slate floor in the adjoining hyphen. As an extra precaution rock salt was always kept by the immense fireplace. It is furnished and equipped to represent a mansion kitchen of the period.

On the landing is a Shaw musical clock that can play eight tunes. An English Chippendale gaming table and chairs grace the game room. While music and dancing entertained guests in another room, quiet games of whist, loo (an 18th-century forerunner of poker), and chess might have taken place here. You'll also see the bedrooms, boudoir, and drawing room.

The Chase-Lloyd House

Just across the street from the above, at 22 Maryland Ave., is the Chase Lloyd House (tel. 301/263-2723), named for its two earliest and very distinguished owners, Samuel Chase and Edward Lloyd.

In 1769 Chase—a signer of the Declaration of Independence and later a Supreme Court justice—embarked on building a house "second only to that of Charles Carroll of Carrollton," one of the wealthiest men in the country. At the time he was 28 and married to Ann Baldwin. Unfortunately, his dreams were larger than his purse, and in 1771 Edward Lloyd IV, an extremely affluent planter (known as "Edward the Magnificent"), purchased the uncompleted mansion. Lloyd engaged William Buckland to finish the job and gave him a free hand. The Lloyd family occupied the house through 1846, by which time their fortunes were on the wane. Hester Ann Chase, a direct descendant of Samuel Chase, then bought the mansion for $5,000 and lived here until she died in 1875. It passed on to her niece, Hester Ann Chase Ridout, a widow who died in 1886 and bequeathed the property as a home for ". . . aged and infirm women where they may find a retreat from the vicissitudes of life." It still serves that purpose today, and eight lucky women have the privilege of passing their twilight years in this sumpⁿ ous setting. Because of this usage, the house is only open in a limited way to the publⅬ Twenty-minute guided tours of a few downstairs rooms are given between 2 and 4 p n. Tuesday to Saturday. Admission is $1 for adults, free for children under 6.

Most notable features are the elegant entrance hallway extending 45 feet through the entire house and the cantilevere stairway, framed by Ionic columns and leading to the great Palladian window.

In the drawing room, the 200-year-old molded plaster ceiling is original, and the marble mantel is adorned with a carved scene depicting Shakespeare being presented with the key to wisdom by a goddess.

A Charles Willson Peale portrait graces the dining room; on the opposite wall is a portrait in antique gilt frame of Mary Tayloe Lloyd Key, the youngest Lloyd daughter, who married Francis Scott Key in this house in 1802.

Paca House

Another great Annapolis Georgian mansion was the home of the governor and signer of the Declaration of Independence, William Paca, at 186 Prince George St., between Maryland Ave. and East St. (tel. 301/263-5553). Built between 1763 and 1765, Paca House was for 59 years absorbed into a hotel called Carvel Hall. In 1965 the hotel was demolished and preservationists fought successfully to save the remains of Paca House from wreckage.

Today the house is fully restored to its 18th-century appearance and is used as a guest house for distinguished foreign visitors. Over 80% of the original woodwork is intact. It is open to tourists Tuesday to Saturday from 10 a.m. to 4 p.m., on Sunday from noon to 4 p.m.; the gardens are open Monday to Saturday 10 a.m. to 4 p.m., noon to 4 p.m. on Sunday (till 5 p.m. on Sundays May to October). Forty-minute house tours are given throughout the day. Admission is $3 for adults, $2 for students, free for children under 6; if you'd like to see the gardens as well, it costs another $1 for adults, 75¢ for students.

The informal and main parlors are painted in a rather intense shade of Prussian blue favored by Paca. The latter is set up for a card game. In the hall is an engraving that was presented by Congress to signers of the Declaration of Independence. The enclosed porch is an unusual Elizabethan feature not usually found in Georgian homes. It leads to the typically 18th-century stone-and-brick-walled garden with its terraces, waterways, Chinese-style Chippendale bridge, and intricate parterres. Restored based on architectural studies, historical garden records, and a Charles Willson Peale portrait of Paca in his garden, it contains a charming two-story pavilion and cold bath house. There's also a small museum dealing with the archaeological excavations and reconstruction of the house. And a wilderness garden features wildflowers of the 18th century. The tour includes the upstairs sitting room (wherein is a John Shaw linen press, one of several Shaw pieces displayed in the house), the upstairs passage, and bedchambers.

The Victualling Warehouse

An 18th-century building housing an Annapolis Colonial maritime history museum, the Victualling Warehouse, 77 Main St. at Compromise St. (tel. 301/268-5576), was confiscated from its British Loyalist owner during the Revolution and used to store military supplies and provisions. Open daily from 11 a.m. to 4:30 p.m., it today houses exhibits on ship chandlery, sailmaking, shipbuilding, and the iron industry. Other exhibits include a model of Annapolis in the mid-18th century constructed after careful research. Admission is 50¢ for adults, 25¢ for children 6 to 18 (under 6, free). It's one of three State Historic Buildings in town, the others being the **Barracks,** at 43 Pinkney St. (quarters for Revolutionary soldiers which are restored to show the primitive lifestyle they endured), and the **Tobacco Prise House** at 4 Pinkney St.—a typical 18th-century warehouse containing an exhibit of implements used in Maryland's tobacco trade. Both of the latter are open weekends only from 11 a.m. to 4:30 p.m. mid-April to mid-October only.

St. Anne's Church

The first church constructed on this site at Church Circle was the State Church of England in the late 1600s. Both William Paca and Samuel Chase were vestrymen. The current St. Anne's parish (tel. 301/267-9333) still uses a silver Communion service that was a gift from King William III. The third structure built on the site (in 1858–1859), it contains an altar screen made in Oberammergau in the 1920s and an 1893 Tiffany window of St. Anne and the Virgin. In the entryway you'll find a self-guided tour leaflet. The church is open daily from 7 a.m. to 6 p.m. (tours are given by appointment). Sunday services are held at 7:30, 8:45, and 11:15 a.m., in summer at 7:30 and 10 a.m.

Harbor and Bay Cruises

Annapolis's restored historic waterfront area around City Dock is the starting point for Chesapeake Bay cruises offered by **Chesapeake Marine Tours,** Slip 20 (tel. 301/268-7600 or, from D.C., 202/261-2719). A fully narrated 1½-hour scenic bay cruise aboard the 149-passenger *Rebecca Forbush*—an authentic Chesapeake oyster-buy boat—departs Wednesday to Sunday, weather permitting, from mid-May to Labor Day at 1:30 and 3:30 p.m. Sights along the way include the United States Naval Academy, beautiful waterfront homes on the Severn River, Greenbury Point Radio Towers (the U.S. Navy's primary communication network), the Thomas Point Lighthouse (a national historic landmark), the Eastern Shore country described by James Michener in his novel *Chesapeake,* bayfront homes and waterfront at Bay Ridge and Tolly Point, Back Creek (home of many of Annapolis's sailing fleets), and the Annapolis skyline. There's an airy upper deck and an enclosed lower deck with large windows offering panoramic views. Snacks and beverages are served on board. Adults pay $7 and children 2 to 12 pay $4. There are other tours offered as well, ranging from a 40-minute harbor tour to a seven-hour "Day on the Bay" that includes a three-hour visit to the quaint town of St. Michaels.

The Shiplap House

Dating to 1713, this one-time colonial inn at 18 Pinkney St. is the second-oldest surviving building in Annapolis. It was built by a man named Benjamin Tasker and became known as the Shiplap House because of the shiplaps used in its exterior siding. Different owners ran it as an inn, lived here, or used it as a tavern through 1844 when the heirs of Benjamin Tasker regained the property. In 1877 it was sold to Frank B. Mayer, a noted Maryland artist. By 1920 it was a multi-family tenement. Historic Annapolis purchased the structure in 1957, along with two adjoining parcels of land on either side that had belonged to the original site. It is now being restored and will open as a sightseeing attraction sometime after this book goes to press. The first floor will be a museum focusing on 18th-century tavern life. Contact the Visitor Center for details.

The Banneker-Douglass Museum

Housed in the former Victorian-Gothic Mount Moriah African Methodist Episcopal Church, one-time home of a free black congregation that gained its charter in 1803, the Banneker-Douglass Museum, 84 Franklin St., between Church Circle and Cathedral St. (tel. 301/269-2894), is named for two eminent black Marylanders. Frederick Douglass (1817–1895) was a famed abolitionist, orator, and editor of his own newspaper, *The North Star.* (Lincoln called him "the most meritorious person I have ever met.") Benjamin Banneker (1731–1806) was among the team of surveyors who laid out the city of Washington, D.C. You'll see a letter from Banneker to Thomas Jefferson about the injustices of slavery on display here. The museum presents cultural exhibits on the history and contributions of Afro-Americans to Maryland and the nation, as well as occasional African themes such as the recent "Design at the Center of Life—Objects of Use in Everyday African Life." An exhibit that will be on during most of the course of this book is "In Search of Benjamin Banneker," a show of artifacts from archaeological digs at his home site which will also shed light on his life and his role in America's history. A permanent exhibit on the third level, Herbert M. Frisby Hall, documents the adventures of the second black man to go to the North Pole. Other permanent features are six oil portraits by New York artist Hughie Lee Smith of abolitionist Harriet Tubman, Banneker, Douglass, Carl Murphy (originator of the *Afro-American* newspaper), civil rights activist Lily Carroll Jackson, and Supreme Court Justice Thurgood Marshall. A gift shop on the premises features Afro-American art, posters, and crafts; African art objects; and books on Afro-American and African themes. Open weekdays from 10 a.m. to 3 p.m., Saturday noon to 4 p.m. Admission is free.

Guided Tours

Historic Annapolis, Inc., a nonprofit organization founded in 1952 to protect the town's historic landmarks from demolition and incompatible redevelopment, offers walking tours departing from their headquarters in the Old Treasury Building on State Circle (tel. 301/267-8149). Their guides are especially knowledgeable. A 1½-hour basic tour of Annapolis landmarks, including the State House, William Paca Garden, the Naval Academy Chapel, and St. John's College, costs $4.50 for adults, $2.50 for students ages 6 to 18 (under 6, free). There are many other options, including custom-tailored tours focusing on your special interests. Some are specially geared toward young children; they get to examine 18th-century artifacts such as a tricorn hat and a chamber stick. The kids will enjoy themselves, and while they're at it you'll have time to explore Annapolis sights that won't hold their interest. Call or come in to the office to discuss the wide-ranging offerings of Historic Annapolis.

An extensive itinerary of tours is also offered by **Three Centuries Tours of Annapolis** (tel. 301/263-5401). Extremely well-informed guides in Colonial attire lead two-hour Early Bird walking tours departing from the Hilton Inn lobby daily at 9:30 a.m. April 1 through October 31; the same route is followed on the Summer Stroll, departing from the Visitor Center at City Dock at 1:30 p.m. daily May 1 through the end of September. The price is $4 for adults, $2.25 for children under 18. The two-hour Colonial Life tour, designed for young people, focuses on 18th-century customs. Children get an opportunity to examine a brick of tea, a tavern pipe, a horn book, quill pen, and other colonial items. The cost is $2.25. There are several other options, including Chesapeake Bay cruises.

ANNUAL EVENTS: Annapolis is the scene of many and varied seasonal happenings the year round. Check at the Visitor Information Center for full details of events during your visit. Of special note are the following:

The annual **Annapolis Heritage Antiques Show** each January brings dealers in period furniture, marine, and American country antiques from throughout the United States.

All segments of Maryland's maritime industry offer exhibits at Sandy Point State Park in early April at the **Marine Trades Exposition.** April also brings the **Annapolis Spring Festival** (late in the month), with parades, crafts demonstrations, and entertainment.

Six days of parades, athletic events, and colorful ceremonies lead up to the **U.S. Naval Academy Commissioning Week,** a graduation celebration the last week in May. Call 301/267-2291 for details.

On a Thursday late in May, **Roses and May Flowers Day** is celebrated at William Paca Gardens (tel. 301/267-8149). Trees are blossoming, and flowers are abloom in parterres and pots. Roses and lilies are on special display, rosepetal punch is served, and a box lunch can be reserved in advance by calling 301/267-6656. There are also talks about 18th-century gardens, and usually, hard-to-find rose plants are sold.

A major mid-June event is the **Annapolis Arts Festival at City Dock,** with live entertainment (bands, clowns, puppets, magic, and bluegrass music), a children's tent, and an indoor/outdoor show of art and crafts. Call 301/267-7922 for details. Admission is charged.

The second weekend in September is highlighted by the **Maryland Seafood Festival,** at Sandy Point State Park on the Chesapeake Bay—great seafood eats and entertainment.

The **U.S. Sailboat and Power Boat Shows** at City Dock in mid-October are the world's largest in-the-water boat shows.

For **Heritage Weekend** a special architectural walking tour is offered on a Saturday and Sunday in late October by Historic Annapolis. There are refreshments, and admission is charged. Call 301/267-8149 for details.

Skipjack oyster fleet races and maritime exhibits are among **Chesapeake Appreciation Days'** fun happenings at Sandy Point State Park the last weekend in October.

Christmas in Annapolis is a month-long celebration each December with dozens of events and other manifestations—a Christmas parade up Main Street, the hanging of wreaths on State Circle lamp posts, the Great Illumination (lighting of the traditional Christmas tree at City Dock, with choral groups singing and Santa handing out candy to children), the lighting of the Christmas trees at the State House and the Governor's Mansion, hunt board buffets, candlelight tours of the State House, community caroling, candlelight pub crawls, traditional Christmas dinners, and much more. Both the Paca and Hammond-Harwood Houses are specially decorated and open to the public for tours and 18th-century food and music.

WHERE TO STAY: Keep in mind that hotel prices sometimes rise beyond what I've quoted here during special events. Bed-and-breakfast accommodations are a viable option in Annapolis.

A particularly lovely choice, which couldn't be more central, is the **Prince George Inn,** 232 Prince George St. (between Maryland and College Aves.), Annapolis, MD 21401 (tel. 301/263-6418). Its four air-conditioned rooms are housed in a century-old Victorian town house and furnished appropriately in period pieces. They're exquisite! Owners Norma and Bill Grovermann have chosen beautiful wallpapers, bedspreads, and curtain fabrics, and decorated each room individually in superb taste. You might draw a turn-of-the-century armoire or bureau, an old wooden traveler's trunk, white wicker furnishings, a brass or Victorian trundle bed, an Oriental rug, or a bay window with leaded glass panel. Both rooms and public areas are further adorned with plants, antiques, and artworks.

You can plan the day's itinerary, use the phone, watch the small TV, or read before the fireplace in Norma's plushly furnished parlor, its sienna walls hung with large gilt-framed mirrors and nautical-themed paintings. Breakfast is served on a glassed-in sun porch, a wicker-furnished screened porch overlooking the garden, or, weather permitting, an outdoor brick terrace. It's a buffet, with a choice of five juices, dry cereal, croissants, fresh-baked muffins, fresh fruit, jams and butter, with tea or coffee. The inn rooms can accommodate only two persons in each, and children under 12 are not accepted. Baths—and very luxurious baths they are, especially the second-floor's deep black tub with gold-plated fixtures—are shared. Rates are $40 single, $50 double. Since Norma runs Three Centuries Tours (details above) she is extremely knowledgeable about local attractions. No credit cards.

A Washington-based firm (see Chapter II for details) called **Sweet Dreams & Toast, Inc.,** P.O. Box 4835–0035, Washington, DC 20008 (tel. 202/483-9191), lists a number of homes in Annapolis. For the best rates and the most choices, contact them as far in advance as possible. All of their listed homes are carefully checked out for comfort, cleanliness, and hospitality.

A similar firm with B&B guest accommodations in Annapolis homes, and even aboard yachts, is **The Traveller in Maryland,** P.O. Box 2277, Annapolis, MD 21401 (tel. 202/261-2233; they have a Washington-based phone number). Room rates, once again including continental breakfast (southern hospitality being what it is, this is sometimes fairly elaborate), range from $40 to $55 single, $45 to $65 double. They have listings throughout Maryland.

Check with the **Visitor Information Center** for additional B&B options; some folks list with them exclusively.

Mrs. George F. Nesbitt rents four charming rooms at a guesthouse called **The Gables,** 1422 West St. (at South Southwood Ave., Annapolis, MD 21401 (tel. 301/263-2010). They're all cozily homey with wall-to-wall carpeting, curtained windows, frilly little lamps, maple furnishings, framed prints on the walls, and stocked magazine racks. The pale-blue room has an Early American chair and an oak dresser; the pink room, a white wicker chair; the green room, an antique wicker chair; the yellow room, a rocking chair. The rate is just $30 to $35, single or double. Each two rooms share a bath. The location, by the way, is about 14 blocks from Church Circle.

There's a moderately priced **Holiday Inn** in town at 210 Holiday Court, off Riva Rd., Annapolis, MD 21401 (tel. 301/224-3150 or toll free 800/HOLIDAY), a tad above the usual budget for this book but a worthy splurge if you're looking for a bit of solid comfort. Its 218 rooms are all being redecorated at this writing, so by the time you arrive everything—carpets, drapes, bedspreads, furnishings, and paint—will be sparkling and new. The hotel is entered via a pleasant terracotta-floored lobby, off of which are a gift shop, a restaurant called Maryland Way (it highlights regional dishes like crabcakes and fried oysters) and an adjoining lounge. Rooms here offer all the requisite amenities—color TVs (with cable stations, a free movie station, and a pay movie station), direct-dial phones, in-room coffee makers, and clock radios. On the premises is an exercise court and a Junior Olympic-size pool (great for serious swimmers) with an attractive sundeck and picnic area. Guests also have complimentary use of a nearby health club with full workout facilities. A washer/dryer is another convenience. At the front desk you can obtain a hair dryer, iron, or any sundries you might have neglected to pack—razors, toothpaste, deodorant, shaving cream, etc. There's no charge. And to further cosset guests, the management throws cocktail parties with complimentary drinks and hot and cold hors d'oeuvres Monday through Thursday nights. Rates are $58 to $62 single, $66 to $70 double, the higher end of the scale for king rooms. An extra person pays $5; children 19 and under stay free.

What used to be a self-styled French country inn has now become **Econo Lodge Annapolis** at 2451 Riva Rd., just off West St., Annapolis, MD 21401 (tel. 301/224-4317 or toll free 800/446-6900). Thus the exterior has more quaint charm than any other branch of this budget chain. Accommodations are housed in a white stucco building with crossbeams and barnwood-shuttered windows. And the lobby has a terracotta floor and peaked beamed ceiling. The new owners have enhanced this entry space with lots of plants; it's used to set up a continental breakfast that is included in rates here. The 168 rooms (nine are Jacuzzi suites) have been recently redecorated in typical Econo Lodge, not country French, style. They have mauve carpeting, oak-look furnishings, and color-coordinated drapes and bedspreads, and they're equipped with all the expected amenities. On the first floor are food and sundry vending machines and a few video games. However, the former are hardly necessary. Dozens of restaurants and shops—including such biggies as Hecht's, Garfinkels, K-Mart, J.C. Penney's, and Sears—are within walking distance. The rates: $49 for one person in a one-bedded room, $53 for two in a one-bedded room, $55 for two people in a two-bedded room. An extra person pays $5; children under 18 stay free. Parking is free.

A second **Econo Lodge** is located at Revell Hwy. (a half mile west of Bay Bridge on Route 50/301), Annapolis, MD 21401 (tel. 301/974-4440 or toll free 800/446-6900). Six miles from downtown Annapolis (no problem if you've got a car), this is a fairly new property with 74 rooms, all identically decorated in rose/mauve color schemes with floral-design bedspreads and one painted brick wall. All amenities are, of course, offered: color TV, air conditioning, direct-dial phone, and tub/shower bath; parking is free, and there are many restaurants nearby.

WHERE TO EAT: Like all towns with a large collegiate population, Annapolis has many inexpensive eateries.

For over a decade locals have been flocking to the **Olde Towne Seafood Shoppe,** 105 Main St., just off Green St. (tel. 301/268-8703). The coffeeshop decor is nothing to rave about—it's sunny and pleasant with hanging plants and brass ship-lantern-style lighting fixtures adding a little charm, but what draws them in is the scrumptious seafood. Genial owner Robert Gates is an avid fisherman who personally catches much of what he serves—the rest is bought fresh from local fisherfolk. Everything is great, but the very best items are Gates's secret recipes: herbed broiled scallops or broiled scallops and crabmeat ($9.99 for either, including soup and a salad). A hearty bowl of homemade clam chowder is $2.19; fish and chips, with slaw, $3.59; stuffed softshell crabs with fries and slaw, $6. Several sandwiches are also offered in the $2.70 to $4.50 range, among them crabcake, softshell crab, fish, and clam. Wine and beer are available. The only dessert is apple fritters.

The Olde Towne is a real find that just happens to be located in the heart of the tourist district right by City Dock. If the weather is nice, take your meal out and have a picnic overlooking the water.

Open daily from 11 a.m. to 8 p.m. No credit cards.

Speaking of picnics, another City Dock establishment, **The Market House,** offers an immense variety of fixings. A historic building, it dates to an 1858 replacement of an earlier 1788 market at this location. Inside are about ten retail operations, including a fish market (raw oysters, clams, and mussels; crab sandwiches, fish 'n chips, fat fries, etc., all in the $3 to $5 range). The Cheese Connection carries about 100 varieties of *fromage* as well as pâtés. And you can also get fresh produce, oven-fresh bakery goods, dairy, burgers, subs, ice cream, burritos, kielbasa, egg rolls, gyros, fried chicken, roasted nuts, and carob trail mix—among other things. Something for everyone here.

Open on Monday, Wednesday, and Thursday from 9 a.m. to 6 p.m., on Friday and Saturday to 7:30 p.m., on Sunday from 10 a.m. to 7 p.m.; October through April a few stalls (including the fish market) are open on Tuesday from 9 a.m. to 6 p.m.

Chick and Ruth's Delly, 165 Main St. near Conduit St. (tel. 301/269-6737), is a mom-and-pop operation started in 1965 by Chick and Ruth Levitt. New

York style, it features fresh-baked rye, cream soda, fresh bagels, and Hebrew National products. The Levitt kids grew up waiting tables here, and son Ted, at 9 the youngest counterman on record, today holds an important position with the family firm. He owns it! And Ted tells me he's grooming his son, Scott Paul, age 6, to carry on the Delly dynasty. The decor is vintage deli—bright orange and yellow, walls lined with photos and caricatures of well-known customers (like George McGovern). The wood-bladed fans overhead have lighting fixtures turned on by pull strings anchored with bagels. And one wall contains an immense map of the world.

At breakfast a bagel and cream cheese is $1.05, a cheese omelet with hash browns and toast runs $2.50, an "eggel" (egg on a bagel) is $1.10, and fresh doughnuts (quite a variety) are 35¢ apiece. Double-sized lunch sandwich specials in the $2 to $5 range are politically monikered: the Golda Meir is lox and cream cheese on a bagel with onion and tomato; the V.P. Bush is ham, turkey, and bacon on rye; and the Pres. Reagan is a six-ounce steak with cheese and onions on a hard roll. Dinner specials are a great buy: half a fried chicken with two vegetables and bread and butter costs $4.95; same price for meat loaf or an eight-ounce T-bone steak. For dessert try a hot-fudge sundae or banana split. Wine and beer are available.

Chick and Ruth's is open 24 hours a day, seven days a week. No credit cards.

Fuddruckers, in the Annapolis Mall Restaurant Park, 175 Jennifer Rd., off West St. (tel. 301/266-8030), is part of a San Antonio, Texas-based budget chain that I'm happy to see spreading to other parts of the country. All branches have spacious, warehouse-like interiors in which items used in meal preparation make up the bulk of the decor. There are sacks of onions, potatoes, and flour; sides of beef, cartons of ketchup and cheese; and jars of pickles stacked up here and there in vast quantities. What you see is what you get. The floor is brown and white checkerboard tile, the walls hung à la Texas honky-tonk, with neon signs. In Texas, however, these signs would advertise brands of beer, but in straight-laced Maryland, that's illegal, so they advertise products like French's mustard and Lipton tea. It all makes for a very comfortable setting, especially the enclosed café area and outdoor seating under umbrella tables. Best of all, Fuddruckers makes great burgers, using quality meat, fresh ground on the premises.

Upon entering you'll get in a cafeteria line to purchase such items as a half-pound burger ($3.65), a one/third-pound burger ($2.95), a steak ($5.25) or a hot dog ($2.50). Accompanying orders of fresh-cut Fudd spuds (french fries), grilled onions, chili, and/or barbecued beans are highly recommended. Then comes the fun part. Having procured the basics, you now proceed to add the frills—at a buffet table laden with shredded lettuce, sliced tomatoes, onions, pickles, relish, jalapeños, salsa, Heinz ketchup, Hellman's mayonnaise, mustard, barbecue sauce, sauerkraut, and big vats of melted cheese, with and without jalapeños. At last, a burger with all the toppings you could want! For dessert there are huge, fresh-from-the-oven brownies, à la mode if you so desire, and your beverage choices include beer, wine, and malteds. You'll never find a better place for family dining.

In summer, Fuddrucker's is open Sunday to Thursday 11 a.m. to 11 p.m., Friday and Saturday until midnight. Closing hours are an hour earlier across the board the rest of the year.

For quick and delicious breakfasts, a good bet is the **Dockside Boulangerie,** 18 Market Space (tel. 301/268-1115), a branch of a well-established (in Washington and elsewhere) French chain called Vie de France. A tiny eatery with about a half-dozen tables, it serves up fresh-baked croissants—fruit, plain, almond, chocolate, cheese, etc.—for breakfast (from 75¢ to $2, the latter filled with ham and cheese). Danish too. Later in the day there are *les sandwiches* on croissant or oven-fresh french bread filled with turkey and cheese, tuna, shrimp salad, roast beef, etc., plus soups and frozen yogurt. It's all affordable.

Open 6:30 a.m. to 8 p.m. seven days a week, till 10 p.m. Friday and Saturday June 1 to November.

One of the most elegant dining spots in town is **Ristorante Remo,** 186 Main St. (tel. 301/263-0949). Its pale pink stucco walls are hung with charming gilt-framed still life paintings and Raoul Dufy prints; soft lighting emanates from shell-shaped sconces; wine racks are displayed; and tables are exquisitely appointed with Villeroy & Boch china. Big bouquets of roses up front and a few roses on each table further enhance the luxe ambience. And for the most part, the prices on the menu—especially at dinner when entrees are in the $12 to $21 bracket—reflect the high-toned surroundings. However . . . at lunch weekdays San Remo offers a miraculously low-priced buffet from 11:30 a.m. to 2:30 p.m., which allows paupers to dine like princes for just $5.95. That price entitles you to all you can eat from a table laden with luscious dishes—hot veal and chicken entrees, minestrone soup, fresh vegetables, salami, cheeses, artichokes, tomato salad, pasta salad, ratatouille, linguine with red clam sauce, scallops in cream sauce, sausage and peppers, beef with vegetables, bread and butter, and, for dessert, fresh fruits with whipped cream. Or you could splurge and order from the tempting dessert display table ($3.95), perhaps a chocolate roulade or raspberry tart with whipped cream. At Sunday brunch an even more elaborate buffet is served from 10 a.m. to 2 p.m. for just $9.95.

Mum's, 136 Dock St., between Craig and Randall Sts. (tel. 301/263-3353) for many years looked like a California fern bar. But a recent renovation has changed its look to sleek art deco, with lots of neon including a kitschy tableau of King Kong climbing you-know-what. The new furnishings are rust and green banquettes lined with pots of (what else?) mums. As for the rest, floors are terracotta, walls are stone, and there are rough-hewn beams overhead. The upstairs front room overlooks the waterfront; it's separated by a dance floor from the skylit back room. The ambience is most congenial.

Almost everything on the menu is in the $4 to $6.25 range, including quiche, fish and chips, a crabcake sandwich served with potato skins and slaw, burgers, omelets, pasta salad, and a hot pastrami sandwich. For dessert there are pies—pecan, Oreo fudge ice cream, key lime, and chocolate mousse. Specialty drinks like a banana Mum—made with fresh bananas, cream, and rum—are also featured.

Open Monday to Friday 11 a.m. to 2 a.m., Saturday 8 a.m. to 2 a.m., Sunday 10 a.m. to 2 a.m.

One of my favorite Annapolis restaurants is the extremely charming **Crate Café,** 49 West St., between Church Circle and Cathedral St. (tel. 301/268-3600). For openers, its very walls are painted in shades called watermelon ice (the palest of pinks) and hung with beautiful framed art and botanical prints. Furnishings and lighting fixtures are rattan, and fresh flowers grace every pink-clothed table. The back room has exposed brick walls and homey curtained windows. Background music is light jazz, and the entire scene is permeated by sunlight in which many plants thrive. There are a handful of café tables out back.

The fare is healthful but not of the Adele Davis orthodox variety. For $5.60 you can create your own salad or sandwich, selecting all you want from nine varieties of breads, 16 salad fixings (mushrooms, sprouts, celery, carrots, crumbled bacon, etc.), seven meats, eight cheeses, and a dozen homemade dressings. À la carte, sandwiches run the gamut from hot roast beef au jus on fresh-baked roll ($5.25) to whole-wheat pita packed with sprouts, Jarlsberg cheese, tomato, slivered almonds, artichoke hearts, and tarragon mayonnaise ($4.95). About eight fresh-baked desserts (sumptuous delights all) are offered daily—chocolate cream pie, banana-walnut cake, etc. A glass of wine with your meal is $2.25.

The Crate Café is open weekdays from 8 a.m. (a good place for your morning croissant and coffee) to 9 p.m., on Saturday from 11 a.m. to 9 p.m., on Sunday for champagne brunch—sometimes with live chamber music—from 11 a.m. to 3 p.m.

One last dining choice is **Dimitri's,** 164 Main St. (tel. 301/269-5666). Just across the street from the above-mentioned Chick and Ruth's, it too is a mom-and-pop operation run by Nicholas and Christine Fotos along with their two sons and a daughter. The decor is pleasant—terracotta floors, exposed brick walls with barnwood wainscotting, *Casablanca* fans suspended from a cream-colored pressed-tin ceiling, and Breuer chairs at matte-topped Formica tables. And the fare is fresh, nutritious and health conscious. At breakfast, for instance, you can get a huge fresh-fruit plate of whatever is in season, with a scoop of cottage cheese, for $3.25; on my last visit it was heaped with strawberries, pineapple, grapefruit, and melon wedges. Of course, you can also get the usual bacon-and-eggs breakfasts here, dry cereal, croissants (from Vie de France), and danish, but your orange juice is fresh squeezed, coffee is fresh-ground vintage Colombian, your toast can be seven-grain bread, and if you prefer tea to coffee, you might select Earl Grey, English breakfast, or country apple, among others. At lunch try a sandwich of avocado, sprouts, cream cheese, and lemon-oil dressing on seven-grain bread. If that's too California for you, sandwich options also include roast beef and turkey breast, both of which meats are cooked fresh on the premises. There are salads too, and Greek specialties like spanakopita—spinach, feta cheese, and dill wrapped in phyllo—served with a salad. All the above-listed items are under $5. Try Christine's homemade baklava for dessert. Open weekdays from 7 a.m. to 3 p.m., on weekends till 4 p.m. At weekday lunches, there's cafeteria service only; waiter service is offered the rest of the time. No credit cards.

For drinks only, head over to the **Afterdeck** behind the Hilton at 80 Compromise St., between St. Mary's and Newman Sts. (tel. 301/268-7555). An outdoor waterside café, it offers the best bay views in town, and a mirrored wall further enhances the marine ambience. You can sit here sipping daiquiris and piña coladas at Perrier umbrella tables, and gaze out at the boats and ducks in the marina. Frequent entertainment is provided—usually piano or guitar music. Many yachts pull in here—about half the clientele consists of boat owners. At night the cherry trees on the Afterdeck are lit by tiny lights. This is one of the most relaxing spots in town. Open daily from noon to 1 a.m. spring through fall, weather permitting.

NIGHTTIME MISCELLANY: In addition to some above-mentioned live-music spots in restaurants, Annapolis nightlife offers a few other notable spots.

The **King of France Tavern,** in the historic Maryland Inn, Church Circle at the top of Main St. (tel. 301/263-2641), often features jazz greats like Betty Carter, Mose Allison, and Charlie Byrd. There are shows nightly (local talent on Monday). Ticket prices range from about $2 to $12, depending on the performer. Reservations are essential, preferably several days in advance. Light fare—cheese and fruit plates, onion soup au gratin, and crudités (in the $3 to $6 range)—is available, as of course are drinks.

Also check out the **Colonial Players,** a theater in the round located in a converted blacksmith shop at 108 East St. just off State Circle (tel. 301/268-

7373). An amateur theater, it features actors from the Baltimore and Washington area in shows like *Deathtrap, Agnes of God,* and *The Dining Room.* Ticket prices are $4 to $8. The box office is open Tuesday to Saturday from 7 to 9 p.m., on Sunday from 6 to 8 p.m.

7. Baltimore: The Inner Harbor

Just an hour from Washington, D.C., and en route to or from home for many of you, Baltimore is a city in the throes of rebirth, and her revitalization centers around the famed **Inner Harbor.** The traditional center of the city, this port on the Patapsco River, a tributary of Chesapeake Bay, was established in 1729. In 1965 a private, nonprivate corporation was formed to develop 240 acres surrounding Baltimore's Inner Harbor. To date over $775 million has been spent in this effort, and more than half as much again is budgeted for future construction. There's already more than enough here for a very full day of varied activities, all of which are described below.

VISITOR INFORMATION: And, of course, in all of Baltimore there are dozens of additional sightseeing options ranging from Babe Ruth's birthplace to Edgar Allan Poe's grave. Though they're not covered in this guide, which is meant as a day's excursion to the harbor area, you can get details on all Baltimore sights, events, and accommodations by writing in advance to the **Baltimore Office of Promotion and Tourism,** 34 Market Pl., Suite 310, Baltimore, MD 21202 (tel. 301/837-INFO, a 24-hour phone number).

There's also an information kiosk adjacent to the Light Street Pavilion, and a **Visitor Center** at the Inner Harbor is in the works at this writing.

GETTING THERE: To get to Baltimore, take I-395 north to Pratt St., make a right and another right at President St., where you'll find a huge parking lot offering the best all-day parking rates around ($3 all day; elsewhere you might pay as much as $8.50!). Bus (via Greyhound and Trailways) and train service (Amtrak) are available if you have no car.

INNER HARBOR SIGHTS: All of the below-listed attractions are located around the harbor and within walking distance of one another. Proceed in order and you'll save a lot of footwork. But should you get weary, just hop a water taxi ($1.25). Between 11 a.m. and 11 p.m. Sunday to Thursday, 11 a.m. to midnight Friday and Saturday (mid-April to mid-October, weather permitting), they make very frequent trips, stopping at all major attractions.

The National Aquarium

Of all the Inner Harbor sights, the aquarium is my great favorite. Since its opening in 1981 this seven-level complex at Pier 3, 501 East Pratt St. (tel. 301/576-3810), has attracted over a million visitors annually. It is home to over 5,000 specimens, representing some 500 species of fish, birds, reptiles, amphibians, invertebrates, plants, and marine mammals. The exhibits are along an easy-to-follow spiral route. They include an **Atlantic Coral Reef**—a 13-foot-deep, doughnut-shaped 335,000-gallon tank, the largest exhibit of its kind in the U.S. Here reside a 100-pound tarpon, a Hawksbill turtle (an endangered species), and bonnethead sharks. More sharks can be seen in the **Open Ocean,** including sand tiger sharks over 8½-feet long weighing 250 to 350 pounds; they share their 220,000-gallon tank with two species of rays and other large gamefish. Accord-

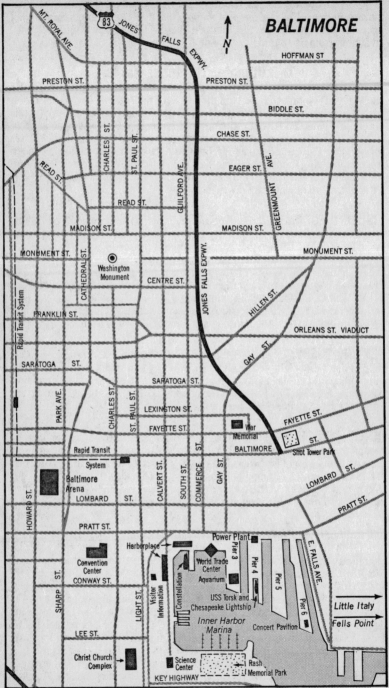

BALTIMORE

N

ing to Bob Jenkins, director of husbandry and operations at the Aquarium, sharks "don't deserve the nefarious, sometimes gruesome reputations they have." Stories of their vicious natures, he says, are greatly exaggerated. They do, however, have from 5 to 15 rows of teeth, and when a tooth is lost a new one moves up to replace it within a week! (I think that's rather ominous.) A 260,000-gallon **Marine Mammal Tray** houses two bluish-gray female beluga whales from the Hudson Bay area of Manitoba, Canada. Feeding times (they eat herring and capelin, a smelt-like fish) are posted at the information desk. In the steamy **Tropical Rain Forest,** a simulation of a South American jungle with about 400 species of tropical plants, you'll view 30 species of fish (including piranha, nearly 100 brightly colored tropical birds, and a pair of two-toed sloths. In the **Habitat Theater** you get to rest a while at an eight-minute multimedia program called *Chesapeake: A Bay at Risk;* it's about how concerned citizens can help preserve the bay. A 70,000-gallon **rock pool** provides an outdoor home for numerous harbor seals and a pair of rare gray seals. Try to see it at feeding time, daily at 10 a.m., 1 p.m., and 4 p.m. Other exhibits deal with feeding habits—how an electric eel uses electrical impulses to locate and stun food. In "Maryland: Mountains to the Sea," four living exhibits depict Maryland habitats—an Allegheny Mountain pond, tidal marsh, coastal beach, and the Atlantic shelf. And kids will love the **Children's Cove,** a hands-on exhibit where they can handle horseshoe crabs, starfish, and urchins. There's also a display of living corals on the third floor.

A new Marine Mammal Complex on adjacent Pier 4 is in the works for the future.

The National Aquarium is open mid-September to mid-May from 10 a.m. to 5 p.m. with extended hours till 8 p.m. on Friday; the rest of the year it opens at 9 a.m. and there are extended hours till 8 p.m. on Friday through Sunday. Admission is $6.75 for adults, $5 for senior citizens, $3.75 for children 3 to 11; under 3, free.

The World Trade Center

Though at 423 feet this 30-story I. M. Pei-designed pentagonal building does not rival New York's World Trade Center, you will want to ride up to the 27th-floor observation deck to enjoy spectacular harbor views and see hands-on displays and multimedia presentations on Baltimore's history, neighborhoods, and architecture. It's a good orientation to your Inner Harbor visit. Hours are 10 a.m. to 5 p.m. Monday to Saturday, noon to 5 on Sunday; spring and summer closing is later on weekends. Admission is $1.50 for adults, $1.25 for senior citizens and children. Call 301/837-4515 for further details.

Harborplace

Like South Street Seaport in New York and Faneuil Hall in Boston, Harborplace, the hub of the Inner Harbor at the corner of Pratt and Light Sts. (tel. 301/332-4191), is yet another of those ubiquitous Rouse developments with all the familiar earmarks. Its two glass-enclosed, glass-canopied buildings contain 14 restaurants and sidewalk cafés, 20 gourmet food markets, 46 additional specialty eating places, and 80 shops. The **Pratt Street Pavilion** offers the bulk of retail outlets—Pappagallo, Laura Ashley, Crabtree & Evelyn, Benetton, a bookstore, clothing stores, toy store, etc. The shops, arranged along colonnades, are skylit on the second level. The **Light Street Pavilion** is more food oriented. Downstairs is the Colonnade Market featuring purveyors of produce, fish, meat, and dairy foods. In the two-story Trading Hall you can purchase wines, baked goods, gourmet foods, and tobacco. Upstairs is the Sam Smith Market with an ever-changing array of gift items and such sold from kiosks and colorful pushcarts. Wares are likely to run the gamut from handcrafted nautical items to baseball collectibles, from hand-blown glass sculpture to computerized horoscopes, from pottery to unusual hats. Also on this level is the **Food Hall** with a wide variety of international eating places; it's designed as an indoor park. More about eating later.

That's just the bare bones of these buildings; hours of browsing and buying are possible here. And my curmudgeony attitude aside, they are attractive and pleasant with chrysanthemum-bordered trees under skylights and colorful banners aloft.

Shops are open Monday to Saturday from 10 a.m. to 9:30 p.m., from noon till 6 or 8 p.m. on Sunday. Most restaurants and cafés stay open till midnight or later.

Be sure to stop at the Light Street information kiosk to find out about special happenings during your visit. A typical month's activities might include a pistachio-shelling and eating contest, crab races, parades, a rowing regatta, jazz concerts, band concerts, choirs, and aerobics demonstration, and a banana split-eating contest (preferable to pistachio nuts in my book). In summer there are also free Sunday-evening concerts at the **Harborplace Amphitheater** featuring jazz and big-band sounds. In addition there are regular street performers, Santa is on hand from Thanksgiving through Christmas every year to take your gift orders, there are midnight fireworks New Year's Eve, a week of water and land races and contests the third week in May complement Pimlico's Preakness Week, a country fair (square dancing, livestock auctions, sheep shearing, and displays of rural arts and crafts) takes place the second week in October, and Independence Day is celebrated with many special events July 1–4.

Opening shortly after presstime is the new **Harborplace Gallery** with 75 stores (mostly retail, not food) and an adjoining 622-room Stouffer Hotel.

The Maryland Academy of Sciences and Science Center

Founded in 1797 for the "promotion of science," the Maryland Academy of Sciences is the oldest organization of its kind in the United States. In the late 1960s the academy's board began a program to build the Maryland Science Center, which opened in 1976. It is designed not as a repository for scientific artifacts but as a "dynamic tactile environment where visitors can interact with exhibits and participate in a variety of programs and activities." In everyday English, that means there are dozens of hands-on exhibits that kids of all ages love. On the premises is the Davis Planetarium with 350 projectors and a four-channel sound system with 12 loudspeakers; be sure to catch the current show. There are marvelous live science demonstrations throughout the day on special stages, many of them geared to children. And half-hour films on subjects like volcanoes and geology are shown two to four times a day in the Boyd Theater. As for the permanent exhibits, they encompass subjects like perception, energy, Chesapeake Bay life, physics, probability, and of course, computers, the latter with numerous learning games. Part of the perception exhibit includes a distorted room, which is always good fun. And just about every exhibit involves the viewer, whether you're measuring your metric height, designing your own energy policy, catching a falling stick to test your reaction time, functioning as a human battery, or pressing a button on a map of the U.S. to locate our greatest sources of coal, oil, and uranium. An exciting development was the recent opening of a new IMAX theater here with a five-story screen. This is good, educational fun for the whole family.

The center is located at 601 Light St. (tel. 301/685-2370). For 24-hour information regarding current exhibits and planetarium features, call 301/685-5225.

The center is open daily, but hours of operation tend to change frequently. Call before you go. Admission for adults is $4.50 for any one attraction (the museum, the planetarium, or an IMAX film), $6.50 for two, $7.50 for three. Students with ID, senior citizens, and children under 12 pay 50¢ less across the board.

Rash Field Flower Garden

The Rash Field Flower Garden, between the Maryland Science Center and the Rusty Scupper Restaurant, is multi-faceted. It contains a spectacular international square-mile garden with flowers from all over the world. On weekends there are art displays. Free noontime shows for children, Little People's Theater Productions, are presented on Tuesday and Thursday at the Kaufman Pavilion. And there's a playground/sculpture garden for kids, too.

Miscellanea

From early April through the end of October you can rent **paddleboats** in front of the Pratt Street Pavilion. Cost is $7.50 an hour, $4.25 for a half hour.

A variety of **harbor cruises,** some including lunch, dinner, Sunday brunch, and/or musical revues, are offered by Harbor Cruises (tel. 301/727-3113). Details at the Light Street Pavilion kiosk.

The U.S. frigate *Constellation,* the first commissioned warship of the U.S. Navy, launched in 1797, is docked at the Inner Harbor, and a self-guided tour is offered at $1.75 for adults, $1 for seniors, 75¢ for ages 6 to 15; under 6, free. The U.S. Navy's signal book and regulations, still serving as basic procedure, were written on board by the frigate's first captain. The ship participated in the War of 1812, saw action against the Barbary pirates, was the first U.S. warship to enter the inland waters of China in 1842, guarded merchant ships in the Mediterranean during the Civil War, was used as a training ship in Annapolis, and transported food during the Irish famine of 1880.

If touring ships appeals to you, also check out the **Baltimore Maritime Museum** in front of the Aquarium (tel. 301/396-5528).

WHERE TO EAT: The problem is not where to eat at the Inner Harbor, but where not to eat. Concentrate your energies on the **Harborplace** pavilions, which abound with gastronomic goodies of every variety. At the Light Pavilion alone you can purchase a Greek salad, stuffed potatoes, Polish sausage, stuffed shrimp, raw oysters, pastrami on rye, barbecued chicken and ribs, a bagel with cream cheese and lox, chili, croissants, quiche, pizza, egg rolls, tropical fruit drinks, moussaka, and tacos—and top off a meal of any of the above with caramel apple cake from Ms. Desserts and Häagen-Dazs ice cream. It's all sold at retail outlets here, and there are indoor tables and chairs overlooking the water where you can enjoy it in the upstairs Food Hall. However, my inclination is to pass up these exotic fast foods eaten with plastic utensils off paper plates and opt for a real restaurant meal. It's more restful, and after traipsing around the harbor attractions, rest is definitely called for. Here again you have a wide choice, and at lunch especially, most of the restaurants are reasonably affordable.

If you like spicy fare, you can't do better than the **Tandoor** at the Pratt Street Pavilion (tel. 301/547-0575), a restaurant that also has a branch in Georgetown. At lunch, entrees like lamb biryani—that's lamb marinated in herbs and spices and cooked on saffron rice, tandoori chicken, and curried ground beef with peas and hard boiled egg are in the $6.50 to $7.50 range. The Tandoor is strikingly attractive within—a setting of orange-clothed tables, hanging plants, and cut-brass lamps overhead. There are also tables on an awninged balcony overlooking the harbor.

Another good choice in this pavilion is the **Taverna Athena** (tel. 301/547-8900), also with water-view seating. Here white stucco and Mediterranean blue furnishings and Greek music create a suitable ambience. Lunch options include stuffed grape leaves ($5.95), moussaka ($6.50), a souvlaki sandwich ($4.95), and a feta cheese omelet ($4.95). There's baklava and Greek coffee for dessert.

Over at the Light Street Pavilion is a branch of the **American Café** (tel. 301/962-8400), which you may have visited in D.C. Sandwich and salad combinations—like chicken tarragon with water chestnuts and toasted almonds on croissant, served with dilled cucumber salad ($6.50)—are featured. See Chapter III for further description.

A greater number of affordable items are offered at the **Soup Kitchen** (tel. 301/539-3810), another eatery with al fresco water-view seating. An eight-ounce bowl of homemade soup served with bread and butter is just $2.95 here; a Caesar salad, $4.95; a cheese plate—New York cheddar, French brie, and Danish havarti, served with sliced apple—$5.50. Both the Soup Kitchen and the American Café offer reasonable prices at dinner as well as lunch.

There are several other restaurants in both pavilions that merit consideration. You'll see them when touring the buildings and can determine which you find enticing and affordable. At dinner, entree prices at the majority of Harborplace restaurants are usually $10 and up. That's the time to purchase from the above-mentioned food stands and enjoy a picnic dinner over at Rash Field.

Want to get out of the harbor area for a bit? Head over to nearby Little Italy for lunch at **Trattoria Petrucci,** 300 South High St. at Fawn St. (tel. 301/752-4515). It's a cozy place. The front room has a beamed ceiling and exposed brick and stucco walls hung with turn-of-the-century Campari posters. The smaller back room is painted in pale peach and has a pressed-tin ceiling. In summer, there are awning-shaded café tables on the street enclosed by flower boxes. Dinner here's very pricey, but at lunch you can order pasta dishes like tortellini opera (in a rich meat sauce flavored with rosemary, basil, oregano, tomatoes, carrots, onion, and celery) or paglia e fieno (pasta with ham and peas in a cream sauce) for under $5. The bread served with your meal is excellent. There are also sandwiches stuffed with veal parmigiana, meatballs, or Italian sausage in the $2.50 to $4.25 range, and veal and chicken dishes—such as chicken breast stuffed with prosciutto, broccoli, and cheese—are $7 to $8. The antipastos, hot or cold, are also good choices. You might order one with a glass of wine for a light meal followed by a dessert of homemade amaretto cake topped with fresh whipped cream and toasted almonds. Everything is made from scratch, including the pasta.

Trattoria Petrucci is open for lunch Monday to Saturday from 11:30 a.m. to 3 p.m.

Another only-at-lunch option is **Something Fishy,** 606 South Broadway at Fleet St. (tel. 301/732-2233), in Fell's Point, another area close to the harbor where restaurants cluster. It's fronted by an oak-floored pub with café-curtained front windows, a handsome oak backbar, cream-colored pressed-tin walls, and a pressed copper ceiling—a lovely plant-filled dining and drinking area. The main dining room is what owner Stevi Martin describes as "nautical-Victorian"; it's furnished with oak pub tables, wainscotted cream walls are hung with marine-themed lithographs and prints, there are stained-glass windows, and a wooden mermaid with torchiers in hand serves as an overhead lighting fixture. Also up front is an actual fish market, providing fresh fish and seafood for your meal. If you like, you can choose your lunch from the counter, perhaps a filet of bluefish, which will then be sauteed in lemon butter sauce and served with Lyonnaise potatoes and grilled zucchini ($7.50). Less expensive is a fish sandwich ($4.75); I had fresh softshell crab on a recent visit and it was superb. Or you might opt for a cold pasta salad tossed with fresh scallops, shrimp, mussels, and clams in a sour cream dressing ($5.50). There are delicious soups like cream of crab, salads with tangy dressings made with grated fresh cheeses and Dijon mustard, and oven-fresh desserts like white chocolate mousse cake. Everything here is homemade using the best ingredients. Premium wines are offered by the glass.

Lunch is served daily except Monday from noon to 3 p.m.

WHERE TO STAY: Baltimore's so close to Washington, you don't really need to spend the night here. The following listing is more for pleasure than practicality.

Though it's a bit of a splurge for budget travelers, the **Shirley Guest House,** 205 W. Madison St., at Park Ave., Baltimore, MD 21201 (tel. 301/728-6550), will so enhance your visit here that it's well worth a little something extra in the green goods. The only trouble, in fact, is the place is so lovely you might find yourself wanting to hang about rather than getting out and seeing the city. Owner Roberta Pieczenik (who also owns the highly recommended Kalorama Guest House in D.C.) has converted a five-story Victorian brick building into a gorgeous hostelry, decorated in the best of taste and offering superb service that is friendly rather than high-falutin'. Actually, "converted" is the wrong word. The building was constructed in 1880 to serve as a "proper gentleman's hotel," and it has always been an inn or boarding house. Upon arrival, you're greeted by one of the Shirley's charming hostesses with a glass of sherry in the parlor. And this parlor happens to be a beautiful room with wainscotted walls covered in period reproduction fabric, furnished with turn-of-the-century pieces including an Edwardian mahogany breakfront, an oak pedestal table by the bay window, and plush, comfortable sofas. It even has a working fireplace. Many plants, including potted palms, make the setting even homier, and classical music, which is played throughout the day, contributes to the serene atmosphere. Not surprisingly, you'll often find guests mingling down here. Books and magazines are provided, as are local restaurant menus and brochures on Baltimore attractions. And a hostess is on duty in the parlor throughout the day to provide any assistance you might require. Continental breakfast—croissants, sweet rolls, muffins, bagels, juice, and tea or coffee—is also served here each morning between 7:30 and 10:30 a.m.

There are 27 rooms in the house, nine of them suites with living or dining rooms. Some have kitchenettes. Once again, they're impeccably appointed. A typical chamber here will have 15-foot ceilings, pale peach walls with sections of period wallpaper, mauve carpeting, a beautiful fireplace mantel, lovely muted-rose silk curtains, and a brass bed with white eyelet quilt. Homey touches are likely to include framed old photographs on the mantel, candlesticks in beautiful holders, ceramic figurines, and silk flower arrangements. There are also ficus trees and fresh flowers in every room. The feel is completely residential, and that includes modern comforts and amenities, often missing in charming guesthouses. A color cable TV is concealed in a handsome mahogany armoire, and you also get air conditioning, a direct-dial phone, clock radio, and in-room bath. Public areas are delightful as well, the halls decorated with Edwardian botanical prints and the like. You can ascend to your room via a grand staircase or ride the old-fashioned European-style lift.

At this writing Roberta is completing work on another building around the corner at 716 Park Avenue which will add another 10 rooms and a connecting garden courtyard (al fresco breakfasts will be an option by the time you read this). The new building's rooms are decorated in a manner very similar to the above described, but some are a tad less luxurious (only because room proportions aren't as grand), and will be a bit less expensive. Also, it's not yet decided whether phones and TVs will go into new building rooms, so check on facilities when you reserve. The Shirley is just 12 blocks from the harbor.

Rates, including morning breakfast and evening apéritif, are $45 to $75 single, $50 to $80 double, $5 for an additional person.

Chapter X

THE ABC'S OF WASHINGTON

AIRPORTS: The Washington area is served by three major airports. Closest is **Washington National Airport,** just across the Potomac in Virginia 3½ miles from downtown. It handles domestic traffic only.

Dulles International Airport, one of the most modern air terminals in the world, services international flights. It's also located in Virginia, about 25 miles from the city. About the same distance from downtown, the **Baltimore-Washington International Airport** is located in Maryland between Washington and Baltimore.

AIRPORT TRANSPORTATION: Taxi fare from Washington National to a central point like Metro Center (12th and G Streets NW) is about $7; from Dulles, about $30; from Baltimore-Washington, about $40. National Airport is right on the Blue and Yellow **Metro** lines, and courtesy van service is provided between the airport terminal building and the station. A company called the **Airport Connection** (tel. 685-1400 or toll free 800/431-5472) runs buses between the Capitol and Washington Hiltons and Baltimore-Washington Airport. The company's buses also ply the routes between five D.C. hotels and National and Dulles Airports. Details in Chapter I.

BABYSITTERS: **B.L. Lee & Associates,** (tel. 783-8573), is a licensed agency that has been serving the District for three decades. Most of the sitters are older women who have been working at the agency for many years. Rates are $4.50 per hour for one child, 50¢ an hour for each additional child of the same family. You also have to pay the sitters (all live in the District) round-trip transportation costs (bus or train coming, or both ways during the day; cabfare going home at night). Don't wait till the last minute to think about a babysitter; the agency takes calls from 9 a.m. to 5 p.m. weekdays only. Most hotels and motels also keep lists of babysitters or provide a service.

BUSES: **Greyhound** and **Trailways** connect just about every U.S. city with Washington. The former has a terminal at 1110 New York Ave. NW (tel. 565-2662), the latter at 1st and L Sts. NE (tel. 737-5800).

CONGRESSPERSONS: To locate your senator or congressional representative, call the Capitol switchboard (tel. 224-3121).

DENTAL REFERRAL SERVICE: Phone 686-0803 weekdays from 8 a.m. to 4 p.m.

DIAL-A-MUSEUM: 357-2020 is the Smithsonian's number for recorded daily information on all its museum's special programs and activities.

DIAL-A-PARK: Call 485-PARK to find out daily events in the National Capital Regional parks.

DISTANCE FROM MAJOR CITIES: Washington is 240 miles from New York City, 40 miles from Baltimore, and 600 miles from Chicago and Atlanta.

EMERGENCY COUNSELING: The **Northern Virginia Hotline** (tel. 527-4077) serves the entire D.C. area as a listing and referral service and crisis-intervention center. They're equipped to help with problems like depression, loneliness, contemplation of suicide, child abuse, sexuality, physical health, material needs, drug and alcohol abuse, marital dilemmas (or problems with significant others)—just about anything, really.

HOSPITAL EMERGENCY WARDS: **Georgetown University Hospital**, 3800 Reservoir Rd. NW (tel. 625-7151), and **Georgetown Washington University Hospital**, 901 23rd St. NW (entrance on Washington Circle; tel. 676-3211), are both excellent. Head to the one nearer you in an emergency.

HOTEL TAX: In addition to your room rate there's a 10% sales tax and $1 per room per night hotel tax in the District. At Virginia hotels you pay just 4% sales tax and 5% hotel tax. In Maryland it's 5% sales tax and 5% hotel tax.

MEDICAL REFERRAL SERVICE: The Medical Bureau's physician referral service can put you in touch with any kind of doctor. Call 872-0003 weekdays between 9 a.m. and 4 p.m. Closed from 1 to 2 p.m. for lunch.

METRORAIL/METROBUS INFORMATION: Call 637-7000 to find out the most convenient bus and/or subway routes between any two points in the District, suburban Maryland, and northern Virginia. The service operates from 6 a.m. to 11:30 p.m. daily.

PHARMACIES (24 HOURS): At **Peoples,** 14th St. and Thomas Circle NW, at Vermont Ave. (tel. 628-0720), you can not only get a prescription filled but buy basic groceries, small appliances, and much else.

POISON CONTROL CENTER: 625-3333 is a 24-hour emergency hotline.

POLICE/FIRE/AMBULANCE EMERGENCY: Dial 911.

TELEPHONE AREA CODES: Washington, D.C., is 202; much of Virginia is 703, though Richmond, Charlottesville, and Williamsburg are 804; and all of Maryland is 301. Many Virginia and Maryland numbers are local calls from the District, and you don't have to dial an area code.

TICKETplace: Why spend $40 for seats at the Kennedy Center when you can get them for $20? TICKETplace, F Street Plaza, between 12th and 13th Sts. NW (tel. T-I-C-K-E-T-S), sells half-price, day-of-performance-only tickets to most major Washington-area theaters and concert halls. See Chapter VI for details.

TIME: Call 844-2525.

TOURIST INFORMATION: The Convention and Visitor Association's **Tourist Information Center,** between 14th and 15th Sts. on Pennsylvania Ave. NW (tel. 789-7000), knows all, tells all. Open 9 a.m. to 5 p.m. daily from mid-April to the end of September, Monday to Saturday the rest of the year. Dial 737-8866 for a recording of events of interest to tourists.

TRAINS: Trains coming into Washington, D.C., arrive at historic Union Station, Massachusetts Ave. and North Capitol St. Union Station conveniently doubles as a Metro stop. Call **Amtrak** toll free at 800/USA-RAIL.

WEATHER: Dial 936-1212.

Date_____

FROMMER BOOKS
PRENTICE HALL PRESS
ONE GULF + WESTERN PLAZA
NEW YORK, NY 10023

Friends:

Please send me the books checked below:

FROMMER'S $-A-DAY GUIDES™

(In-depth guides to sightseeing and low-cost tourist accommodations and facilities.)

☐ Europe on $30 a Day $13.95	☐ New Zealand on $40 a Day $10.95
☐ Australia on $25 a Day $10.95	☐ New York on $50 a Day............. $10.95
☐ Eastern Europe on $25 a Day $10.95	☐ Scandinavia on $50 a Day........... $10.95
☐ England on $40 a Day.............. $11.95	☐ Scotland and Wales on $40 a Day..... $11.95
☐ Greece on $30 a Day............... $11.95	☐ South America on $30 a Day $10.95
☐ Hawaii on $50 a Day............... $11.95	☐ Spain and Morocco (plus the Canary
☐ India on $25 a Day $10.95	Is.) on $40 a Day $10.95
☐ Ireland on $30 a Day............... $10.95	☐ Turkey on $25 a Day............... $10.95
☐ Israel on $30 & $35 a Day $11.95	☐ Washington, D.C., & Historic Va. on
☐ Mexico on $20 a Day $10.95	$40 a Day $11.95

FROMMER'S DOLLARWISE GUIDES™

(Guides to sightseeing and tourist accommodations and facilities from budget to deluxe, with emphasis on the medium-priced.)

☐ Alaska $12.95	☐ Cruises (incl. Alaska, Carib, Mex,
☐ Austria & Hungary $11.95	Hawaii, Panama, Canada, & US) $12.95
☐ Belgium, Holland, Luxembourg $11.95	☐ California & Las Vegas $11.95
☐ Egypt............................ $11.95	☐ Florida........................... $11.95
☐ England & Scotland $11.95	☐ Mid-Atlantic States $12.95
☐ France $11.95	☐ New England....................... $12.95
☐ Germany $12.95	☐ New York State $12.95
☐ Italy............................. $11.95	☐ Northwest $11.95
☐ Japan & Hong Kong $12.95	☐ Skiing in Europe $12.95
☐ Portugal (incl. Madeira & the Azores) . $12.95	☐ Skiing USA—East $11.95
☐ South Pacific...................... $12.95	☐ Skiing USA—West $11.95
☐ Switzerland & Liechtenstein $12.95	☐ Southeast & New Orleans............ $11.95
☐ Bermuda & The Bahamas............. $11.95	☐ Southwest......................... $11.95
☐ Canada $12.95	☐ Texas............................. $11.95
☐ Caribbean $13.95	

TURN PAGE FOR ADDITIONAL BOOKS AND ORDER FORM.